Lifting The Day

Published in 2021 by
Unicorn, an imprint of Unicorn Publishing Group
5 Newburgh Street, London W1F 7RG
www.unicornpublishing.org

ISBN 978-1-913491-57-4
10 9 8 7 6 5 4 3 2 1

Designed by Felicity Price-Smith
Printed by Fine Tone Ltd

Lifting The Day

a lockdown exhibition

Mary Collis

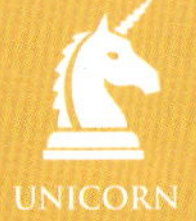

UNICORN

Mid-March 2020 was when our whole world quite suddenly turned upside down.

For me it happened in one afternoon: travel to the Cape with a friend, suddenly off. Airlines shutting down. I put away the suitcase.

Temperature-taking and hand-washing became obligatory wherever one went, and then came the (anti)social distancing. I kept my eye on the Worldometer to see the low numbers rising in an effort to justify the word 'pandemic'. Threatening lockdowns for healthy people – isn't 'lockdown' a term used in jails? Within days we were 'past the point of containment'. I wrote that phrase down so as not to forget it.

Six days later, on 21 March, Kenya had seven cases of the coronavirus. My world as I had known it was completely different. Already there was talk about vaccines and we were all frightened. That same day, I posted my first painting on Facebook. There was no thought in my head other than to 'lift the day' for myself and any friend who cared to look at it. I thought I would be posting for two weeks.

This digital record of my work grew in a miraculous way. Much of my earlier painting had been recorded on dusty old transparencies. Suddenly, long forgotten works came to light from all over the world, as kind collectors sent me photographs taken with their phones. Seeing the paintings again brought back memories of how they came about, where they were painted and of people and friends long out of mind. Daily, I looked forward to the comments, thrilling conversations reminding me to look back with joy. I made new friends. Some people were very special to me, they never missed a day without comment and I often had chats on the side with them. I found to my surprise that my paintings are all over the world. I had forgotten so many of them. Interesting and often erudite conversation ensued. We covered the history of contemporary painting, as well as different methods of working, media and composition. There were discussions on colour and synesthesia. It was a daily lift to my day, a warmth. I met much kindness and consideration, as well as a realisation of the amount of work I have done. I am grateful to all of you who followed me on this journey. A huge thank you. I only stopped 243 days later, because we were permitted to finally travel to the Cape.

Thank you, my darling daughter, Mia Collis, for your help and support and for showing me how to transform this whole digital diary into a book. Without Mia's labour of love, this project would have remained forgotten on Facebook.

Day 1

I haven't had an exhibition
in a while, so I am going to
have one here...

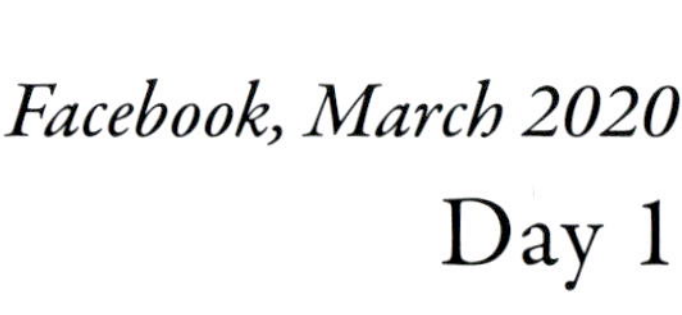

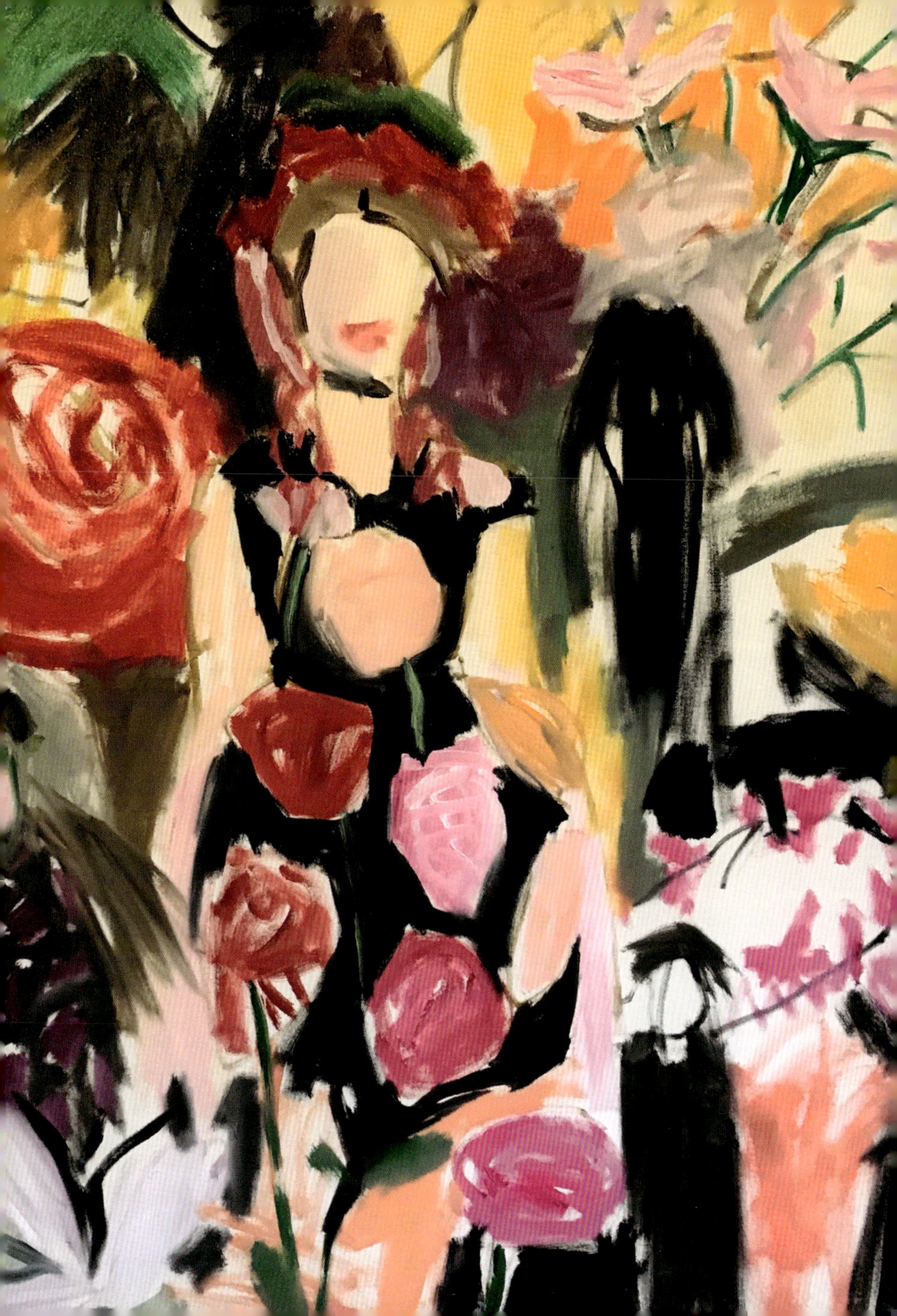

Day 2

Part of this vessel was in the RaMoMa (Rahimtulla Museum of Modern Art) Collection. After it was broken, I fixed it with gold leaf and added a piece by Anselm Croze. It now adorns my lounge.

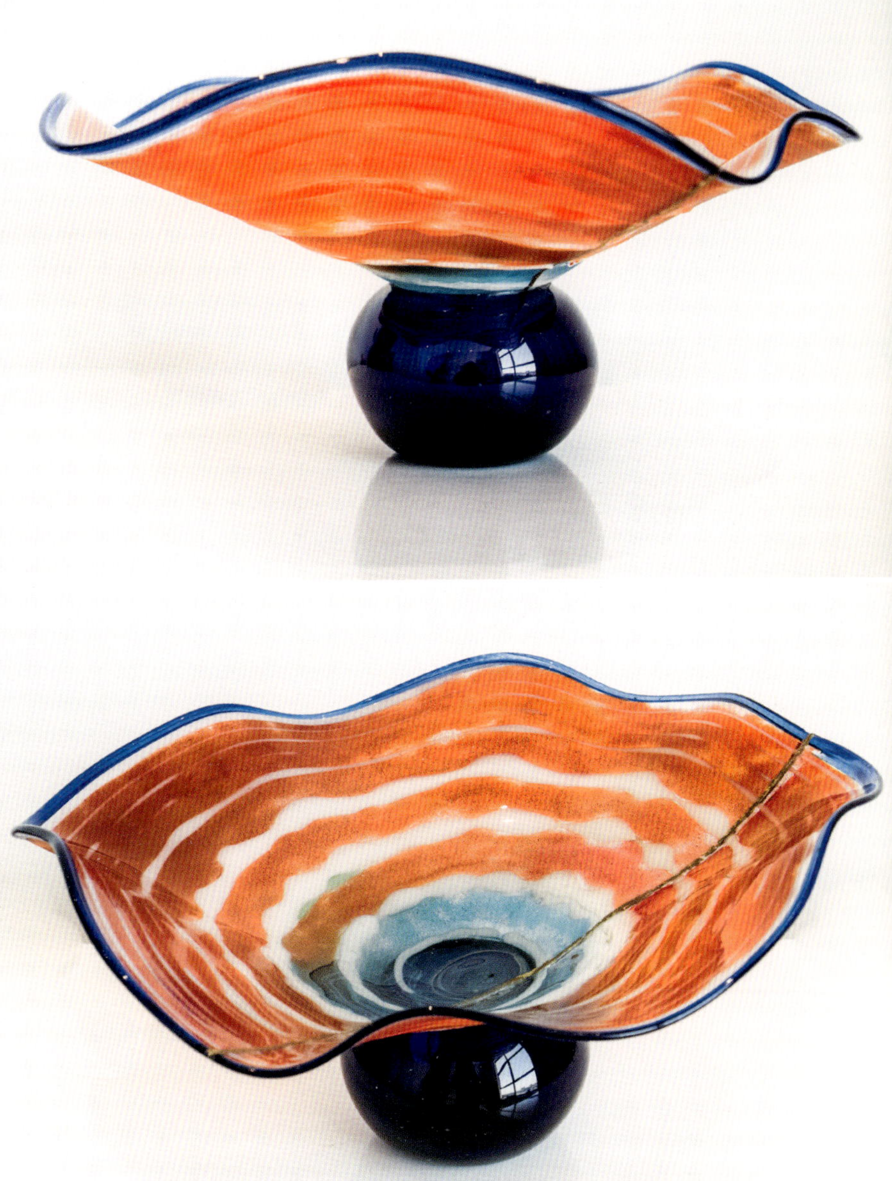

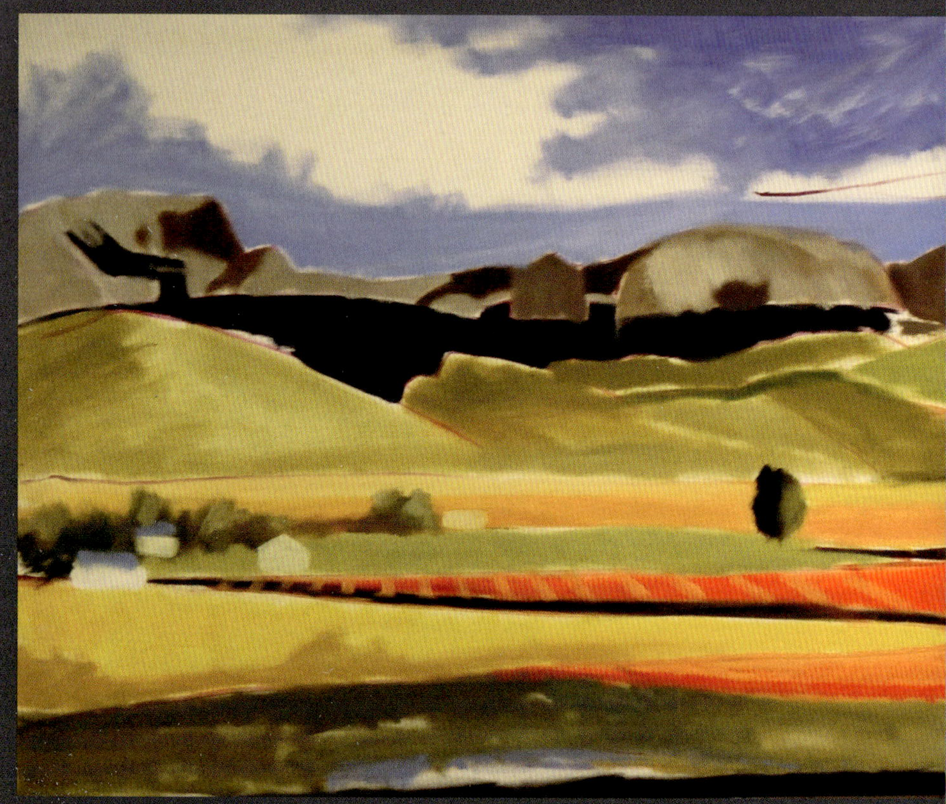

Day 3

This painting of the Hex Valley in the Western Cape was a commission. It filled a corner which gave it an interesting perspective. Unusually for me, I painted it from a photograph, being mindful that we see with two eyes, while the camera has one.

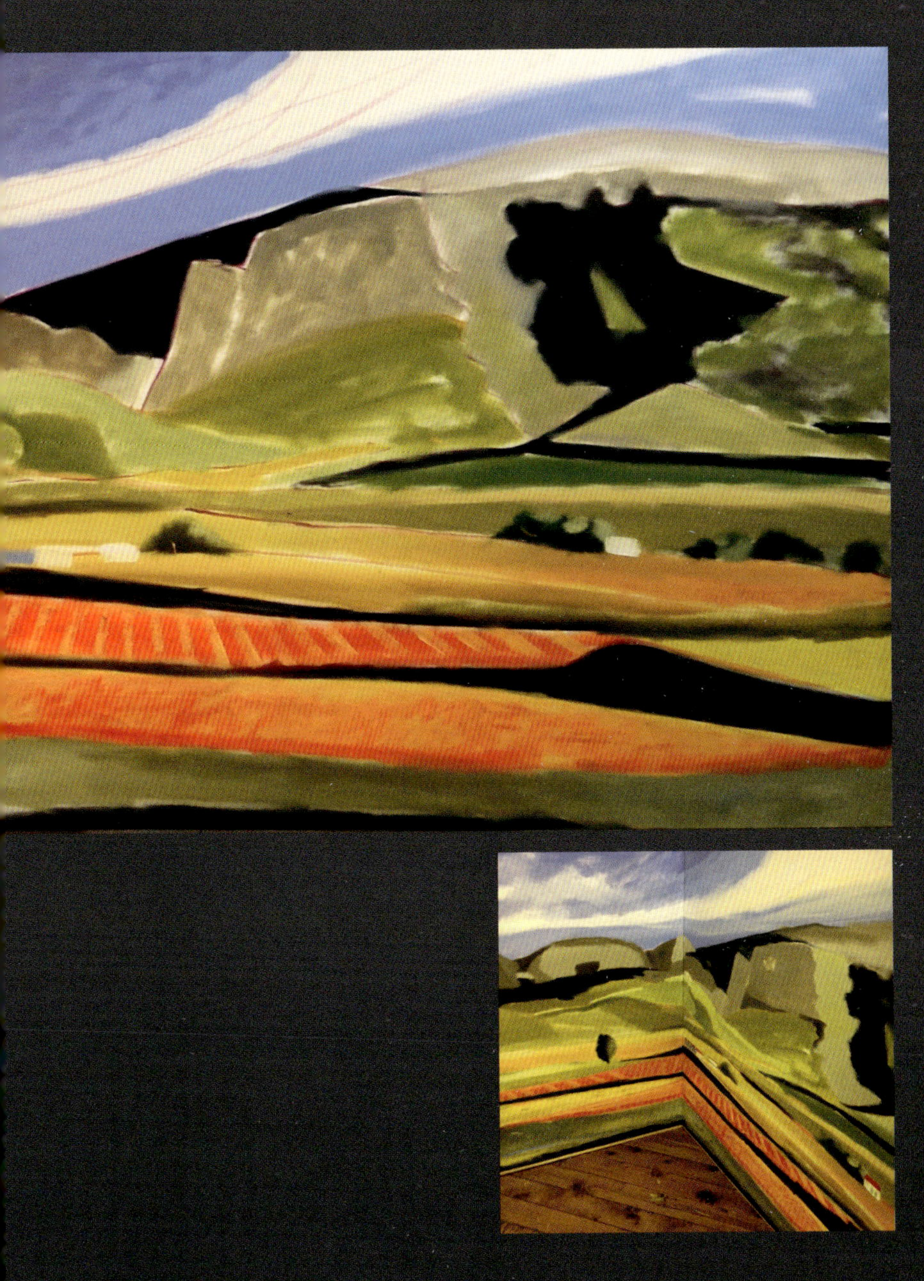

Day 4
Early Morning at Lewa

I was lucky to be staying with Jane Craig at Lewa, Kenya. Sophie Walbeoffe and I were painting there together, a wonderful week. The photograph of this painting was taken when the paint was wet and still on the easel – you can see the grip of easel at the top.

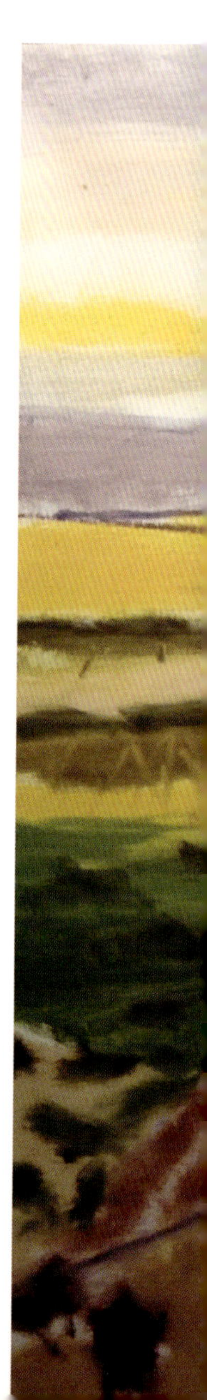

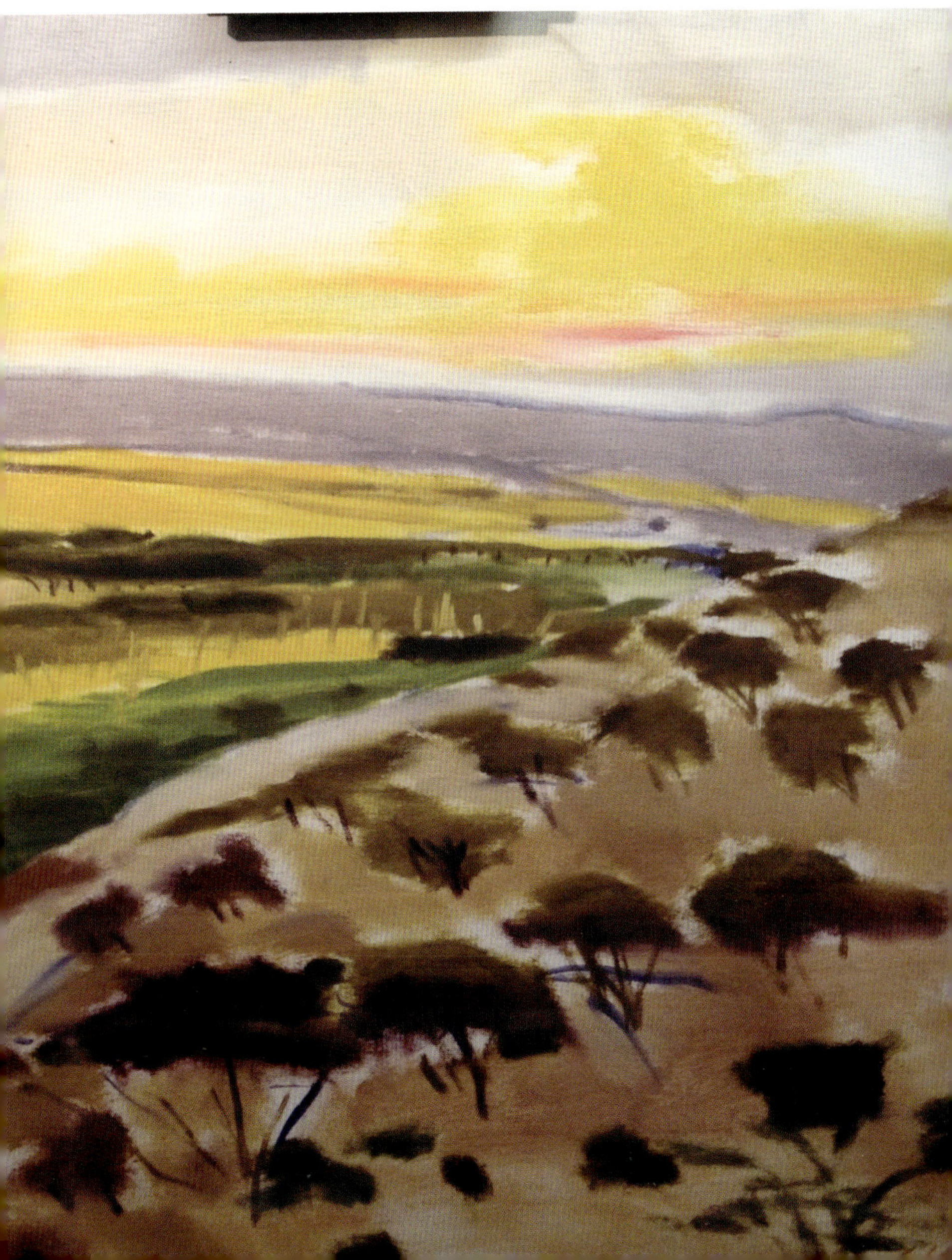

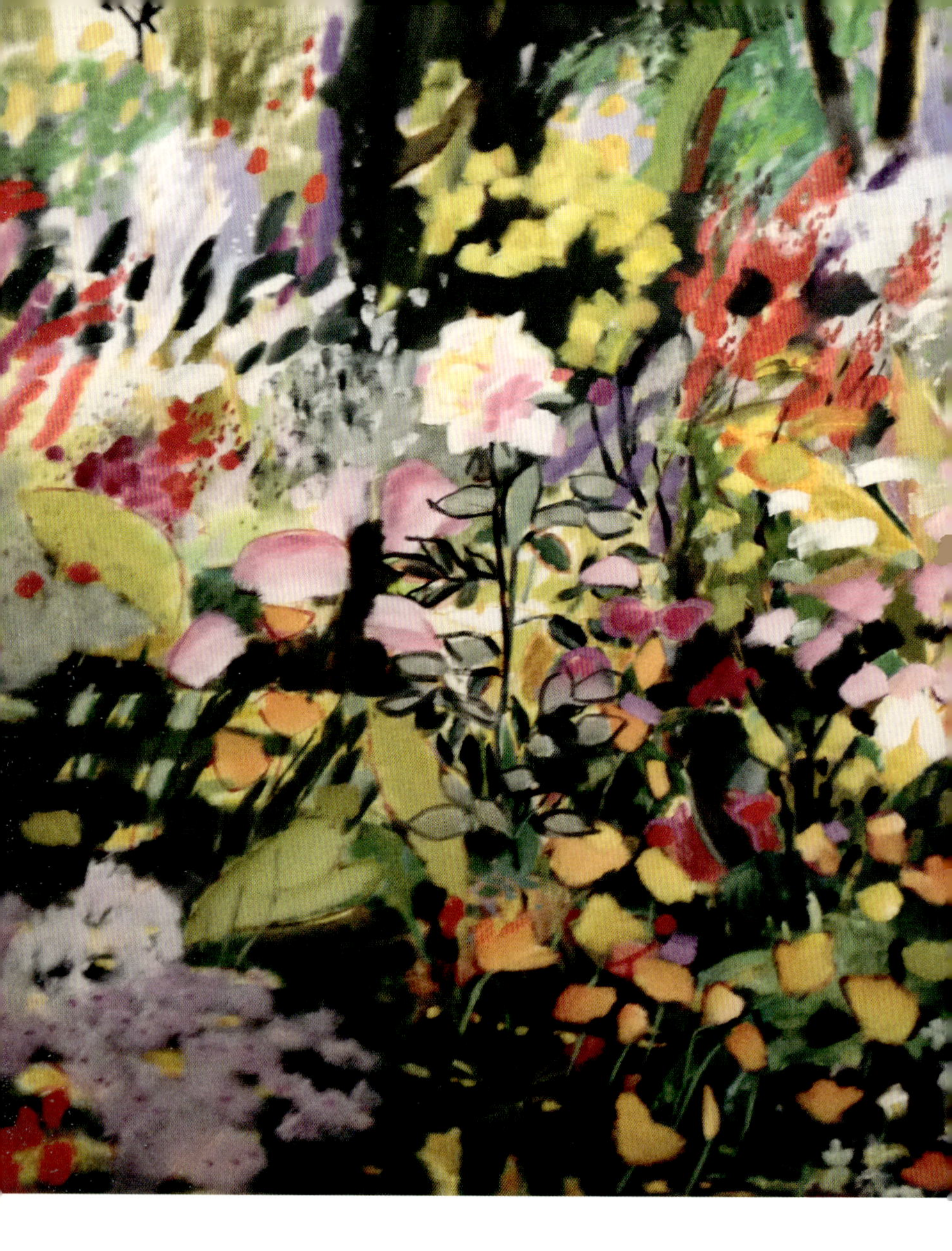

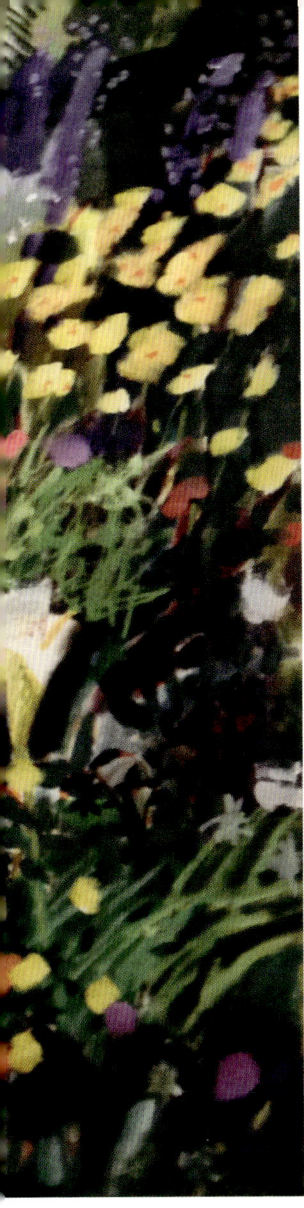

Day 5

Here's an old chestnut. It was painted
outside my former studio in our
garden in Kibagare Valley, Nairobi.
When painting gardens, I look for a
focal point, often a rose.
The painting was bought by dearest
friends Carol and George Zibarras,
and I often see it above their fireplace.

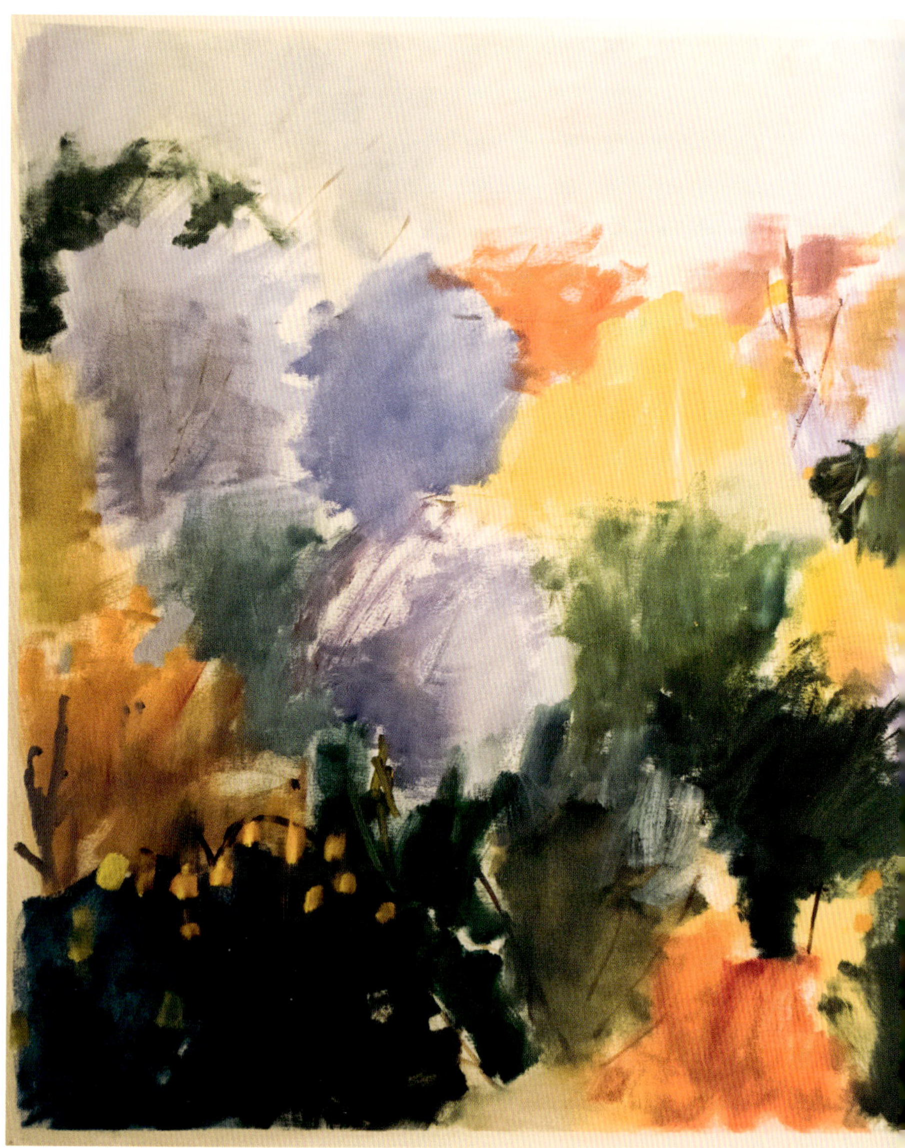

Day 6
My Valley

There are quite a few in this series
of large works painted in October
in Nairobi when all the trees are in
blossom: jacaranda, nandi flame,
grevillea, erythrina abyssinica (bright
red), phicas. Can anyone tell me what
the yellow ones are?
This is an oil on canvas, painted in an
immediate way (as one would paint
a watercolour), allowing the white
canvas to show through and no layers.
It was bought by favourite friends,
Alec and Christine Davis, who have
collected my work over the years.

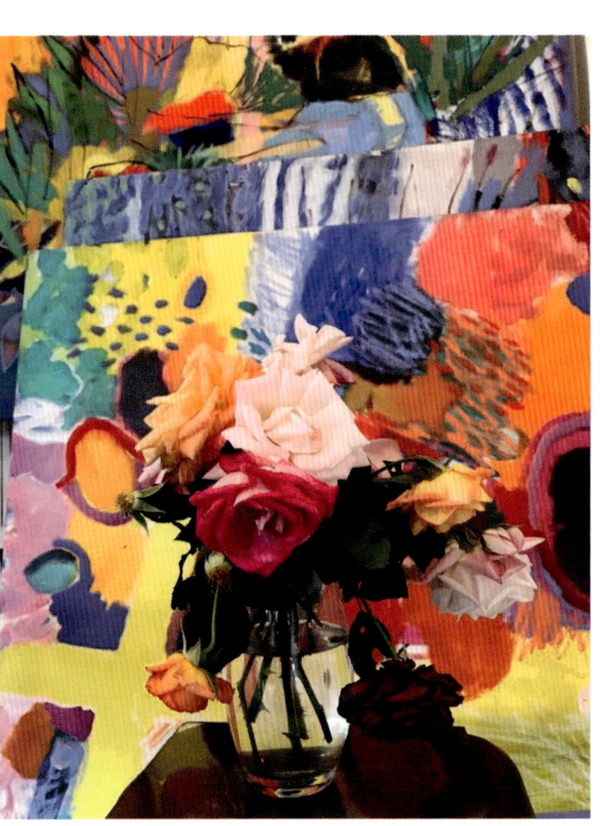

Day 7

A photograph taken by my daughter Mia, a professional and multi-international award-winning photographer. Last year Mia Collis won first prize in the portrait section for *National Geographic*. This vase of garden roses is set against stacked work in my studio. I think this is a great ending to this week, which has been all about colour. Colour lifts our spirits. Next week's exhibition will be about horizontals.

A desolate salt lake in the Rift Valley
where temperatures range from 90º
to 110º F. My shoes melted painting
this one, due to standing on the salt.
It is difficult to paint the heat and
some in the series look like winter.
In the private collection of great
friends, Hal and Lis Wackman, at
their residence in Washington, USA.

LAKE MAGADI, KENYA

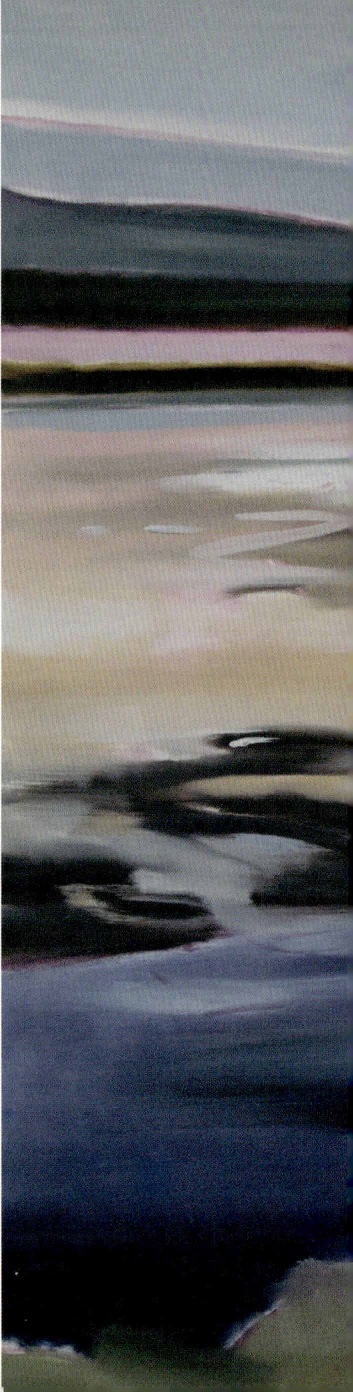

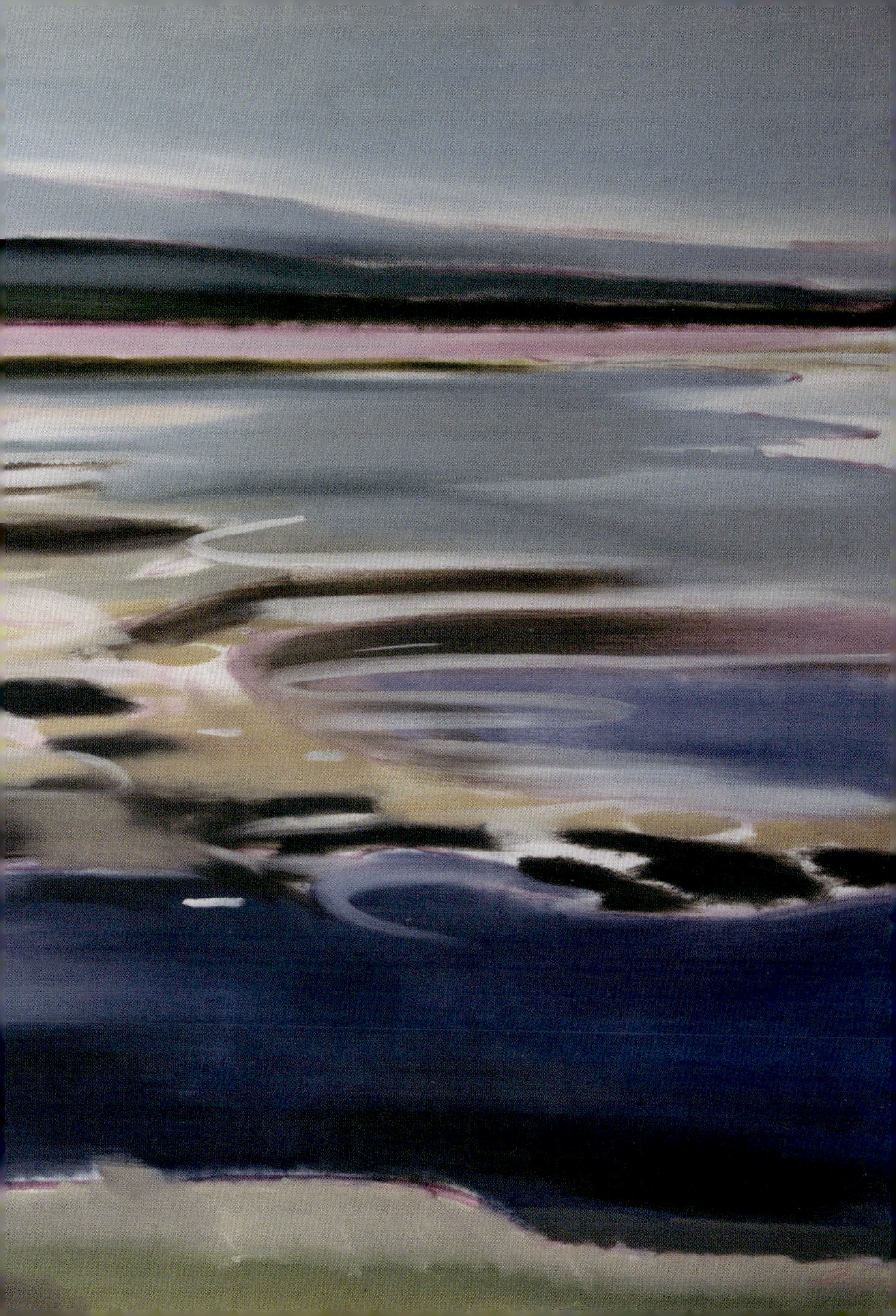

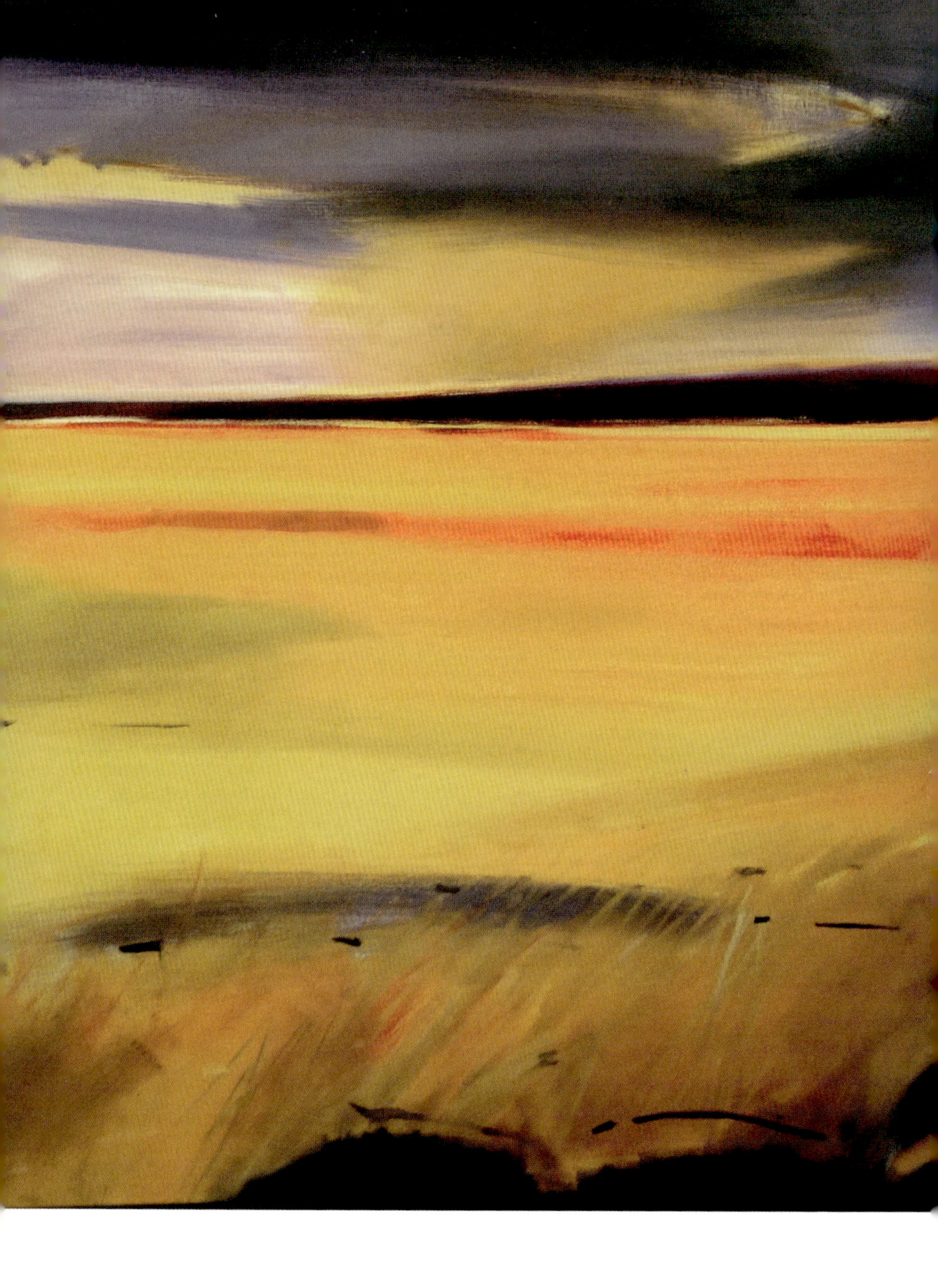

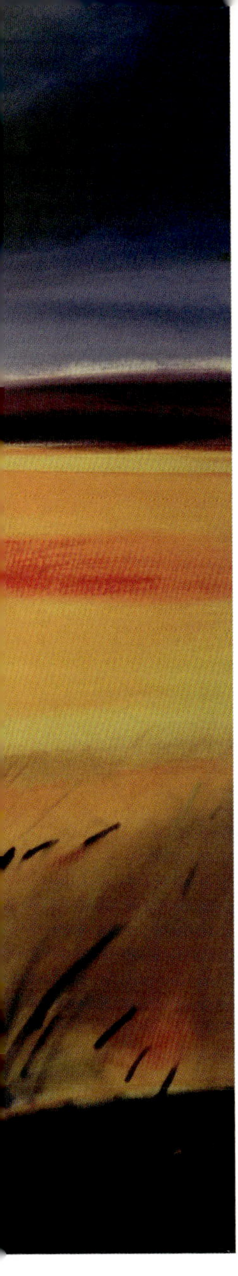

A super commission from Caltex Oil to
produce a top-quality calendar of six pages.
I was sent all over East Africa, lovely for
me. I painted twelve, 52 sq inch works
on a collapsible stretcher designed by my
engineer husband, so that I could roll each
canvas after I finished working on it, and
then stretch another immediately.
I exaggerated what I saw in the Serengeti,
taking inspiration from a photograph and
cover from the threatening sky.

SERENGETI

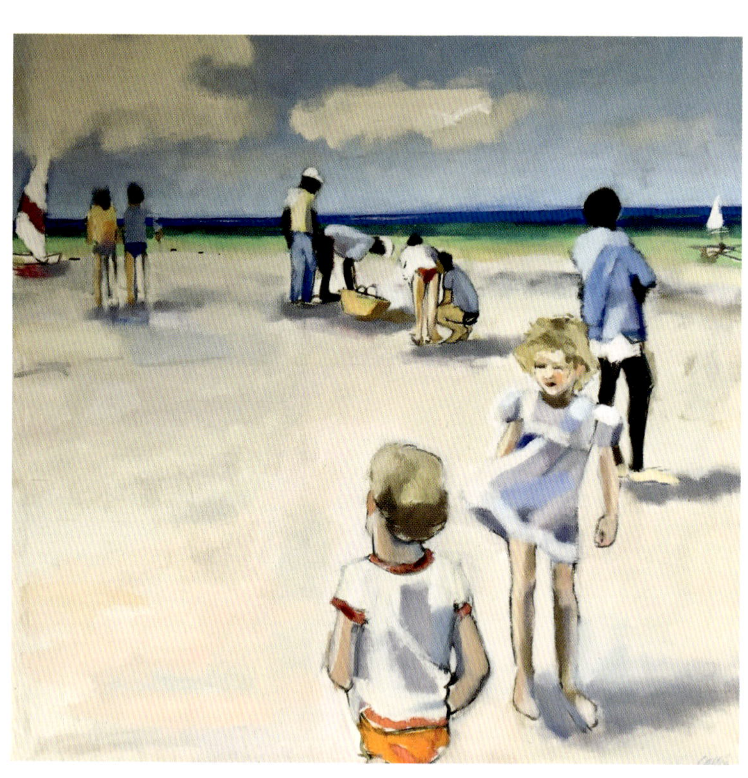

This is a very old painting, as you can see from my
two children, Fabian and Mia, in the foreground. I like
to think that the expression on my daughter's face
shows the brightness of Diani Beach and the heat.
This is part of two works. It is said that East Africa
has the best beaches in the world. Diani is a straight
beach, 4 miles long, with a reef which ensures the
turquoise water and no sharks. When I was a child
we spent our summer holidays in October at Jadini
Hotel on Diani Beach. My father would hire two little
airplanes to transport a family of six and we would
land on this beach. This practice was banned just
before Kenya became independent in 1963.
The painting is owned by Minnie Rabb-Conquest in
the UK who writes to me and tells me how happy it
makes her feel. How gratifying is that?

DAY 11

This week is about horizontal lines.
Painted in the studio, one of several on the
same subject of the 'feeling' of standing in
the shallows of the incoming tide and really
looking at the movement of the water and
remembering its warmth. The Indian Ocean
on the equator is like a warm bath.

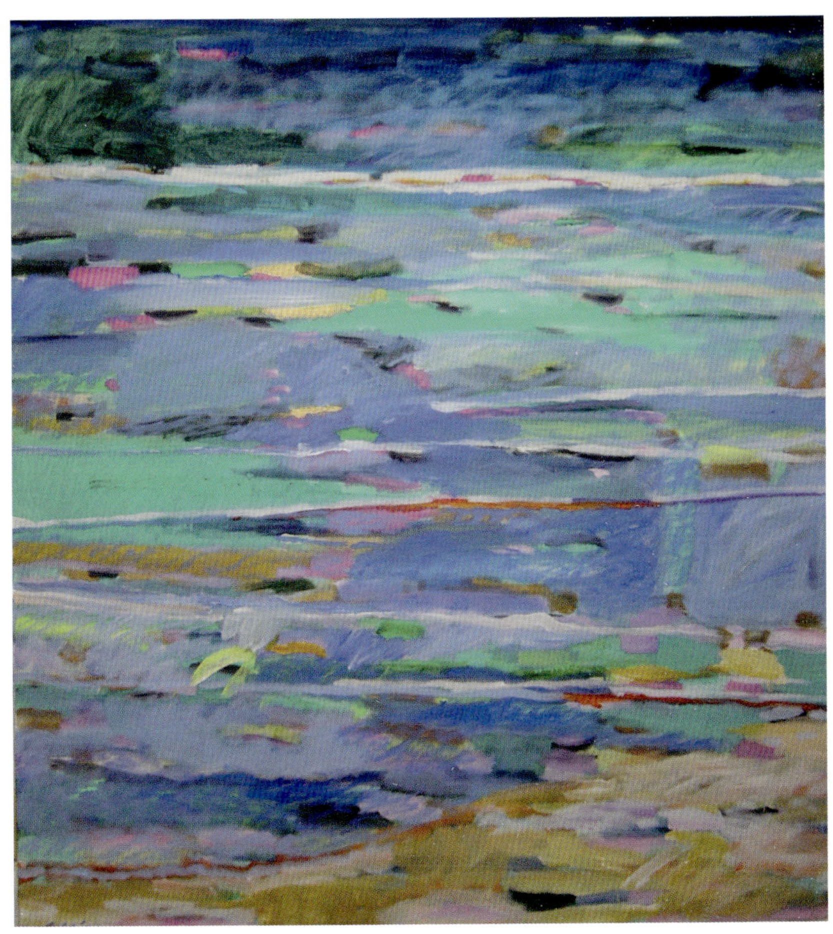

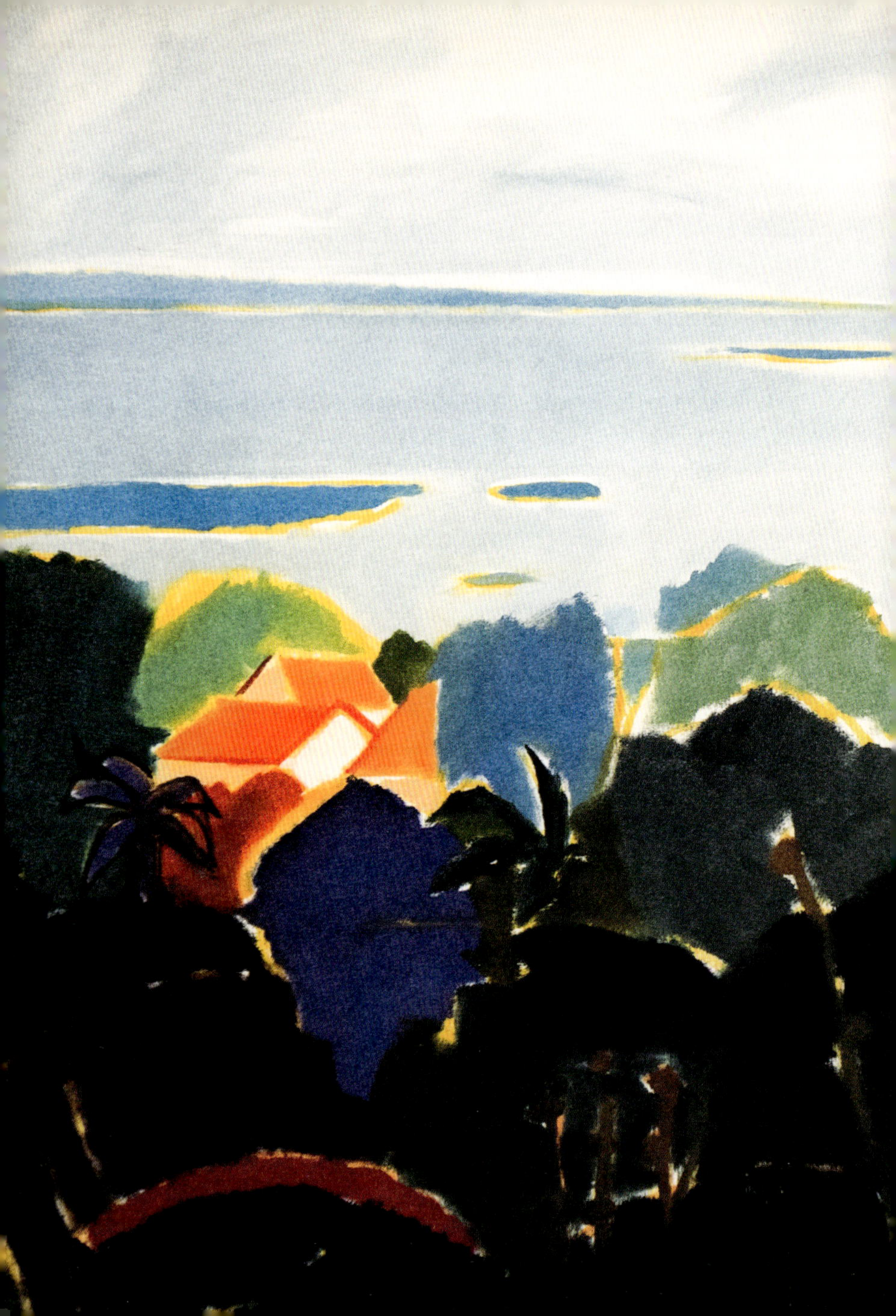

The slope on Lake Victoria's horizon
(the largest lake in Africa) stops
at the golden section.
This is no accident. It balances
the colourful roof tops in the left
foreground, also at the golden mean.
It is a little trick to push the viewer's
eye around the picture.
This is one of six paintings for the
Caltex calendar commission, painted
in Entebbe, Uganda.

I am posting this for interest, as it is not the best painting.
There are so many friends here. Monica (the Troup family's
wonderful ayah) is dead-centre, controlling everyone as
she used to do. My children Fabian and Mia, the entire
Troup clan, Polly, Nancy, Texas and their mum Marjorie,
Sally my sister and Alan my husband, in the foreground.
Holidays on Diani Beach, south of Mombasa were the best.
Much later Monica came into my studio, put her hands on
her hips, exactly like here, and said, 'Is that me, Mrs Collis?'
All of us suffered the most terrible grief when she died,
she was one of the most wonderful people in the world.

FAMILY HOLIDAY

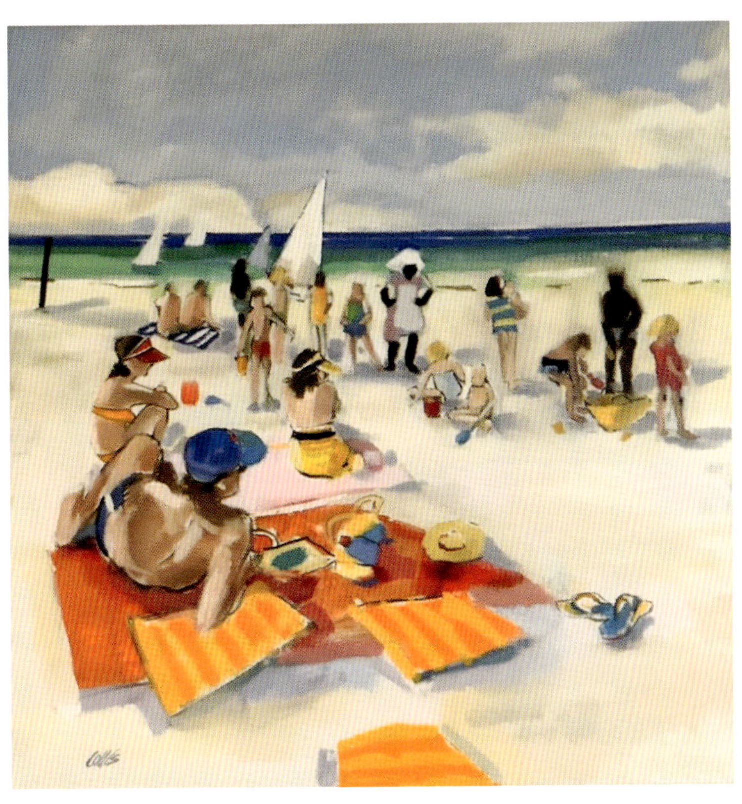

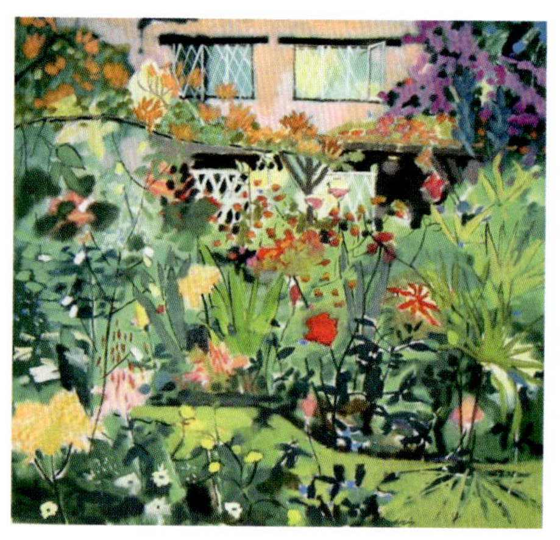

JACKIE MCCONNELL'S GARDEN

I was lucky to paint in Jackie's garden for about
two years before she so sadly died of cancer.
Her garden was unique and quite unlike any
other. It was an organised jungle of exotica and
plants of great rarity mixed in with the common.
Here there are two loose horizontals, to give some
order to the complete chaos, and the red rose at
the golden section (both ways) gives a focal point.
I like the bougainvillea in the top right corner,
a complicated colour to paint.
It reminds me of Nietzsche: 'Without chaos we
cannot give birth to a dancing star.' Words of
great comfort which are appropriate to all of us at
this unprecedented moment in time.

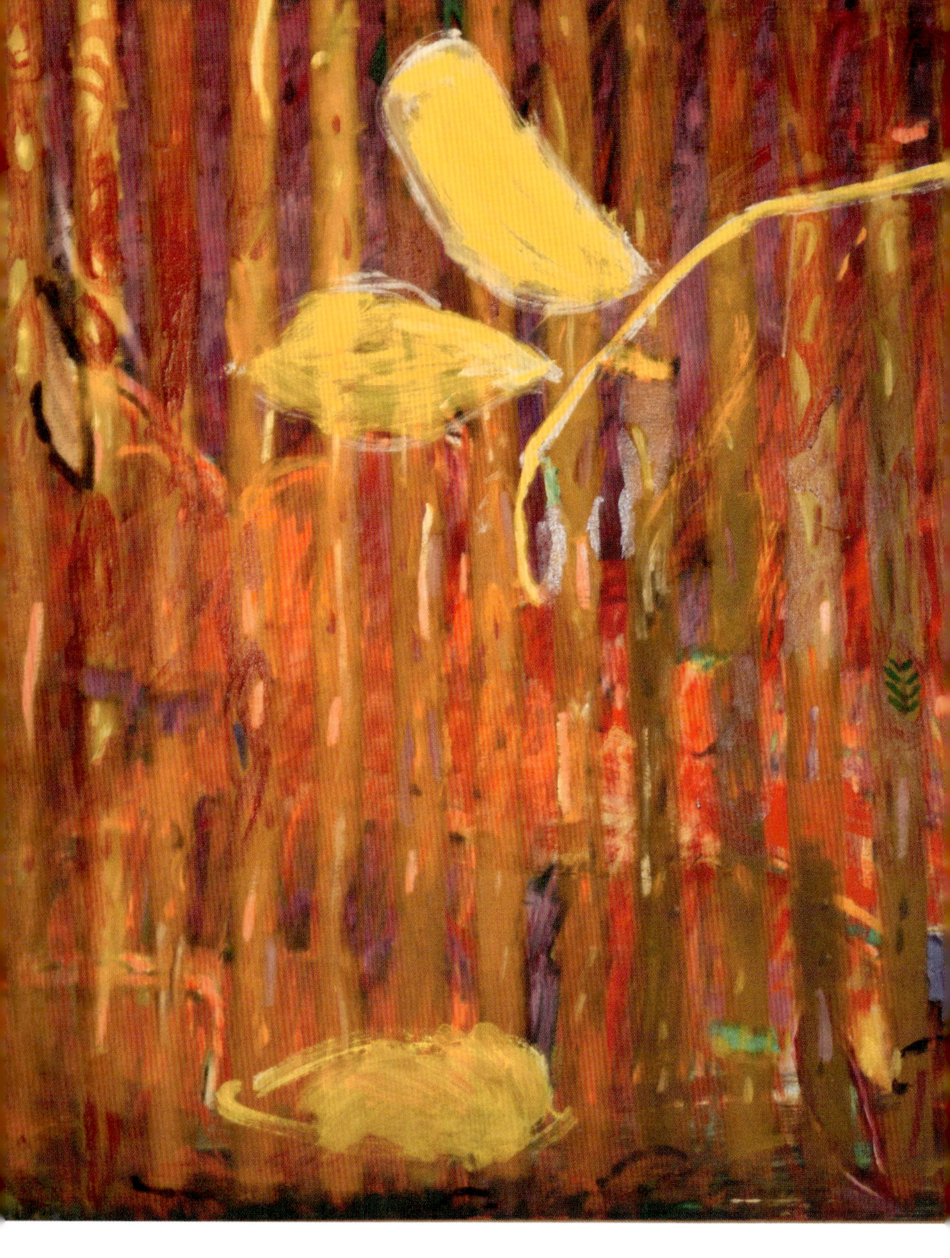

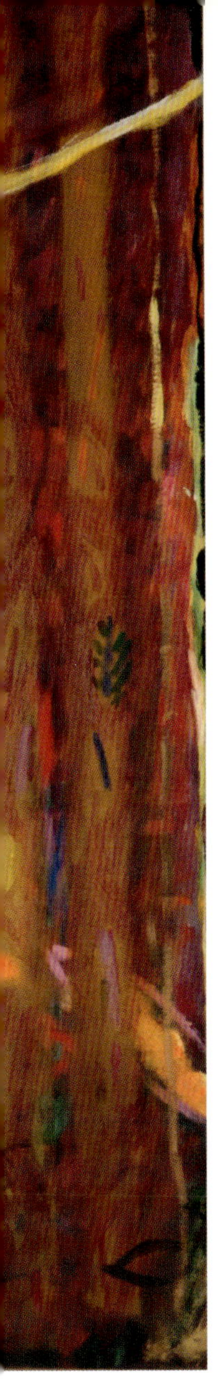

Day 15

Autumn at Monticello

I was travelling in the back of a car
from Washington, DC to Charlottesville,
Virginia. Being an African, I had never
seen such an autumn before. This was my
impression of the colour as we whizzed by
the beech and oak trees. Overwhelming
red, oranges and yellows passed at great
speed. I added the large yellow frond
much later, a memory of swishing through
the leaves as we walked round the outside
of Monticello, Thomas Jefferson's house in
Albemarle County.

My travelling companion, Doria Block,
swapped this painting with me for one of
her Ellsworth Kelly lithographs. She left it
back to me in her will. I've had it printed
on to silk organza and made into scarves,
and so I quite often wear it.

The painting now resides in my home
and reminds me of my great friend Doria.

Day 16

Bollywood is the title of this diptych.
Sometimes the size of the painting
grows as it is being worked on and
another canvas alongside becomes
necessary. I was thinking of Henri
Matisse and his cut-out *L'escargot*
(*The Snail*). I saw it for real in the Tate
and realised that Matisse adds a bit of
'ugly' to his works, which enhances his
colours. The background colour here
is made up from all the sediment that
falls to the bottom of the jar when one
cleans the brushes in turpentine.
I think it enlivens the pure colours
and makes them dance. They most
definitely move about when looking
at the large canvas, like a dance scene
in a Bollywood film. This coming week
is about my abstracts.

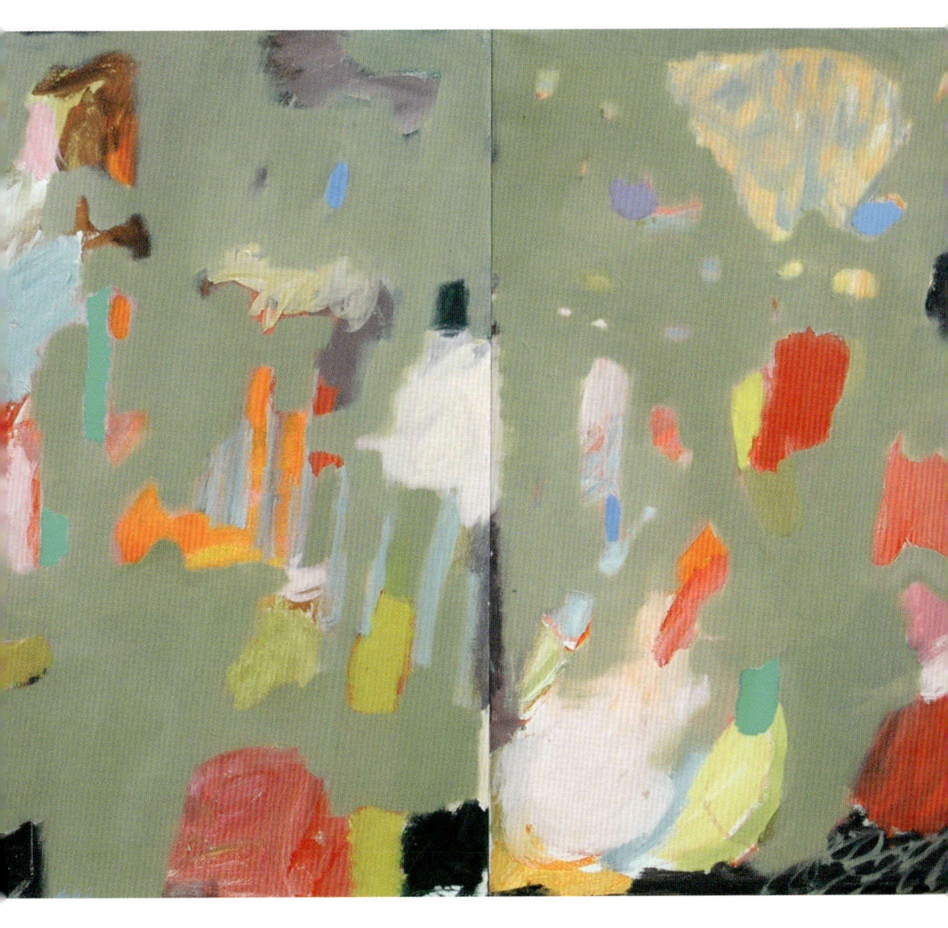

Day 17

50 Shades of Matrimony

I have so many gold tubes, pots
and jars of different golden
colours, I thought I would use
the whole lot in one painting.
I am unsure if this work is
finished. However, I did show
it at our Golden Wedding lunch
celebration. Our great friend,
the Safari guide and raconteur,
Don Young, gave this painting
its clever title, perfect for the
occasion. He was guest of
honour at the lunch and spoke
about the great romances of
East Africa: Isabel and Richard
Burton, Samuel and Florence
Baker. The painting has a life of
its own. It changes at different
times of the day and night,
depending on the light.

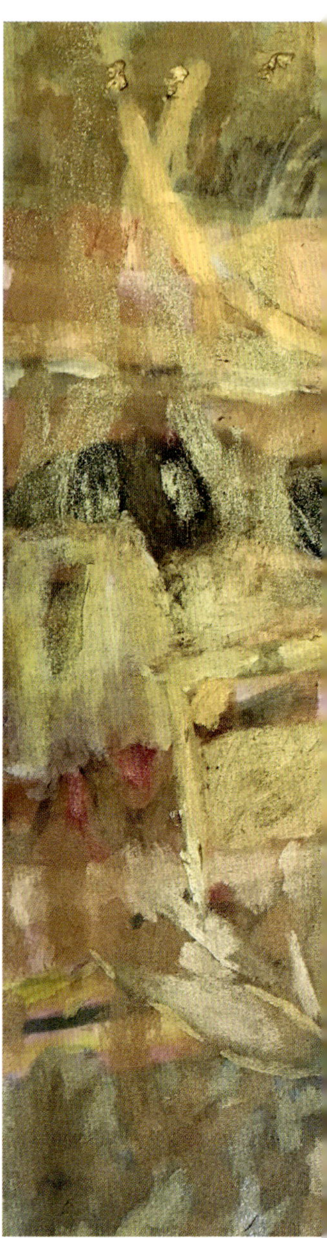

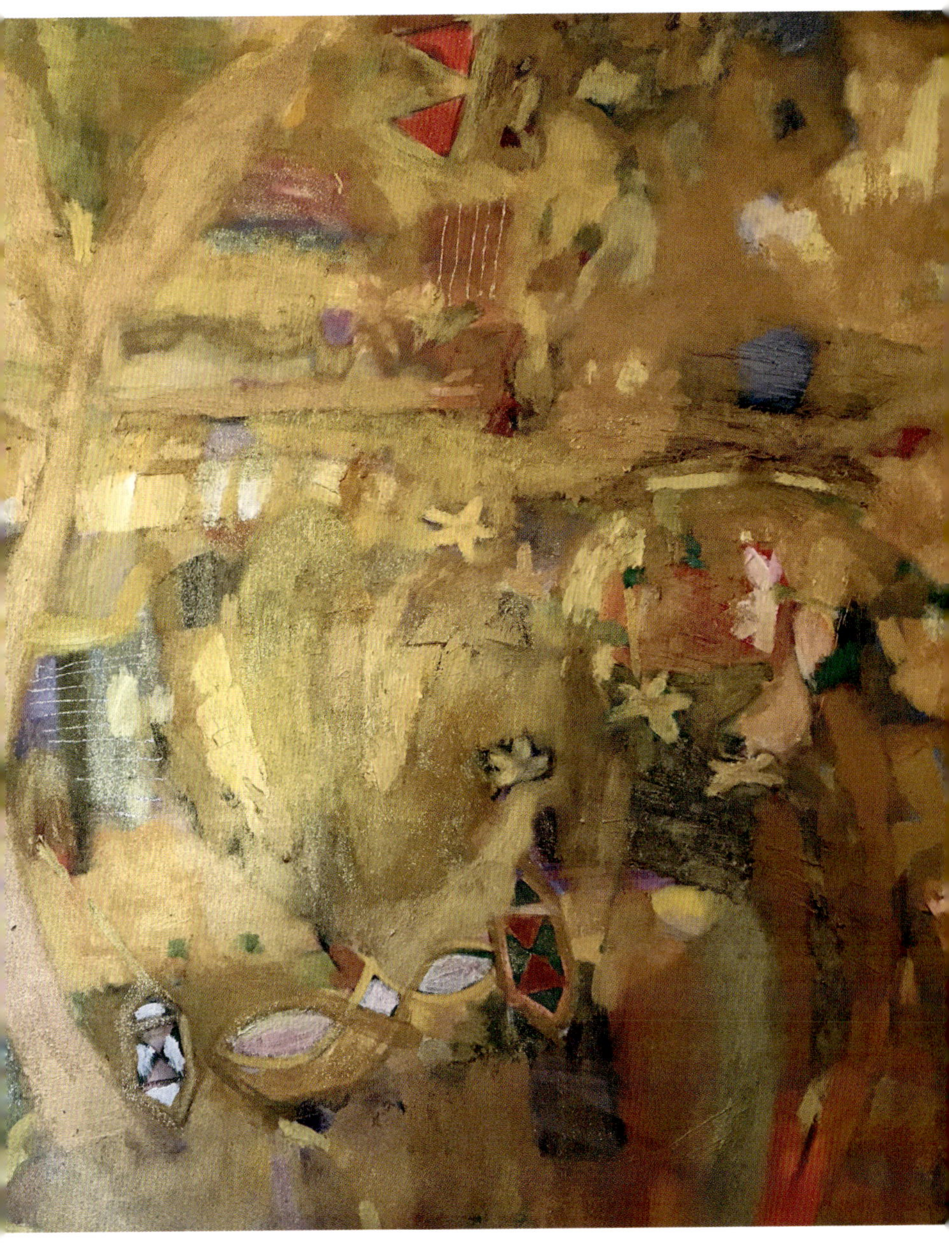

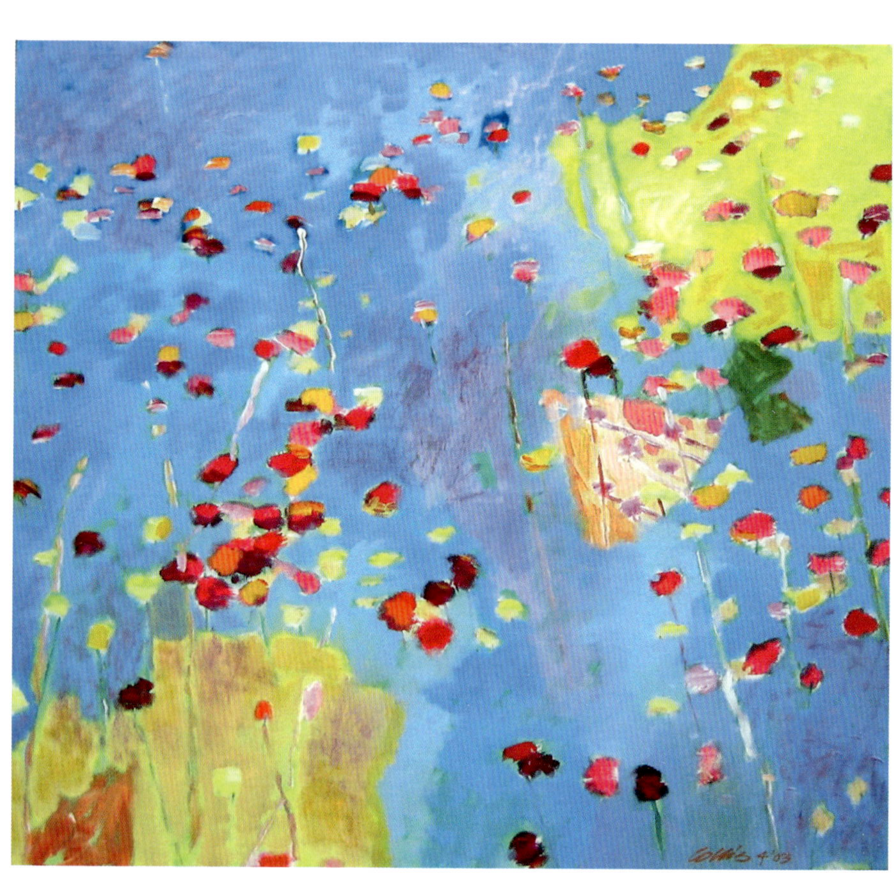

Day 18

Roses over the Tigris

This was painted on the day that George
Bush and 'company' went to war with Iraq
over the 'weapons of mass destruction'
accusations. Half-a-million American
families have lost a loved one so far.
It is appropriate for our present situation,
with the Coronavirus pandemic.
The composition was inspired by a lovely
painting that I admired but unfortunately
cannot remember where. It was quickly
bought by the collector Anis Pringle,
who has many of my works.

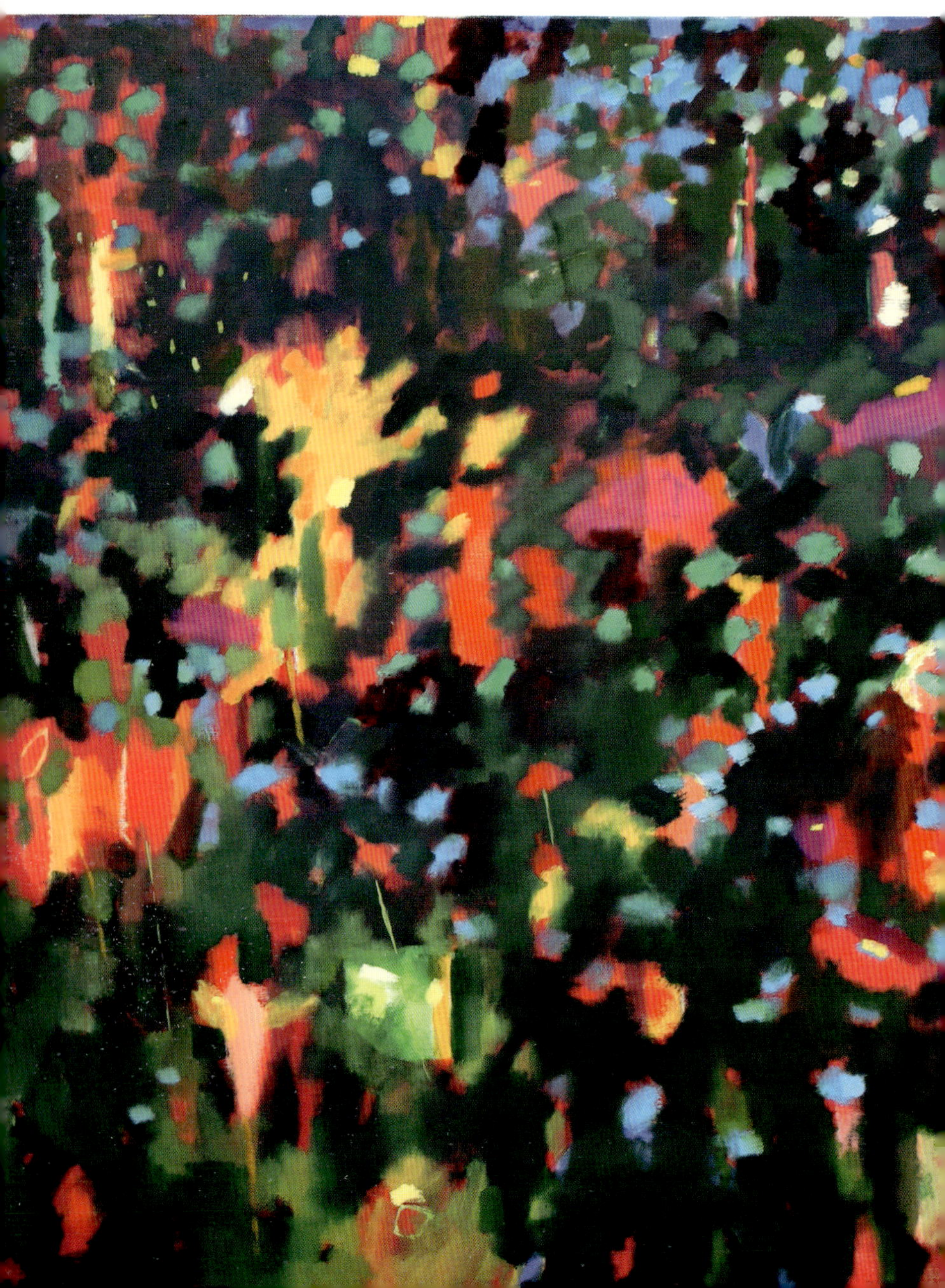

Day 19

Midnight Shamba

This one probably does not really belong in this week's category of Abstracts'. Not much about it really. 'Shamba' is a Swahili word for garden. I was painting in a shady garden which suddenly went into deep shadow in the late afternoon, and so I began painting out the colour with deep viridian and Hooker's greens. In reality, the colour disappeared completely in the shadows, I hadn't the heart to lose it all. There is a loose horizon, one-third from the top of this painting, where it changes focus and gives the work its stability.

Day 20

This is the first painting I have shown
from the massive series, 'False Bay', which
currently comprises about 600 small works
of both paintings and photographs. I work
on these paintings when I am in South
Africa overlooking the beautiful False Bay.
I have very ambitious plans for the series.
I am showing this now because it resides
in Nairobi in the eminent collection of
Frank Whalley, the much admired and
erudite art critic in Kenya.
My ambition for this serious sequence
(as I regard it) increased greatly with
Frank's purchase of this painting.

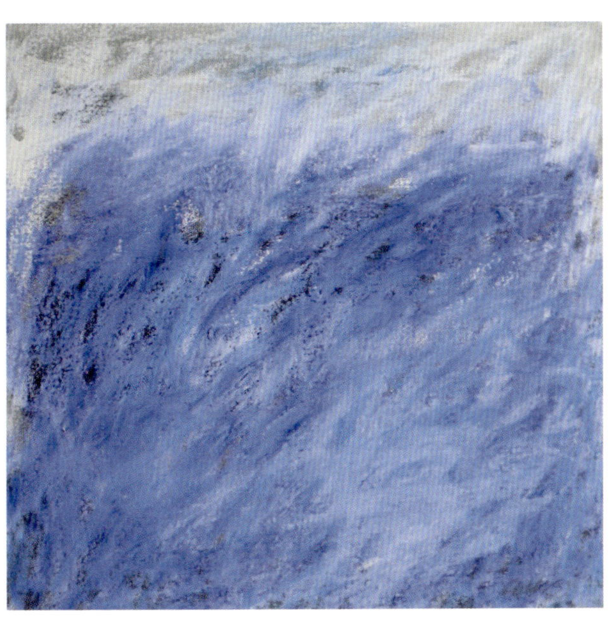

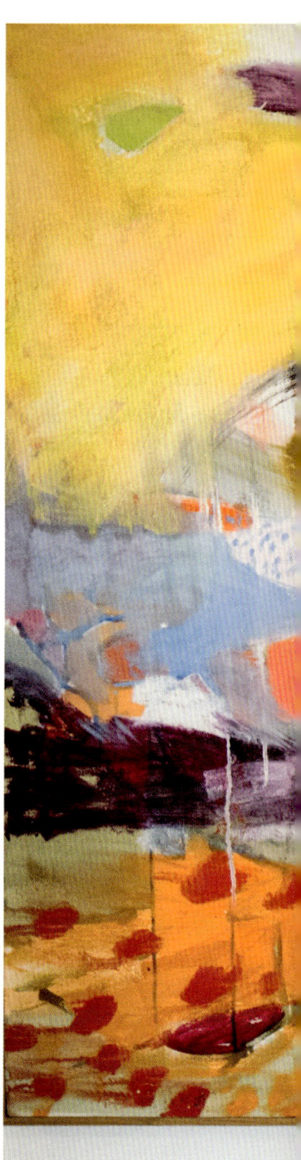

Day 21

I end the week (10 April 2020) on a personal note. This is my husband, Alan, toning in with an abstract painting *Reading*. It may be of interest to see roughly the size of the paintings that I am comfortable with. Next week will be landscapes.

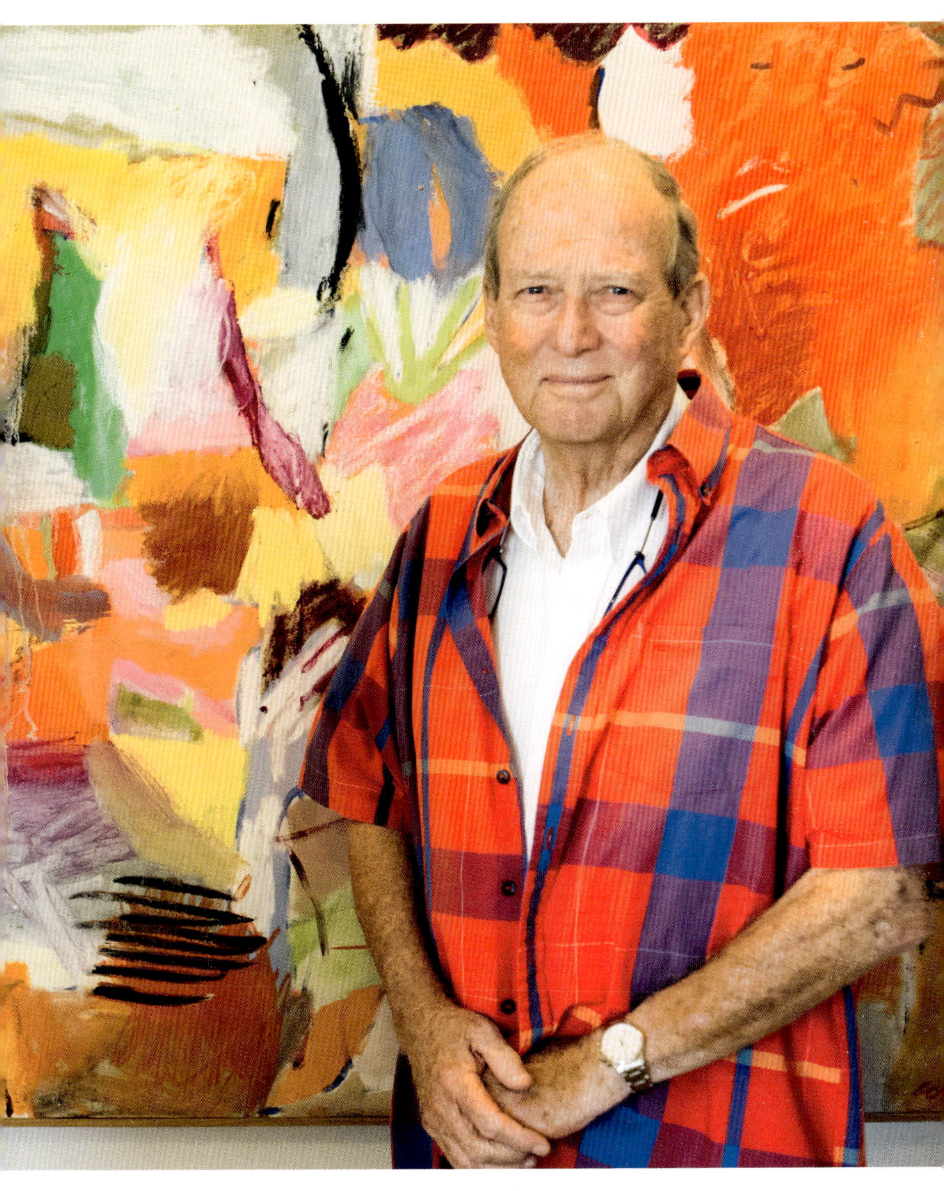

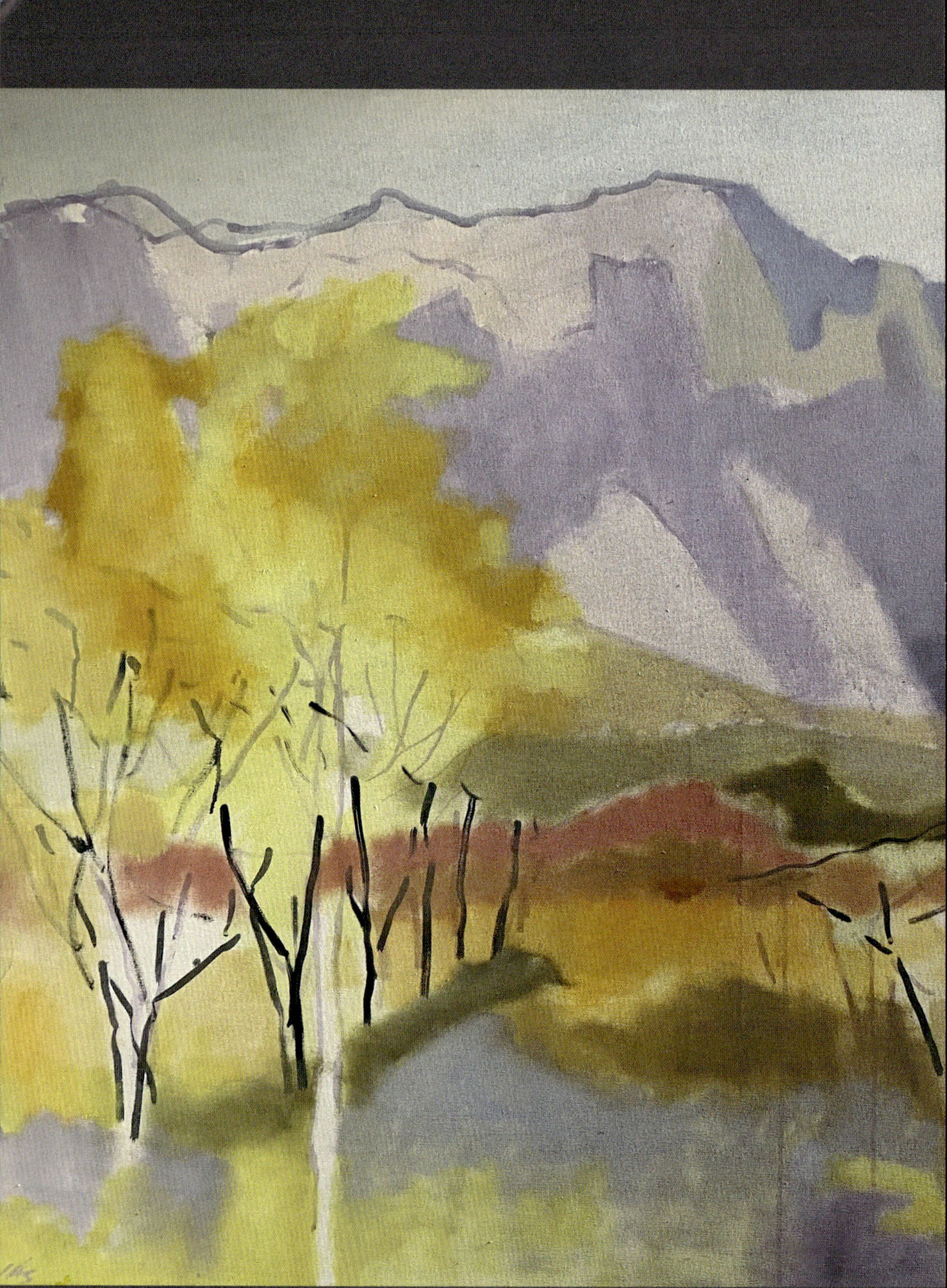

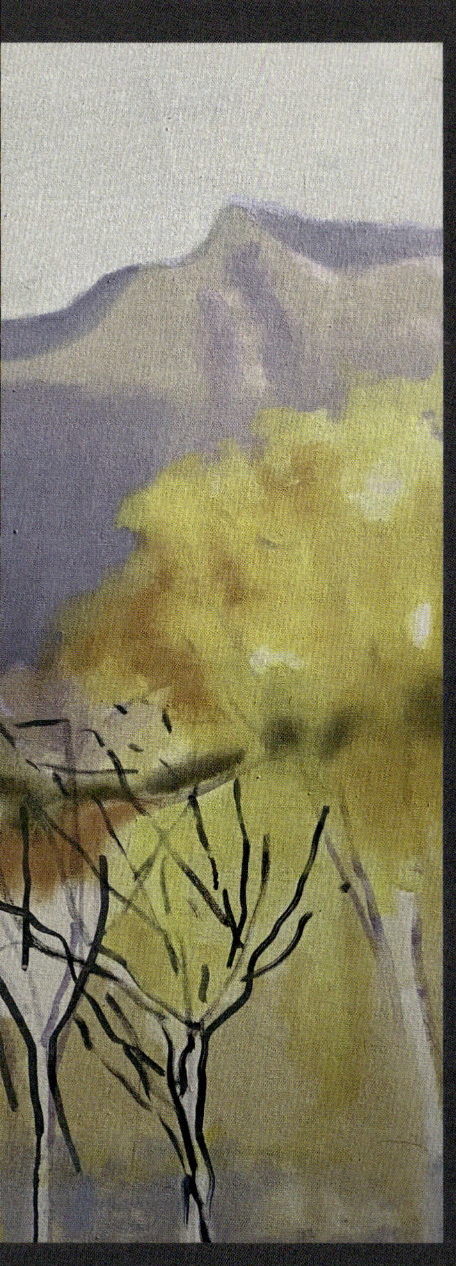

DAY 22

Views driving into Cape Town
from the south along the M3
between Wynberg and Claremont.
A rehash from many photographs
and memory. The colours in this
temperate climate are much
softer than on the equator.
This is going into autumn.
The collector Thomas Wright
bought this painting from my
studio; he liked the fact that it
was slightly unfinished. He has
the largest collection of my work.

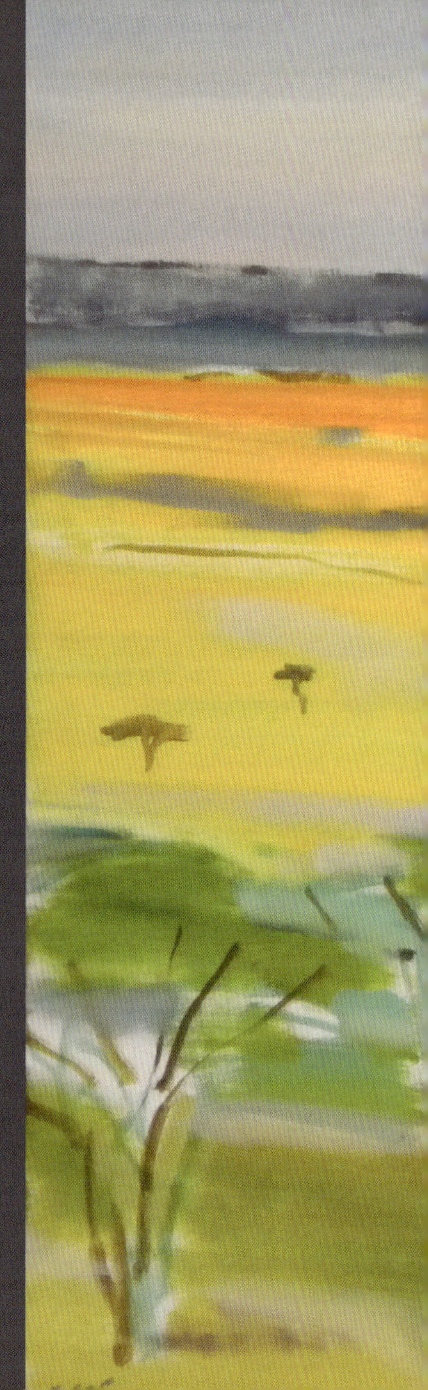

DAY 23

A beautiful early morning in Lewa.

*'Cadmium and translucent
Indian are splendid glowing
yellows, invaluable for such
subjects as a gorgeous sunrise.'*
Alexander Theroux

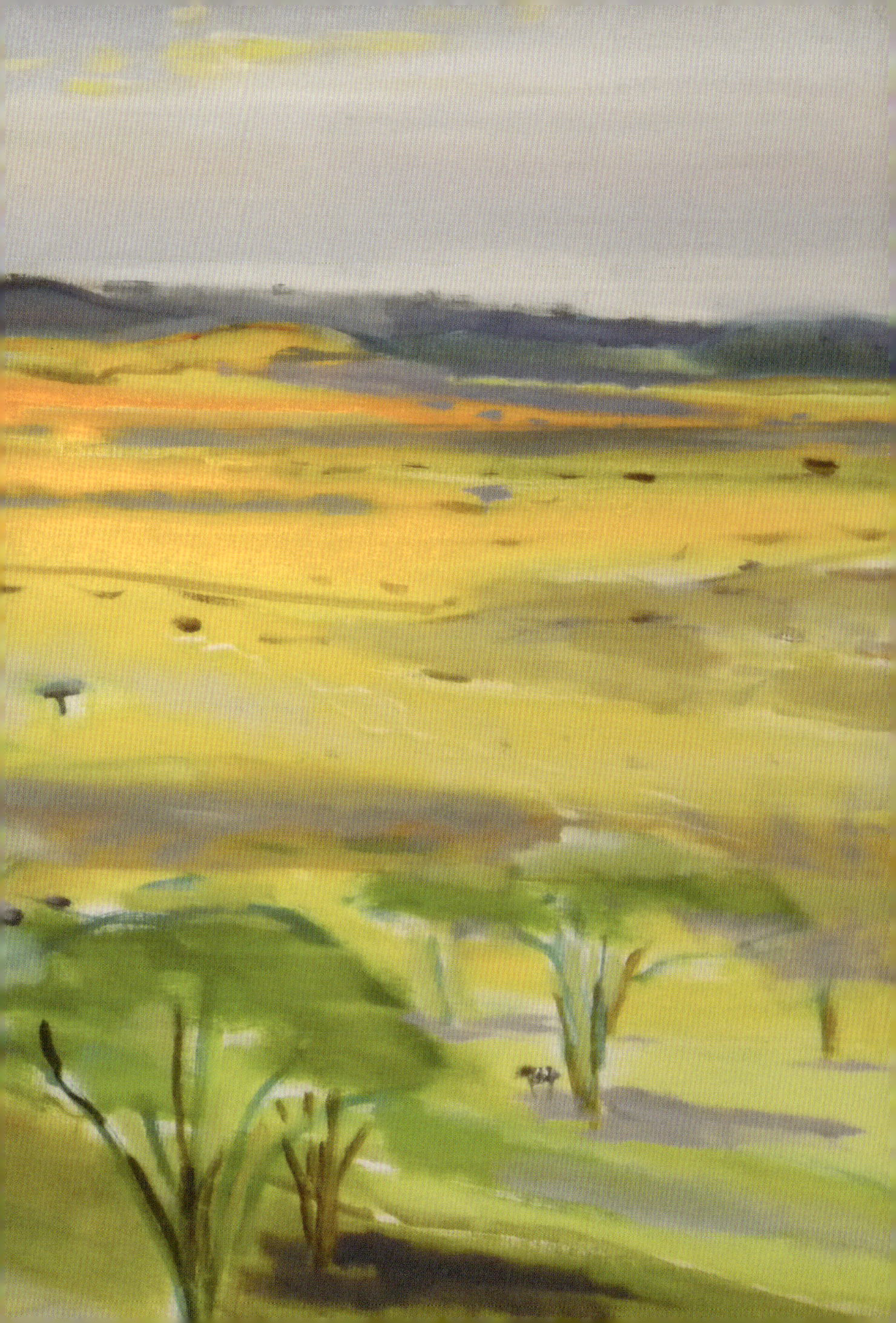

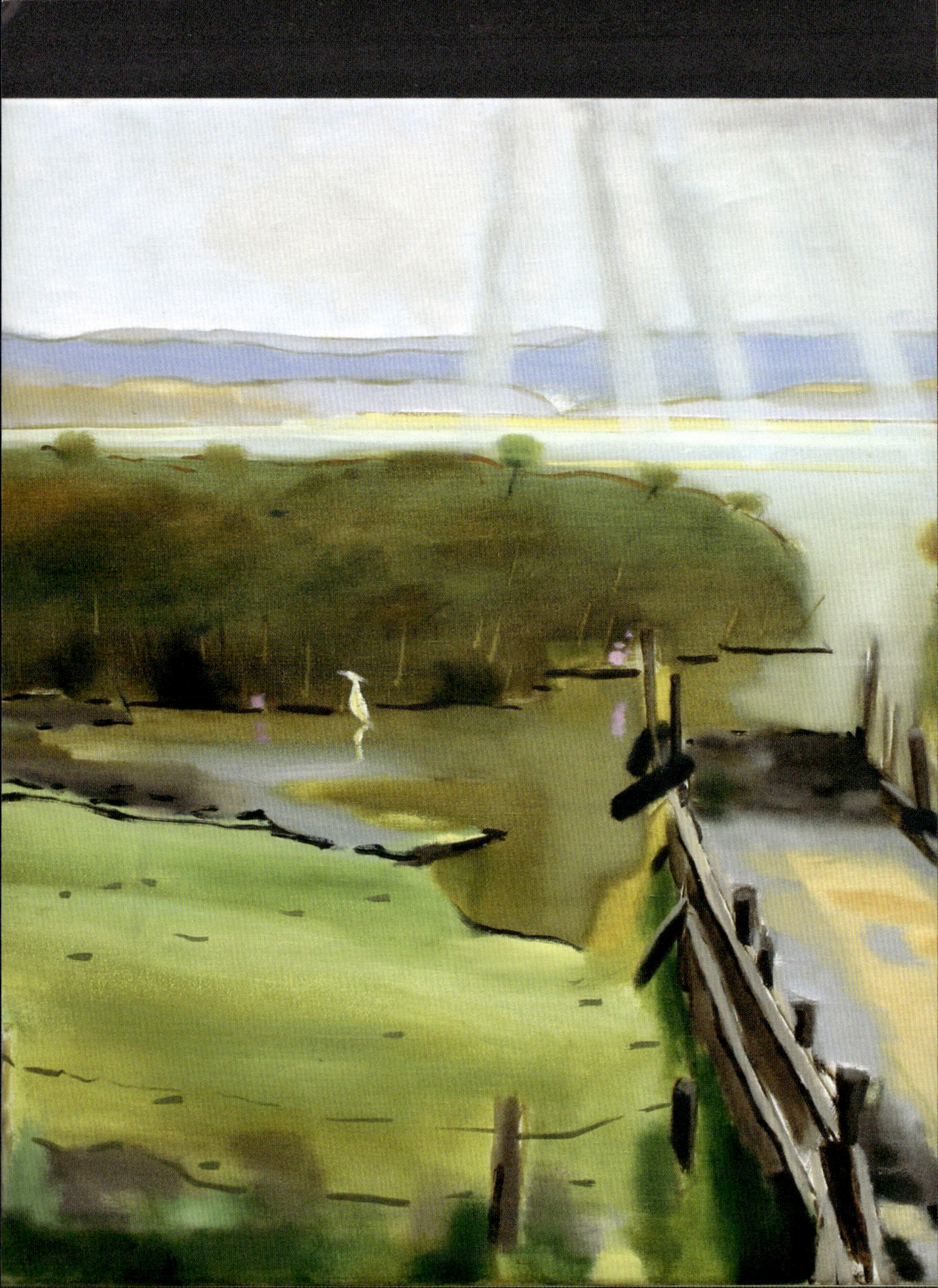

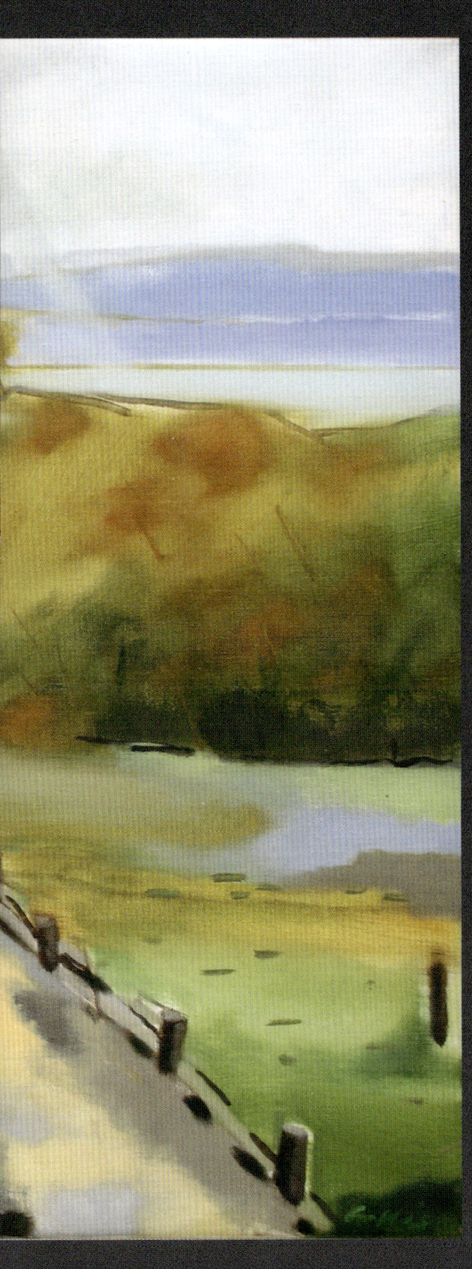

DAY 24
JACK'S JETTY

Lake Naivasha in the very early morning, with the sun's rays in the gap and the foreground yet to light up. The birds are there in the shadows awaiting breakfast. This is a favourite spot of mine, I have painted often from here. I will show more of them in the coming days.

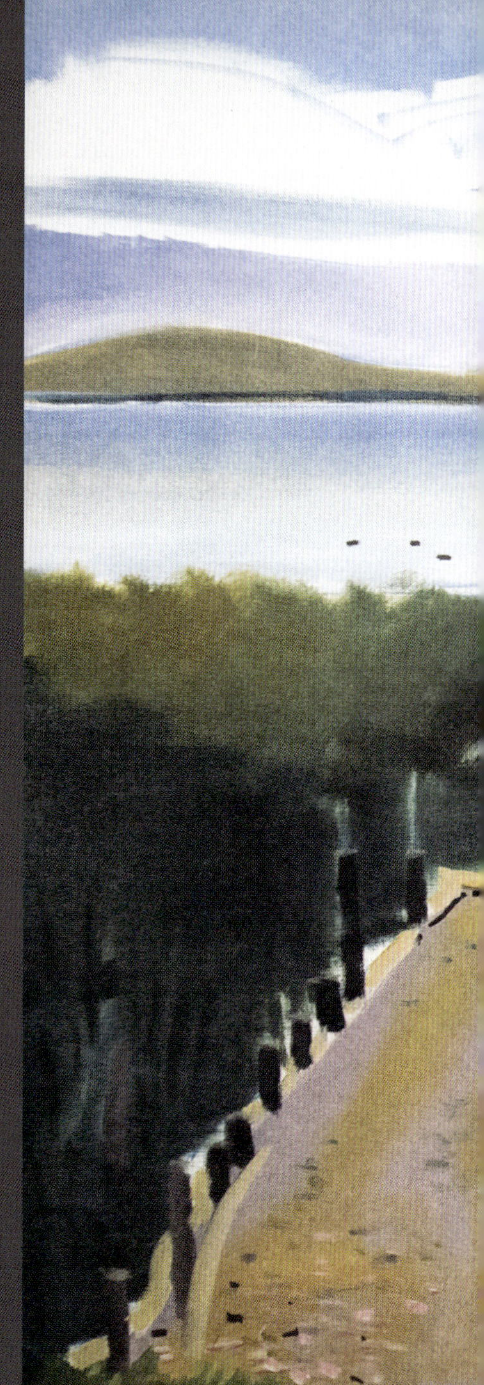

DAY 25

Jack's Jetty again, with the jetty on the left, at midday, when we stand on our shadows. This was another of the Caltex calendar pictures. One of my children pointed out that I had missed the hippos, so the little spots in the lake were quickly dotted in with a long paintbrush whilst she watched.

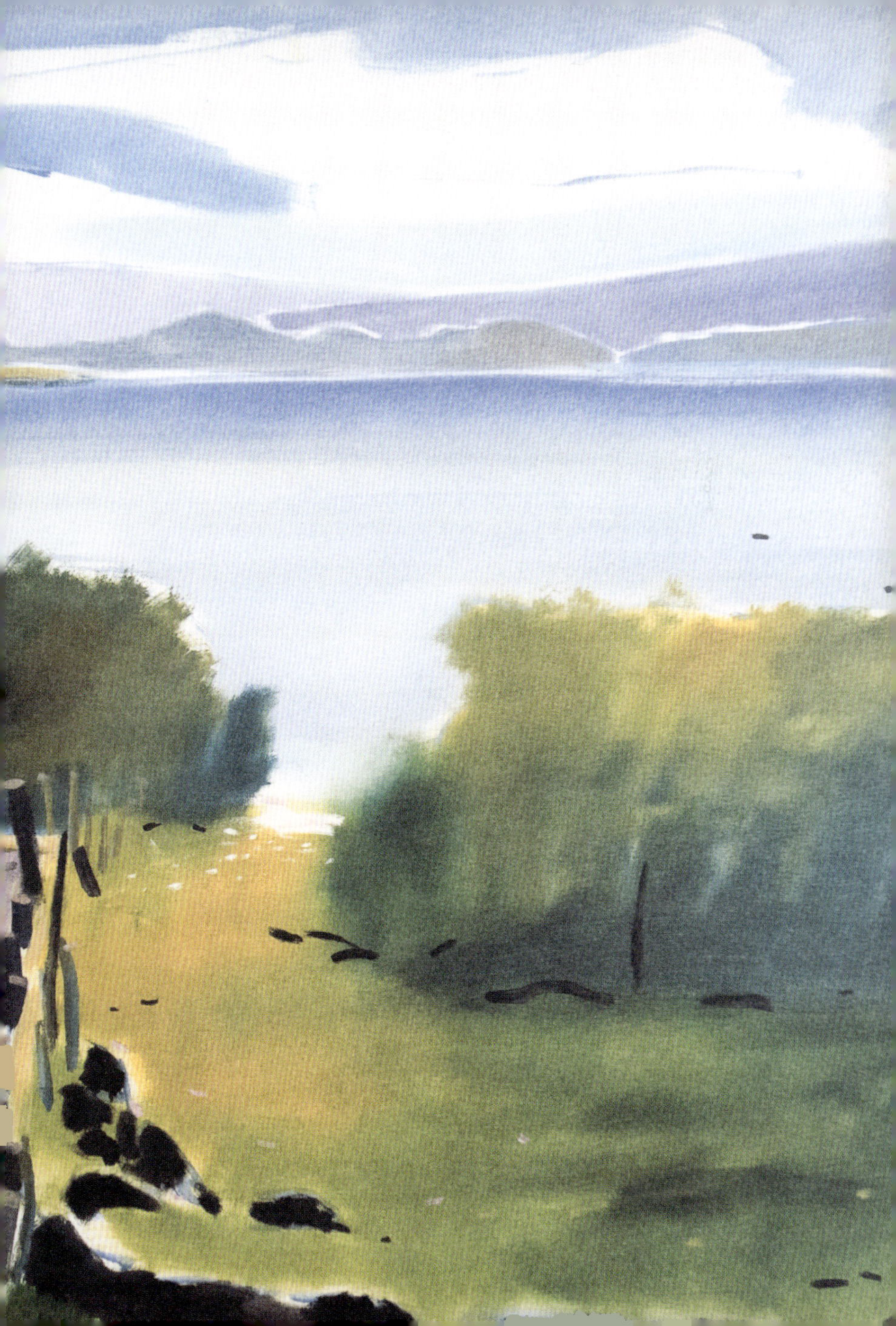

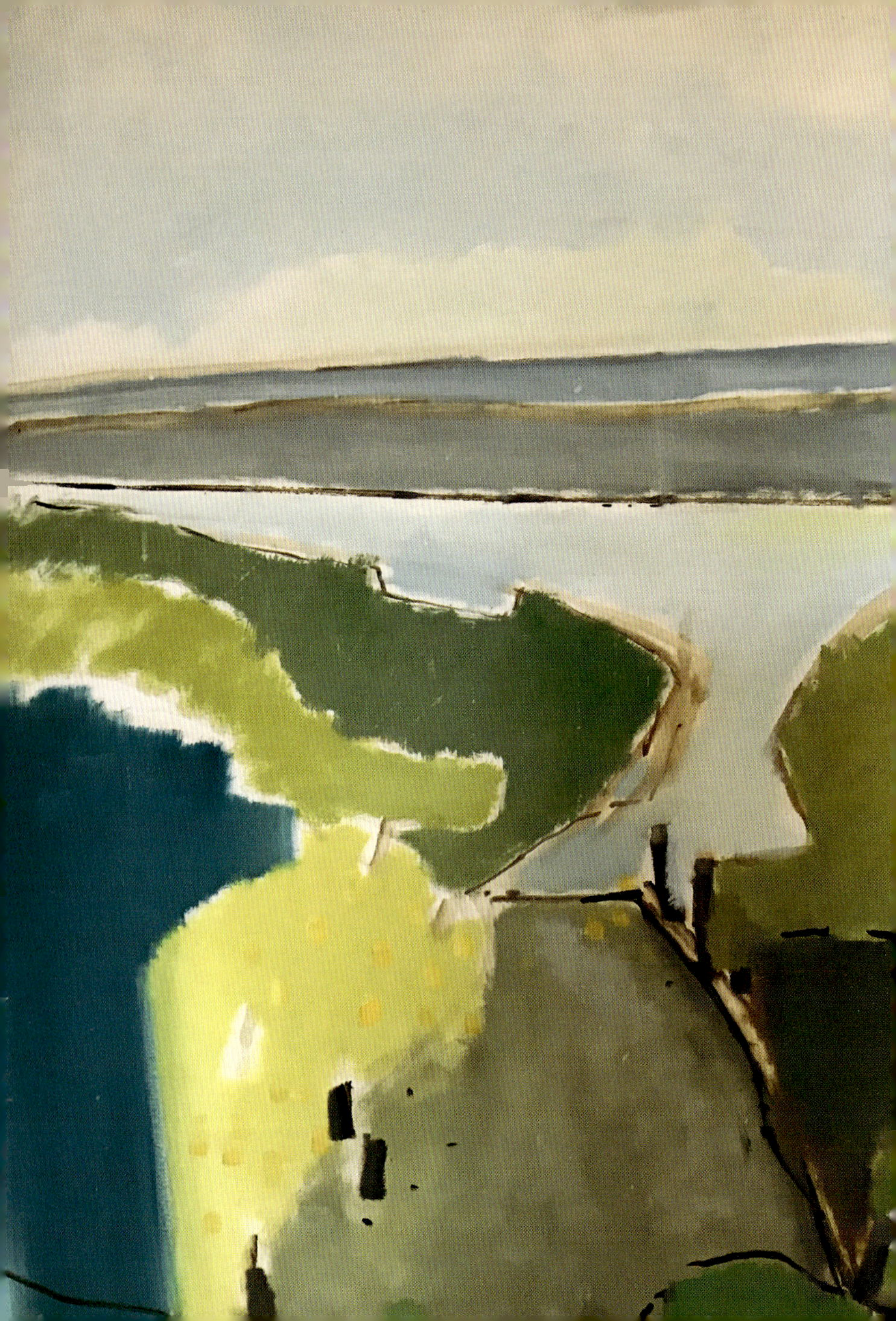

DAY 26

Jack's Jetty again. Milton Avery is one of my very favourite of painters and one of America's great artists. He influenced Rothko and was a friend to all the Abstract Expressionists whilst remaining committed to representation. I often think about him and when I am completely familiar with a view like this one, I can approach it differently, thinking entirely about shape and composition. After Avery died, his wife Sally remarked that one tube of every colour had lasted his whole life. Doria Block bought this painting and left it back to me when she died. She also bought me the most comprehensive book on Milton Avery's work and life. She was the most wonderful friend to me and I miss her and our conversations about art and music. This was the view of Lake Naivasha from the bottom of her garden.

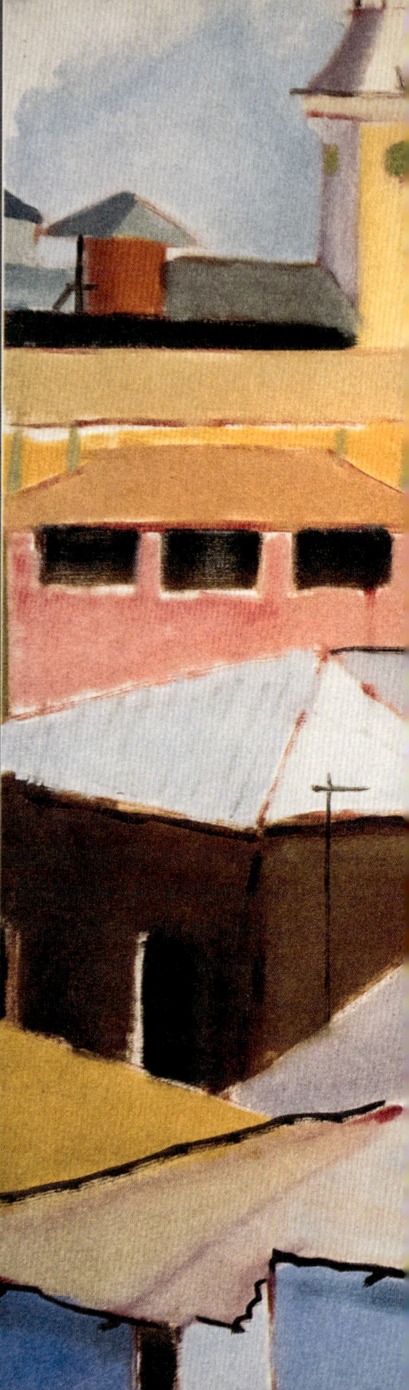

DAY 27
THE HOUSE OF WONDERS, ZANZIBAR

The Caltex calendar commission. Painted from the rooftop of Emersons in Stone Town. I spent four days up there, so there are a few paintings with different views from that spot. My travel agent, Glynn Rogers, came with me. Zanzibar was emerging from years of a communist government that had almost shut down the whole of Tanzania. I remember listening to the music of hammers and whistling and a happiness of hope, even though it was so different to my memories as a child, being taken through the 'gold bazaar' by my father Bernard Kampf. The tiny little gold shops were exotic, as we weaved our way through the winding streets. The goldsmiths weighed the gold, dripping over the display cases. A thrilling memory for a ten year old.

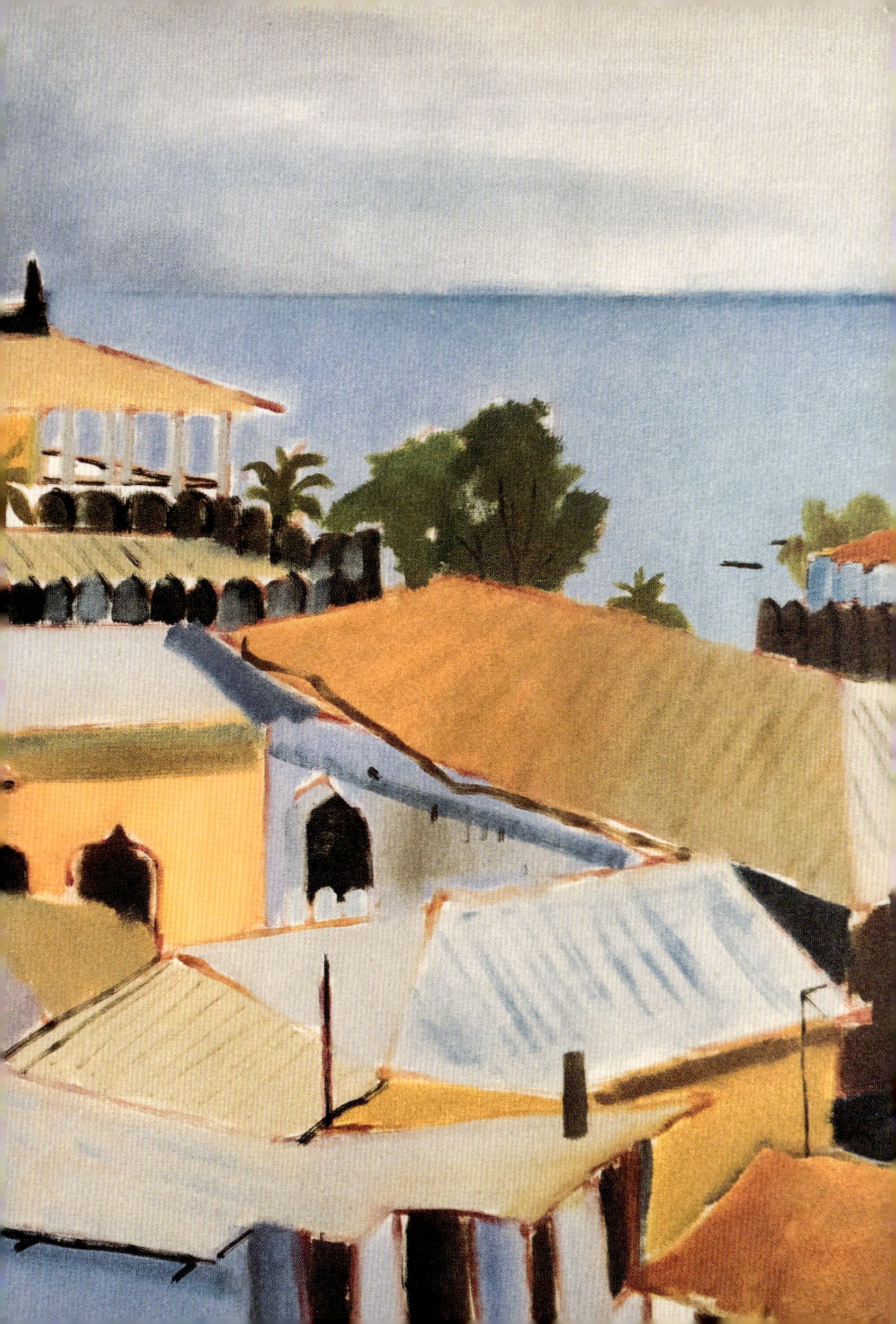

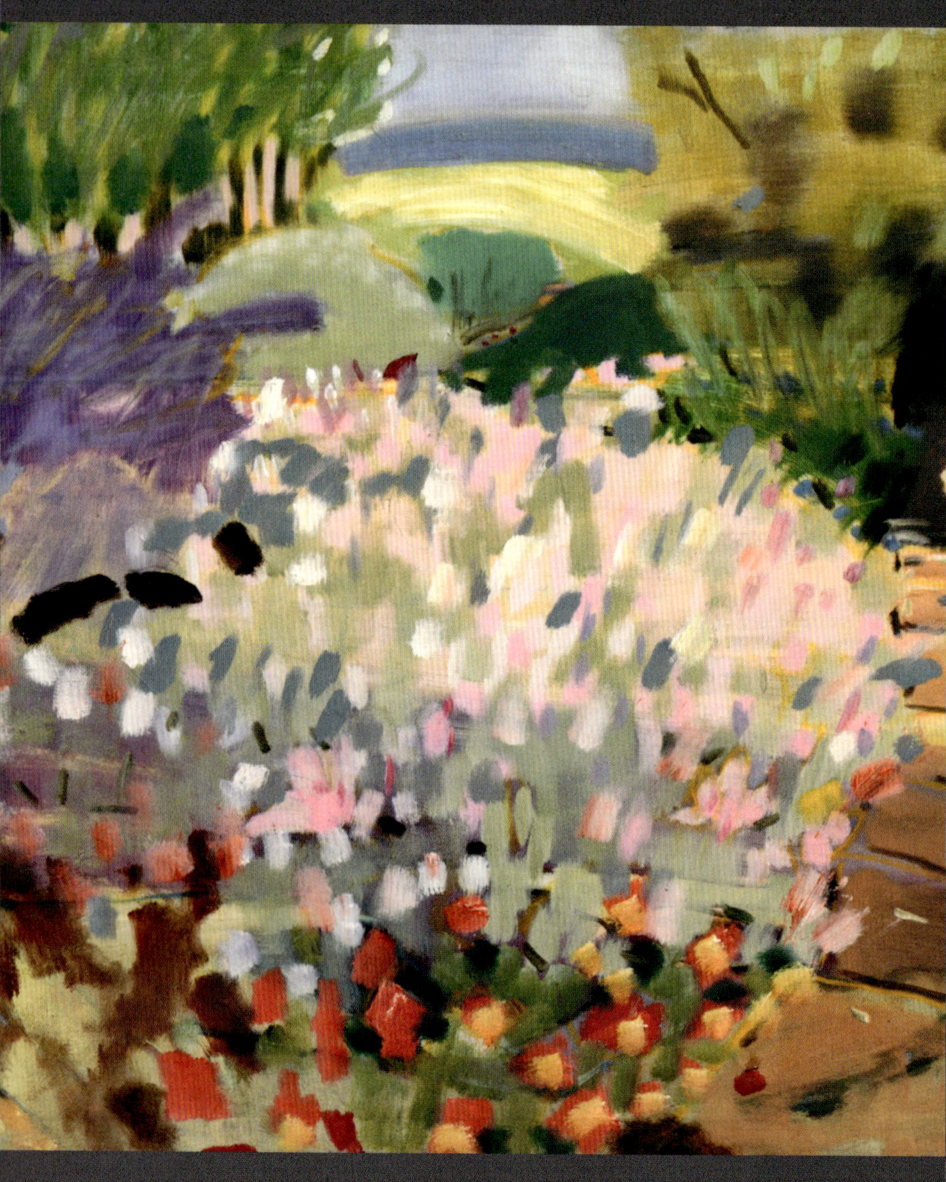

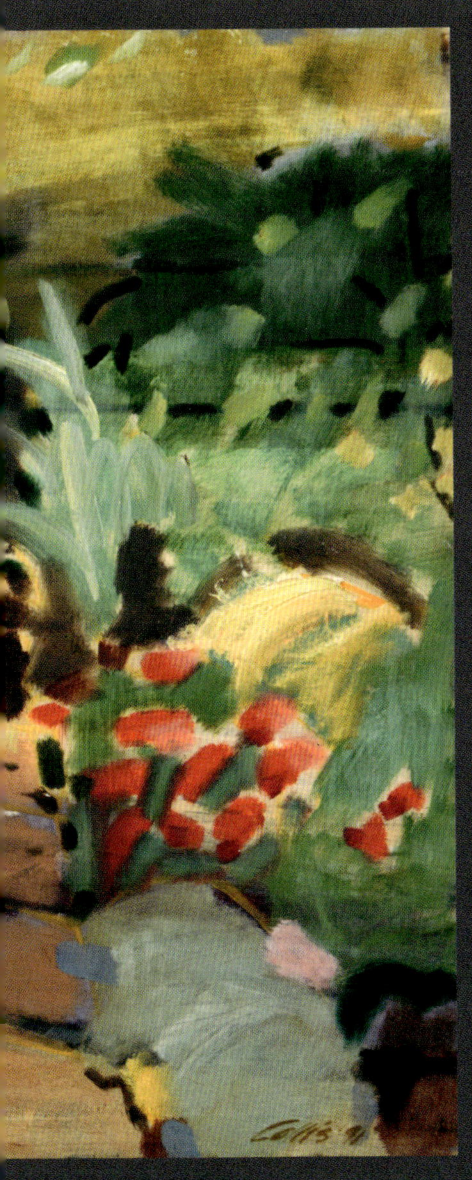

DAY 28
THE SECRET GARDEN

Painted in 1991, this is the first from the massive series called 'Erica's Garden', after Erica Boswell and her exquisite garden in Limuru. The path in this work leads to a little secret hiding hole in amongst the bushes. One of the unexpected joys I have had with this online exhibition is being in touch with long-lost friends.

Chris Whiteman owns this painting, and he sent me this perfect copy, as only he could, as he used to photograph all my work before the digital camera. He lives in England now and according to Facebook we share many similar observations. This is the last of the painted landscapes this week, and over the next seven days I intend to show my drawings, something that I have never done in public.

Day 29
Red Pepper

It looks like a simple drawing.
It started off as a monoprint with a
red splodge. I love that look of flat
squashed colour that a monoprint
bestows on absorbent paper. There is
always room for 'a happy accident'.
I added the green core, then the white,
still using the glass to transfer to the
paper. Lastly, I drew with a brush
directly on to the paper.
I am very fond of Ellsworth Kelly,
he was a master of the single line.
I met him once at an opening in
London and said that I had two
of his lithographs. He said, 'I had
no idea I had work in Africa.'

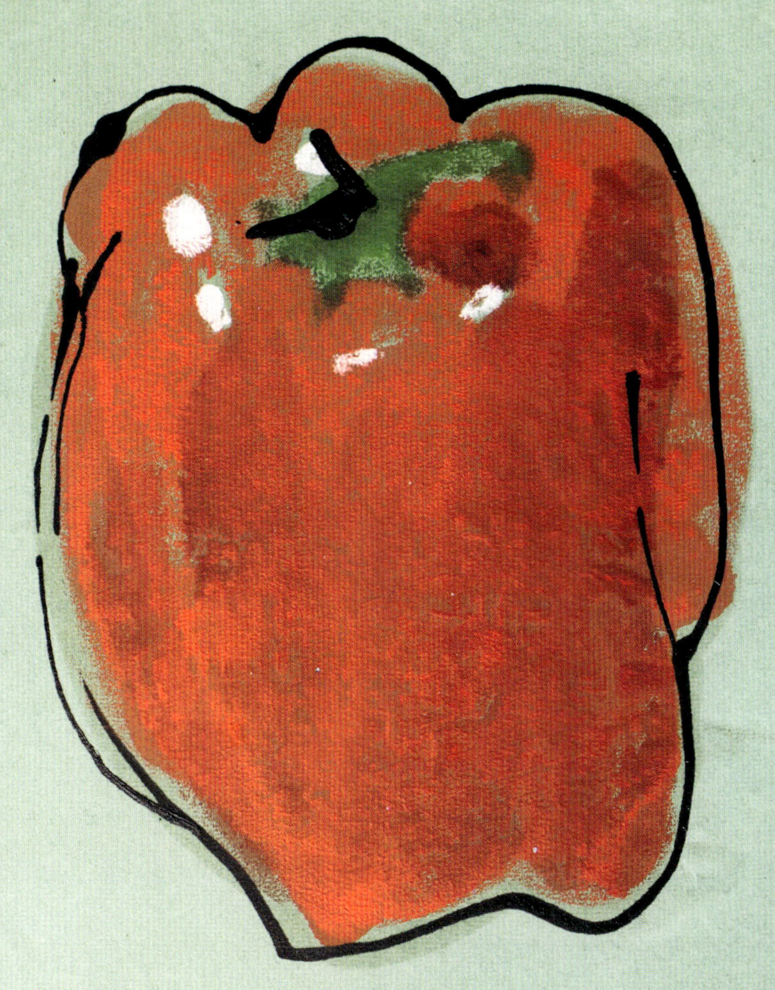

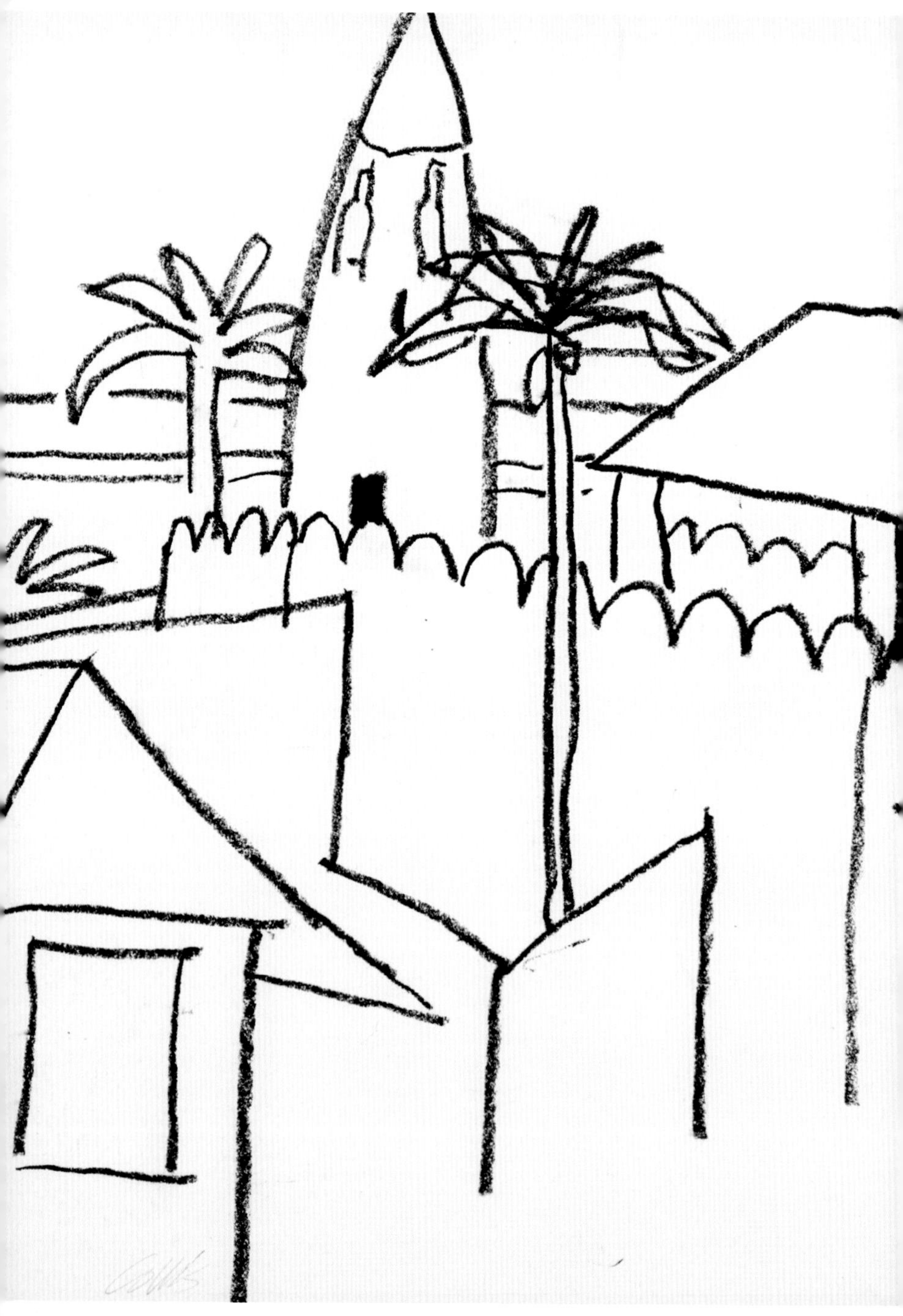

Day 30

Quick sketch of Lamu.
I like this drawing because it
adheres strictly to the golden
section in every quarter, third or
half. It is what I call one of those
lucky accidents.
I like the messy palm tree, as it
gives some relief from the line.
I believe composition is the single
most important feature for any
work on paper or canvas.

Day 31
Pansies in a Box

I was excited when these pansies arrived, I had to draw them before planting. I squared up the large handmade paper, expecting to get perhaps a few works out of the project. It did not happen. I rarely plan successfully. Now, looking at it years later, perhaps it was a good idea? This is an enormous drawing, which was rescued by Mia who stopped me making a bonfire of the drawings when we were moving house. My darling daughter documented everything with her camera. There was so much unseen work. It took her a week to photograph it all and number it. A labour of love. It is still in storage.

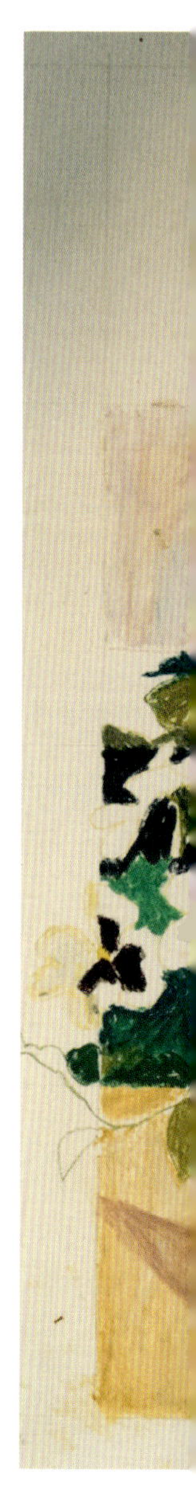

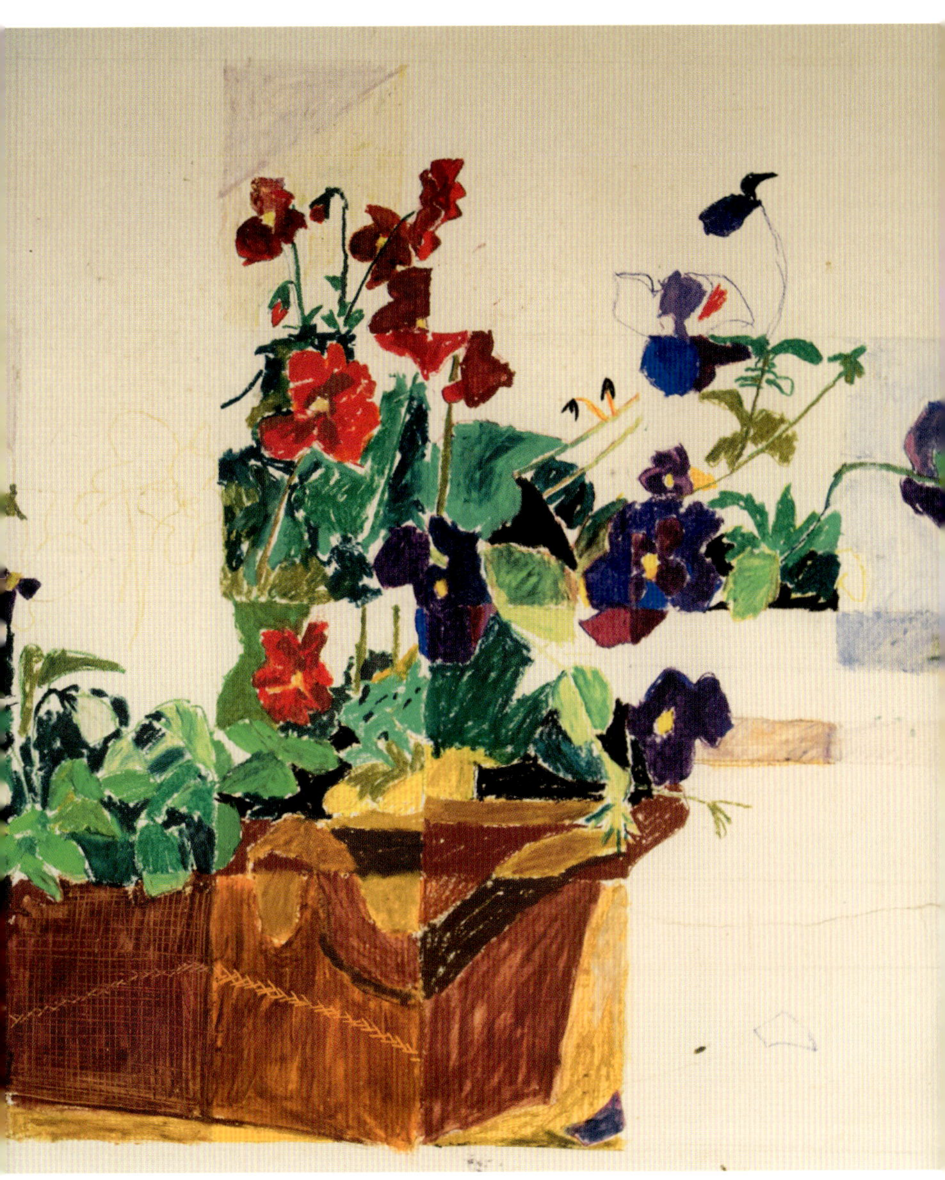

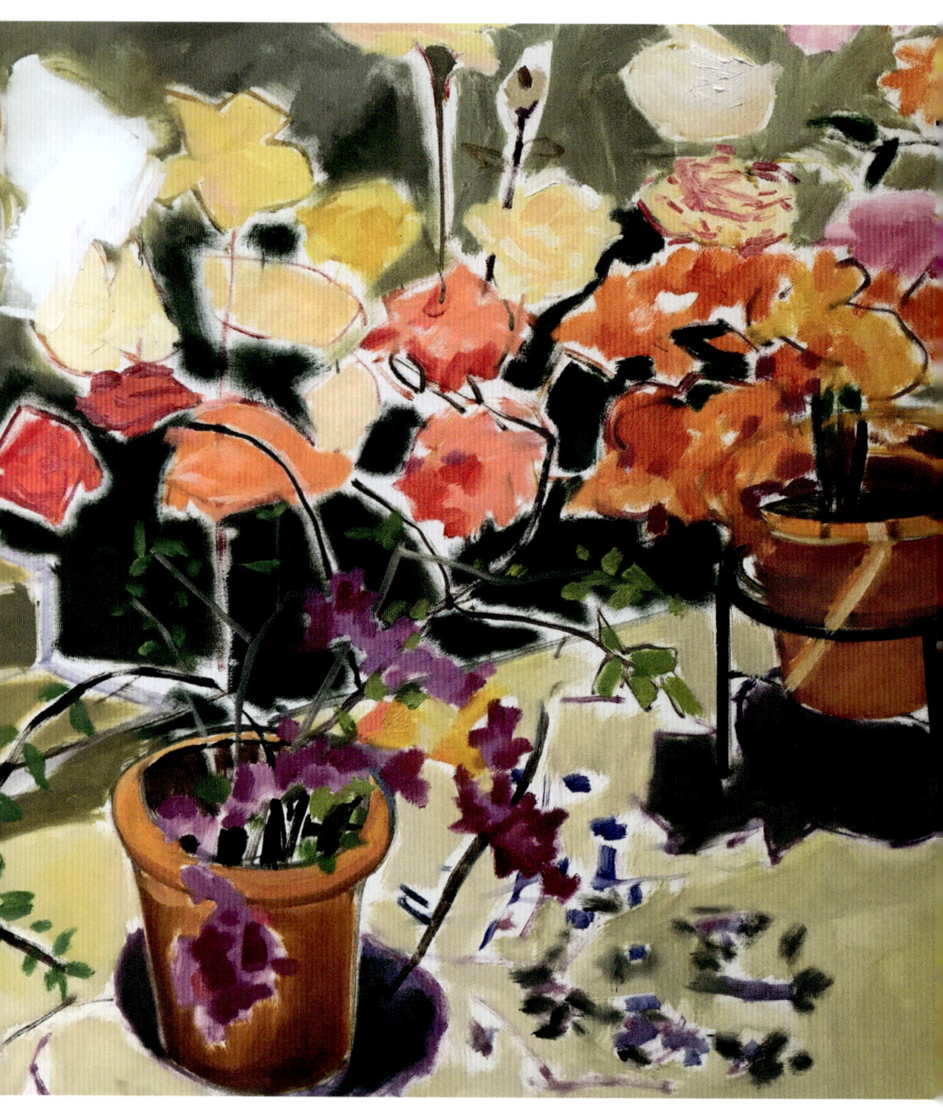

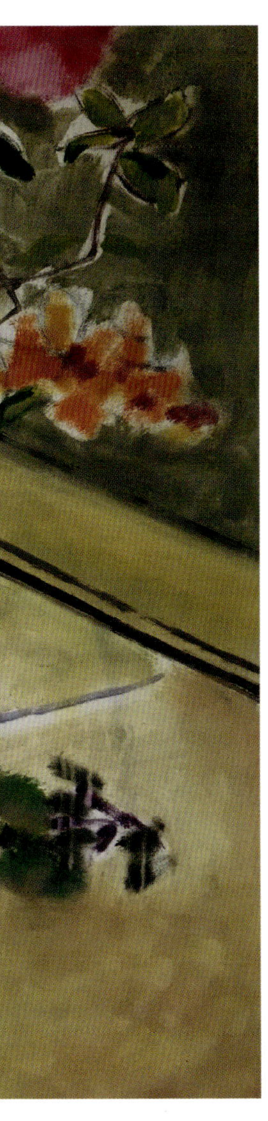

Day 32
Pots and Pinks

Pots and pinks and the importance
of getting the drawing right for a
painting. I use a very long brush
to draw, the length of two brushes
so that I can stand well away from
the canvas – about 3 ft with the
extension of my arm. I liked the
drawing aspect of this work, so left
the painting mid-way, although the
subject really was the colour.
It was a difficult view, looking down
on the paving stones. The roses were
grown by my daughter-in-law Jilna.
She has green fingers, among
her many talents.
The painting is in my studio.

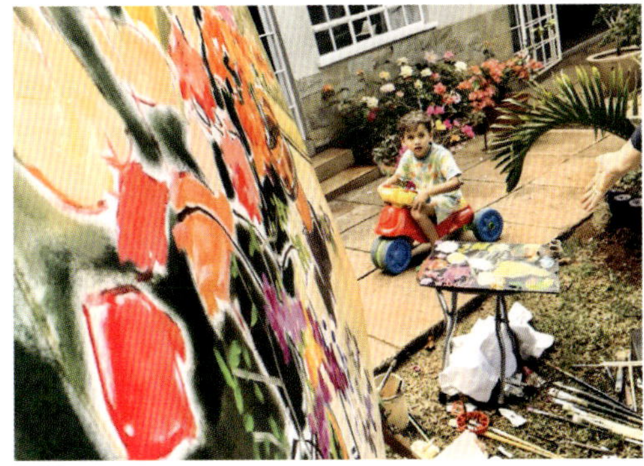

Day 33
Untitled drawing

I was thinking of Josef Albers and his series 'Homage to the Square', in particular, *Ascending*, where the yellow square ascends into the blue, although his yellow starts lower on the page and there are two blues and an off-white that draws the colour up. I like to think that the top of this yellow table recedes, giving the drawing a perspective.

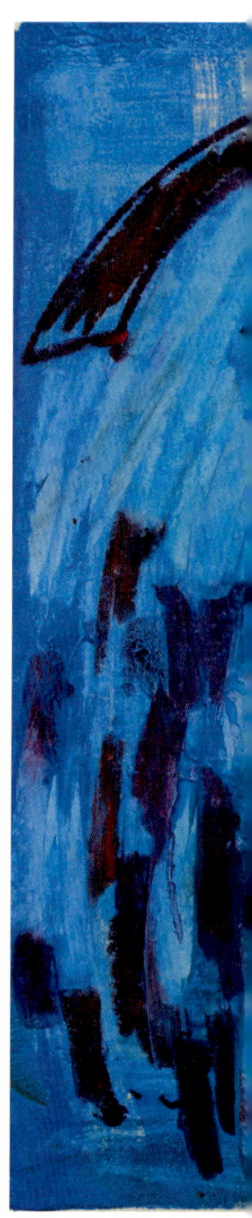

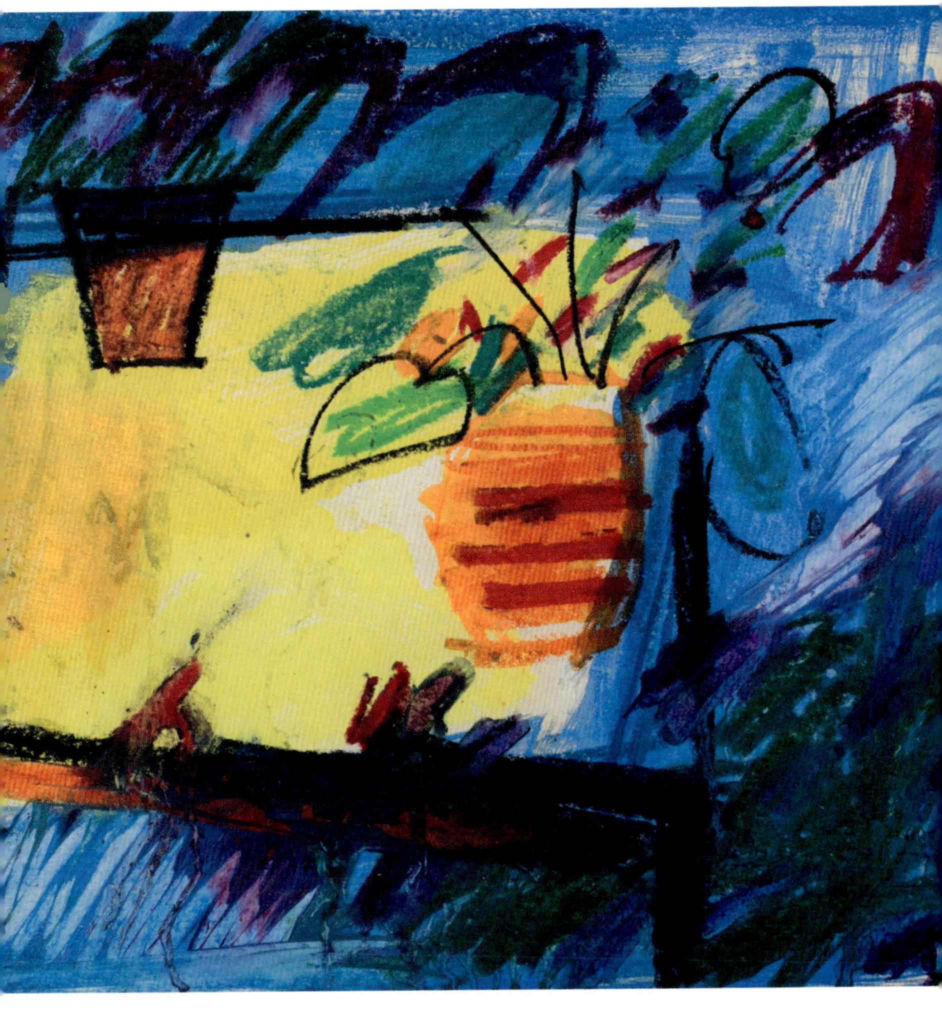

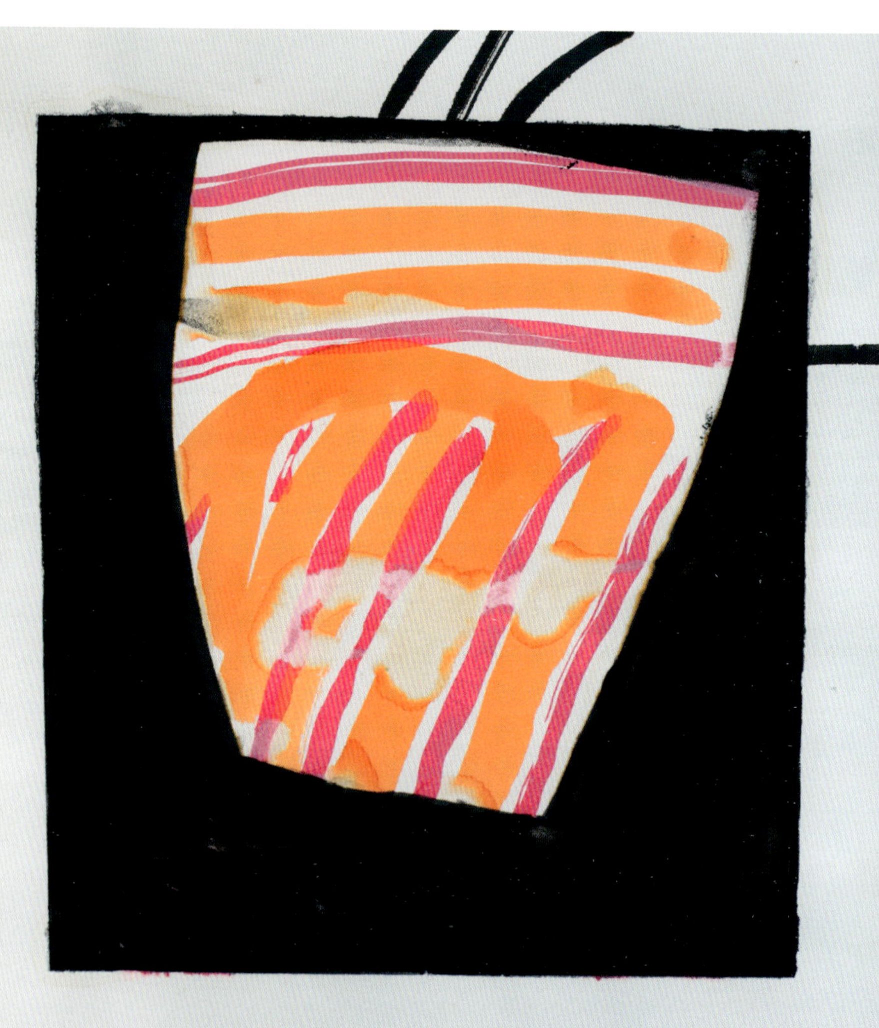

Day 34
Untitled drawing

This drawing was done using
acetone on absorbent handmade
paper. Joseph Beuys produced a
pencil and oil sketch on paper which
I love, titled *Dance of the Shaman*.
It inspired me.

Day 35

Last day of the week of drawings,
ending up with something personal.
My daughter Mia photographed
me in my studio when I was sorting
all my work on paper. She was too
late to save this self-portrait, so she
made a portrait of her own.
Next week will be about
stripes and grids.

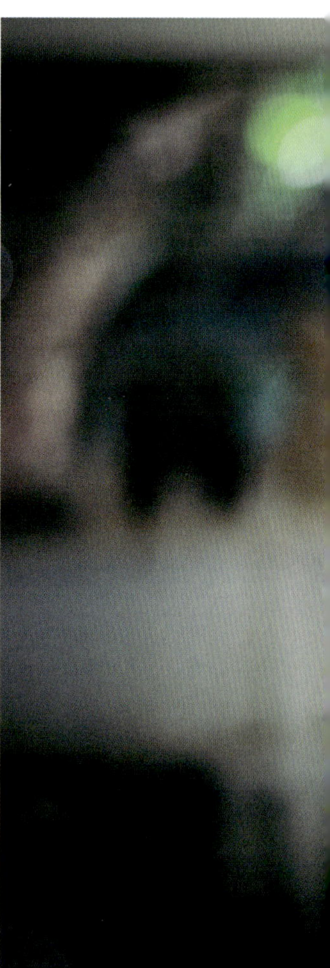

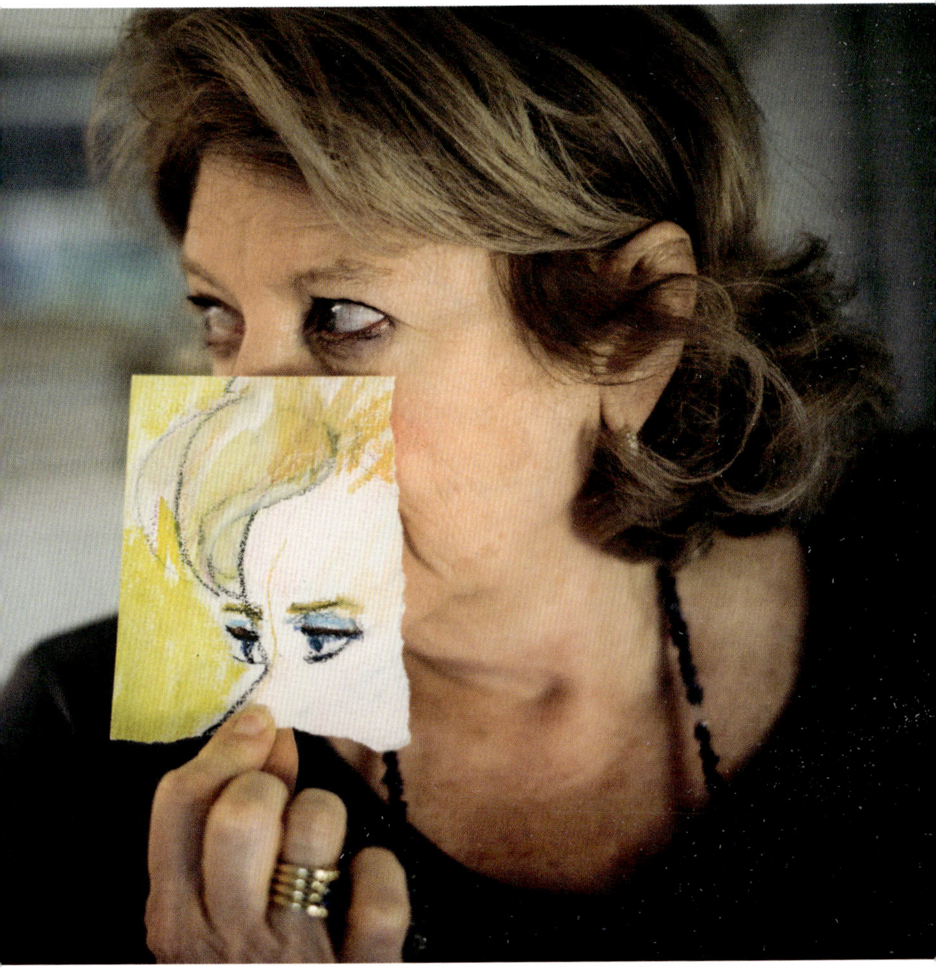

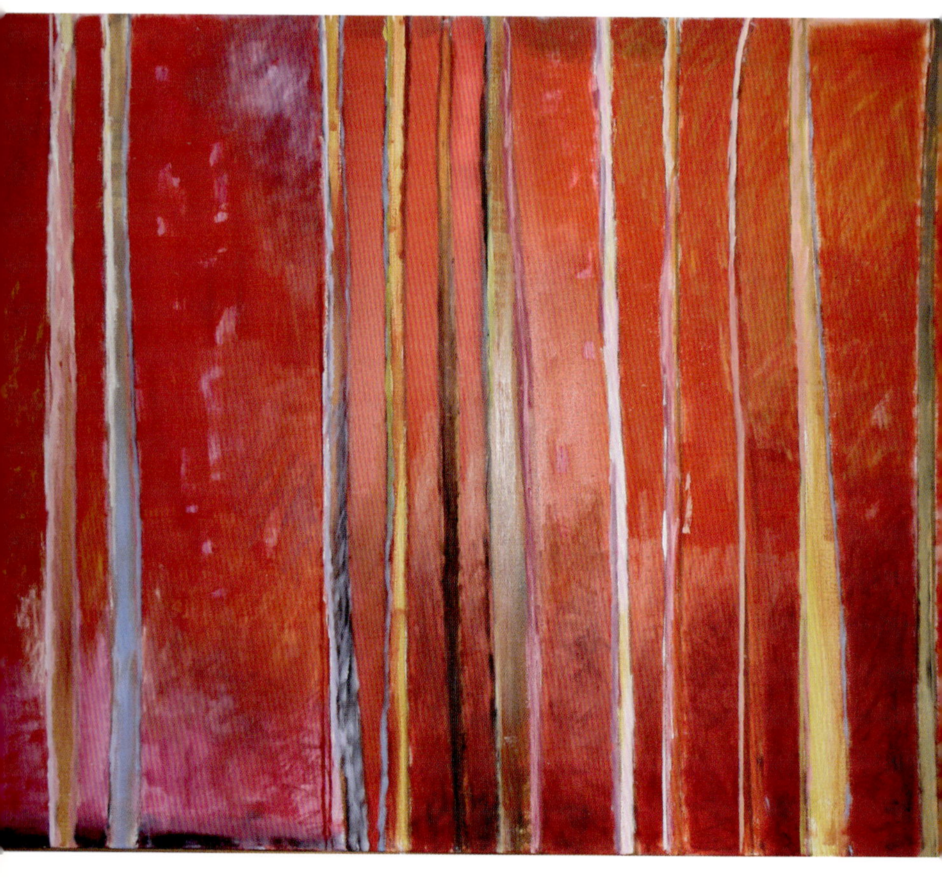

BY HIS STRIPES
WE ARE HEALED

It is strange how deeply colours seem to penetrate one. This is part of a recurring theme, 'The Spiritual Truths'. My great friend Julia Doig owns this work and I was honoured when she bought it, as Julia is a deep one. Not an easy painting and it dominates a room. I think it is an appropriate work to show at this time whilst we are all under lockdown and awaiting a healing of the world and ourselves. I like to think that this very large abstract can change the viewer's inward state to a meditation. One of my favourite quotations is from Kandinsky, who said, 'Red without boundaries, like a trumpet sound in the mind, goes straight to the soul.'

ONE LILY, ONE LIFE

This is the significant main work in this entire series, which consists of soap stone, glass and metal, as well as numerous works on paper and canvas. The sequence happened shortly after my father died. I had an exhibition coming up and no work to show. One solitary lily was growing outside the studio. The bulb had been given to me by Donna Reid, a visiting American friend, on the day my father died. She has no idea what her gift did for me. I plucked and twisted this lily every which way for several monoprints and discovered the washed-off lily was also another impression. When all the paper was around me on the floor, I had a huge subject for a body of work. The work in this series was leading me. The 'washed' rectangles are the life after death. The stamen produces the pollen on the live rectangles, and represent time ticking away. There is much to this massive series which revealed itself to me as more and more lilies were painted as they grew outside the studio.
In the end the series covered the history of art as well as the life, well lived. The series was exhibited in Kenya and Holland.

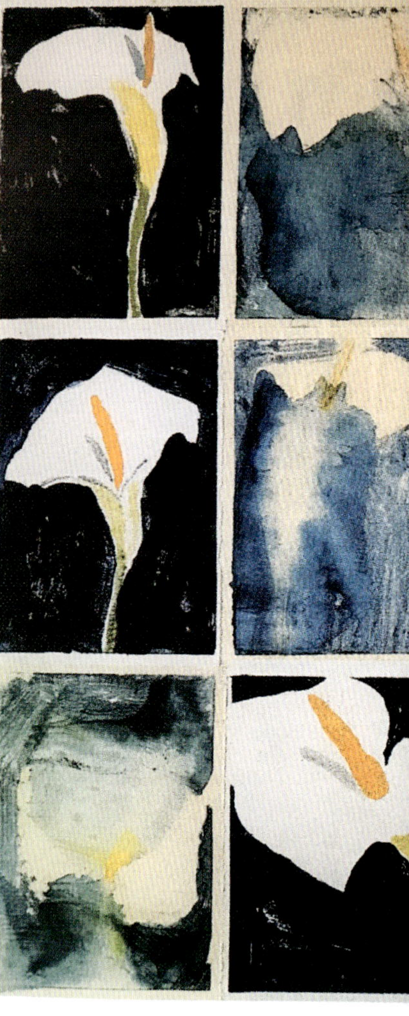

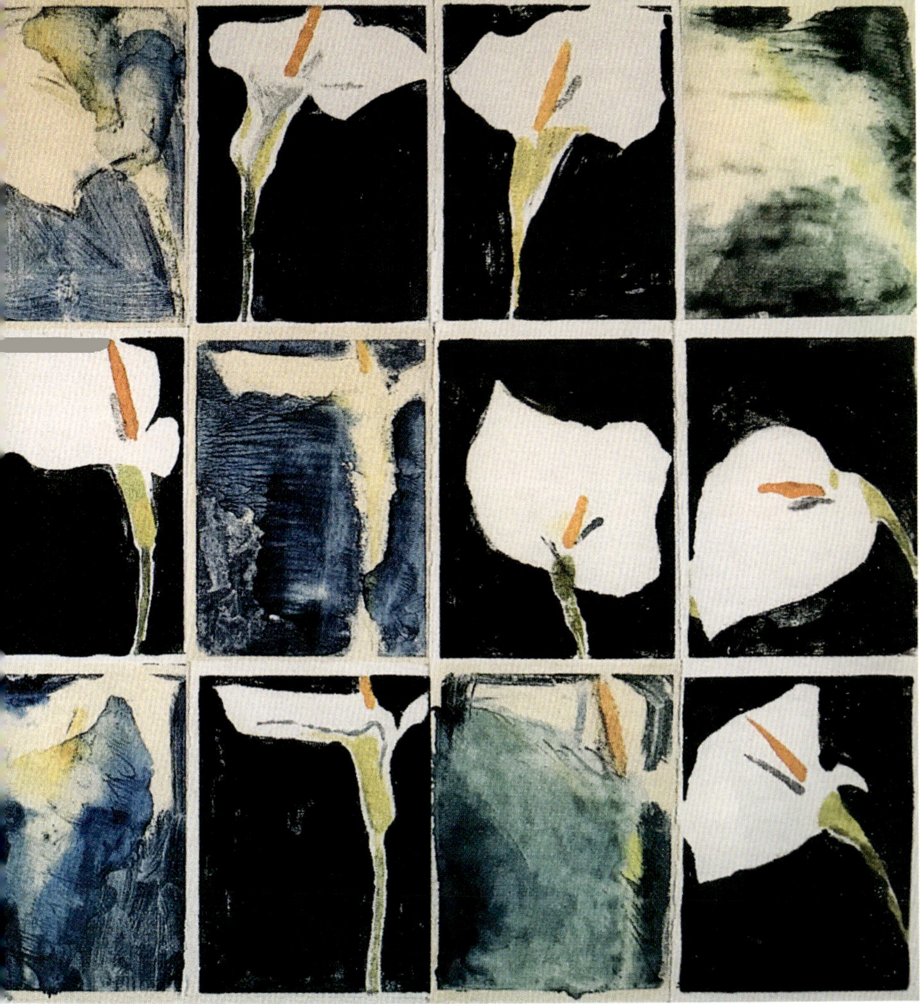

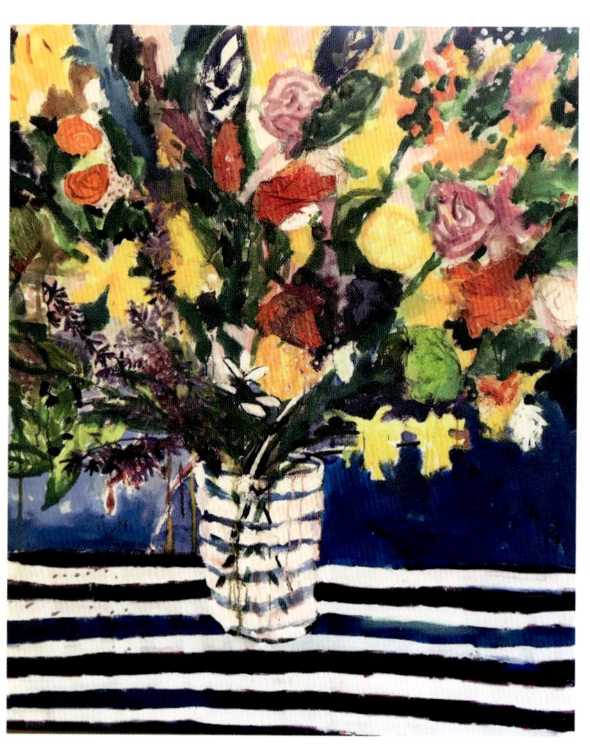

UNRULY FLOWERS IN A VASE
50 X 45 IN

I am swinging wildly from one serious
subject to beauty. It has always been the
beauty in life that motivates me most.
This is a week of 'stripes and grids'.
The stripes at the bottom of the painting
bring a stability to a disorderly top, mixed
media, made from my acrylic pallet on
kitchen paper, stuck on to the canvas any old
how, and flowers evolve around the lumps.
I like the lemon smack on that mystical
proportion of the golden section.
This is owned by an ex-Swiss Banker,
Veronique Su, who has become a valued
friend and now has a few of my works in
a gloriously modern home built especially
to show her collection of art.

'FALSE BAY' SERIES

A second day of this massive series (the first was Day 20 – 9 April). Thus far there are approximately 600 small works of paintings and photographs. This is our view when we are in Simon's Town in the Cape. Every day, I work on one; oils on canvas, 10 x 10 in. I marvel how every day each moment is new. Picasso said, 'Every time you look, it's different.' Who is the creator? What happens that makes this view different every moment? Why is my response singular? Who is in control here? Big questions, go on and on. And photographs, to be slotted in amongst the paintings are as dissimilar as these. This particular group of nine were auctioned, to attract interest. They are in Dubai. I have huge ambition for this series.

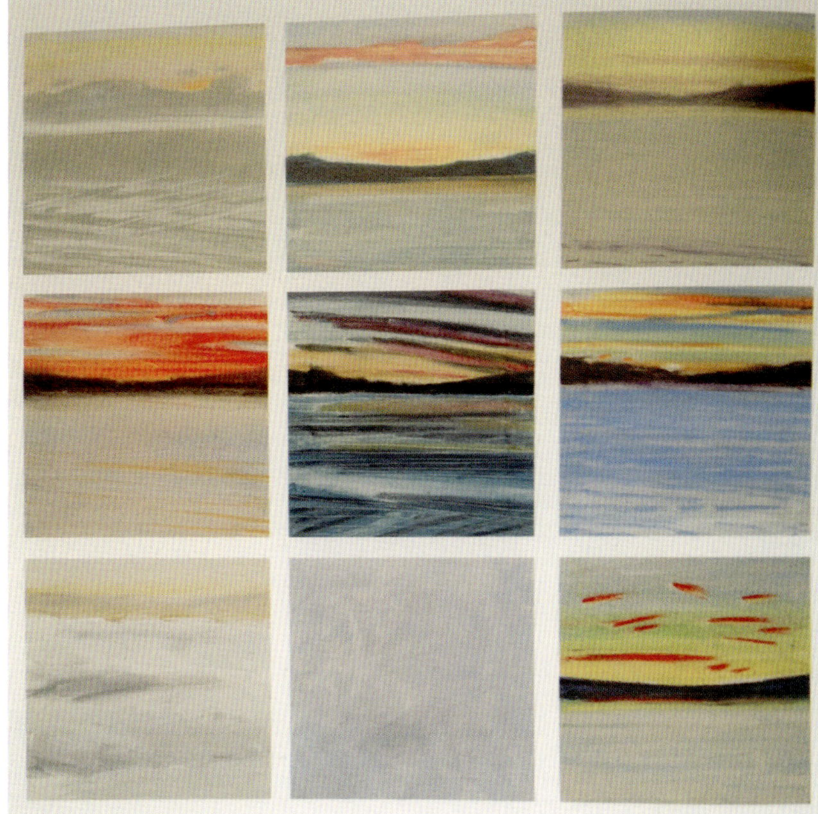

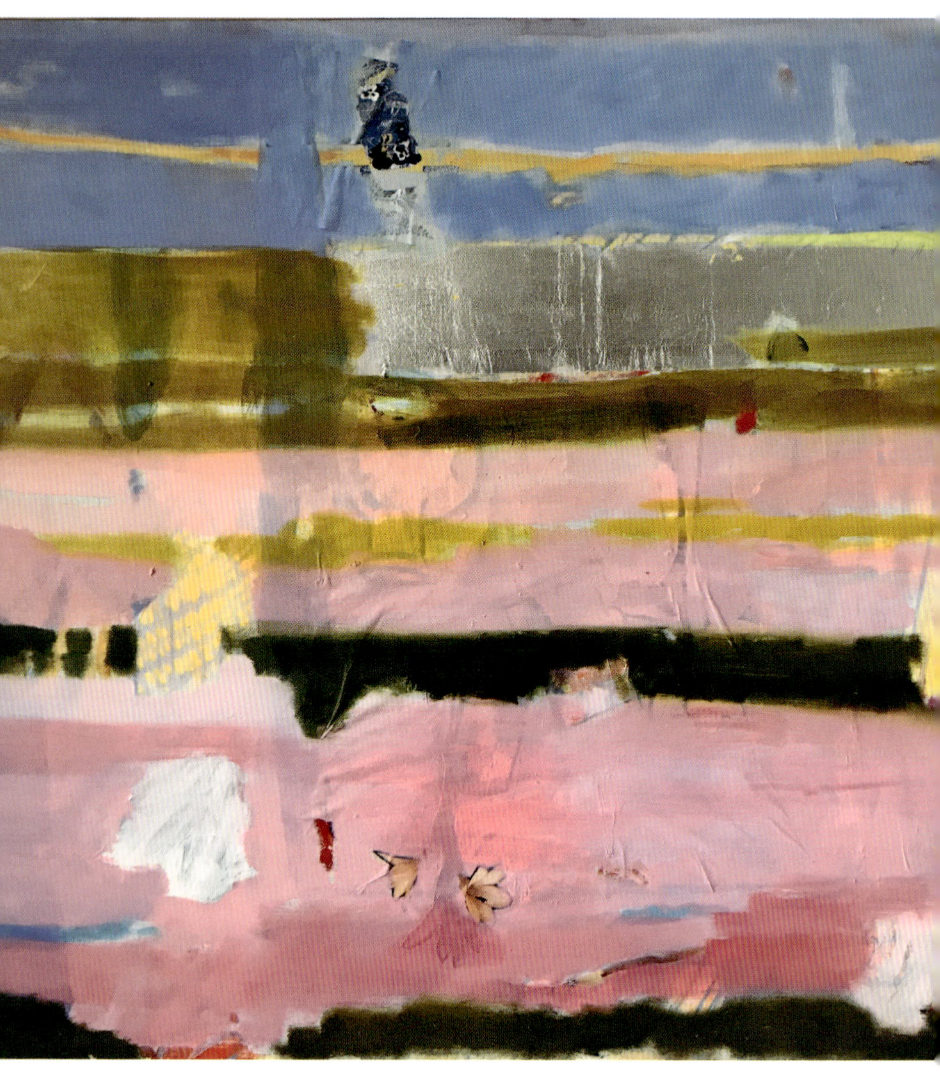

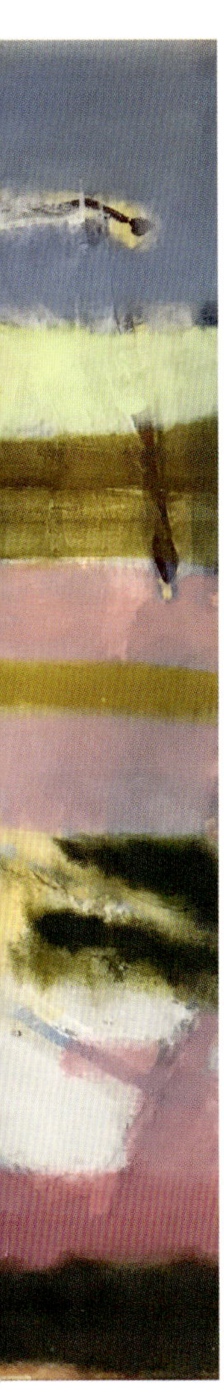

DAY 40

WABI SABI

Both life and art are beautiful because they are impermanent. When nothing is certain, everything is possible. A markedly potent sentence at this time, 2020. This is a recent work and hangs in my entrance.

DAY 41

HIBISCUS

I am including this in the week of grids and
stripes, as this painting is more about the grid
than the hibiscus itself. An ancient technique
of enlarging a work, though in this case the
'becoming bigger' became the subject.
Each square is a painting in itself. My thought
was to give myself inspiration, abstracting
the squares. How extraordinary to discover
that in each square, there is the golden
section, the divine proportion 1.618 ... we
humans are wired to see it.
I have noticed that I signed this work twice!
The signature is as important a part of the
painting as any other mark and, in my view,
it needs to be hidden. I think I hid the first
one a little too well.
This large work found a beautiful home
with José and Rusa Saldanha, in Portugal.

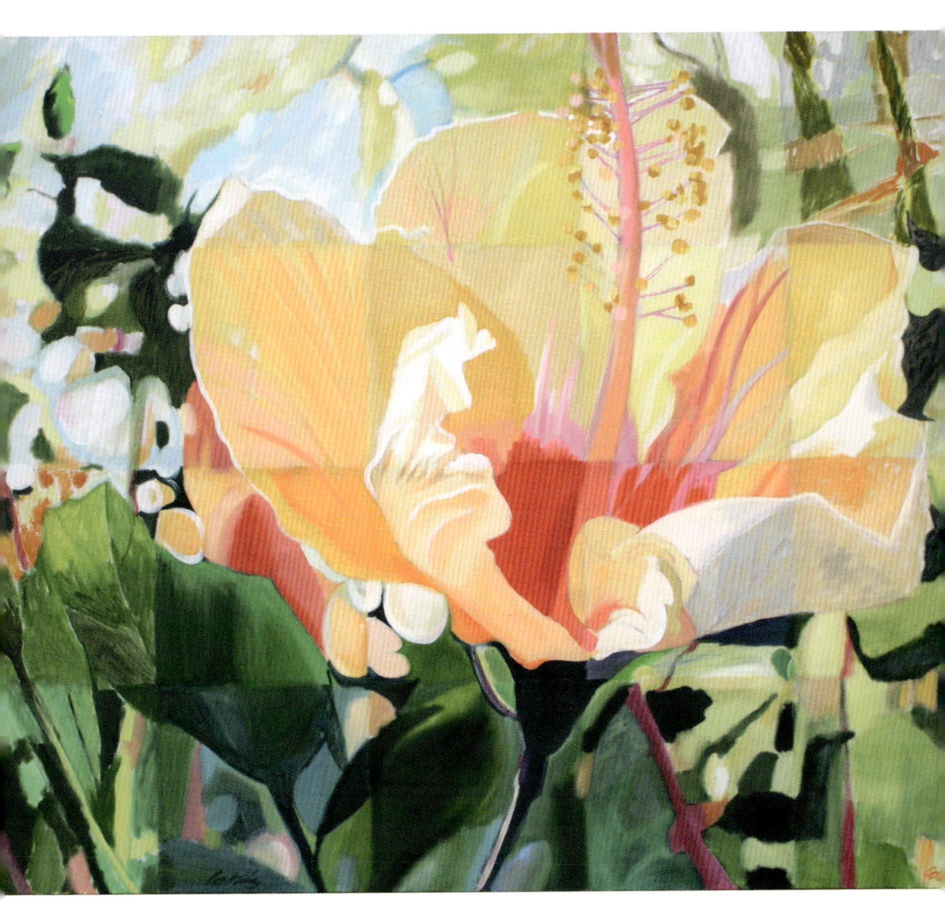

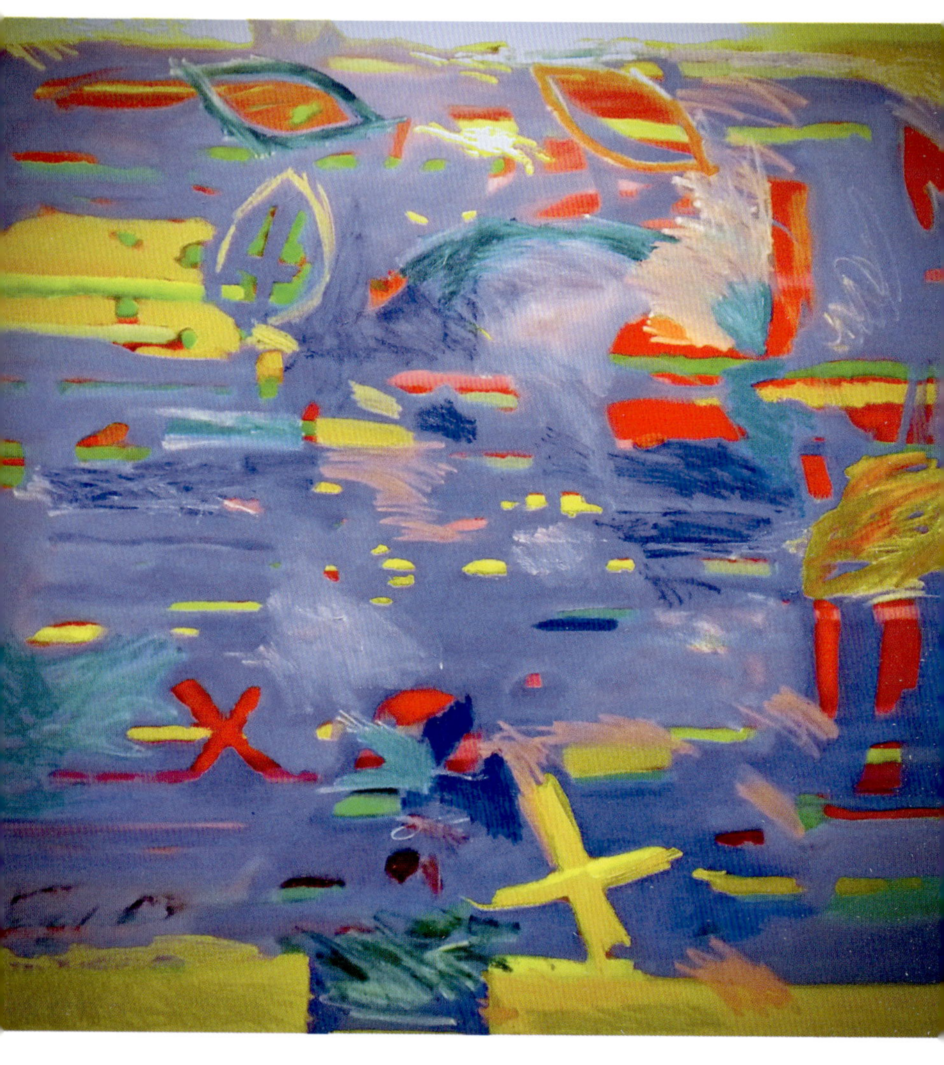

A COLOURFUL SIGH

This is after the painter Cy Twombly, who excites me whenever I see his work. For those who know him, you will wonder how this work was inspired by him. It is in the mark-making, though Twombly rarely used any colour other than black, grey, off-whites, umbers and an occasional bloody red blob and a splash of pink. His work transports me into the present moment. I can barely breathe round them. Shaun Parker, a fellow artist and great friend, bought this painting of strong primaries, a difficult one to hang, and a difficult one to reproduce here. I apologise if the colours are too high a register.

Day 43

Flamingos on Lake Nakuru, Kenya

I painted this more than forty years ago in the late 1980s. It was a chilly day and the pink of the flamingos was very pale along the water's edge. This online exhibition has put me in touch with collectors whom I still know well, with past work, forgotten long ago. This painting resides in England and was bought by Mike and Sheila Barker. In the next few days, I am going to show some of their collection.

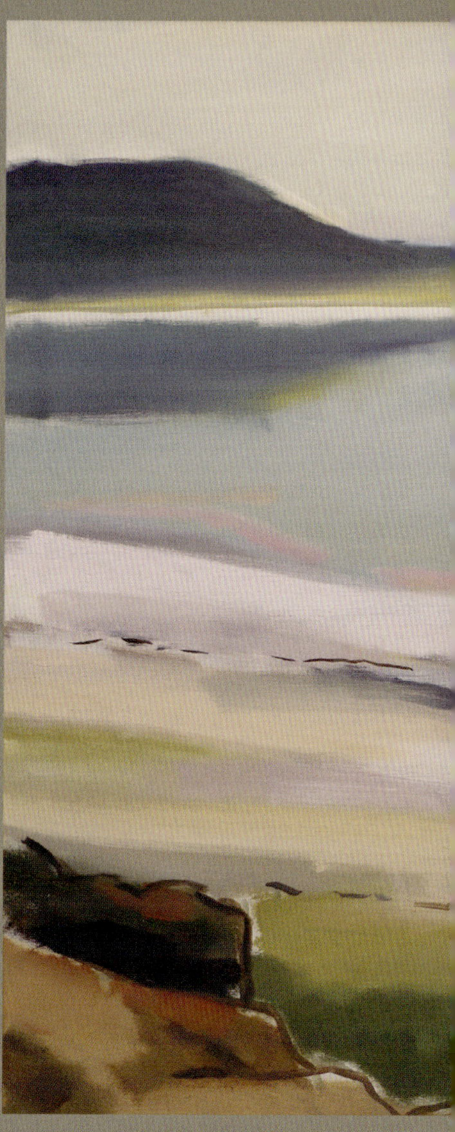

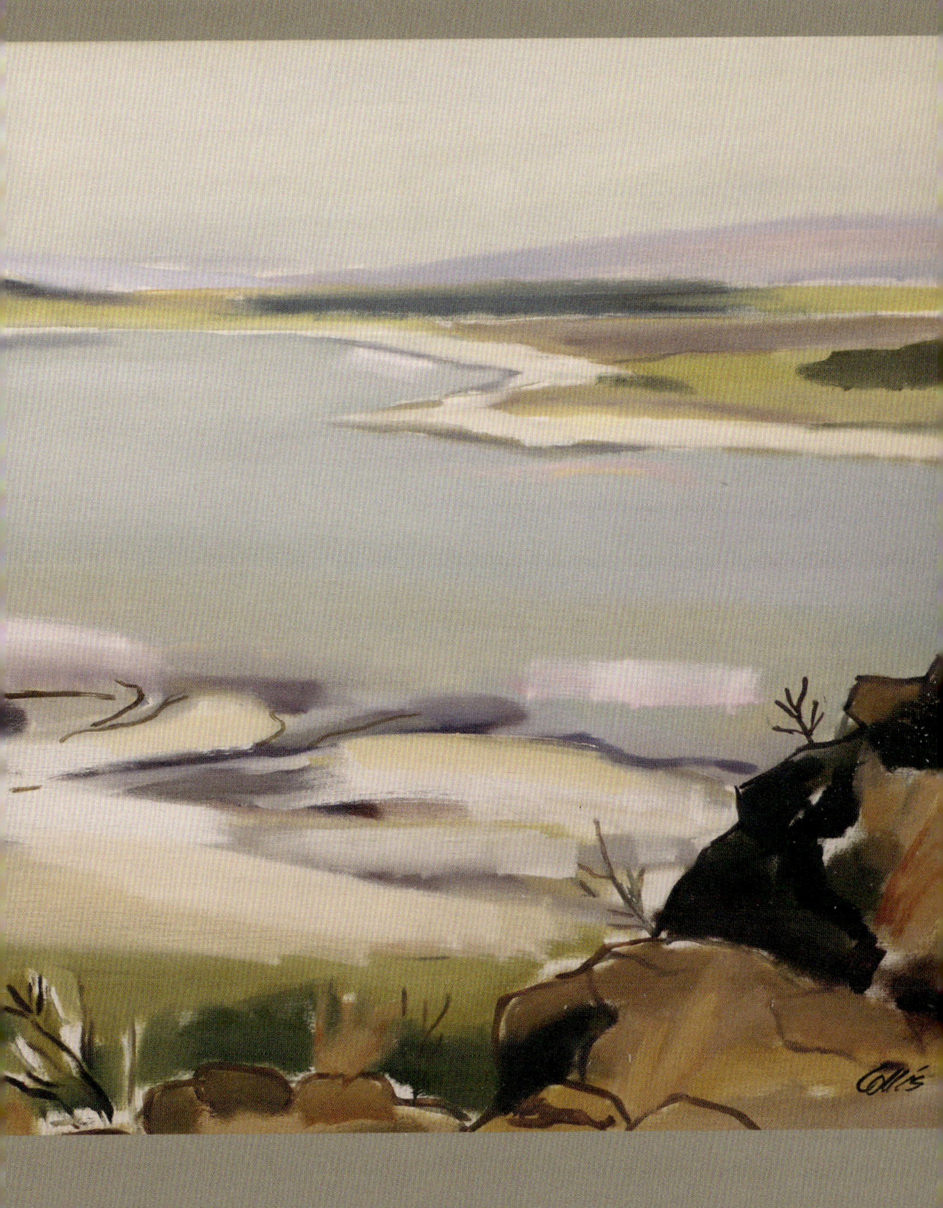

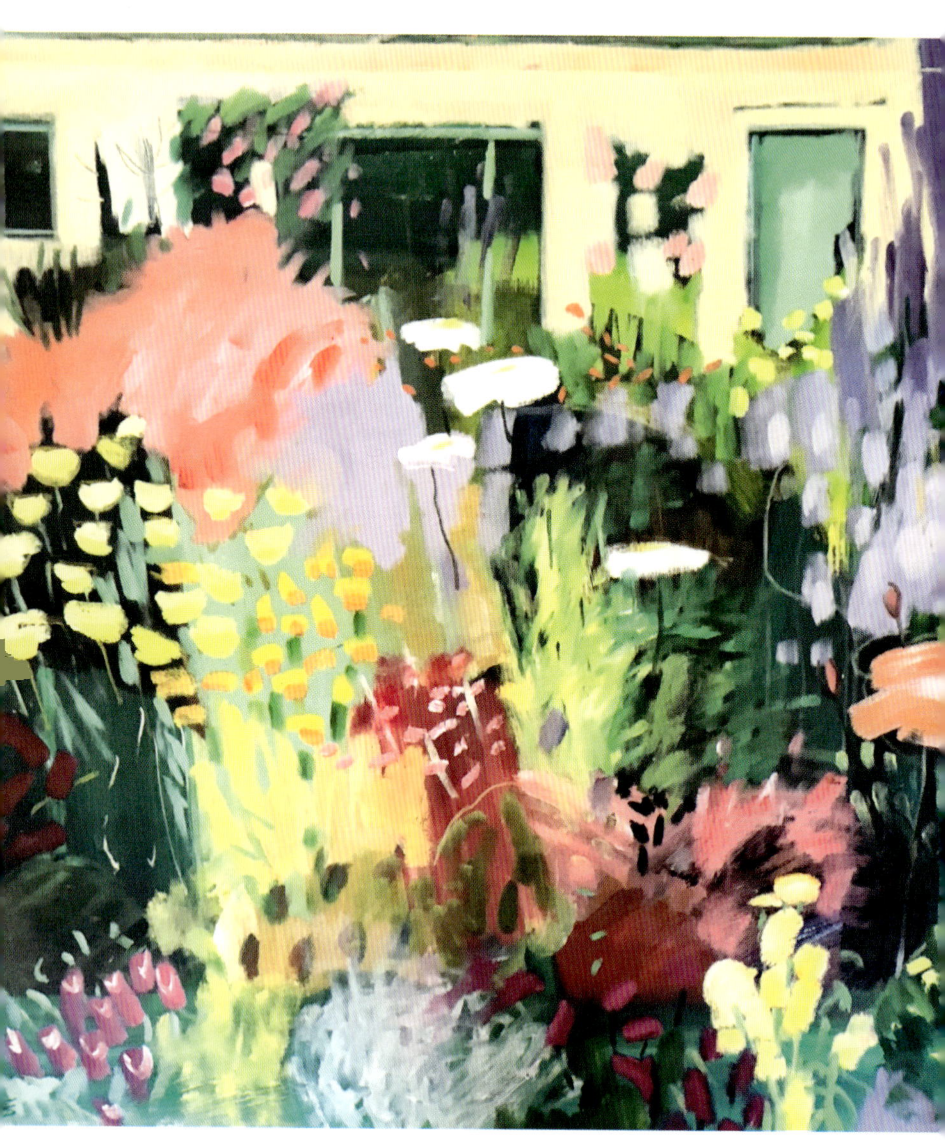

Day 44
'Erica's Garden' series

This garden was Erica Boswell's beautiful place in
Limuru, Kenya. It wasn't huge, but everything in it
was in bloom all the time. To my dismay, whilst I was
painting, the gardeners would dig out a crop of poppies
that would 'almost' be over, and a moment later there
would be marigolds in their place. Constantly changing,
I was always in wonder and greatly appreciative.

I spent many years painting her garden. Erica was as
pretty and sparkling as her surroundings. Encircled
by beautiful things in the house, family photographs
everywhere and a library that extended down a long
corridor, inside this part of her house painted here.
She would take no credit for the garden, always telling
me it was Graham, her husband, who had planned and
planted it. Graham had died many years earlier.
Collection of Mike and Sheila Barker, Nairobi

Day 45

A beautiful Arab town on the North Coast of
Kenya. A painter's paradise. I welcome a canvas
that has not worked, as you might see in this
case, as I will paint another work over the one
below and allow all the happy accidents to come
through to the new one. I seriously consider
the painting beneath, turning it upside down,
anticipating what will show through.
In this case the geranium pink that peeps through
the windows comes from what is underneath.
It was most probably bougainvillea. The colours
lead the eye into the real bougainvillea in this
painting, and because of the magenta windows,
did not need to be overstated.
Collection of Mike and Sheila Barker, Nairobi.

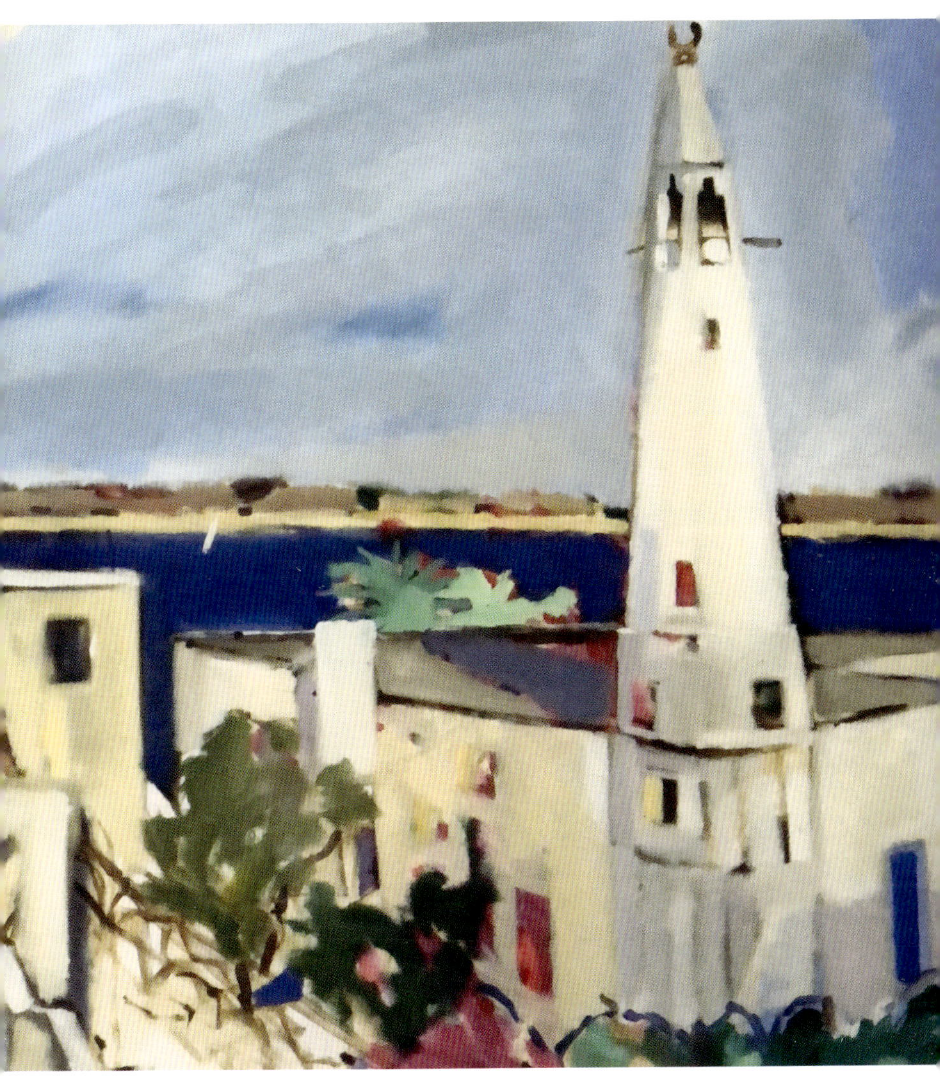

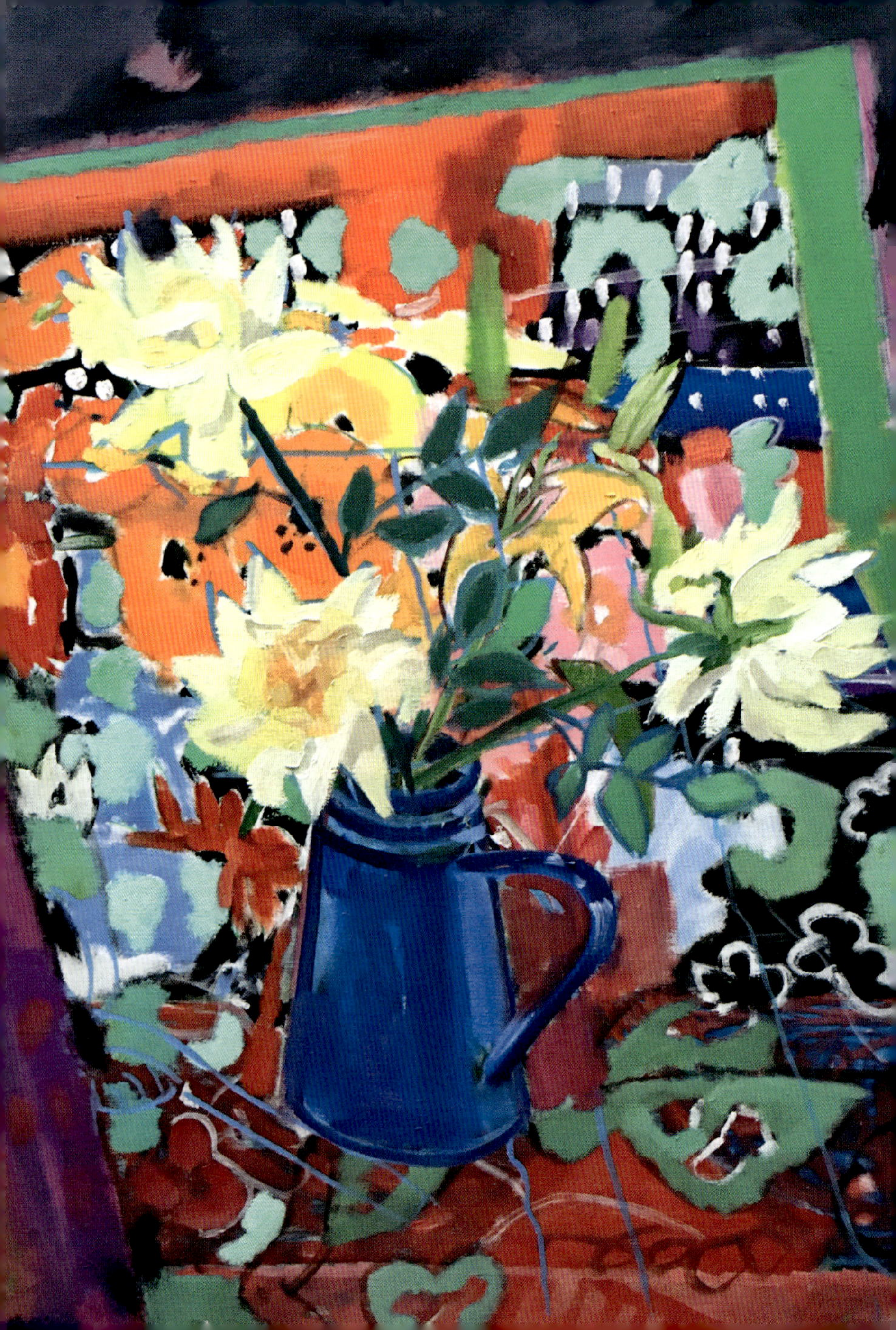

Day 46
Blue Jug on a Philip Sutton Scarf

I love the English painter Philip Sutton, born 1928.
His work is playful and colourful. He travelled the
world to assimilate colour, spending time in Fiji and
on the Great Barrier Reef. His kaleidoscope of hues
came from invention, so very clever and admirable
to absorb that into one's being. I am different.
My colours come through my eyes and I can retain
an exact shade for months in my head, but pulling
it out and painting it alongside others without a
visual reference is very difficult for me. A deep bow
to Philip Sutton, for his spontaneity comes directly
from his soul. His scarf is a wonderful backdrop for
this blue enamel coffee pot and three garden roses.

I had forgotten this work completely. Thank you,
Martin Thomas, for the reminder and sending this
to me. Martin and Theresa Thomas in the UK bought
this painting from my studio whilst it was still drying.

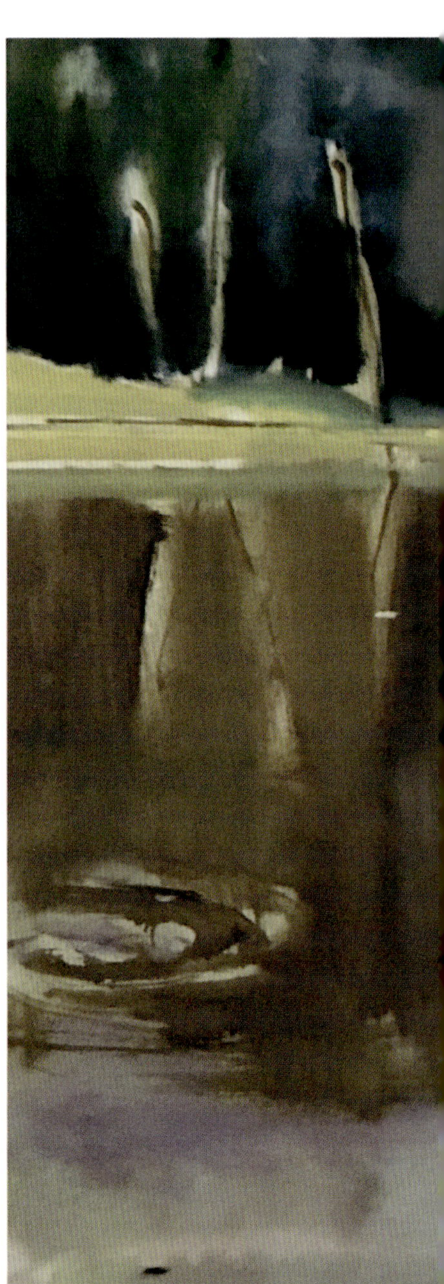

Day 47
Lake on Windsor Golf Course, Kenya

A large oil on canvas, painted on
a grey day and it rained. I might
have abandoned it before it was
quite finished, a gift, for it became
a postcard and travelled the world.
This painting resides in Guildford,
England, in the collection of
Martin and Theresa Thomas.

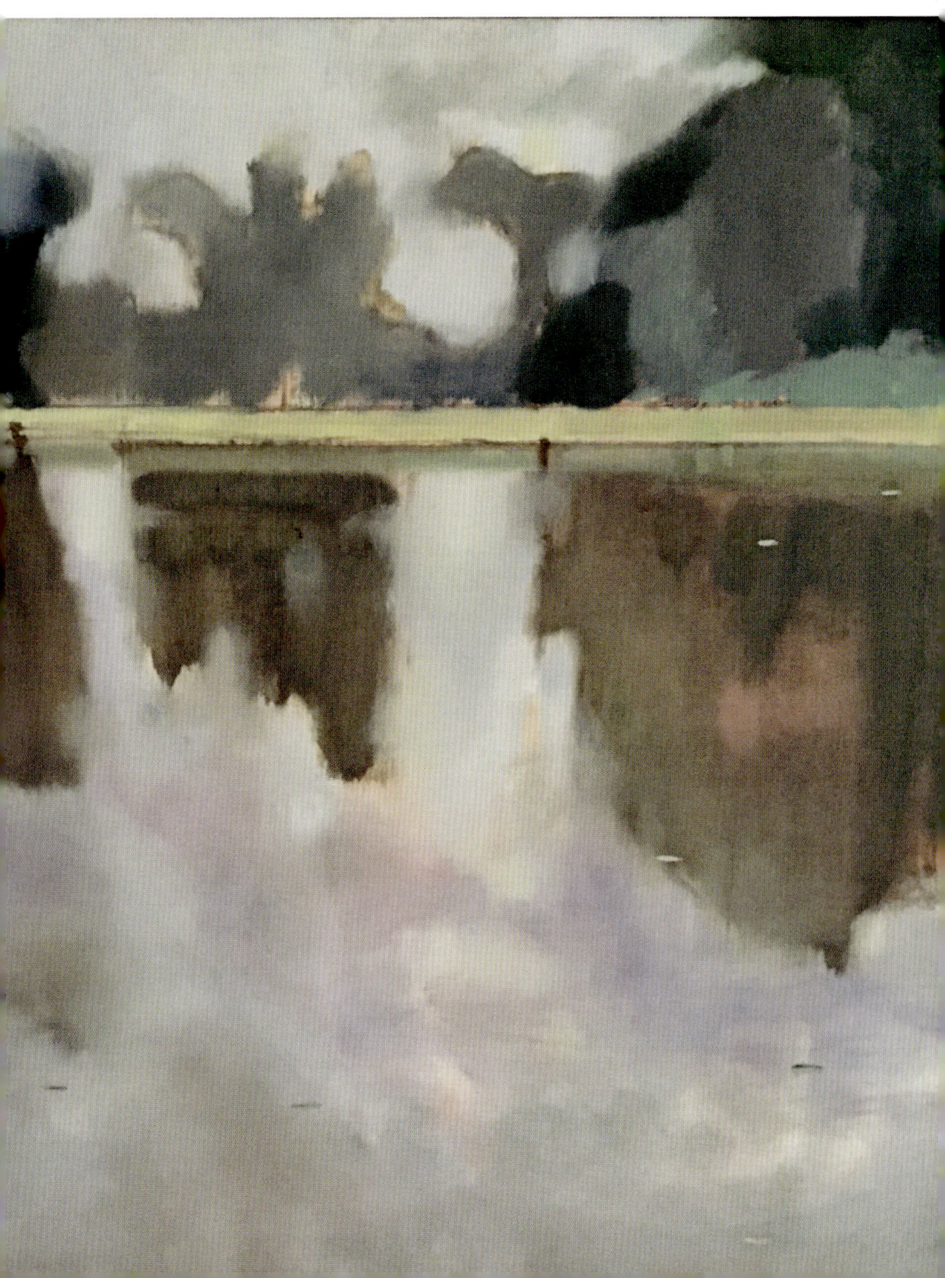

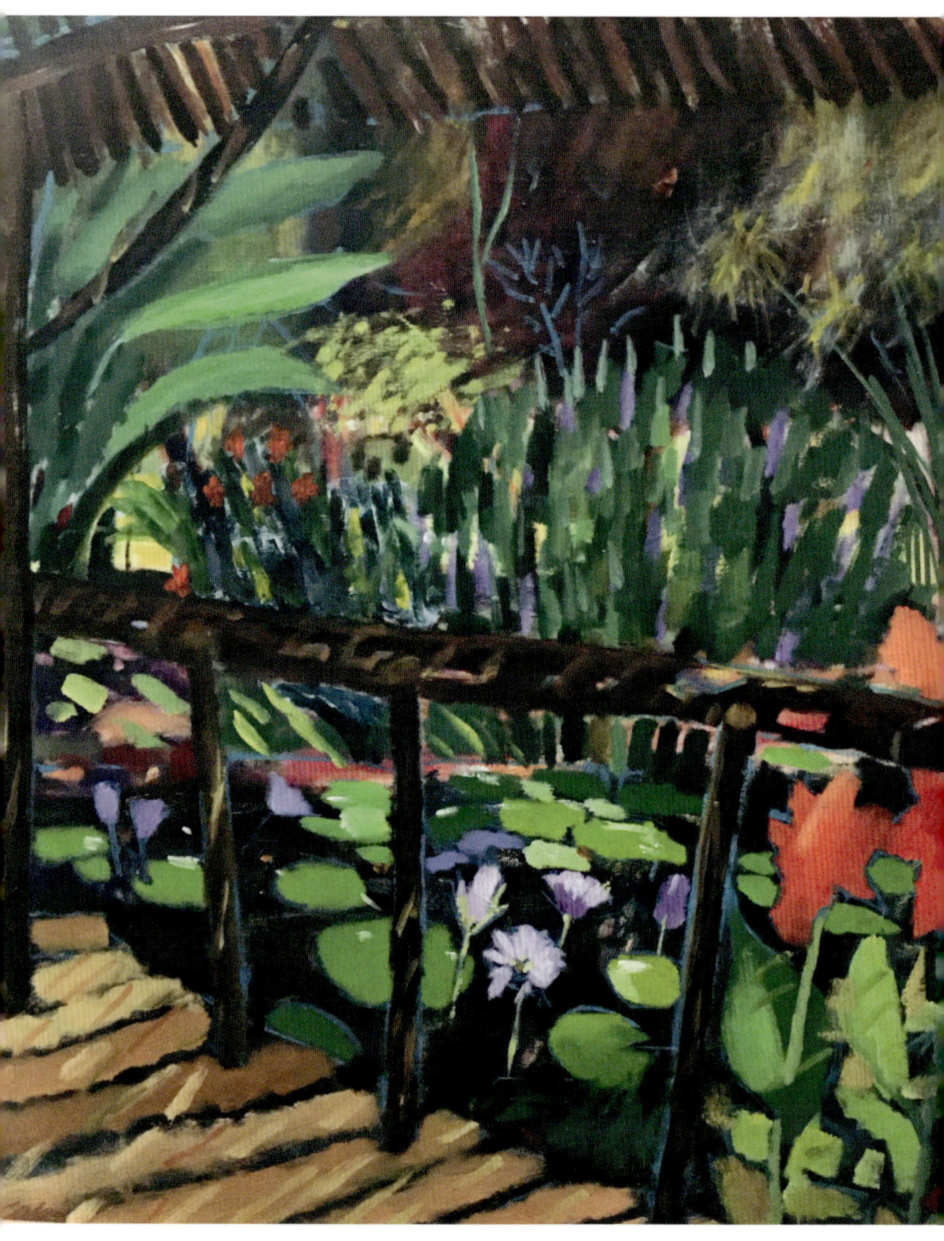

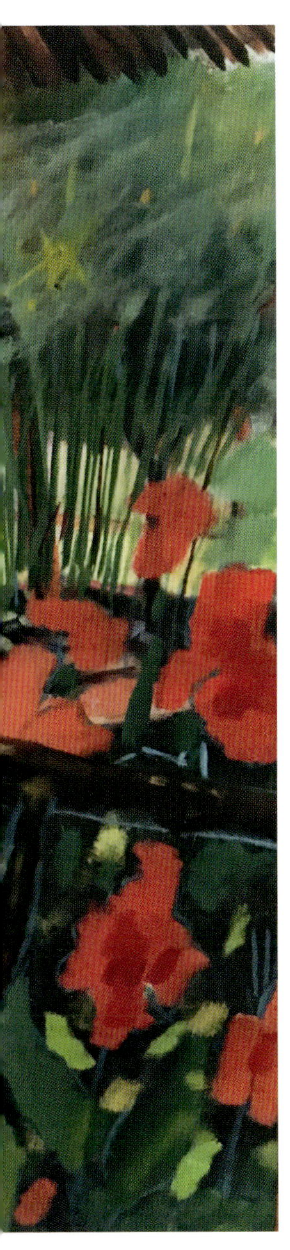

Day 48

Rosslyn River Garden, Nairobi

One of many painted in this beautiful garden. Lauren and Paul Mackenzie, professional gardeners, have this enormous flat area with a river running through the middle. Quite recently Lauren dug up the entire park, altered the whole layout and replanted, so this dark view and the little covered bridge has gone, along with the shade. I remember I was not satisfied with this work when I had finished it. Too dark for me.

Thomas Gray wrote these beautiful words 300 years ago,

Full many a flower is born to blush unseen,
And waste its sweetness on the desert air.

Martin and Theresa Thomas saved this one. And I forgot completely about it until last month, when they sent it to me.

Day 49

One of the very last of the series from
Erica Boswell's garden in Tigoni, Limuru.
I painted there every week for about
five years. Erica had died and her spirit
and mine went out of the garden.
The wrought-iron chairs look lonely.
The little green island is still there, giving
the flowerbed a stability, the flowers are
more common.
This was bought by Heinz and Theresa
Schmed, who visited my studio and took
the painting back to their home in Zurich,
Switzerland. I am flattered by them,
they have six of my works.

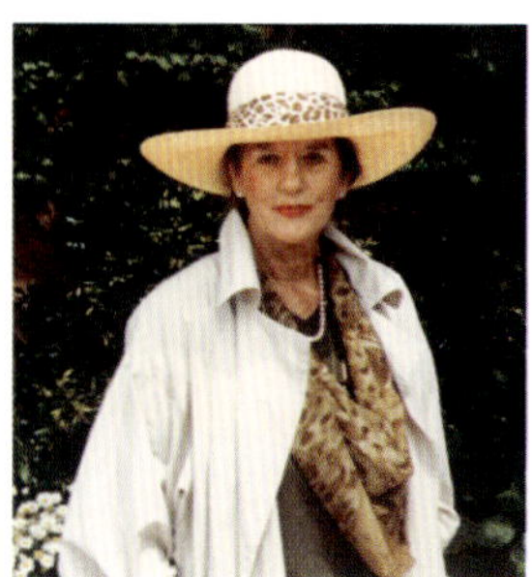

Erica Boswell was beautiful, indeed, as this
picture will attest, taken towards the end of her
life. She was generous and funny and her house
was filled with visitors. I had many meals with
her and coffee, always, in a beautiful cup, on a
silver tray. She owned a lovely dress shop called
JAX in downtown Nairobi in the 1960s and
'70s. She was a fashion icon in Nairobi and we
all benefitted from her eye. Erica's garden was
the closest to heaven one could be on this Earth.

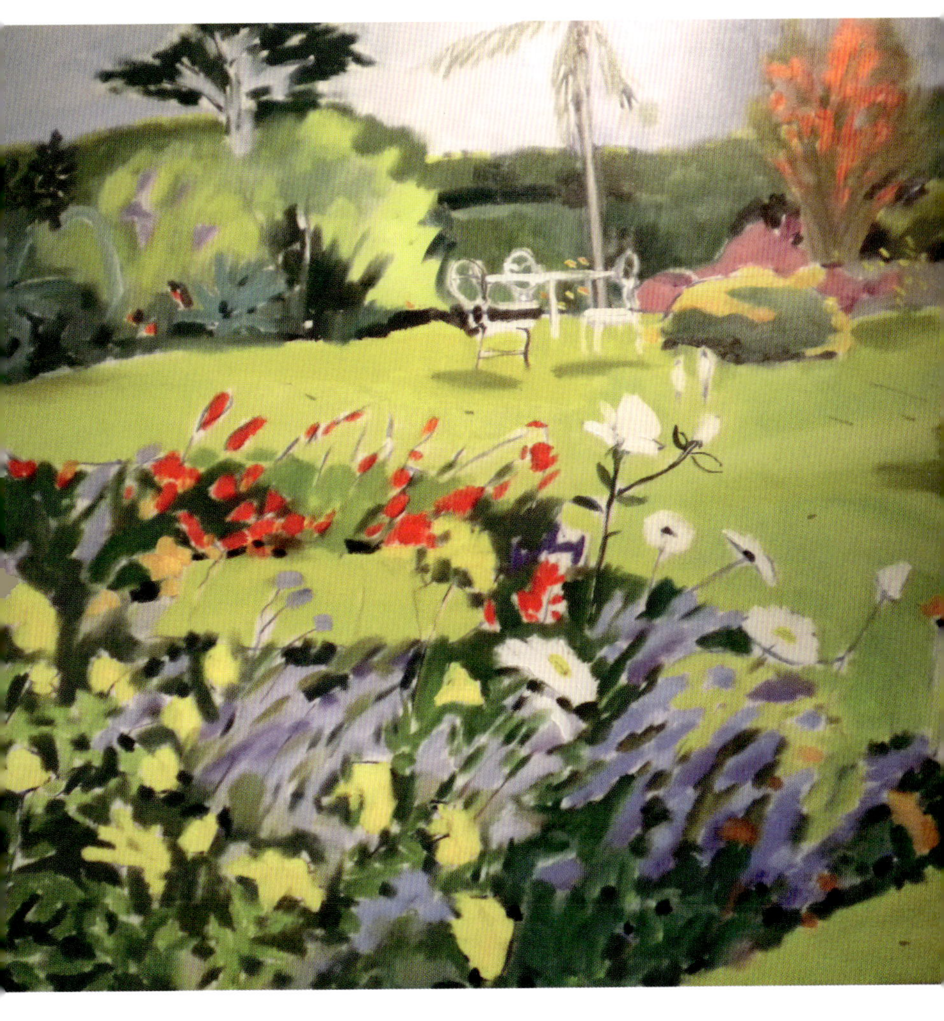

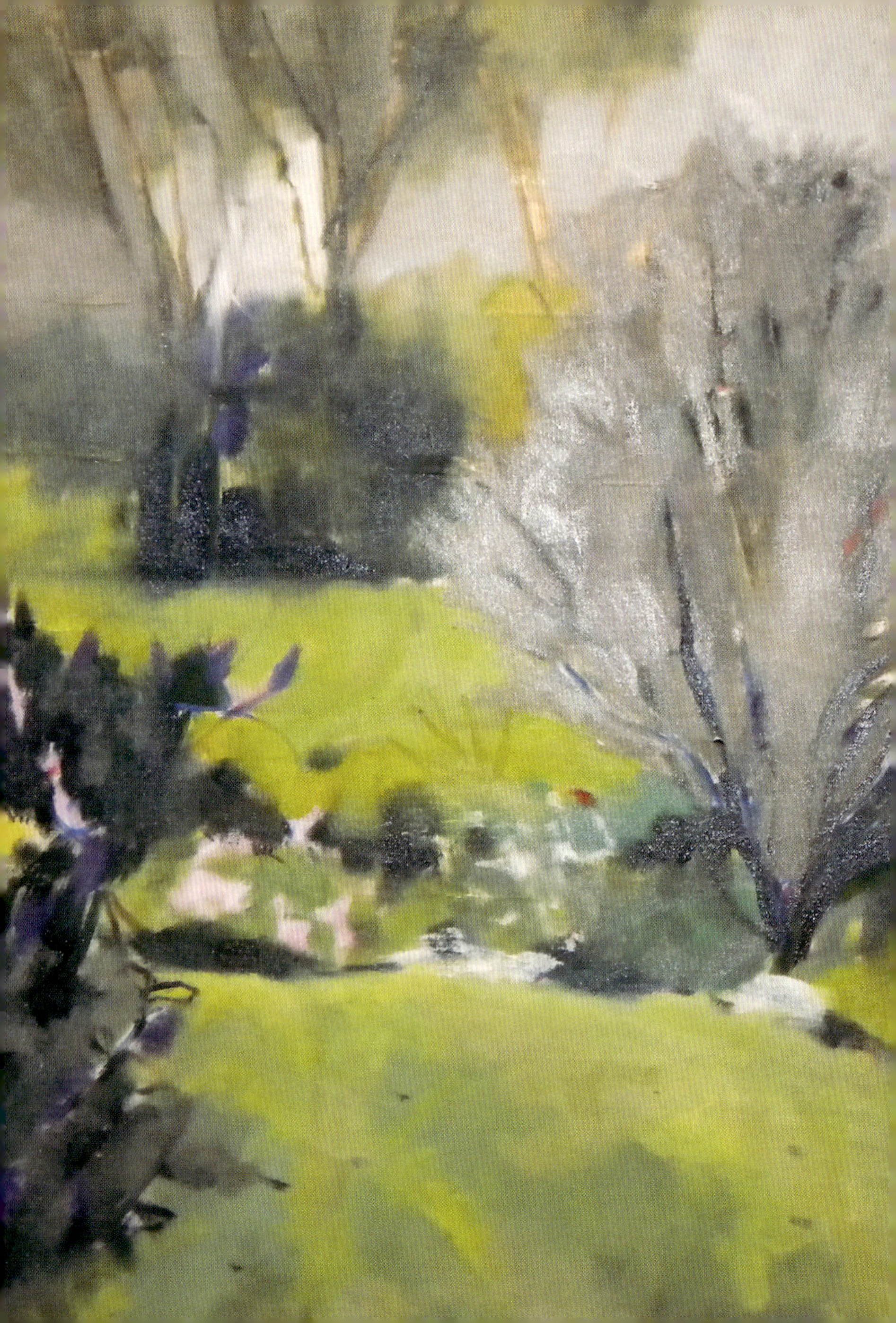

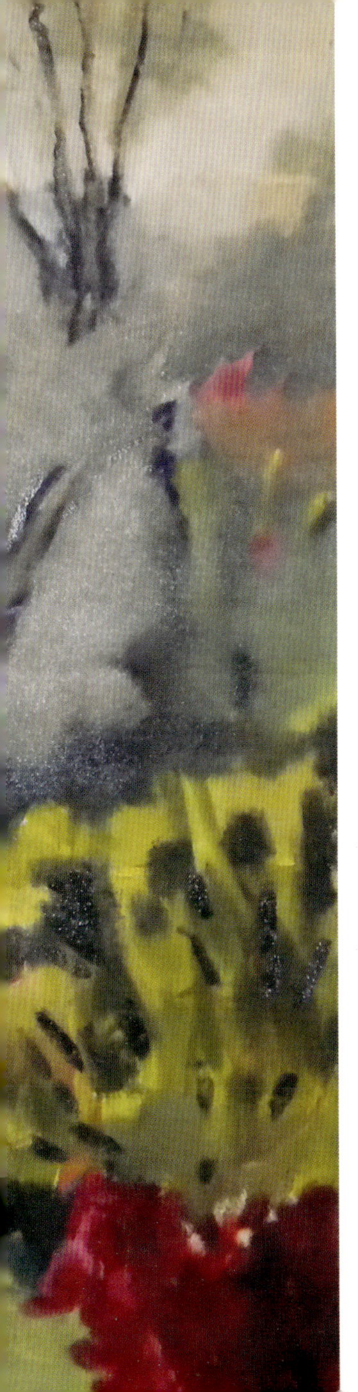

Day 50
Gray Day in
Pat Dixon's Garden

After Erica died, I continued to paint in other gardens in Limuru. The ground in Limuru is the richest, a deep red fertile soil (an Indian Red in my paint box) full of nutrients that one can practically see with the naked eye. Every garden going towards the top of the Rift Valley has this thick, powdery red earth. A stick put in the ground to hold up against a weak stem will blossom in this soil. I painted this whilst it was raining, which accounts for the weak look of the grey paint on that bush next to the yellow.

Day 51
Warm Sea

This very large painting found a beautiful
new home in the collection of Carlo and
Adriana Van Wageningen. I was thrilled when
they bought it, as they had built their dream
house and it was like the full stop to the
interior of their lounge. It hangs beautifully.
This work is primarily acrylic with some oil
on top. Acrylics give me a gauche mark which
I like. I am not in control, for it has a soapy
feeling on the brush. This is a memory of
standing in the Indian Ocean which was like a
warm bath on a very hot afternoon. We had
flown down to Mombasa for twenty-four
hours only and I was marvelling at the pea-
soup look and the feel of the ocean around
me. It was a challenge to make a warm
painting out of cold colours.

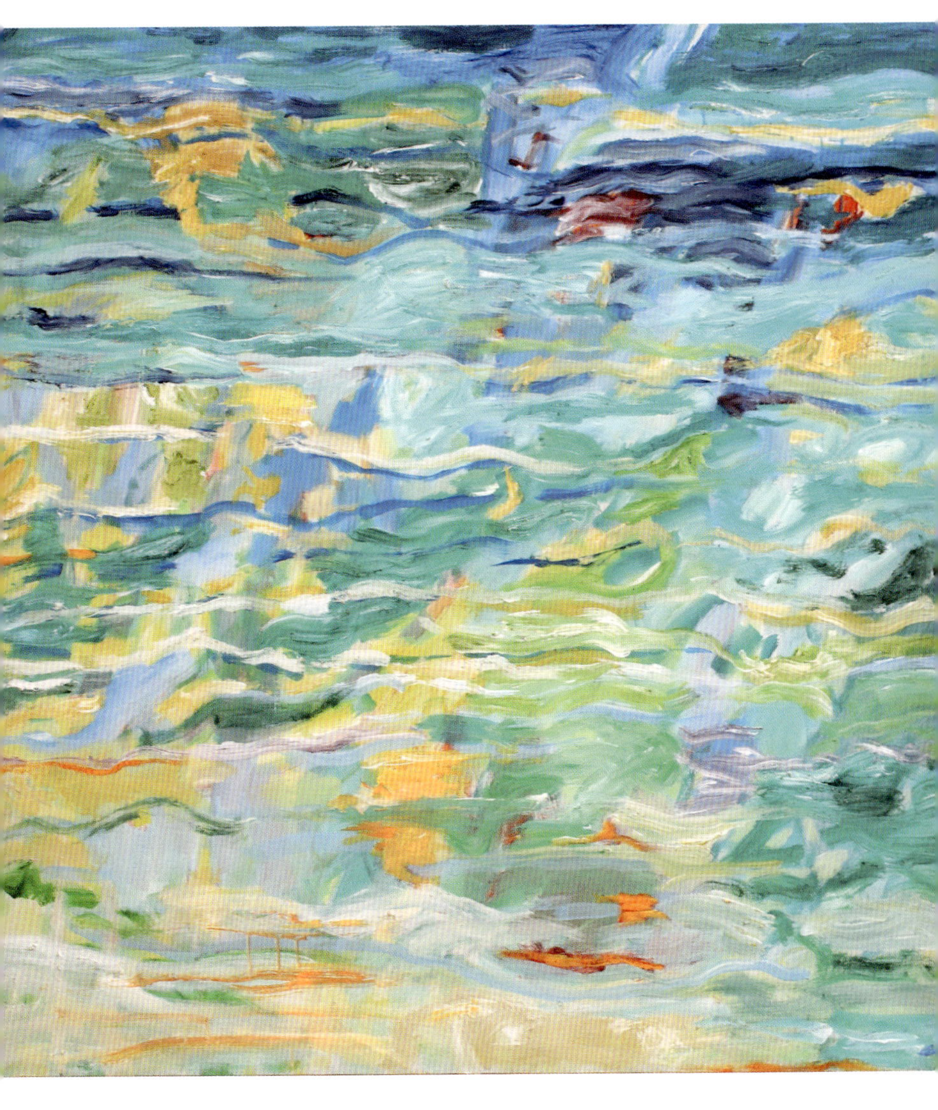

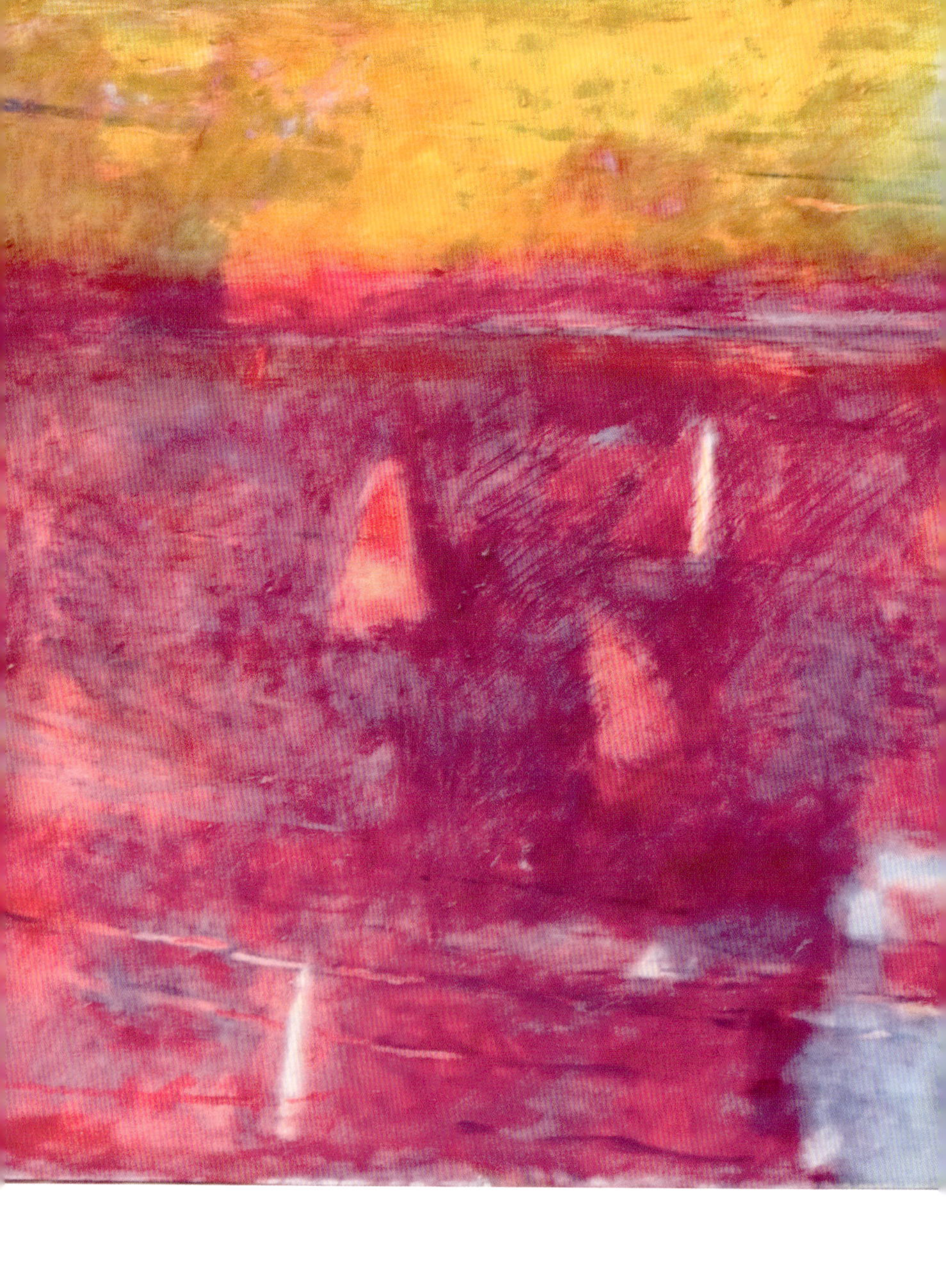

Day 52
Last of the Light,
False Bay

4 x 5ft

I was very wretched when I sold this sunset, as it was one I would have liked to have kept. It has that feeling at the end of the day before the light goes completely and the energy, the earth and the colours vibrate, and one contemplates the source of love and illumination. Collection of Jay Mehta, Mumbai

Day 53
Autumn Movement

A large mixed media landscape, it was sent
to me by Lauren Mackenzie. It is in her house
in London. One of her sons took this photo.
The brushstrokes rain down, like falling
autumn leaves. Squishy Sennelier oil sticks
are wonderful to use.

Jesus said, 'I have cast fire upon the world,
and look, I am guarding it until it blazes.'

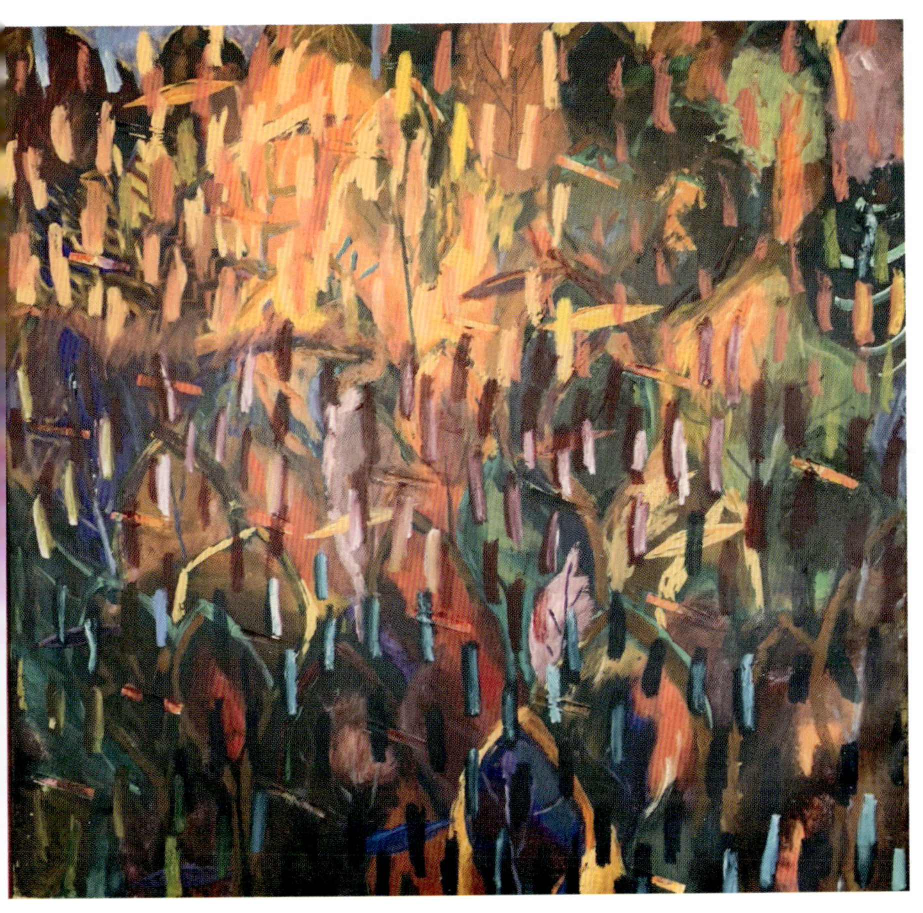

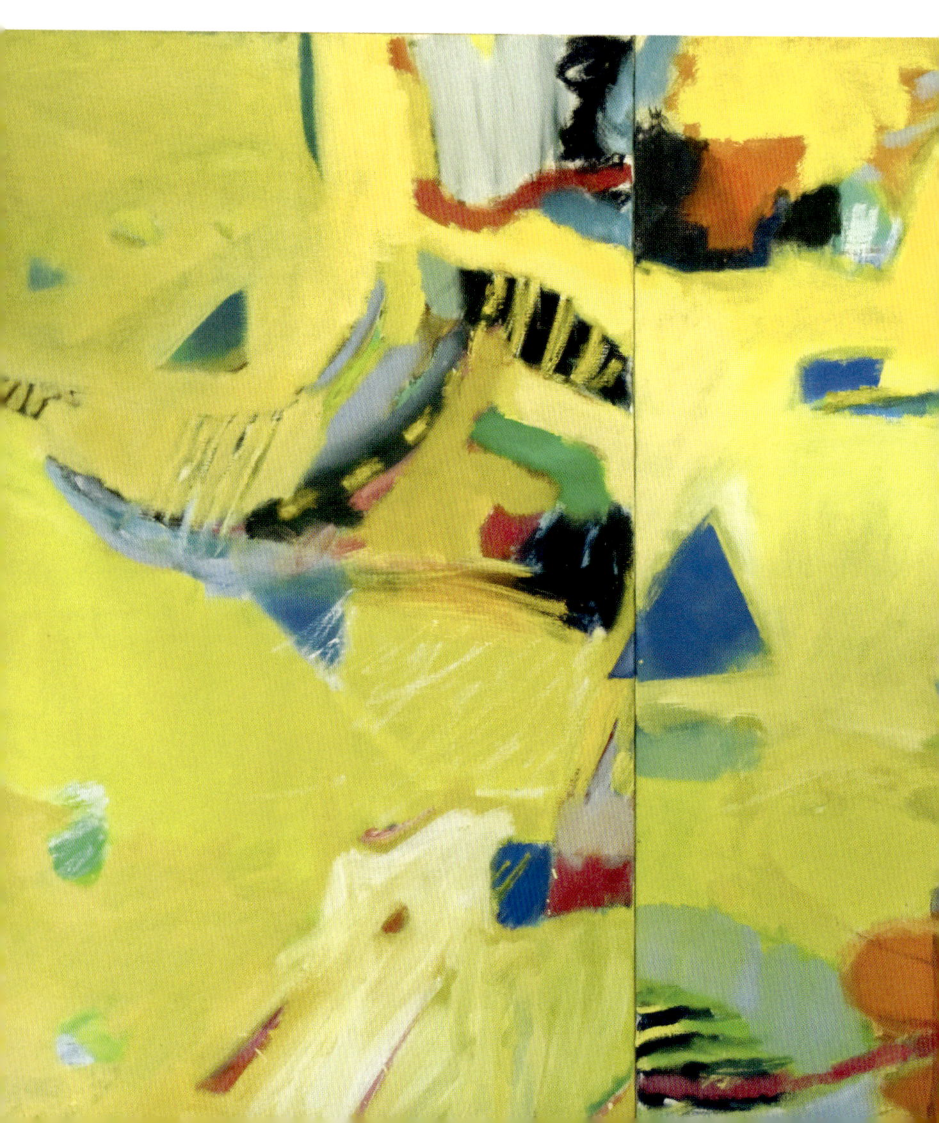

Day 54
More Sand

Armantine Aurore Dupin, best known
by her pen name George Sand, was
the subject of a number of my works
between 2000–07. I have no record of
who bought it. It is one of those rare
works I wish I had kept.
There is something about the forms,
 the spaces and yellow background
having a perfect balance, and I was
pleased. This diptych was sold by
RaMoMA (Rahimtulla Museum
of Modern Art), Nairobi, a rapidly
expanding concern changing the face
of art in Kenya.
Carol Lees and myself were at the helm.
For a few thrilling years I felt I was
making a difference in my world.
During those ten years, when my energy
was focused on the greater good, my
own painting career took a tumble.

Day 55
Out of the Blue
Mixed media

An Yves Klein Blue and a subject title
I often use as I paint the ocean in
South Africa. The Atlantic is much
deeper and darker (more like this
blue here) than the Indian Ocean,
which is predominantly turquoise.
How mysterious? Sails and crosses
float in this blue space, along with a
few fronds from my idol Matisse.
Collection of Henry and Heather Davis

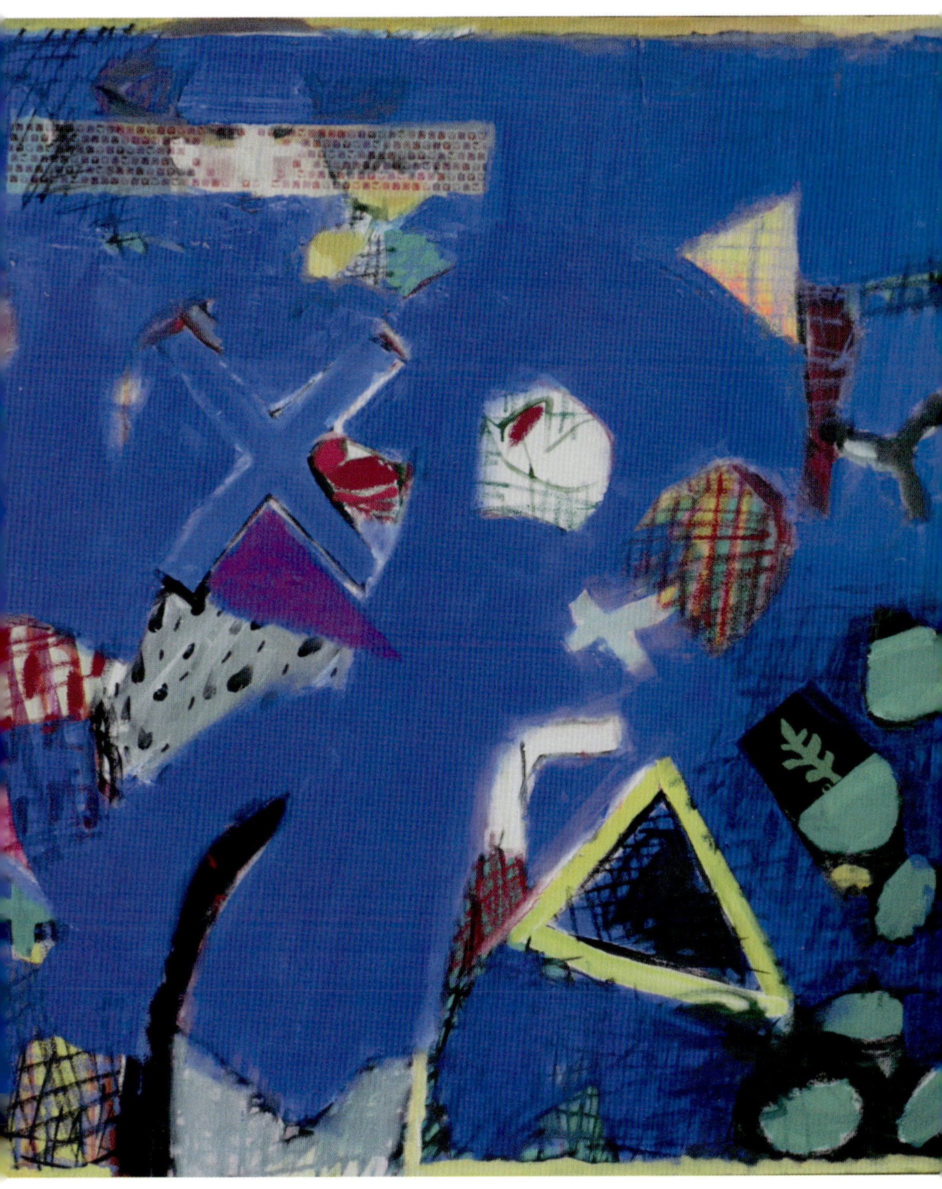

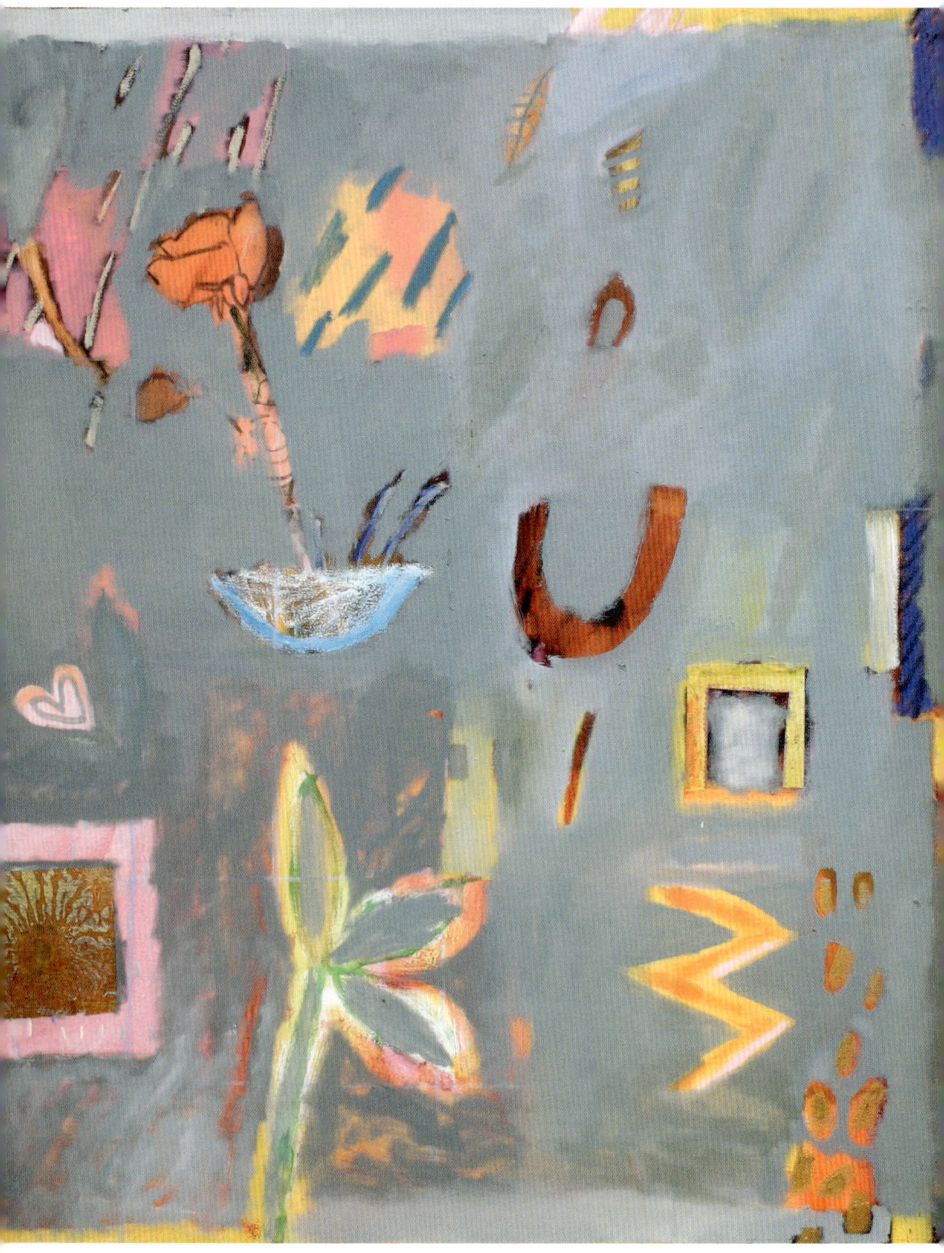

Day 56
Meza

I like the way Elizabeth Blackadder, the Scottish painter, pushes objects round her table or a tray and pays so much attention to the 'social distances' in between. The two greys in this work make the colours vibrate. Every painting needs a bit of ugly. This work evolved slowly; it has much indecision going on beneath. Collection of Diana Bird

Day 57 – 16 May 2020

This article appeared today in the *The EastAfrican*
by the art critic, Frank Whalley.

Life under lockdown continues apace and artists are filling in their enforced bonus time in many wonderful ways.

A few are trying to drown out the whole miserable experience with sleeping draughts of vodka and Night Nurse; others are thinking about getting down to a bit of work, eventually; some are actually painting, drawing and sculpting in their studios.

But Mary Collis, an artist for more than 50 years, has seized the opportunity to document her past output and show it as an evolving exhibition on Facebook.

And that means moving from easel to laptop to catalogue more than 2,500 paintings, drawings and prints, many now in collections worldwide.

So far, Collis is up to 50 – one for each day of the lockdown at the time of writing.

With each posted painting comes its title, media and an explanation of what prompted the work, where and how it was made and anything else she thinks a reader might find useful.

Collis plans to extend the series into a book that will both catalogue her major works and become a helpful manual, with examples, for young and emerging artists.

It is a bold idea and would be a useful adjunct to the region's art history as well as a handy teaching aid.

Looking into the artist's Facebook page, I was struck by the variety of her practice; a loose Realism, Abstracts, essays into Post-Impressionism (always the strongest sellers, she told me ruefully) Pop Art and throughout, her enthusiastic use of colour – one of the hallmarks of her work. Interesting too is the variety of her subjects... gardens, land and seascapes, portraits, flower pieces, still life, paintings of wildlife, children and even telling drawings and prints of the vegetables from her garden; all are grist to her mill.

"I paint my life and all that surrounds me" she explained.

What is perhaps unusual is the facility she brings to each subject.

Her original garden has now gone although the memories remain.

For many years based in Nairobi's Loresho suburb, the artist, a Kenyan citizen, moved a few years ago to a large apartment in the Westlands area of the city and set up her studio in a friend's garden, surrounded by the plants and flowers she loves.

Appropriately, if Collis had to choose just one subject from the myriad it would be flowers, "because of the colour", she said.

Probably running a close second would be the stream of minimalist seascapes she paints of the view from her second home, an apartment overlooking False Bay, near Cape Town.

Each just 25 cm by 25cm, these are made on her balcony that looks across the bay, facing east into the rising sun.

Each takes her about 20 minutes to

complete and so far, she has painted around 450 of them, plus taken 150 or so photographs of the same scene; sea, horizon, and sky with differing emphasis on each and sometimes with a glimpse of mountains. Collis argues they are in fact one painting, albeit one with so far some 600 facets, and she is hoping a museum will one day show this series, hung floor to ceiling only inches apart, providing an immersive experience.

(The Post-Impressionist Paul Cezanne, known as the Father of Modern Art, managed "only" 60 paintings of the many moods of Mont Sainte-Victoire, and that was considered obsessive.)

The many drawings by Collis are particularly interesting in that while recognisably by the same hand as the pared down seascapes they are even more spare, often a single confident line doing double duty in describing the form as well as the depth of the subject.

A great fan of the American abstract expressionist Ellsworth Kelly, Collis is often content to define her subject – plant, vegetable, a single leaf – with an incisive sweep of line that suggests volume and weight with the minimum of fuss.

The artists applies the same skill to her Pop monoprints (paintings on glass that are then pressed to paper, reversing the image) and sees the same value in, say, the reductive Red Pepper reproduced here as she would in a gorgeously painted garden view.

For her, composition is the key and she has destroyed many works in which the subjects are not either balanced or harmonious.

In a busy painting you can correct any imbalance with a flurry of strokes elsewhere, whereas her more austere practice demands a skill acquired over a lifetime of effort. It is those works of hers that I admire the most.

MAGAZINE

Galleries

Artist Mary Collis spends lockdown documenting more than 2,500 of her works and posting them on Facebook as an evolving show and also a useful teaching a

Pop goes the easel as Net hosts a class act…

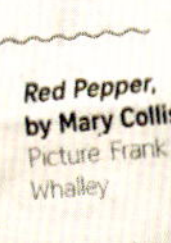

Frank Whalley
Special Correspondent

ife under lockdown continues apace and artists are filling in their enforced bo-

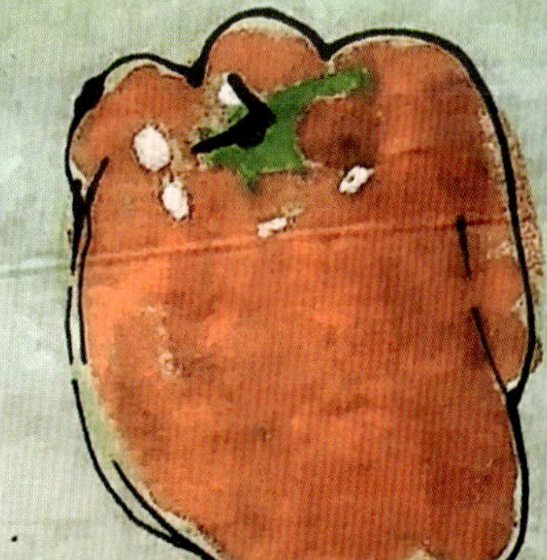

Red Pepper, by Mary Collis.
Picture Frank Whalley

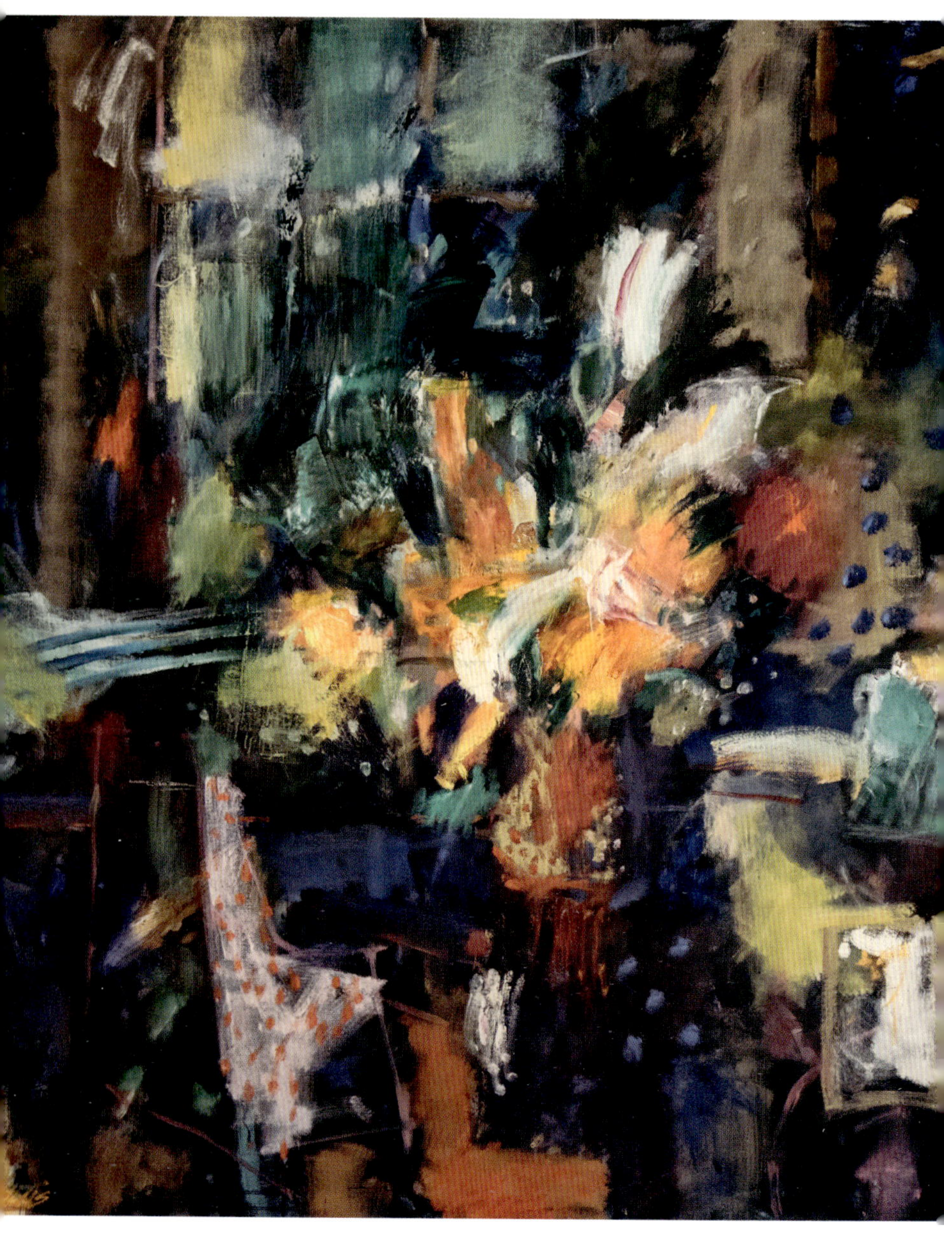

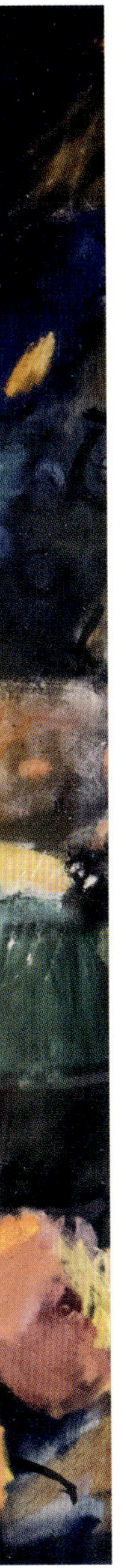

Day 58

Interior with Flowers

A dark painting is difficult for me.
The floor leads the eye in and the wall
gives a stability. Howard Hodgkin
paints wonderful interiors and I was
clearly looking at his work and have
painted his dots. Sometimes less is
more, there is no edge to the table but
one can see that there is one.

*'God, how I ricochet between
certainties and doubts.'* – Sylvia Plath

Collection of Duncan and Aru Willets,
Nanyuki, Kenya

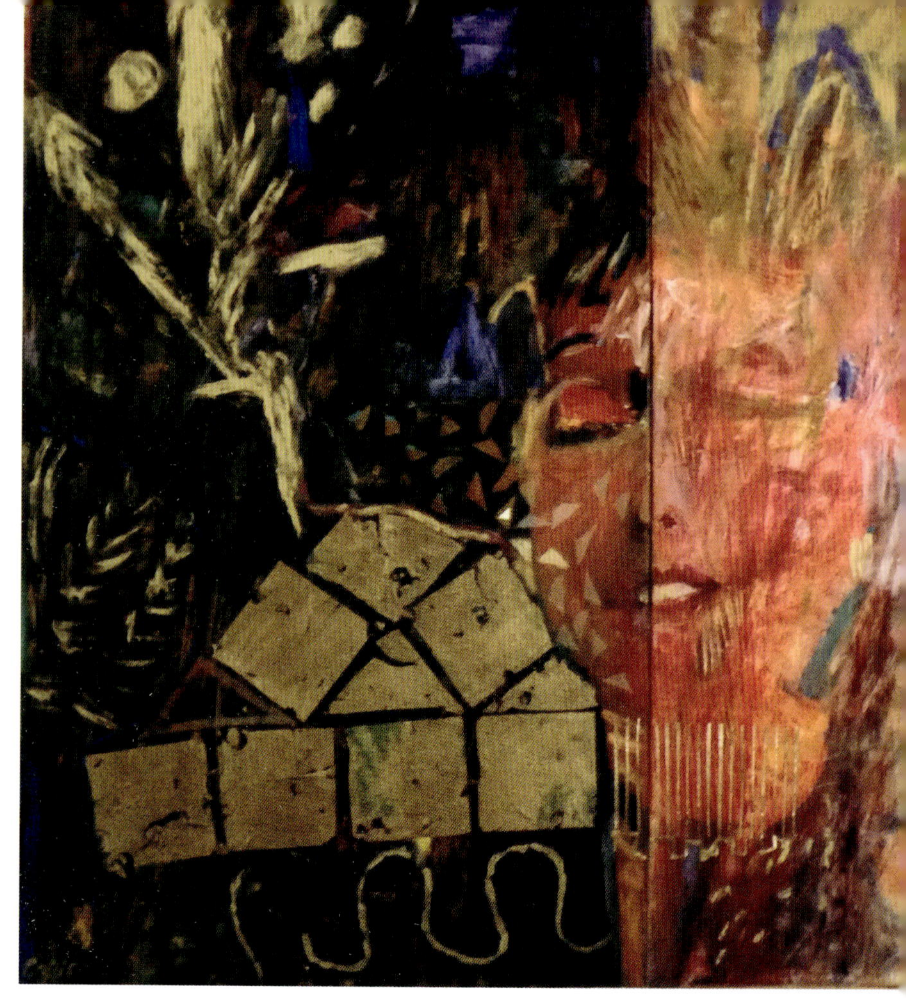

I don't think I titled this, as it sold so quickly. Clearly I was
thinking of 'Judith III, Mrs Blochtauer'. There is lots of
gold paint and gold leaf, and I have used some of Klimt's
symbolism. I love Gustav Klimt (who doesn't?) This red

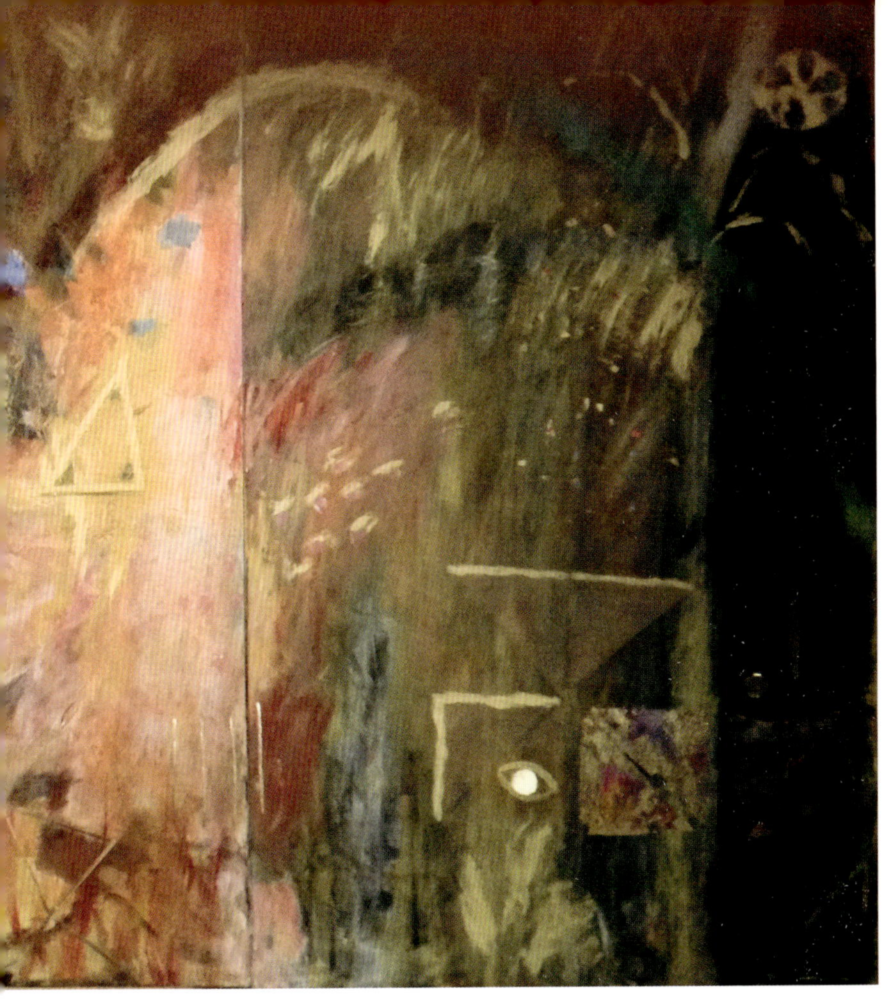

face does not begin to emulate the way he paints his flesh, with downward strokes of palest blue over Naples yellow and pinks. For ages I gazed at his forest in Birkenwald with my nose practically on the canvas in the Musée d'Orsay. He was a masterful colourist with an extraordinary feeling for light and his brushstrokes make me heady. Collection of Anis Pringle.

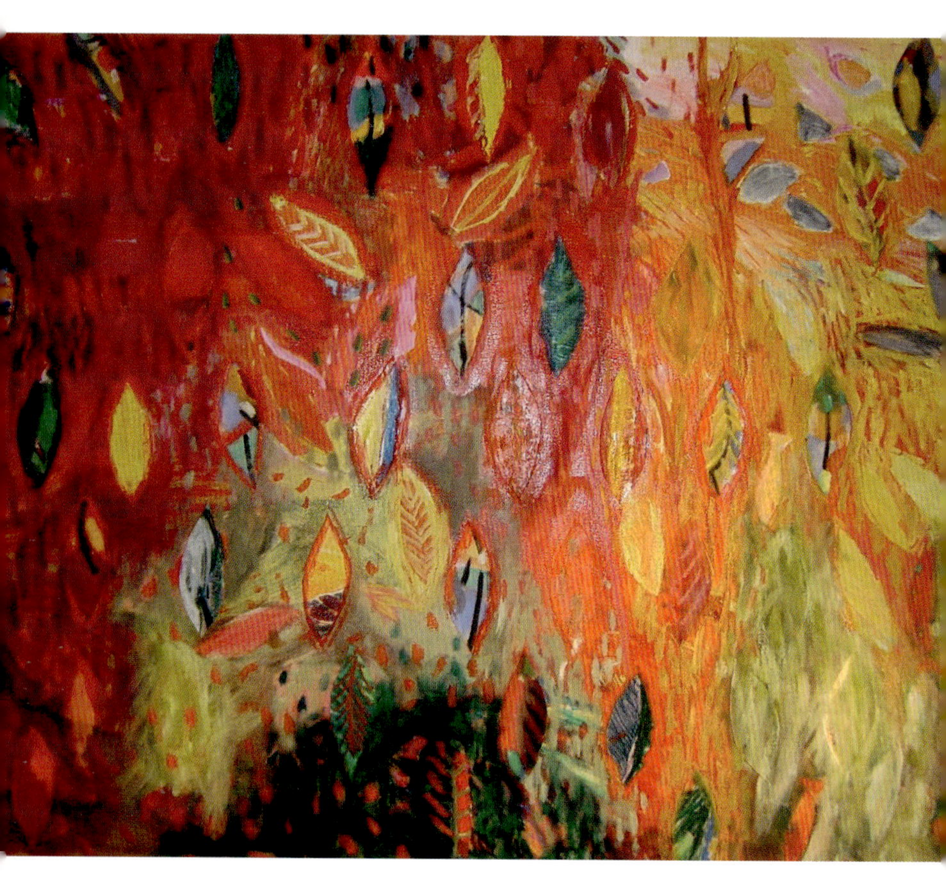

Day 60
Red Rain 1

One of those large paintings
that evolved, with much going
on underneath. It's not the best
photograph of it, as there is a distinct
flash about the middle. However, it is
one of my own personal favourites,
which I reluctantly let go. It graced
the cover of the art magazine
MSANI, Swahili for 'artist'.
The work is of mixed media, as some
of the leaves were collaged from other
paintings. Maintaining a brilliant red
is not easy, as red if overdone (like a
steak) has a tendency to go brown.

Day 61
Another Red One

'If I do live again,' wrote Oscar Wilde, 'I would like to be as a flower – no soul but perfectly beautiful.' He wasn't completely certain about geraniums, a lovely but common flowering plant: 'Perhaps for my sins I shall be made a red geranium.' From Alexander Theroux, *The Primary Colours*. His book is a constant source of inspiration for me.

My friend Julia Doig, who now lives in Loughborough, bought this painting sight unseen directly from the Facebook lockdown exhibition. When I posted it, I was still changing my mind about it, unsure if it was finished. With the help of Julia's eye, it came to a sudden end.

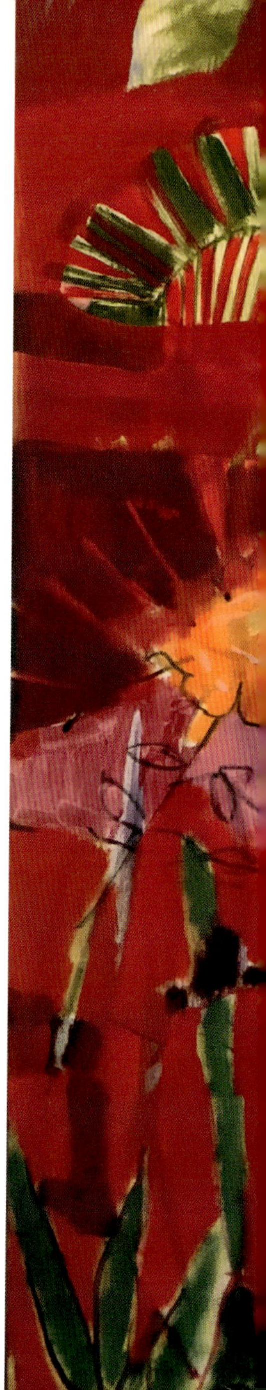

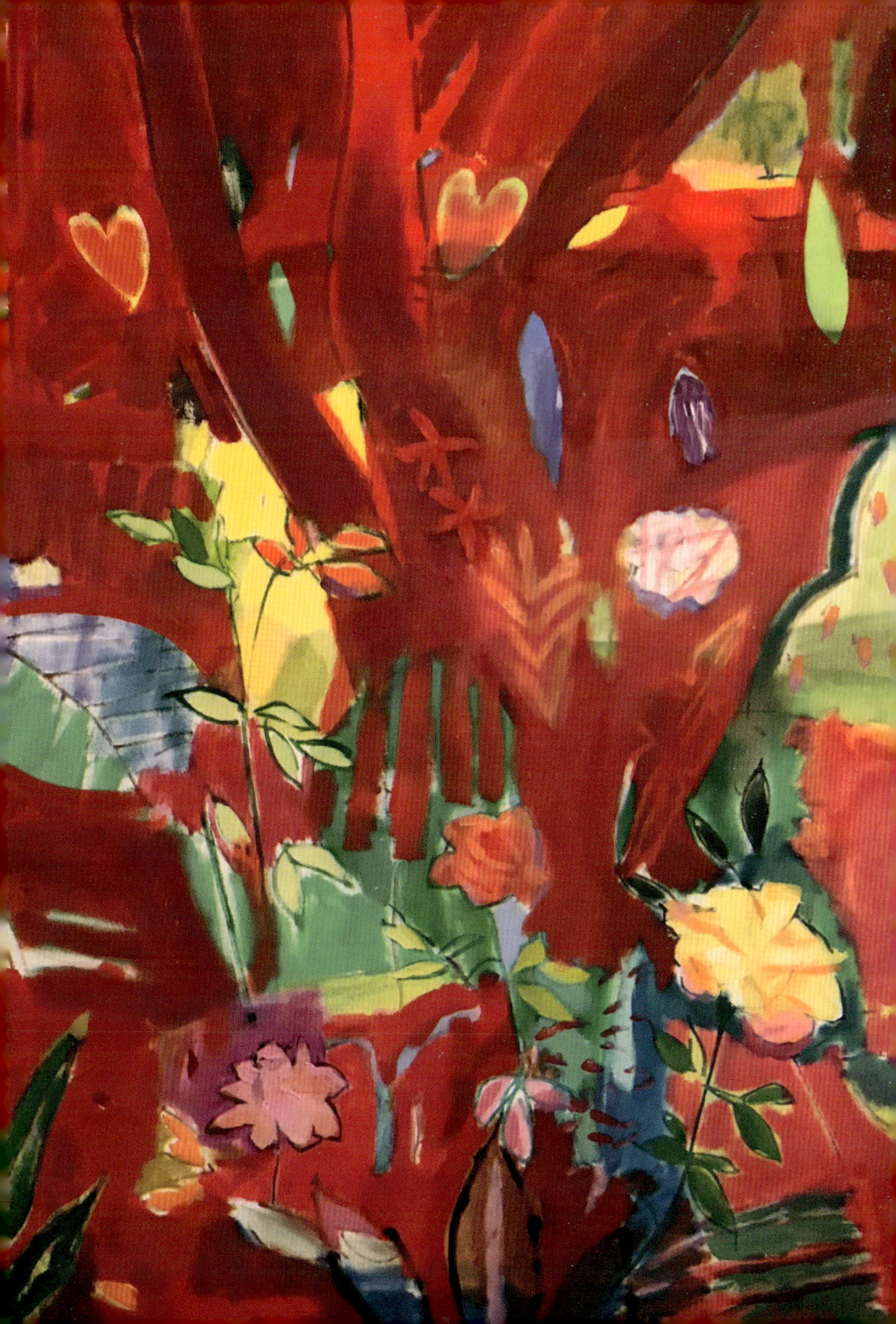

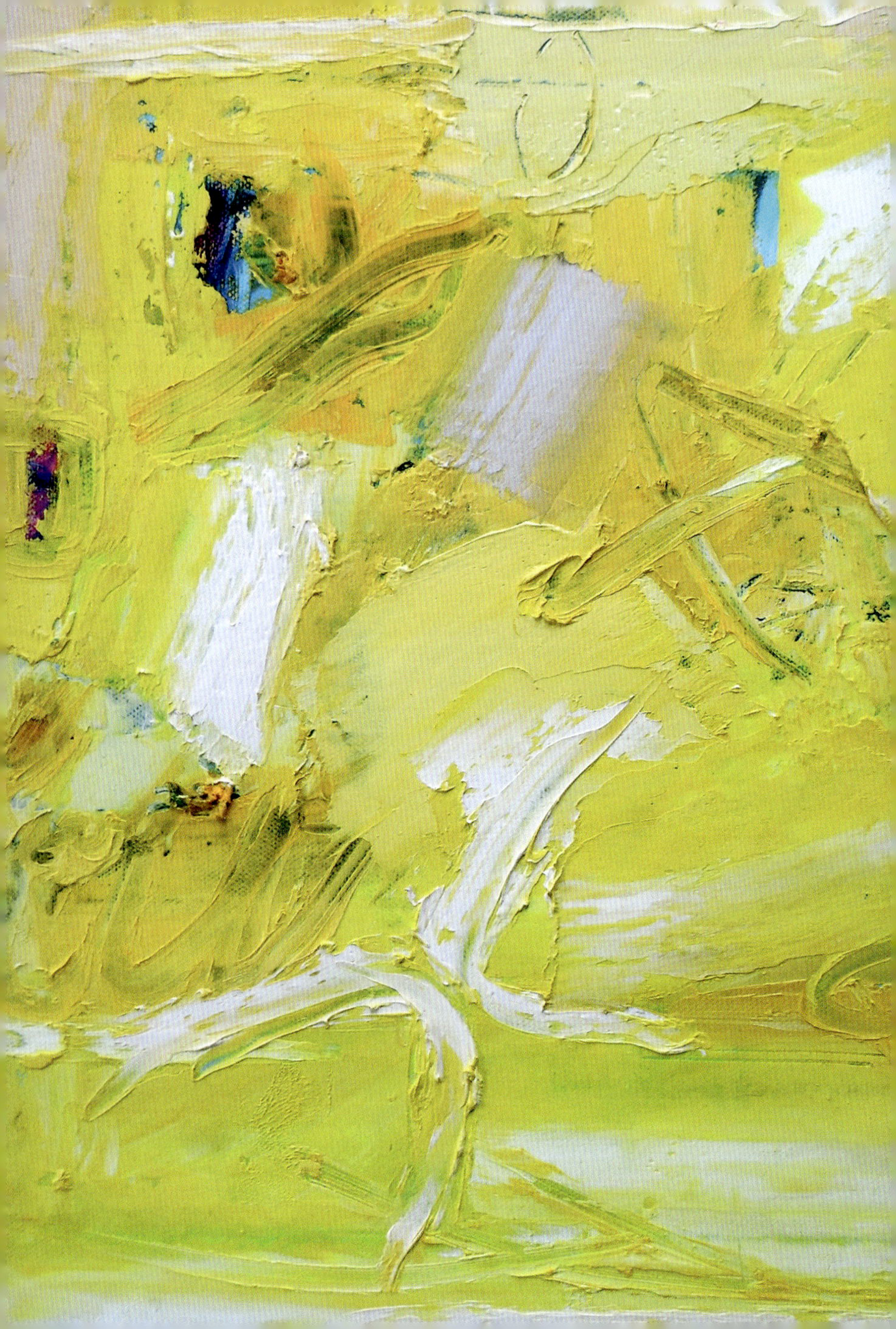

Day 62

Yellow is joy and luminous.
I like to think this lifts the spirit,
as it is so joyful. Its energy is in
the brushstrokes and I used a
pallet knife.
The crosses force the eye round
and on the complementary lilac
the eye rests. A good abstract
can be hung any way round,
and I change this one round on
my wall, in the Cape. It amuses
me to do so. No one else in the
household ever notices.

Day 63
Swimming

The painter Sean Scully is interesting to me.
He paints stripes, only stripes, and he
paints them in the most painterly way.
He has a huge influence over many artists.
This is a small work which is one of many
in a series I painted about fifteen years
ago. I like it because it has an action of a
swimming gala and movement, opposite
and complementary colours. During this
pandemic time, Scully has done something
interesting, he has introduced a black
square over his stripes, which he calls 'Dark
Windows' to acknowledge the dark times.
In the collection of great friends
Jan and Azmina Janmohamed, who have
many of my paintings.

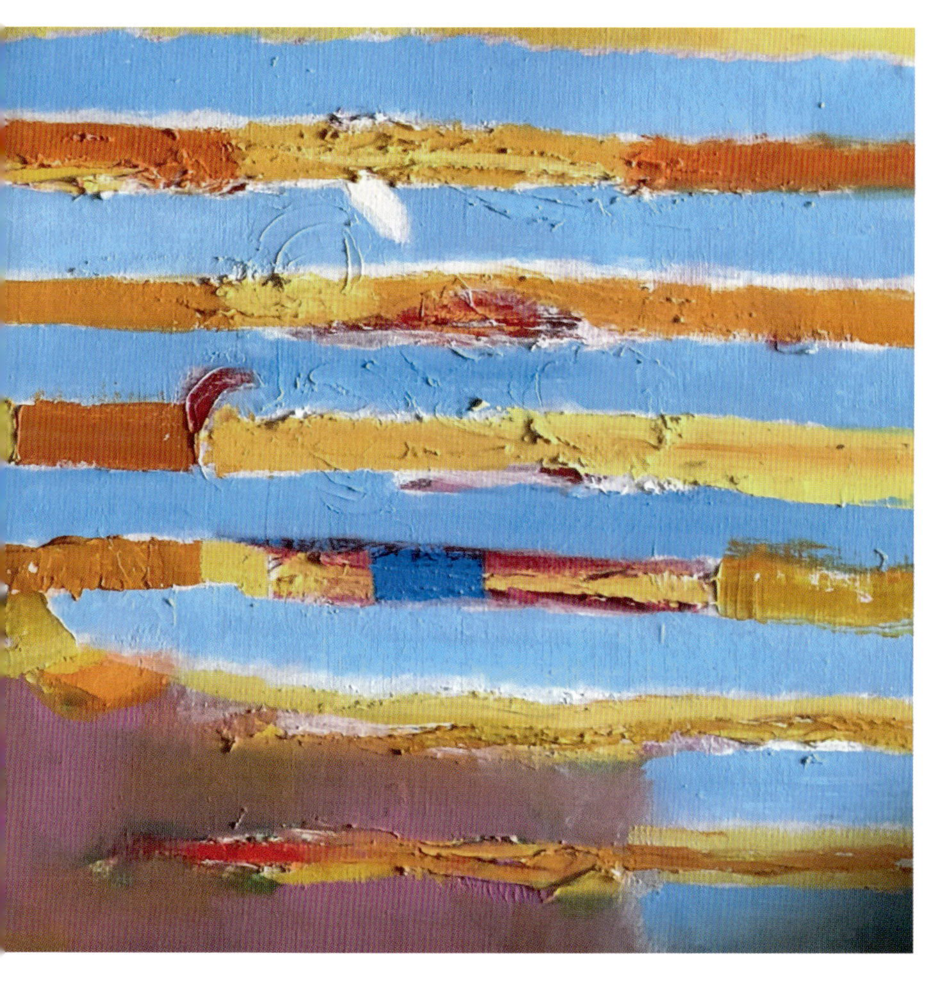

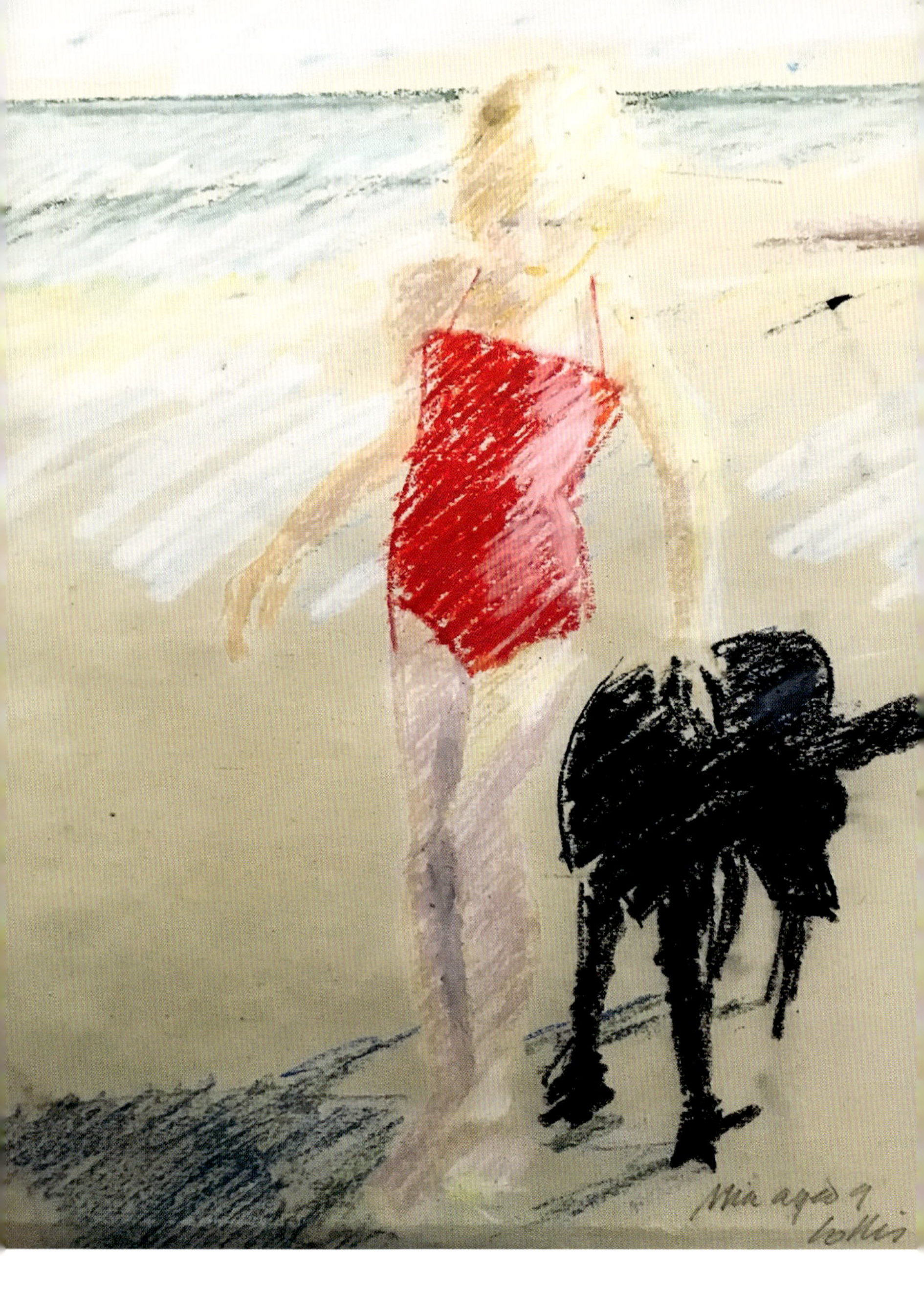

Day 64
Mimi

I visited my daughter Mia today
and found this long-forgotten
sketch on her wall. I can tell by
the light and the shadow it was
about an hour before midday,
on the beach at Msambweni,
south of Mombasa.

Day 65
Another Red Shift

The dark red arch holds the two sides of this
canvas together. I look to the contemporary
American artist Susan Rothenberg, with her
jabbing brushstrokes often indicating movement
through time. She is far more marginal in her
admirable paintings than my red shift here.
Her compositions take up a minimal space on
her monumental canvases and yet her punching,
stabbing brushwork takes over the space. She is
so distinctive, so admirable, so idolised by me.
This work resides in the Netherlands.

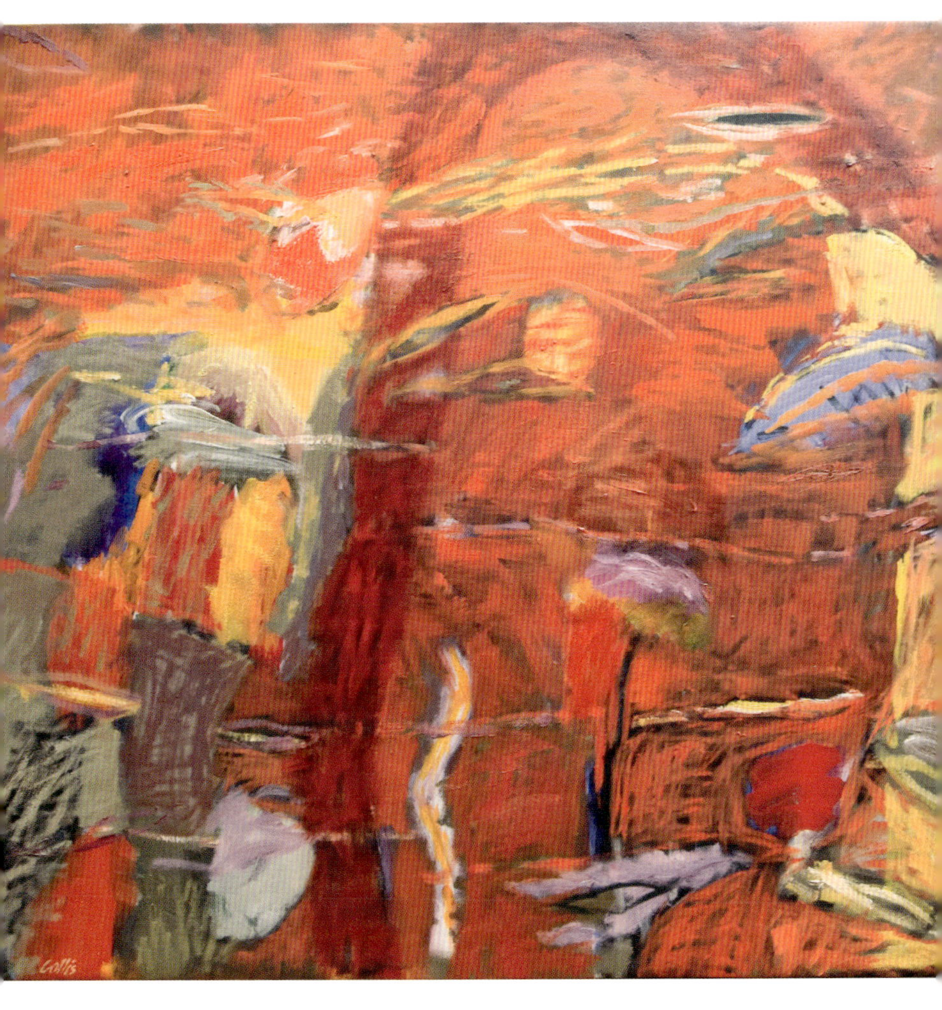

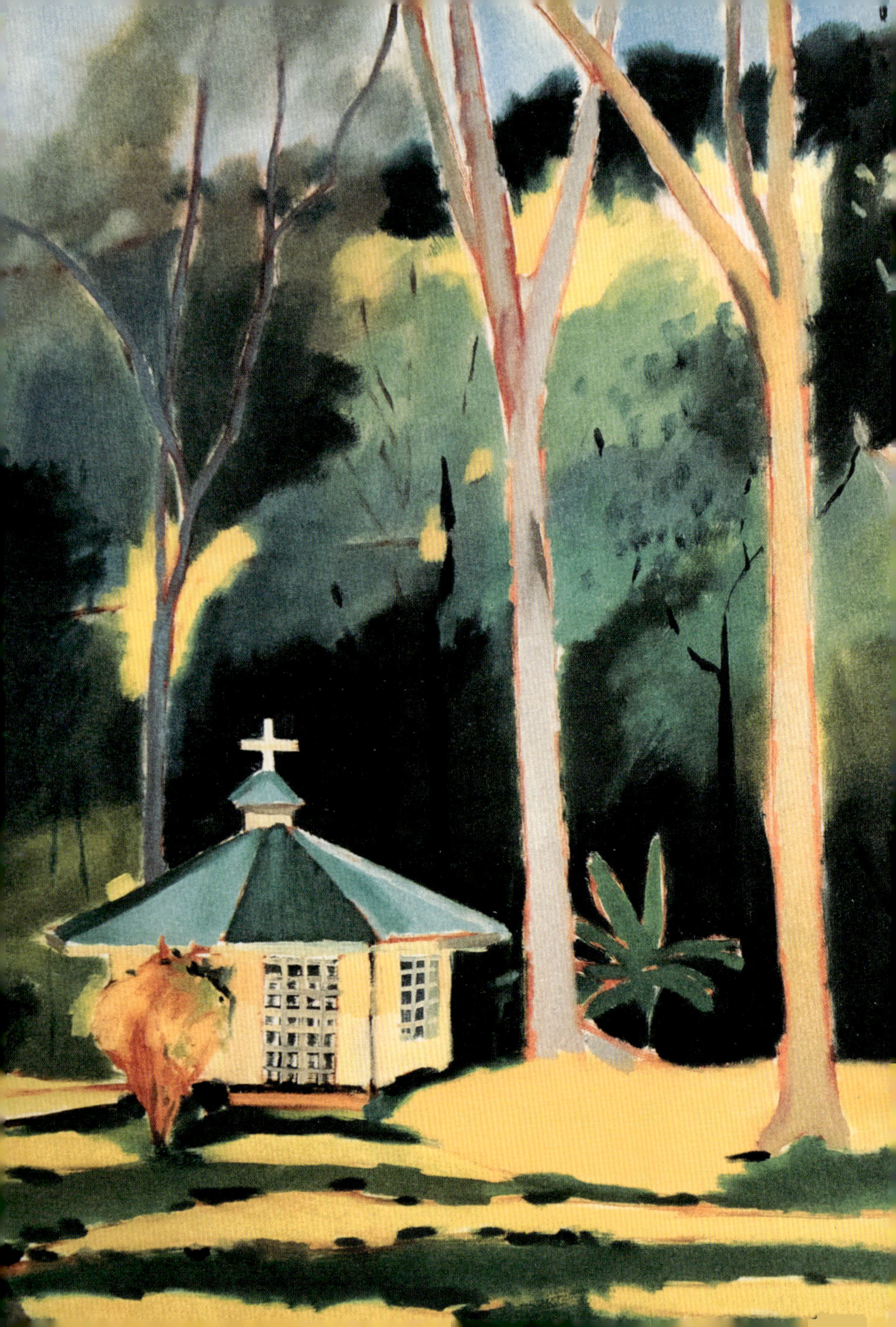

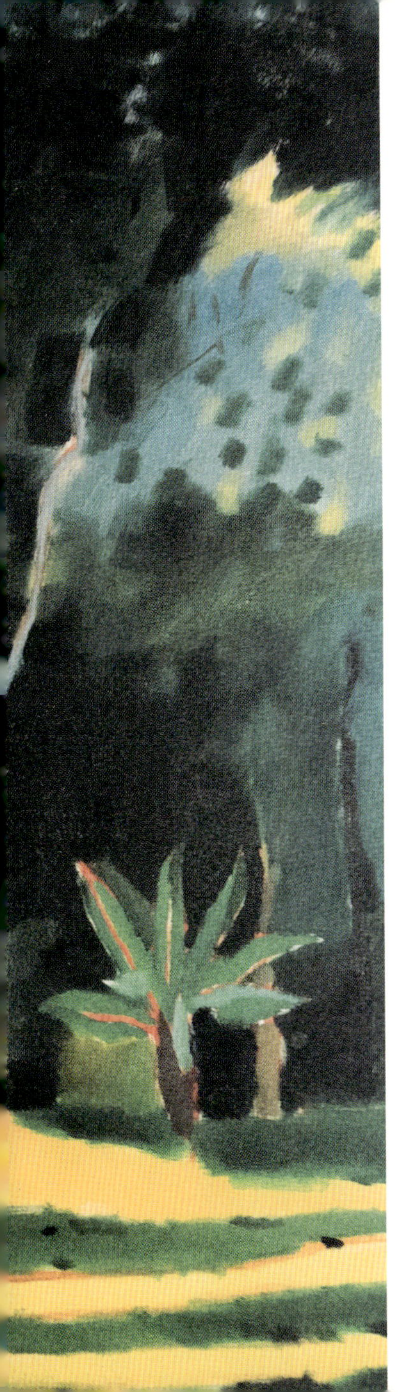

Day 66
Rondo Retreat, Kakamega Forest, Western Kenya

A beautiful place to be for peace and quiet in the middle of the forest, sadly being decimated at a horrible pace. Two families went there when our children were small. Lovely walks through the trees have left me with a memory of a complete feeling of peace. Painted for the Caltex calendar.

Day 67
Cityscape

I see there is a new series about Ned
Kelly on Netflix, which reminds me of the
Australian painter Sidney Nolan, who made
an extensive series of paintings after Ned
Kelly. Nolan is a wonderful landscape painter
and he would put this shocking black figure
with a square head and a rectangle where
the eyes should be, so the viewer can see
through the mask into the painting.
My friend Doria Block knew Sidney Nolan.
I don't remember thinking much about him
when I was painting this, but perhaps I had
been looking at his work with her?
Collection of Mike and Sue Bristow, London

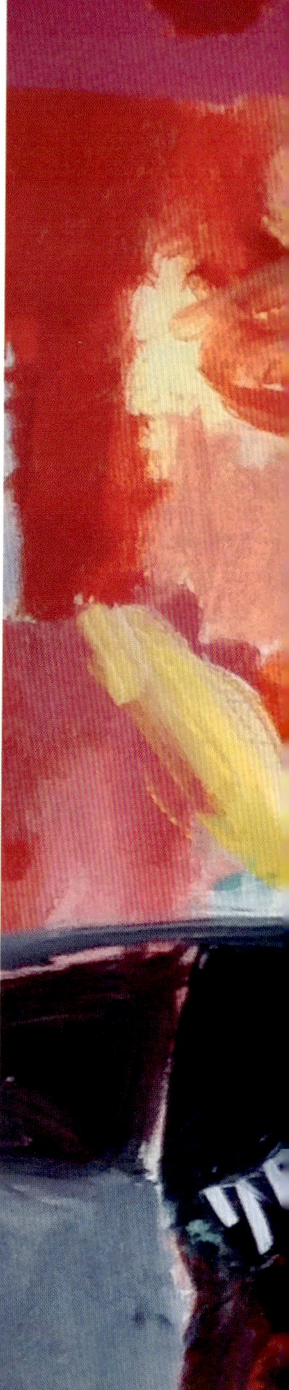

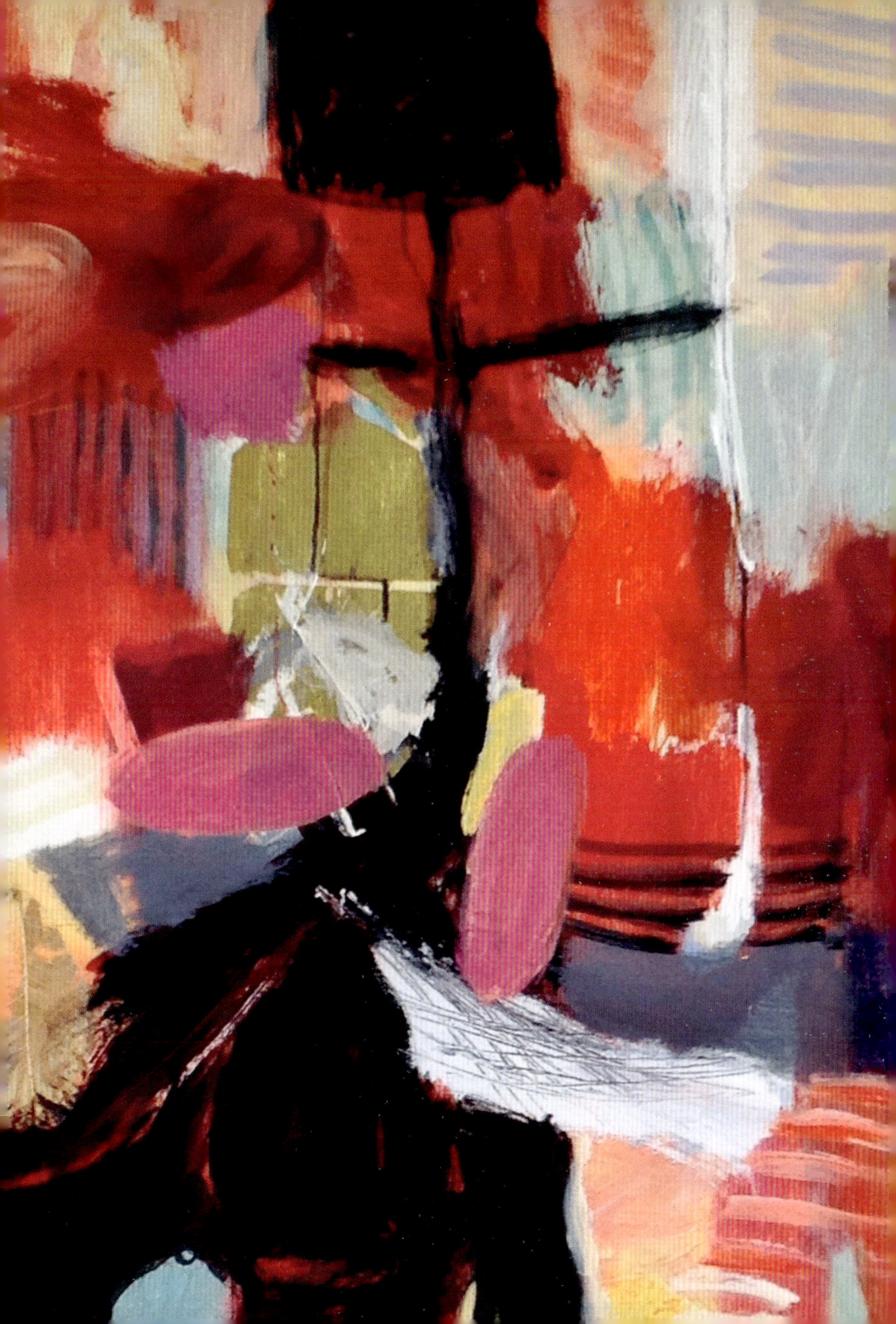

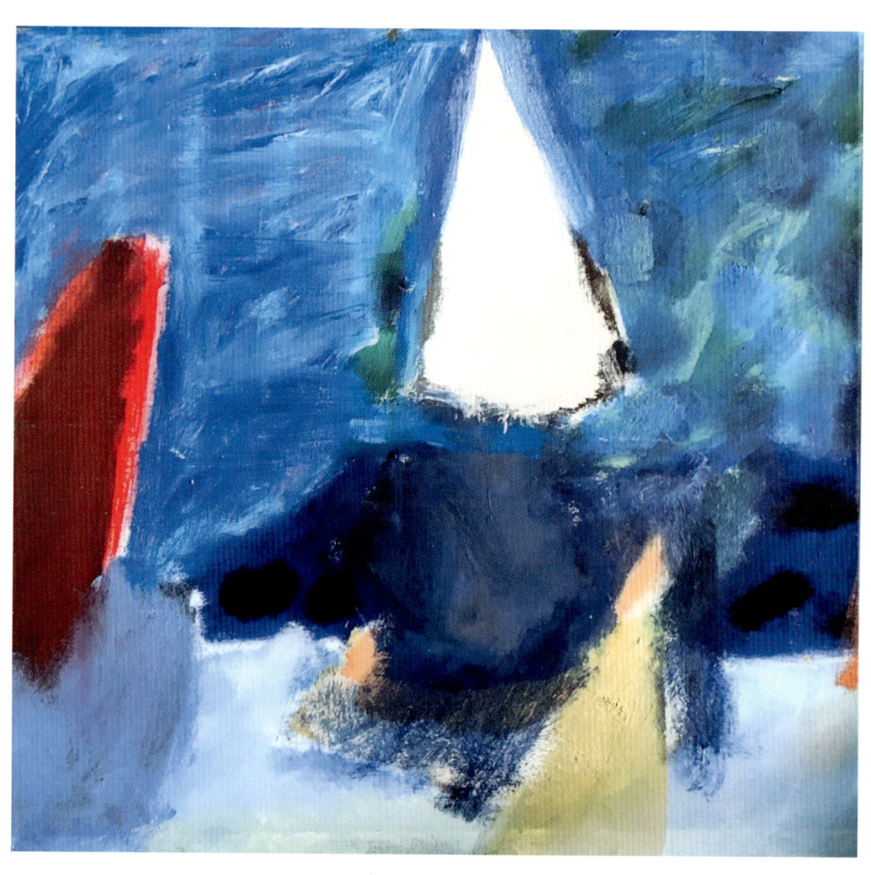

Day 68
Sailing

This small but dense painting is favoured.
It sits on a very thick stretcher like a brick.

*I think I can see a boat floating white
in the mist, and my heart opens*
Estrella by L.L. Barkat

I had a moment letting this go, although
it went to great friends. Collection of
Jan and Azmina Janmohamed, Nairobi, Kenya

Day 69
Moving Perspective
of Vase on Table

At the time I was painting these grids,
I was thinking very much about Paul
Cézanne and his 'moving perspectives',
the way one can see the background
move against the still subject by a mere
movement of the head. Cézanne forged
the way in his deconstruction of his still
lifes, where one becomes more aware of
the table on which his apples are placed,
despite the fruit being the subject of the
work. This vase was a beloved clay pot
I painted, and one of my red paintings is
behind the yellow roses in the vase, sitting
on the glass dining room table, with the
chairs all moving about.
Collection of Mike and Sheila Barker, Nairobi

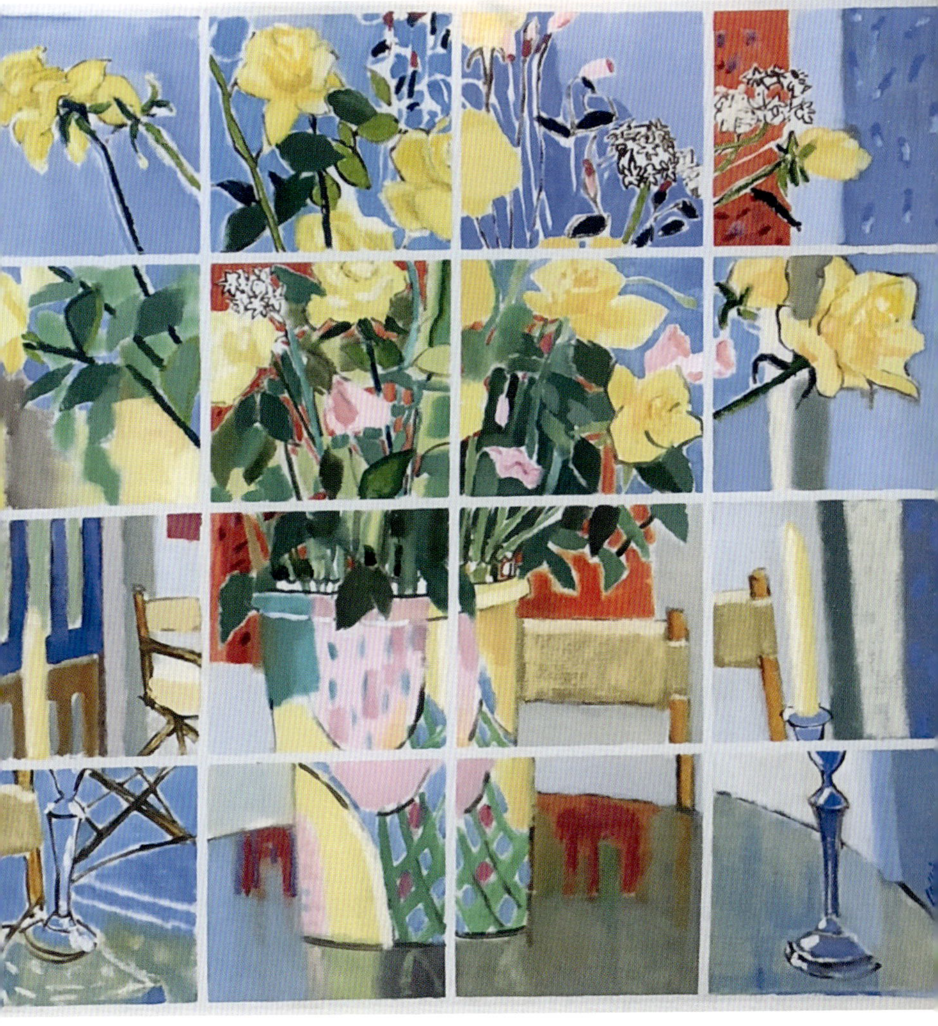

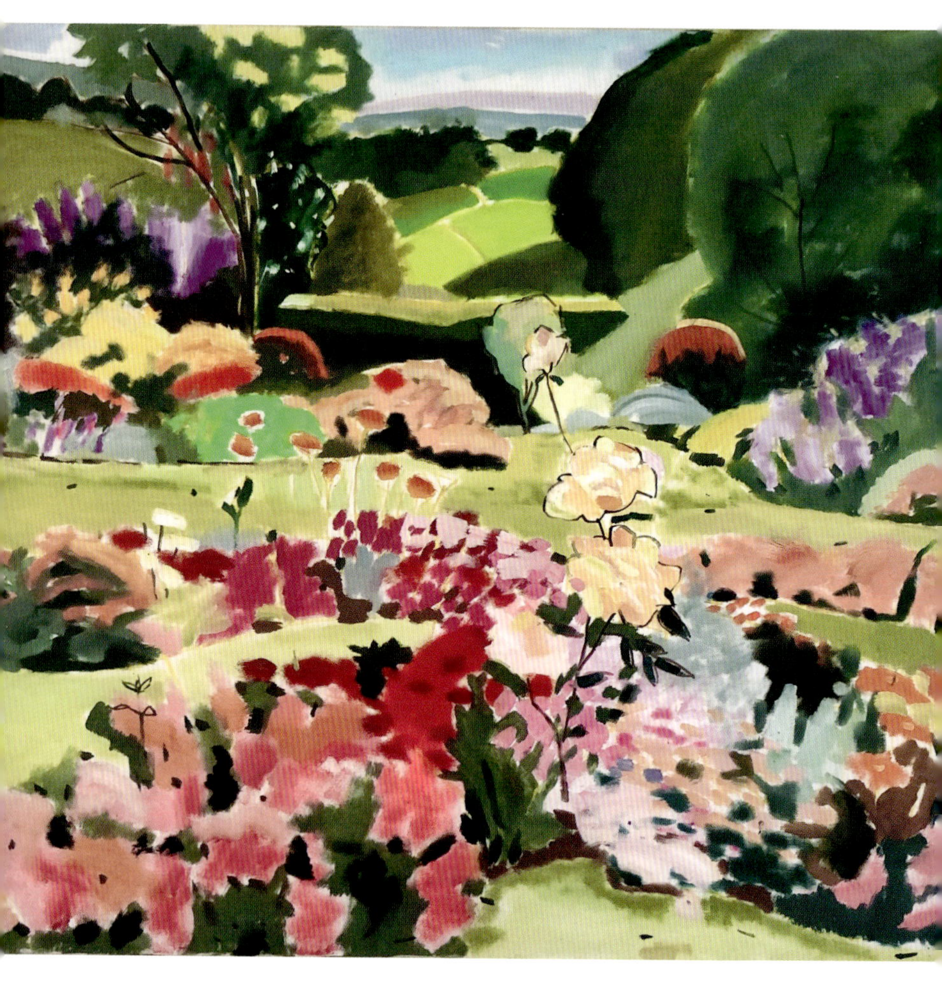

Day 70
**The Long View
'Erica's Garden' series**

This online exhibition has been a splendid
and surprising occurrence for me. There
were no expectations when I began,
other than to uplift everyone's day during
lockdown. Today Lindsay, Erica's daughter,
kindly sent me these photos of her mother's
garden in Tigoni. With my back to the house,
this is the view that Erica woke up to on a
clear morning. You can see the garden was
not huge, and it sloped downhill with a view
of the tea field over the hedge at the bottom,
and on to Nairobi in the distance.
I was attracted by those beautiful pinks in
the left foreground and the rose (of course)
that anchors so many of my paintings.
Collection of Lindsay Alice Boswell, France

Day 71
A Walk in the Park

The first work painted in my new
studio after we moved downtown,
over an old painting. Fireworks,
oranges and the red hot pokers and a
cool blue path. I like to think one can
stand inside this painting in one's mind.
A large canvas for a small space in a
hut in a friend's garden, currently my
studio. I am looking for a bigger atelier.

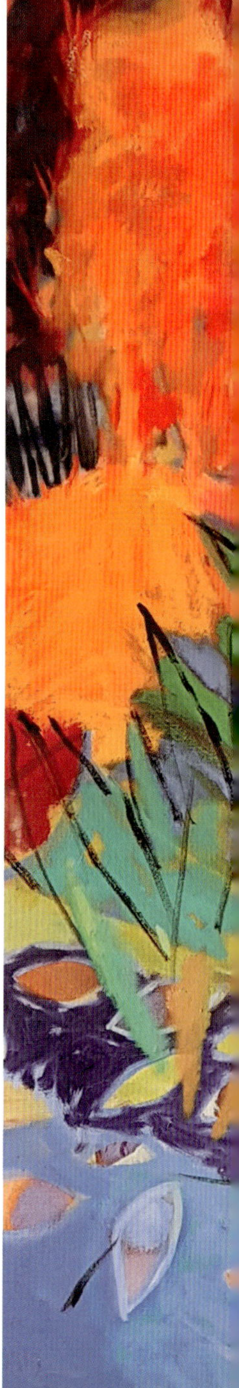

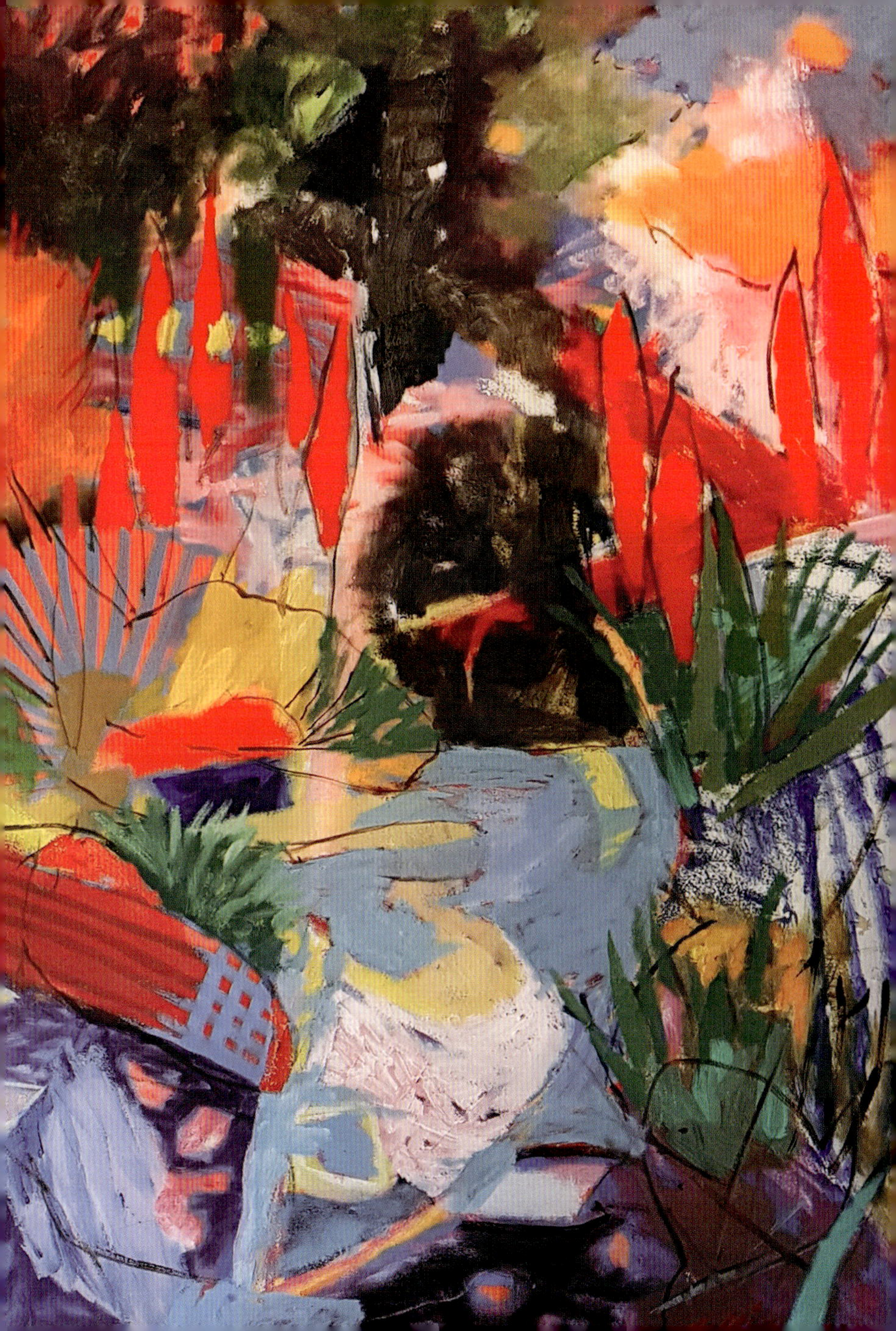

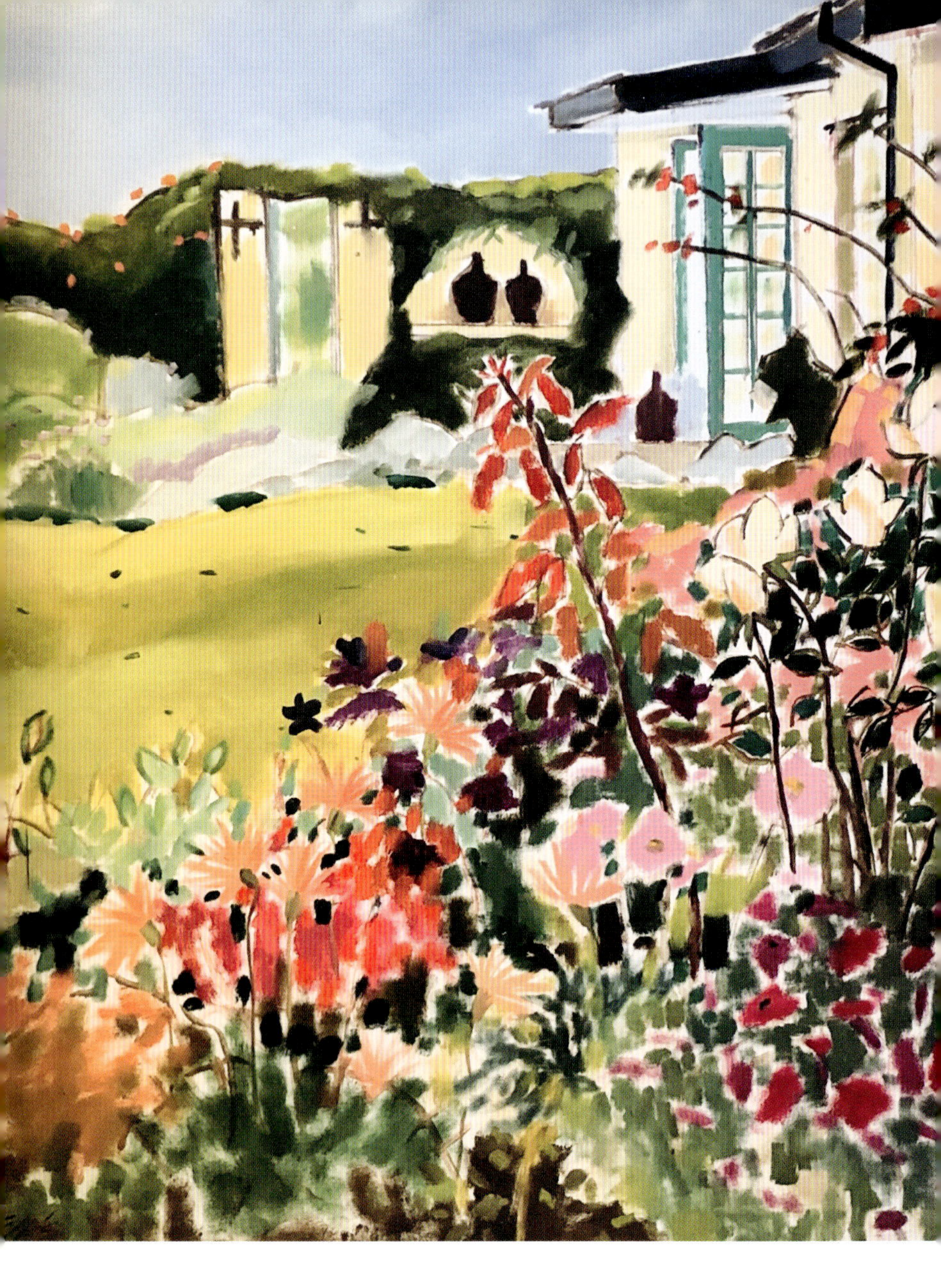

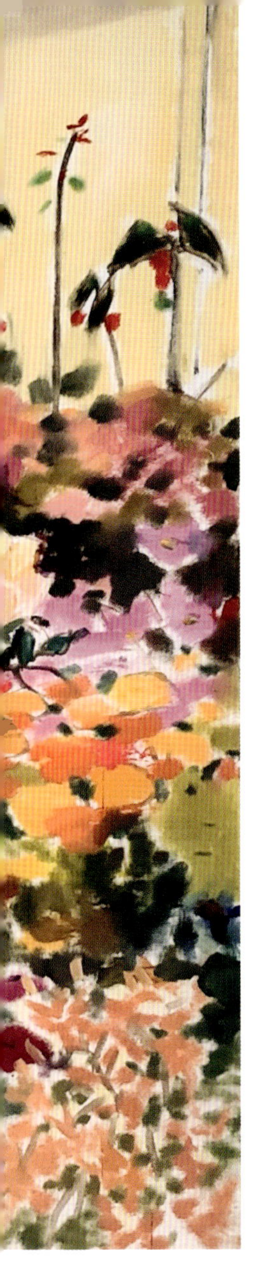

Day 72
Erica's Garden
'Erica's Garden' series

Looking at the house – all the converging
lines meet on that divine proportion, the
golden mean – where the front doors were
always open with a welcome. Painted over
midday, again, where everything sits on
its shadow. And the rose bush gives some
stability to the flowerbed. Every bush was
in flower in Erica's garden, all the time.
No sooner was the flower 'over', it would
be removed and replaced. Erica had a large
nursery adjacent to the garden and two
knowledgeable shamba men.
I am grateful, for this forgotten work was
sent to me by Erica's daughter, Lindsay
Alice Boswell, who lives in France.

Day 73
Jackie McConnell's Garden

This is the second one I have shown from Jackie's exotic
jungle, the first is Day 14. This is of the side of her house,
where she had created a little more breathing space. I
am pleased with this composition, where the path of the
exotic flowerbed leads the eye to the open window. In
my mind's eye I can see the beautiful Jackie looking out.
My friend Sarah Withey photographed this in Sonja's
house in Nanyuki.
Sonja and David Parkinson saw this in my studio,
just before they moved to their new home in Nanyuki.
The move was such a wrench to all who knew them
in Nairobi. A few years later, David was tragically
murdered, most probably by poachers, as he had
stopped a lorry loaded with elephant tusks. Terrible
things like that have happened to good people in Kenya.
Photo by Sarah Withey

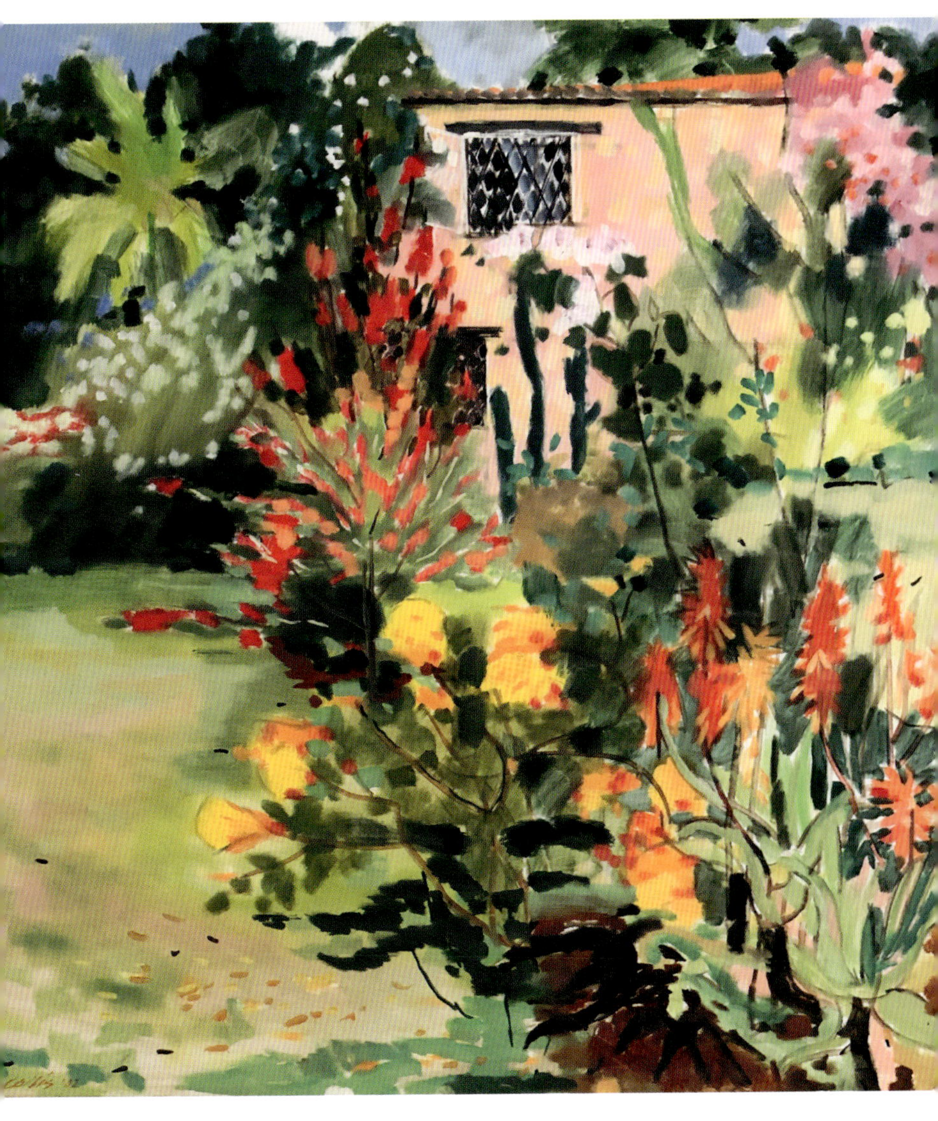

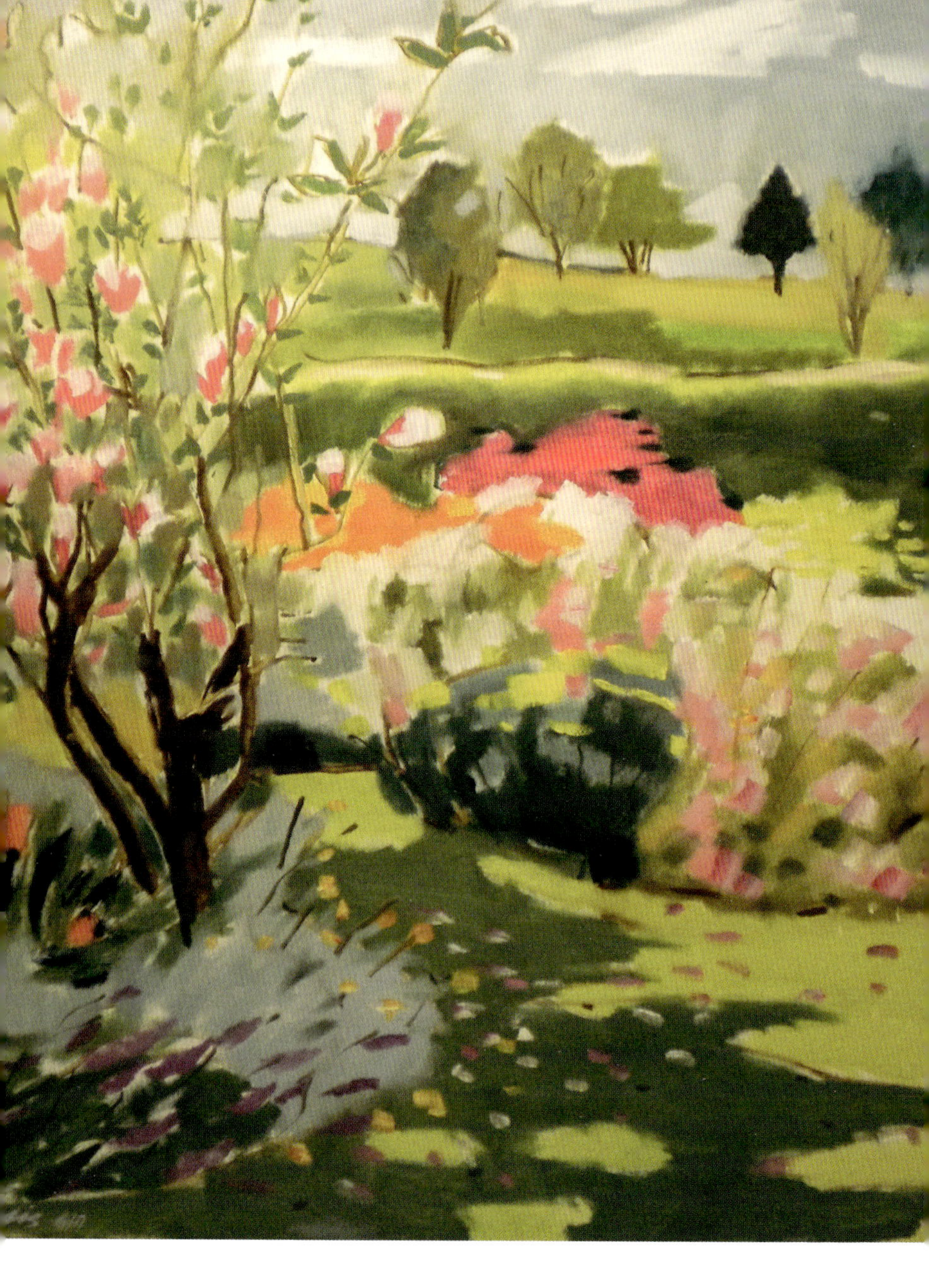

Day 74
After Midday at the Bottom of Erica's Garden
'Erica's Garden' series

Over the hedge looking towards Nairobi from Limuru, Tigoni. It is manicured to the bottom of the garden, with a beautiful apple tree in full blossom. The field of tea over the hedge and, further on, in front of the trees, is invisible to my eye from this low level. Collection of Jan and Azmina Janmohamed.

Day 75
Cannas

This large work was the penultimate
painting in my first series. Painted about
thirty-five years ago, at the very end of
the whole 'Canna' sequence, which was
the best year for that plant in East Africa.
Abundant, colourful and numerous, in thirty
years they have never been the same until
this year ... I am watching them now.
This painting hangs in a marriage parlour
in Holland. I like to believe that it brings
joy to the ceremony.

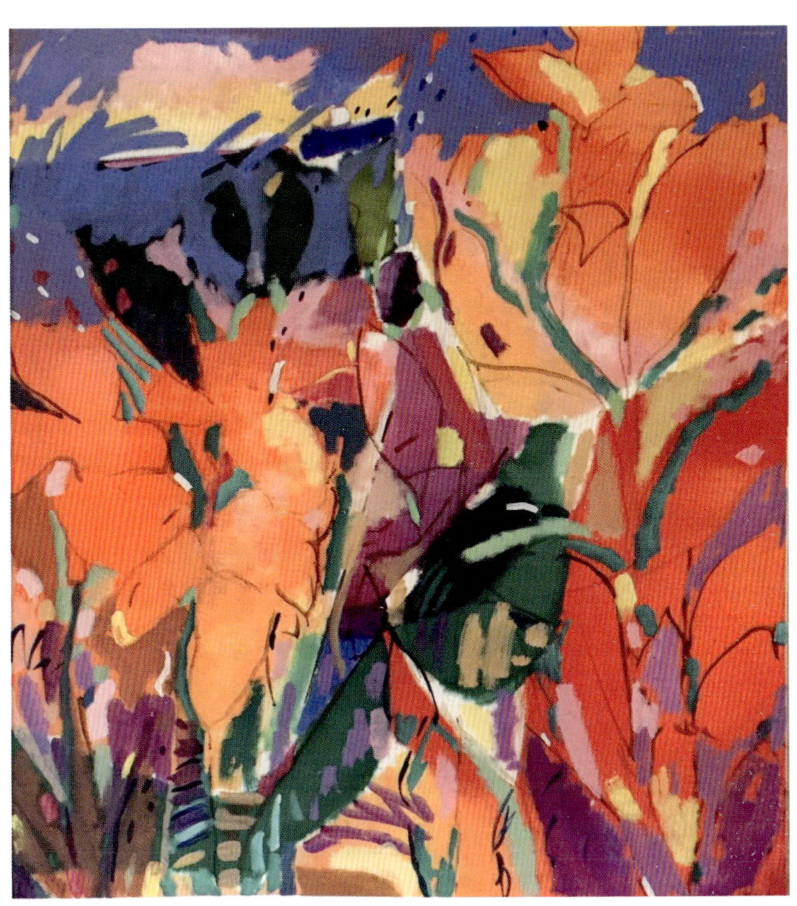

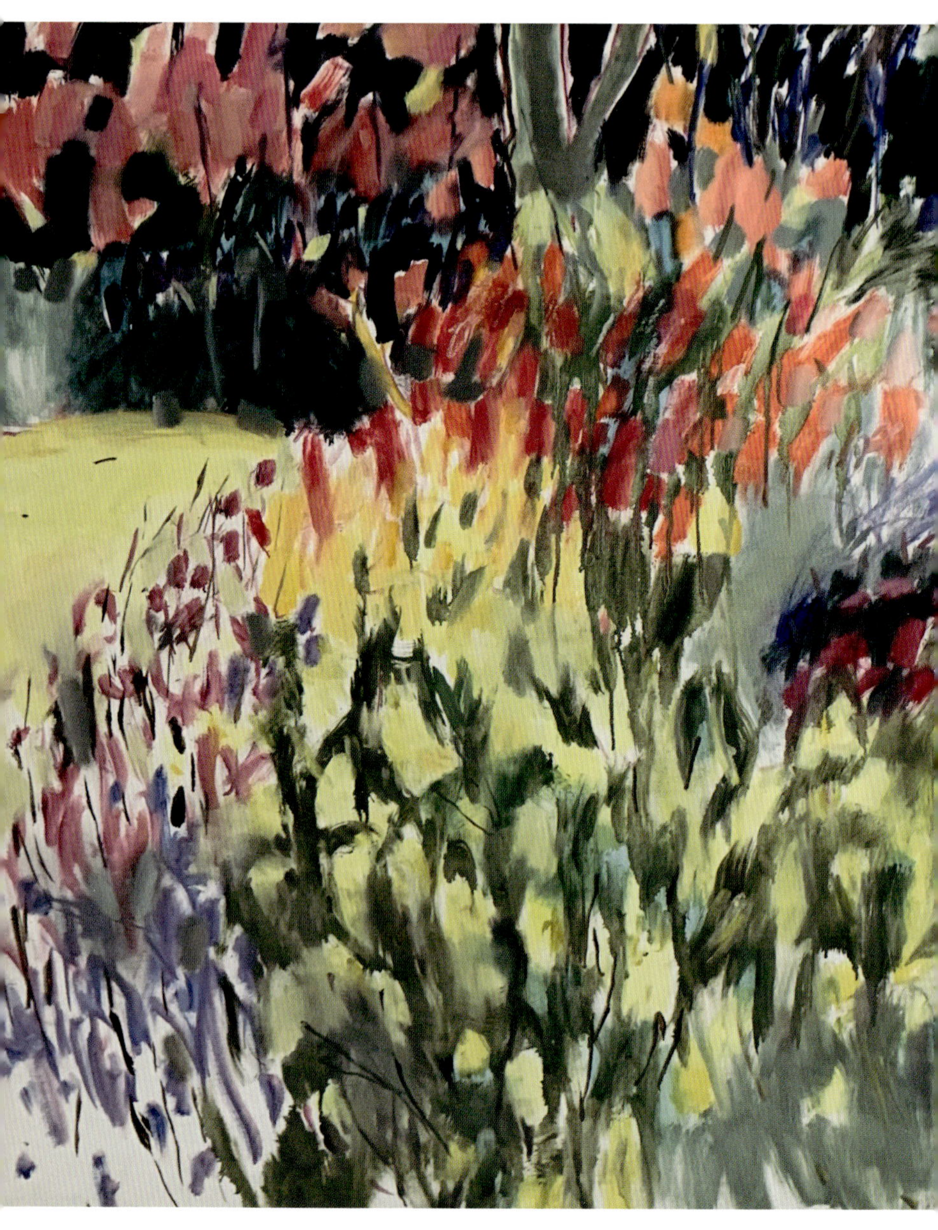

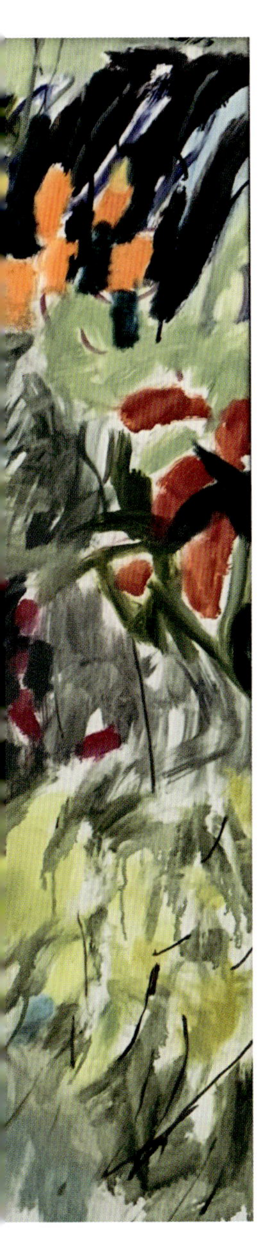

Day 76
Garden in Thika, Kenya

A large canvas painted with diluted oil,
it looks a bit like a watercolour. I must have
painted this a long time ago when the cannas,
top left, were at their very best.
I was pleased to sell this to Celia Macpherson,
who is a fabulous ceramicist. It is always a
compliment when an artist buys one's work.
I have one of her beautiful pots which I treasure.

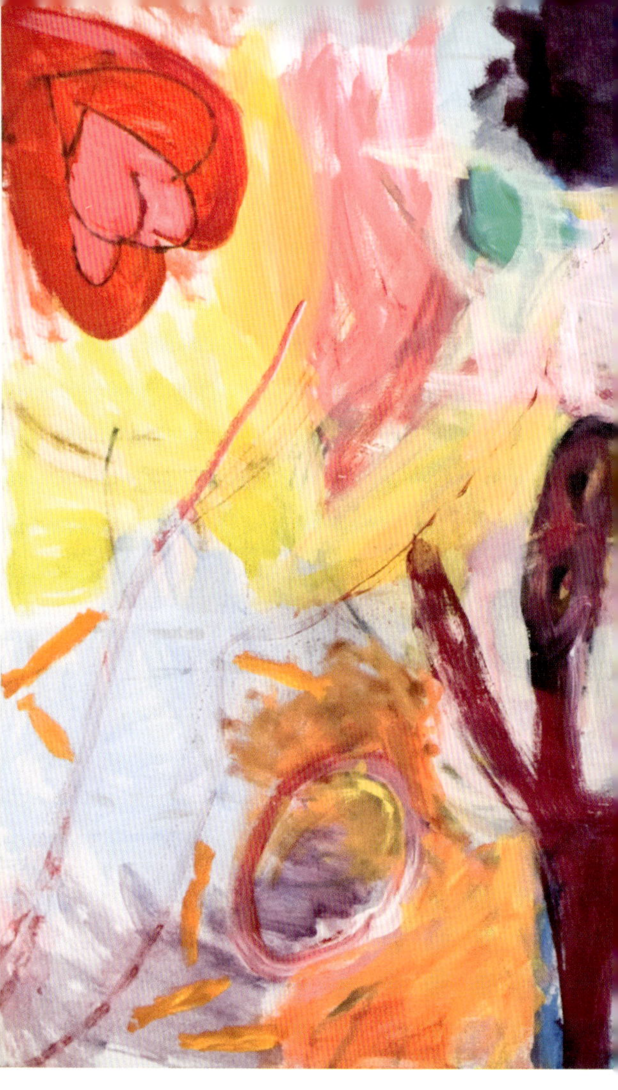

Day 77
Powerful,
Pink,
Passionate,
Painting

A commission that I very much enjoyed, this painting was to hang in a bedroom above a double bed and is the same 6 ft width. I liked the fact that the title was given to me by the client in advance of the work. It is one of those paintings where one can let one's imagination roam. It was rejected but it lived happily in my lounge for a long time

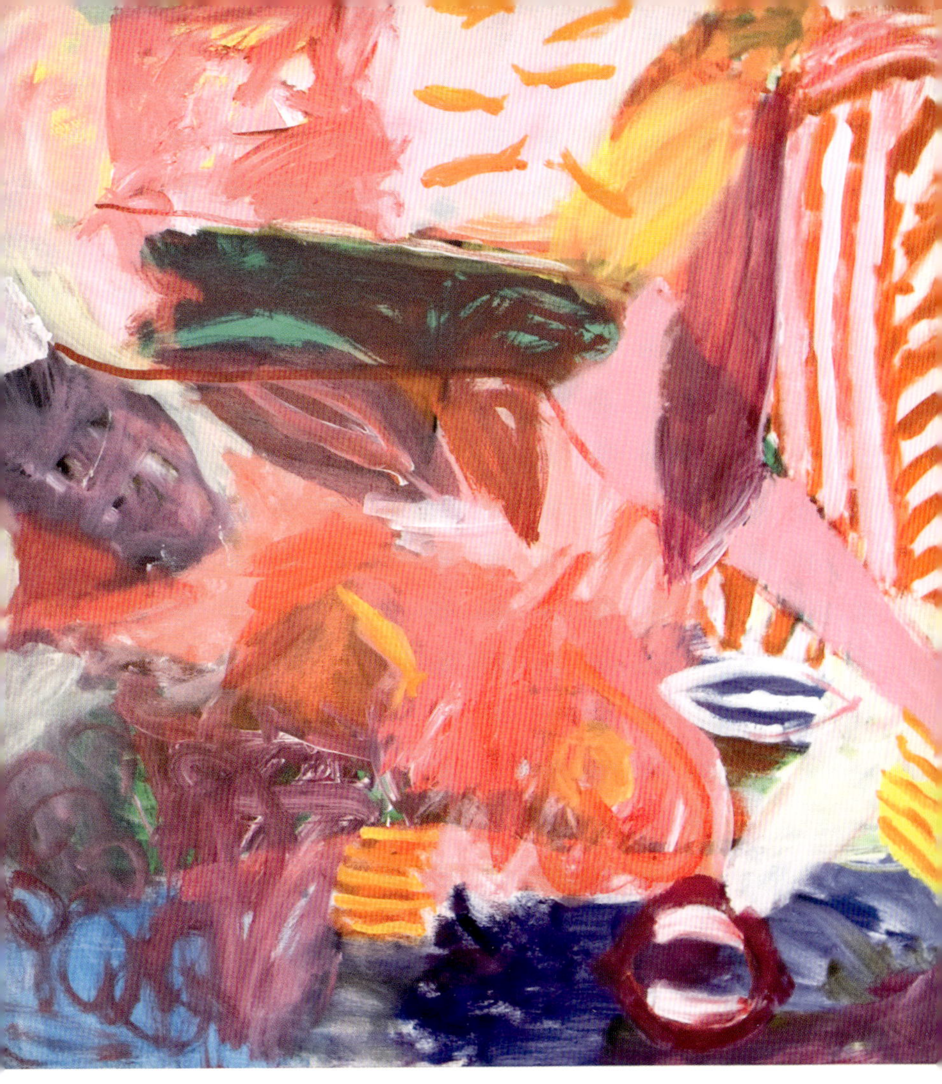

before it was bought. In the meantime, I had it printed on chiffon and
made into scarves, and printed on a heavy linen suitable for furniture.
I shall show some of the results tomorrow.
It was shown in a prestigious exhibition called 'Islands of Creativity'
curated by Dr Gonda Geets at the Safaricom Centre, Nairobi, 2010.

A chair designed
by Jutta Gavida.
Five chiffon scarves
from Collis Paintings.

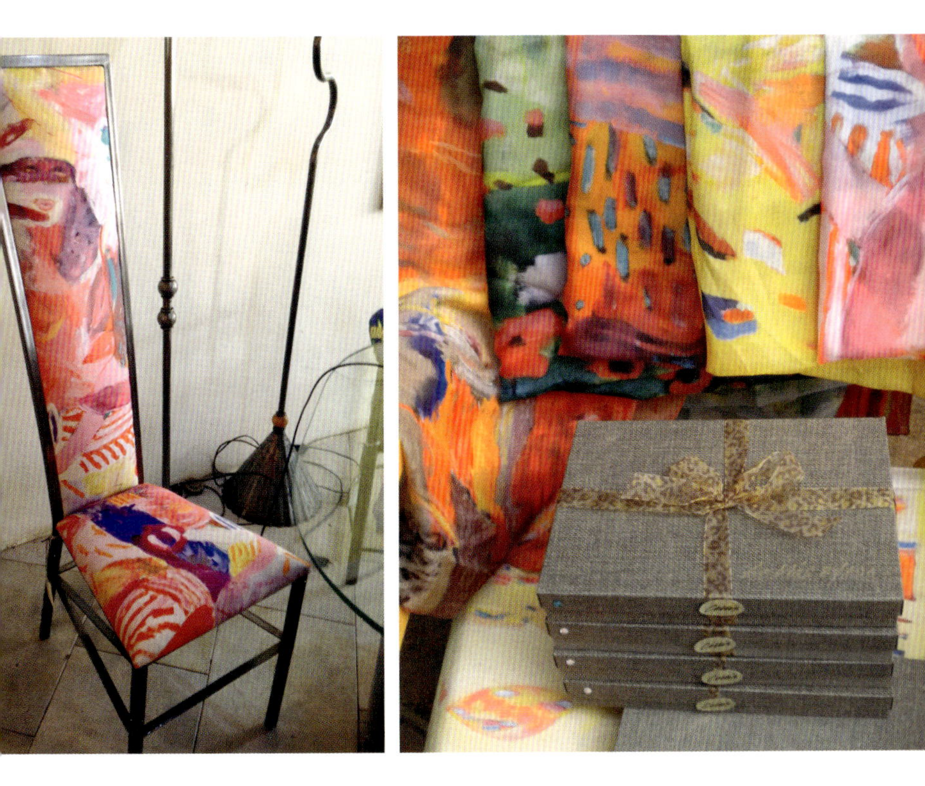

Day 79
Kimono

Something different ... I have had a lot of
mileage out of this quick sketch. It has been
enlarged to 5 ft high, printed on to canvas and
it looks splendid in both an office in Nairobi
and a beautiful bedroom in a modern home.
It has more of a presence, being larger than the
original. It has been printed on to thick silk and
made it into a lovely scarf, and friends have made
other creative garments with it. Not much more
I can say about this, other than I love it.
For fear of sounding a little whacky, this was
sent to me at the end of a long day when I wasn't
thinking and I had a blue brush in my hand.
The day before I had been life drawing a lovely
girl holding a fan.

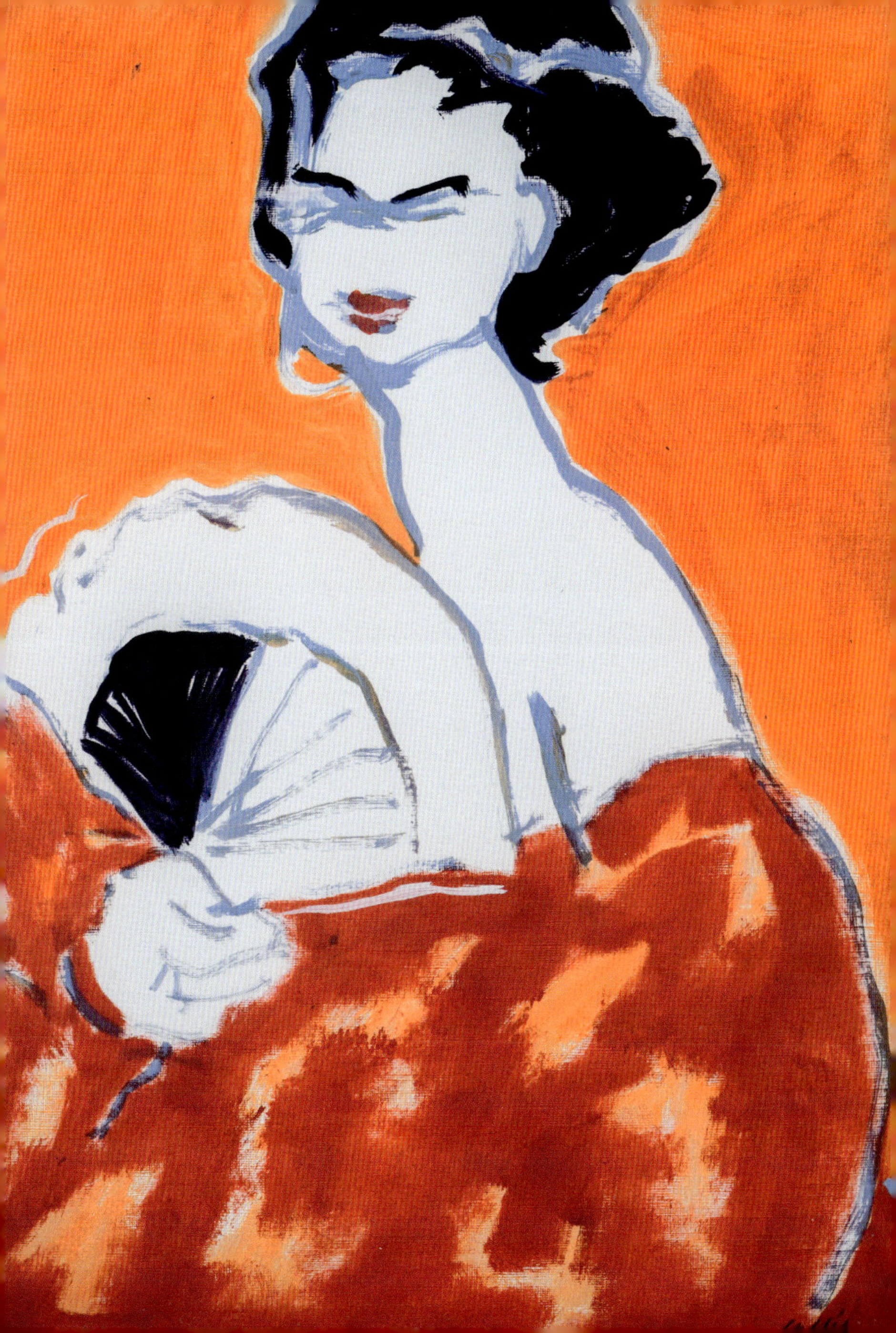

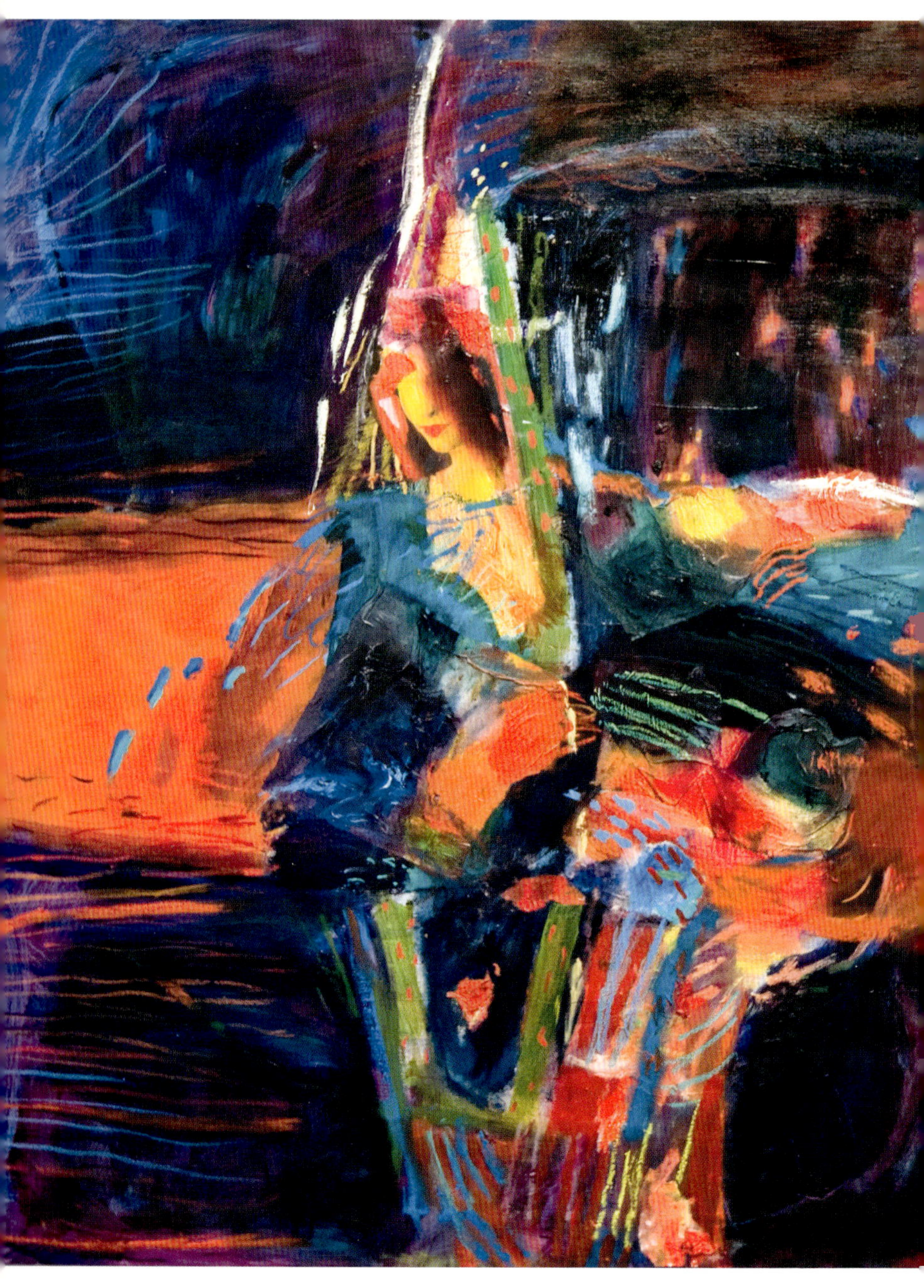

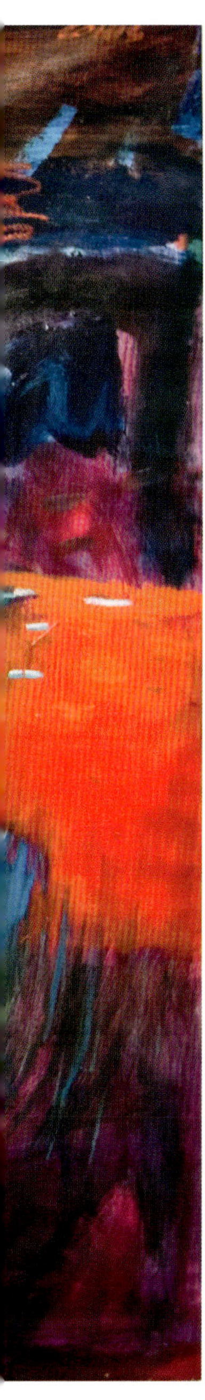

Day 80

Kimono
oil on canvas

To add the mouth and the nostril was a huge decision and I am still unsure if it was correct. It turned this colourful abstract into a figure. However, I do like the fact that the painting told me what to do. Kenneth Noland once said, 'We want the appearance to be the result of the process of making it – not necessarily to look like a gesture, but to be the result of real handling.' There is a Scottish colourist called Barbara Rae whose works are breath-taking, and I look at her when I need some inspiration. Collection of Nimu and Chandu Gidoomal, who have bought my work many times.

Day 81

Life Drawing

Somebody asked me if I ever draw
a figure? Here's one. The model is
very thin. I got quite carried away
by the blanket beneath.

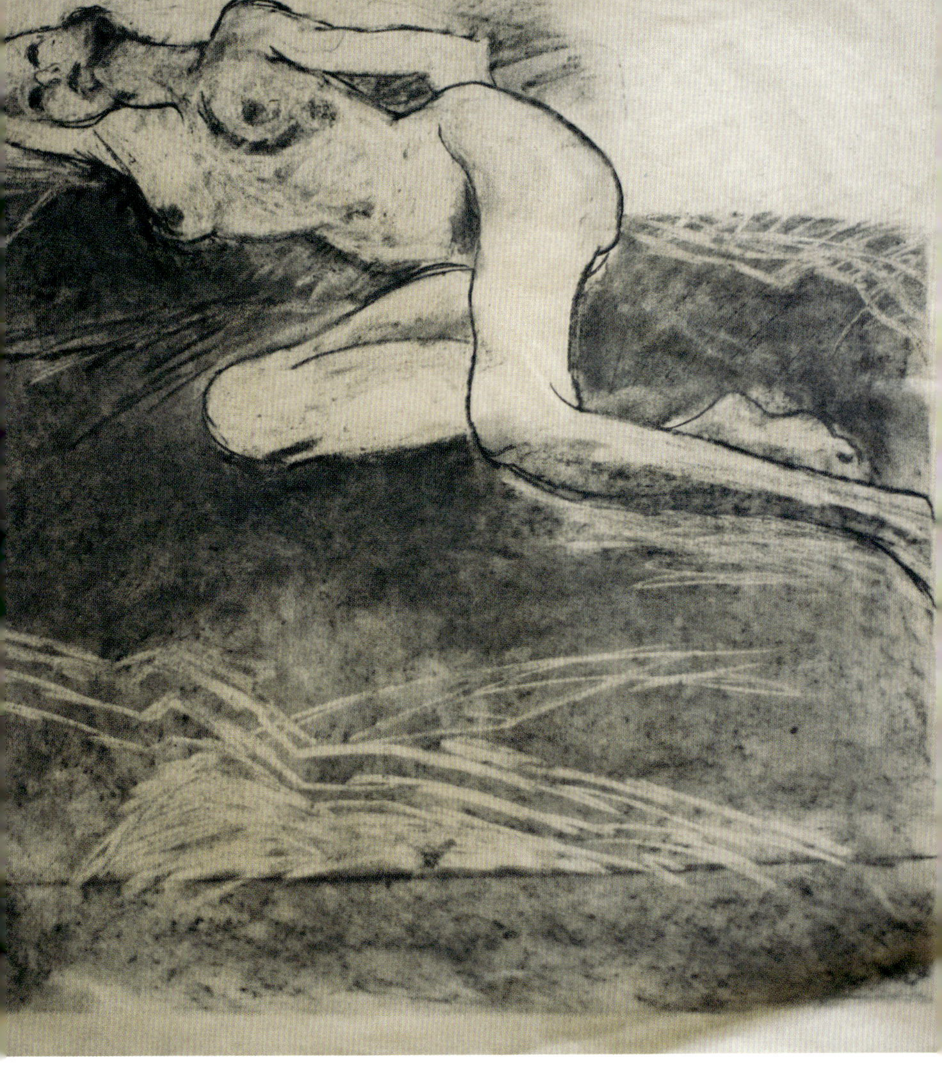

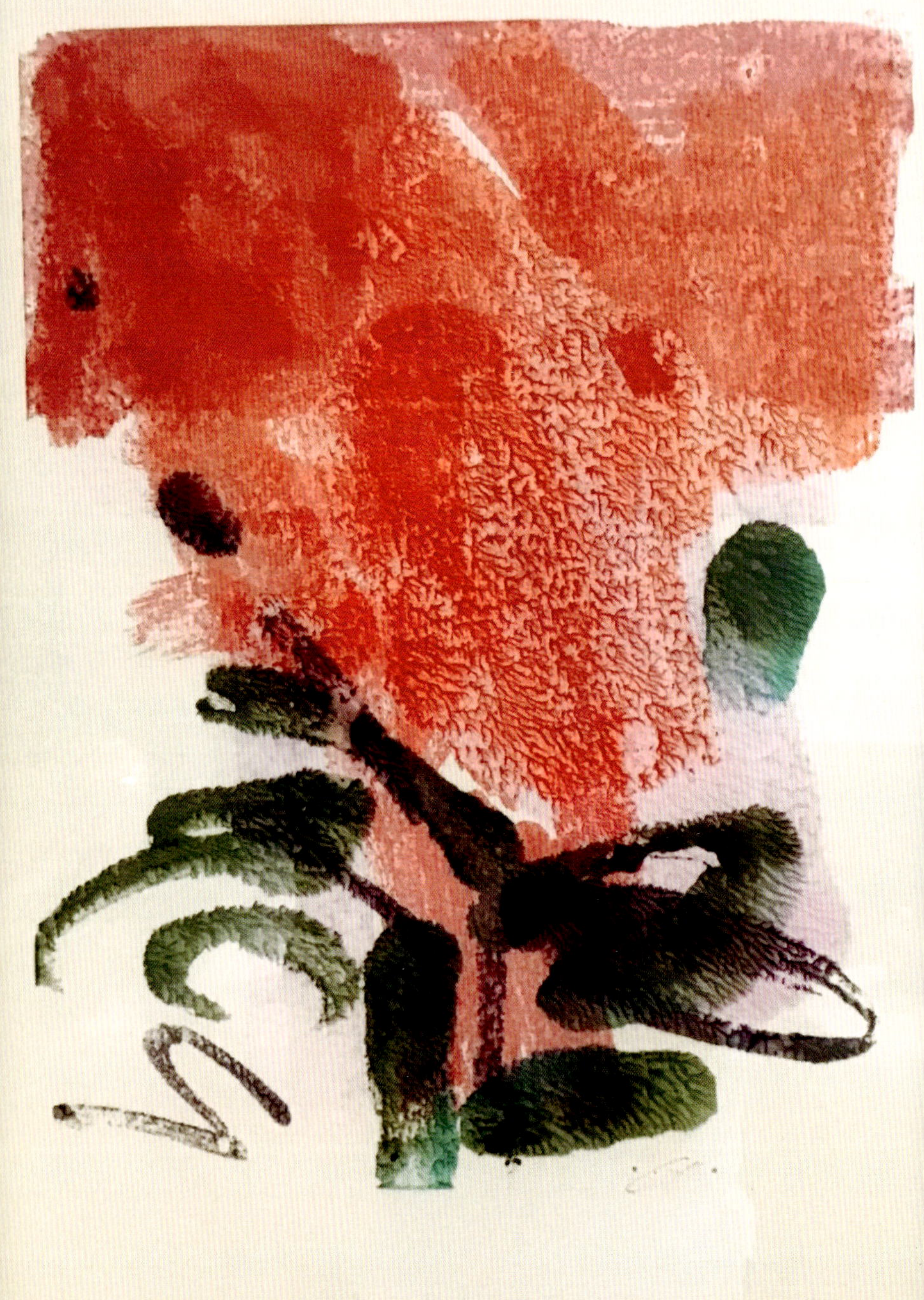

Day 82

I thought this monoprint, which followed the two Kimono works (Days 79 and 80), was suitable this week. It has a look of the Far East, although it was loosely based on the canna flower. It belongs to my sister Elizabeth (Liben) Valaperta in Texas.

This is something I have never done before! This is the painting I have worked on today, 11 June 2020. Unfinished. No idea where it is taking me. It started off as usual with a canvas on which I clean my brushes from the previous weeks. I always have at least three of these on the go. Sometimes they suggest a way forward, as this one did this morning. I kind of like it, it's a bit pretty though I know it has some way to go.

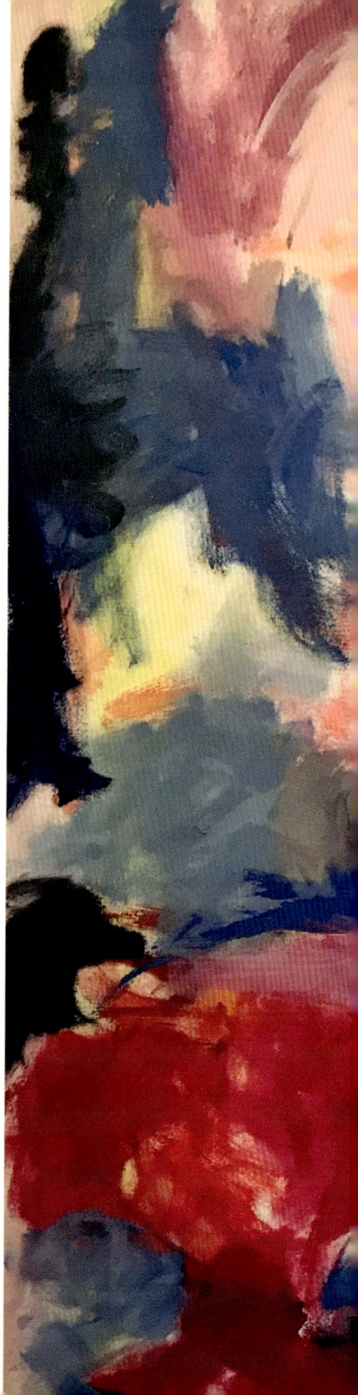

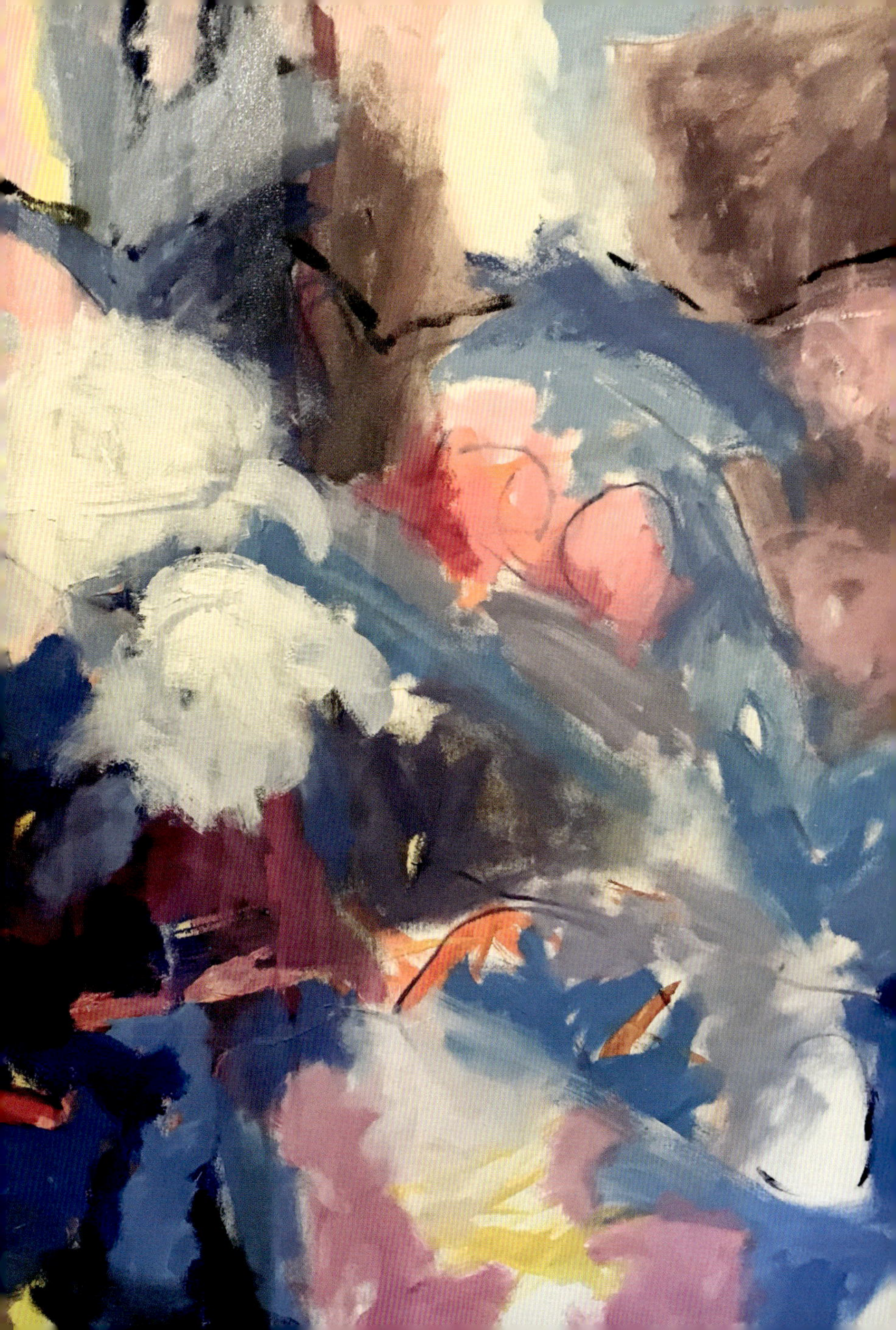

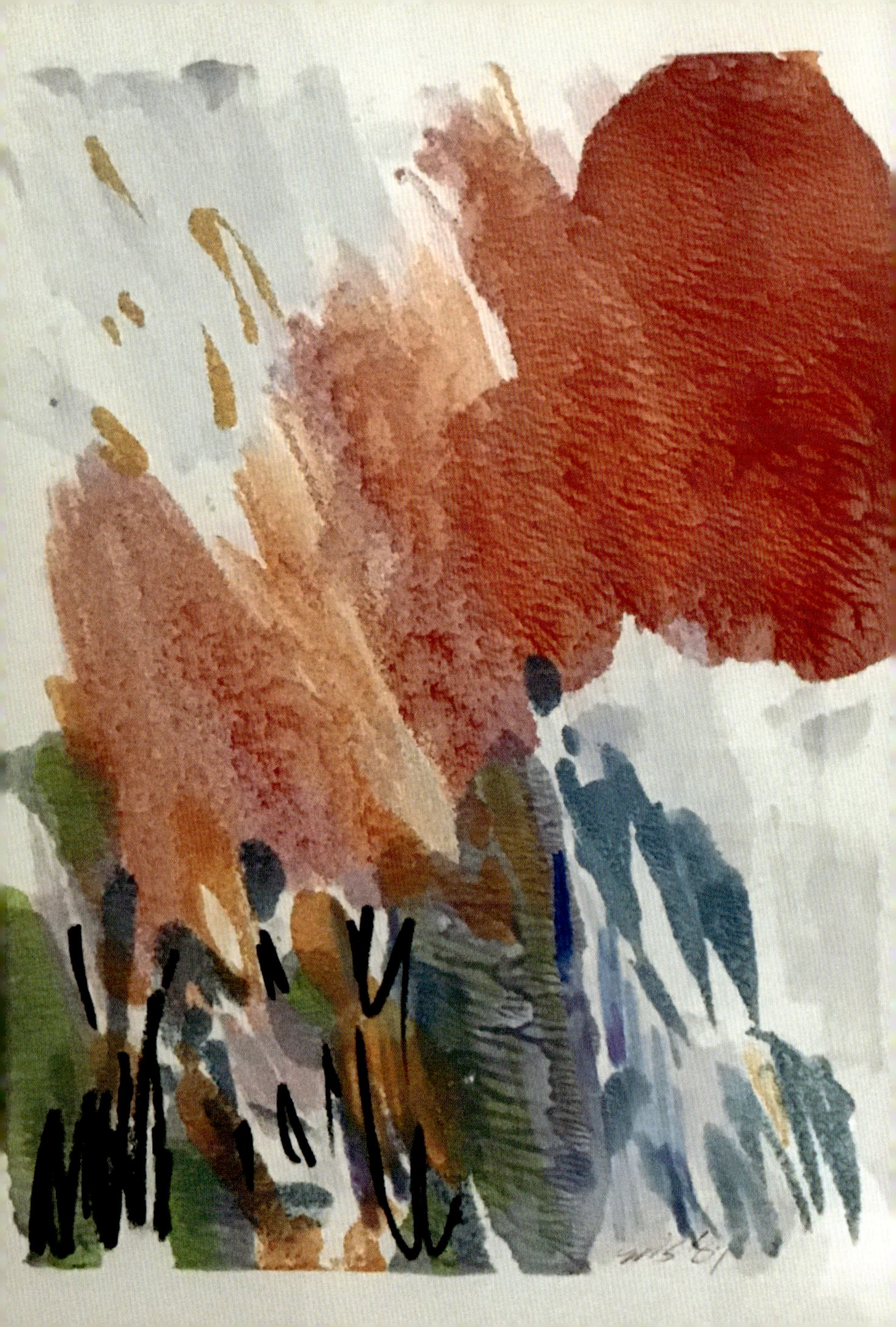

Day 84

More Cannas,
monoprint

Although this looks like a watercolour,
it is actually an oil on handmade paper.
The technique is of painting on to
glass and taking an impression on to
the paper, one colour at a time,
squashing the paint on to the paper.
I like the 'happy accidents' this
method inspires. Collection of
Mario and Elizabeth Valaperta, Texas

DAY 85
COLOUR CHORDS

This last week I have posted some different works that
some will not recognise as mine. This one is part of a
series that kept me busy one year, painting 'music'.
This three-dimensional painting represents the sound
and vibration of a chord (quite low). Painted on to
plywood, cut into strips and re-assembled as the sound
goes on, it has no clear edges, and the waves look a
lot like the flow. Sounds have colours if one thinks
about it, greys and blacks are booming, low, deep
and ponderous. I stopped this series when the pieces
of wood were too numerous in my studio and I felt
overwhelmed by them.
Our great friends, Alec and Christine Davis, bought this
one. I am grateful to them, for they have consistently
bought my work over all the years, having a large and
very varied collection spread around two countries
and three households.

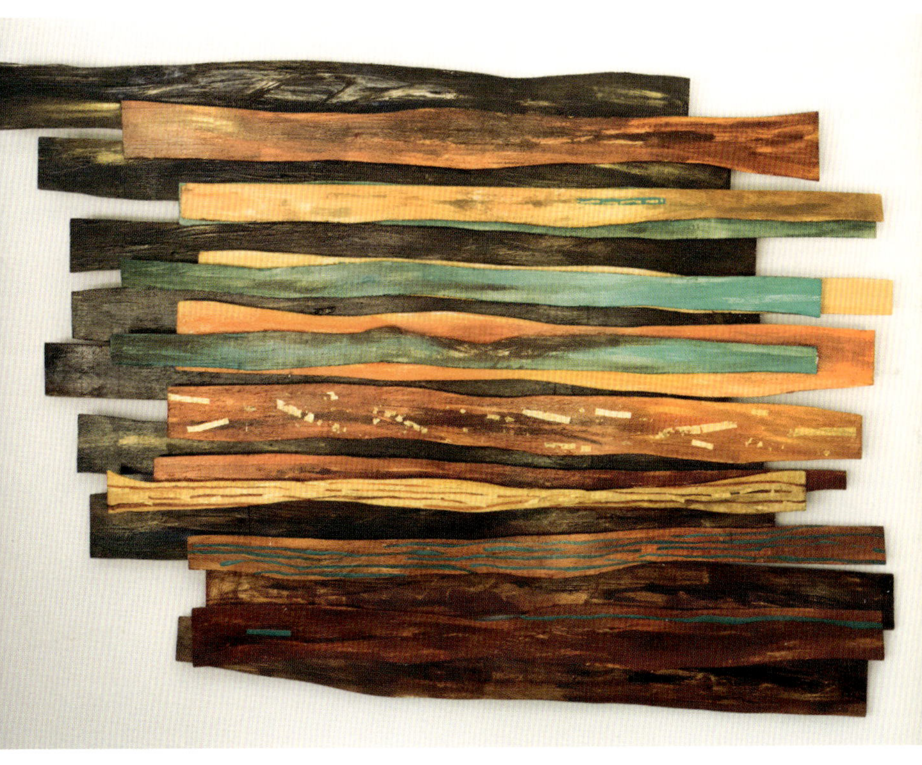

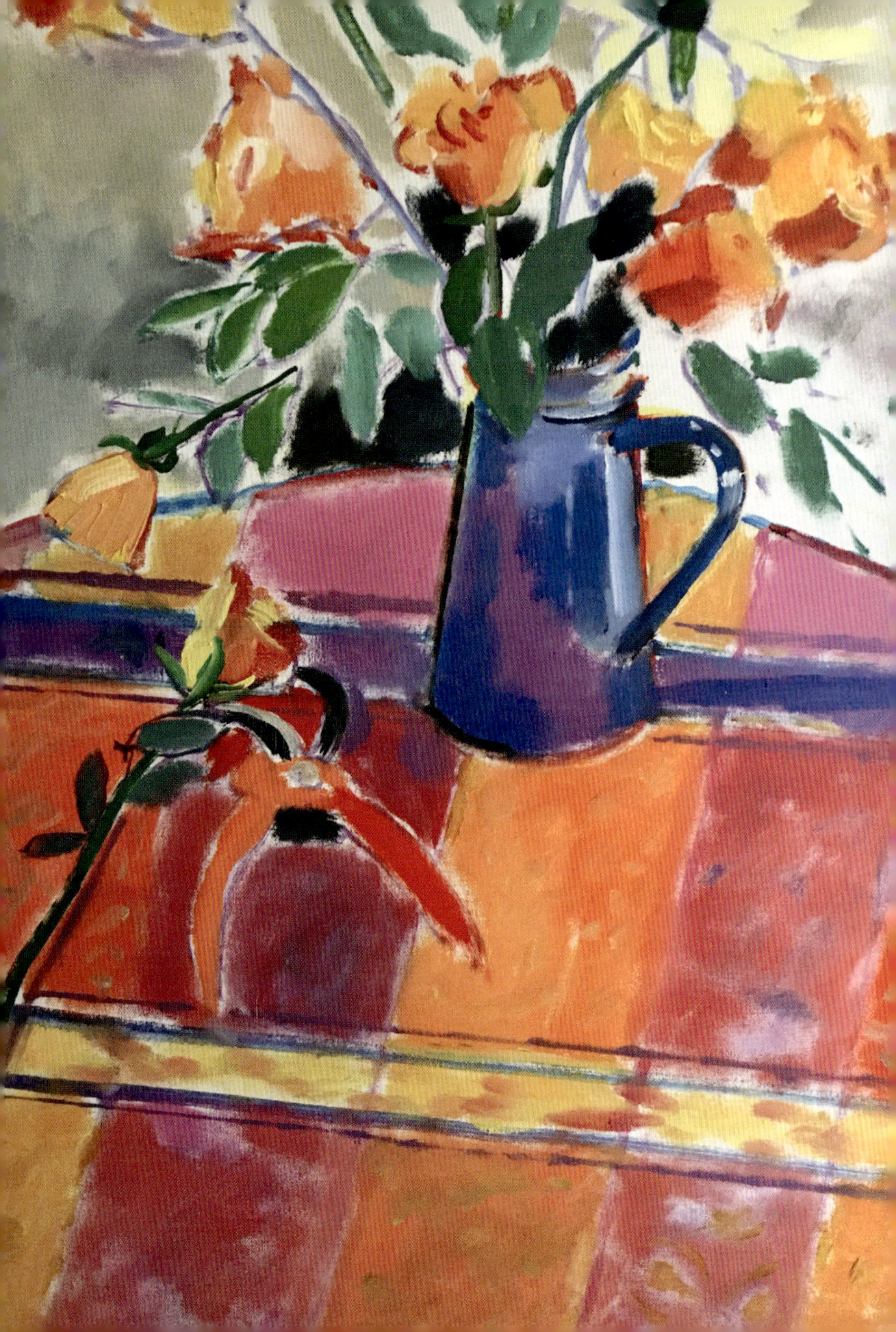

DAY 86
STILL LIFE WITH BLUE JUG

The colours in this still life were carefully chosen
to get the maximum result for a demonstration of
painting on a Saturday morning in the Westgate
Shopping Mall, Nairobi. This was the mall where
sixty-seven people died during a terrorist raid
by Al Shabab. Orange against blue and magenta,
colours that sizzle against each other.
This painting took an hour to do, planned ahead.
Collection of Martin and Theresa Thomas, UK

DAY 87

Painted in situ at the Orchid Society Exhibition in the Sarit Centre, Westlands, Nairobi. These beauties had arrived that morning from Singapore and were arranged in the vase. I could not resist them. The work was auctioned.

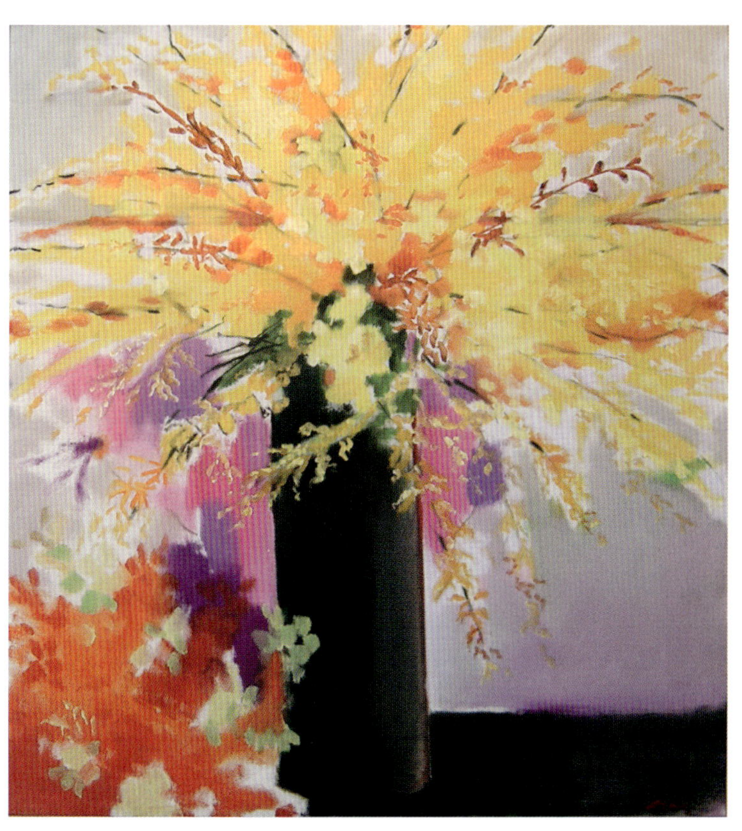

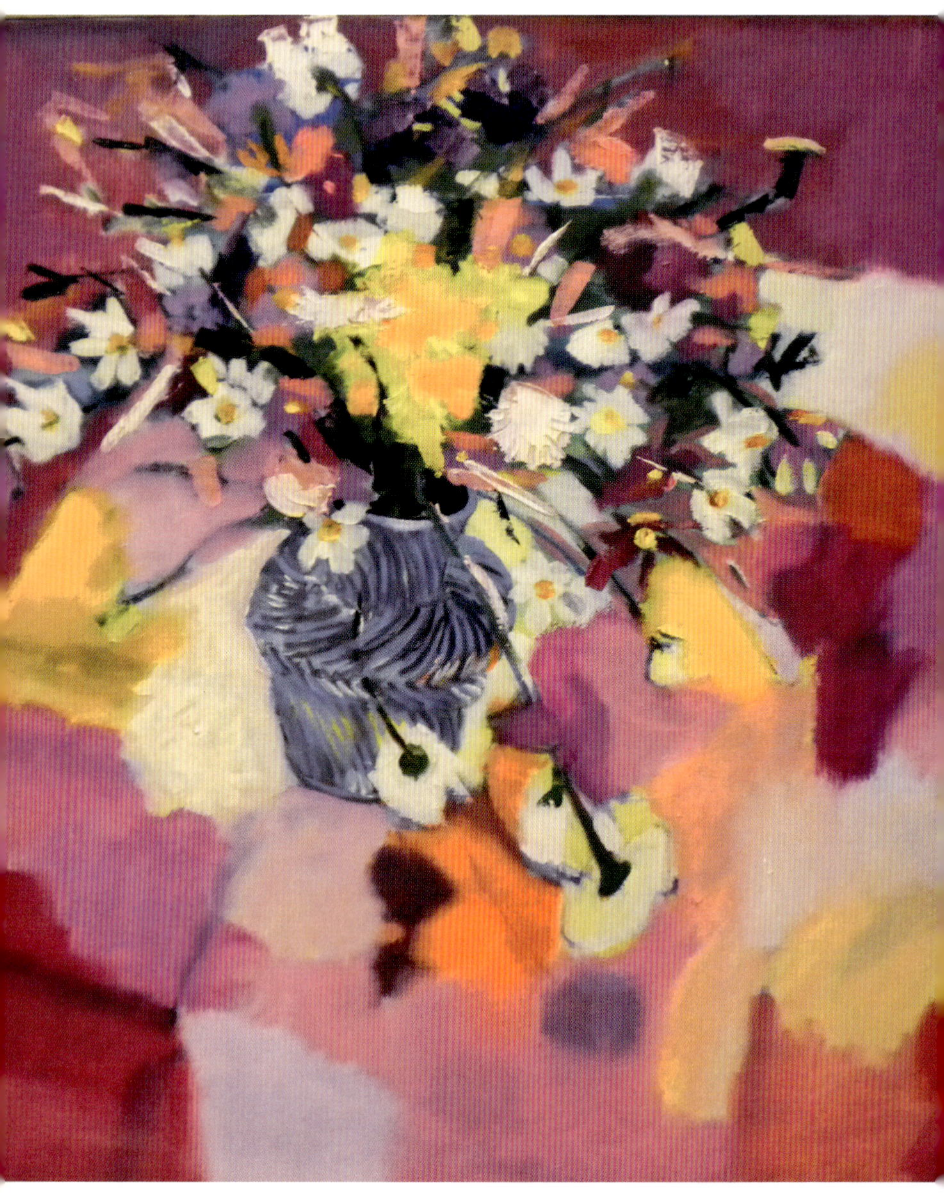

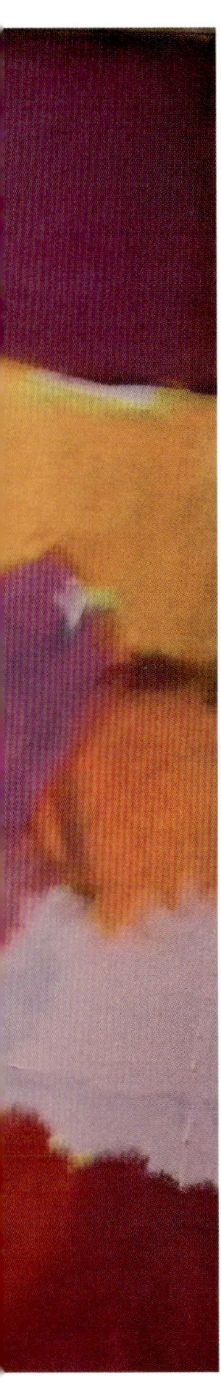

DAY 88
BALMORAL STILL LIFE

In Alexander Theroux's *Primary Colours*,
I found this sentence which I thought was
very entertaining, 'The Queen's favourite
flowers, it is well known, are long-stemmed
pink carnations, and the lipstick she wore on
the day of her own coronation in 1952 was
concocted especially for the occasion to
go with her long crimson and purple robes:
it is a gentle red with blue undertones and
is known as the Balmoral lipstick.'
Collection of Alec and Christine Davis, Nairobi

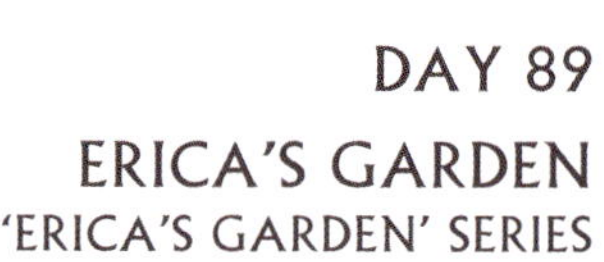

DAY 89

ERICA'S GARDEN
'ERICA'S GARDEN' SERIES

This scribbled oil is one of the very late
works, the result of having painted
the garden so many times. I love
Pierre Bonnard's paintings, where
he practically mixes the paint on the
canvas, which is what I have tried to
do here. A colour is altered by another
laid down beside it or on top of it.
In Bonnard's work he would have a
dark area to hold it all together,
so I am unsure if I succeeded here.

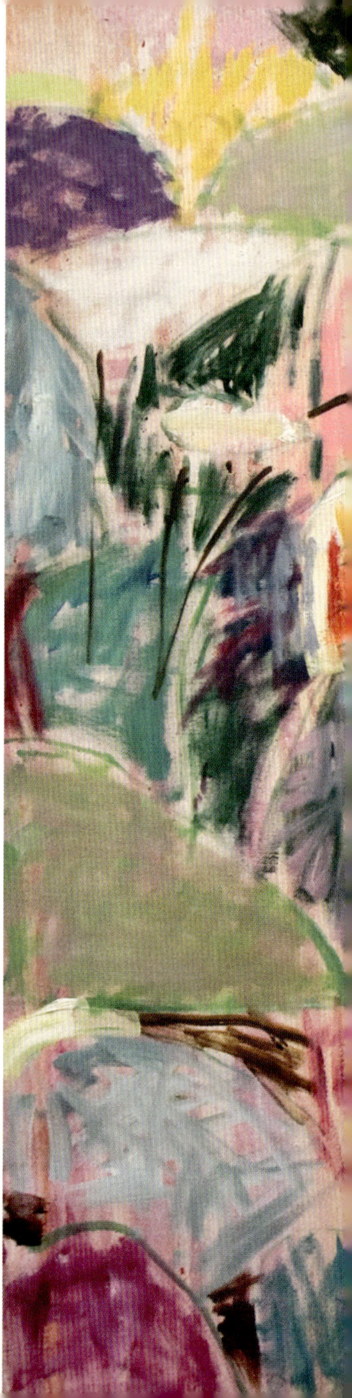

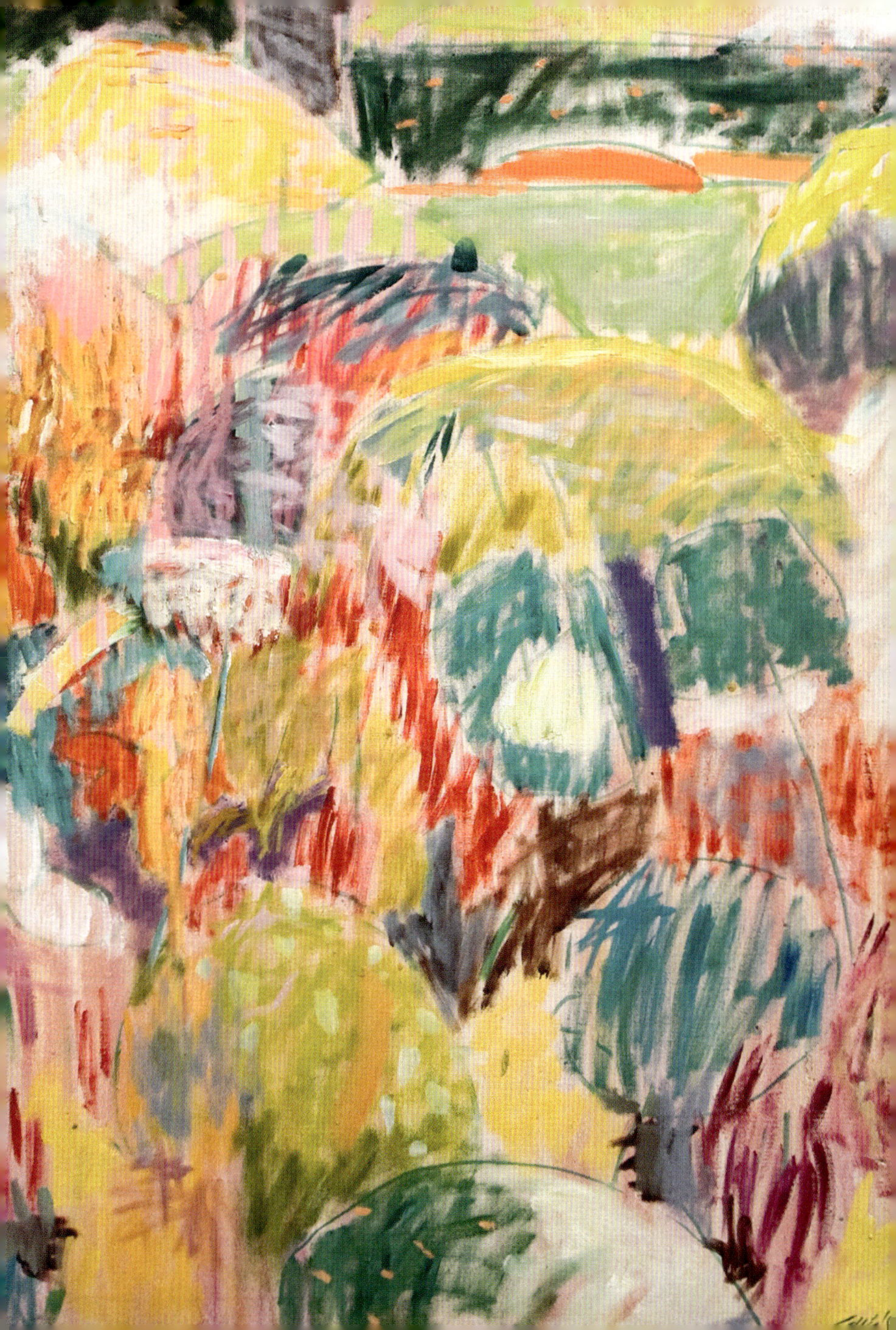

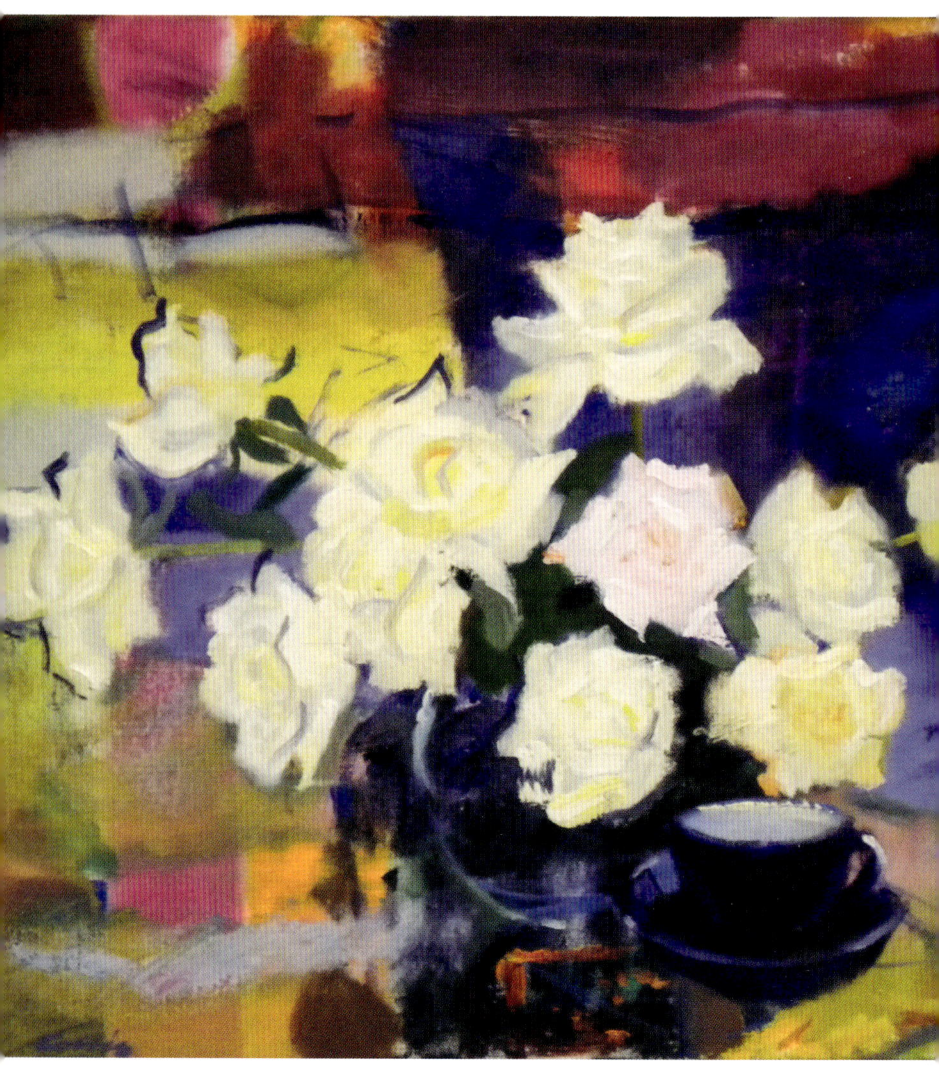

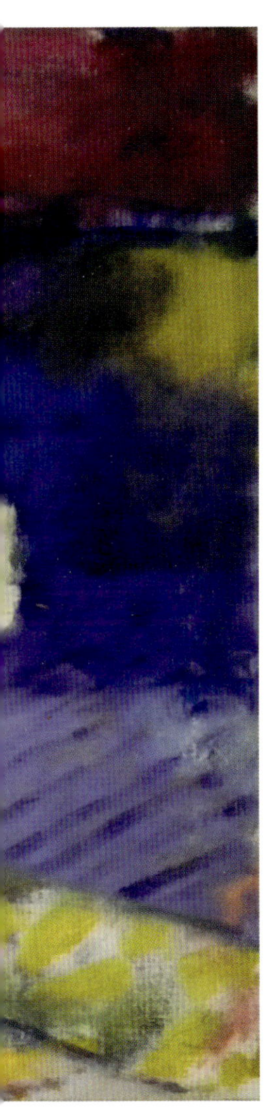

DAY 90
TEA & ROSES

A special still life, I think. I like the composition.
I was painting with my artist friend, Sophie
Walbeoffe, in her studio, her teacup and her
lovely garden roses. Occasionally we paint the
same subject together. I love to daub with
another artist, especially Sophie. Our conversation
is happy and sparkling and we discuss what we
are doing in a language only artists can have with
one another. It was painted over an old painting
and I allowed a lot to show through; there are so
many unplanned parts that appeared by magic.
The trick is to spot them when they happen and
not to paint them out.
Frank Whalley, the art critic, bought this
from me, confirming it was special.

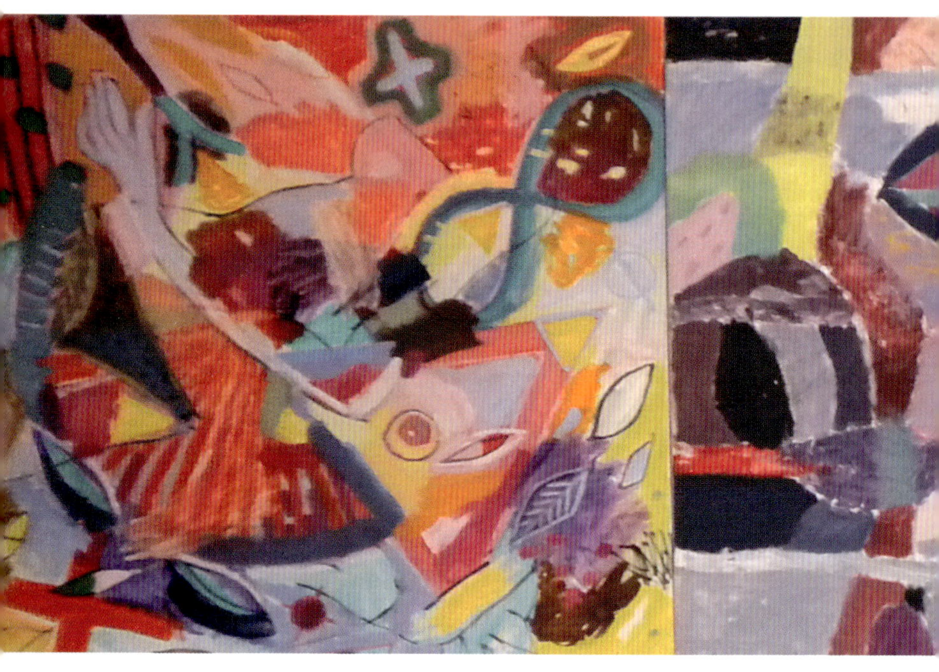

DAY 91
BODY, SOUL, MIND

This triptych spread the entire length of my dining
room. I would practice Qi Gong in the same room with
my friend Sue Canny Davison, and we would discuss
its meaning and symbolism, sometimes for hours.
The configuration in our new space was entirely
different. So, on a whim in my new tiny studio
I split up the canvases and painted on top of them.

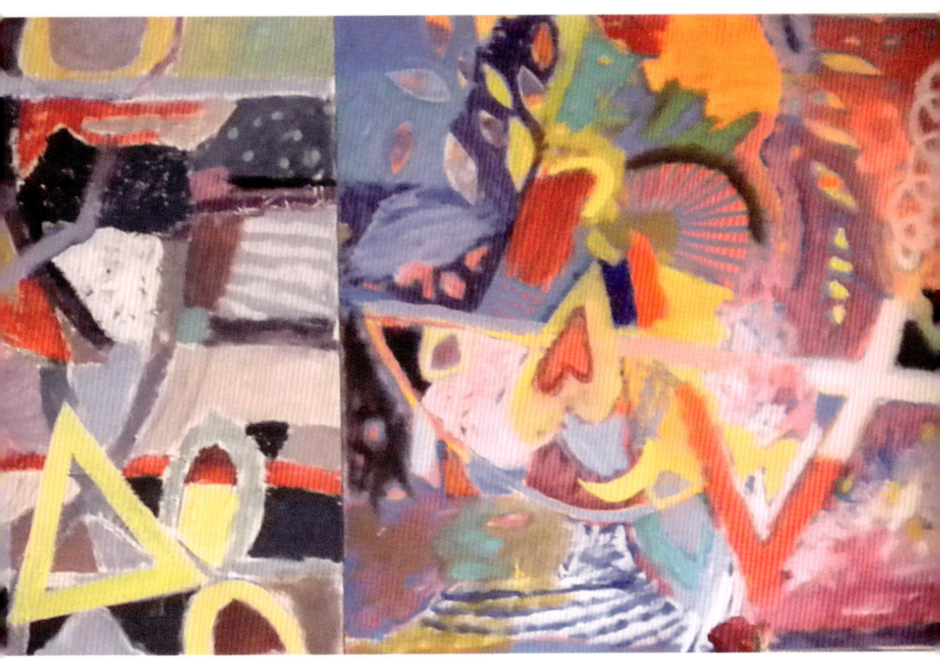

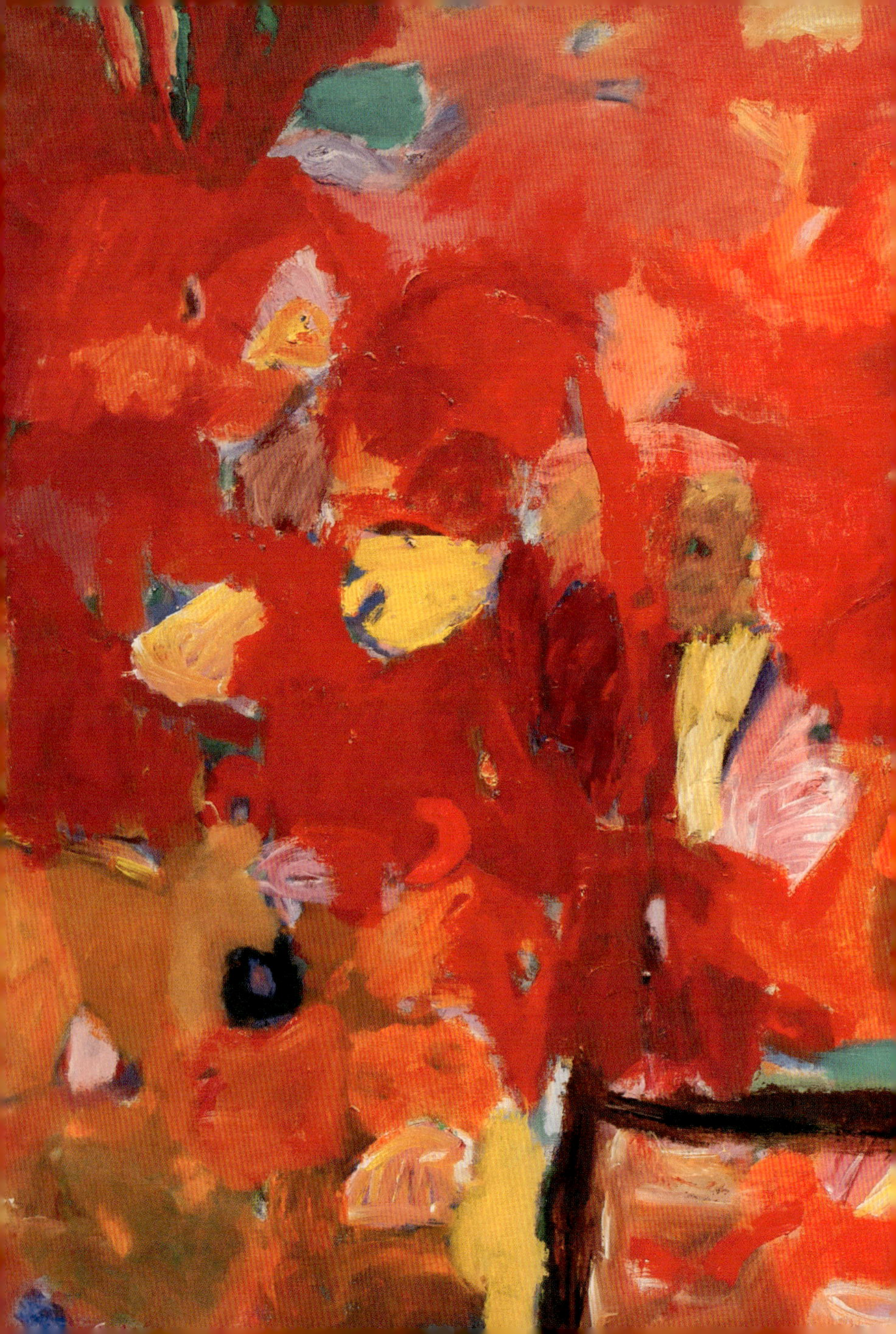

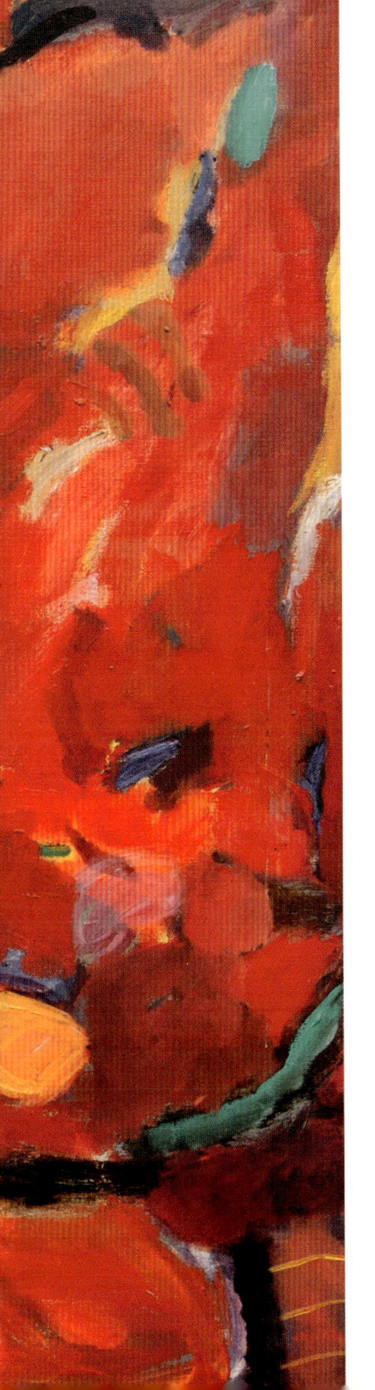

Red Letter Days

Prior to this title, this very large 6ft square abstract had another title. It was called *Death of the Clown*. You may be able to see that this painting was like a wrestling match for me. It went on and on, and at one stage it developed a clown's face with bulbous nose which I could not get rid of. Best efforts, he kept reappearing. I exhibited it at least twice in former lives.

Many people have to see pictures or objects in these works and express them, which sends me to the studio to quickly eliminate them.

This huge work found a wonderful purpose-built-for-art modern home, where it hangs in splendour. I love the lady who bought this, all the art in her home is fabulous. Veronique Su lives in Kenya now after working for a Swiss Bank. Kenya is lucky to have people like her living here. She has a successful community project and is making a difference.

False Bay series

I marvel how each day, every moment is new.
This is a third showing of this massive series,
the first being Day 20 and the second Day 39.
Thus far the series numbers approximately
600 small works of paintings and photographs.
This is my view, when I am in the Cape.
These are oils on canvas, 10 x 10 inches.

Picasso said, *'Every time you look, it's different.'*
Who is the creator here? What does this?
Why is my response different? Who is
in charge? Big questions go on and on.
Photographs, too, to be slotted in amongst
the paintings are as dissimilar as these.
This particular group hangs in my bedroom
in Simon's Town.

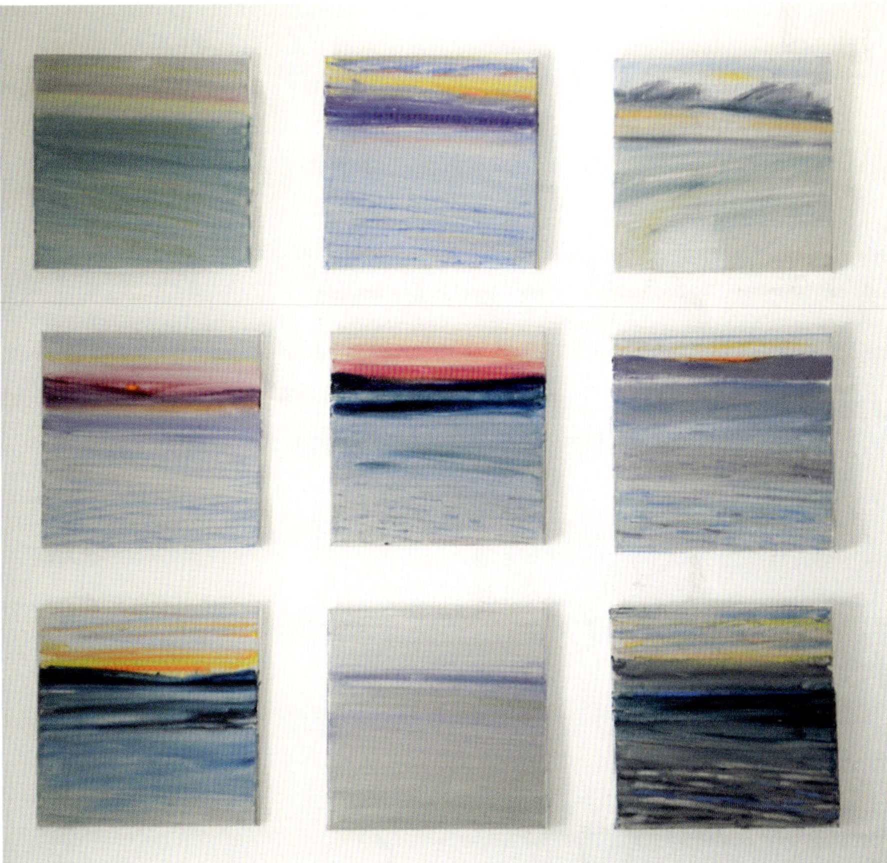

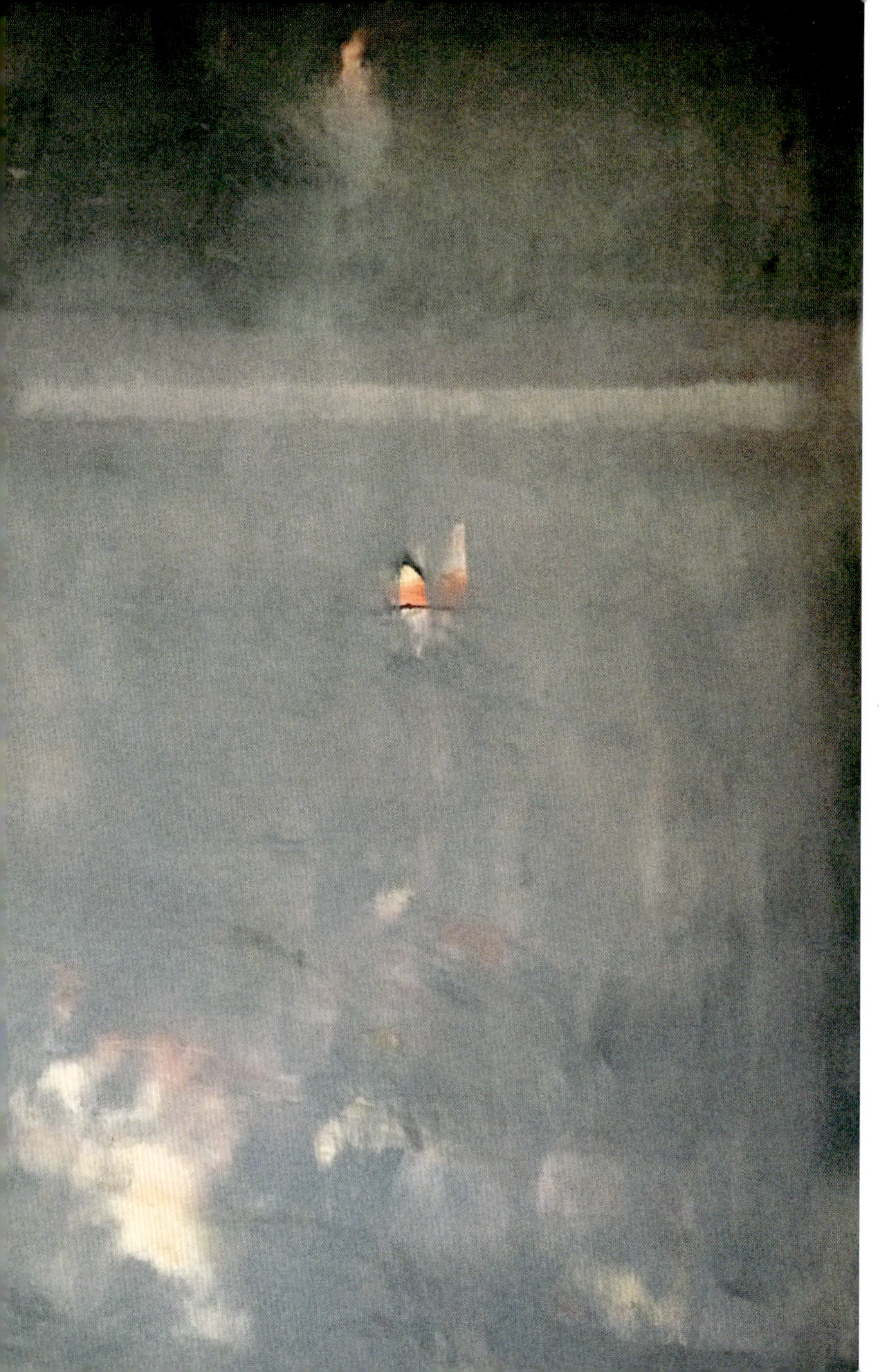

The Dream

A painting about a dream of water and a butterfly.
The dream must have shaken me to paint such a
thing a long time ago and I barely remember except
the feeling it left me with, which is clearly still here.

Chuang Tzu in a dream became a butterfly,
And the butterfly became Chuang Tzu at waking.
Which was the real – the butterfly or the man?
Chuang Tsu And The Butterfly by Li Po

Mark Rothko is my favourite painter. I get lost in
his works, although his paintings use these dark
colours that can bring one down to a deep sadness.
This work of mine is quite the opposite I think,
uplifting greys, the sea and a butterfly.
Collection of Terry and Gayle Davidson, Nairobi.
Gayle tells me this work has evoked much conversation.

Windows

Painting still life with
Sophie Walbeoffe in her
studio. Green pears on
a yellow plate and two
china horses. Wonderful
colour lilies in a vase.
My still life was a failure,
so I covered the bits I did
not like in the sediment
the dirty brushes make
when washed down
in turpentine, as it
has every colour in it.
My thinking is it must
harmonise with them all.
Although there are two
illustrated windows here,
I like to think that every
colour you see is poking
through a window.
Collection of Bruni Tiffin,
Phnom Penh, Cambodia

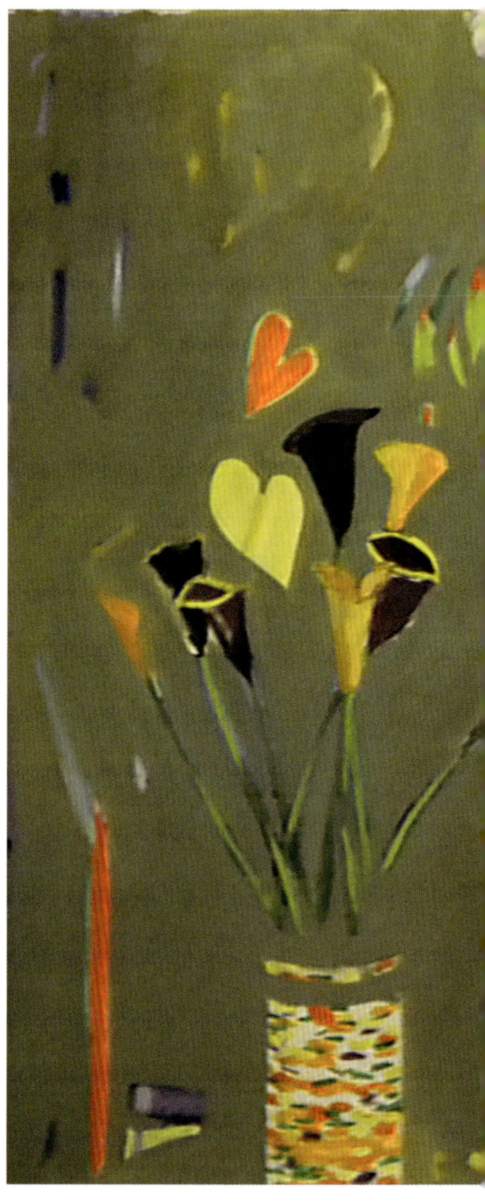

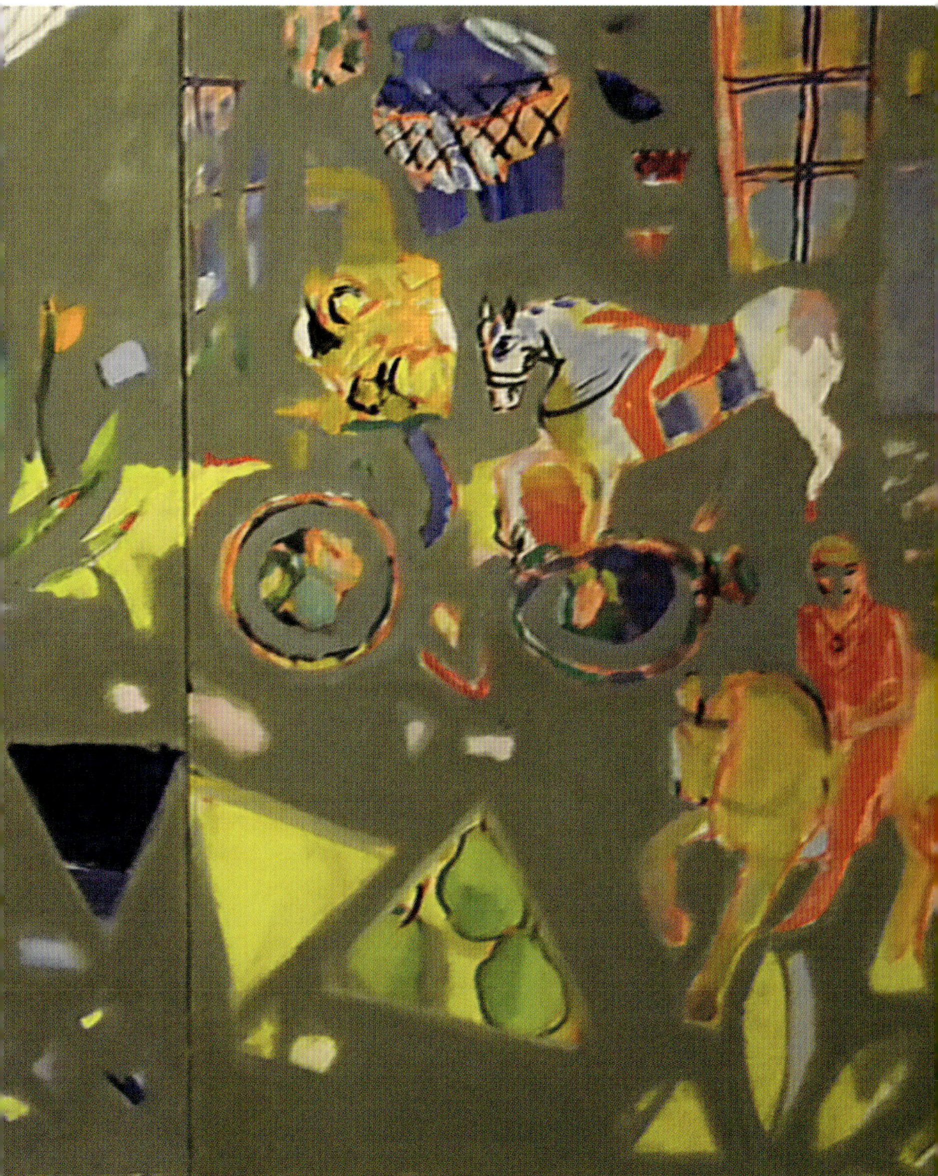

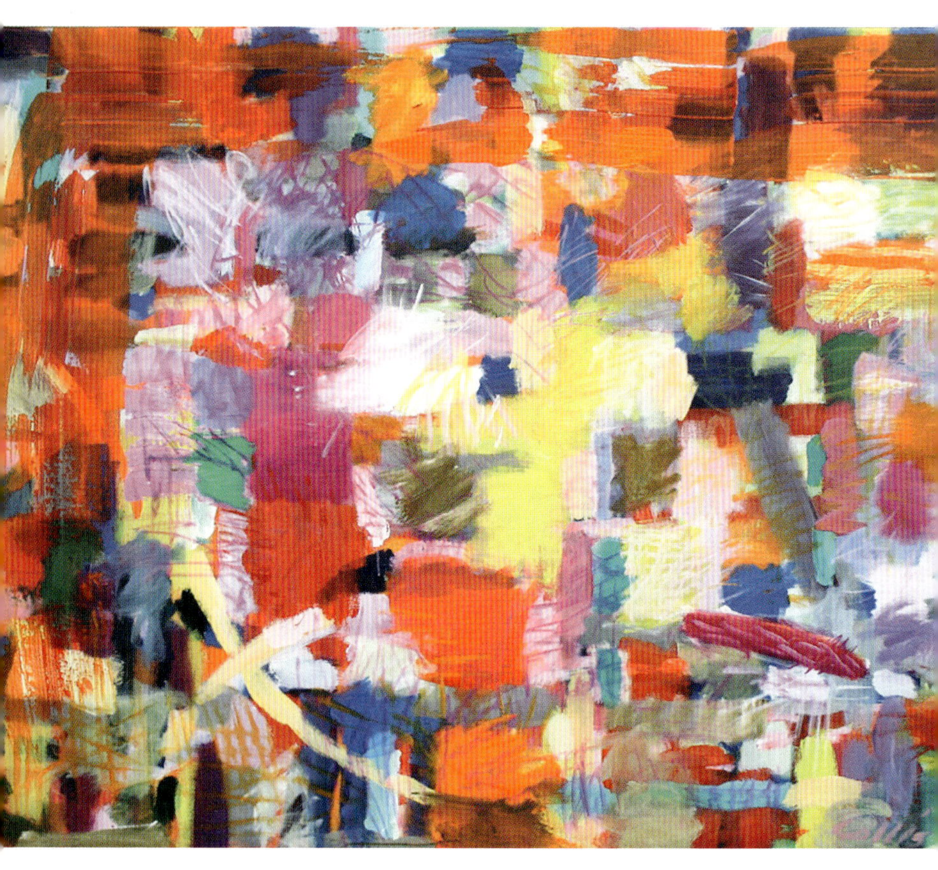

Bollywood II

The second of this series, the first being Day 16.
Kenya was blessed with a wonderful painter from
Holland who chose to live his last years in this
country on a tiny island north of Lamu. Hans Seuren
was a friend and would visit me when he was in
Nairobi. He loved to sit on our veranda looking at
the forest, so different to his surroundings of sea
and coast near the Arab town. He married a girl
from the village and had a son. He would paint huge
abstract canvases on the flat roof in the hot sun.
I regarded him a Gauguin figure and a genius.
His canvases got darker after he lost both his wife
and his son to malaria, and about a year later he
died of a broken heart.
I painted this after the memorial for Hans and I
borrowed his brushstroke. I called it Bollywood, as
I like to think of him surrounded by dancing colours.
Collection of Sean Walwyn, Toronto

Grass

Outside my studio a lawn of
green grass was surrounded
by ornamental Japanese
cherry blossom, which
shed when the wind blew.
Verdures and other beautiful
plant life against the green
was always a subject for me.

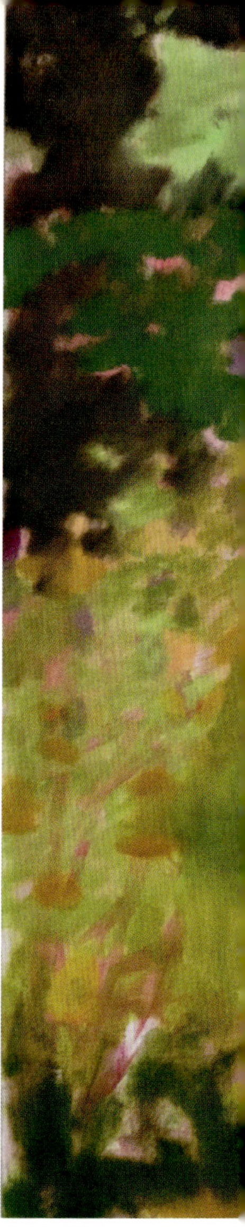

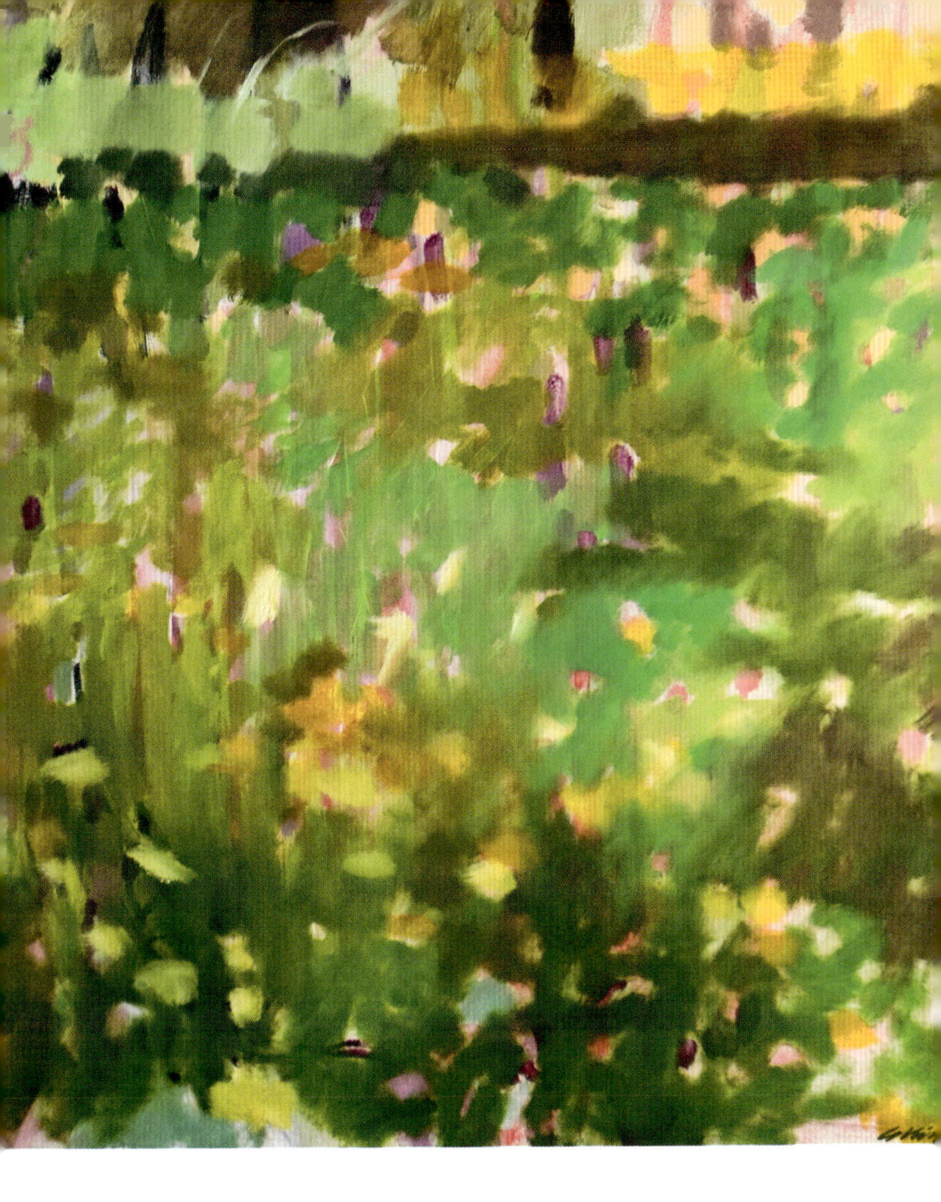

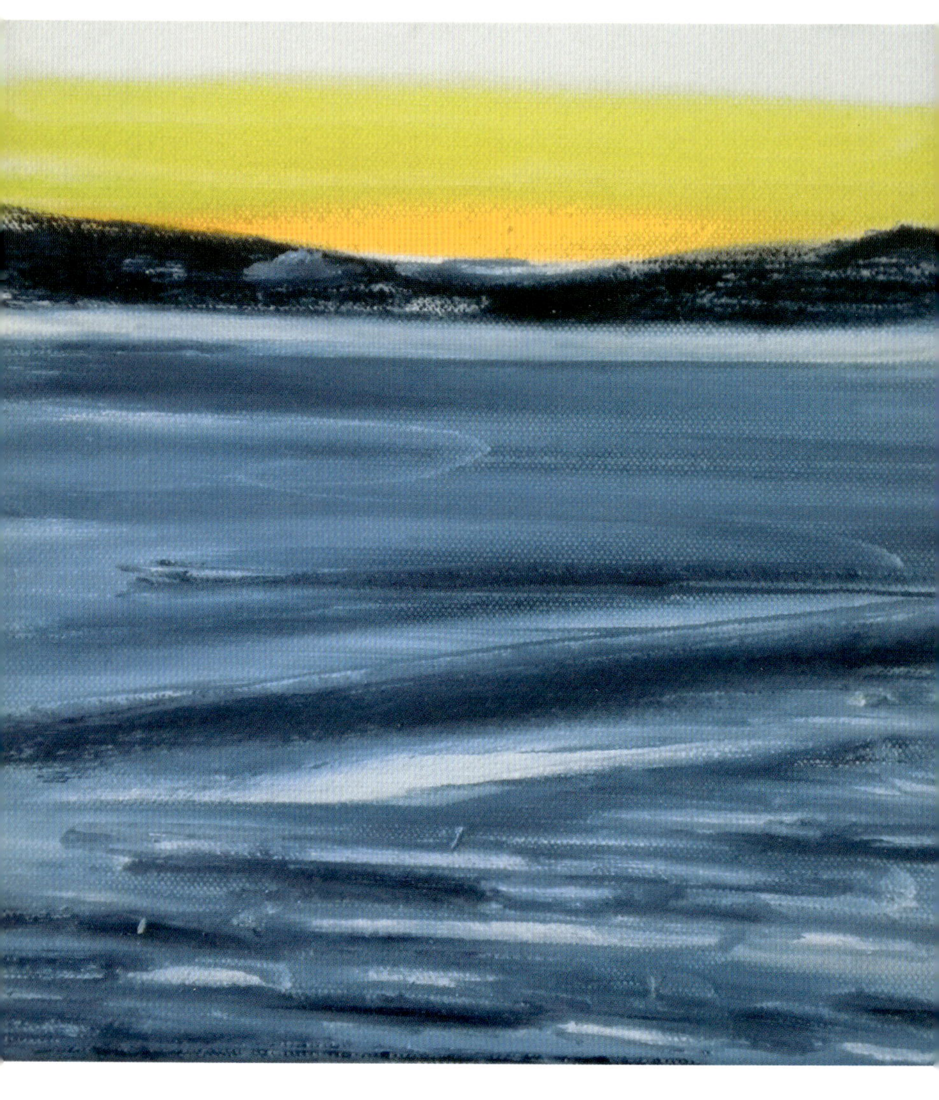

Early Start, 'False Bay' series

I thought I would end this week of abstracts
with another from the 'False Bay' series,
technically not an abstract. Each of these
works (there are 600 at the time of writing)
is numbered, the time and date is logged on
the back, titled and signed. The titles have
been one of the most difficult things to think
about in this large series. This *Early Start* was
easy, as there is a little speedboat, if you
look carefully, that goes out at daybreak
every morning taking tourists to Seal Island,
where they can witness the early morning
breakfast of the sharks.

Day 99
Blue Gums

The Nairobi National Museum had an interesting exhibition called Tree Life in July 2011, curated by the artist well-known for her trees, Camille Wekesa. All in all, there were twenty painters, a glass artist and several sculptors showing diverse work in wood and a photographer. It was well curated and carried an environmental message. This was my contribution, inspired after a walk in the Karura Forest, known as the lungs of Nairobi, now a life-saver for the residents of this city during this time of many restrictions. There are extraordinary women who have been responsible for saving this forest for Nairobi, chief amongst them was Wangari Maathai who was awarded the Nobel Peace Prize for her Green Belt Movement. Professor Maathai died shortly after the exhibition in September 2011. We Kenyans are indebted to her.

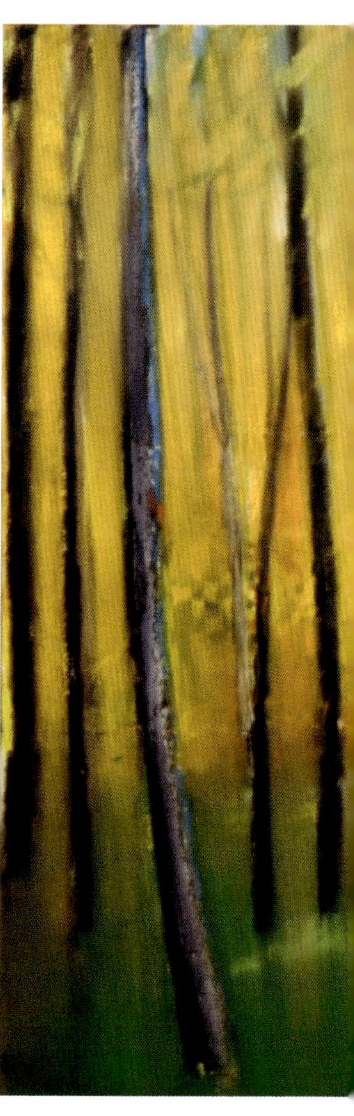

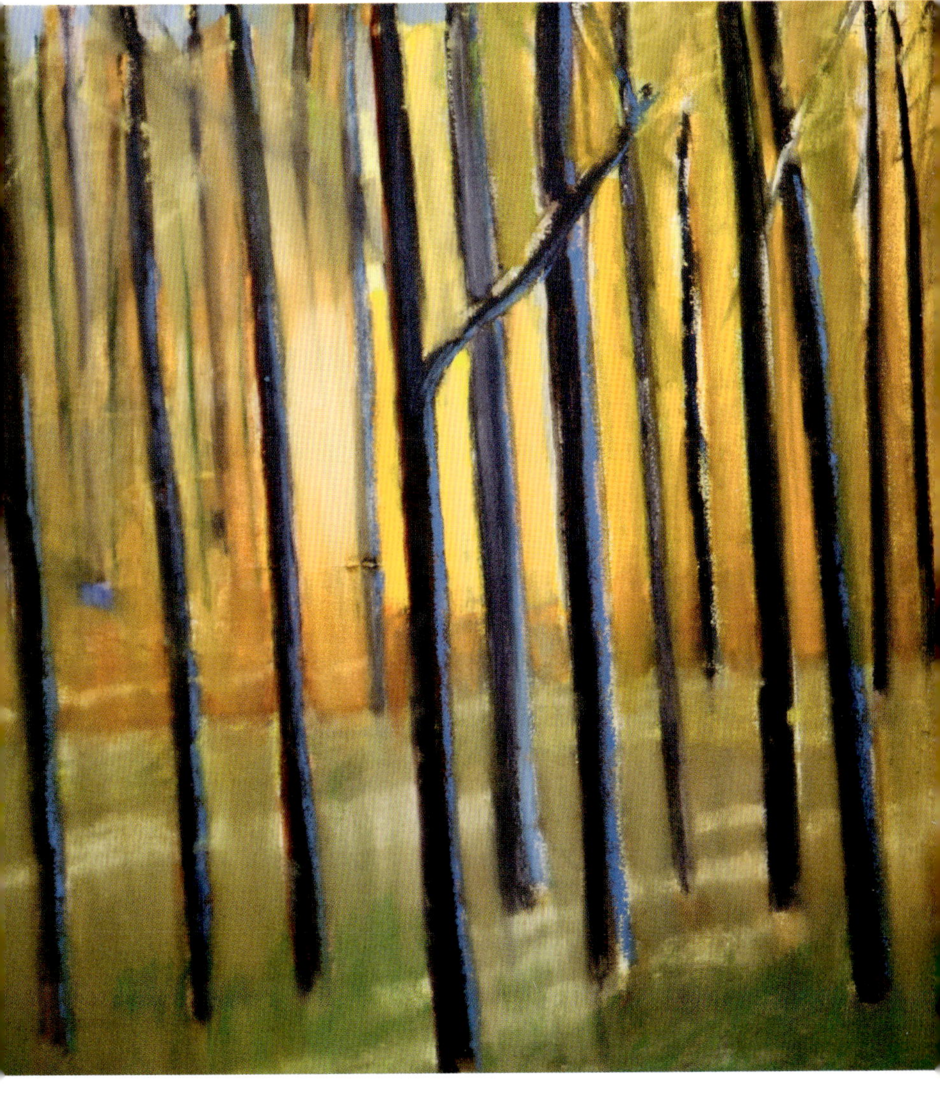

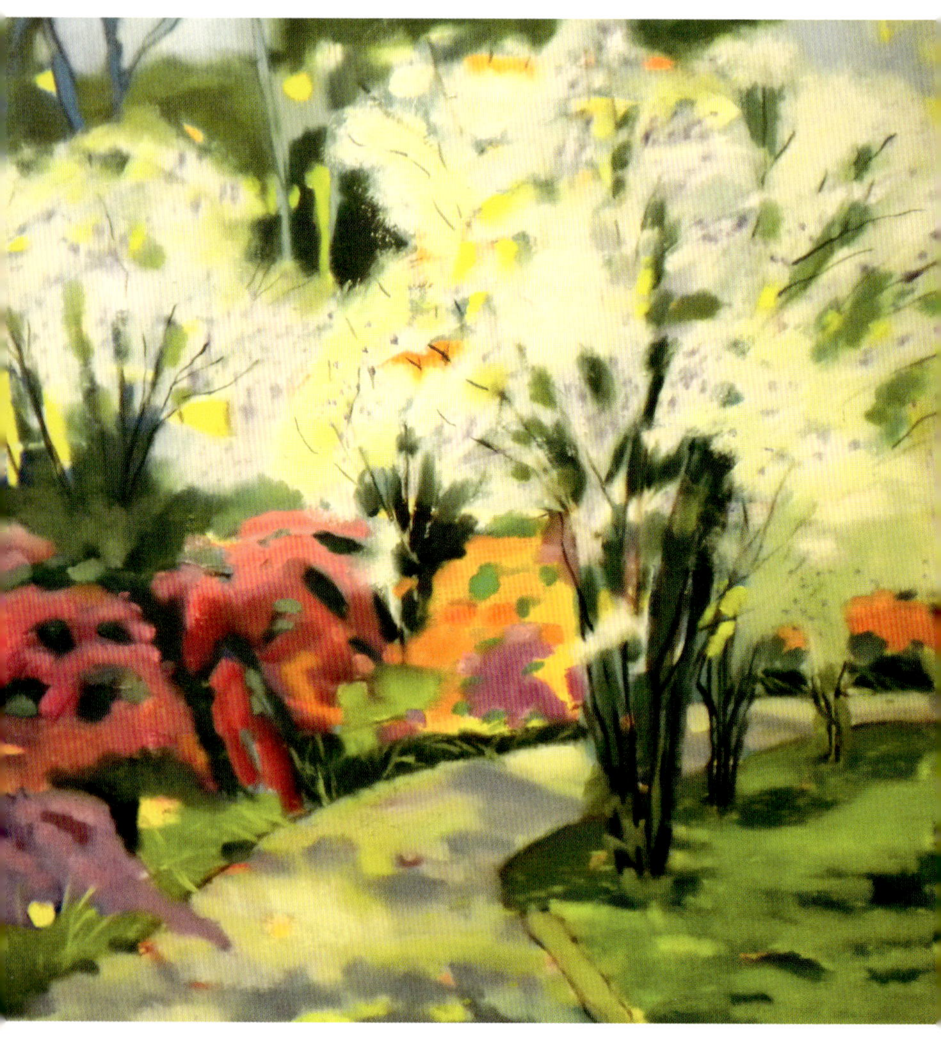

Day 100

'Yesterday, Today and Tomorrow' series

We lived in Kibagare Valley, Loresho for forty years and
this was our drive up to the house, though it did not
always look like this, it was seasonal. Trees are the subject
for this next week. 'Yesterday, Today and Tomorrow'
are more shrubs than trees, and I saw them like this one
colour, only once, almost all white.
I painted them often over the years in different moods.
The perfume was intoxicating. Beneath the bushes, which
latterly I asked the gardener not to trim, were about five
different colours of bougainvillea. The shadows tell me
it was about 2pm. Looking at this gives me some regrets
about moving to an apartment in town.

This picture numbers one hundred days since Covid-19
began, a whole season. Time to move on again.

Day 101

Today Up My Drive

'Yesterday, Today and Tomorrow' series

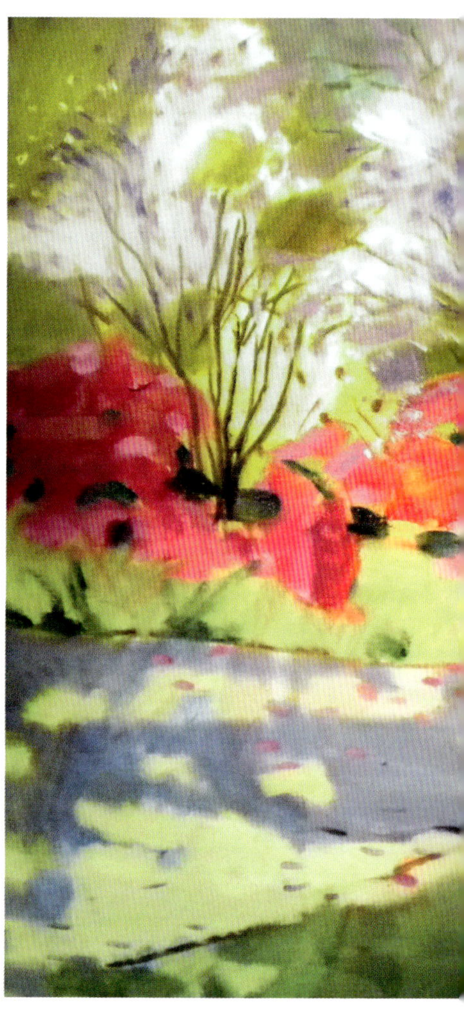

Same view as the previous painting, Day 100, titled *Tomorrow Up My Drive*, though quite a different year and late afternoon. The flowers start off purple, then gradually fade to lavender and then white. This painting was bought by my dear friend Sue Canny Davison, who lived very close by and we often spent time together. At one stage she would come every day and we would practise Qi Gong and then paint in my studio, located to the left of this drive. I can smell the Yesterday ..., Today ... and Tomorrow ... as I write. The Latin name for this fragrant shrub is *Brunfelsia*.

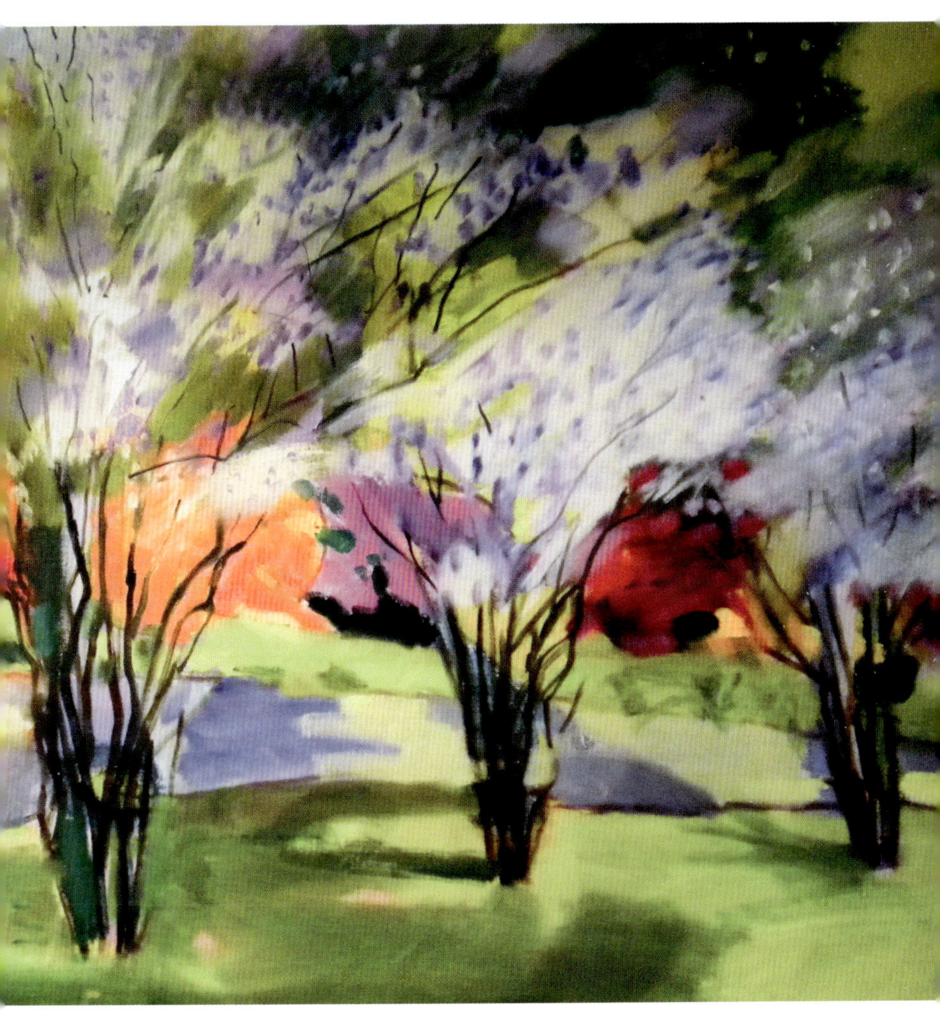

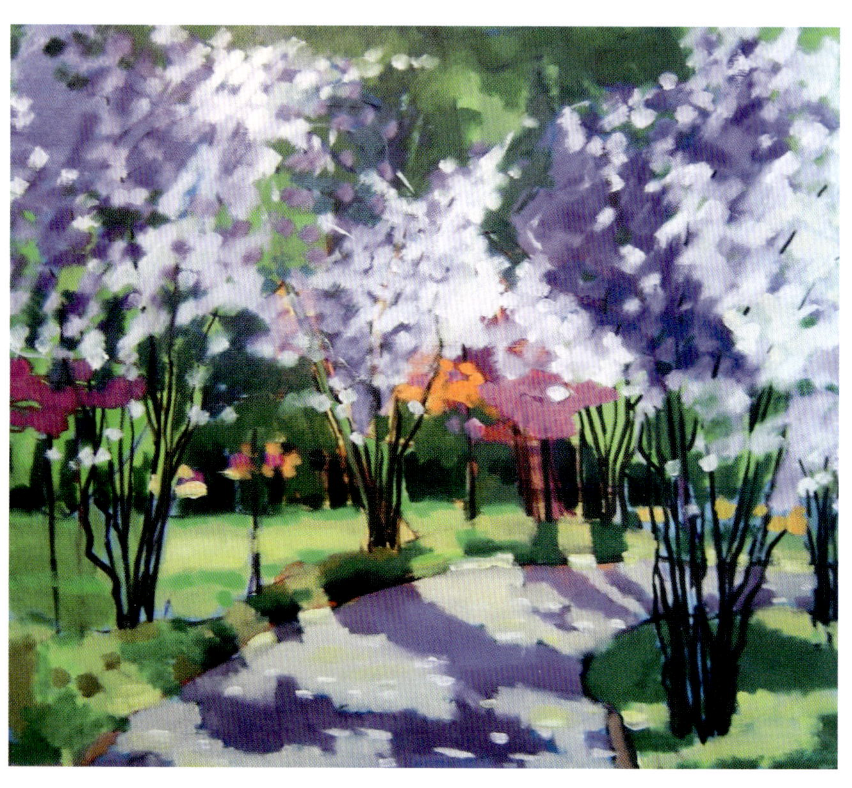

Day 102
Yesterday Up My Drive,
'Yesterday, Today and
Tomorrow' series

This must have been an earlier year to the
other two paintings, *Today* ... and *Tomorrow* ...
as there is no bougainvillea, it was planted later.
Captured at midday when the trees are standing
on their shadows at the equator.
Collection of John and Diana Sawers,
Durban, South Africa.

Day 103
Further Down the Drive

Rendered early afternoon.
I've painted looking down to the
gate and looking up from outside
the gate. I've stood beneath the
avocado tree that I planted by the
side of this picture, and painted
the bougainvillea, horizon-like,
straight on. There were so many
trees in the Kibagare Valley,
I have only just noticed that in
these last four paintings there
is no sky. I must say during
this Covid time, when we are
ensconced in a twelfth-floor
apartment, I miss the garden and
putting my toes in the grass.
My sister Elizabeth Valaperta,
who lives so far away in Houston,
Texas has this work.

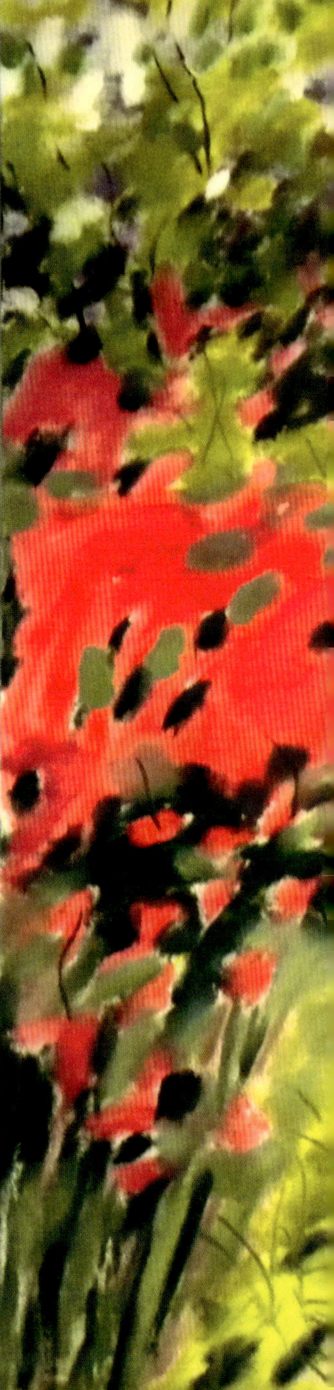

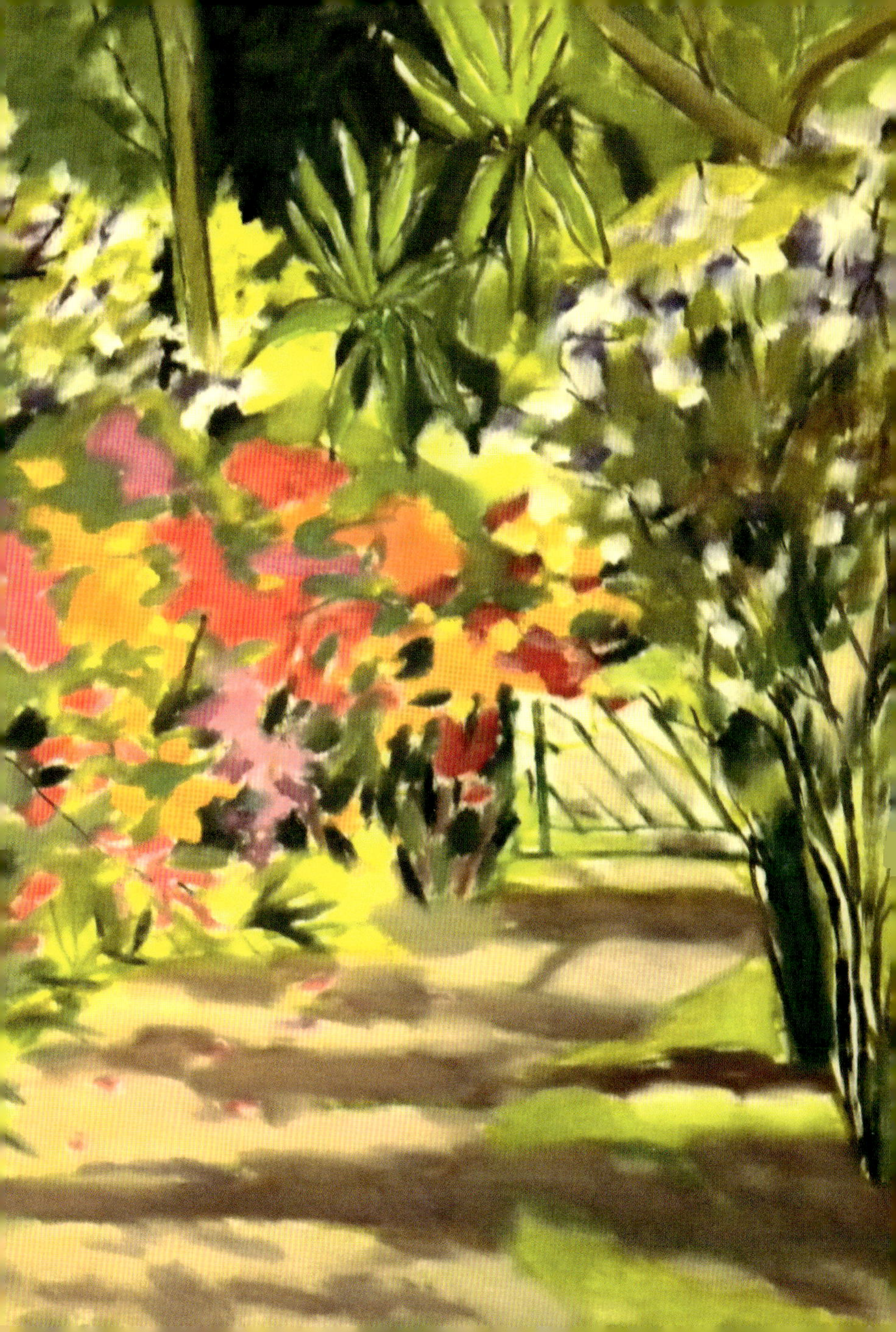

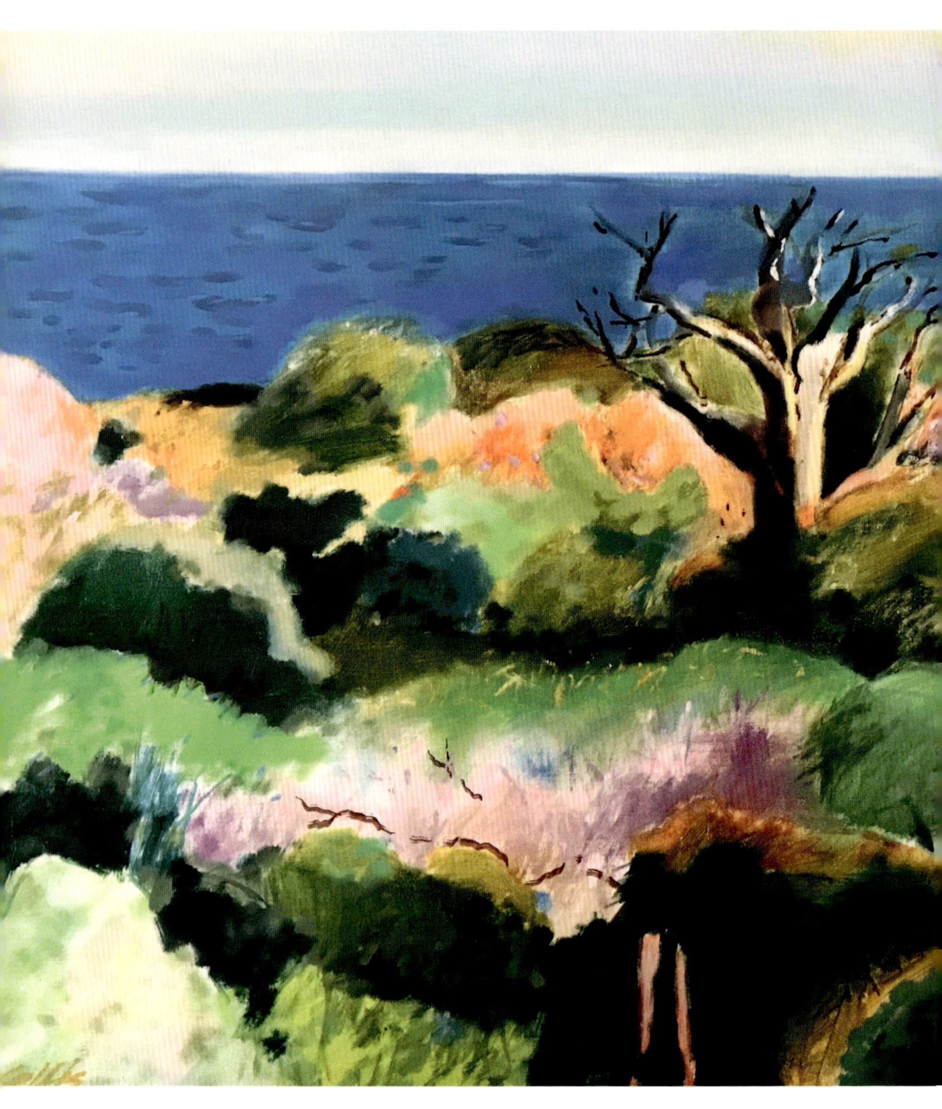

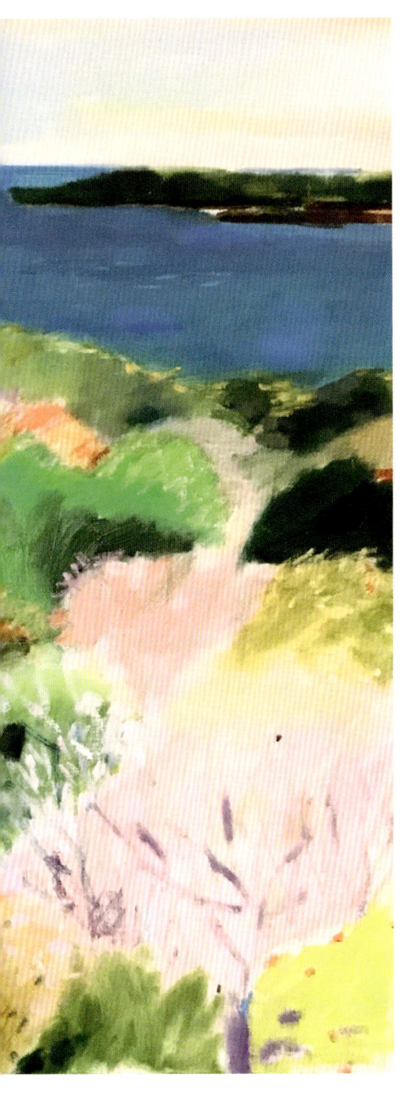

Day 104
Early Evening at Mida Creek

As this week has been about trees, I thought I would extend it to this baobab and the riparian land that is at the gateway to Mida Creek, Watamu on the north coast of Kenya.
This is one of four canvases which hang in a large block painted at very different times of the day. This series was all about the light.
Private Collection

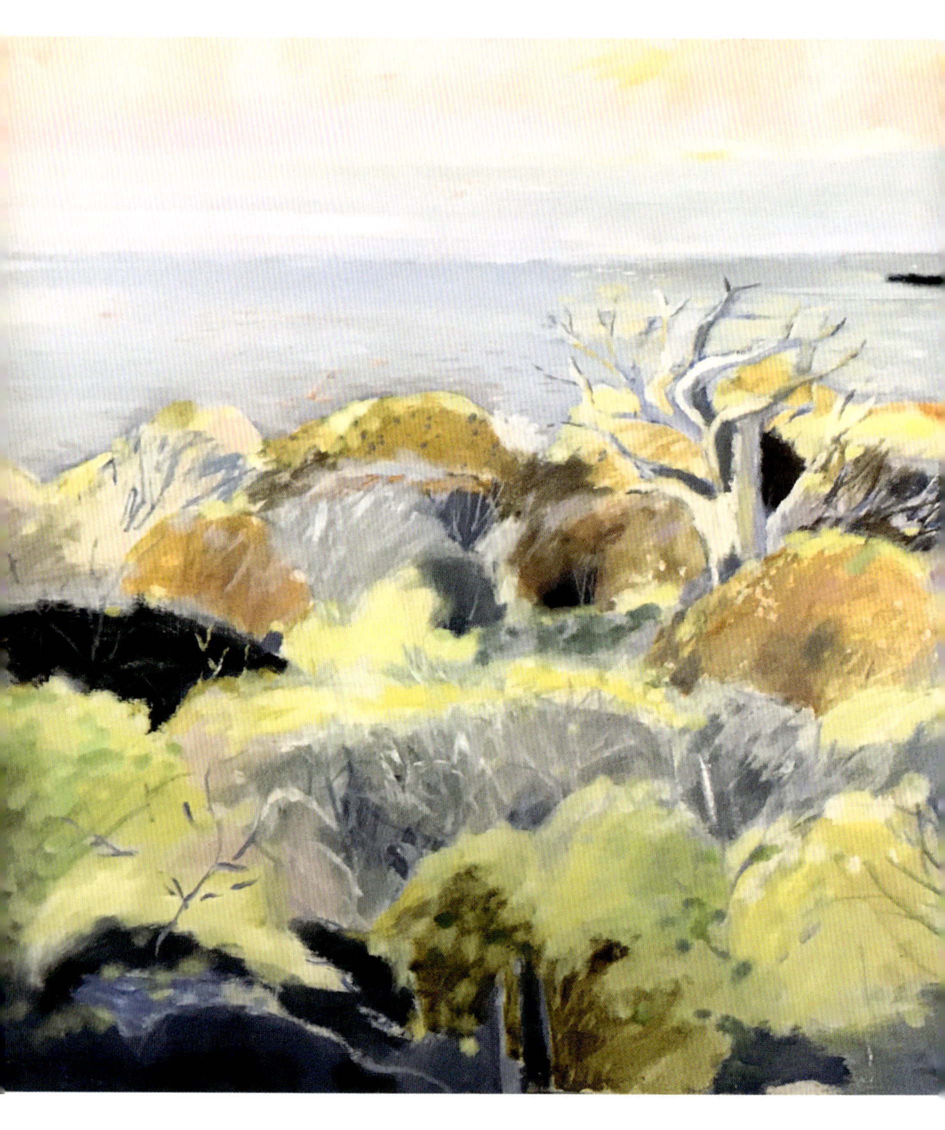

The baobab at the entrance
to the creek, before daybreak,
with gorgeous soft pale colours,
including the sea, and a feeling
that all is fresh and right with
the world. This was painted on
the third floor of a magnificent
plantation house with an upstairs
veranda around all four sides.
I would have loved to have been
there longer than the week and
paint all the views.
Private Collection

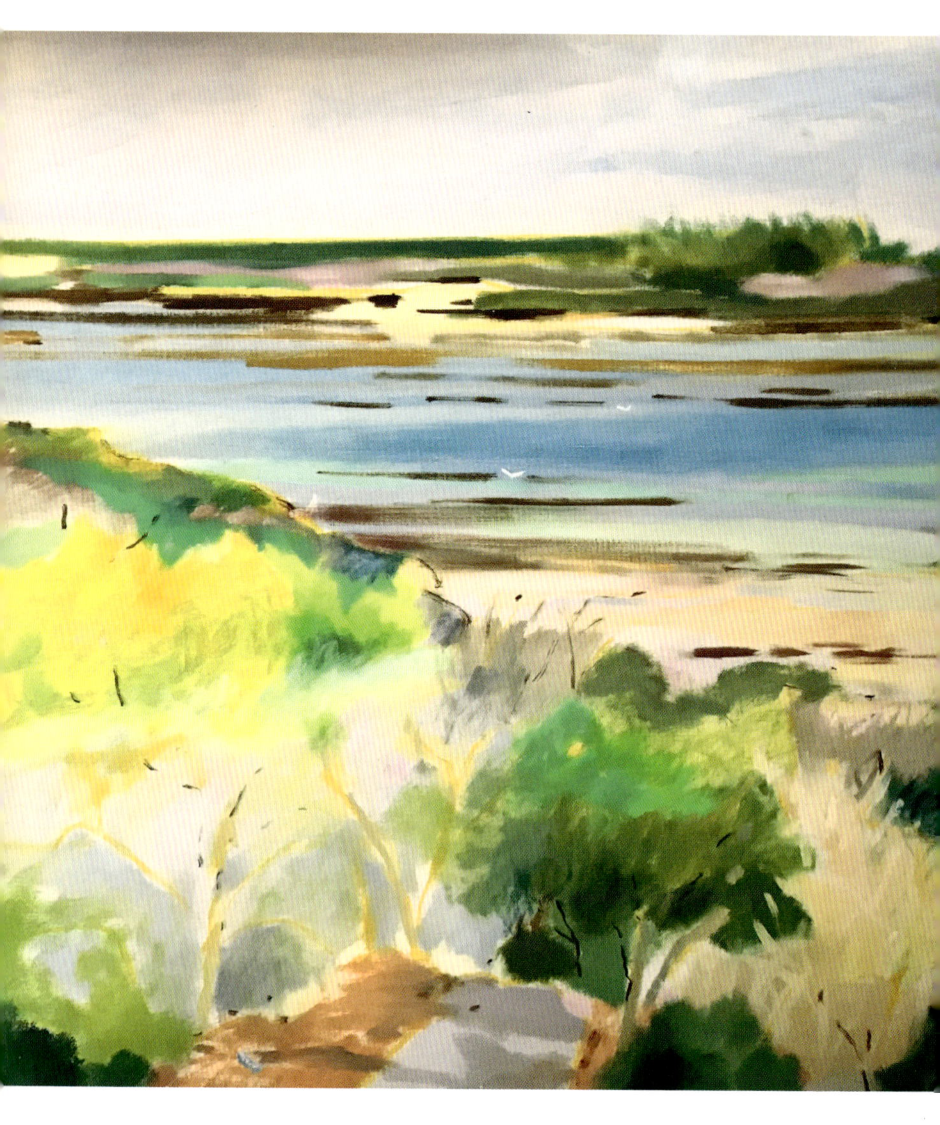

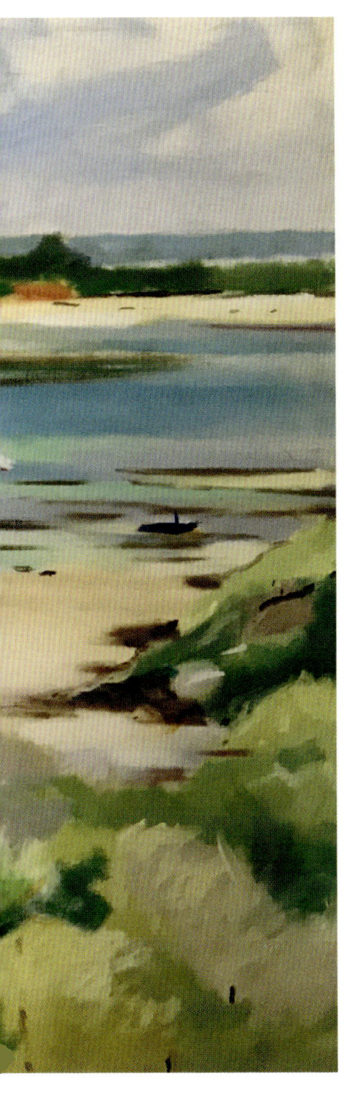

Day 106
Entrance to Mida Creek
at Low Tide

One of the four works that lead
up to the quadruple canvases,
a little further round the entrance
to the creek, midday and at a very
low spring tide. One can clearly
see the beach on the other side
of the creek. I like to think you
might feel the heat? Little stirs
at that time of the day. I note that
there is a rust-orange splodge
near the horizon, which connects
to the path in the foreground.
It holds the eye. If you put your
finger on it, the painting dies,
as there is little else vertically
to hold one's interest.

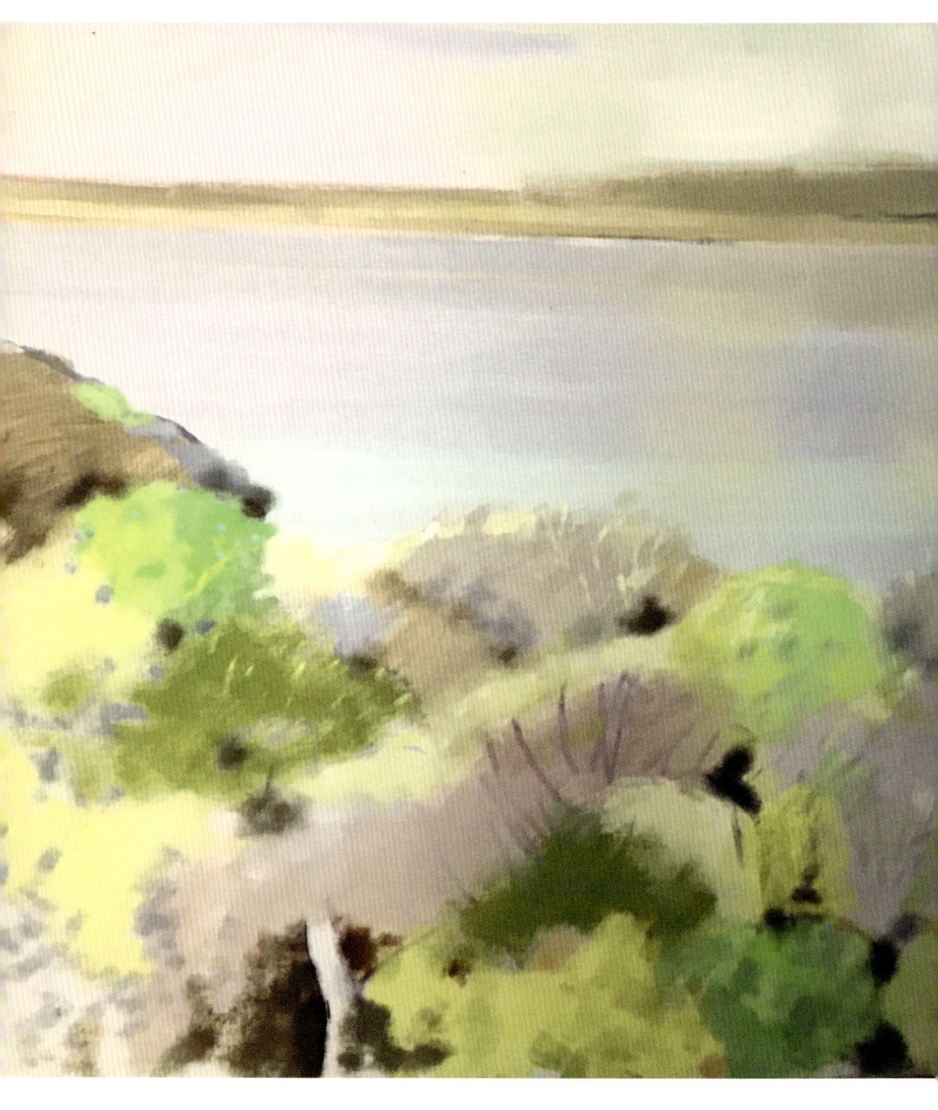

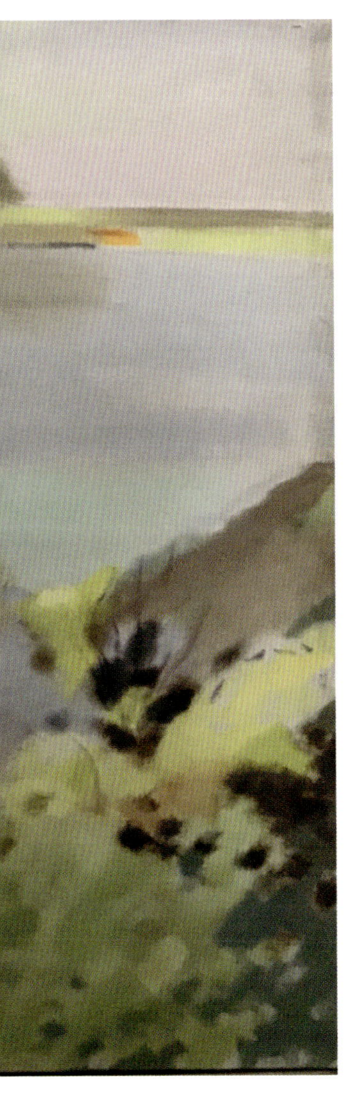

A flat painting, with the early morning light coming from the east. It is so different, yet this is exactly the same view as yesterday's low tide. I like the reflection in the water from the other side of the creek. Very subtle vertical lines, which make the composition easier. I felt this was an uninteresting work on its own, which is why I decided to put all four canvases together.

Two diptychs one above the other. A huge creation, it hangs in splendour in the entrance to the collector's house in Nairobi.

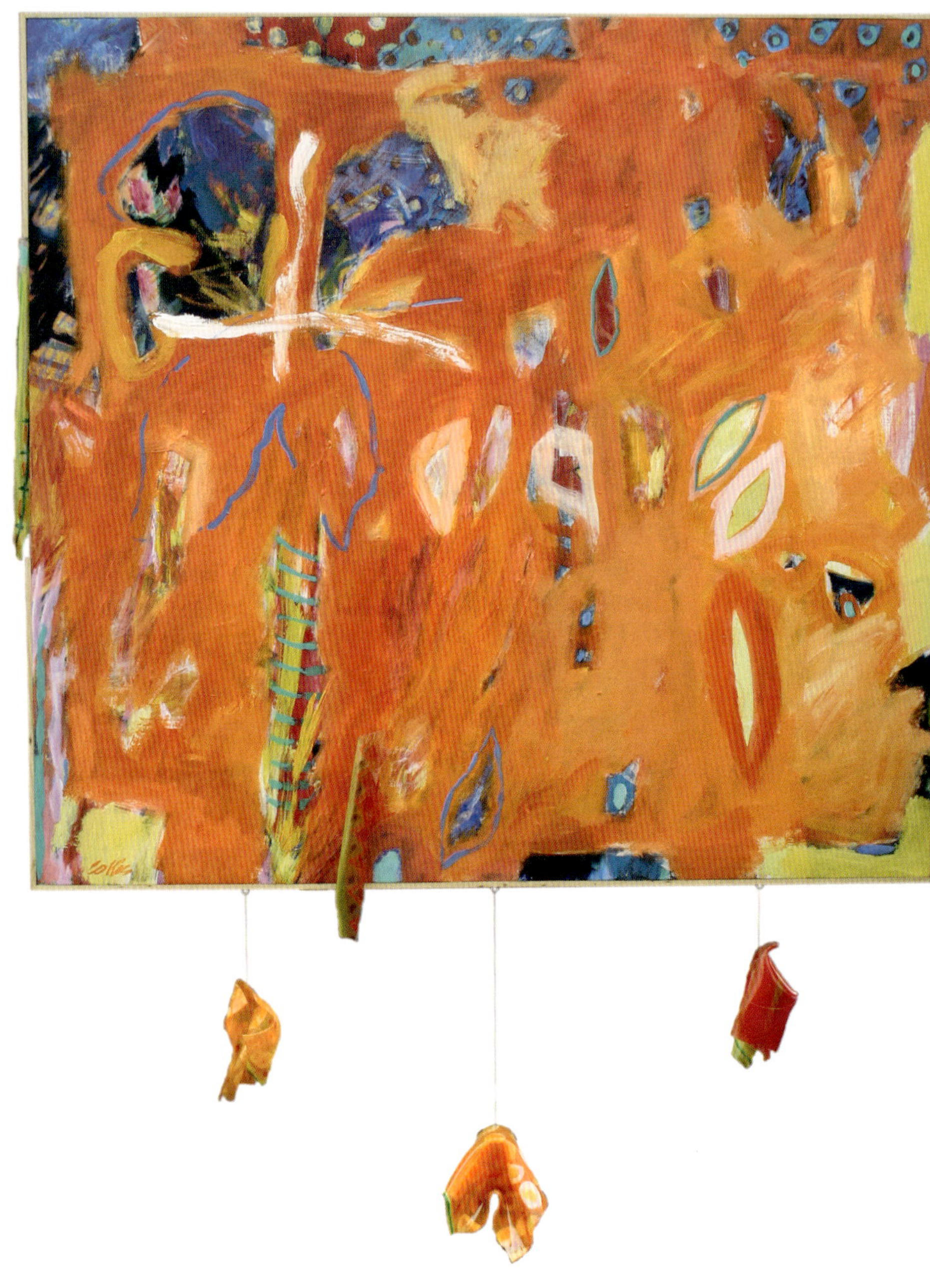

Kenya Burning

This was painted during the time that
the environmental and political activist
Professor Wangari Maathai was protesting
about the construction of a 64-storey
building Robert Maxwell wanted to erect
in Uhuru Park called the Times Media
Trust Business Complex. I had this vision
of Kenya being a beautiful butterfly and
falling to pieces. I painted on Perspex with
acrylic, cooked it over a flame to melt it
into shapes and attached the shapes to the
sides and the foot of the canvas.
This was bought by HE Ambassador for Switzerland
Dr Ralph Heckner and Dr Ilaria Macconi Heckner.

A Colourful Sigh

A 6-ft square canvas, after Cy Twombly,
a favoured painter. I gaze at his work in
wonder, it has to be seen for real. One of
a kind, he scribbled a unique path and
did not give a damn about the critics who
scratch their heads. My lines here have
a rhythm and are uniform and naturally
have a bit of colour. Granted, nothing as
free and admirable as my guru, mentor,
swami who sometimes worked in the
dark. Imagine an artist being that brave.
Perhaps that is the ultimate freedom?
My work was bought by the art critic
Frank Whalley. Frank is one appraiser
who absolutely gets Twombly.

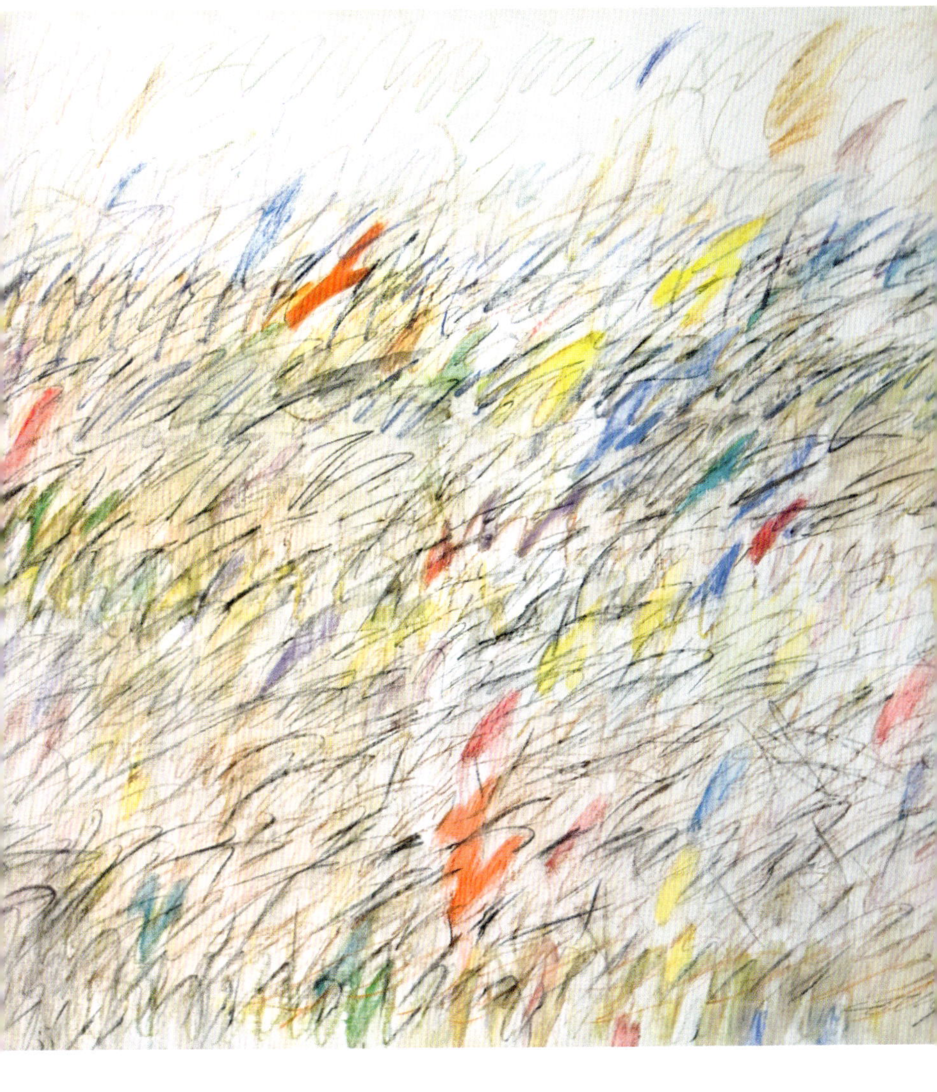

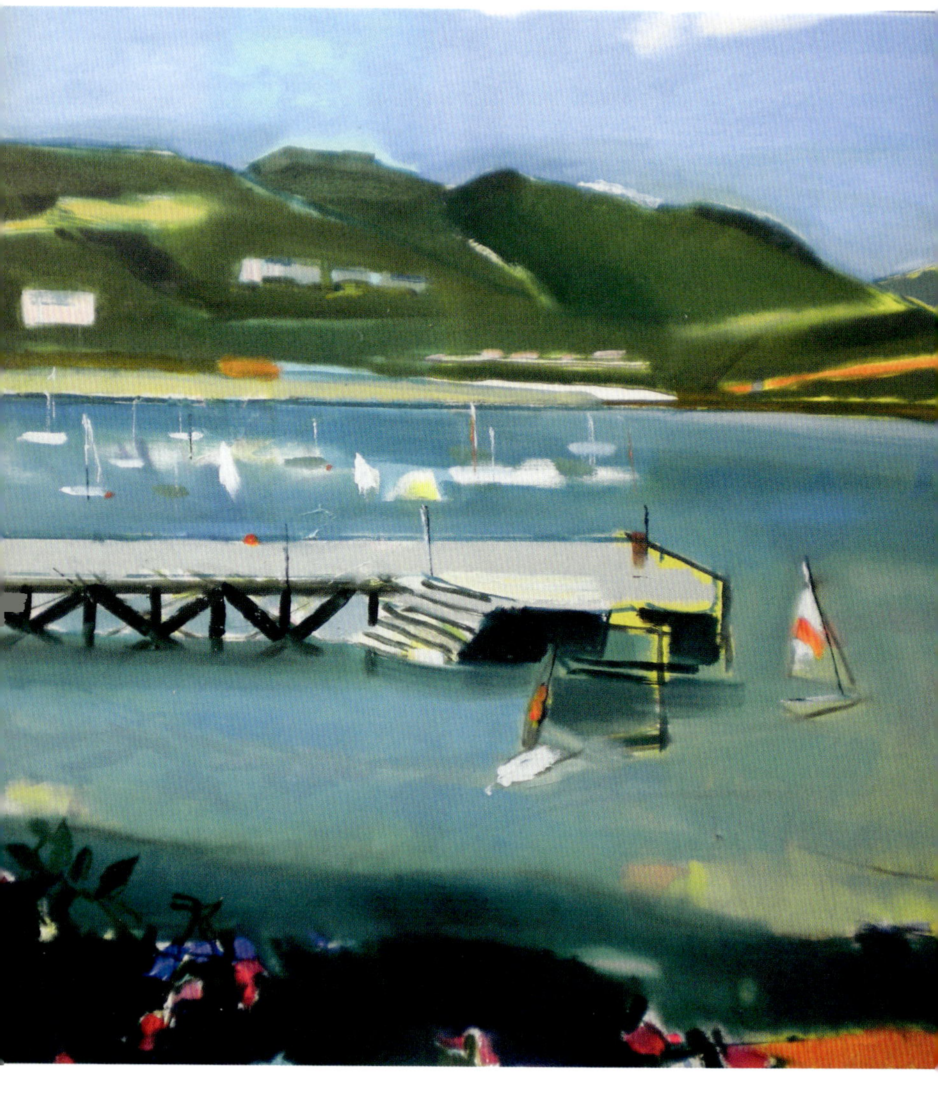

Simon's Town Jetty

I had an audience whilst
painting this in the Jubilee
car park, standing next to the
famous statue of Just Nuisance,
a Great Dane, treasured by the
South African Navy.
The view is across False Bay
to our apartment on the hill.
In my own collection.

1995 Artists' Calendar by PrePress

'I paint because I am a lily and I lily in July.' – not an original line but one I have slightly changed and added to, as I like its quirkinesses.

The One Lily, One Life painting came in useful for my artist's page of a very creative and fabulous calendar. PrePress was a different organisation, a group of extremely creative people.

It saddens me how many of the most inventive companies in Kenya have folded, as if they were ahead of their time.

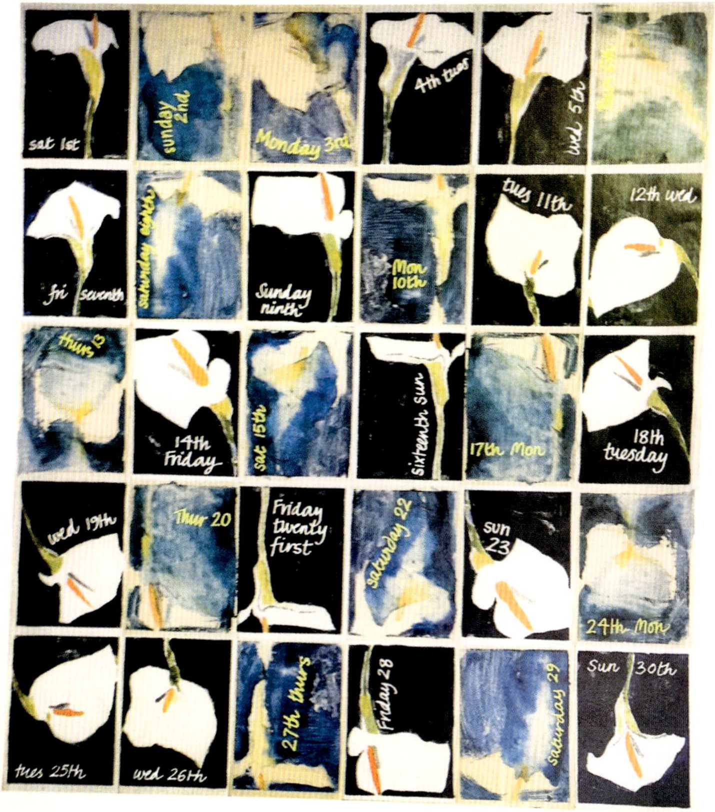

sat 1st   sunday 2nd   Monday 3rd   4th tues   wed 5th

fri seventh   saturday eighth   Sunday ninth   Mon 10th   tues 11th   12th wed

thurs 13   14th Friday   sat 15th   sixteenth Sun   17th Mon   18th tuesday

wed 19th   Thur 20   Friday twenty first   saturday 22   sun 23   24th Mon

tues 25th   wed 26th   27th thurs   Friday 28   saturday 29   Sun 30th

Collis '95

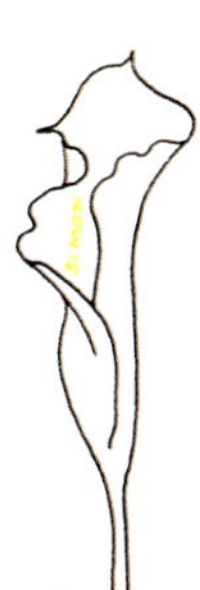

I paint because I am a lily – and I lily in July

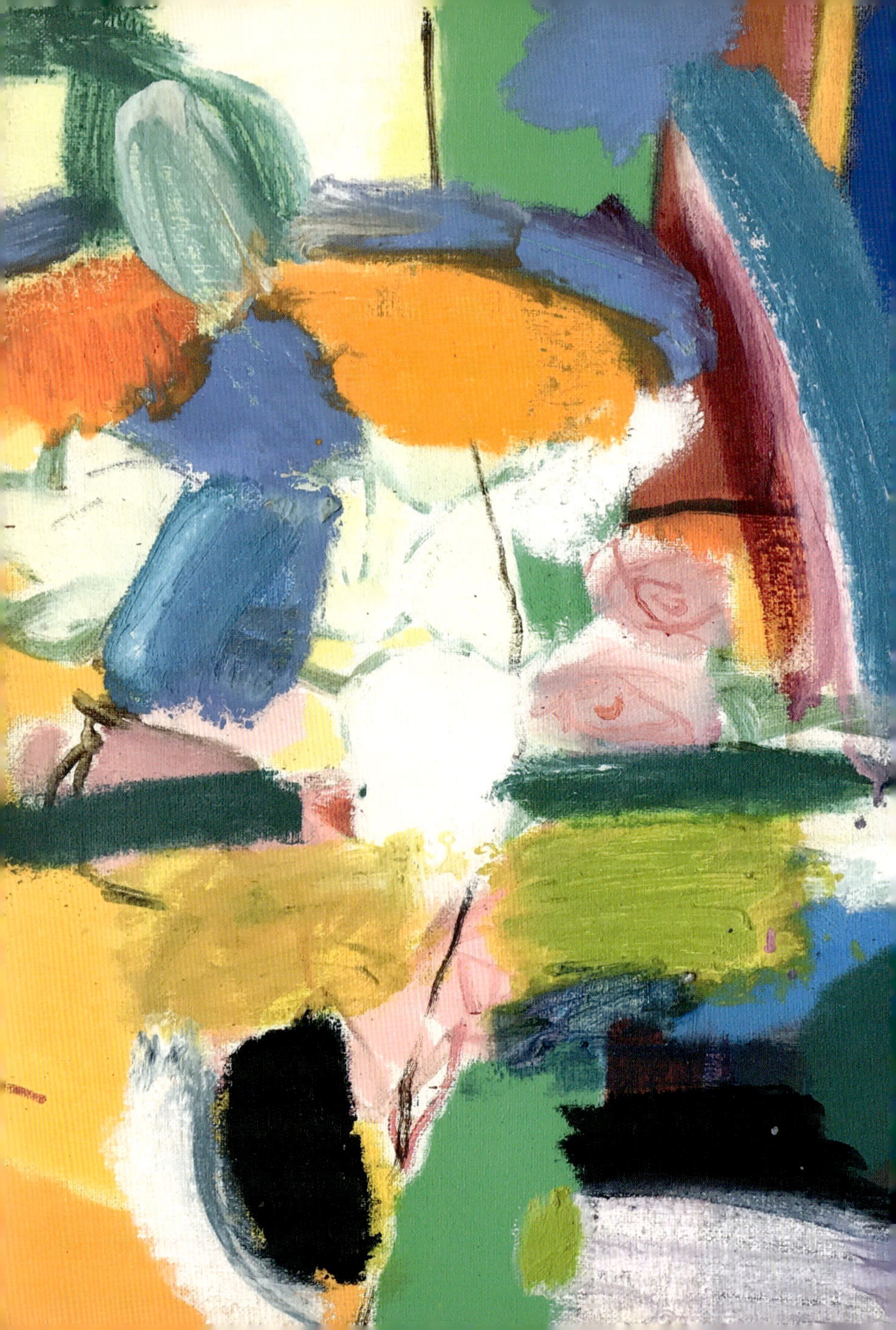

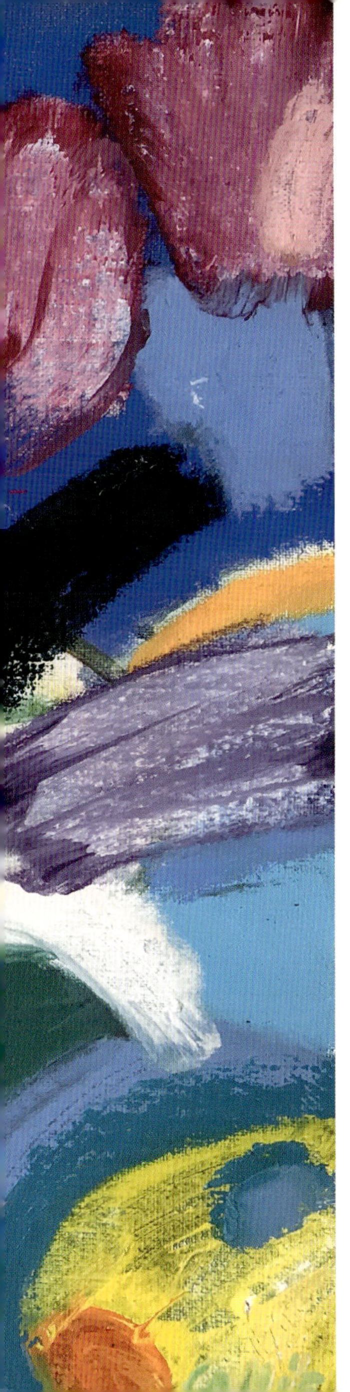

Looking round the Rose Bowl

One of my favourite abstract artists is Gillian Ayres, the British painter who died two years ago in April 2018. I look to her for her energy, colour and shape. She worked on enormous canvases and applied the paint with a trowel. In my view, she was very underrated, although now she has died she will be greatly revered. Fourteen of her huge pieces were tragically destroyed in the fire in the warehouse on the Cromwell Industrial Estate in London. She would throw naming parties for all her friends to 'title' her works after they were finished … so the intention was to resonate with the mood of the works and had nothing to do with the content of the painting. True abstraction.

Day 113
Riotous Assembly

'There are no beautiful surfaces without a terrible depth,' Friedrich Nietzsche, again, always an inspiration to me. His words fill me with wonder. He has influenced generations of philosophers, psychologists, writers and artists.

Liz Pannett first came to Kenya as a visiting artist to the University of Nairobi, I went along to one of her lectures and so looked up to her. I was amazed and flattered when she bought this piece from me. It resides in her home in the New Forest, UK.

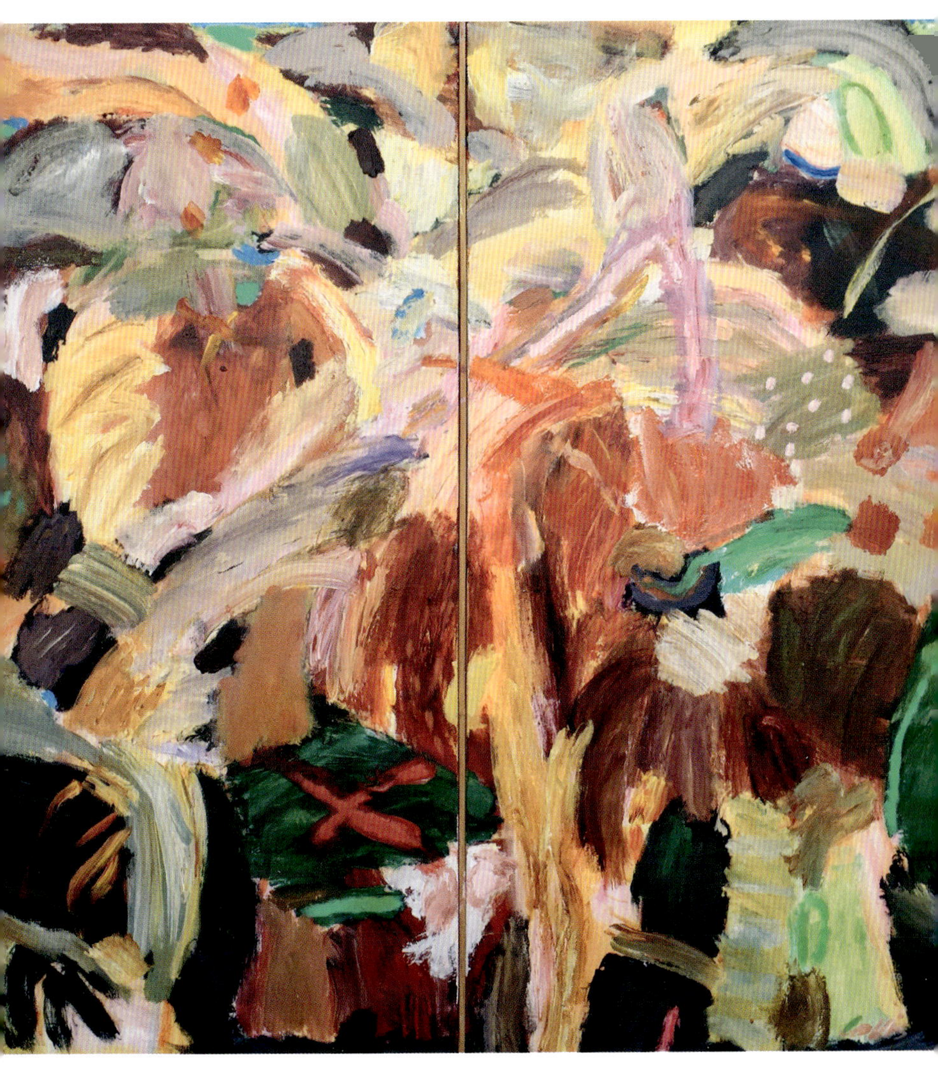

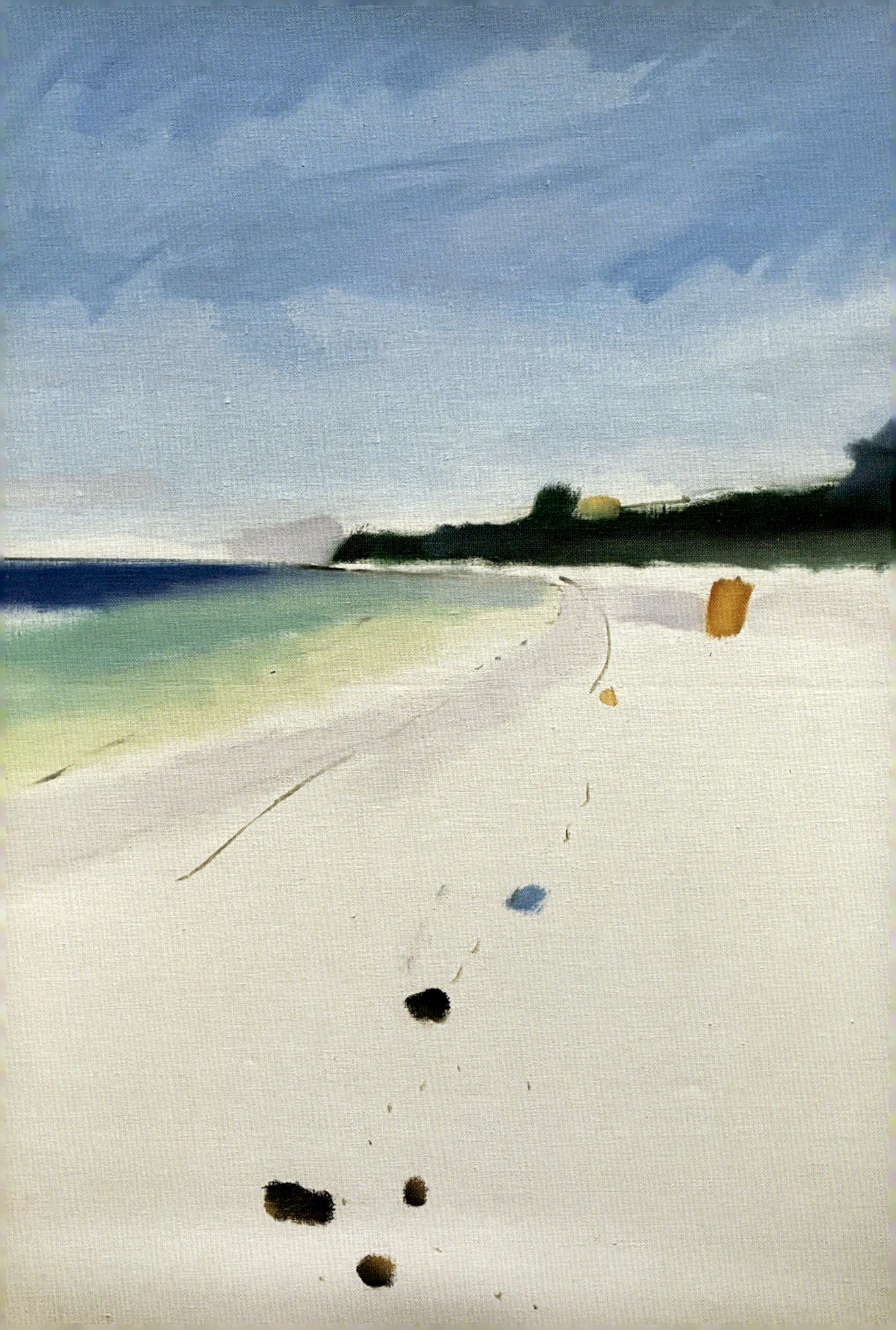

Day 114

Diani Beach,
South Coast, Mombasa

A very early canvas painted in the late
1970s. It was made into my first print.
Twenty years later, I was walking down
Cork Street and I saw a very similar work
in an exhibition of a similar beach, but it
was in Cornwall. I did wonder if that artist
had seen this? I doubted if there is such a
beautiful beach in southwest Great Britain
(I have been corrected on my ignorance).
This is another work with an orange dot ...
because the painting needed 'that'. If you
put your finger on the dot, the painting dies.
I remember that the oil painting took me
about 15 minutes to complete and I had to
ask myself if I was brave enough to leave
the canvas white, without paint.
This painting belongs to Geraldine Dunford.
We used to play on this beach together
as children.

Day 115

Kay's Garden

When my children were small we would often spend the weekend on a farm in Makuyu. My friend, Kay, was a splendid gardener, so there was much for me to paint, and the farm was tremendous with its vistas and cattle.

There are many colour dots in this painting, though I like to think one can see the gladioli, the roses (often on the golden mean to anchor the work), the cannas, large marigolds, periwinkle, lupine and plumbago. One can see from that Indian Red how rich the soil is ... we are blessed in Kenya with virgin red soil, you can see the nutrient in it.

This painting belongs to another splendid gardener, Christine Davis.

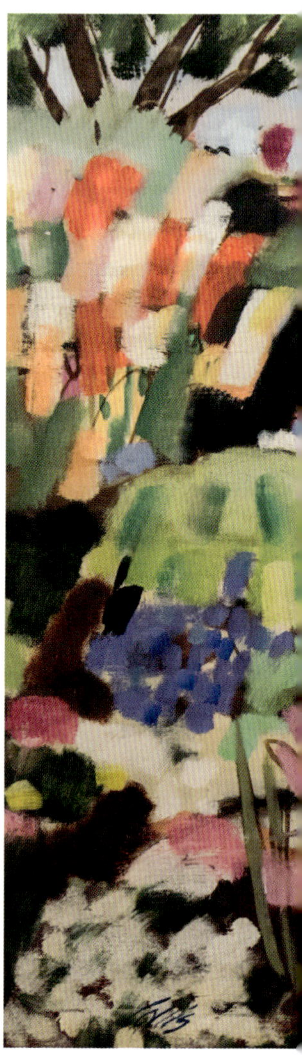

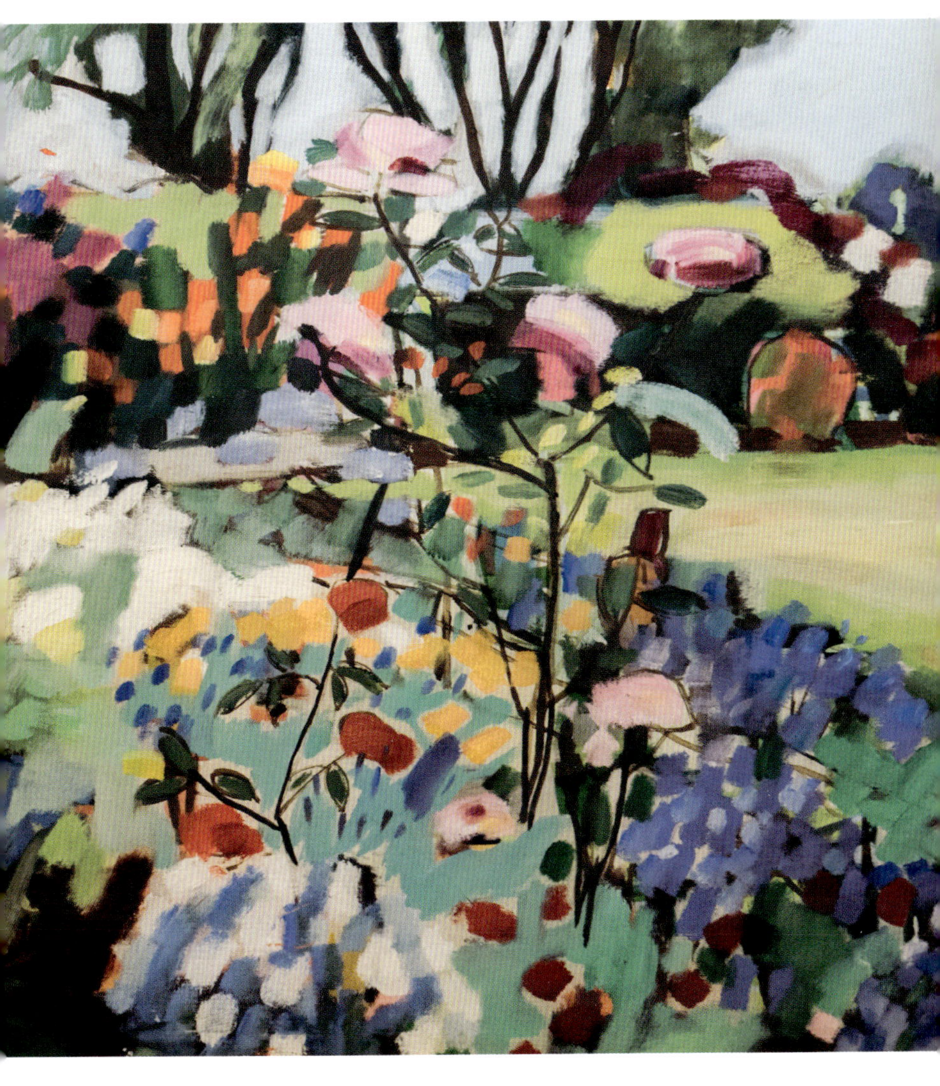

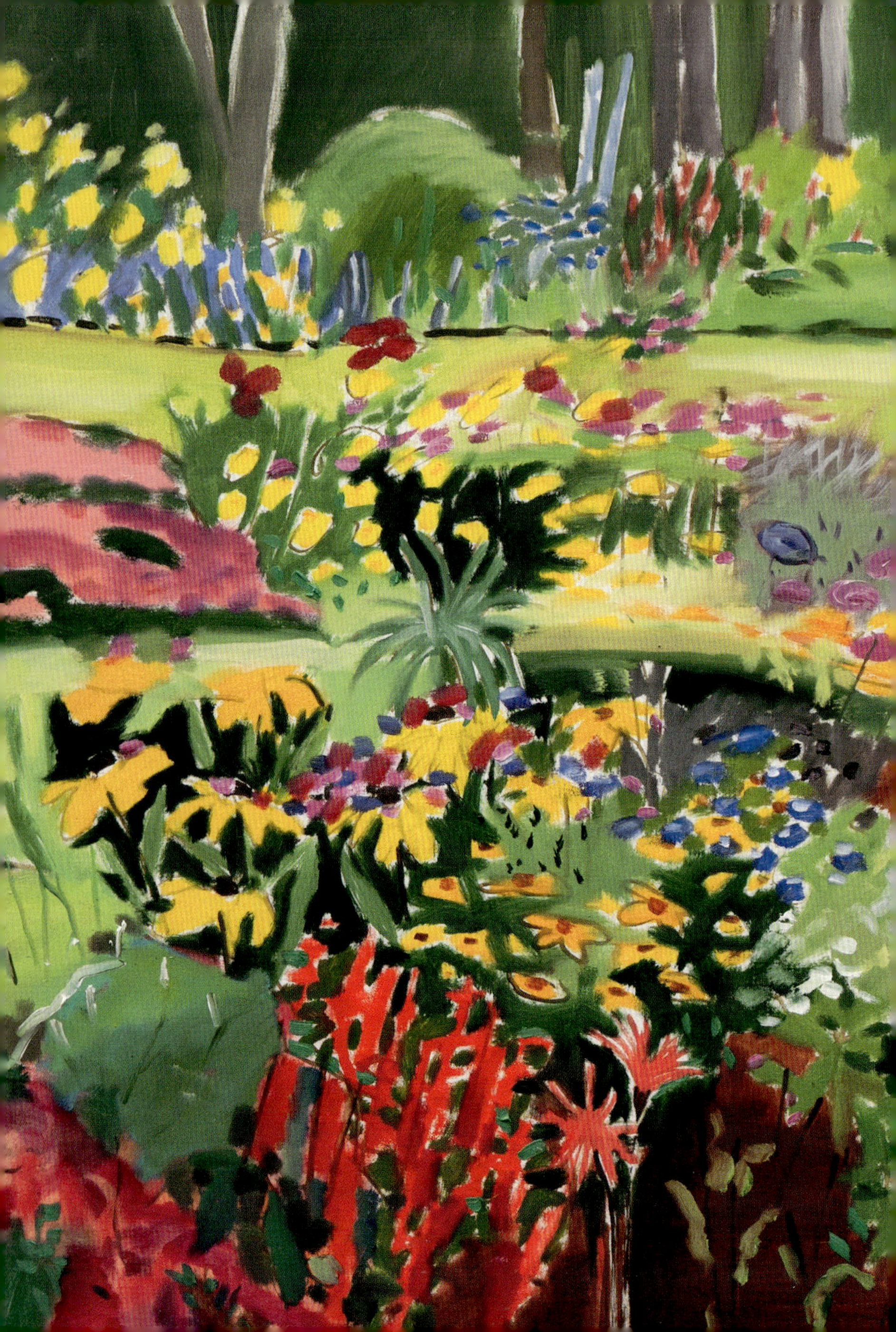

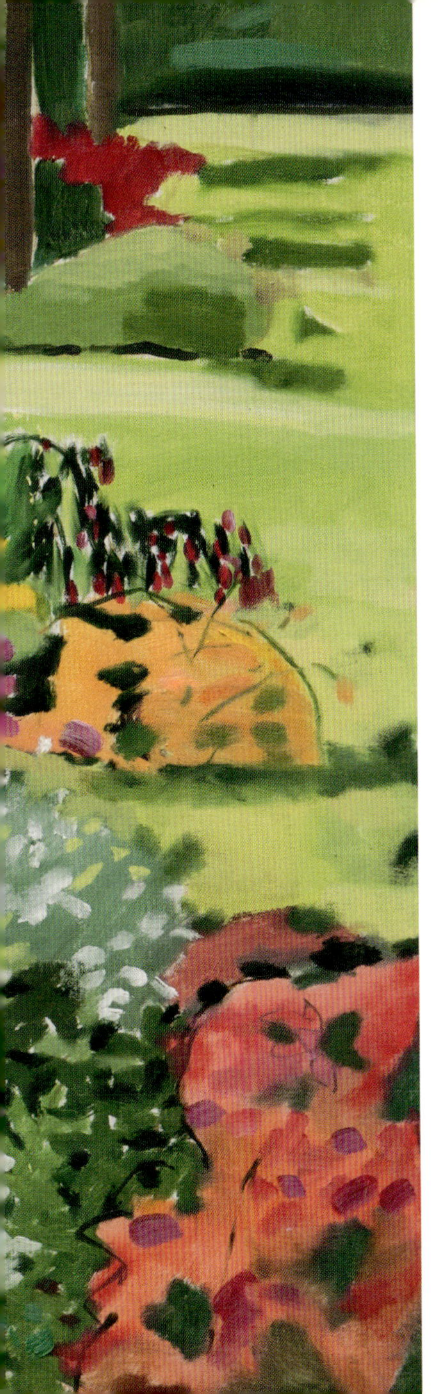

Day 116

Erica's Garden
Erica's Garden series

This garden work was featured in the WPP Annual Report, 'Thirty Years of Communications Services 2014', the fanciest publication of its type I have ever seen. That year the WPP in London used eleven artists from one continent, Africa, and a number of them came from Kenya. Top painters Peterson Kamwathi, Richard Kimathi, James Mbuthia and others were from the Tingatinga School. I was pleased to be included with these eminent painters in Kenya.

Day 117

Aloes

Looking over the aloes towards her sister Janet Hurt's house. In Jackie McConnell's exotic garden there were more different species of aloe than I have ever seen in one place. The following words aptly describe Jackie (I don't know the author), *'Life is a one way ticket. There's no refund if you don't use it all. Take what you can, when you can but be sure to always put back more – than what you have taken.'* Jackie burnt the candle at both ends and left everyone she met with a lasting impression. Her garden speaks for itself.

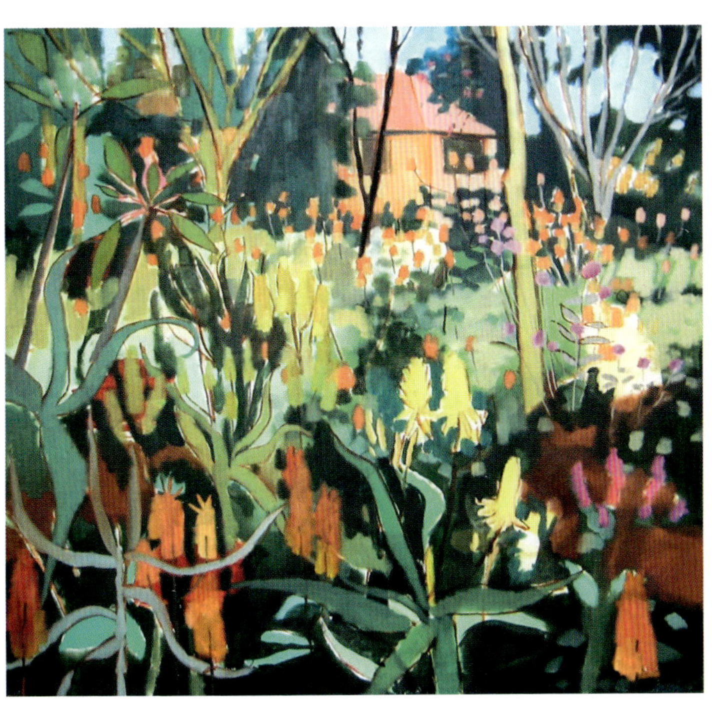

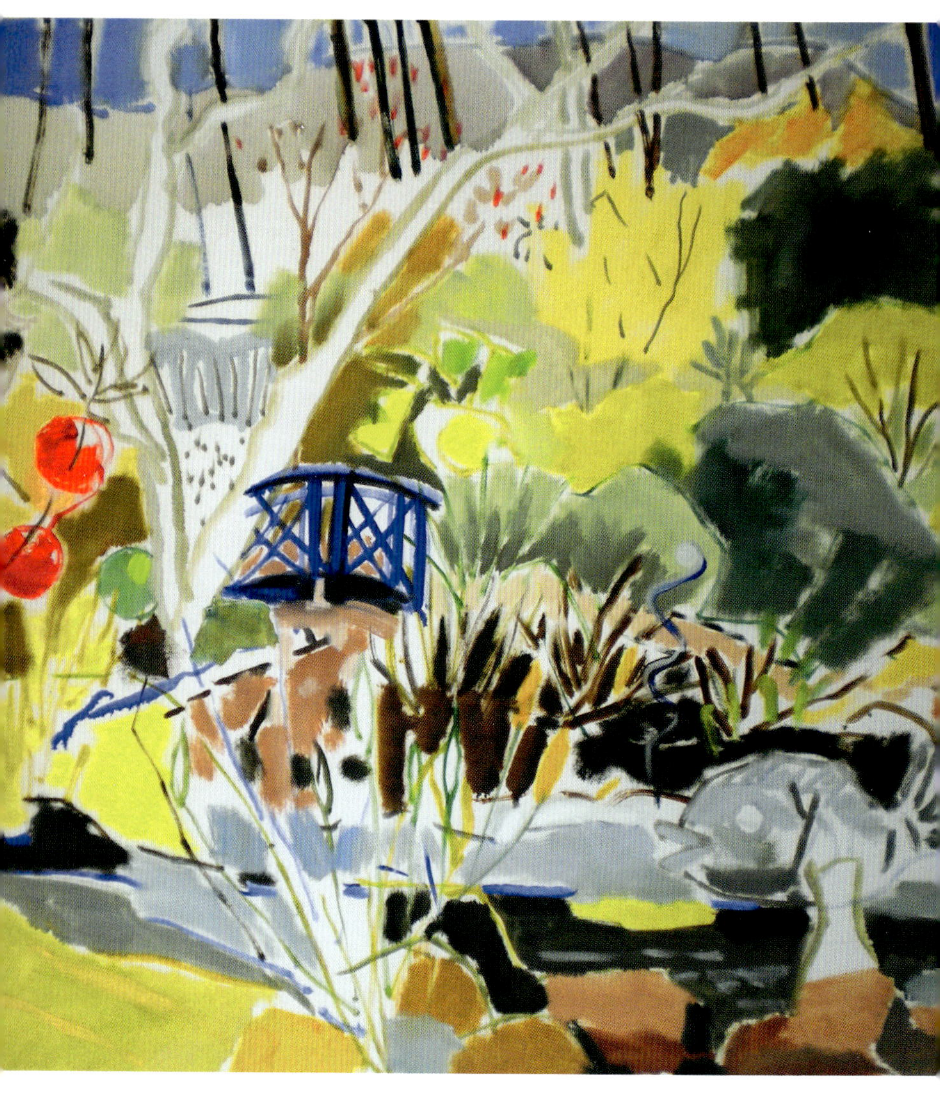

Blue Bridge

Judy Conway bought a smallholding of stony ground in the mountain shadow of Hout Bay, Cape Town. She turned it into another Kirstenbosch (the exquisite botanical garden of Cape Town). I decided to leave this unfinished canvas as the story is told. There are streams and sculpture and ornaments in this garden. Judy is a dazzling artist, as brilliant in her garden as she is with ceramics and painting.

Day 119
Bauhinia

A beautiful thing about our road in Kibagare Valley
was the Camel's Foot Trees (or Bauhinias, their
proper name). From September to November
they are covered in blossom and the road looks
magnificent. The Kenya Power and Lighting
Company would slash the trees once a year in a most
brutal way, as the branches got in the way of the
hanging power lines. Only in Africa do power lines
sag in this dangerous way. It dismayed me to see
the trees so brutally hacked. Then again, they would
seem to thrive despite having their limbs cut off and
flower like anything as if it was their last breath.
Every year I was out on our road painting them.
This one is a half-painting, half-drawing,
a close-up of a couple of branches, with the
blossom in front of my nose.
Collection of Hal and Lis Wackman, Washington, DC.

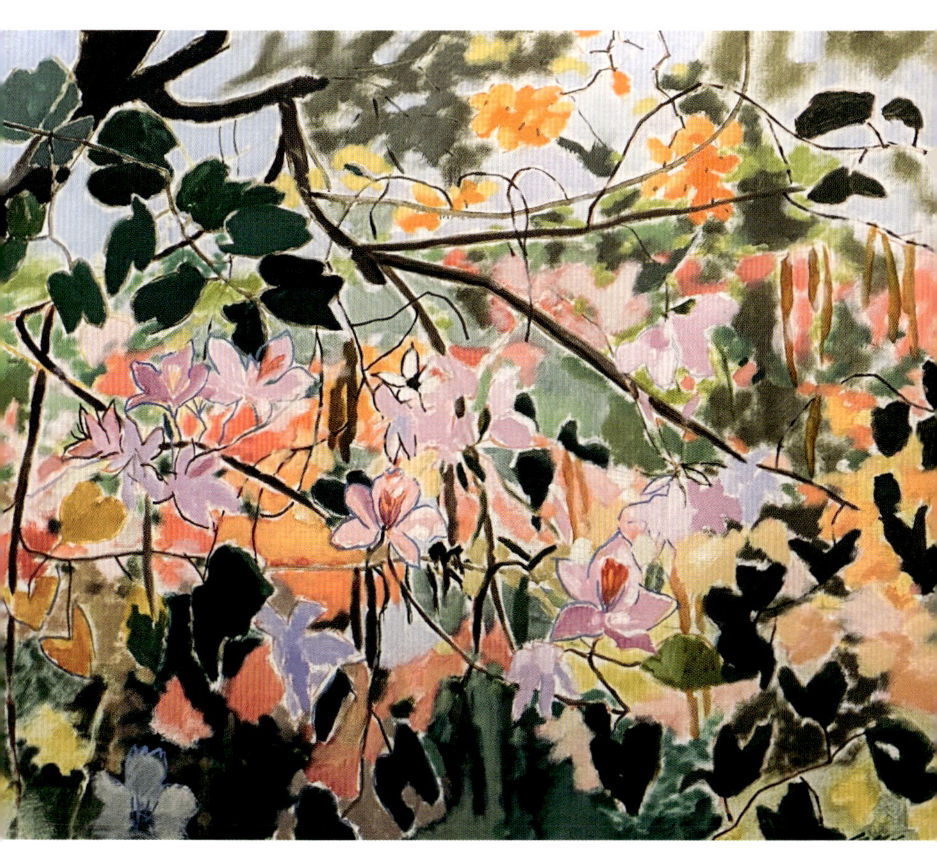

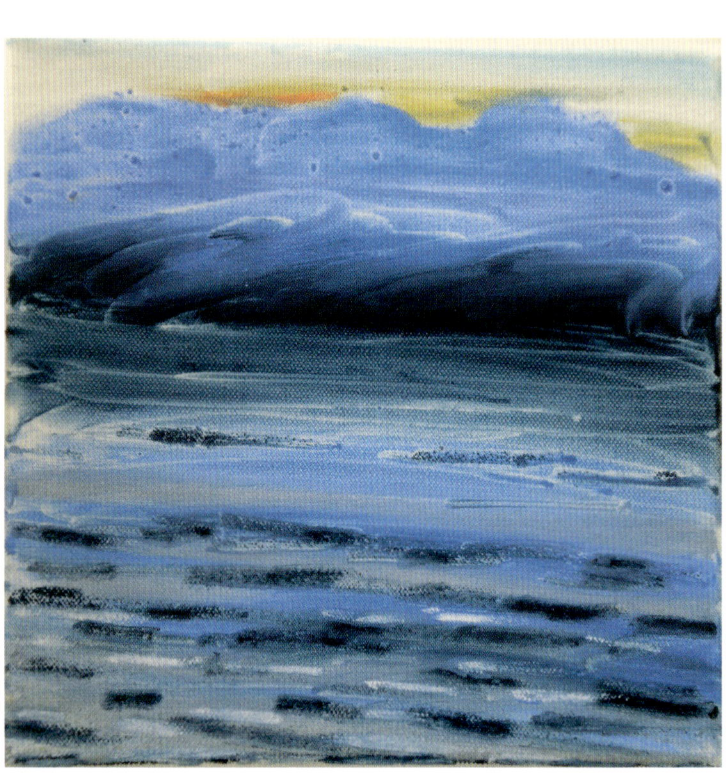

Windy Day on False Bay

Simon's Town has lovely weather, so we
are told. This was painted on 18 July 2020,
after gales and lots of rain. I painted this
one when the wind was howling.
I like to think that I caught the movement and
the sound. Of the something like 600 works
I have of this series, this little one is a favourite.
It is hanging in our kitchen in the Cape,
amongst a row of other 'windy' ones.

DAY 121

Still Morning, False Bay

The morning after all the wind, a very
still, silent morning. I get up before
dawn to paint these small squares.

'Each soul must meet the morning sun,
the new sweet earth,
and the Great Silence alone.'
Ohiyesa, Dakotah Sioux

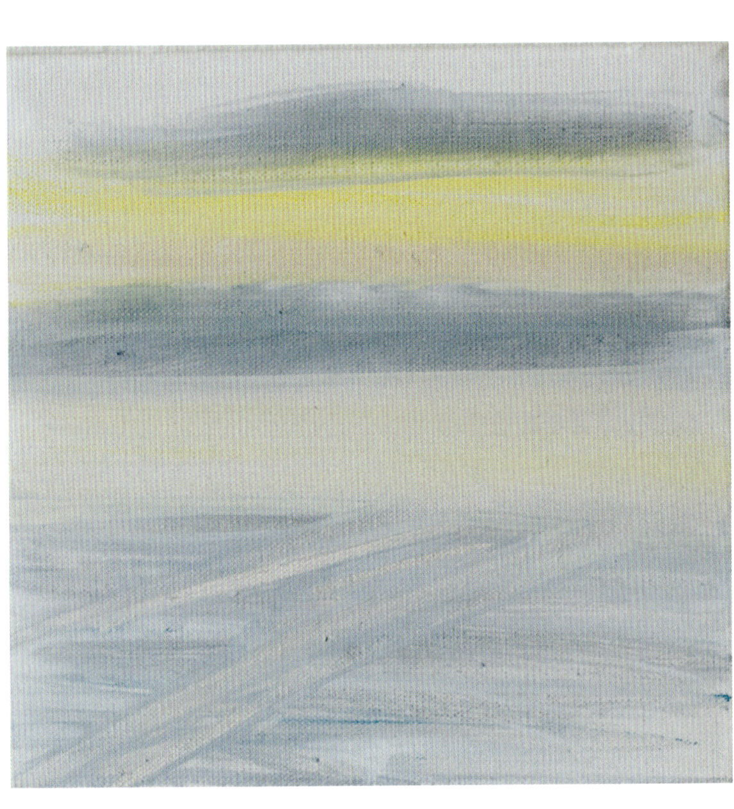

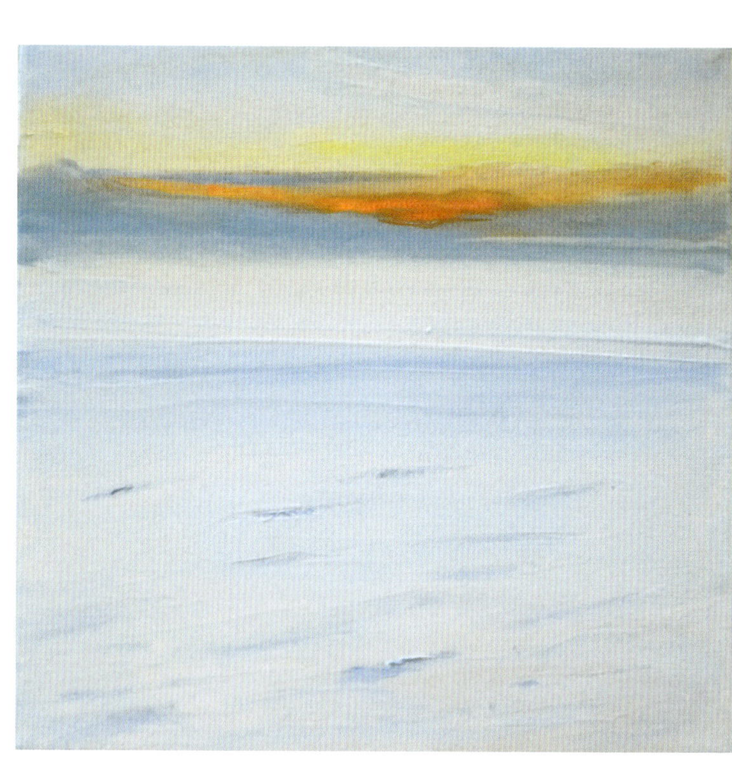

False Bay

A cold, calm, white sea despite
the glimmer of a sunrise over the
mountains on the opposite side of
False Bay. We can see the saddle where
Stellenbosch resides and Pringle Bay
around the corner. My brother-in-law,
James Pringle, is the younger brother of
the very same Pringle clan. Being at the
southern tip of Africa (a long way from
Scotland), it is still a very small world.

Jade Sea, 'False Bay' series

Colour fronts is certainly not my best painting,
albeit the extraordinary phenomena.
I have seen it a few times. It is beautiful, yet
I have a feeling it is inauspicious and menacing.
My clever sister-in-law, Margaret Underwood,
looked it up and wrote this on the Facebook
comments: 'Particles of buoyant calcium
carbonate from the sea floor and eroded from
the cliffs at Swartklip are lifted up into the
water column, changing its colour to jade green.
Wind-driven circulation patterns in the bay
push the front from its original location in a
southerly direction, towards Simon's Town.'

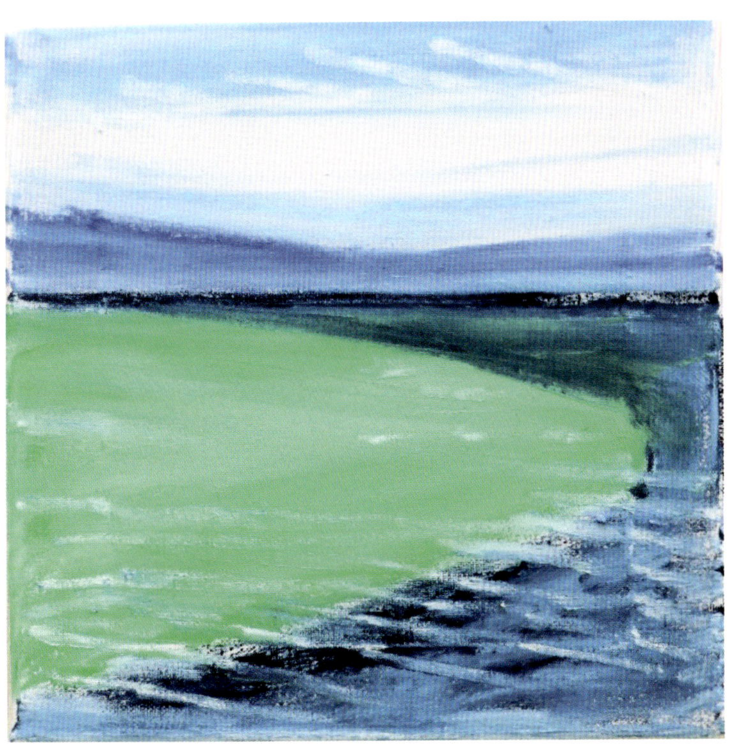

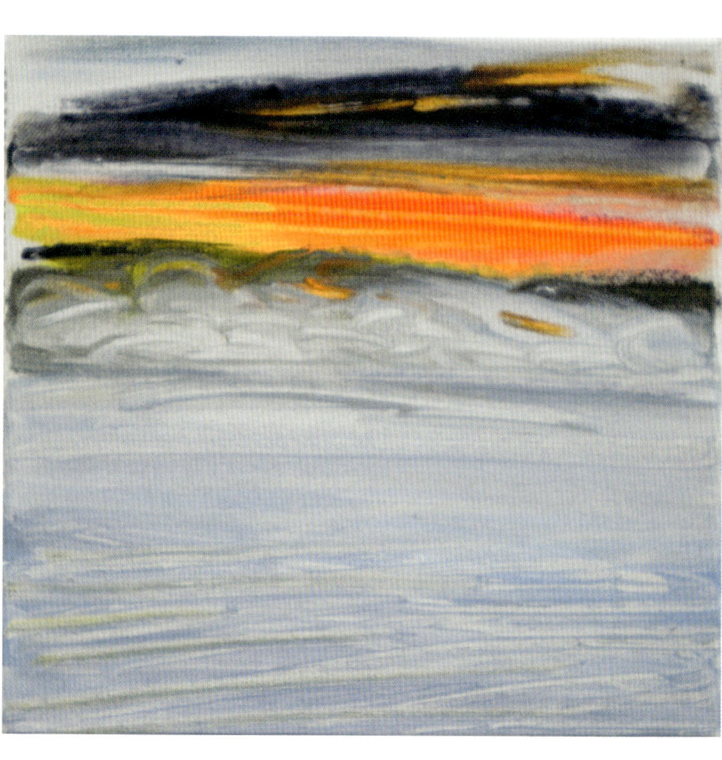

'False Bay' series

'Red Sky in the morning,
shepherd's warning.' And the wind
bellows. Very early morning,
half an hour before dawn. It looks
like the horizon is downhill, with
the cloud on the water, though the
thin grey horizontal line below
gives the work a stability.

'False Bay' series

Last seascape this week. I hope I have not
overdone the same subject, I have tried
to show a variety. Each of these works
are separately titled. I am in East Africa
writing this, and the whole series is in
South Africa, with the titles, date, time
and numbers on the back of each work.
A pink dawn morning and a promise
of a lovely day ahead.

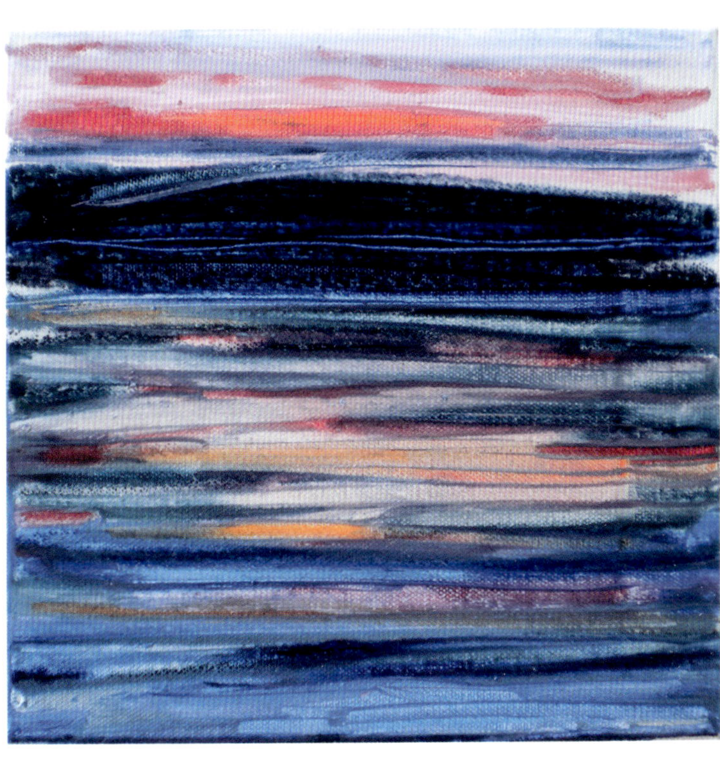

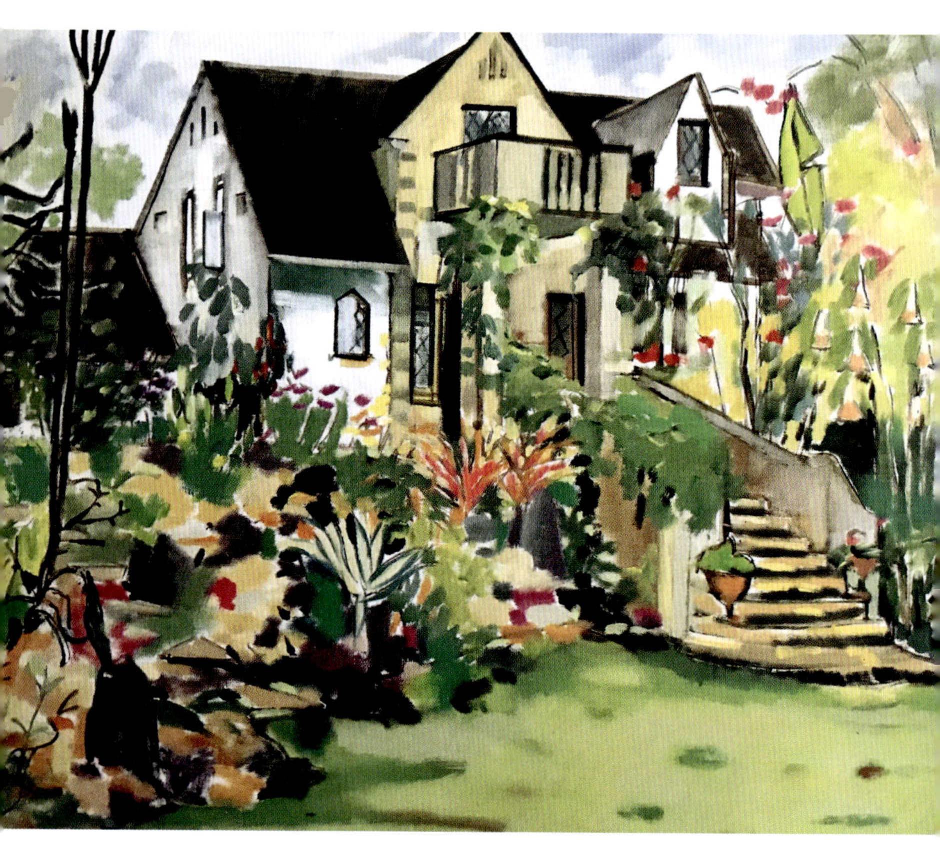

The McConnell House

Another commission of a lovely
home, Charlie and Mouse
McConnell's house, in Karen
(the district named after the
author Karen Blixen, where
she had her farm), Nairobi.
They had this made into a card,
which is why I have a copy.

The poppies in this field were a tribute
to the deaths in the unnecessary war in
the Gulf, George Bush's war.
This painting made a striking chiffon
scarf and shoes. My friend Diana Bird
retired from the retail business and had
my work printed on to different fabrics.
An exciting time for both of us.

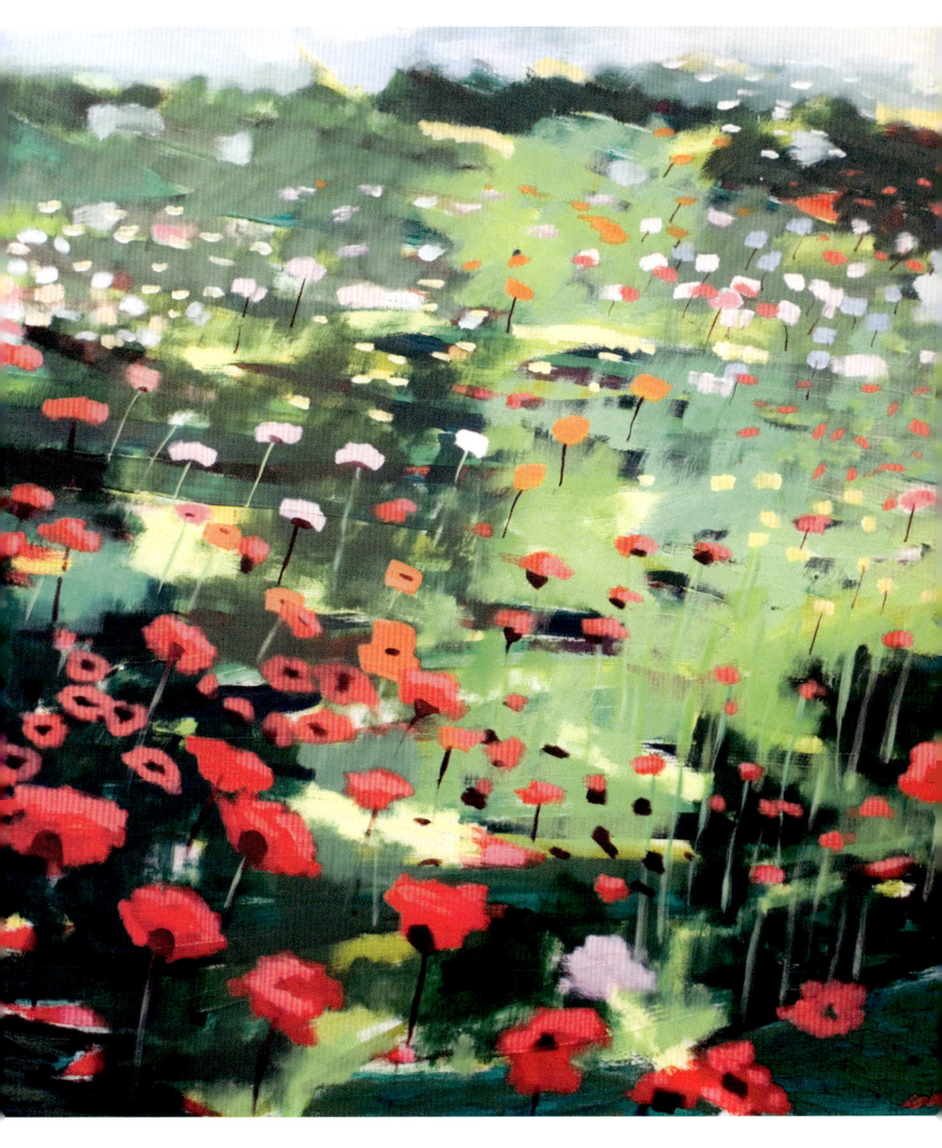

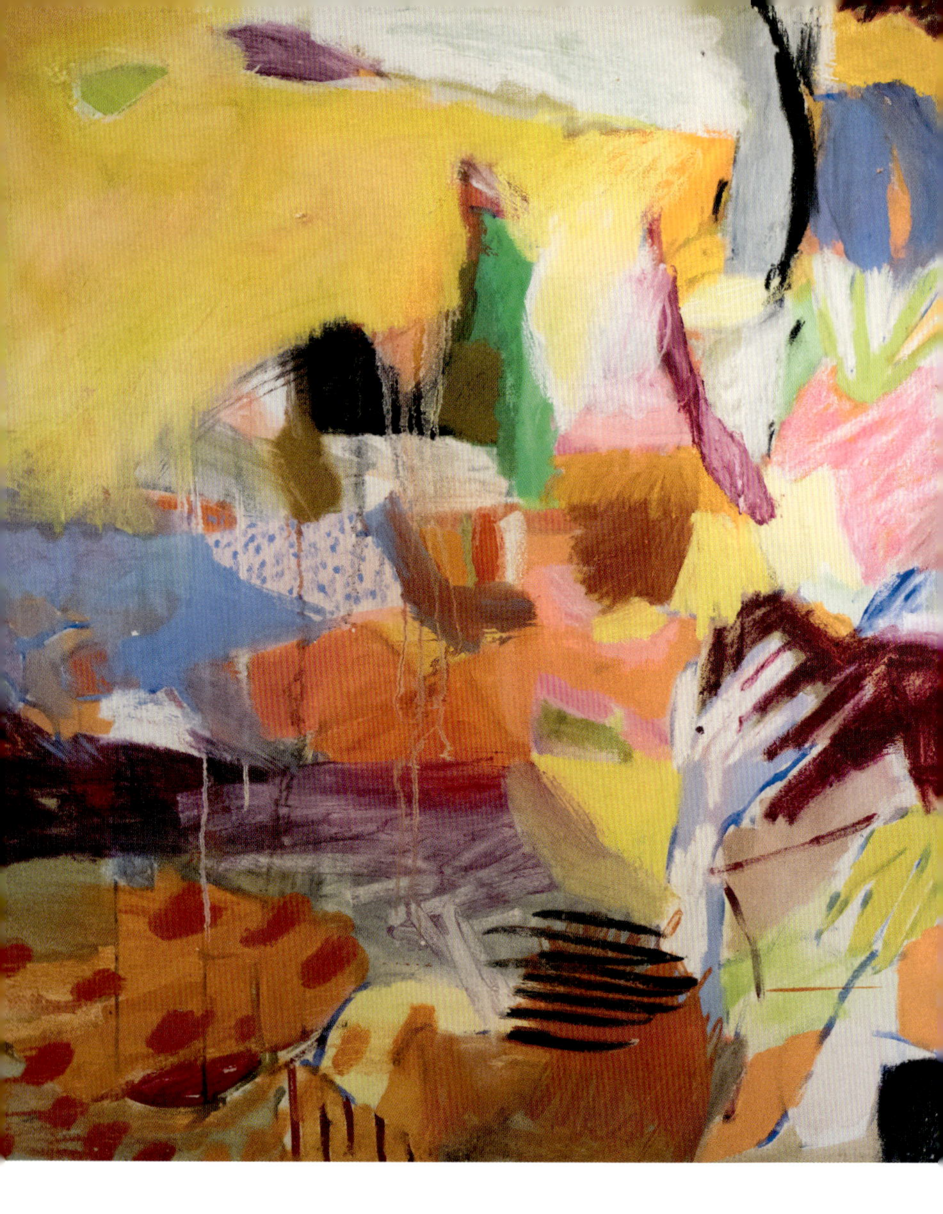

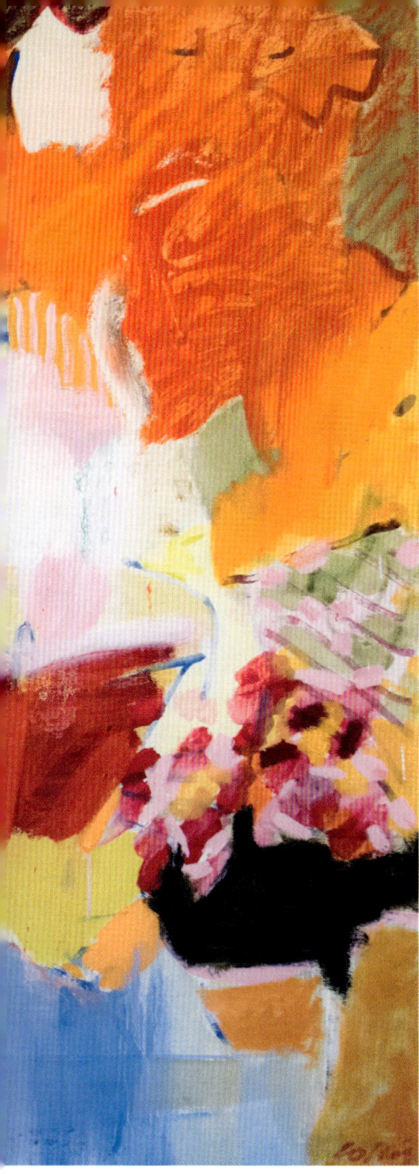

Day 128
Reading

There are some paintings that stay with me for years, usually because no one declares any interest. This one still sits comfortably in our apartment. Semi-illustration, semi-abstract. I like it. I have exhibited it several times.

Day 129

No title on the back of this,
it hangs in our spare room and
is the pair to Day 112 (*Looking
round the Rose Bowl*), both
small paintings. I have been
thinking about Gillian Ayres
today whilst in my studio,
reading a book about her.
I can't help noticing that her
inventiveness came from the
same inspirations as mine – the
American Helen Frankenthaler,
Abstract Expressionist and the
English abstract painter Patrick
Heron. I see both artists in her
work. All three painters create
from that 'still centre', a vital
place to find when working.
Gillian Ayres is the painter's
painter and I love her work.

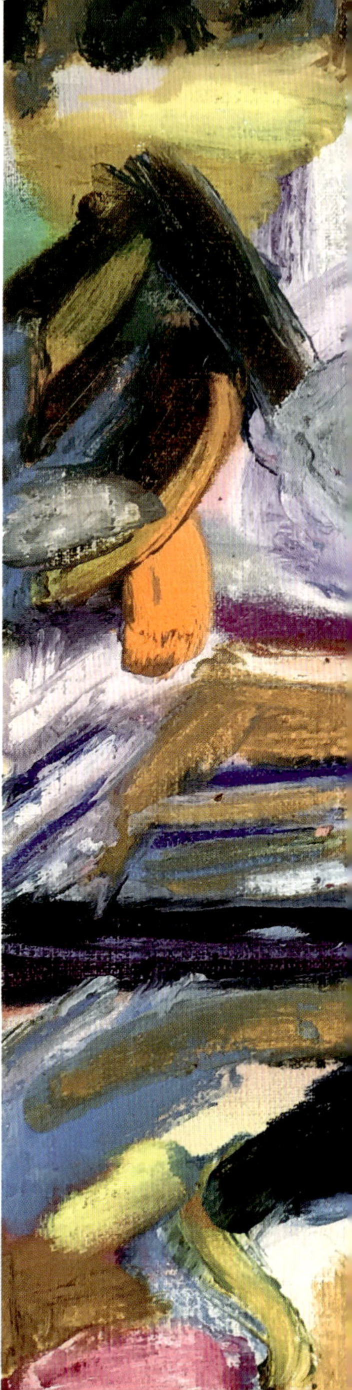

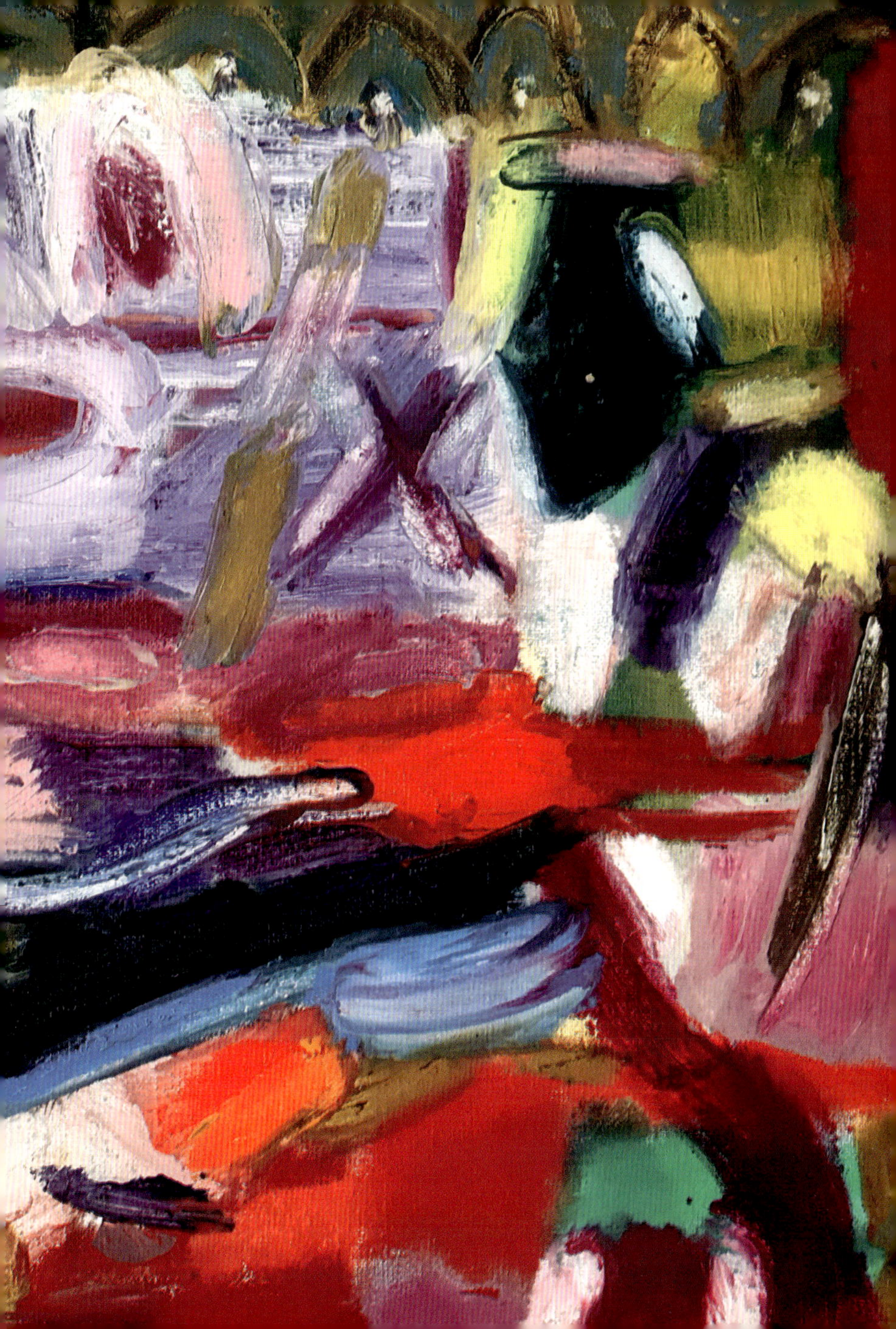

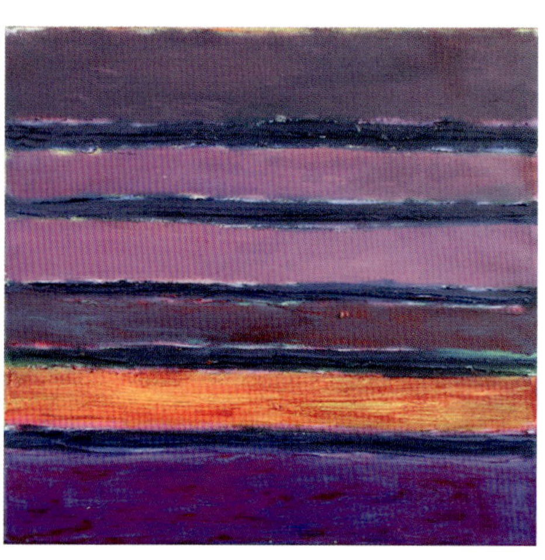

After Sean Scully, who paints
the stripe almost exclusively to
anything else. The Chinese love
him and he was the first Western
artist to have a retrospective of
his entire oeuvre in China.
Every abstract artist has had
a go at works inspired by him,
including me, who did a series
based on the Maasai. I much
admire him and, in particular,
his integrity with the stripe which
he still paints, since the 1980s.

There is an awful lot of it about at
this moment! This was painted for an
exhibition which ran concurrently with the
performance of *The Vagina Monologues*.
It is in the collection of Thomas Wright,
who is one of those special people in
this world to whom I shall always feel
incredibly grateful and indebted.
He has twenty-six of my works.

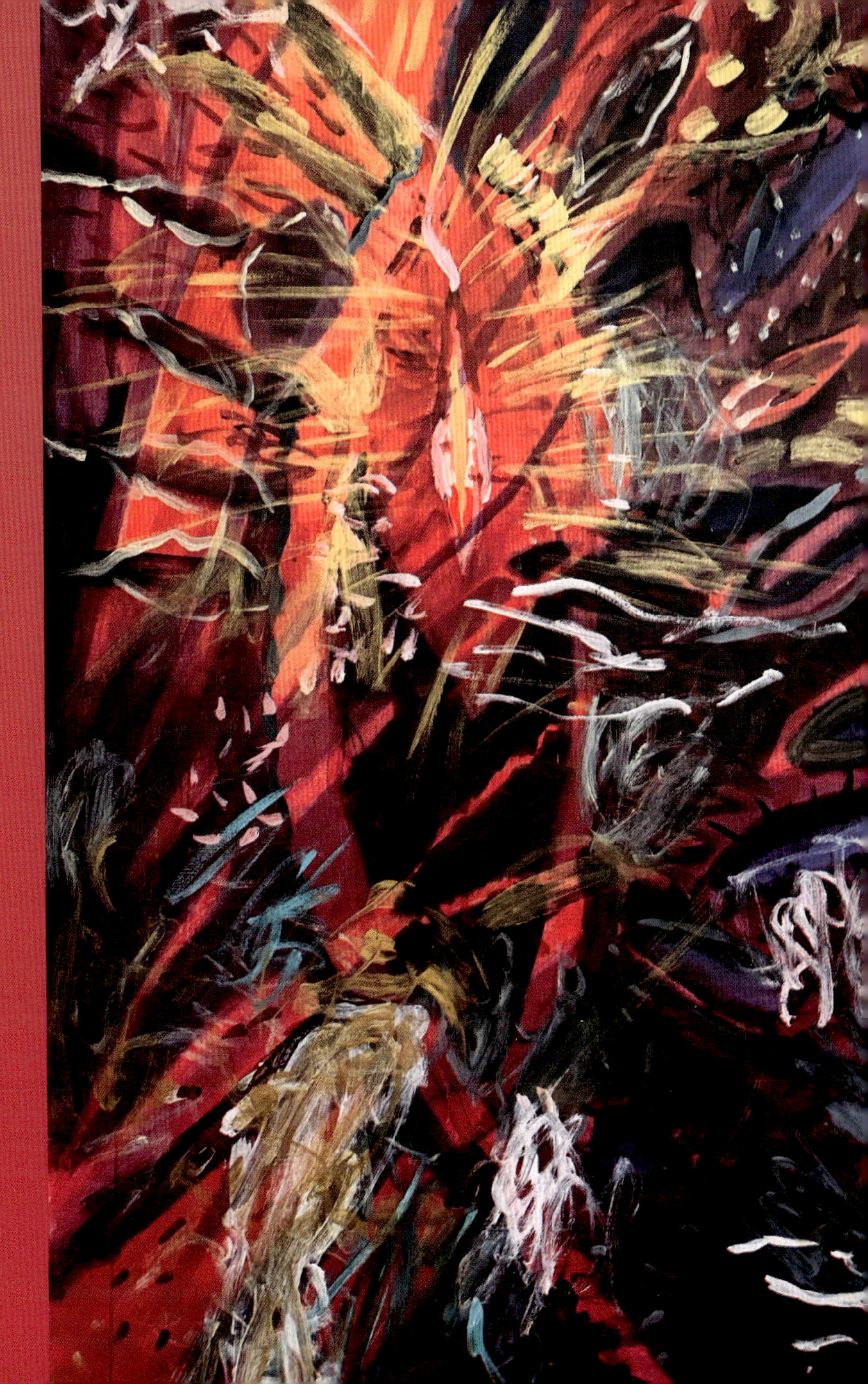

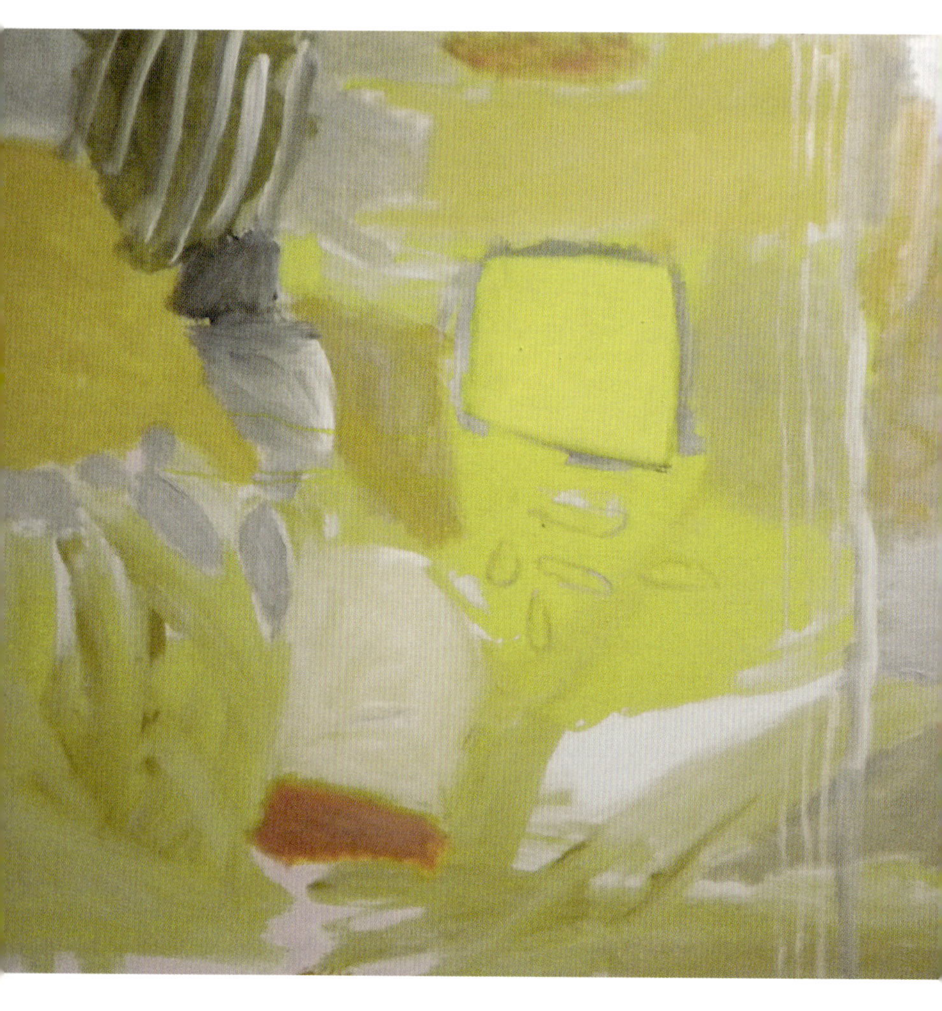

The curator Osei Koffe titled this work.
One of the best and unexpected things
about this online exhibition has been
the forgotten paintings that have
popped up from all over the world.
Many of the works, I am ashamed
to say, I have forgotten, and it is
surprising to see them again.
I was looking at Nicolas de Staël,
the French painter of Russian descent,
born in 1914. He was ahead of his
time. He painted colourfields with
thick impasto, inspired by landscape.
I remember the story … how art
dealers would hang round his studio
to snatch the work as it was done.
He was particularly popular in Britain,
where he inspired artists such as
Roger Hilton and Patrick Heron,
and others from the St Ives School.

A yellow path through the woods.
I like to think it invites you to
meander through the painting.
Collection of Hamish and Jacky Keith,
Nanyuki, Kenya

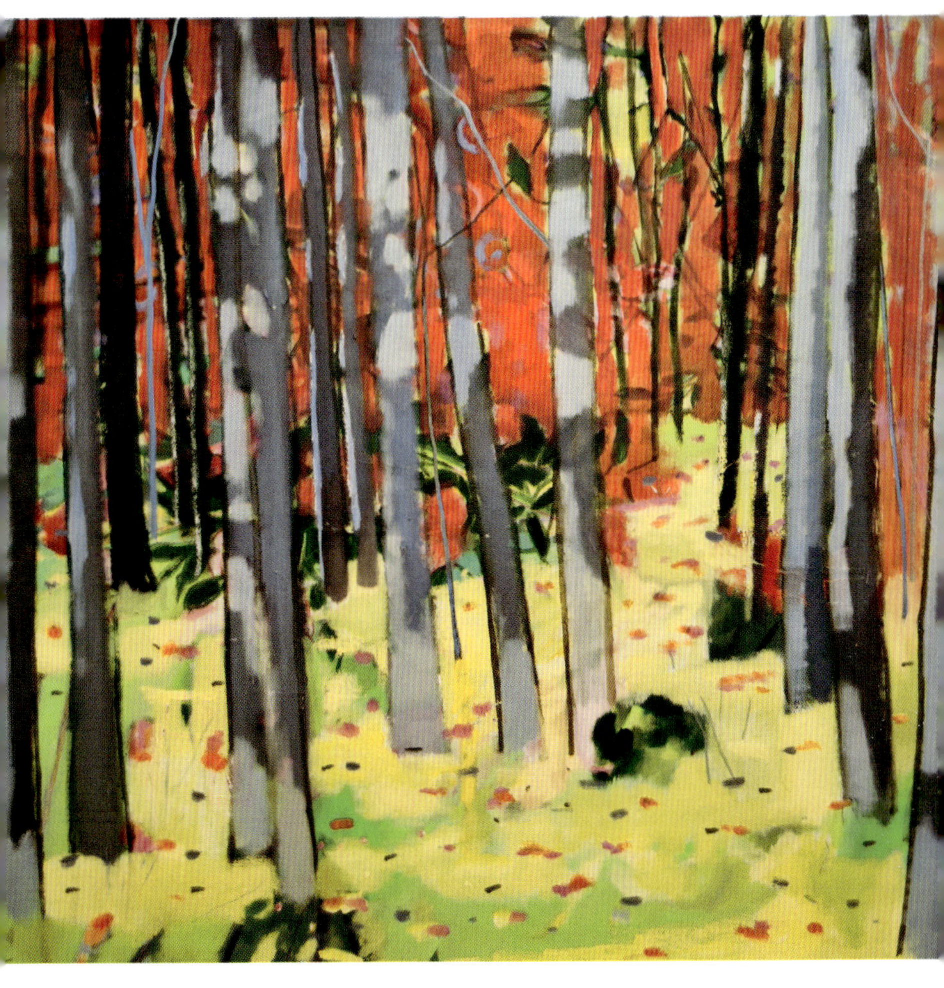

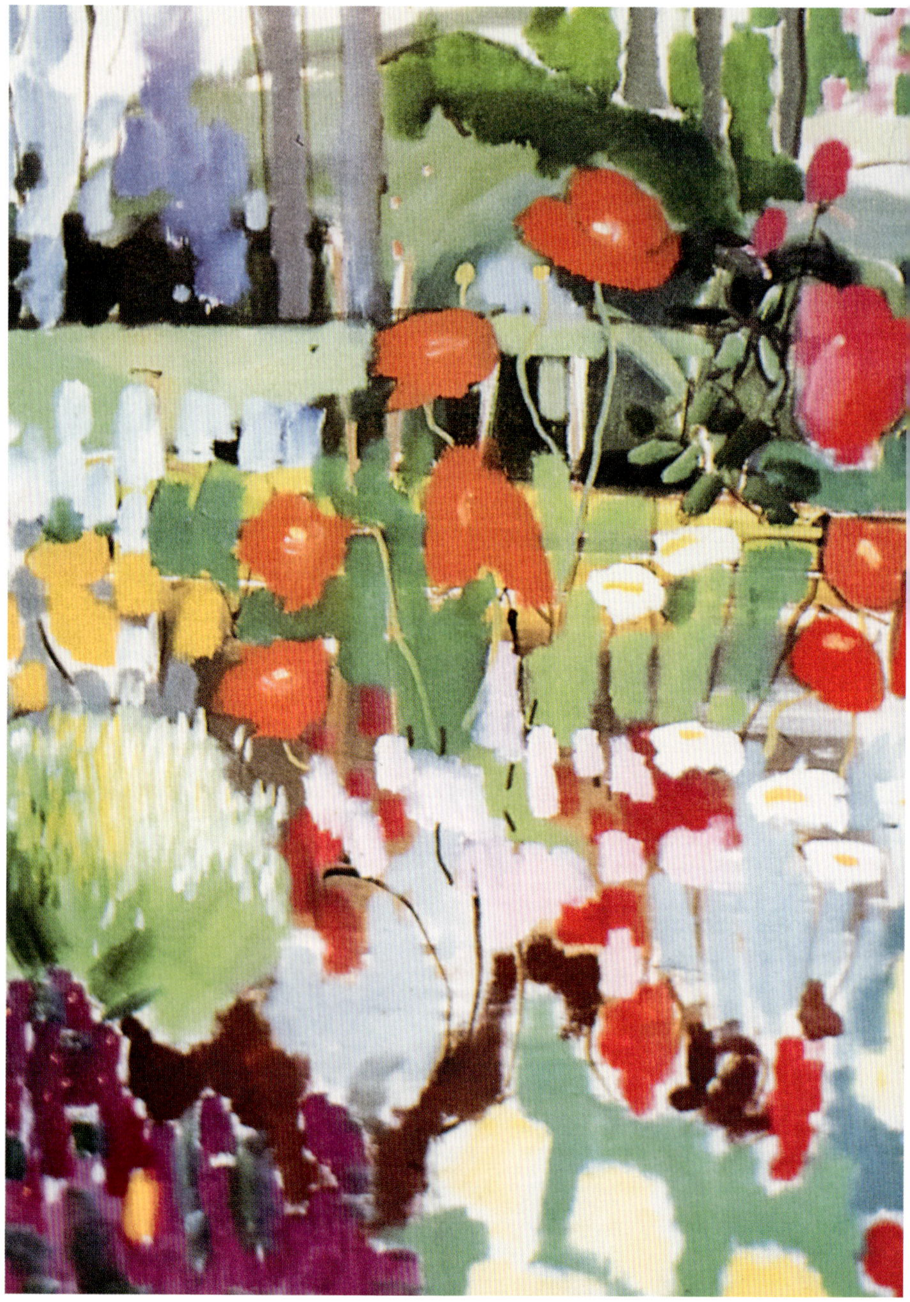

I have had many paintings made into cards,
and this one of poppies in Erica's beautiful garden
was one. The bottom one-third is abstract and the
eye sorts it out because the top is more realistic.
Collection of Nelson and Pirkko Edwards, France

POPPIES
ERICA'S GARDEN
SERIES

A painting weekend in Lamu,
north Kenyan coast.
Orange bougainvillea against a
sunlit wall. A 10-minute sketch
using brushes after a long day
completing a sizeable canvas.

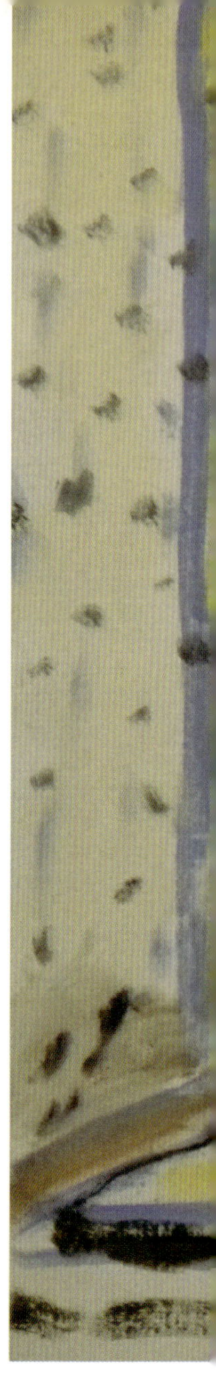

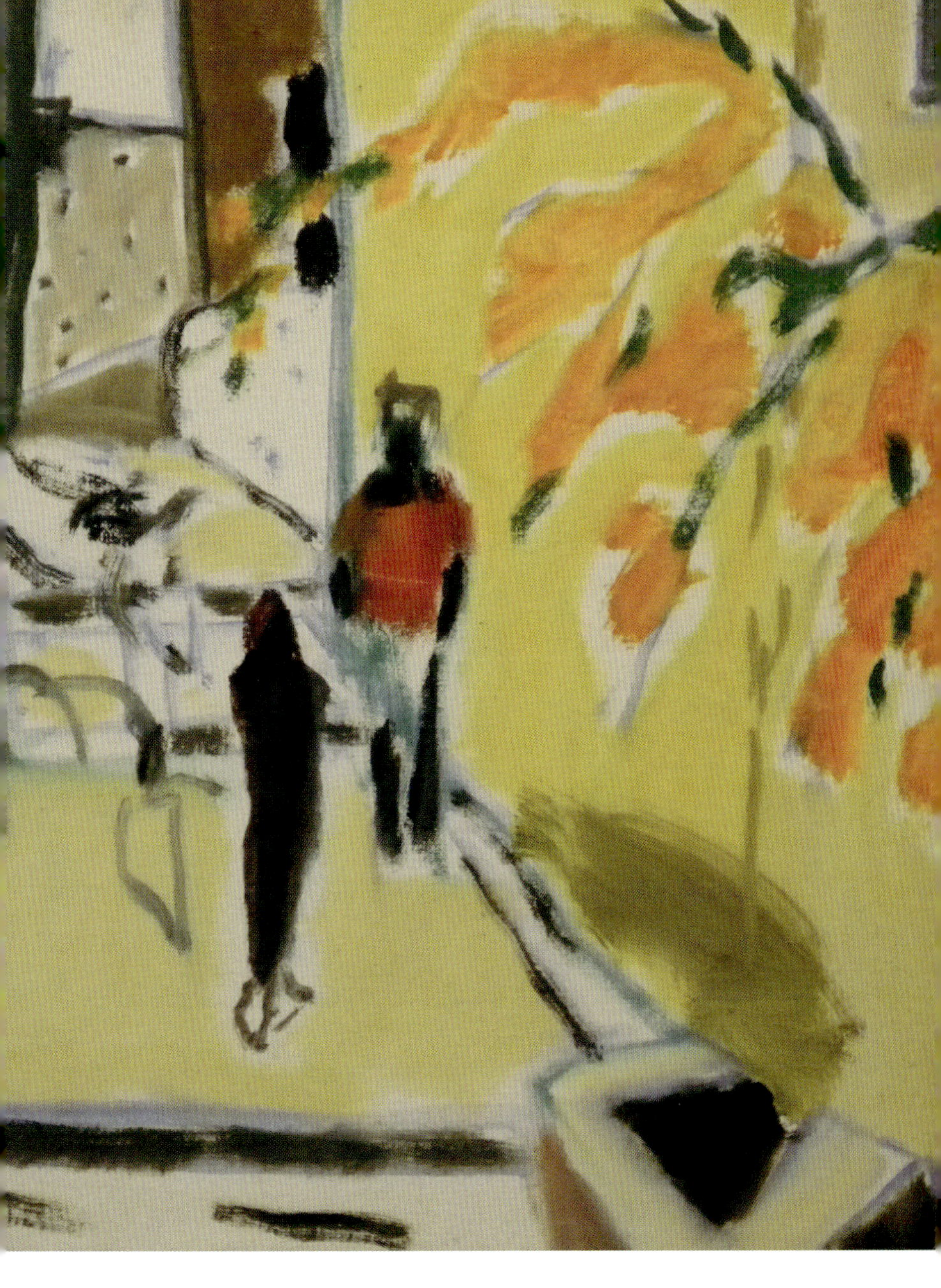

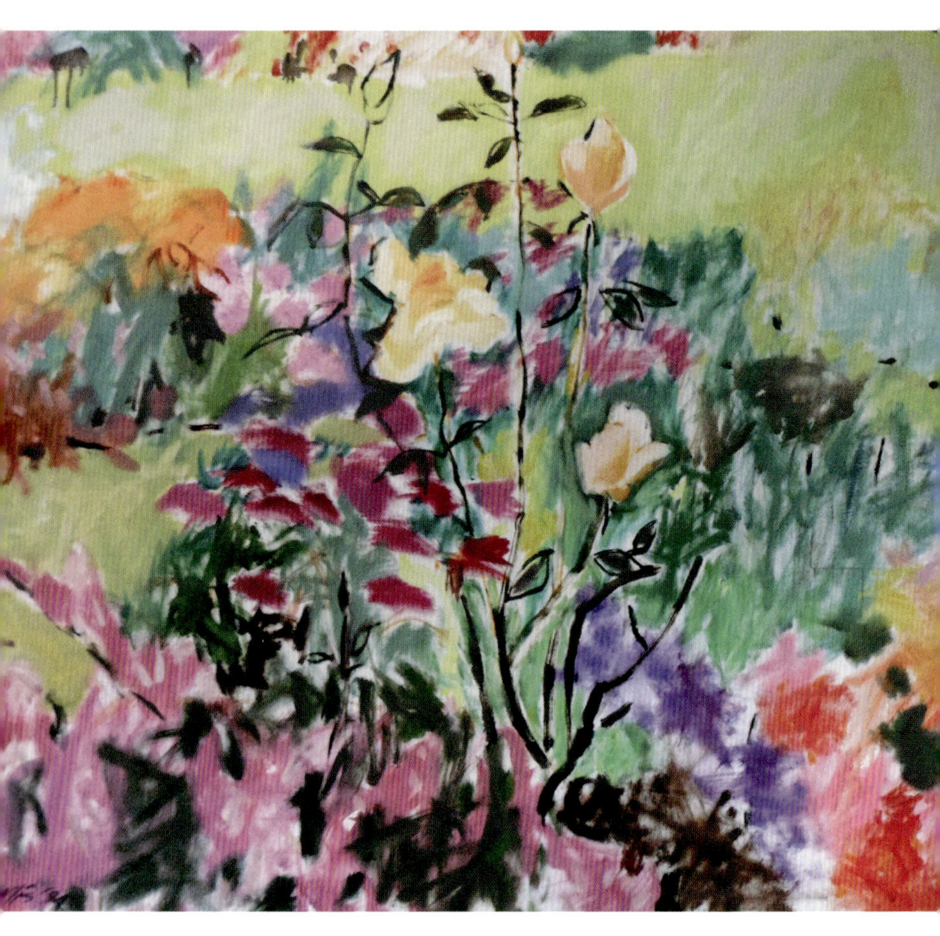

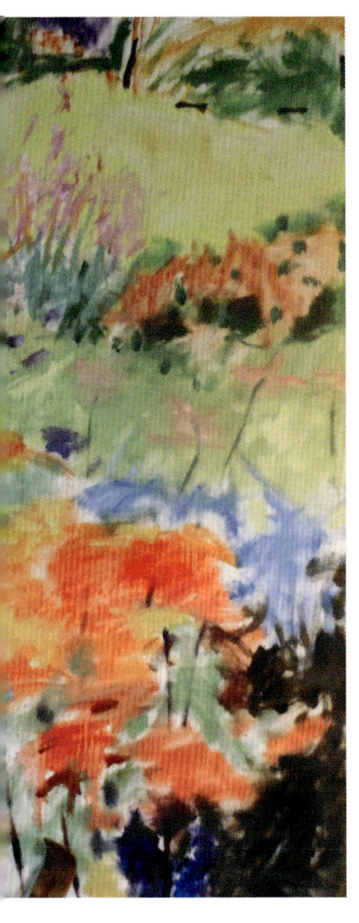

Once again, Erica Boswell's beautiful garden
from my most favourite position, with the
little green island of grass now on the left.
That grass island holds the whole riotous
assembly of colours together, giving both
the garden and my painting a stability,
not forgetting how the rose on the golden
mean anchors the work.
A late painting and a large canvas to paint
outside standing in the sun, the brushwork is
chaotic and the colours are mixed on the canvas.
Judy Conway in Hout Bay, Cape Town has
this work, though it could not compete with
her beautiful garden.
This essential grass island, like a full stop,
where the eye rests, appears in many
paintings in this garden.

ERICA'S GARDEN
SERIES

Limuru Tea Plantation, at the bottom of Erica's garden, over the hedge, with 'the long view' all the way to Kajiado. I painted this with my lovely painter friend Sophie Walbeoffe. The tea pickers work so fast, we asked them to stay where they were until we got them in. And the cross is where the eye rests. There are another seven resting places for the eye in this perspective. Can you spot them?

THE TEA PLUCKERS

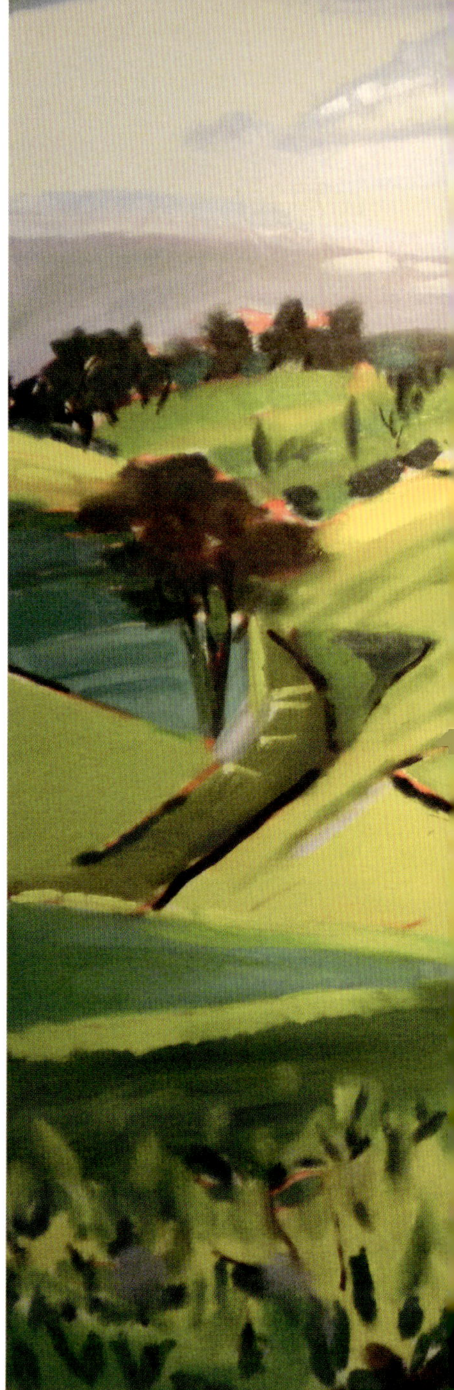

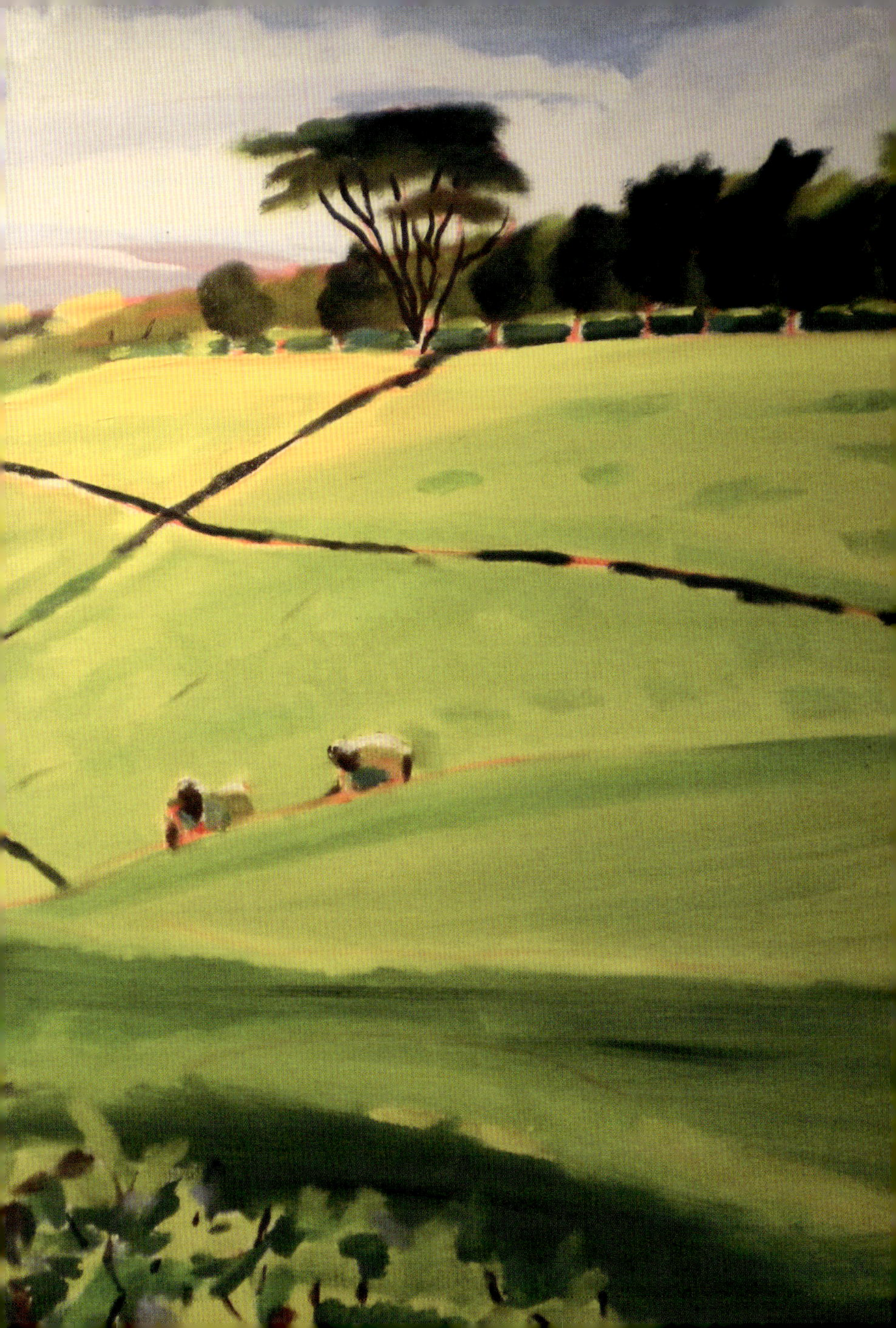

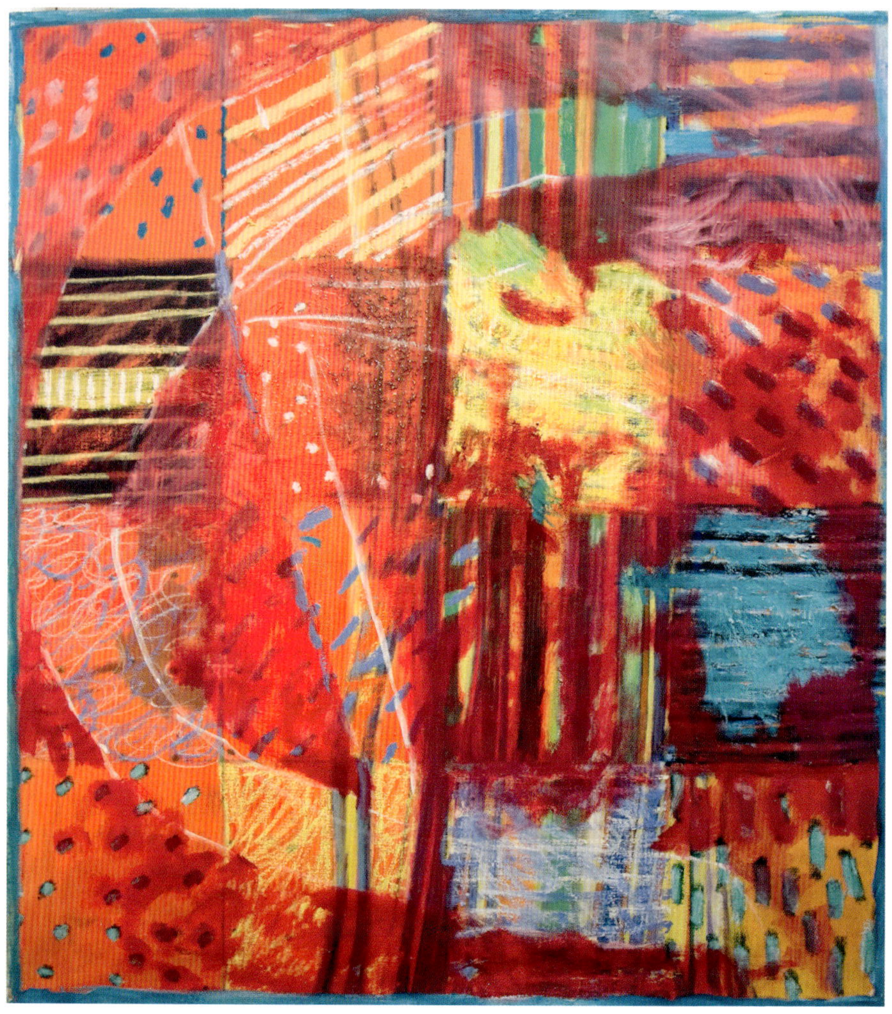

The way I like to paint best is when the painting
paints itself. It's a dialogue with the canvas.

'Look at this little spot,
a thrust of turquoise,
I like the way the colour moves about.
These stripes against the red are luscious.
I wonder what this arch means?
That's a funny yellow shape, think I'll leave it,
it's necessary, it holds the lot together.
Pink upon red a wonderful brushstroke,
hurried and Kline-ish.
Translucence seeks a stable grid
Edged with an aqua ribbon.
Is this my still centre?'

STILL CENTRE

My favourite part of this
painting is the ghostly pale
blue sail. It says much about
the spiritual. And there is a
drain if you care to look.
Collection of Thomas Wright.

SAILING

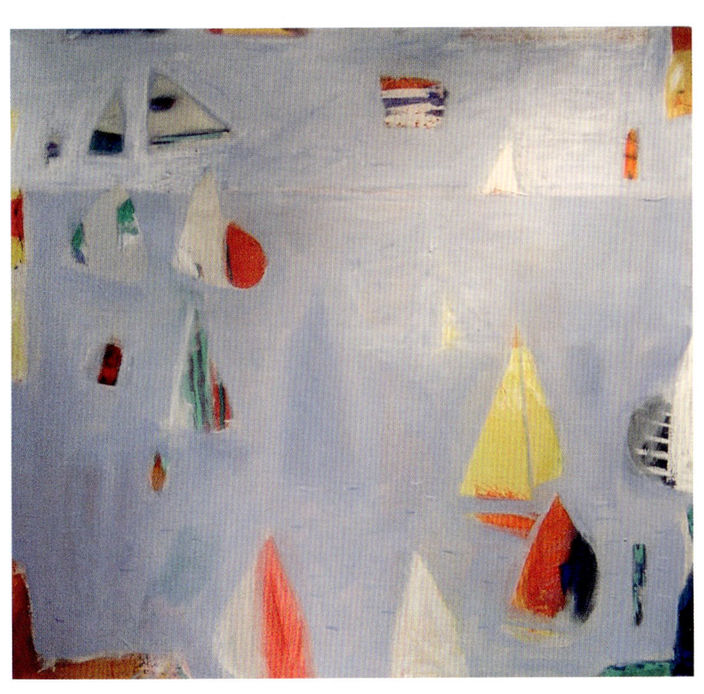

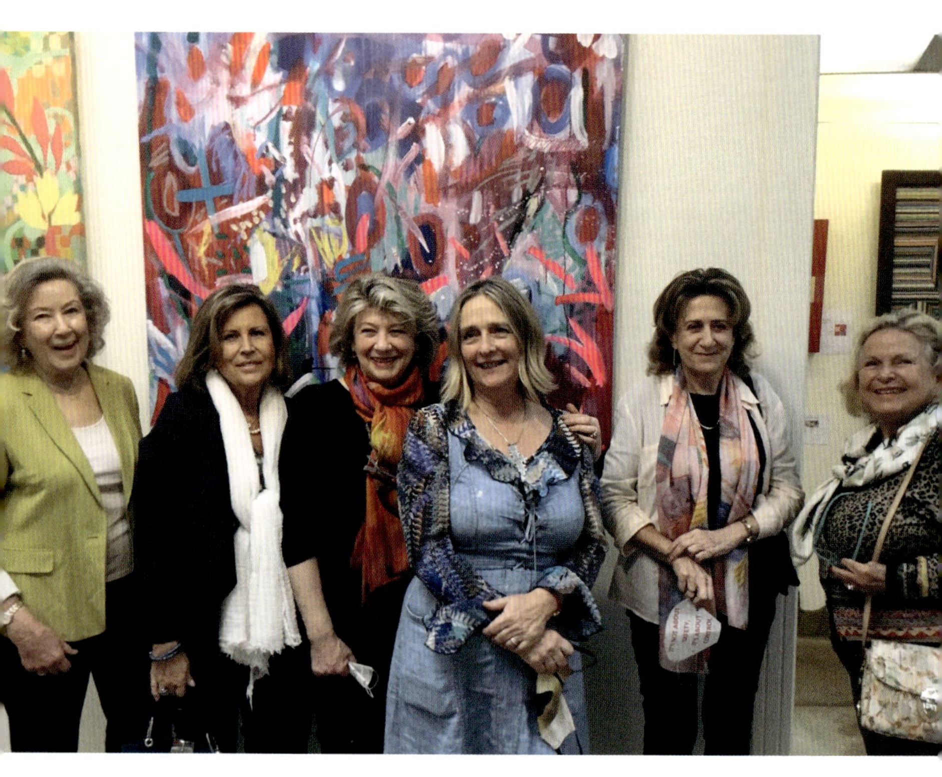

I thought I would post this photo today to 'commemorate' 140 days since this pandemic started. An exhibition, 'Artists against Hunger', was brilliantly organised by the artist Sophie Walbeoffe at the Matbronze Gallery in Langata. We arranged two cars from the other side of town (so we could do the anti-social distancing thing) in order to support Sophie, centre in blue, right next to Sally Kampf (my sister) and Christine Davis, I am centre left next to Adriana Van Wageningen and Sheila Barker far left.
For those who are concerned, our muzzle masks were removed for the photograph!
The exhibition was a magnificent success – three of my friends photographed here bought three large paintings. And a large amount was collected for food for the hungry.

The Golden Rose

The title of this work is to help the viewer
focus on the linchpin in this enormous
painting. It is a 6-ft square work.
I remember when it was in my studio
I would paint another flower when I felt
like it, as the painting would hang there,
beckoning me. Apart from the rose and
the tree, there is almost no other focal
point. I hoped to force the eye around
the whole work and discover new
flowers or pattern each time you look.
Collection of Thomas Wright

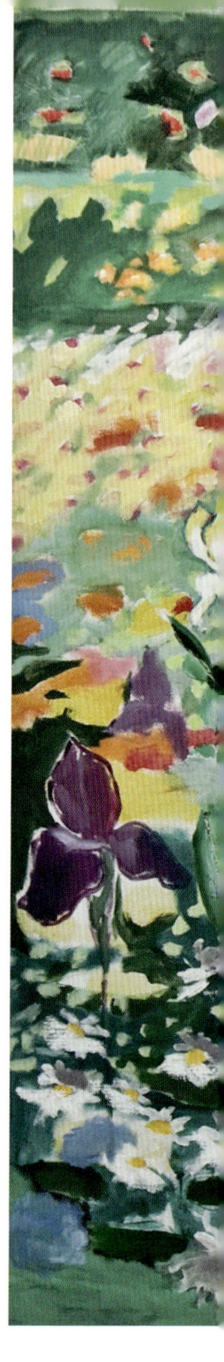

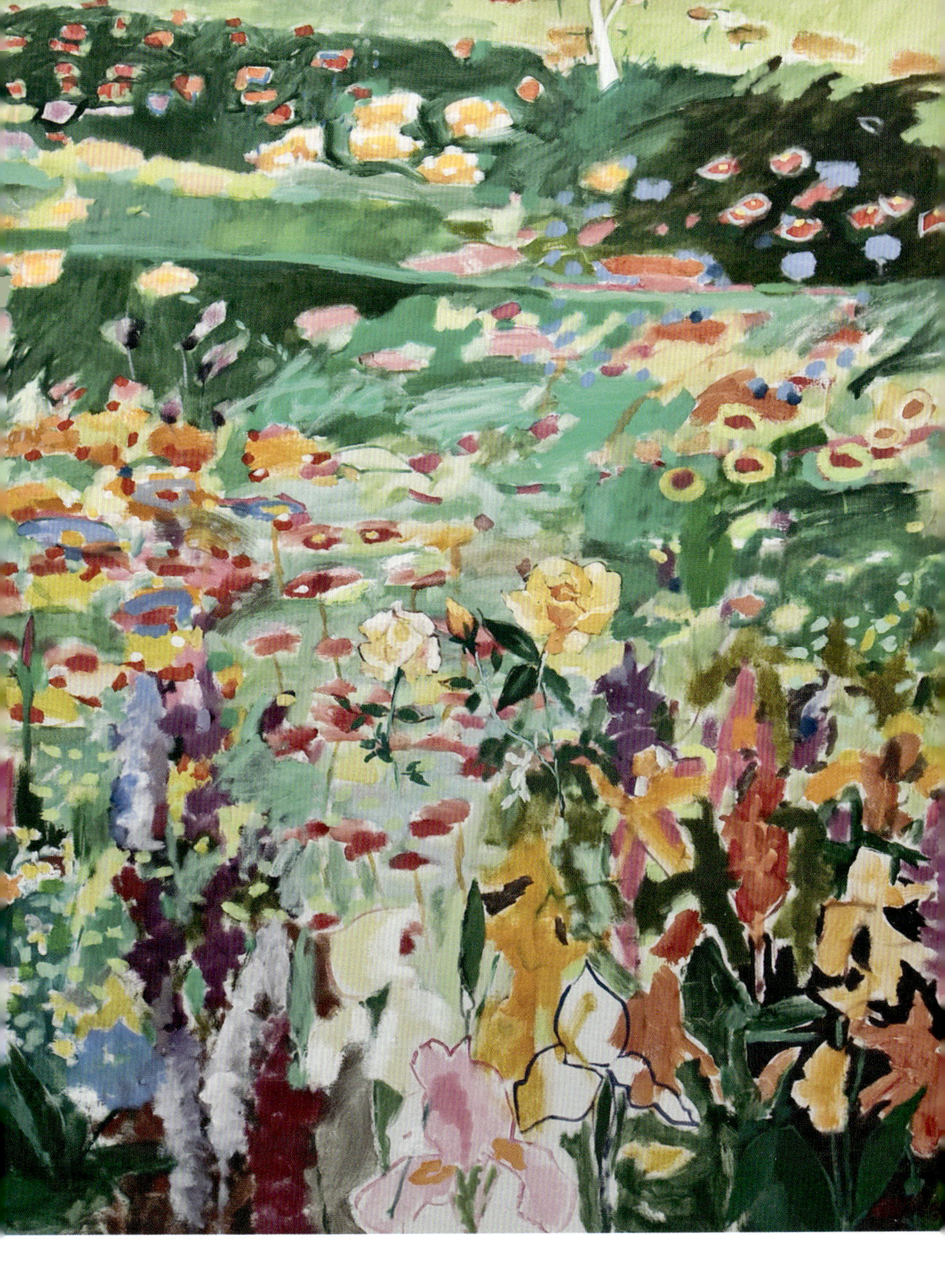

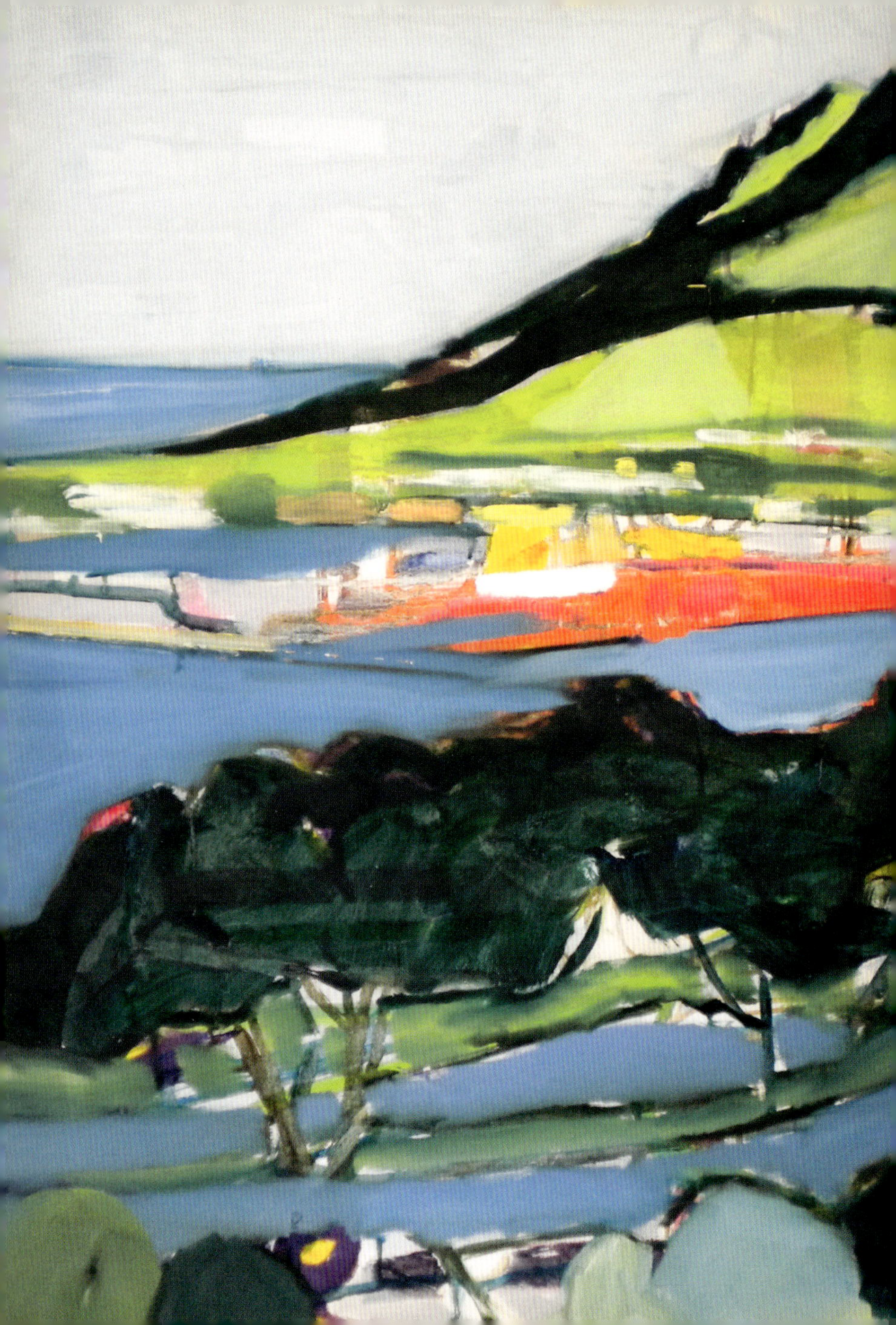

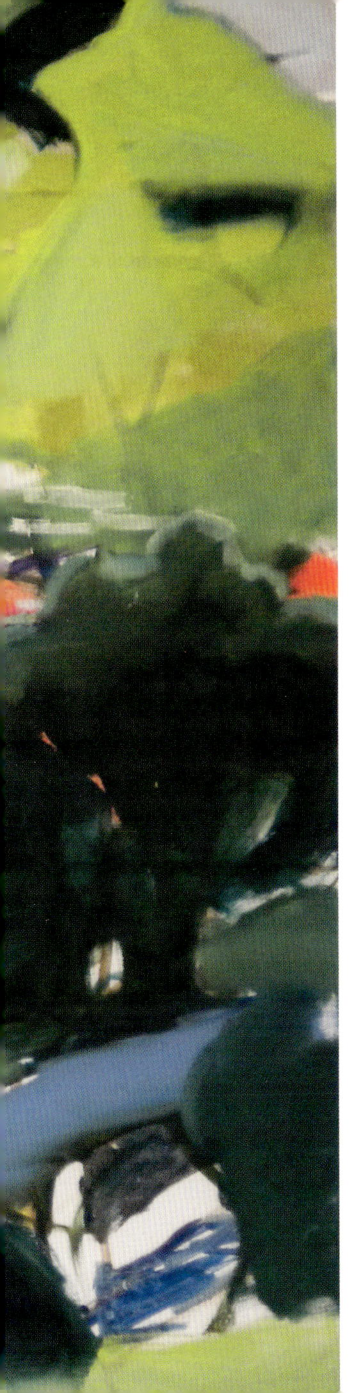

Simon's Town

The postcard view of the town and the naval harbour from our downstairs flat.

Another studio canvas, with a flower added here and there as I felt like it. Ben Okri said, *In Arcadia*, 'Painting is the still life of God's mind. It is the heaven of remembered things, the hell of forgotten things.' Presently there are many canvases hanging on walls around the studio, which require the odd addition (a flurry of irritation) or gentle brushstrokes. Right now during this Covid crisis I have four large abstract works all being painted more or less at the same time.
The painting hangs in Longonot Farm, the home of Jonathan and Henrietta Block, on the shore of Lake Naivasha.

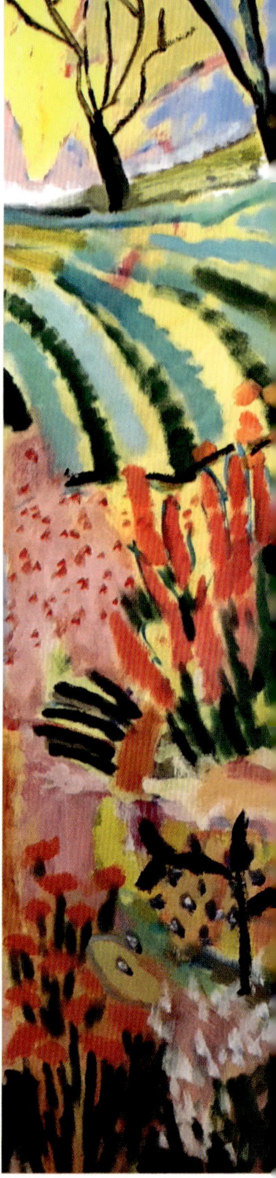

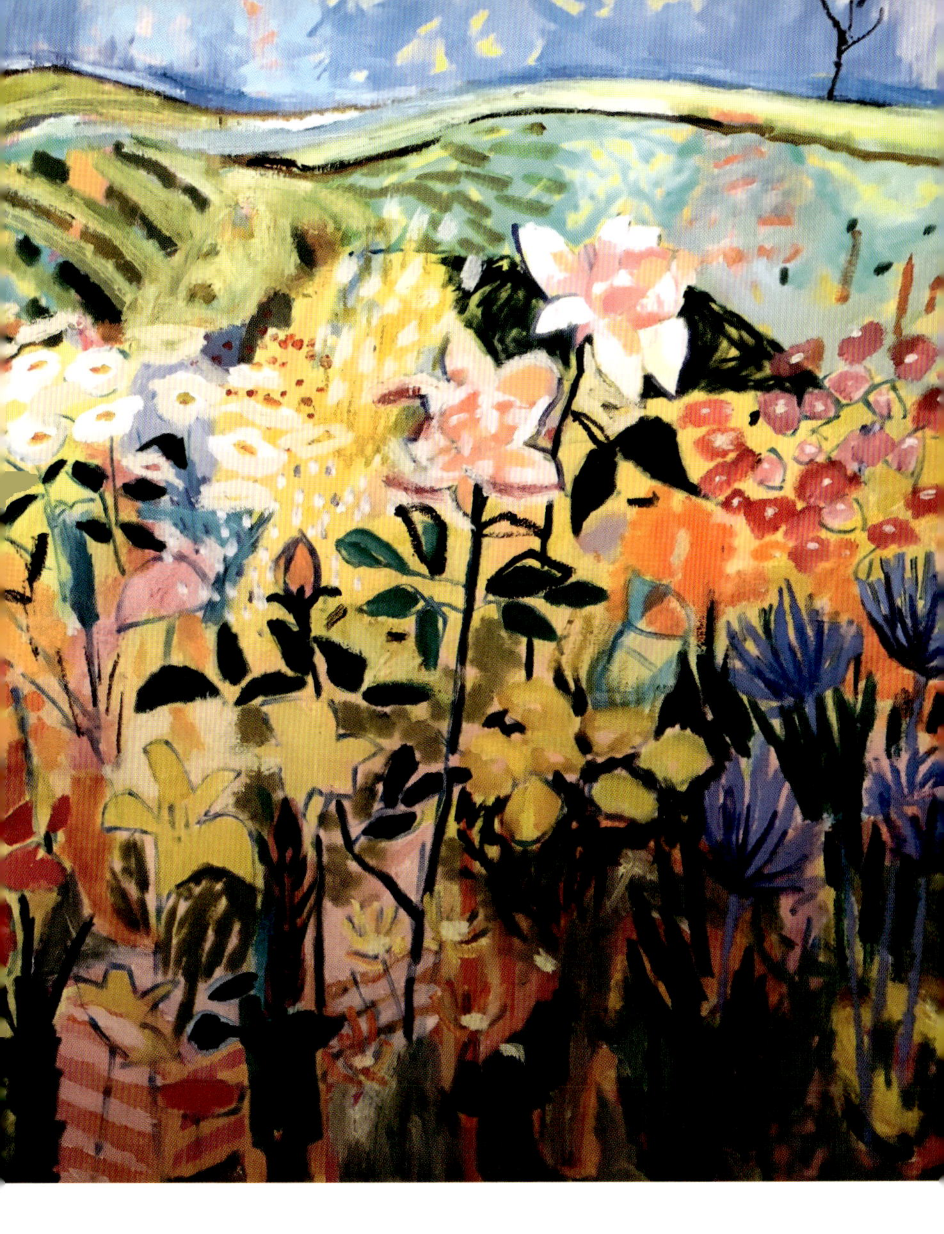

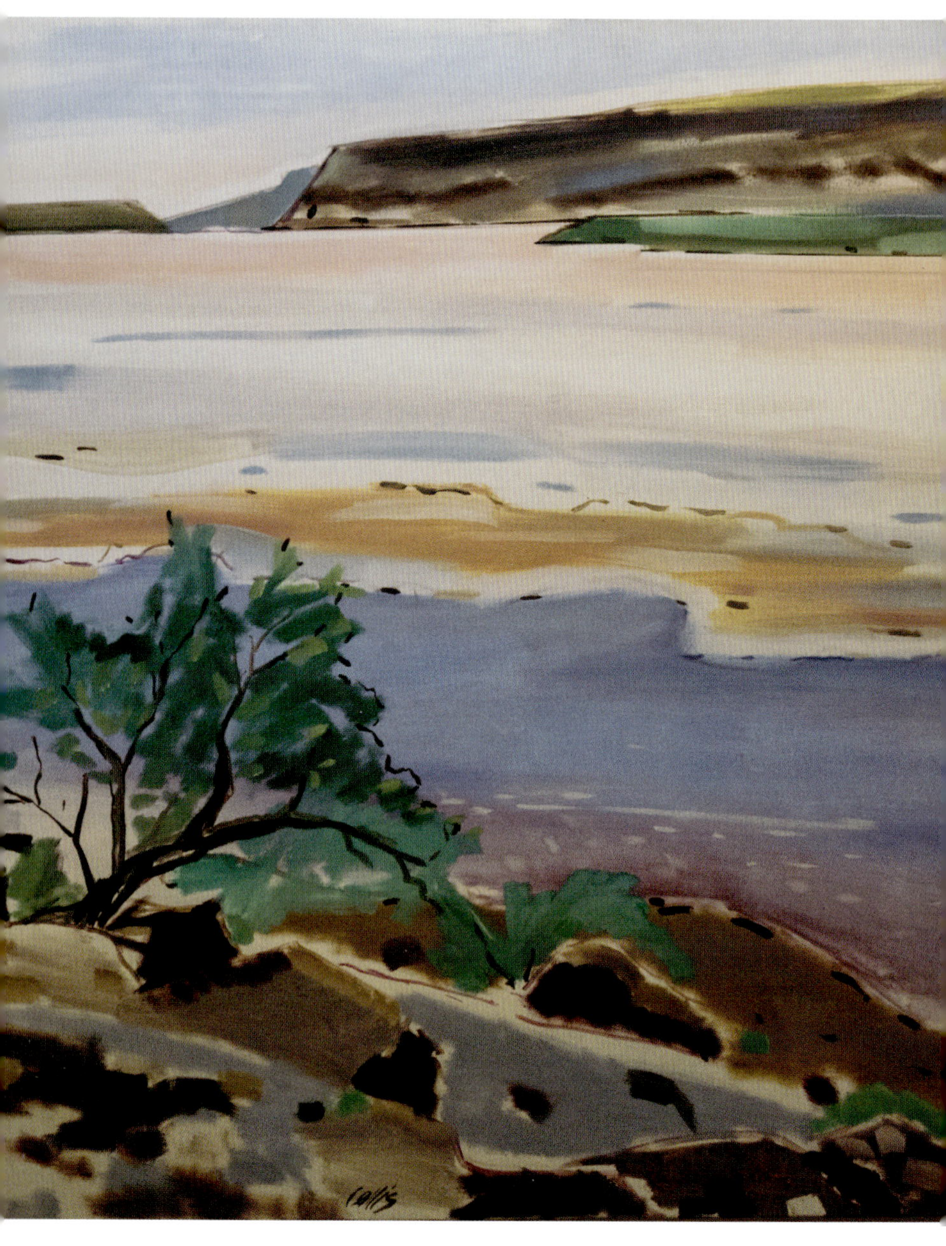

Lake Magadi

A salt lake in the Rift Valley.
I have painted it many times in situ
when the temperatures are in the nineties or
hotter. The dry heat is probably the reason
that the paint on this work is rather thin,
as one cannot be outside for more than
a couple of hours. Sometimes the lake is
completely pink, when it has a little more
water than here, and it is most beautiful.
There is a salt factory collecting the salt
for export. The pale pink-white area is salt.
Collection of Alec and Christine Davis

Interior with Yellow Tulips

A monoprint means one print only.
I love the technique of painting on to glass
and taking an impression, building up slowly,
one colour at a time. Yellow and blue are
complementary colours, gorgeous together.
I think this was inspired by a picture in a
magazine and it hangs in a home as beautiful
as its owner, Sheilah Combos.

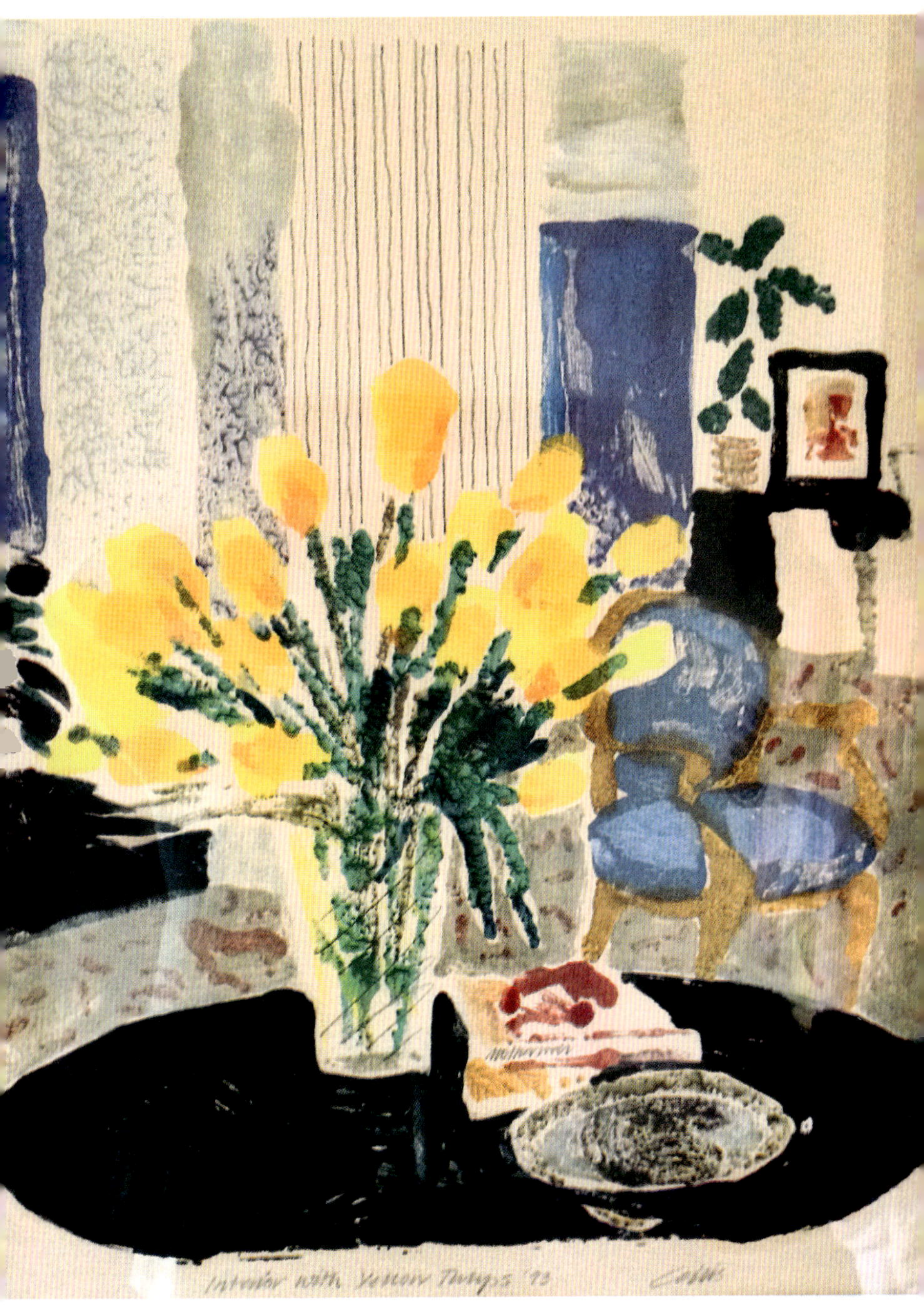

Interior with Yellow Tulips '93

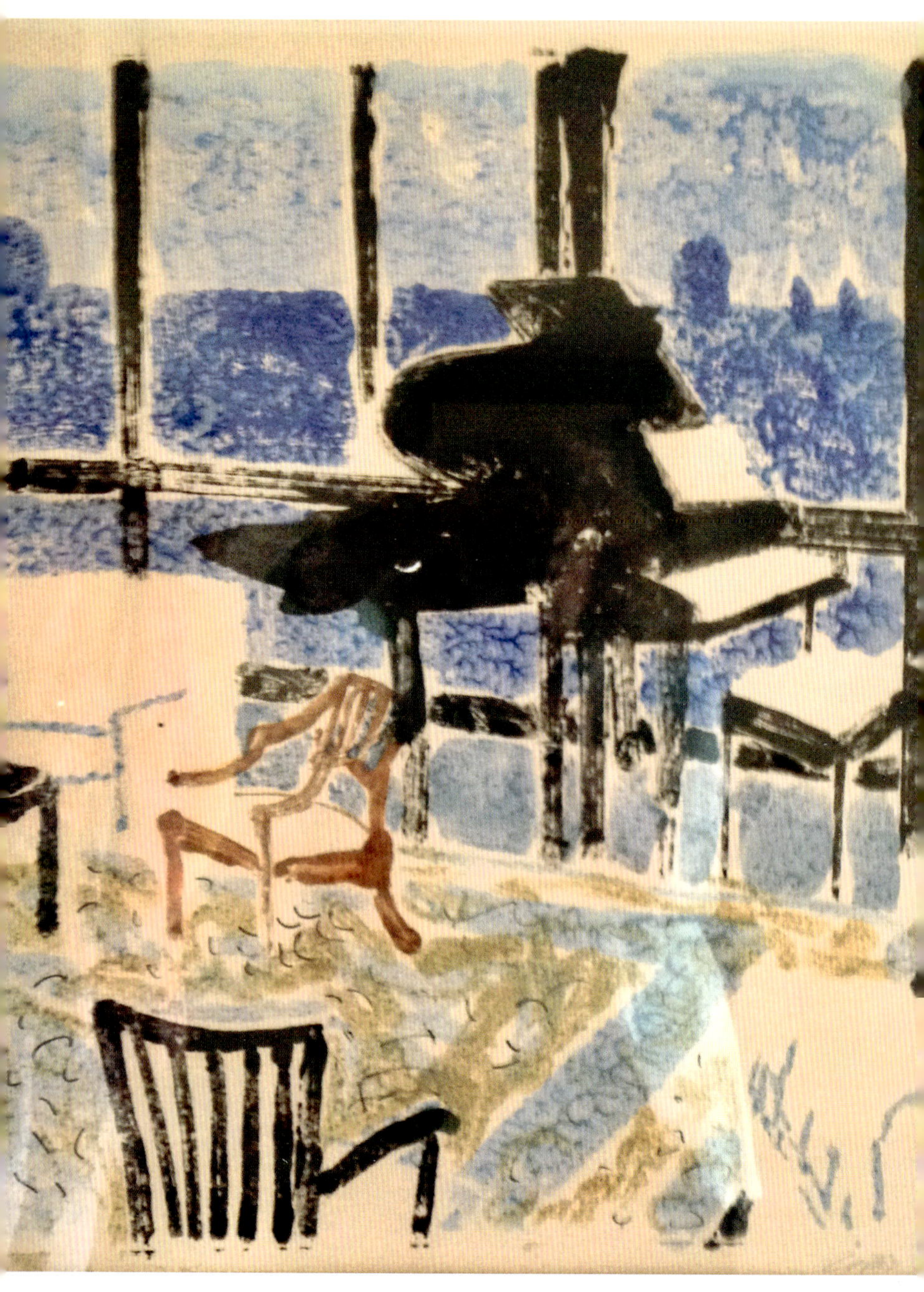

Interior with
Baby Grand Piano

A monoprint on paper, of the same series as
yesterday's interior and owned by Sheilah Combos.
I like the sofa on the white square mid-left.
It is a sofa with four lines.

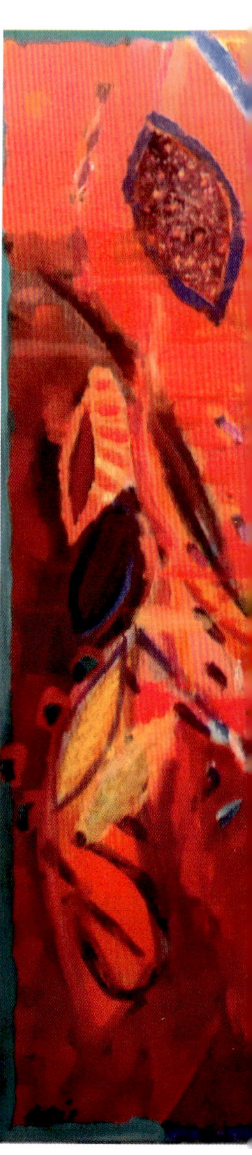

Queen of Hearts or Ruby Throne

Gold and ruby colours, this is a large painting and it resides in Colorado. 'Curiously, a strange phenomenon happens when two rubies are placed side by side: they stain each other, and their singular beauty is immediately lost.' Alexander Theroux, from my favourite book, *Primary Colours*. In the collection of the most special and best friends Marcia and Bill Levy in Colorado.

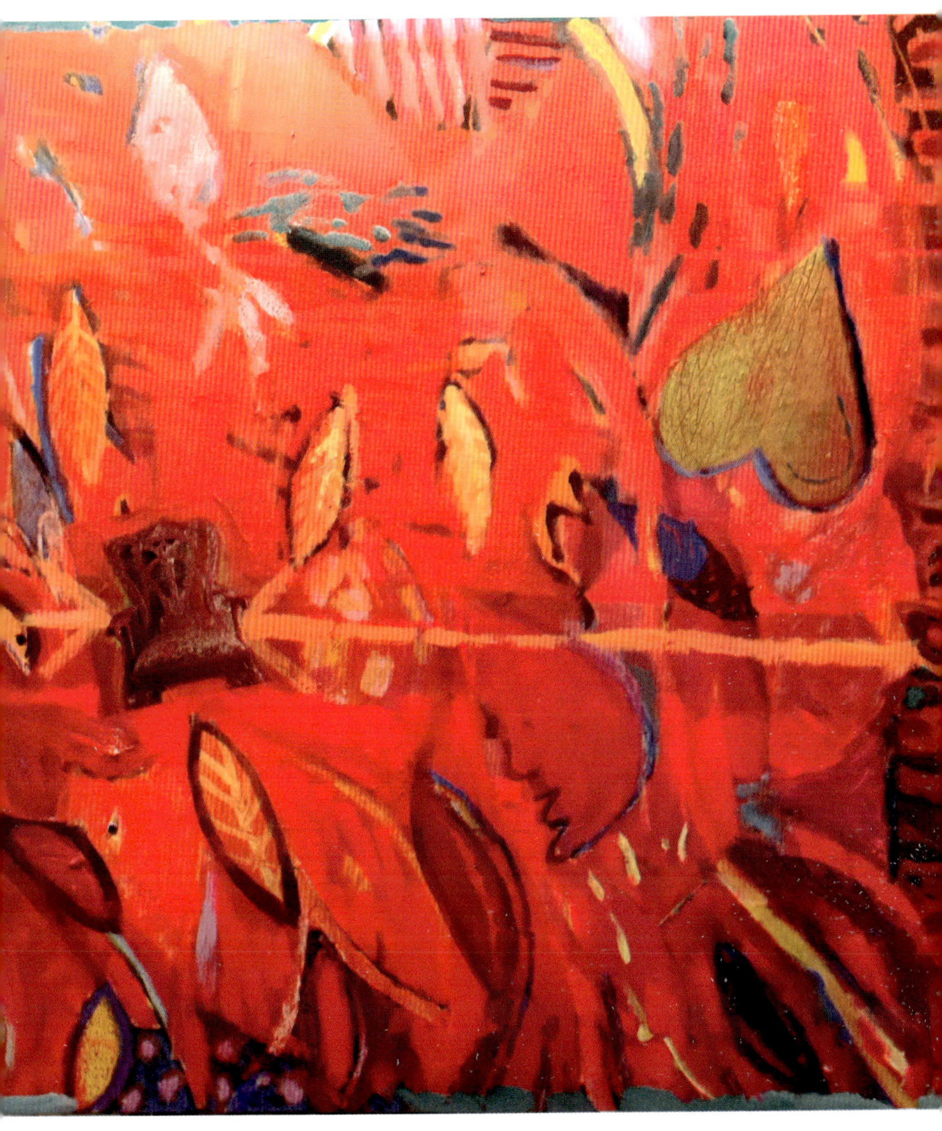

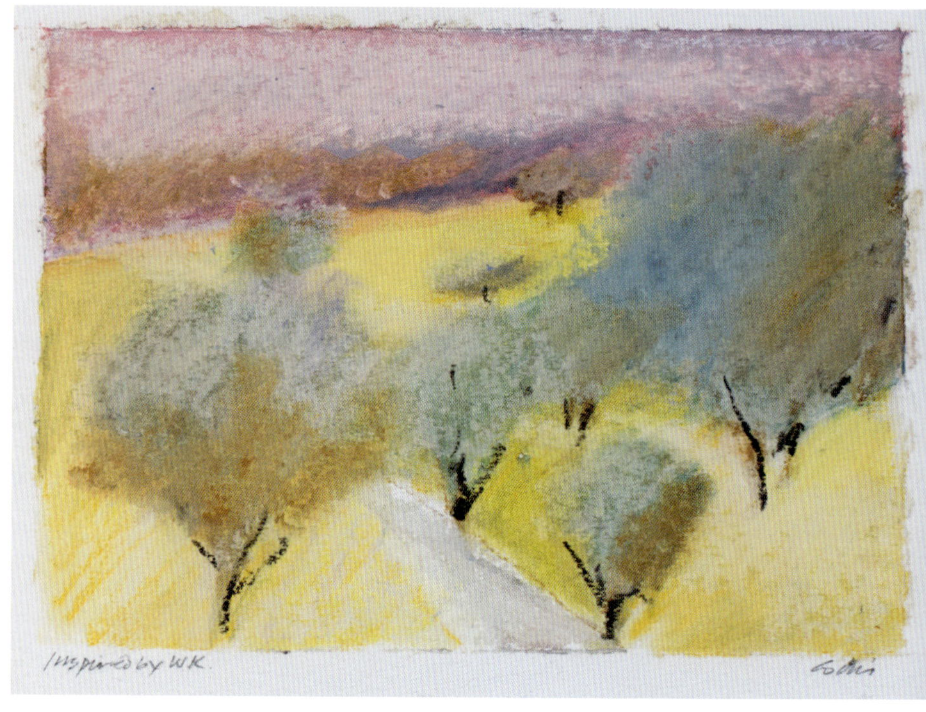

Inspired by W.K.

Day 148

On a day I was lacking inspiration and looking at the American colourist Wolf Khan, who often used pastels. His compositions are minimal and his colours sizzle. I think about him a lot. Doria Block was going to introduce me to him when we were in Virginia. He was away and I was disheartened. His beautiful paintings have only ever been painted to 'lift the day'. There is no angst in him. This is a chalk pastel and I taped the edge of the paper, which when removed gives the work a natural frame and an advantage over unframed paper works. A little tip.

Day 149

Canna

A small pastel work on
handmade paper. I like to think
it has the monumental about it?

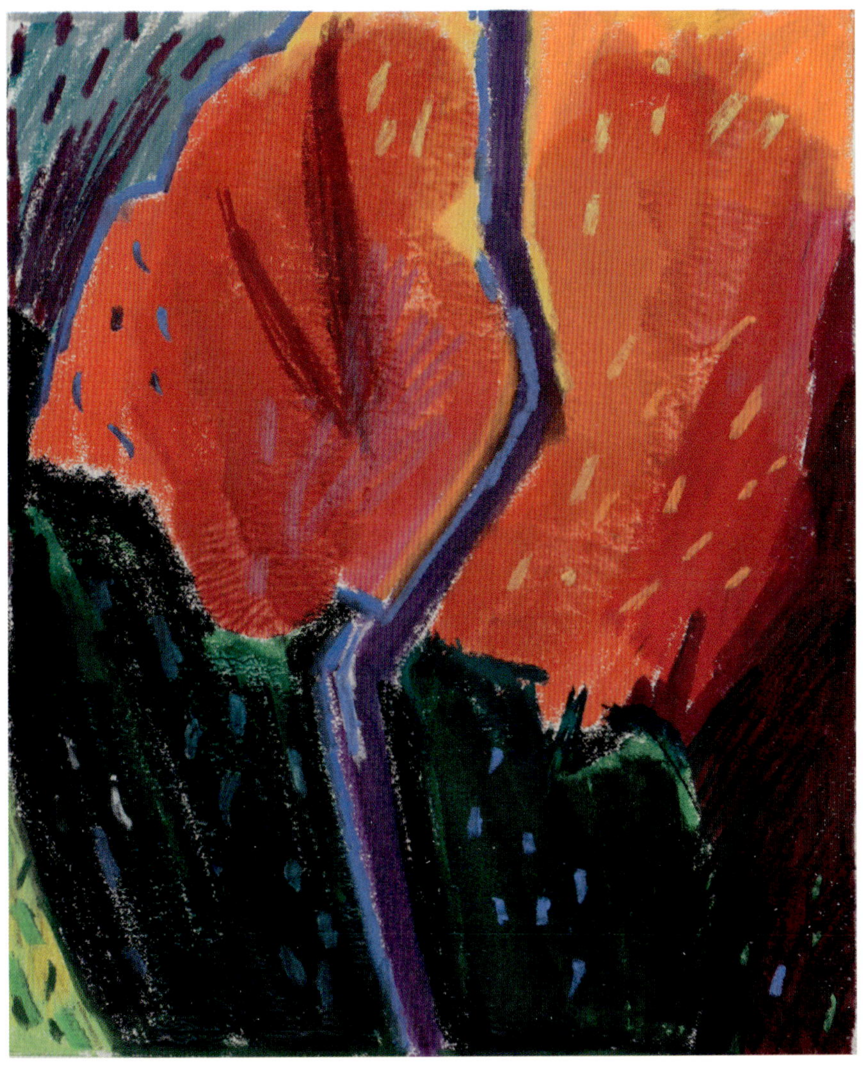

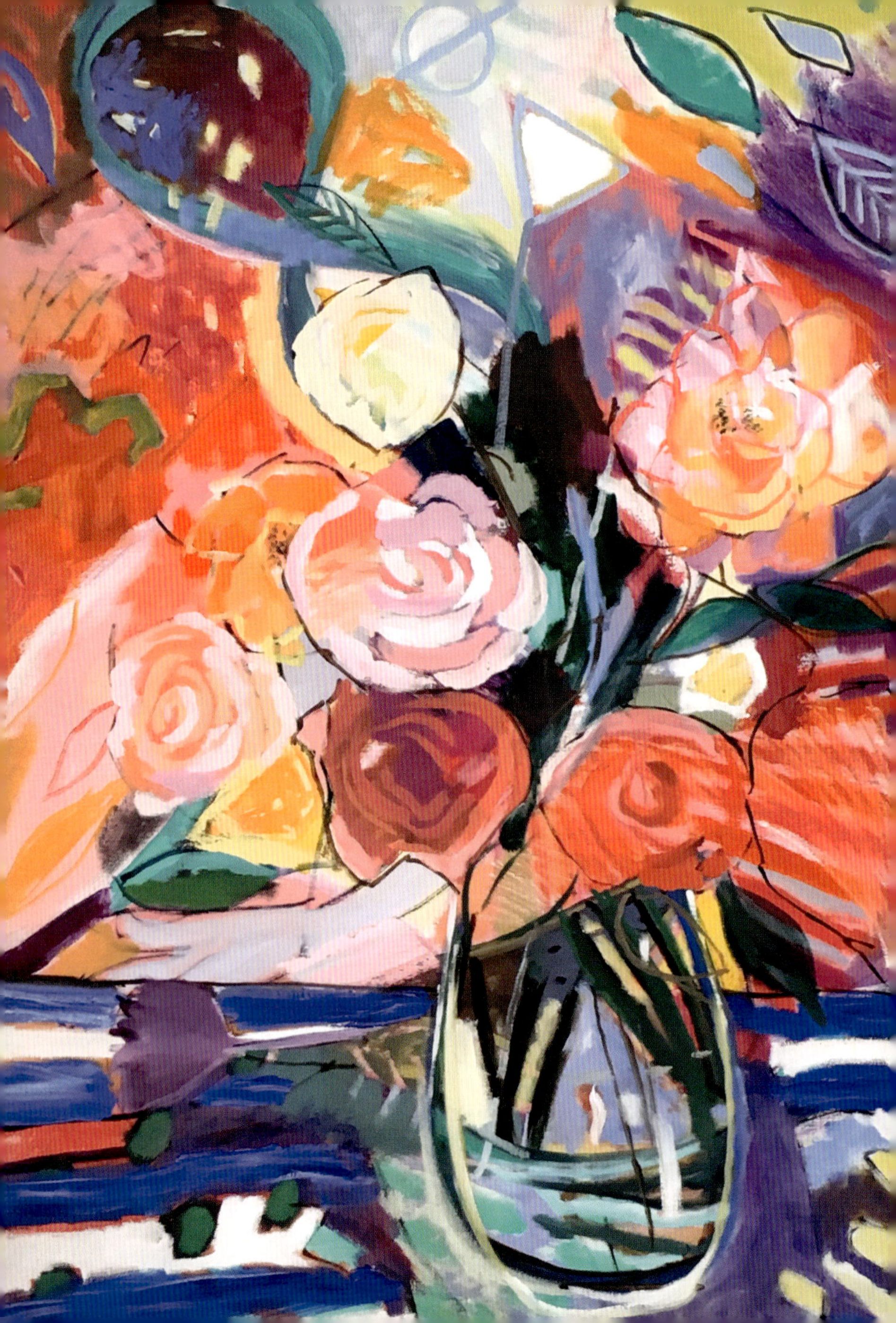

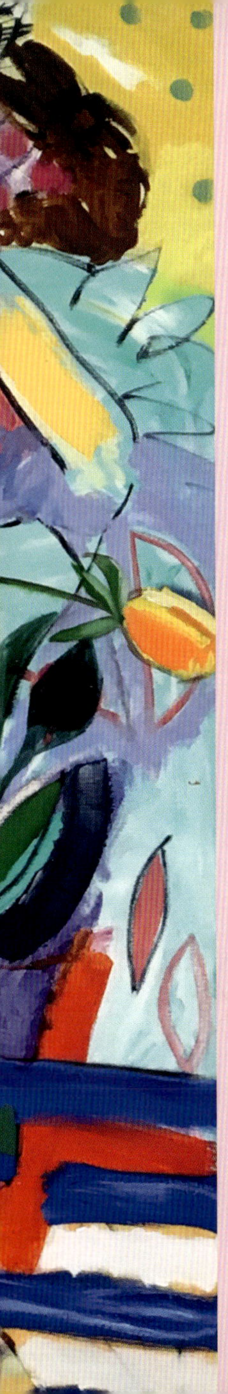

Day 150

Beneath these roses in a vase was a spiritual
painting – see the alpha sign top left.
Its brushwork has added to the final weight.
I have been saving this significant work for a
special day and number. Every now and again
I complete a painting which I know is distinctive.
I finished this in 2018. It hangs in my home and
I have great ambition for it. It has appeared in
the Kenya Arts Diary of 2019 and was exhibited
in that same exhibition. It measures 125 x 116 cm
and is thus far untitled.

Day 151

Androcles

The Born Free Foundation sponsored a project to save
lions, which at that time numbered 20,000. The sculptor
Gakunju Kaigwa made the original lion and one hundred
moulds were presented to artists. Dr Paula Kahumbu asked
me if I would work on the lion that Dr Richard Leakey and
she had sponsored. Furadan, an insecticide for plants in a
luminous pink plastic bucket, deadly to lions and all wildlife,
was (and still is) the culprit in many deaths of countless
wild animals. The chemical got into the human food chain
from the vegetation and topsoil washing into Lake Victoria.
Made by FMC Corporation in Philadelphia, it was sold in
Kenya (banned elsewhere) as an insecticide.
We called our lion Androcles, and attached to his chain are
photographs of all the tragic animals and people who are
affected by this poison. The chain represented the hold
FMC Corporation had over the Kenyan Government.
The lion's mane symbolised all the money that is made
through the sale of the poison. When the lion was
exhibited, he stood on a ground of blue crushed glass,
which looked exactly like the poison chemical in the
luminous pink bucket.

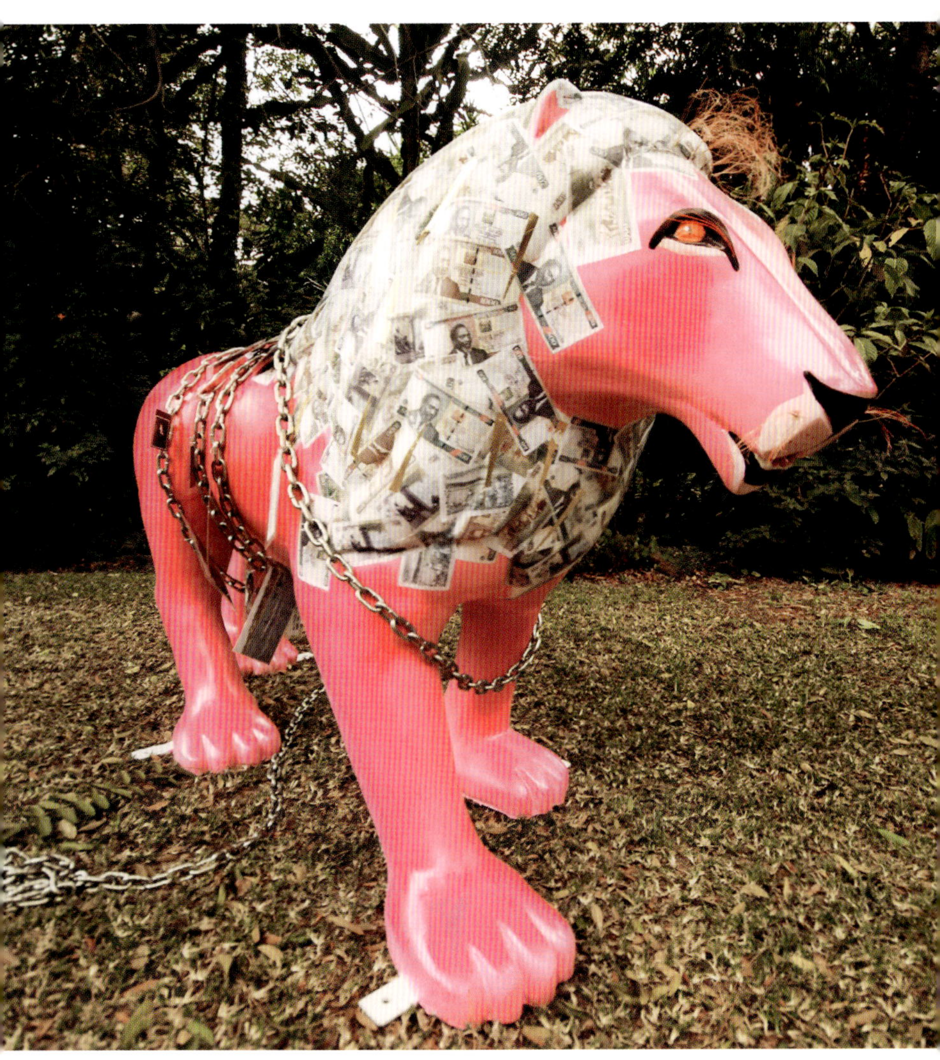

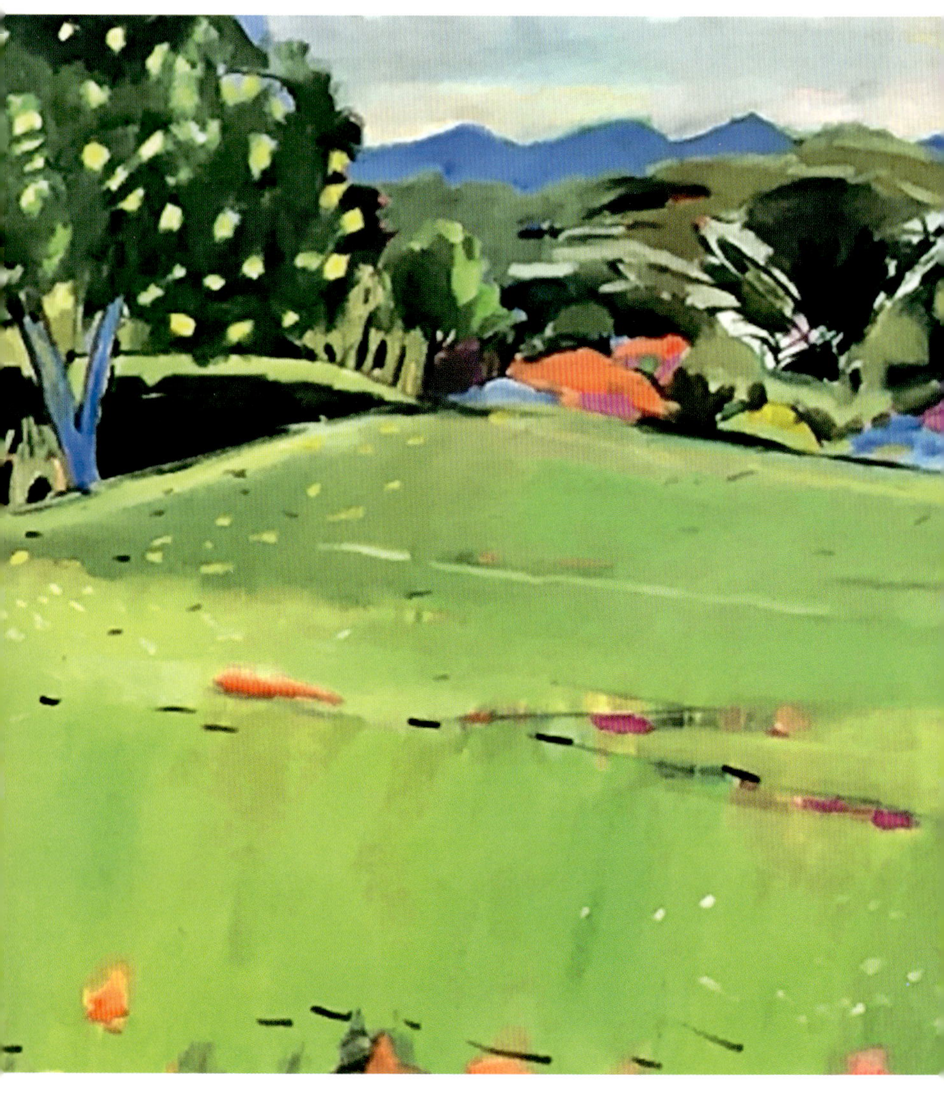

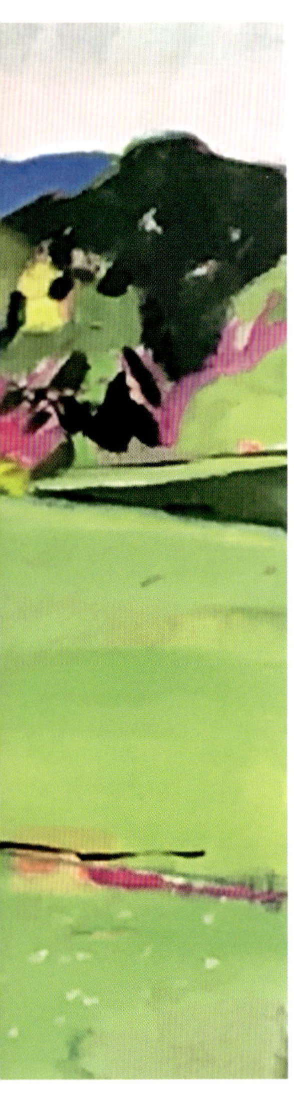

Day 152

Ngong Hills

It took a long time to plan this composition at the foot of Sophie's garden. A dull day and not much colour. An oleander tree with yellow blossom and the five knuckles of the Ngong Hills was the attraction. The ground sloped up to a garden with some colour below, and the hump is on the golden section. I really liked the composition. I would like to paint it all again on another day with much more light.

Frondesecence

From the large series of the same
name. We have enjoyed a splendid
lunch today with our long-time
friends Jan and Azmina Janmohamed.
I thought this large painting looked
so well in situ in their dining room.
It was shown in my exhibition in
London through the well-known
McEwan Gallery, who came down
from Ballater, Balmoral, Scotland
and hired the Mall Galleries to
show fifty of my works in 1988.

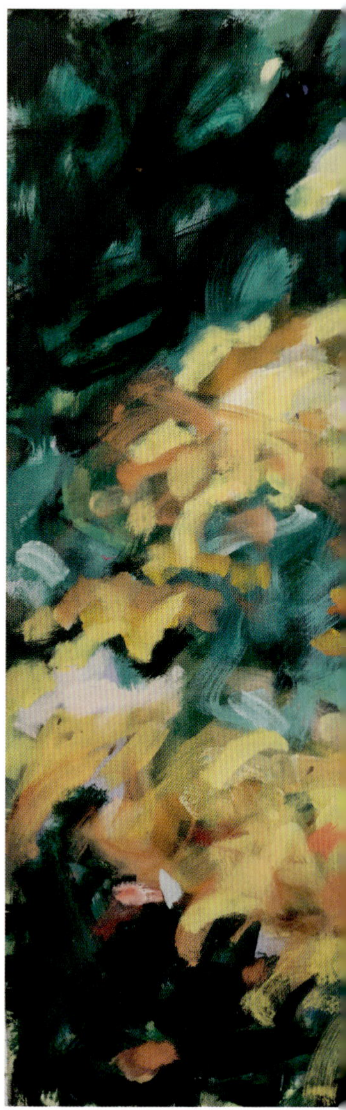

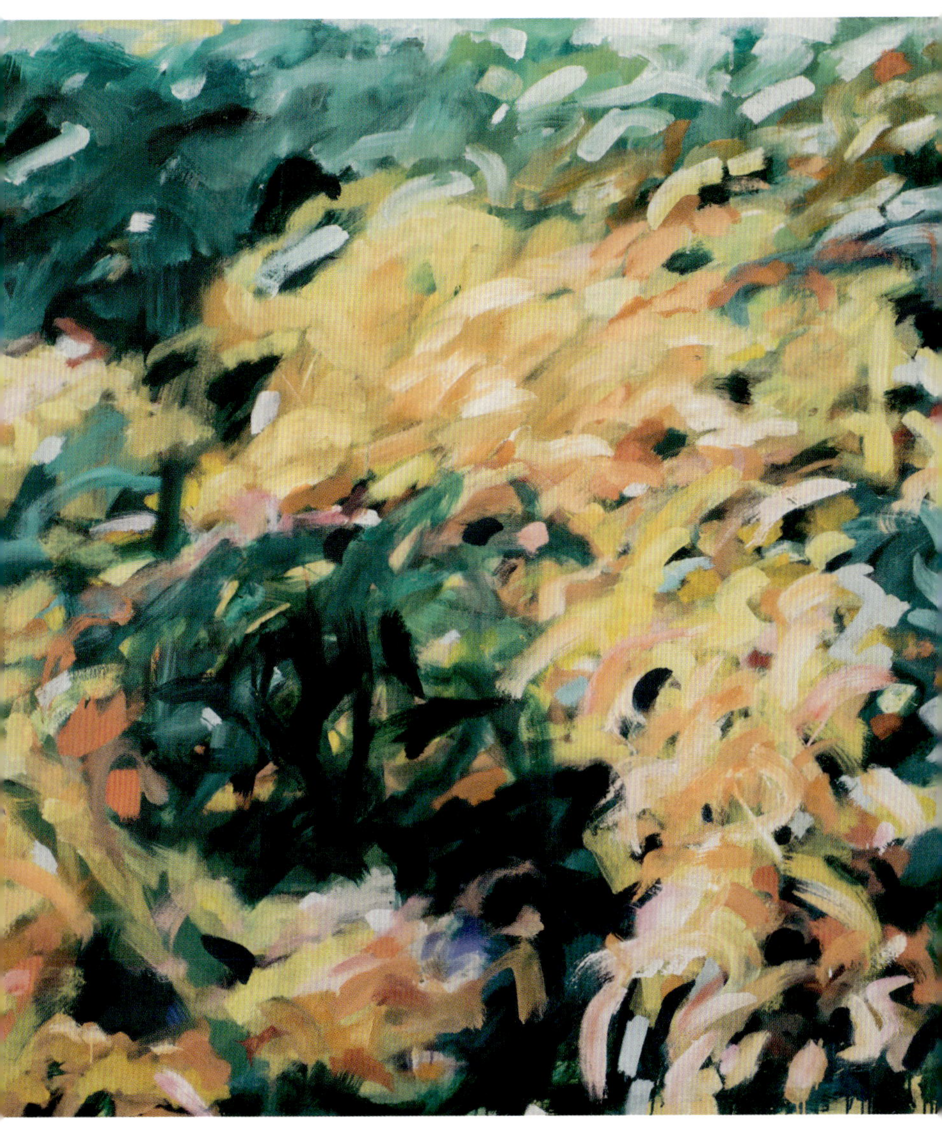

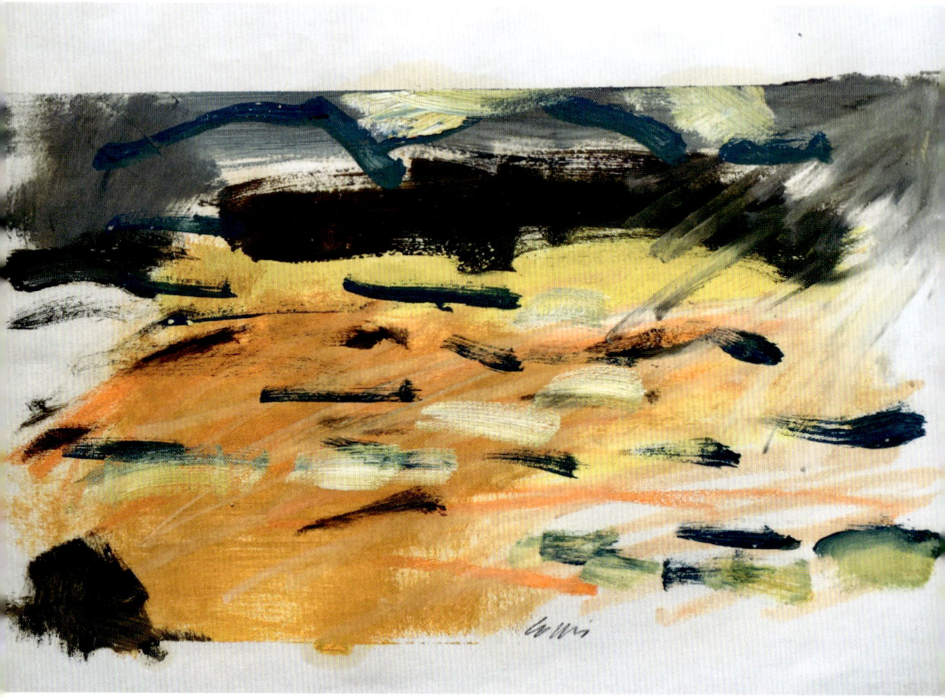

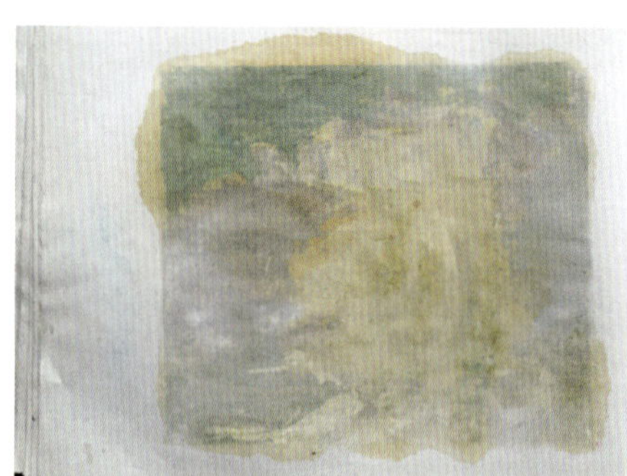

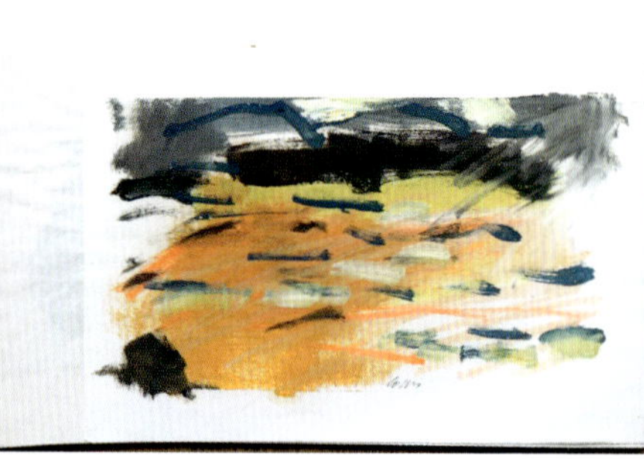

Day 154

In the 1990s I made a few books
of abstract sketches on A3 paper.
This is the Maasai Mara in a storm and
we are going there for a few days to see
the migration (our first trip out of Nairobi
due to the lockdown). I have never shown
this book to anyone. Two decades later,
I am beginning to think it is interesting.
Here is a page.

Day 155
Governors Bend

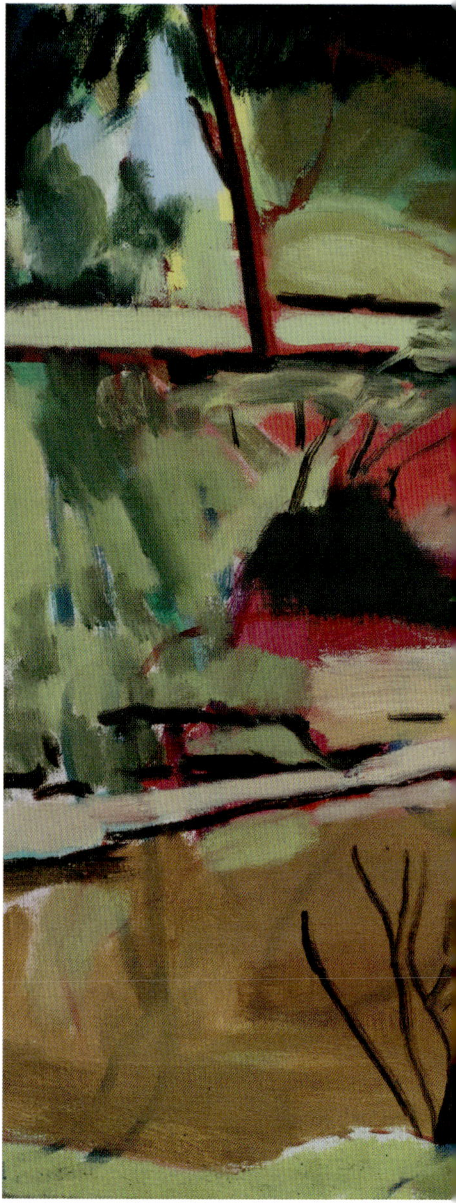

On the Mara River,
painted a few years ago.
At this moment we are
up-river at Il Moran.
The hippos are parked on the
edges of the bank opposite
our tent and game is
abundant. We are here to see
the Maasai Mara migration.

23 August 2020
My father, Bernard Kampf,
died this day in 1993.

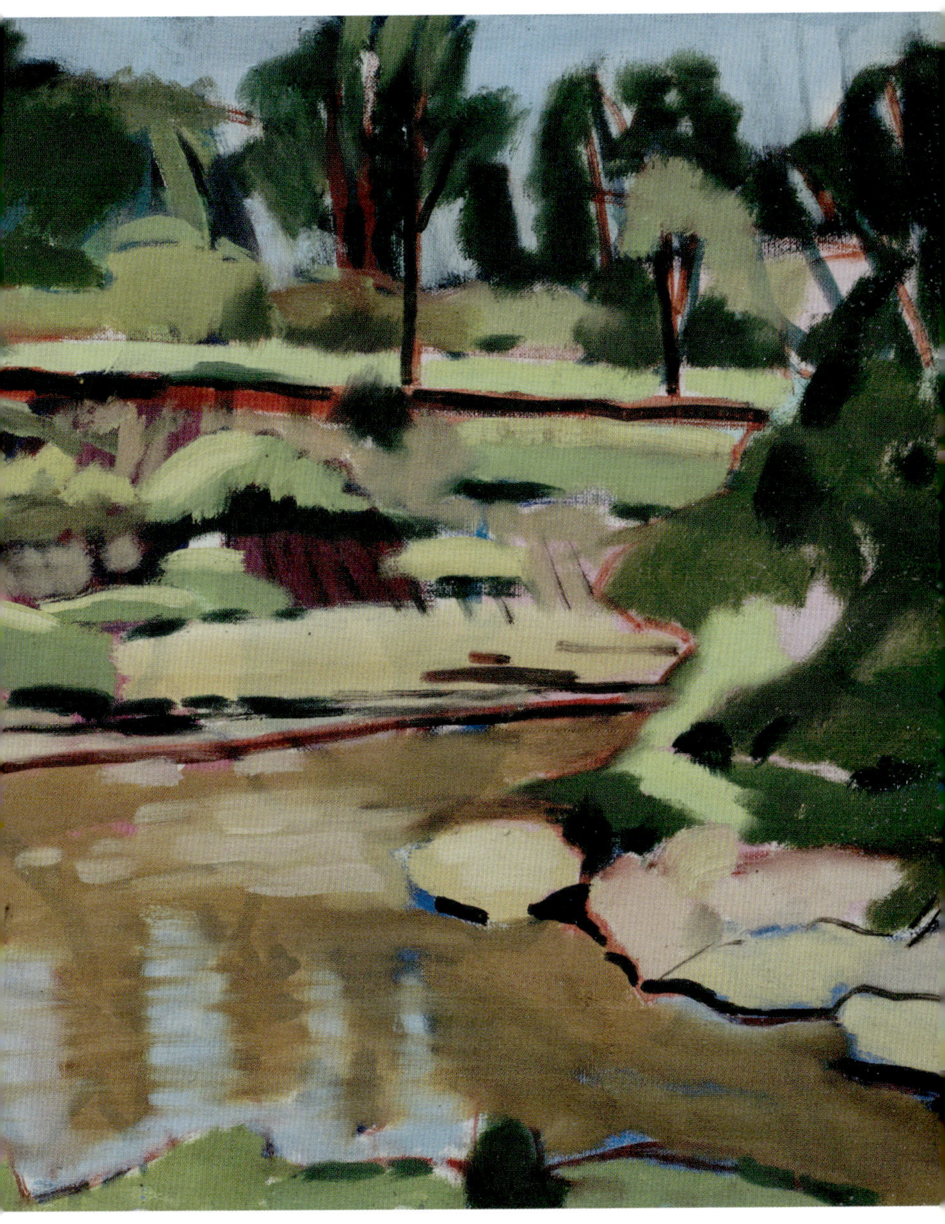

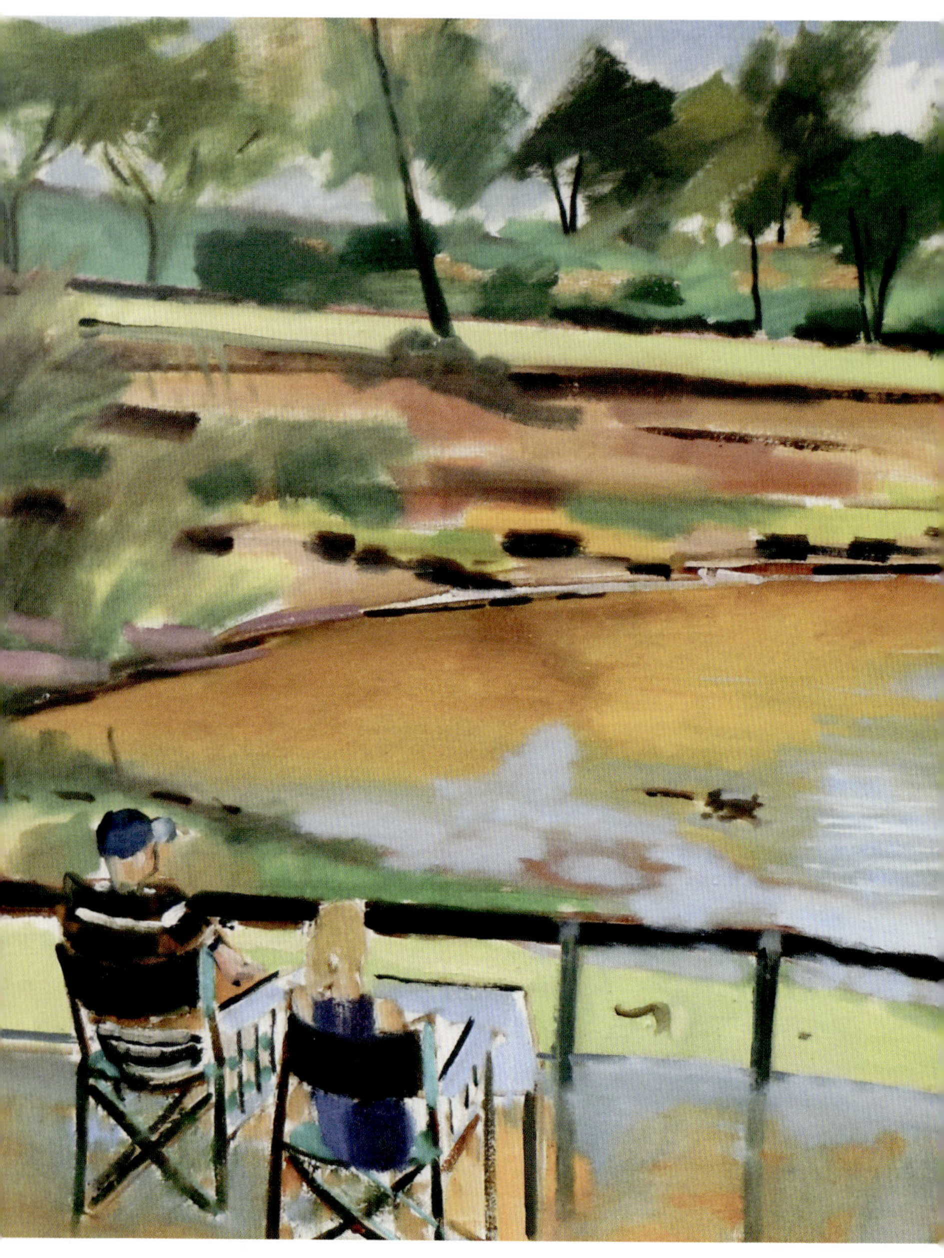

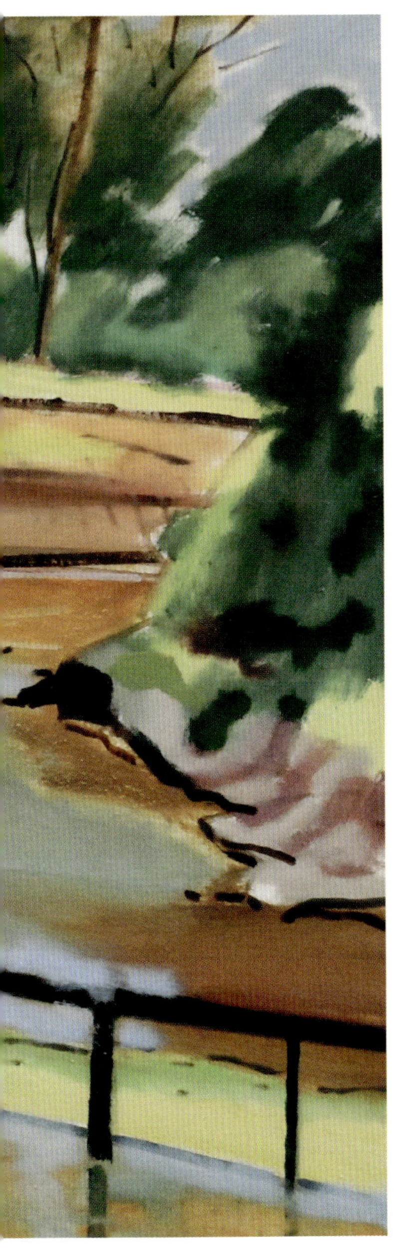

Day 156
Watching Hippos

At Governors Camp on the
Mara River. The migration of
wildebeest and other plains
game from the Serengeti, north
to the Maasai Mara, is a spectacle
I am fortunate to have seen.
This year the animals seemed
more especially abundant.
I wonder if they sensed that
all the humans are locked up?
The Mara can be overrun by
tourists and this year the only
people who were there were the
fortunate residents of Kenya.

Day 157
the way a line can
hold a composition in

From pages of my notebook.
This is appropriate to how we,
the people, are brainwashed.
Just a little line. A little line and
we all obey. Conditioned all our
lives. And in particular now.
Time to think outside the box.
Stop watching the box.
Do journalists investigate
anymore? YouTube another box,
censor those who disagree.
One has to think about the
postings being removed off
YouTube, Twitter and Facebook…
Might they be true? This work
may be old but here is an
appropriate metaphor.

25 August 2020
five months of lockdown.

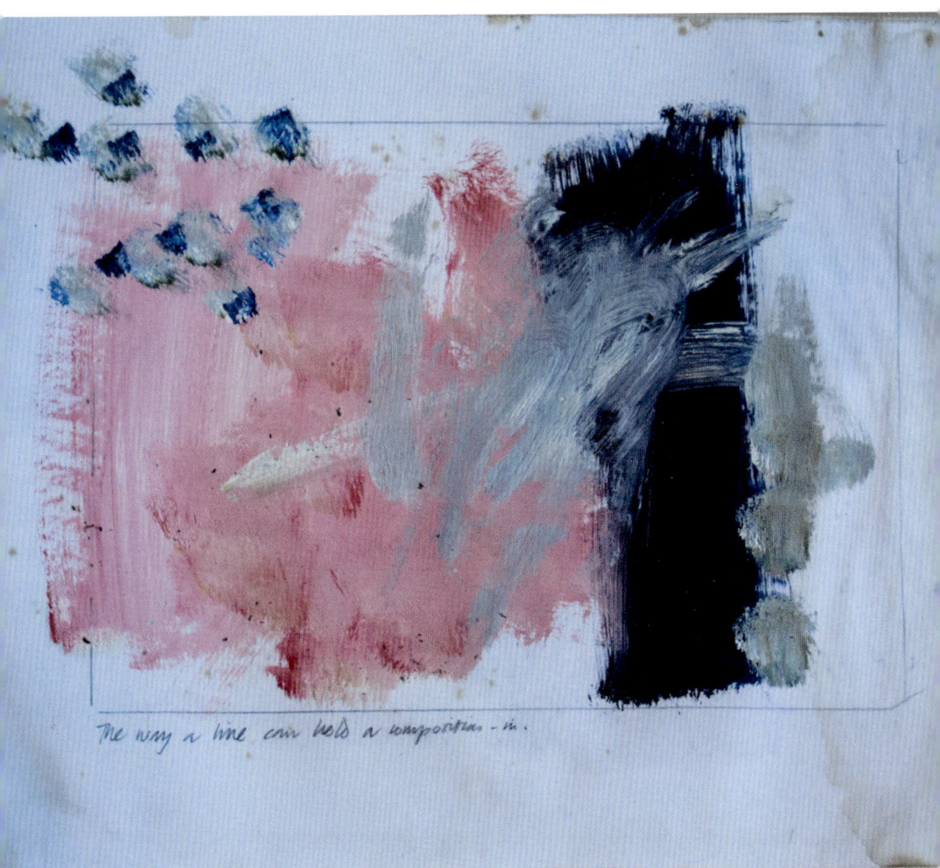

The way a line can hold a composition - in.

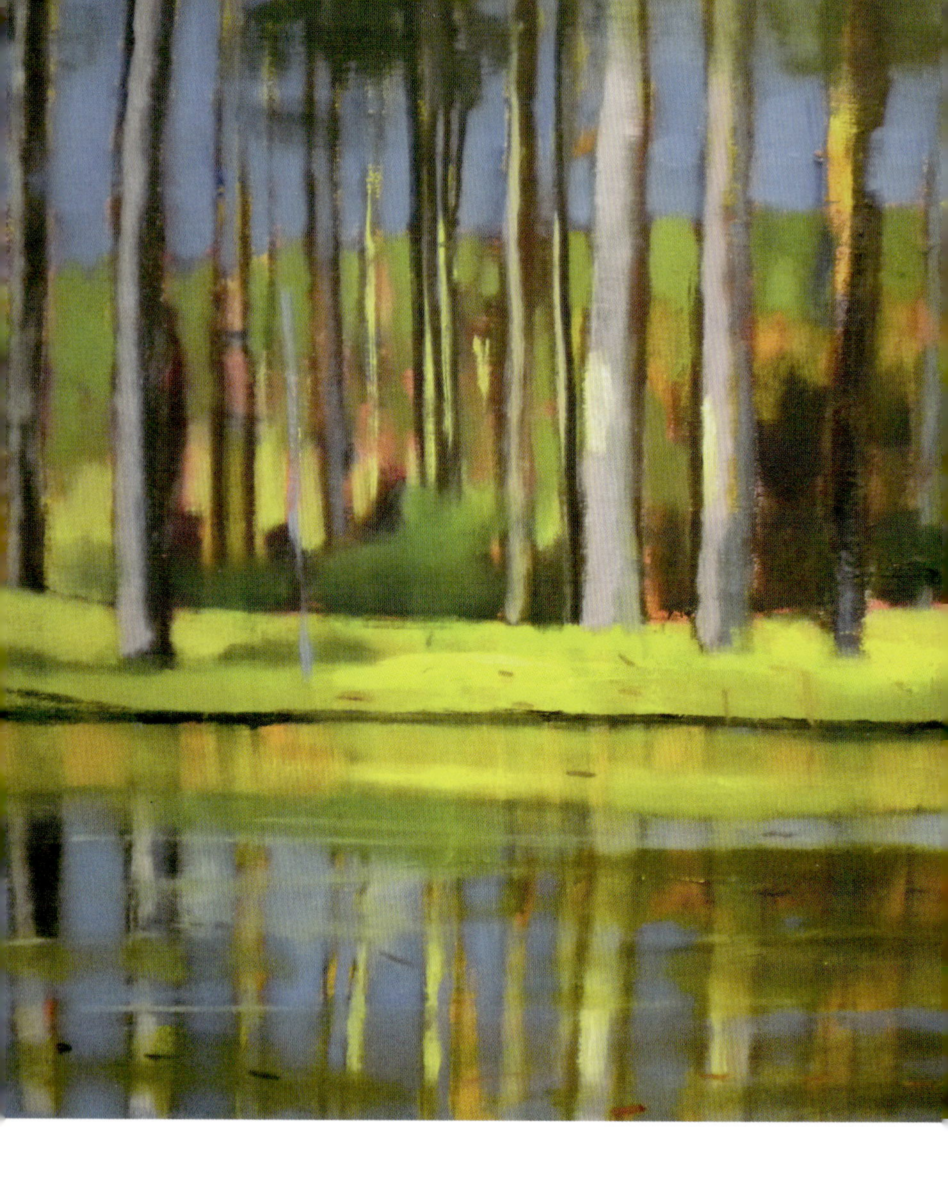

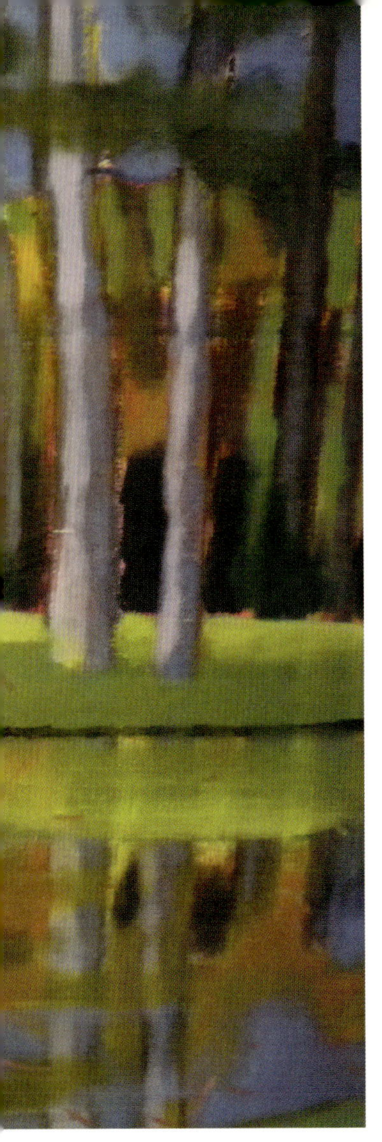

Day 158
Dames Dam

My artist friend Liz Dames has a
dam at the bottom of her garden.
She lives in Karen (the area named
after Karen Blixen) where the
plots are large, usually 10 acres.
There was a singular light that
day, although the lime green is
exaggerated and I painted over
another effort, allowing the reds
to come through the trees.

Whenever I phone my much-loved sister Liben, who lives in Houston, Texas, she sits in front of this work, which was my valley when we lived in Loresho, Kibagare Valley. Ever-changing, the vale was our backdrop for forty years. Now it belongs to Elizabeth. A thousand different greens. I have painted this beautiful Mathari River Valley many times.Our home was on a hump between the two valleys. Many suburbs of Nairobi are on gorges with streams at their feet, as if God parted the land and pushed the earth into waves and rivulets. And the Great Rift Valley was formed.

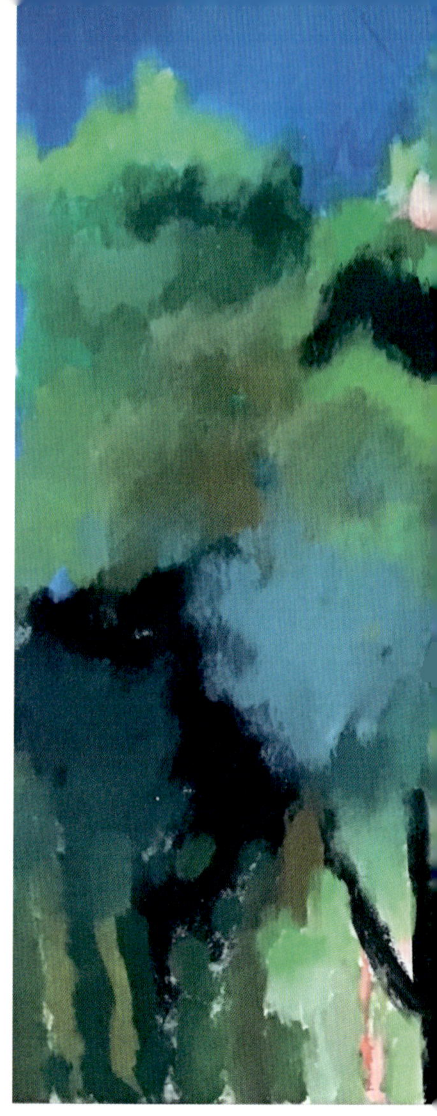

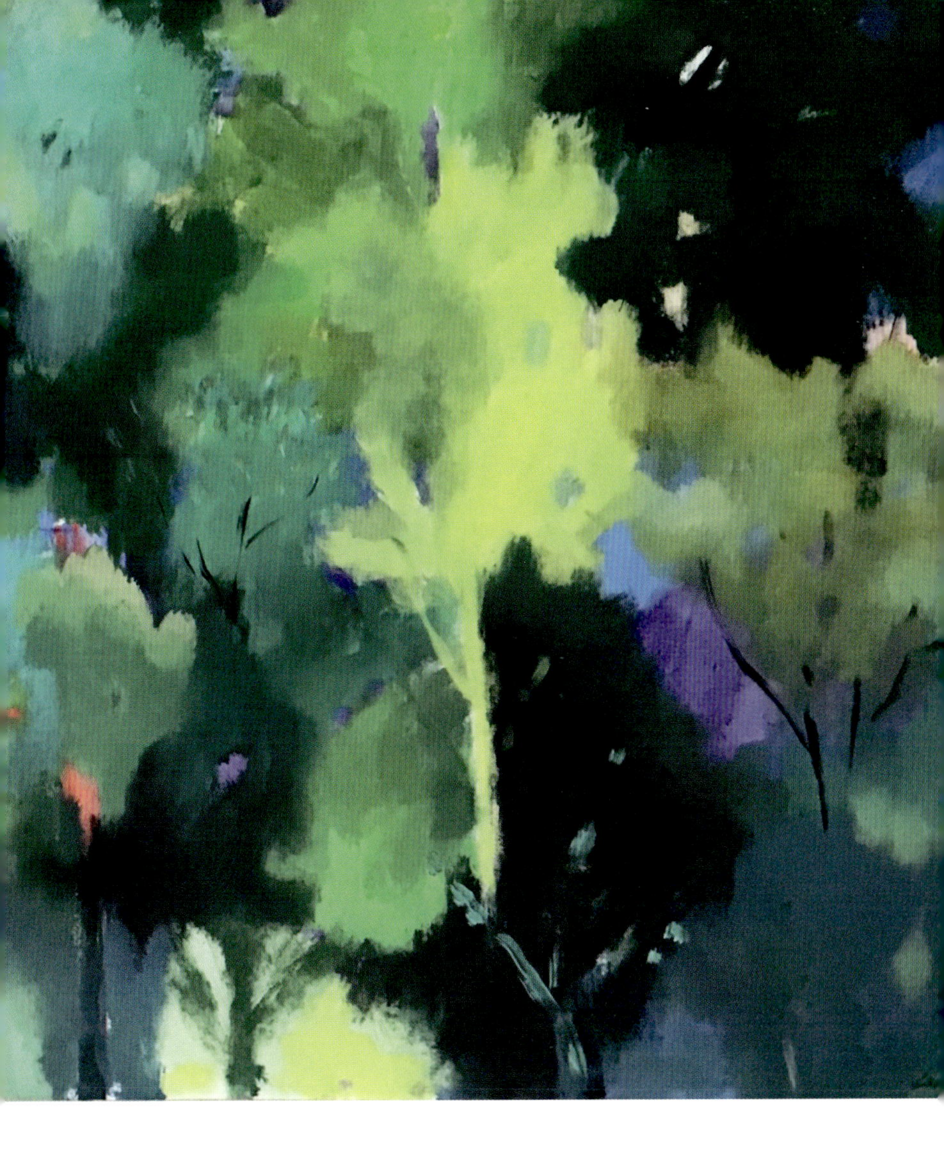

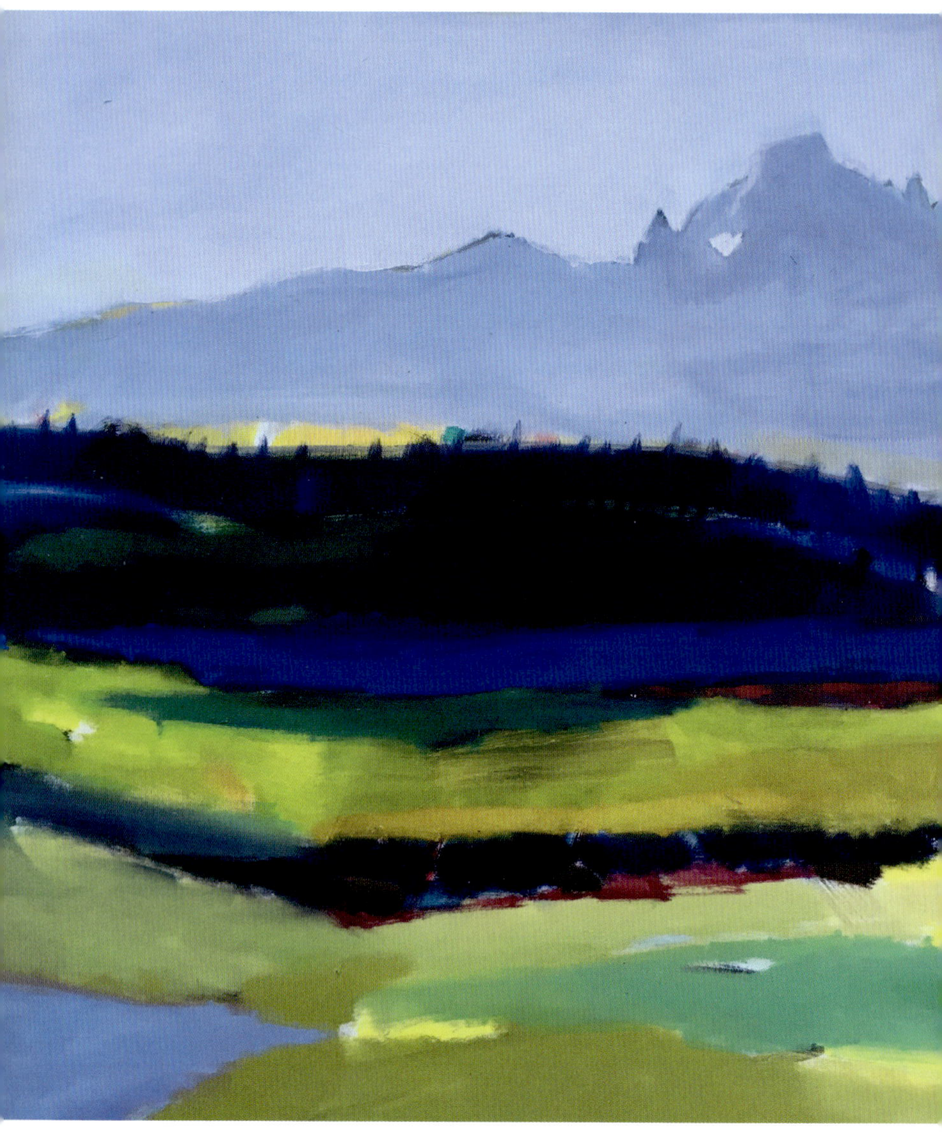

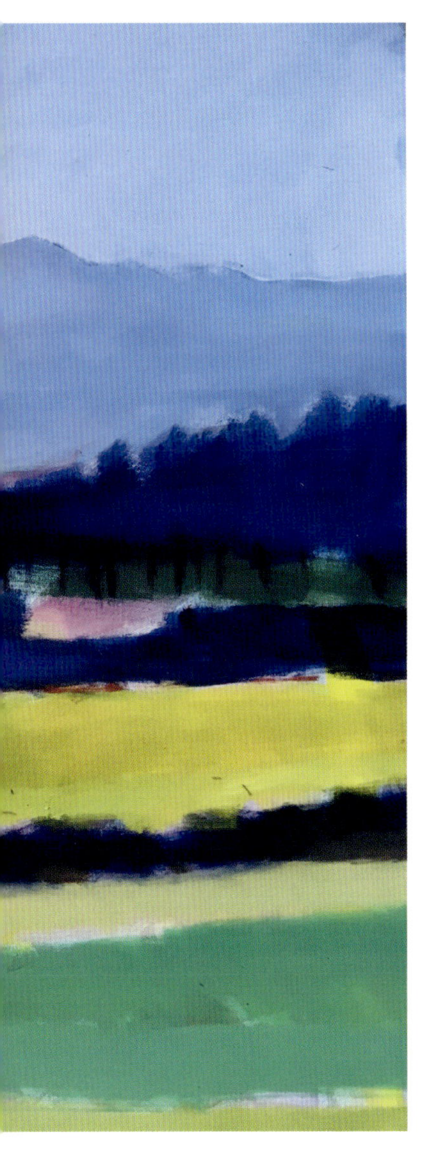

One of four works done over
five days while staying with
my friend Sarah Withey in
Nanyuki, who had the best
early morning view. I would
paint the mountain quickly,
as it could disappear, and
the foreground would reveal
itself over the next two
hours. I admire the Scottish
painter Barbara Rae, and this
foreground is inspired by her.
She gets a depth to her colours
which I struggle to emulate.
There was forest in front and
water on the side.
A wonderful view, different
with each painting. I have
three of them in my studio.
Notice the dip in the dark
horizontal, on the golden
section, which anchors the
whole work. The Yves Klein
blue separates the work but
adds weight to top and bottom,
like a luscious sandwich.

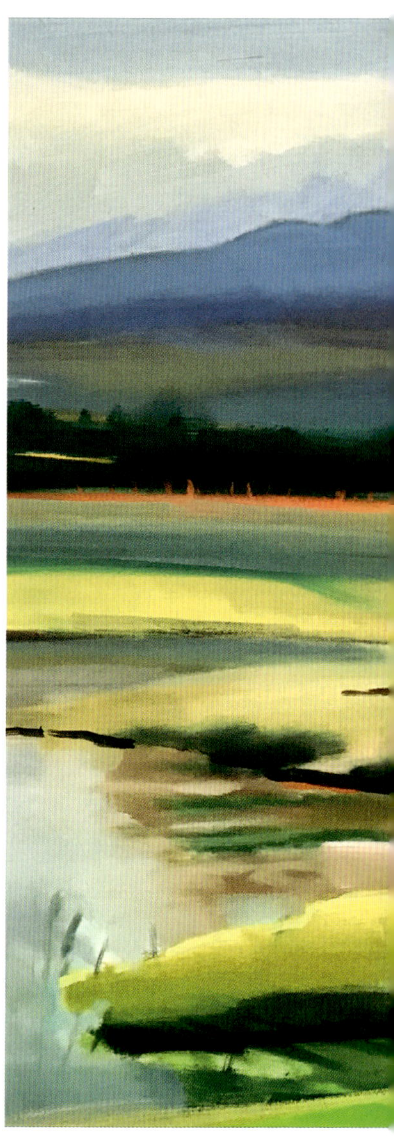

The yellow line under the
blue pushes the mountain
back. There is a dip on the
golden mean, and a zig-zag on
the left side that leads the eye
to the stick in the ground that
crosses the line of the inlet.
The eye rests there and then
goes immediately again to the
mountain. This oil on canvas
resides in Kiota Safari House
in Nanyuki, a very special
place for a weekend.
Collection of
Don and Tina Young

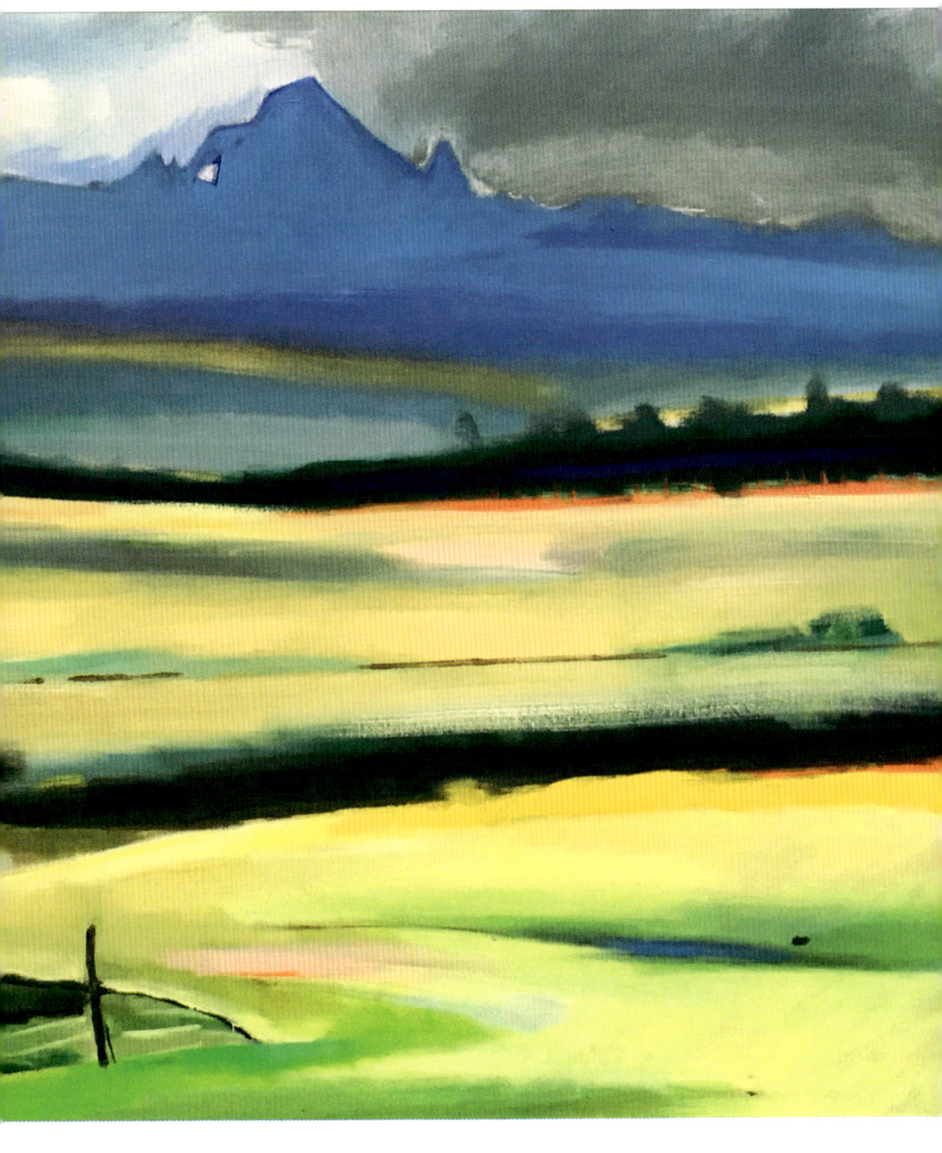

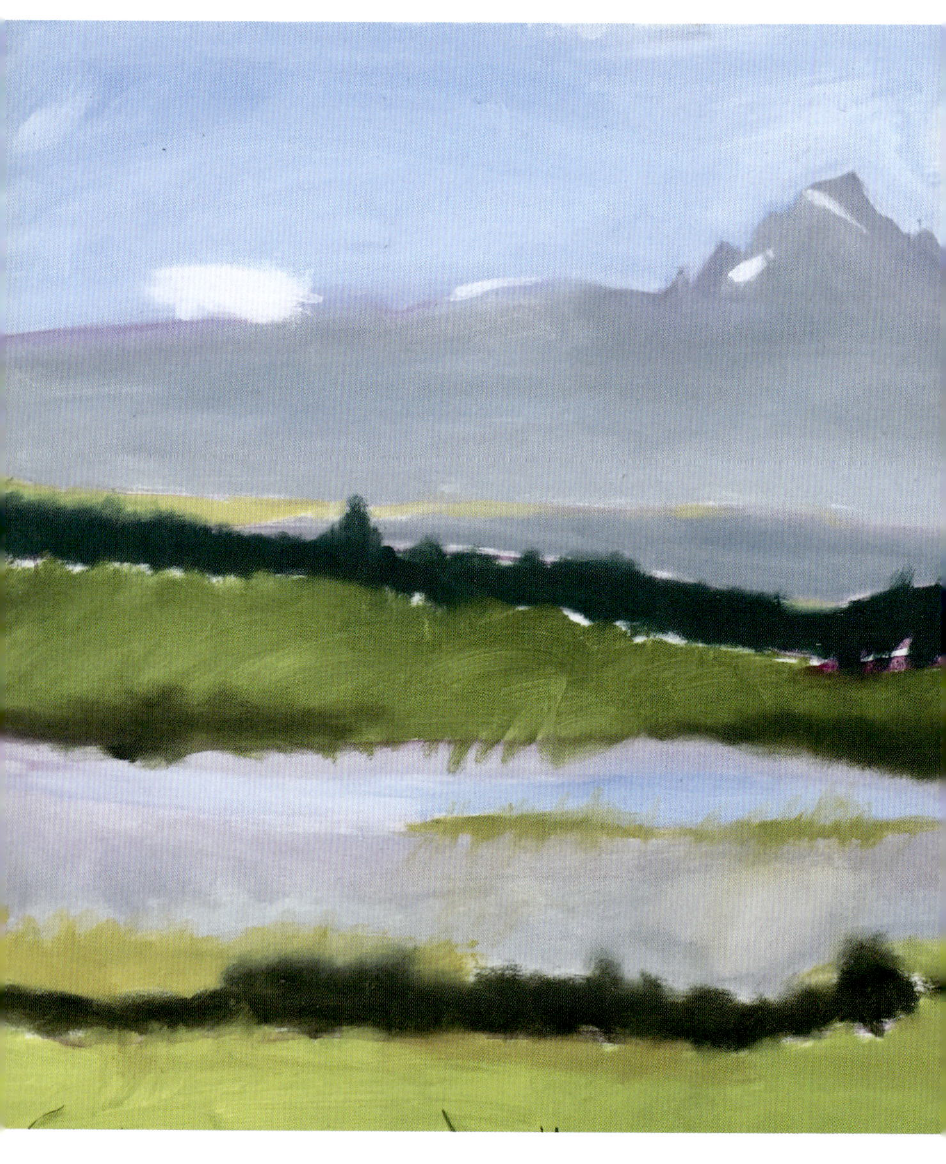

Day 162
Mount Kenya

An early start and the promise
of a bright new day. There is
less colour than in the others,
but a feeling of a nip in the air.
Sunlight sparkles off the glacier.

Day 163
Mount Kenya

An amazing view that
will disappear before
one's very eyes.

The Mountain by Emily Dickinson

The mountain sat upon the plain
In his eternal chair,
His observation omnifold
His inquest everywhere.

The seasons prayed around his knees,
Like children round a sire:
Grandfather of the days is he.
Of dawn the ancestor.

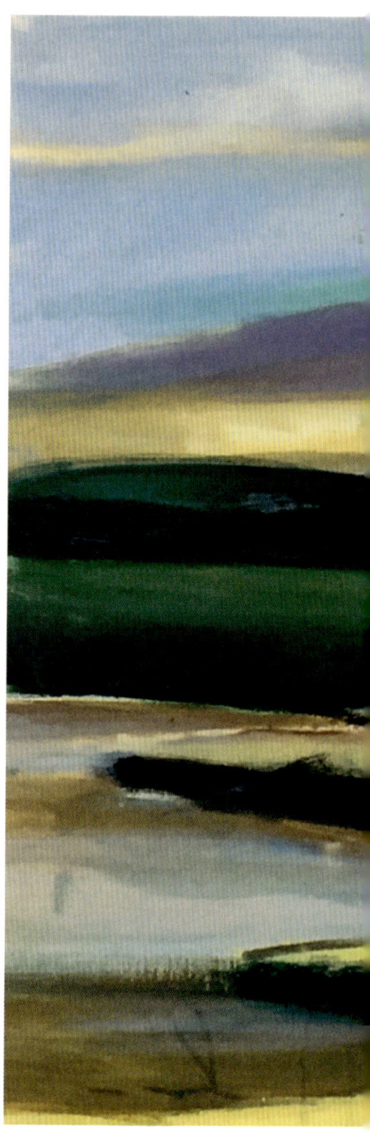

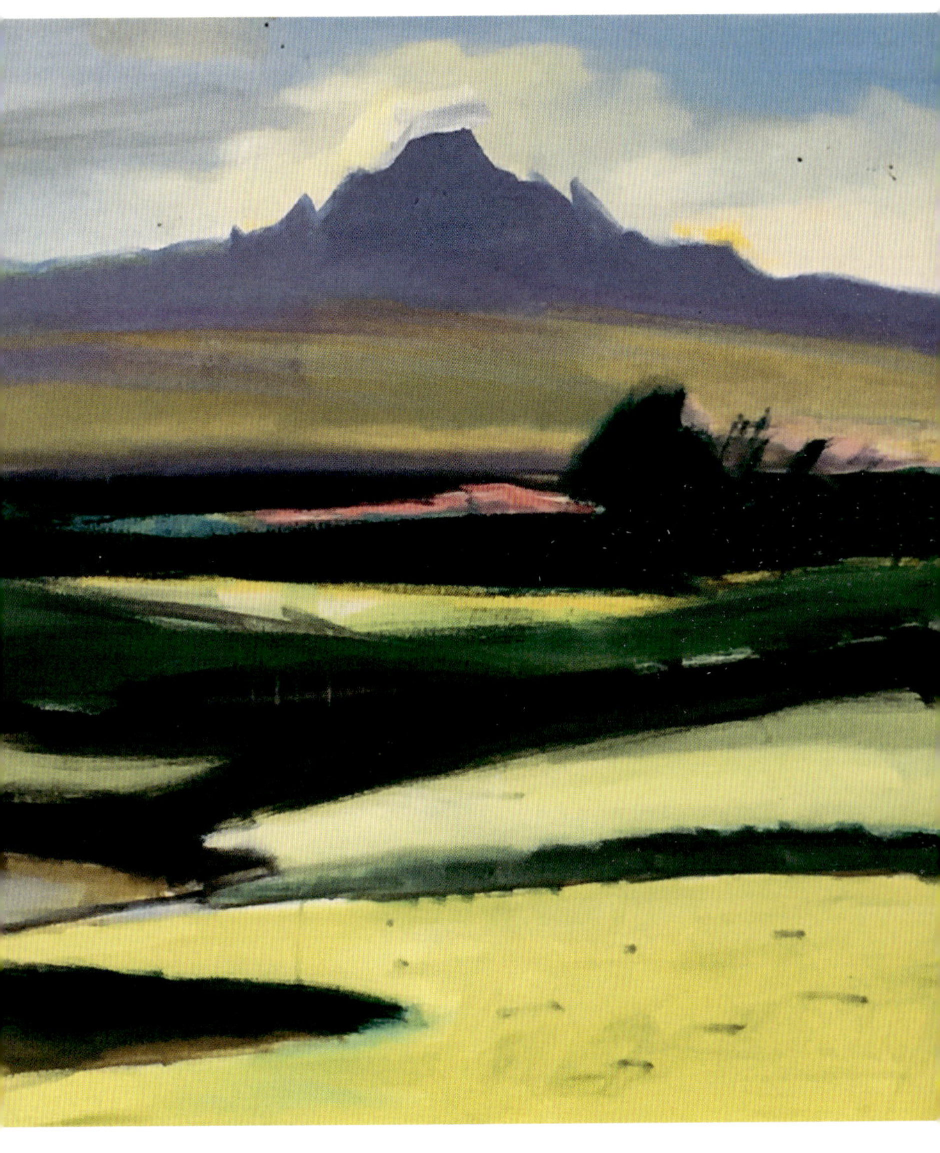

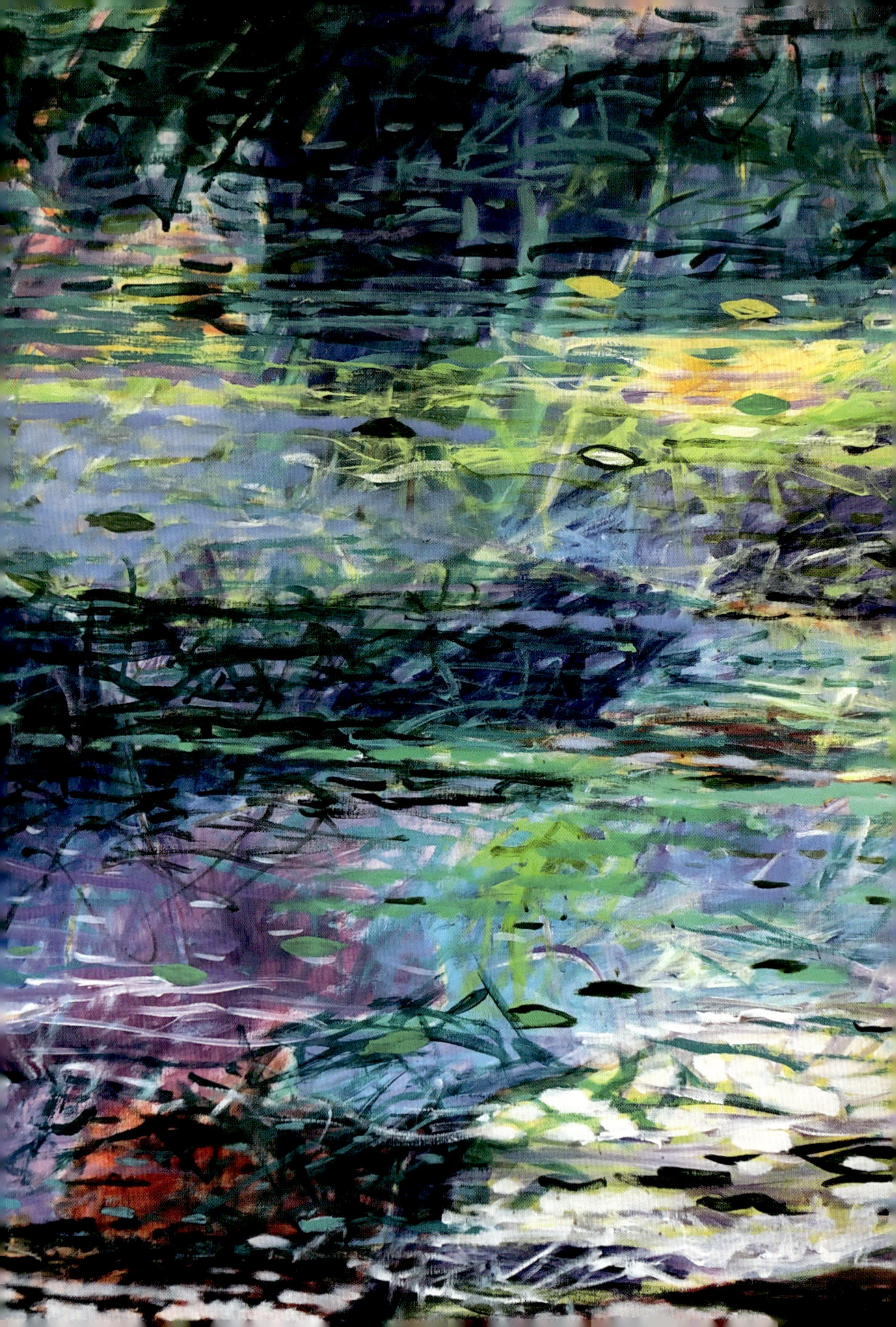

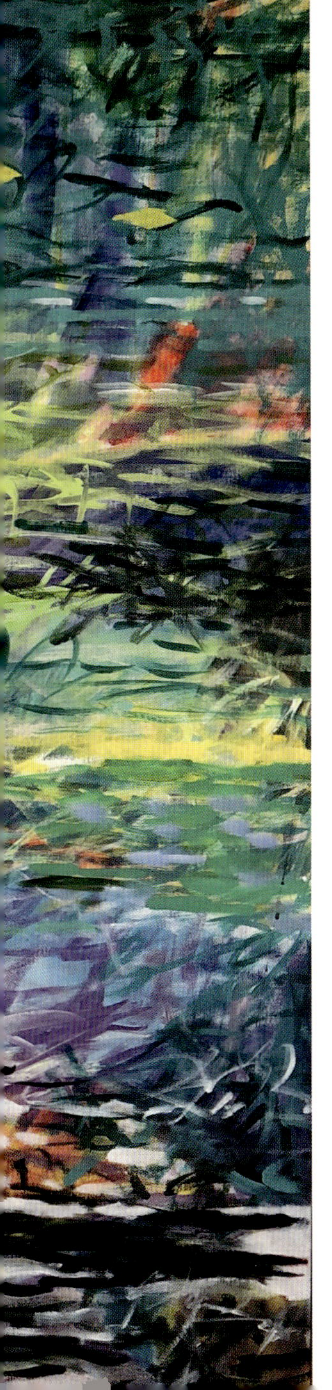

Day 164

Indian Ocean

Colour and warmth. I like the different surfaces in this work – the top surface where there is some seaweed, some reflections beneath and movement of the water, and the bottom with drenched seaweed.

Celia Macpherson sent me this photograph of a long-forgotten painting. I have no record of this one, though I can see it is mine, and Celia, who is a wonderful ceramicist, has quietly collected many of my paintings. It is a lovely thing when another artist buys one's work. Somehow, it is the highest validation.

Now in the collection of Yiota Matsi Epenetos.

Day 165
Powerful Passion

This work was a commission
and I was given the lovely title.
I was in the middle of painting
when a visitor to the studio saw
it and begged to have it.
I figured I would paint a better
one later, and I did.

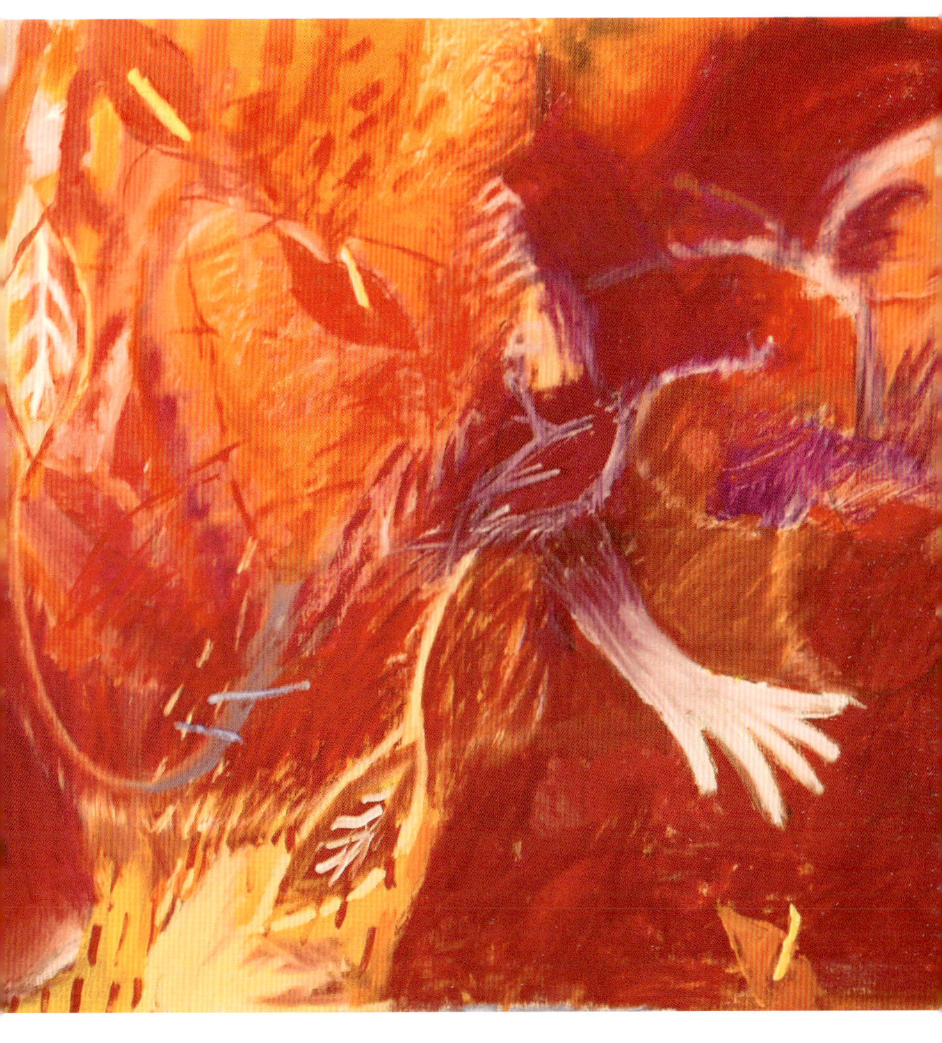

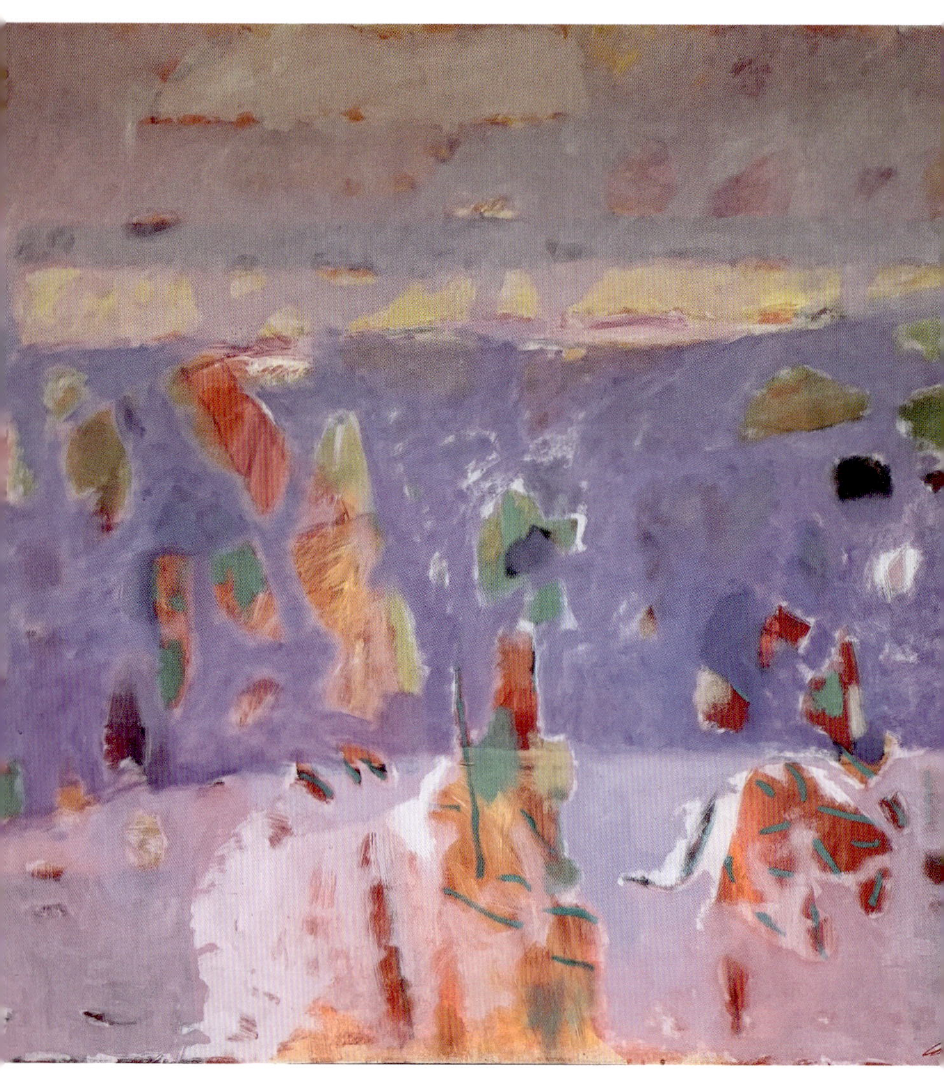

Day 166
Purple Haze

I recollect my feelings before I managed to finish this
work. I was at a loss about how to pull the painting
together. Lilac was the solution. An unusual colour to
go over the whole work – violet, mauve.
Lilac shrubs have a wonderful scent, a small tree of the
olive family. Bright lilac, pale lilac, strong lilac, three
horizontal bands. I am always thinking about Rothko,
his ability to change the viewer's state and the way his
paintings breathe; something about the edges and the
brushstrokes where the colours touch each other.
Celia Macpherson saw this painting, as it was hanging
in my lounge, and I was sorry to see it go, though it
went to a special person who appreciated all that had
gone into it.

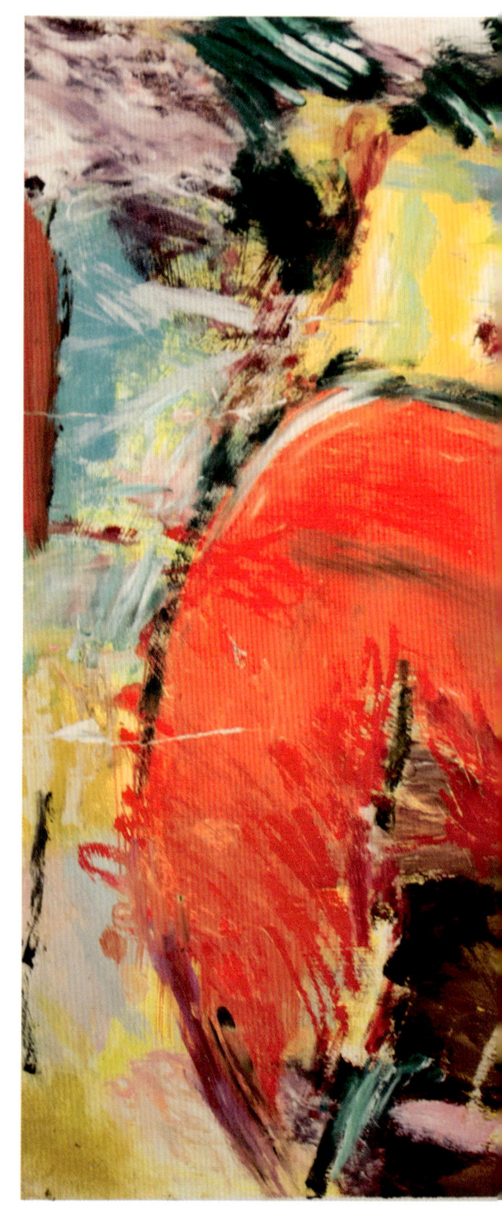

Day 167
Nucleus

Painted at the end of a day
in the studio when the
finish is of no consequence.
On card, very quick and
more than likely using up
all the remnants of the
paint on the pallet.

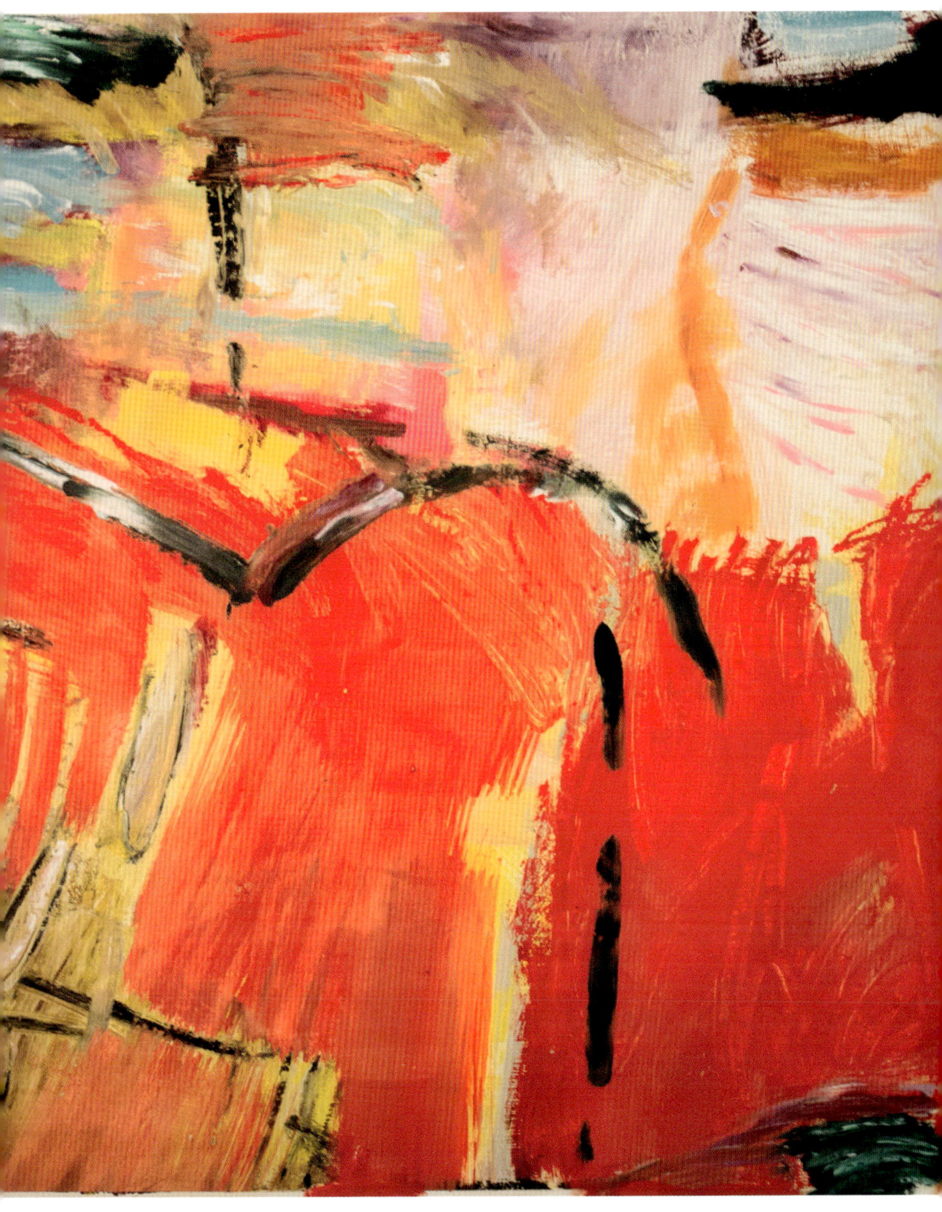

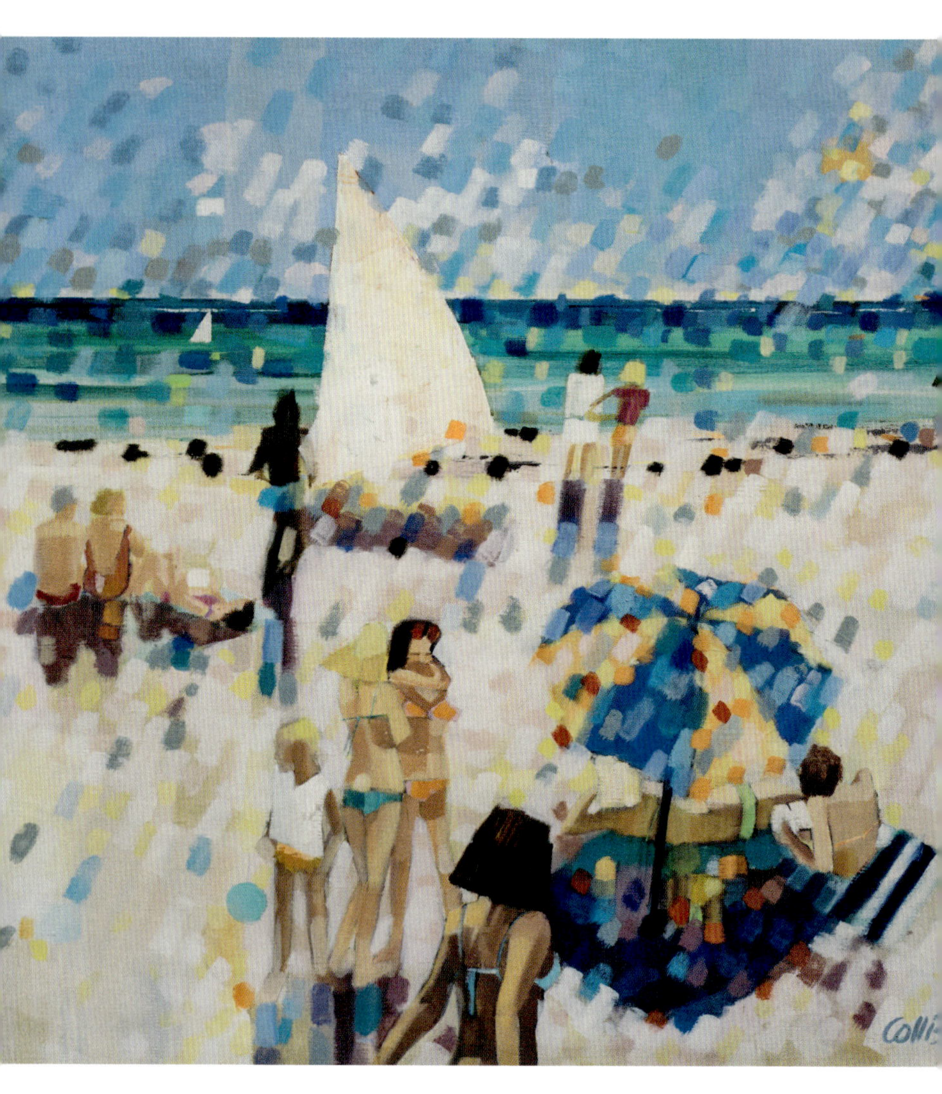

Day 168

Diani Beach

An old chestnut, one of the first very large oils that I attempted. It belongs to my daughter, Mia, who is the little blonde figure on the beach by the lapping waves looking out to sea, standing with her friend Nancy Troup. My son, Fabian, is in the foreground, wearing a white vest.
The central figure in the foreground was based on my sister Liben, who is much blonder but I needed a dark spot there.
I spent ages on the shape of her head.
I never felt that I pulled this painting off, which is probably why the family still has it.

Day 169
Torso

Experimenting with squares was a
short project and an easy 'cheat' to
draw and inspired from a magazine.
These three works (see tomorrow
and the day after) were spotted in my
studio by my friend Christine Davis,
who sees things that I don't necessarily
see myself. She took the works to
London. This has been photographed
with some reflection in the glass.
The work is on card with oil sticks.

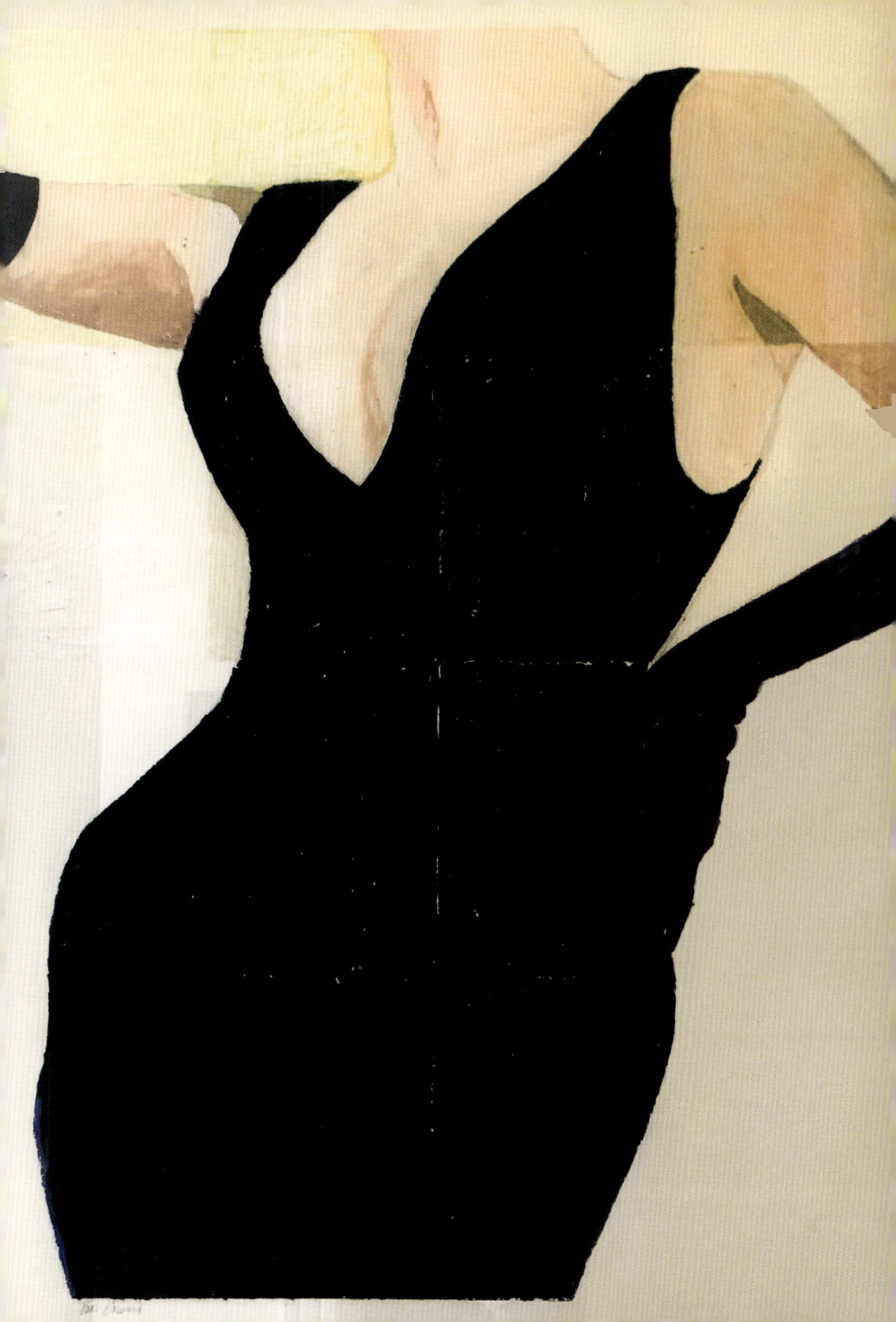

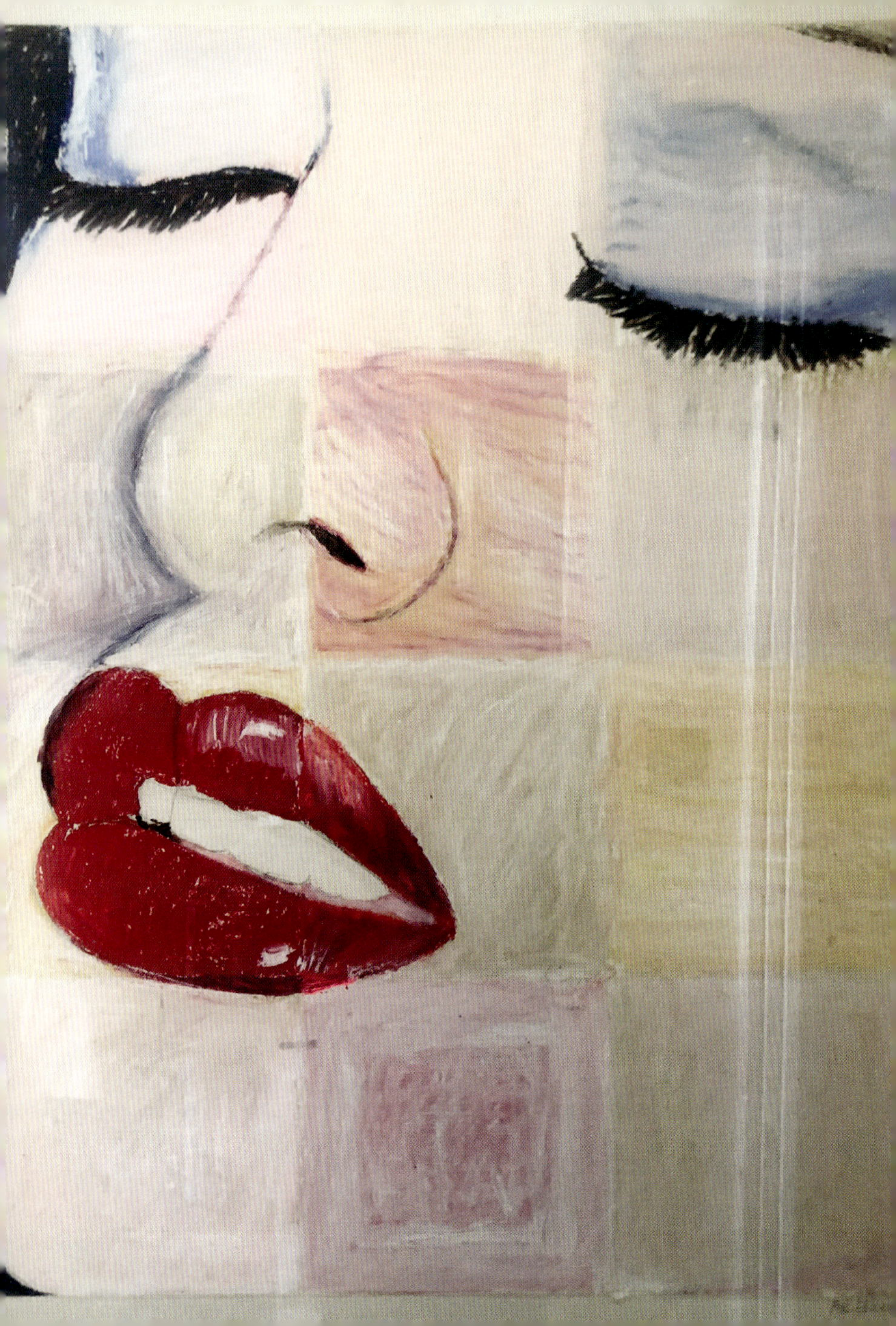

Day 170
More Squares

The same series, of three large drawings with
oil sticks on card. This is the first time they
have been in the public. The symbolism of the
squares' geometric shape represents solidity,
stability and physicality. There are two things
going on here. The squares and the face on
top. Great friends Alec and Christine Davis
bought these works for their son's birthday.
The large drawings are in London.
Collection of Edward Davis, who kindly took
these photographs for me. There is some
reflection from the glass.

Day 171
Another Torso

This time, rectangles. Oil sticks on card.
I have always loved Paul Klee, there is much
to learn from looking at his squares. It is one of
the hardest exercises in art. The shapes within
the grid need not be squares, yet the overall
emphasis should be rectilinear. Light and dark,
an arrangement of chiaroscuro. I used the
rectangles to make the drawing easy.
Collection of Edward and Lorna Davis, London

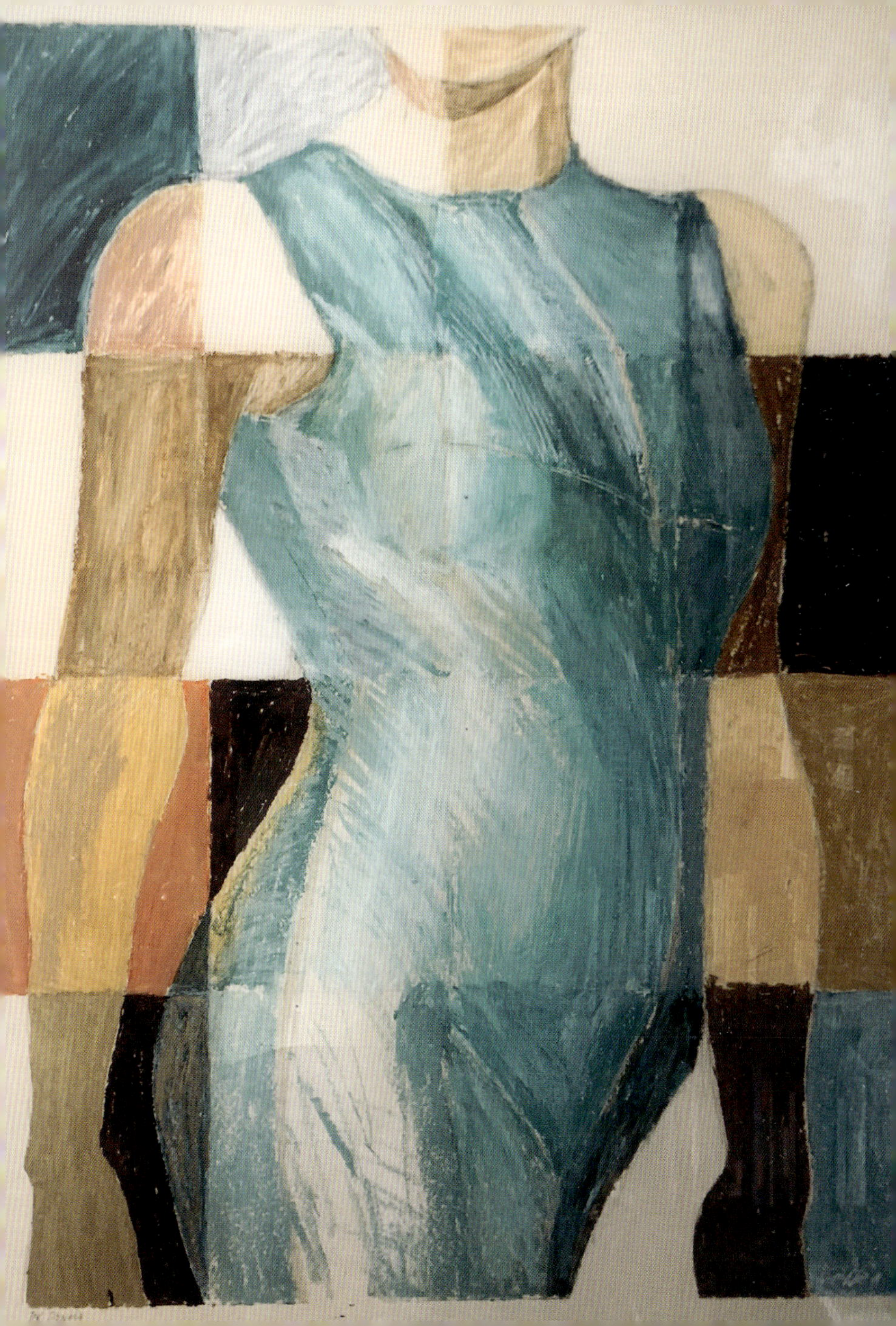

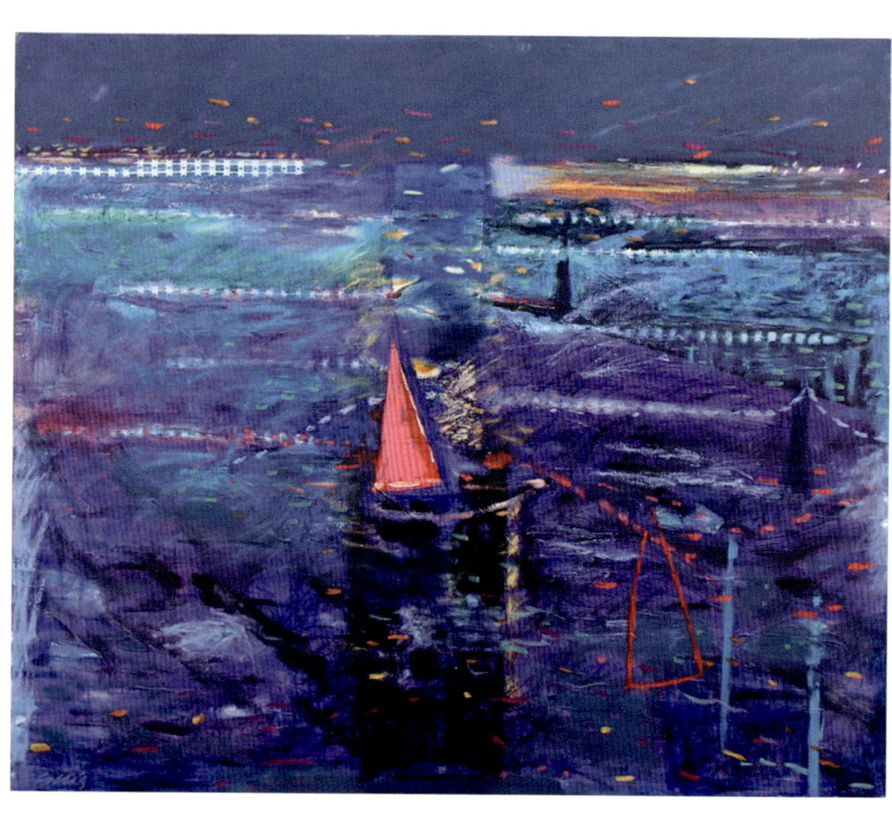

I am missing this wonderful
place this year … of enforced
lockdown. Never in the history
of mankind has there ever been
a quarantine of *healthy* people
for a 'virus'. This was painted
in my studio in Nairobi, a bit of
artistic license, I stuck gold and
silver stars all over it and all
sorts of other bric-a-brac.
In the collection of
Alec and Christine Davis who
have supported me always and
have a very large and most
diverse collection of my work.
Thank you both xx

Day 173
Maasai Mara

Taken from my photograph looking over the basket of a hot air balloon. It was daybreak and the tyre tracks were lit from the side as the sun came up. I was awe-struck by the patterns on the ground.

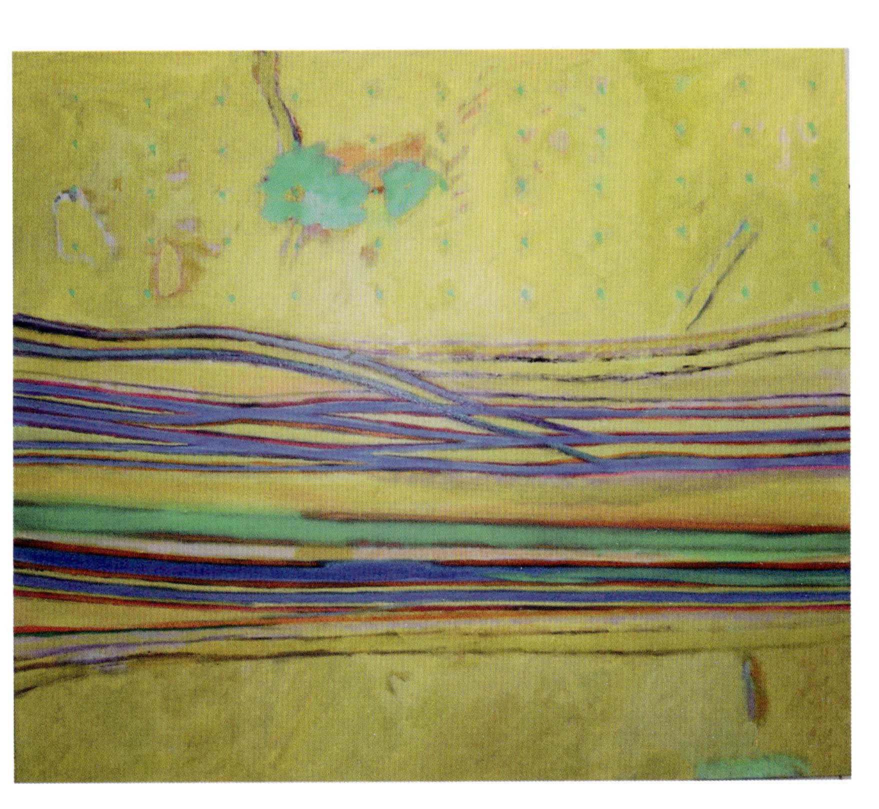

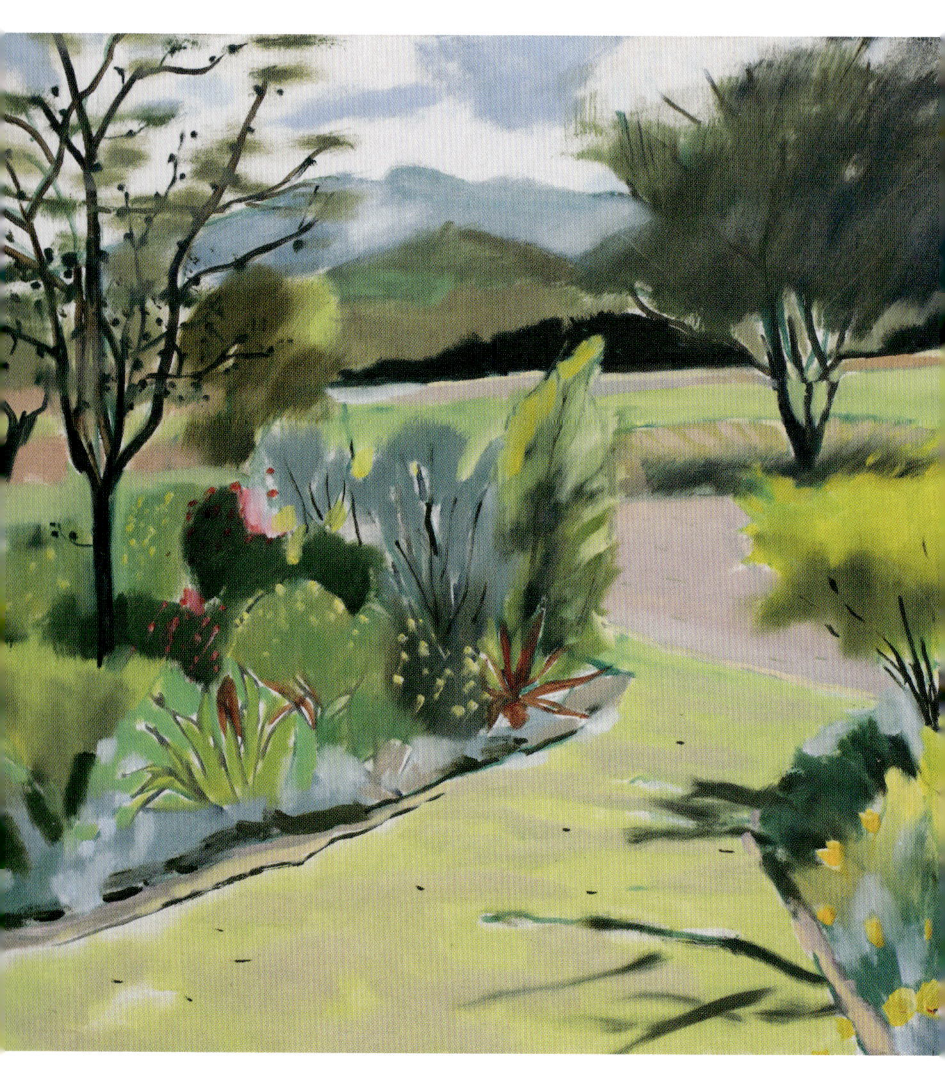

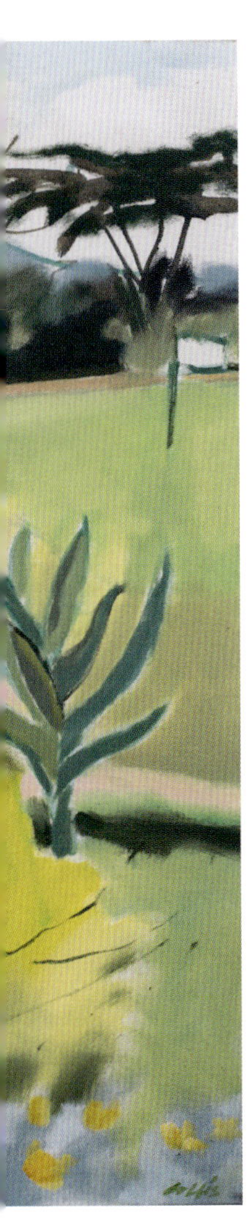

Day 174
14th Green

Painted looking at Green Park Golf Course.
It was the whistling thorn tree that attracted
me, balanced by those cinnamon green bushes
on the right. A golf course is in the middle of the
Rift Valley for those who do not know Kenya.
It was a drizzly day and the blue in the sky was
a bit of artistic license. I grapple when there is
not enough light or colour to excite me, and
this was one of those days.
My lovely, special friend Adriana Van Wageningen
bought this from my studio, although I have just
heard that her son Alex bought it for her, as a gift.
It hangs in a resplendent home which he and his
twin brother, Max, designed for their parents.

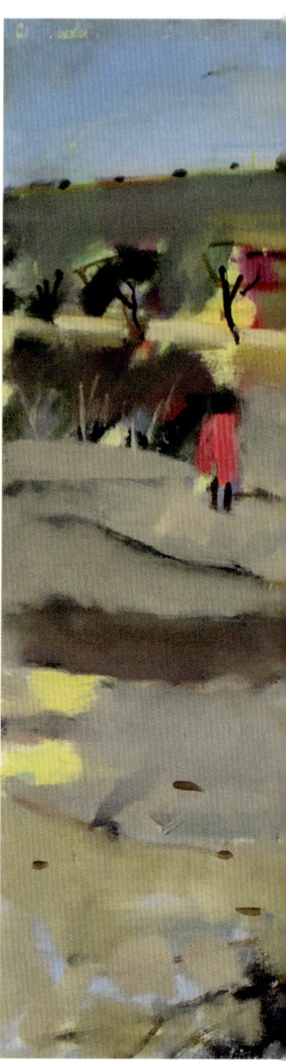

Day 175
Behind the Ngong Hills

On a painting excursion with my painter friend, Sophie Walbeoffe, who paints camels beautifully. This was my first and only camel, and I don't think I was very confident. I painted this over another painting and let the colour shine through. An old trick. Collection of Edward and Lorna Davis

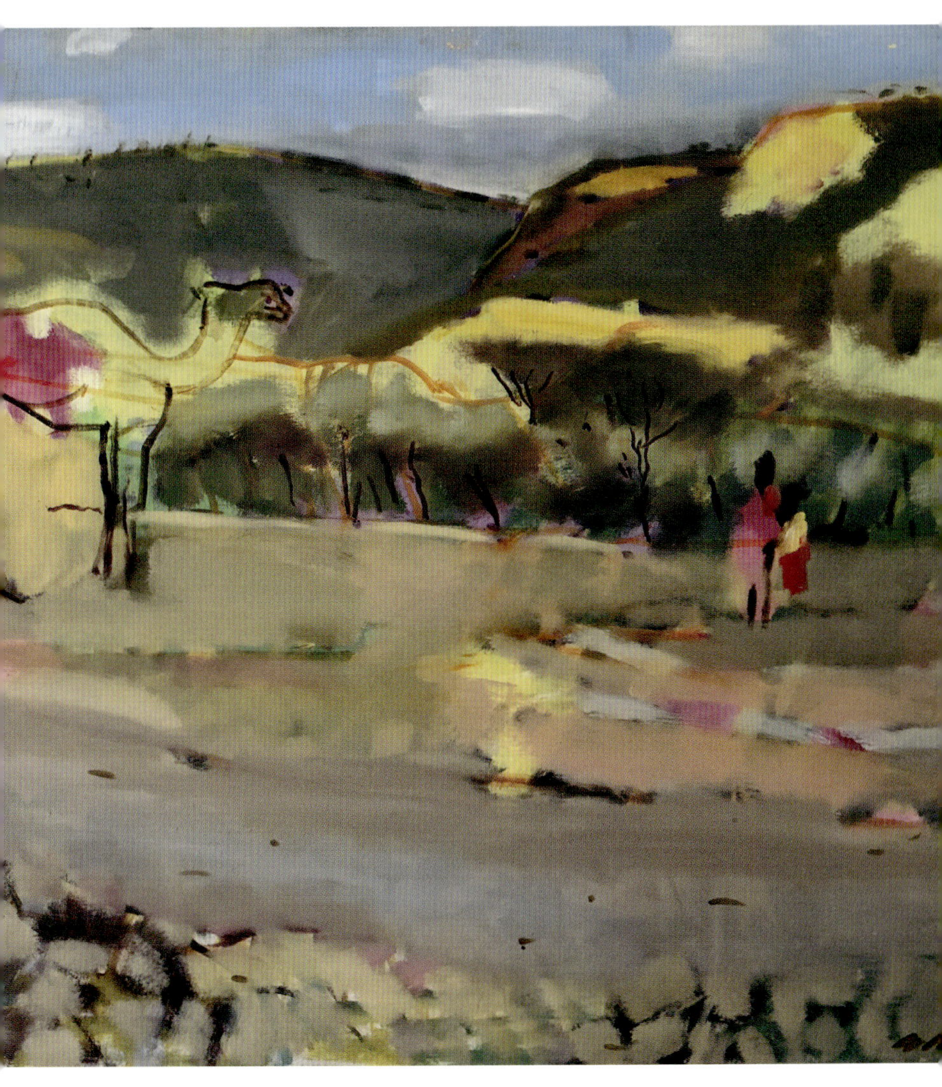

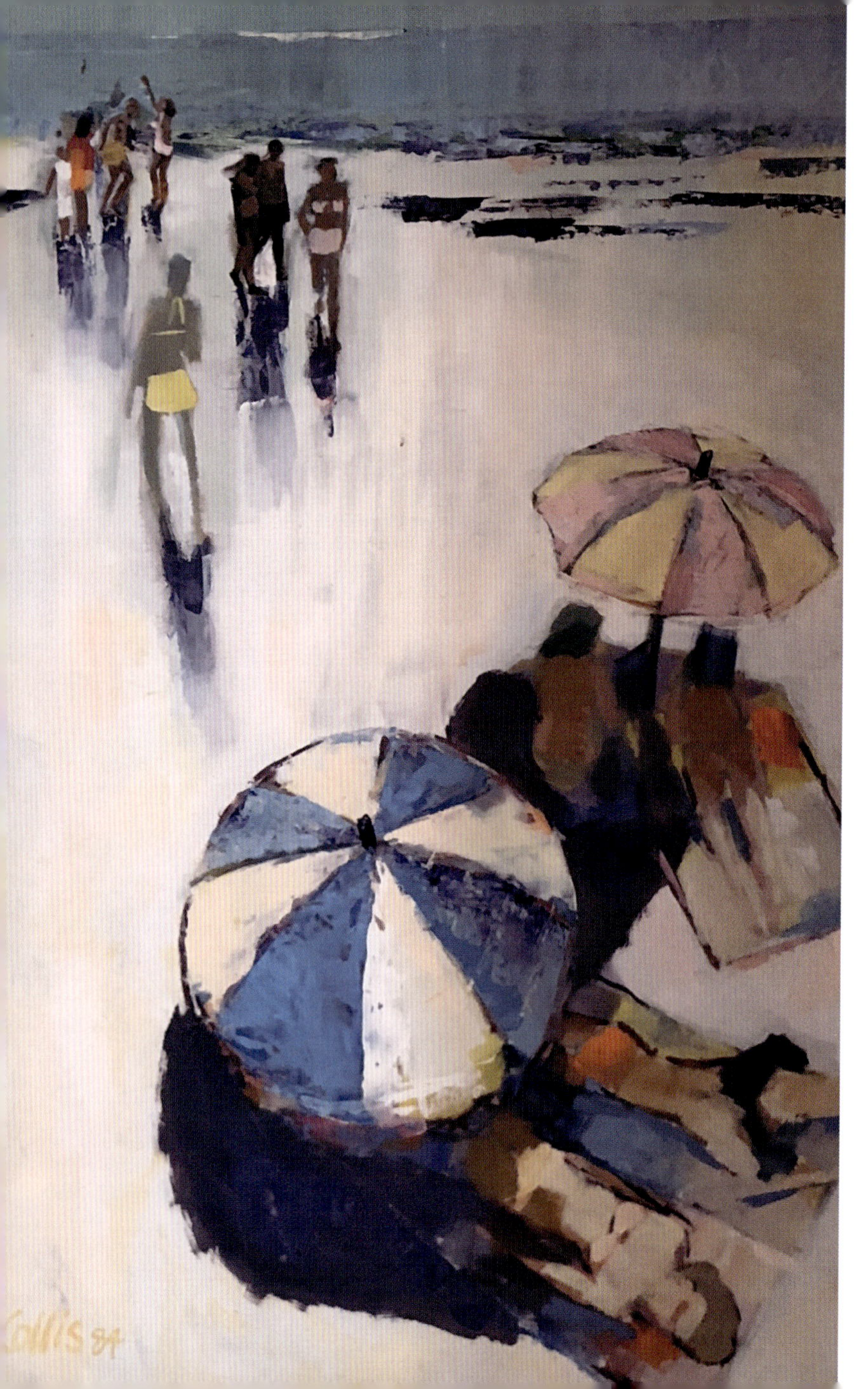

An early painting before I was
confident. I remember I was very
much in the process of learning
and exploring. Some of the figures
are cut out and stuck on to a board.
The painting has lasted well.
Painted in 1984, it belongs to
Mike and Sheila Barker.

DIANI BEACH

This collage resides in my studio.
I have been persuaded by several
friends to leave it alone. Reluctant
at first, it has grown on me. It is of
multiple media with kitchen paper,
handmade paper, sticks from the
garden and acrylics on a board.
I made the glass vase during Anselm
Croze's workshop at Kitengela
(glass works located outside
Nairobi, bordering the game park).
I love that vase and I still have it.
It has appeared in several paintings.
More of an assemblage, the vase is a
wonderful shape which I stuck on
to a thick square of blue 'dahl glass'
found on a shelf when foraging at
Kitengela. Anselm and I had an
exhibition of our glass vessels at
RaMoMA (Rahimtulla Museum of
Modern Art). I remember thinking
it looked like a display at Selfridges.
It was beautiful.

GLASS VASE

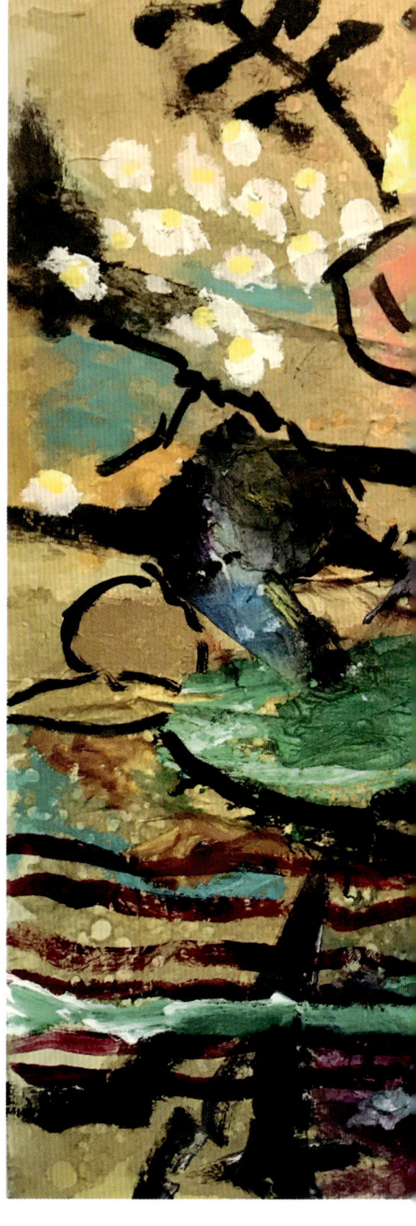

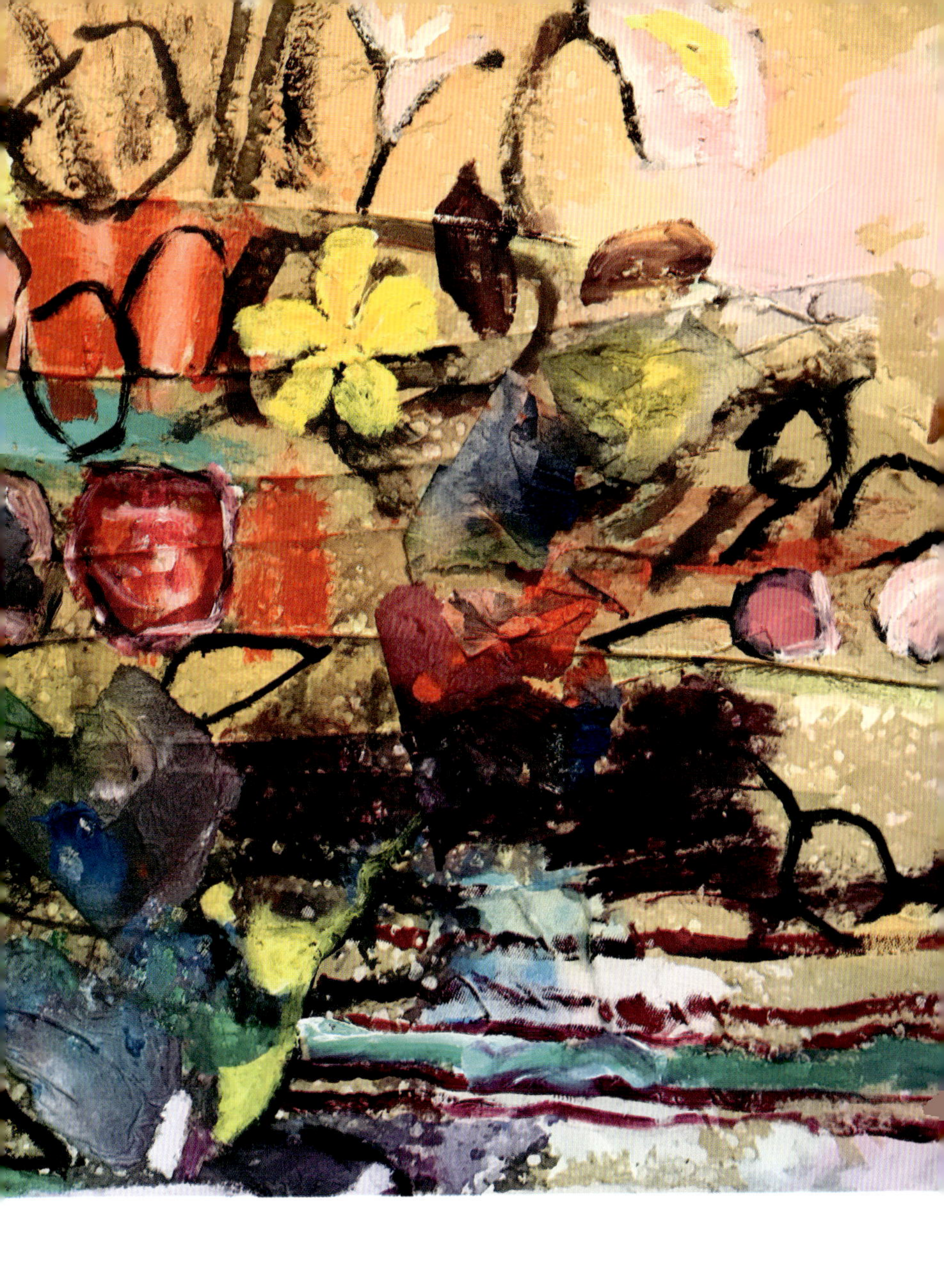

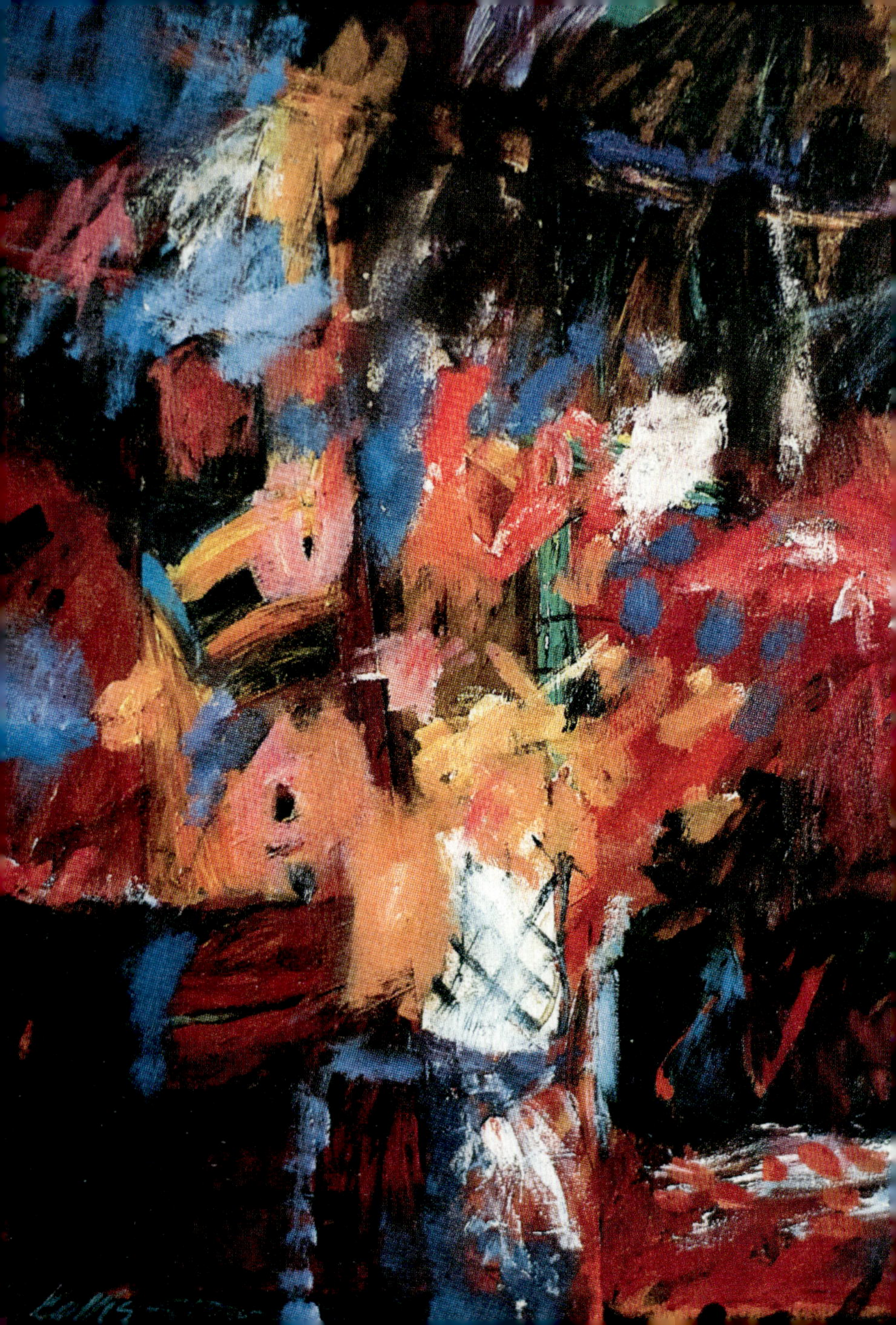

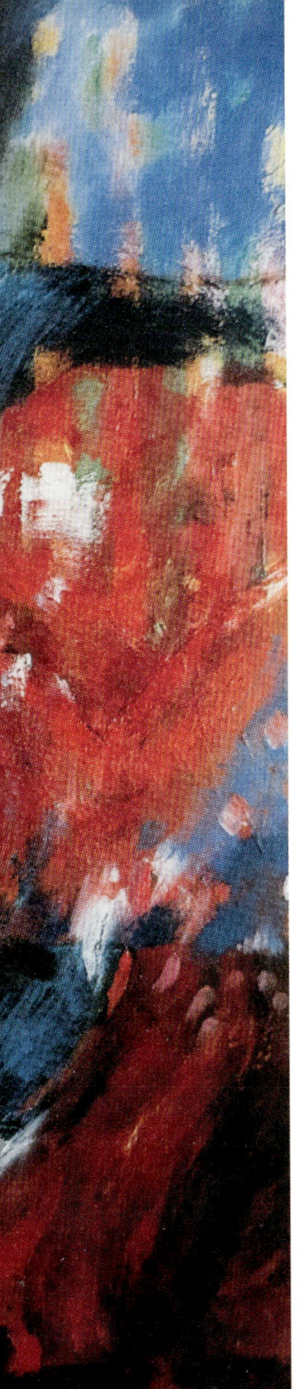

My mother titled this painting,
although she does not know
that. Now aged ninety-eight,
she is brilliant; in another era
she might have been a professor
of English Literature. Instead of
that she regarded bringing up
four daughters her career and,
as her eldest, it was tough.
A hard act to follow and one of
competitiveness every day.
I was rebellious then and am
probably still? I chose a career
that she had no idea about.
When she saw this painting,
she asked, 'Is that a little piece
of cut glass in there?'

My mother died on
30 November 2020. There was
a full moon and a lunar eclipse.
Brenda Clare Kampf 1922–2020

CUT GLASS

You can see the tell-tale island of dry grass behind the central pink roses on one stalk. I have talked about that little grass island in the middle of that often-painted flowerbed, that gives the whole vista a stability. This was a very late painting of that beautiful garden, it came quickly after I had painted well over one hundred of them.

This work borders on the abstract, and is really about directional brushstroke. Paul Gauguin is an artist to look up if you want to see brushstrokes. Many times in those days I would refer to his work. My sister Elizabeth owns this one.

Now here is something frightening! I have just looked at a map which popped up below my painting on the computer screen and it shows me where the painting resides … in Houston! Can you believe that?

SPRING
ERICA'S GARDEN SERIES

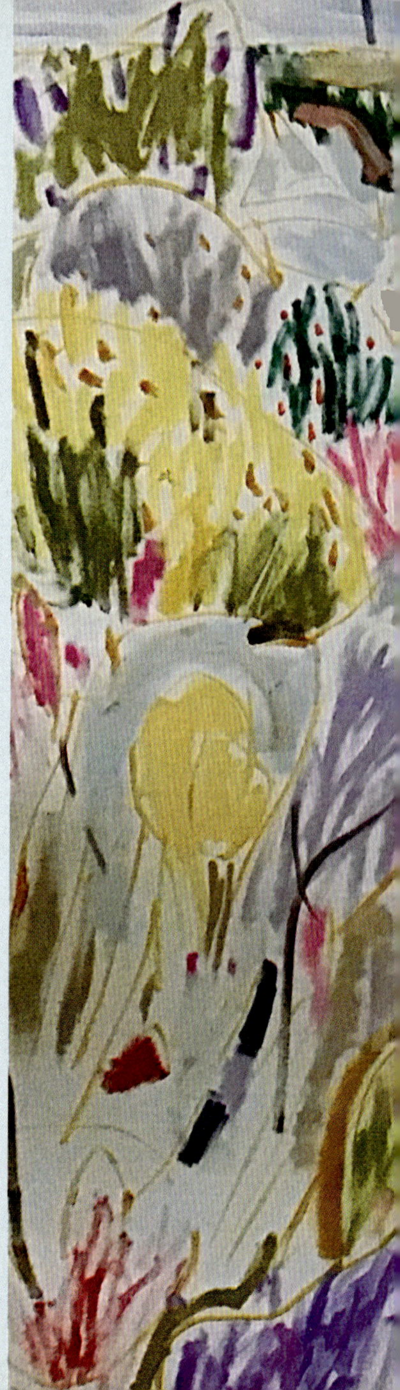

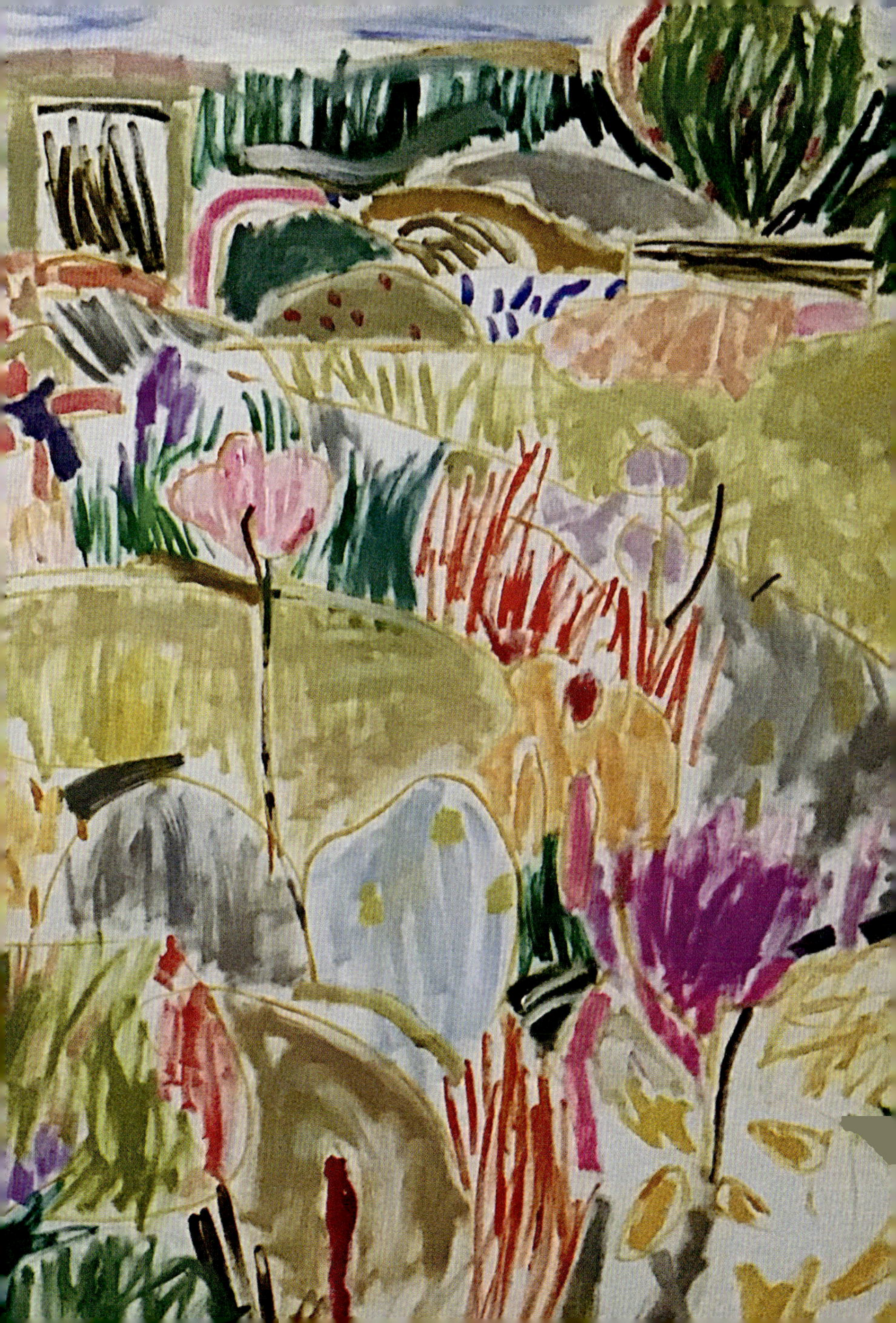

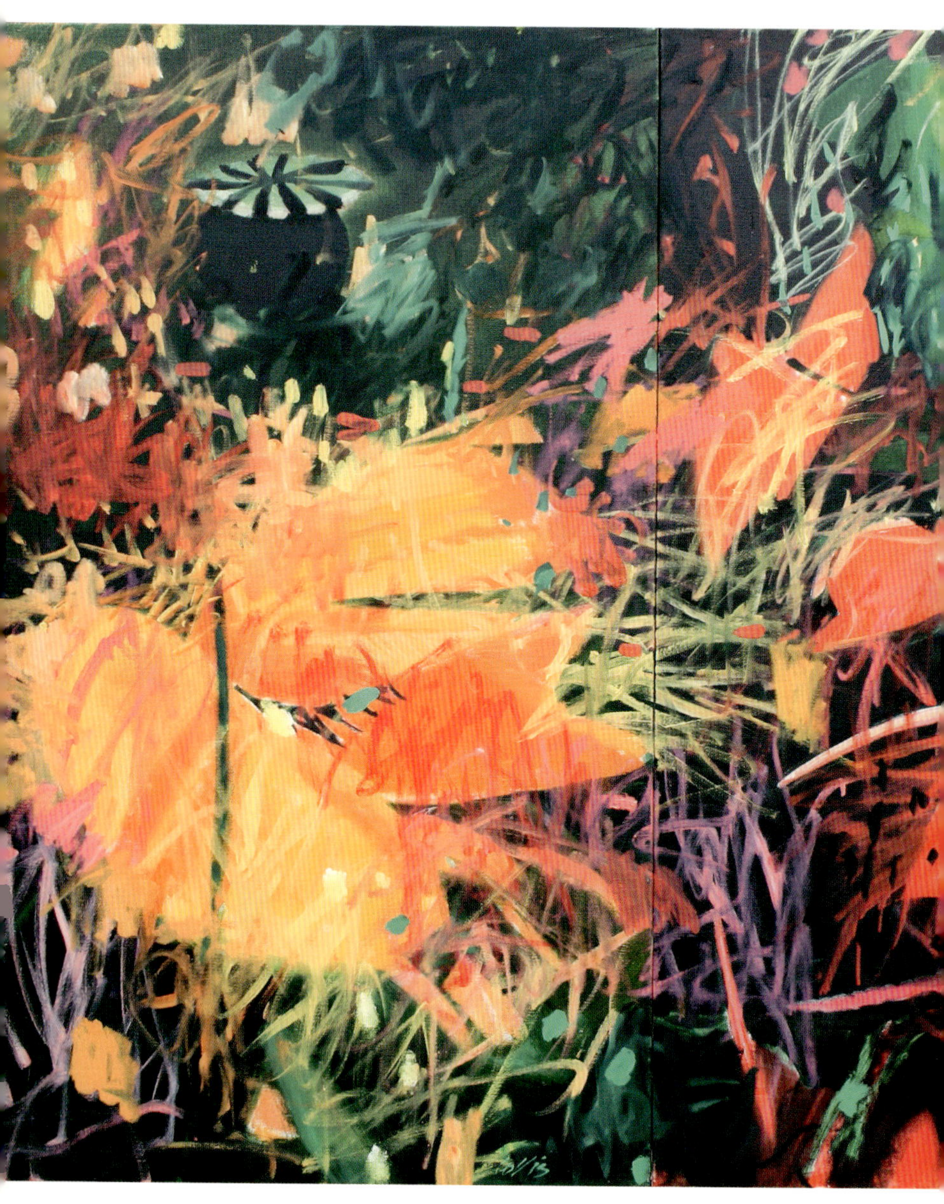

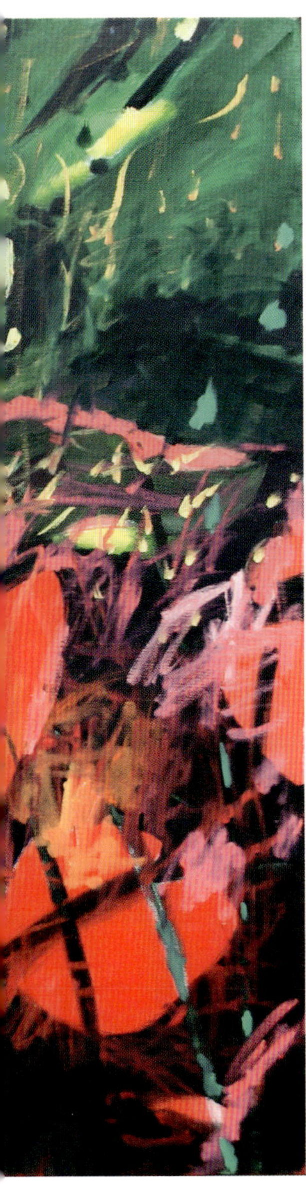

This work is on my website, which is not the easiest to negotiate. I confess to say this painting was inspired by two photos I found. The end result, however, is entirely different. The drawing never worked for me until I scribbled with a brush all over the diptych and the whole static thing began to breathe. I learnt a lot about layering with this work.

www.marycollisartist.co.ke
Private Collection, London

I was inspired to paint this from
photographs in a book of Monet's
garden as it is now. It was rendered
with oil sticks on canvas, which
accounts for the different look,
although it is my usual favourite size,
about 4.6 x 5ft. Many of Monet's late
works were painted as he was losing
his sight, the wonderful blurry
paintings are so different from his
early work. Claude Monet himself
said, 'I would like to paint the way
a bird sings,' and he did.

MONET'S GARDEN

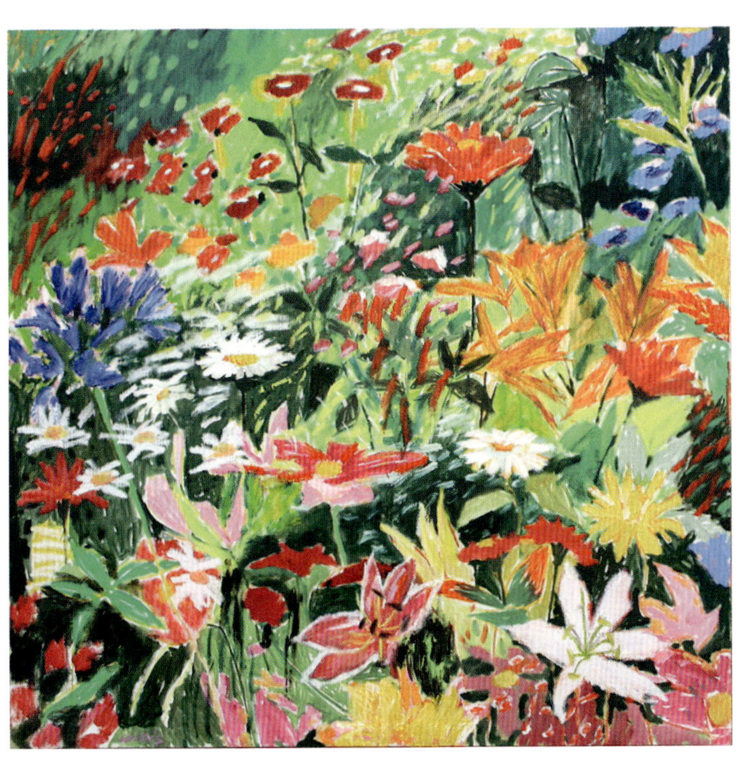

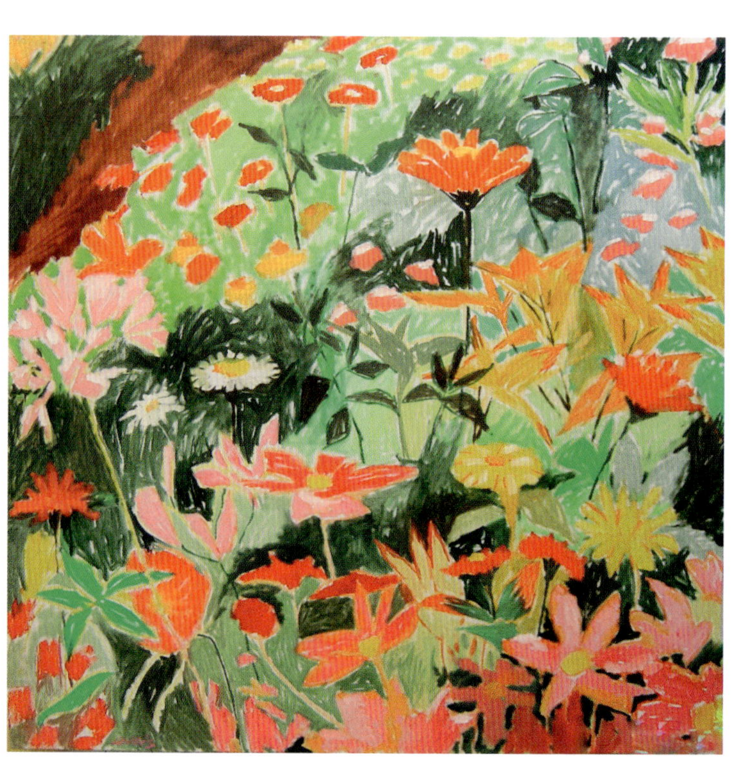

I thought it might be
interesting to see the
difference in a painting
that was lying about in the
studio for a long time. I was
dissatisfied. At last I pulled
it together – see Day 181.

MONET'S GARDEN

Day 183
Buoyant

For those who know Howard Hodgkin,
a great favourite, this is directly inspired
by his always central compositions with
frames. I almost bought a tiny one in the
Serpentine Gallery, which after much
agonising I chickened out of doing, as I
would have been left with nothing in my
account. A poor decision I have regretted
ever since. I love the way he butters
his canvases with the thickest paint.
This work hangs in a small room at the
Muthaiga Country Club and it is for
sale. It is an oil on handmade paper and
framed under glass. Presently unsigned.
It is about 36-in wide.

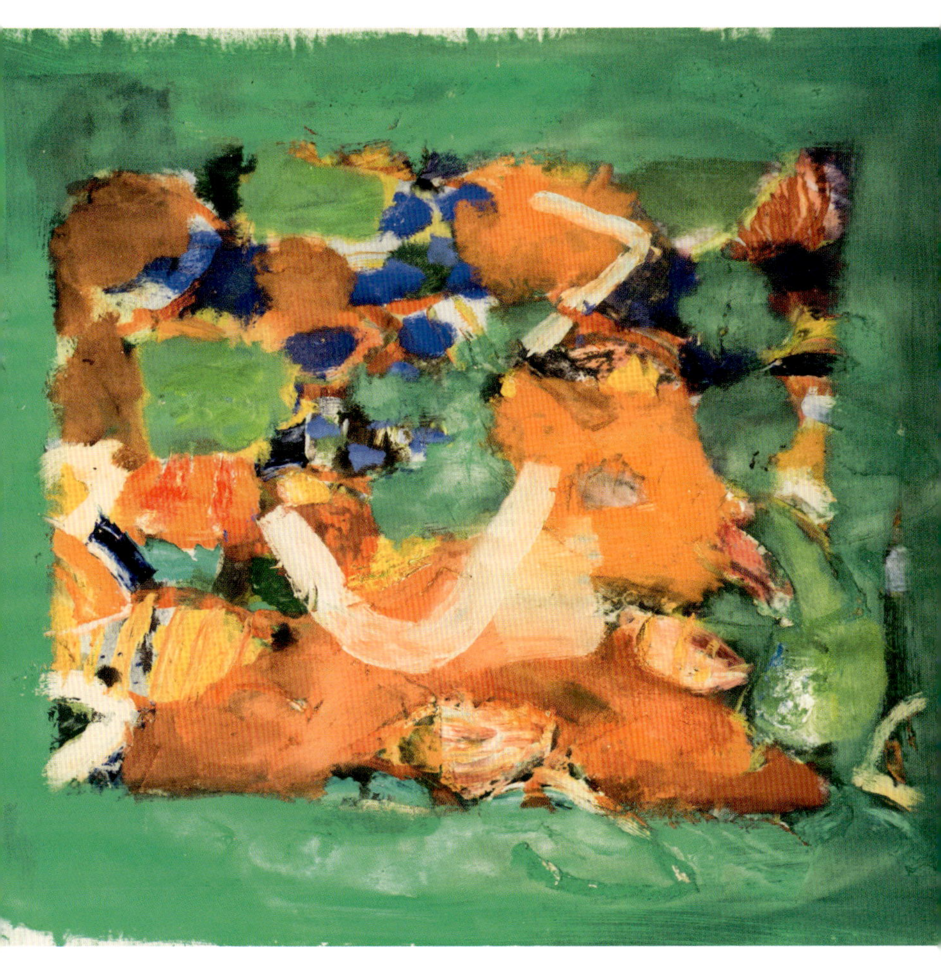

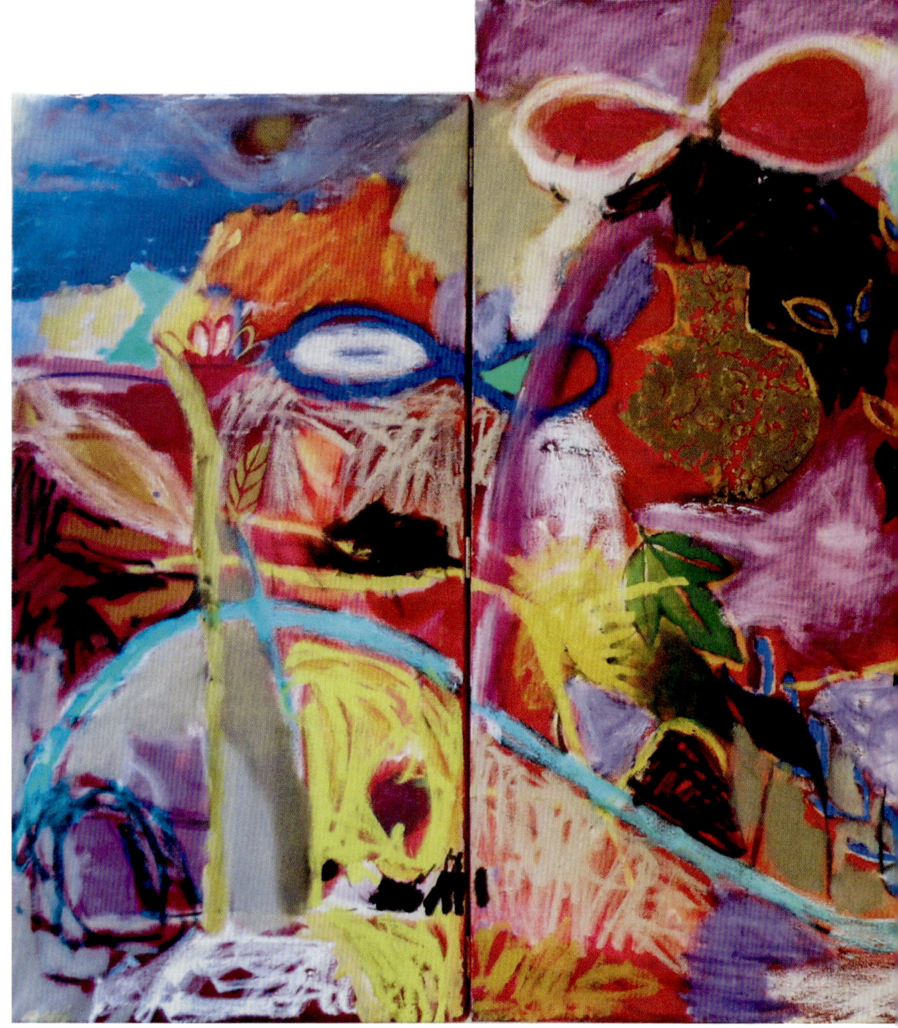

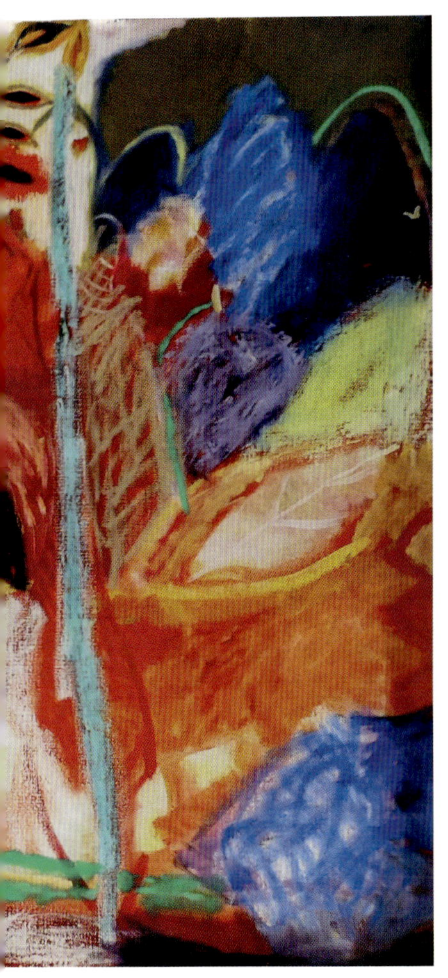

Day 184
All is One

A hinged triptych, intended as a reredos. When on the wall, one can fold in the sides so that it sits like a reredos determining three pieces behind the altar in a church, which usually portrays religious iconography. This was the final painting in the series, 'The Seven Spiritual Truths' (and the one I held on to the longest). There is much meaning going on in this work, and for anybody who is really interested, there is a written essay that accompanies it on my website written by Sue Canny Davison after much discussion with her.

www.marycollisartist.co.ke

Collection of Debbie and David Coulson, Karen, Kenya

Day 185
Canna Love

This 7 ft canvas hangs in
Paul and Lauren McKenzie's
dining room. They run the most
successful garden business in
Kenya. Lauren is an American,
brought up with contemporary
art, and so her purchase of
this large piece was of great
satisfaction for me. Much else is
going on in this painting,
for those who wish to see it.

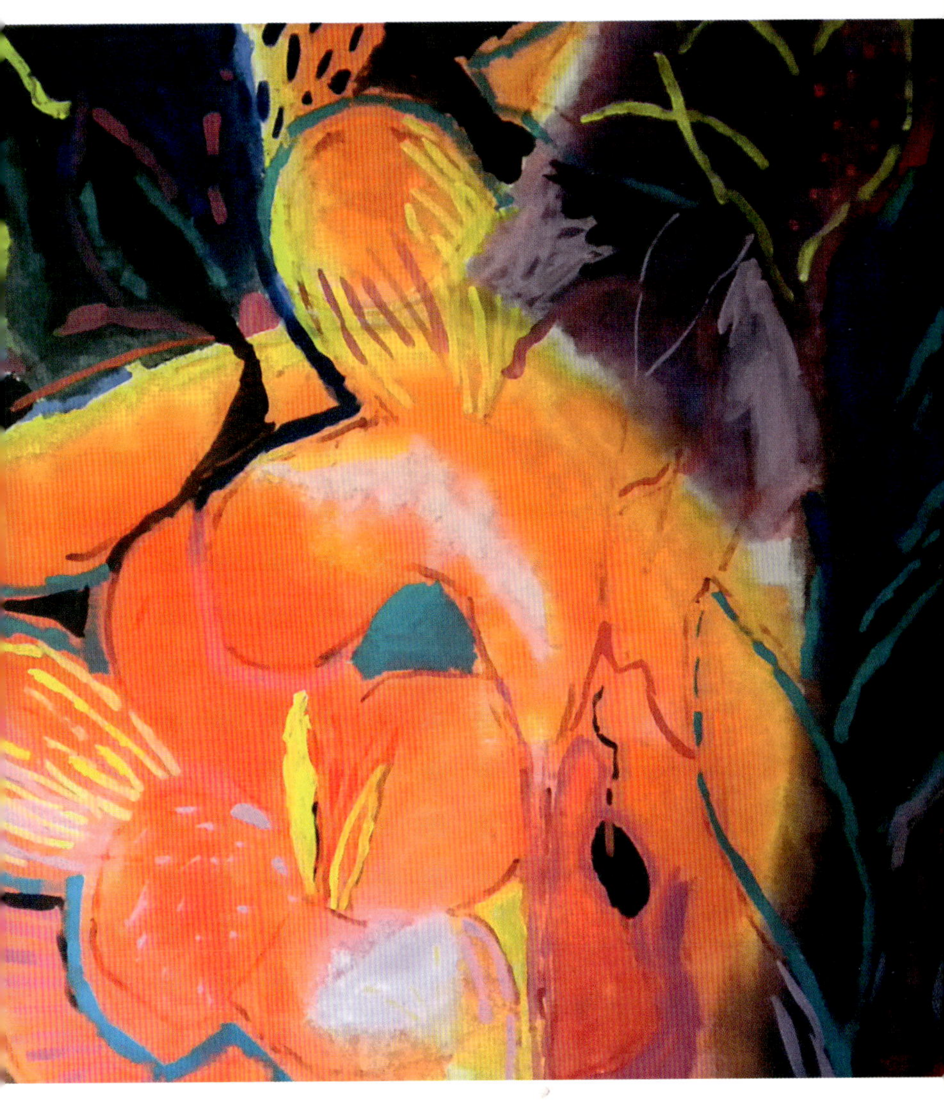

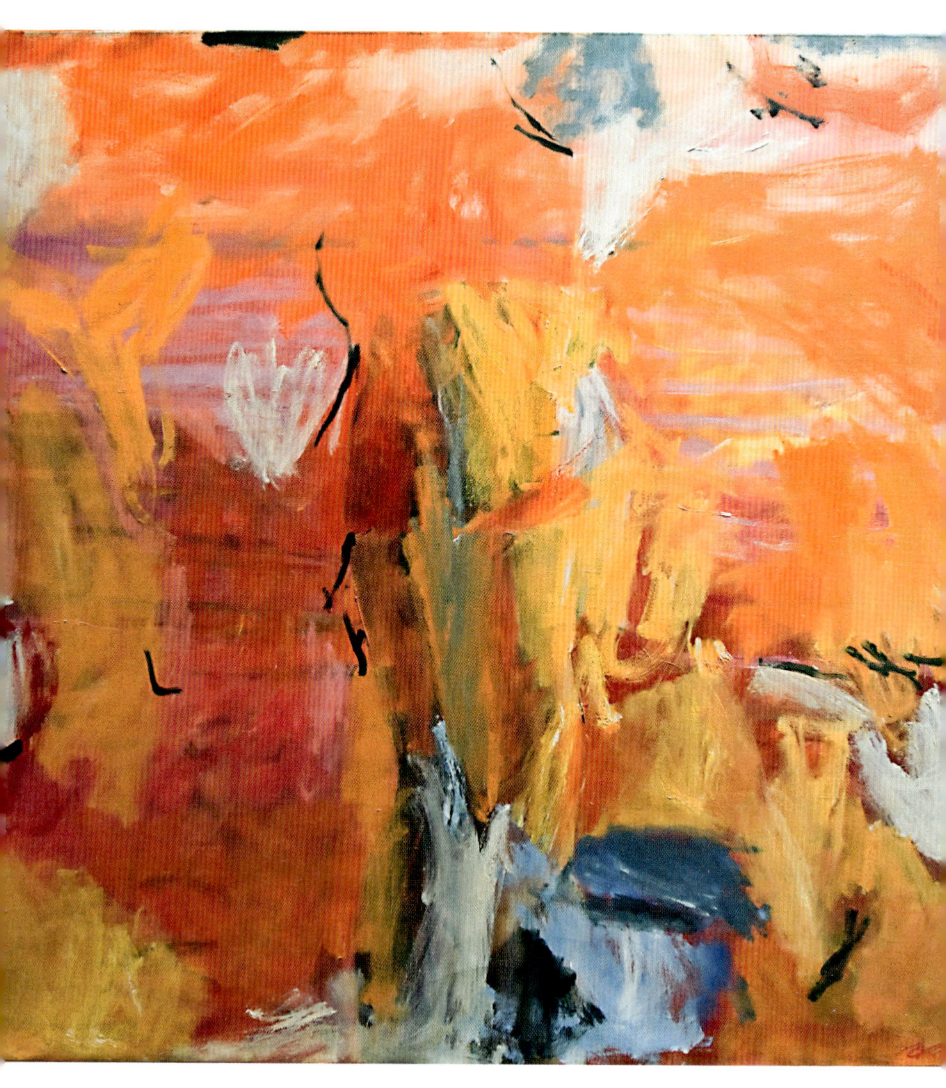

Day 186
August

These are bright colours, however, they are sad for me. My father, Bernard Kampf, died that August and this is the work I painted during that very sorrowful month in 1993. He was born in Kenya in 1913 to Jewish parents, an American father and English mother who lived in South Africa. They were different to the other early settlers. His contribution always involved doing good for the country and its people. He sat on many boards – Nairobi Hospital, the Prince of Wales School, the Agricultural Society, to name a few. He spent his life in service to Kenya, a life well-lived.

More Sand

The sandy colour of this work has something to
do with this title and also the French romantic
writer George Sand herself. Way ahead of
her time, she had many lovers, including the
composer Frédéric Chopin. This work has been
printed on to silk, which made lovely scarves,
and hessian for cushions and covered furniture.
The painting was part of the RaMoMA
Collection in Nairobi, Kenya. Now called EAVAT,
RaMoMA was the Museum of Modern Art in
Nairobi, started by Carol Lees and myself. It
ran for ten very successful years and its forced
closure in 2010 was a tragedy for the art of this
region. Ten years later (at the time of writing),
there is still nothing to take its place.

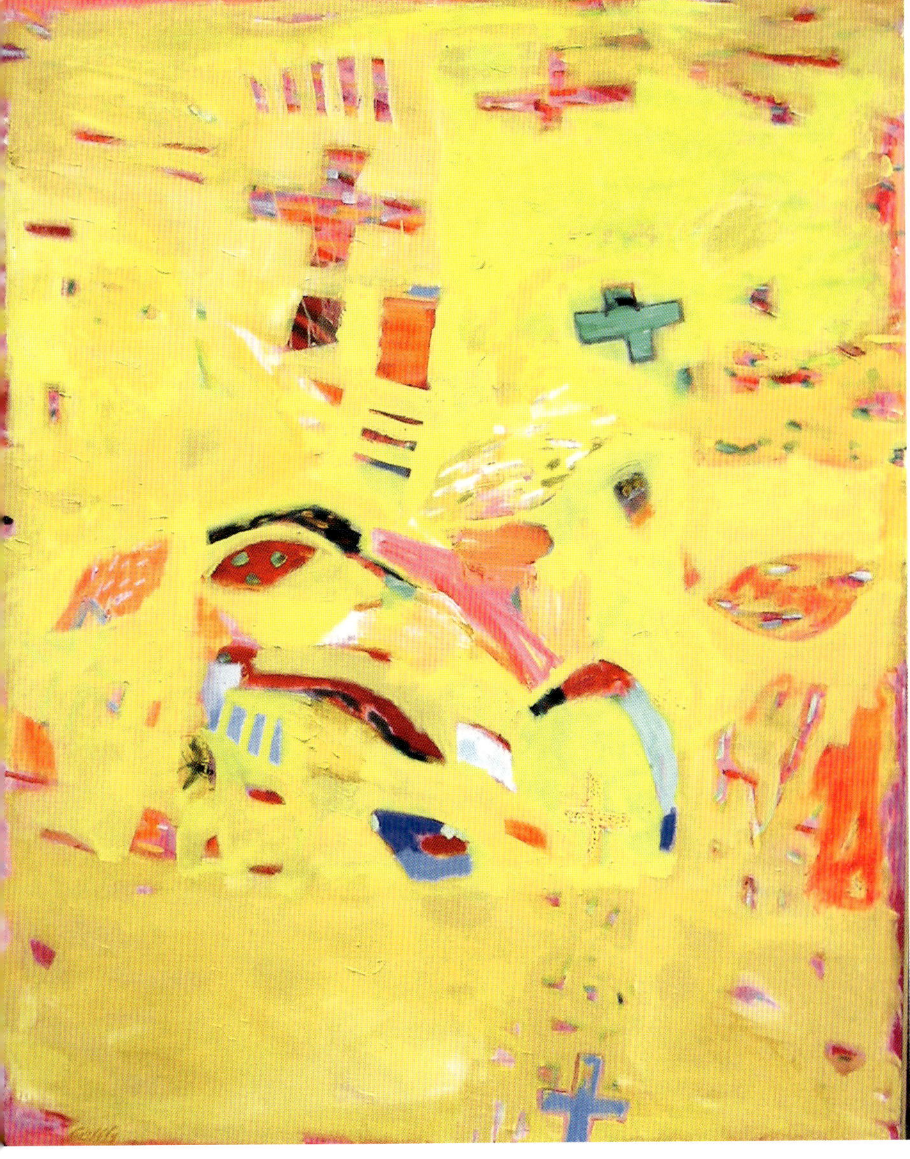

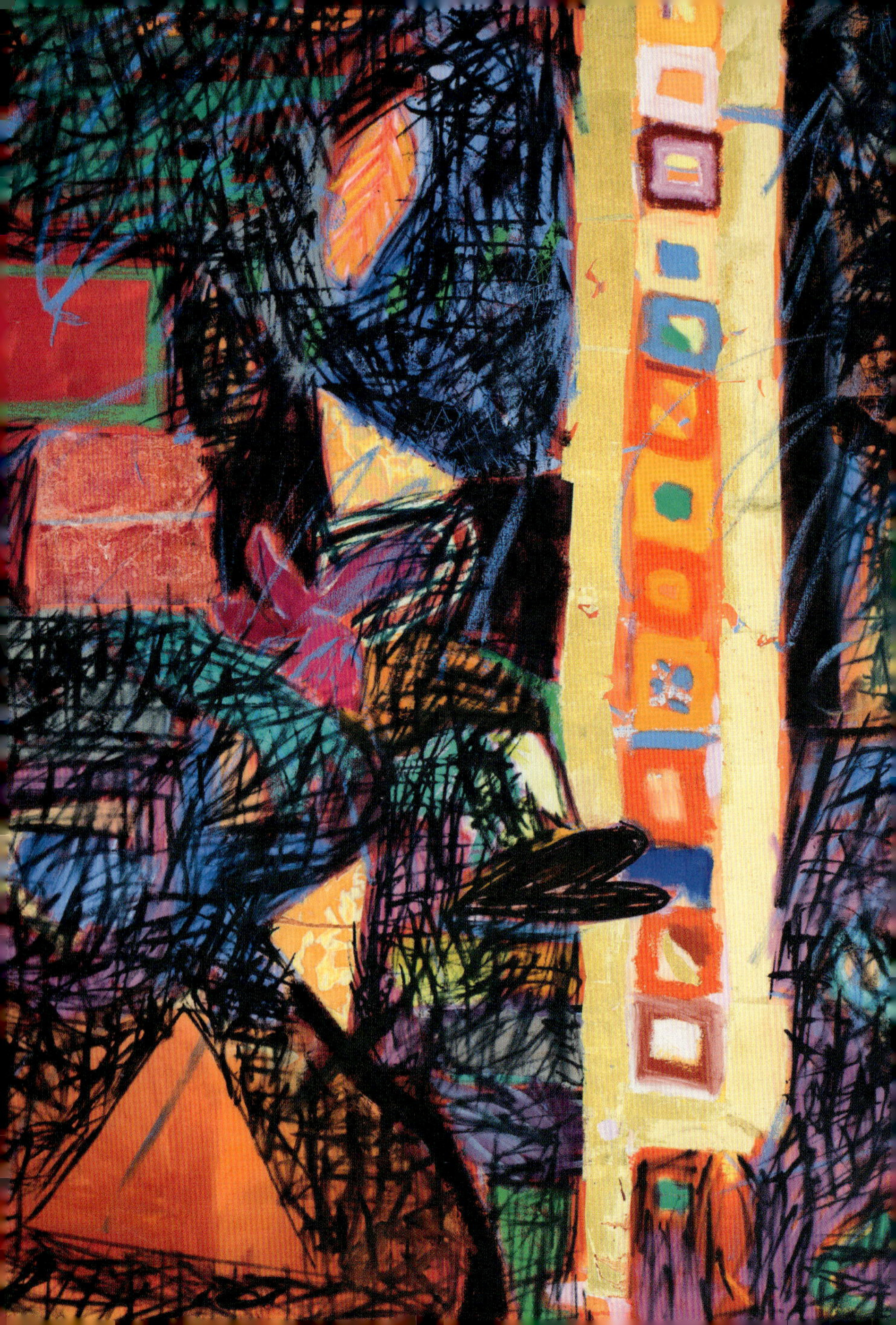

Day 188
Black Heart

This work is after Klimt, although nothing like
him except for the gold strip which is applied
gold leaf (and very difficult to administer).
I got a little lost in this one, and the solution
was to scribble over the whole thing in black.
It hangs here in our home in Nairobi.
A black heart describes someone or something
seen as innately evil or fundamentally corrupt.
I don't think this work has evil overtones,
as the colours balance the black and gold
shoots through. This painting works very well
as a horizontal. I am always undecided how to
hang it and so I change it from time to time to
make life more interesting.

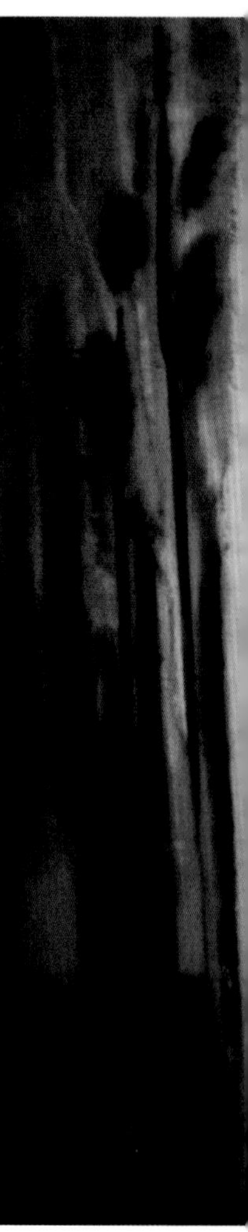

Day 189
First Impressions of the Forest

Painted when Karura Forest, the lungs of Nairobi,
first opened to the public. Near to the entrance,
I think these trees must be Blue Gums?
They are not indigenous.
I gave this painting to Graham Shaw MBE,
who kindly gave me so much of his time to help
me over a contemptible problem. I have never
encountered so much generosity and consideration
and real help in anyone. At the time, I could
not see the wood for the trees.

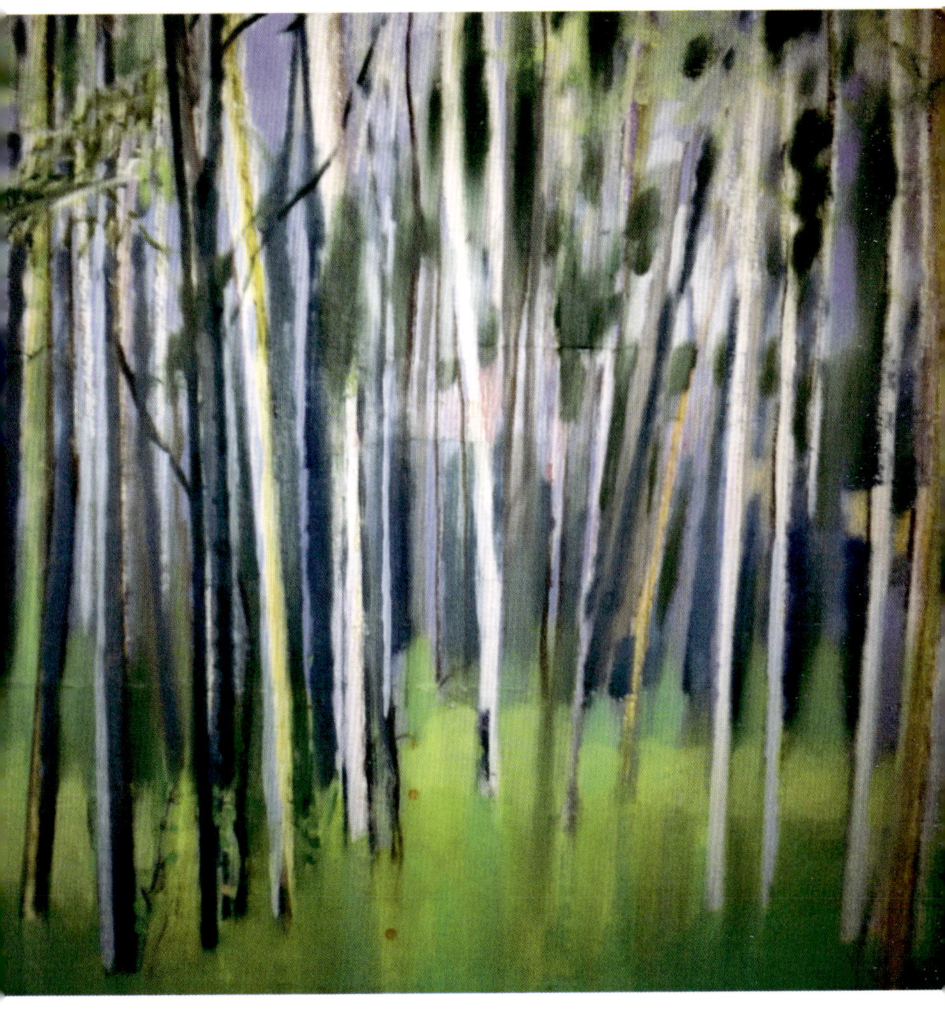

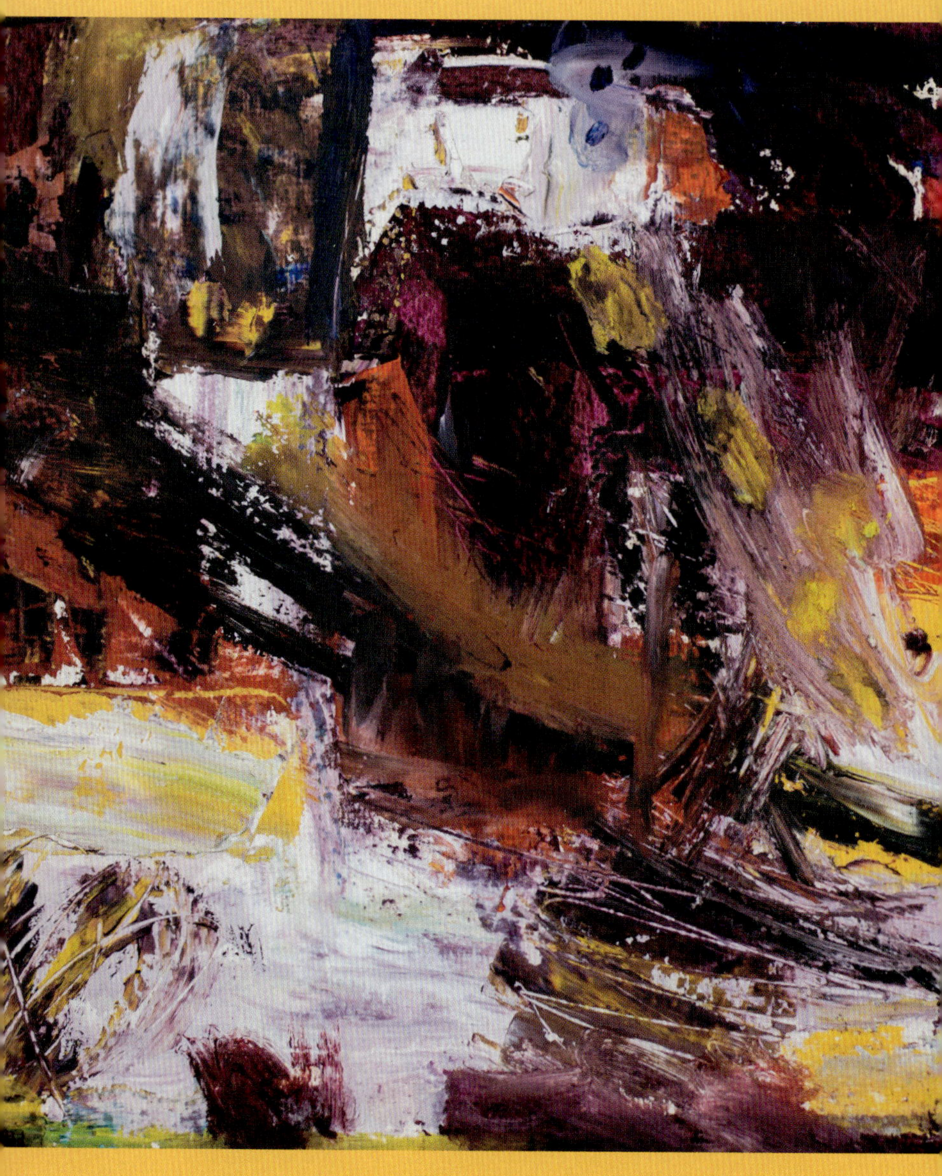

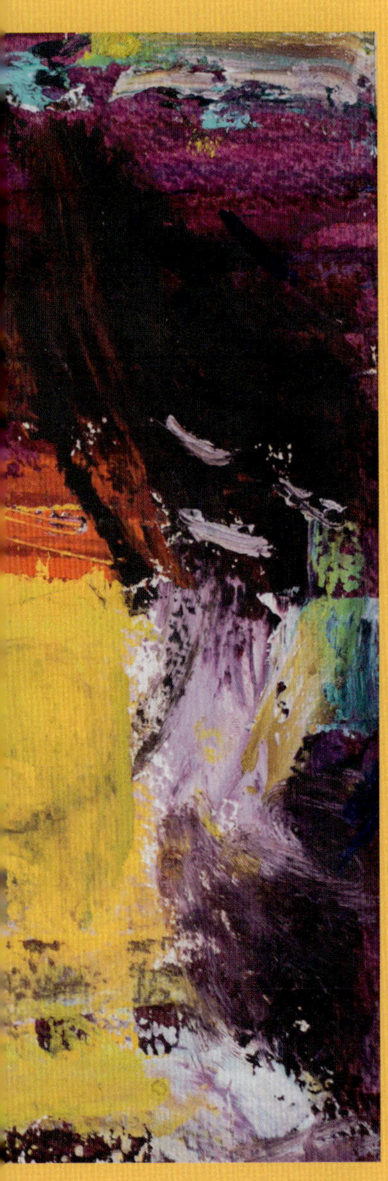

DAY 190

A quick daub to music
at the end of the day, with
the remnants of the oil
paint on the pallet.
The red rectangle holds
the composition.

The Road Home, Loresho

I painted this quiet, pretty road frequently during the forty years we lived in the Kibagare Valley. I can see this one was painted at midday, as the bauhinia and bougainvillea are sitting on their shadows. The picture was made into an attractive limited print in Holland. The printer pre-printed this in a gorgeous yellow hue. I loved it, so made a very unusual decision to go with the yellow, as it seemed to me a different work, all of its own.

Our oldest and dear friends Carol and George Zibarras own the original, which is this one. Carol was unimpressed with the yellow print. However, I matched it with another, *A Blue Road Home*, which looked well when hung together as a pair. Both prints were sold in John Lewis, London.

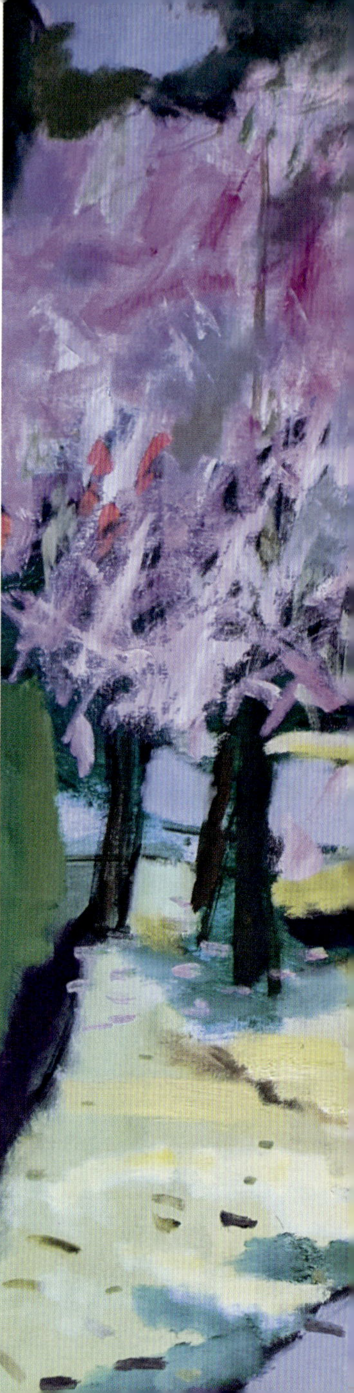

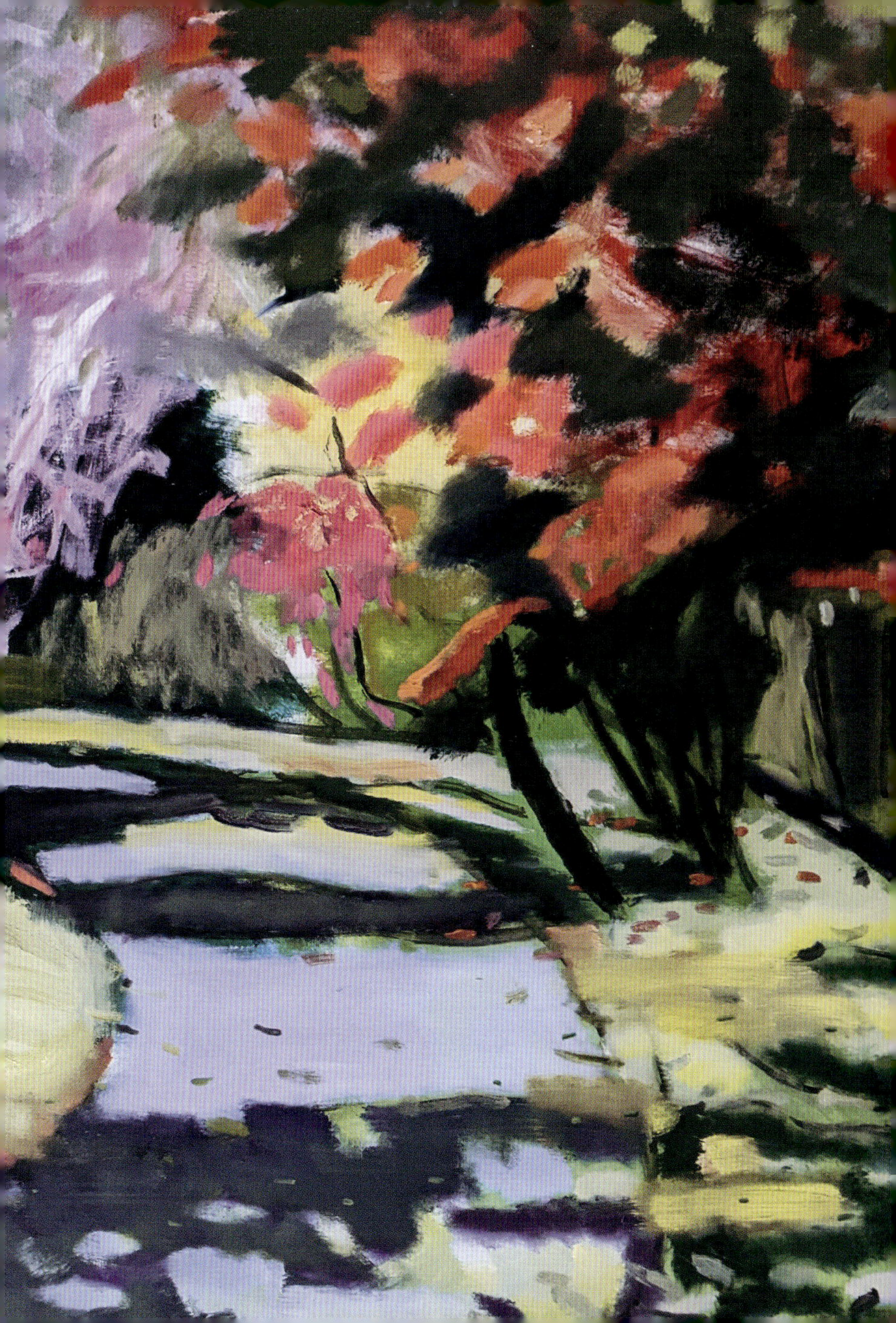

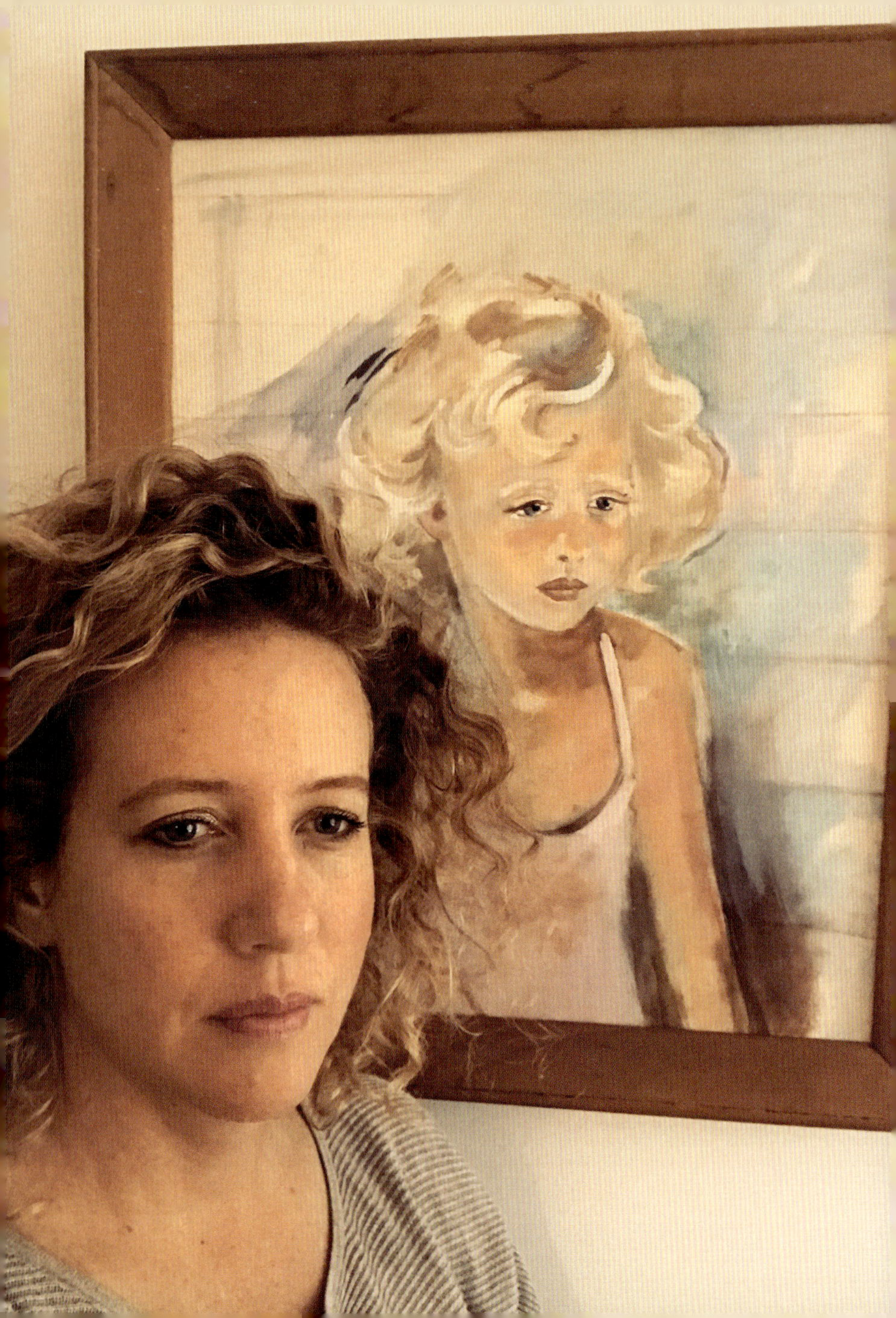

Daughter's Day

The painting is not the best of my
daughter Mia at just four years old,
but the hairstyle is the same, as well as
something about her eyes and mouth.
Today she is photographing a natural
cedar forest on the slopes of Mount
Kenya, following her bliss, always
standing in a field of opportunity.
I am so proud of my accomplished
daughter. In 2018 she won the National
Geographic Portrait prize, and many
other international competitions for
her photo series called 'Sunday Best
at the Weekend Studio', where she
photographed people in Kibera, one
of the largest informal settlements
in Kenya. She photographs for the
Sheldrick Wildlife Trust and produced
a stunning large book, *The Unsung
Heroes*, about the extraordinary,
dedicated people who devote their
lives to help save orphaned elephants.

<u>DAY 193</u>

Sailing

Four brick-like canvases,
painted round thick sides.
I gave it away to somebody who
was deserving. It was one of the
hardest works to give away,
as I loved it and still do. The golden
mean is in every quadrant, and the
brushstrokes are mixed with thick oil
sticks. It has movement and space,
and I feel the motion of the water.
The work belongs to Donna Donahoo,
Vancouver Island.

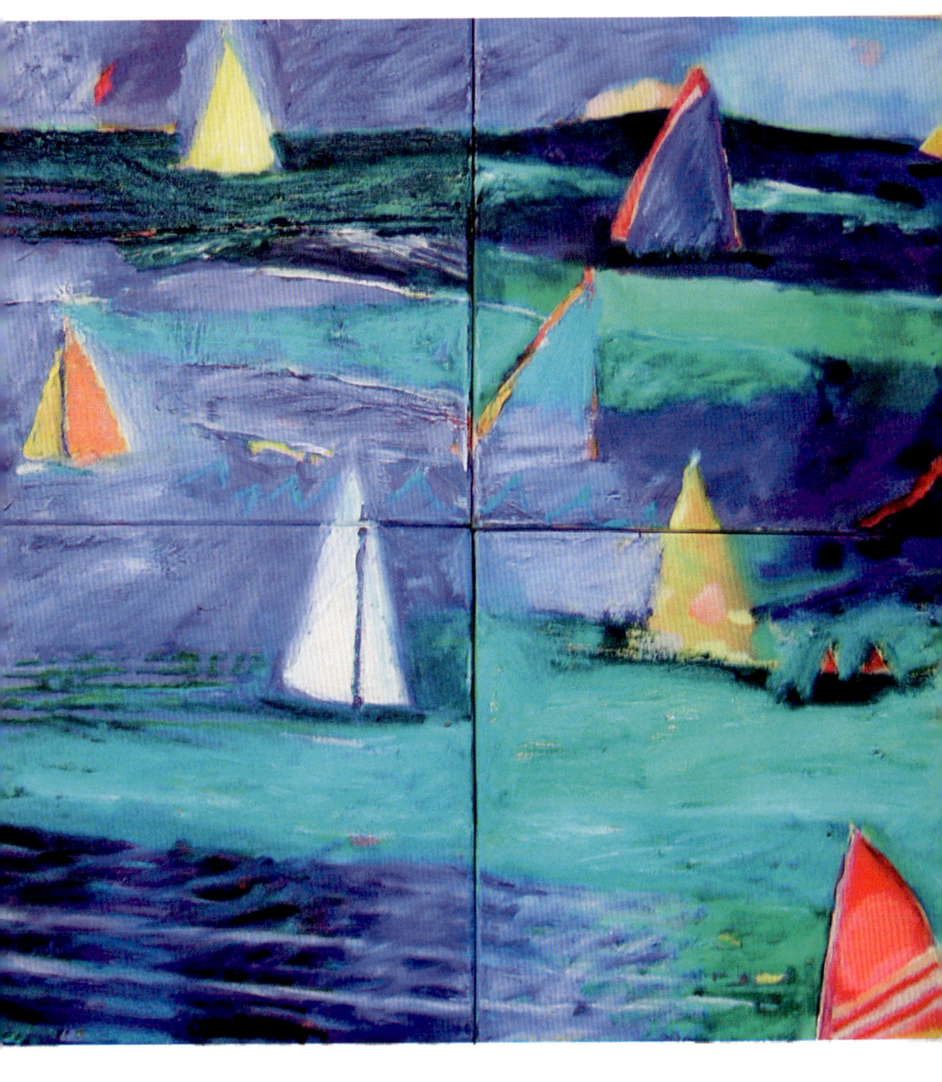

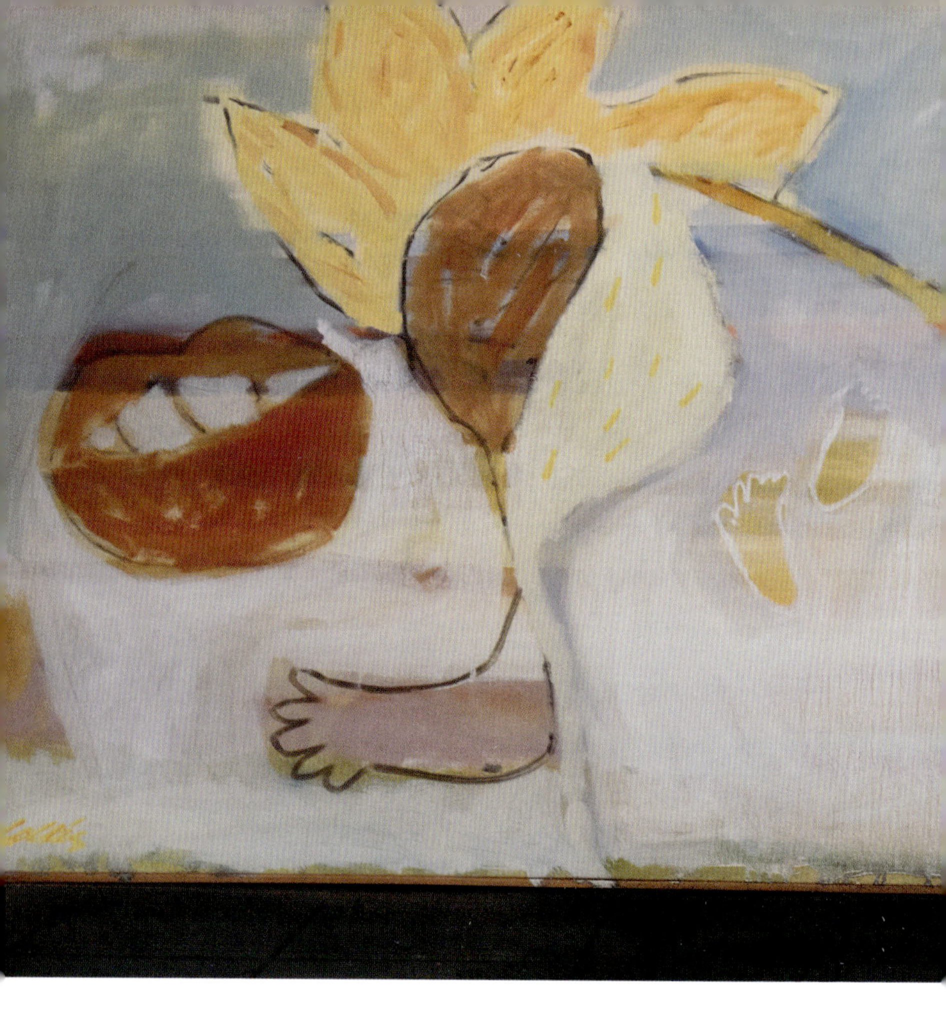

My beloved son, Fabian, a podiatrist, has a very
successful practice and is devoted to his work. He is
pursuing his passion and doing good. He is admired and
respected by his patients, and I, his mother, know that
he is a healer and doing what he was born to do. I adore

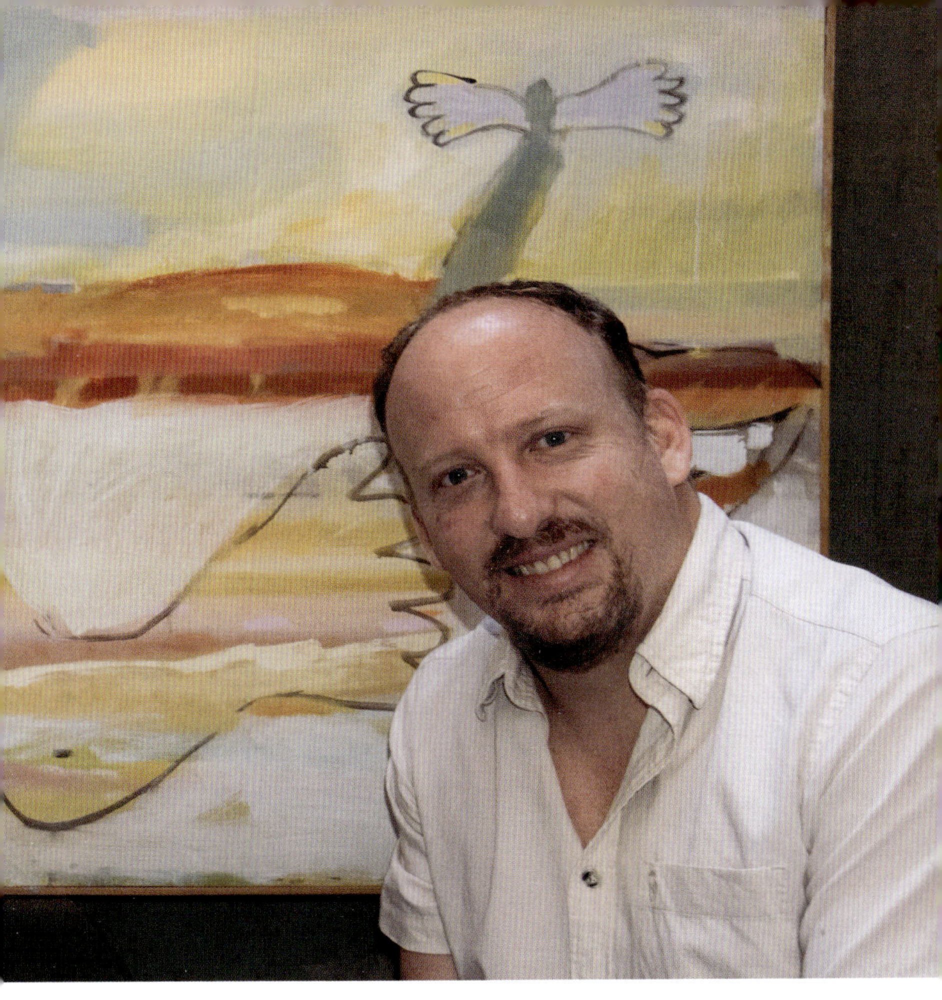

his wife Jilna and my two grandsons Jayden and Dylan. Fabian has brought great joy into my life.

I think he thought he was going to get a landscape when he asked me to paint a picture for his surgery. He was a bit shocked when I came up with this one. It has an obvious title, though Fabian asked me not to mention it!

Wild Flowers

After a day's drive up the
west coast of South Africa,
we saw some spring flowers,
just past Langebaan, a beautiful
phenomenon sometimes
referred to as 'the garden of the
Gods'. The wild flowers come
out from August to October and
this year we are missing them.

Her heart was wild,
but I didn't want to catch it,
I wanted to run with it,
to set mine free.

Atticus

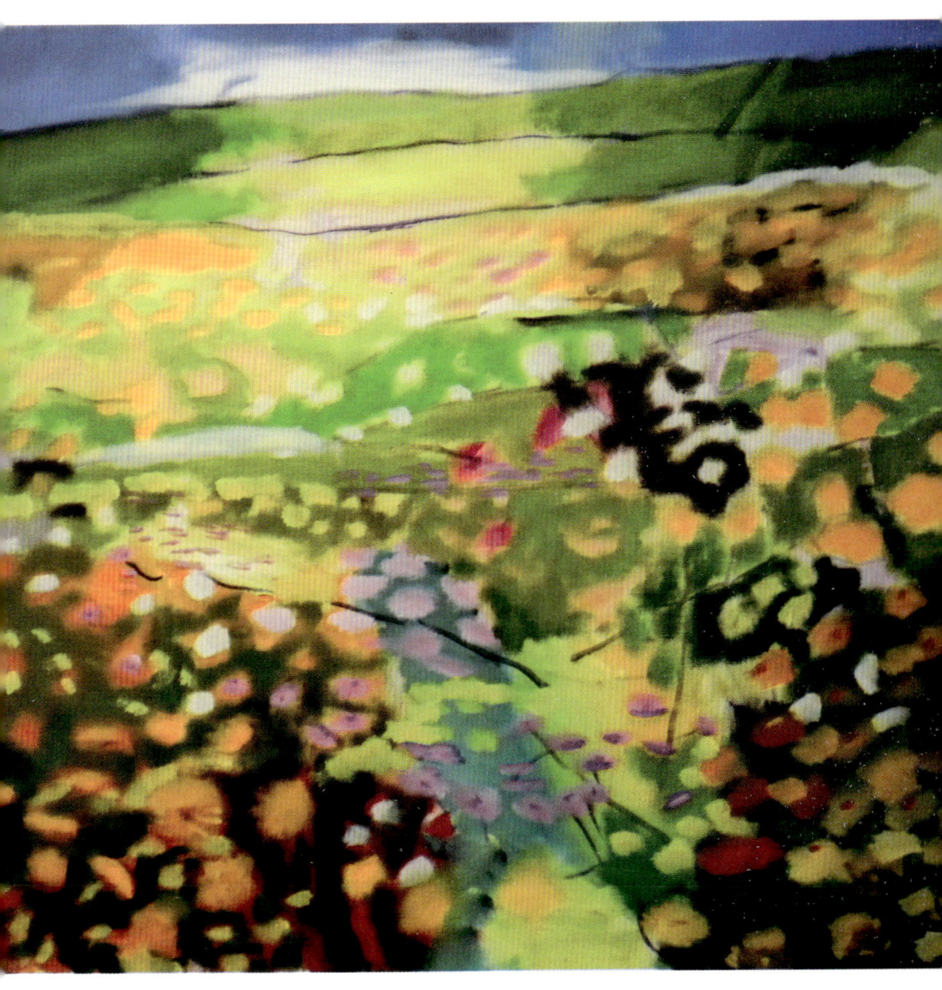

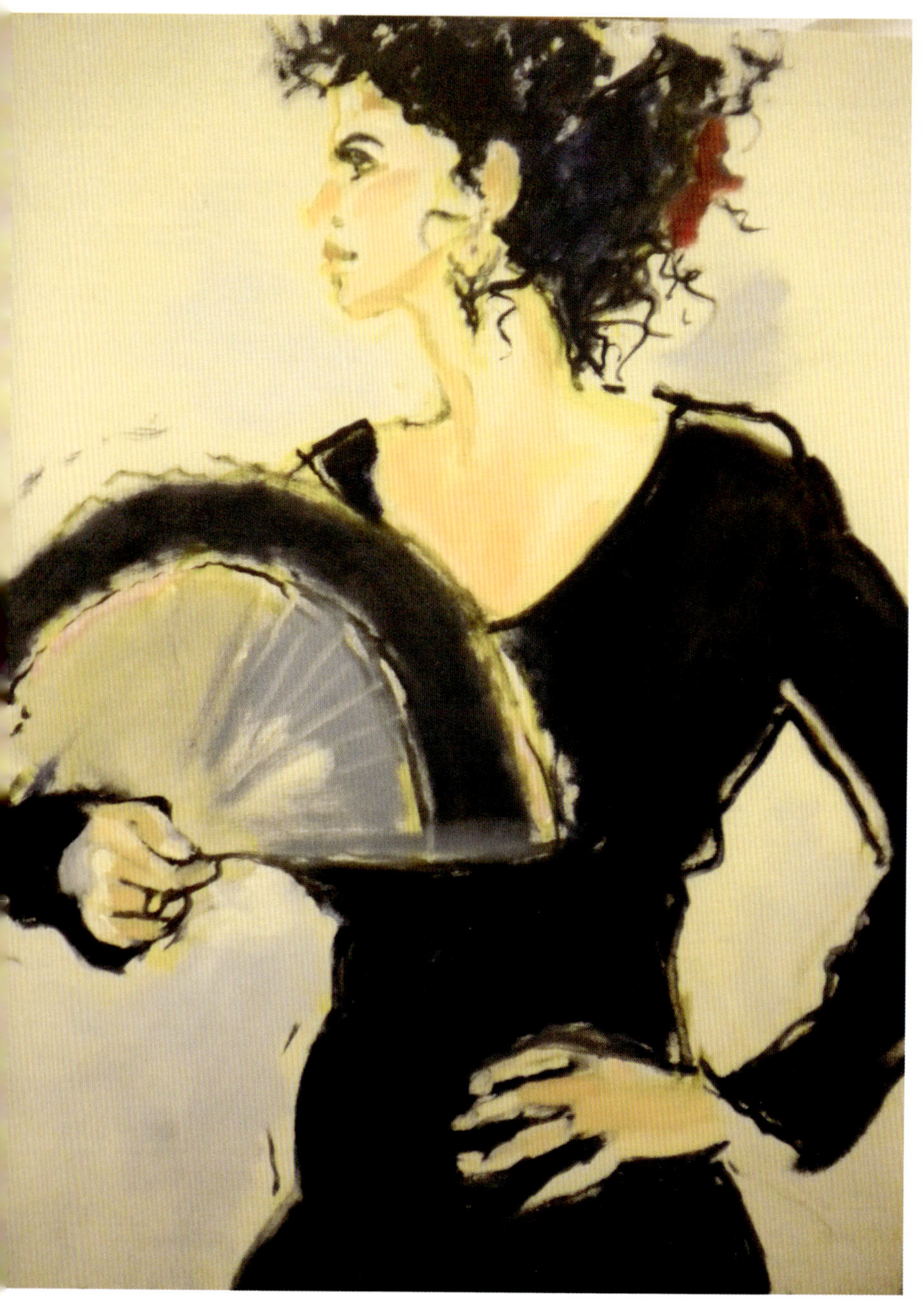

Girl with Fan

A day with Sophie in her studio
with a gorgeous model, which
generated many other works.

Day 197
Winter, Four Seasons, Vivaldi

In the early 1990s I was thinking about
music, about how each sound has colour.
There is a word for this phenomenon,
'synaesthesia'. Chords are interesting, made
up of many notes, often four on the right
hand, and two, three or four notes with
the left. The vibration and sound would
carry and in the case of this series of quick
sketches, how one could paint a whole
season or a movement?
This is one of many works of that time,
which eventually moved into sculpture
with painted wooden strips, so the
sound was not bound by the edges
of the paper and the visual would
move out like the vibration.

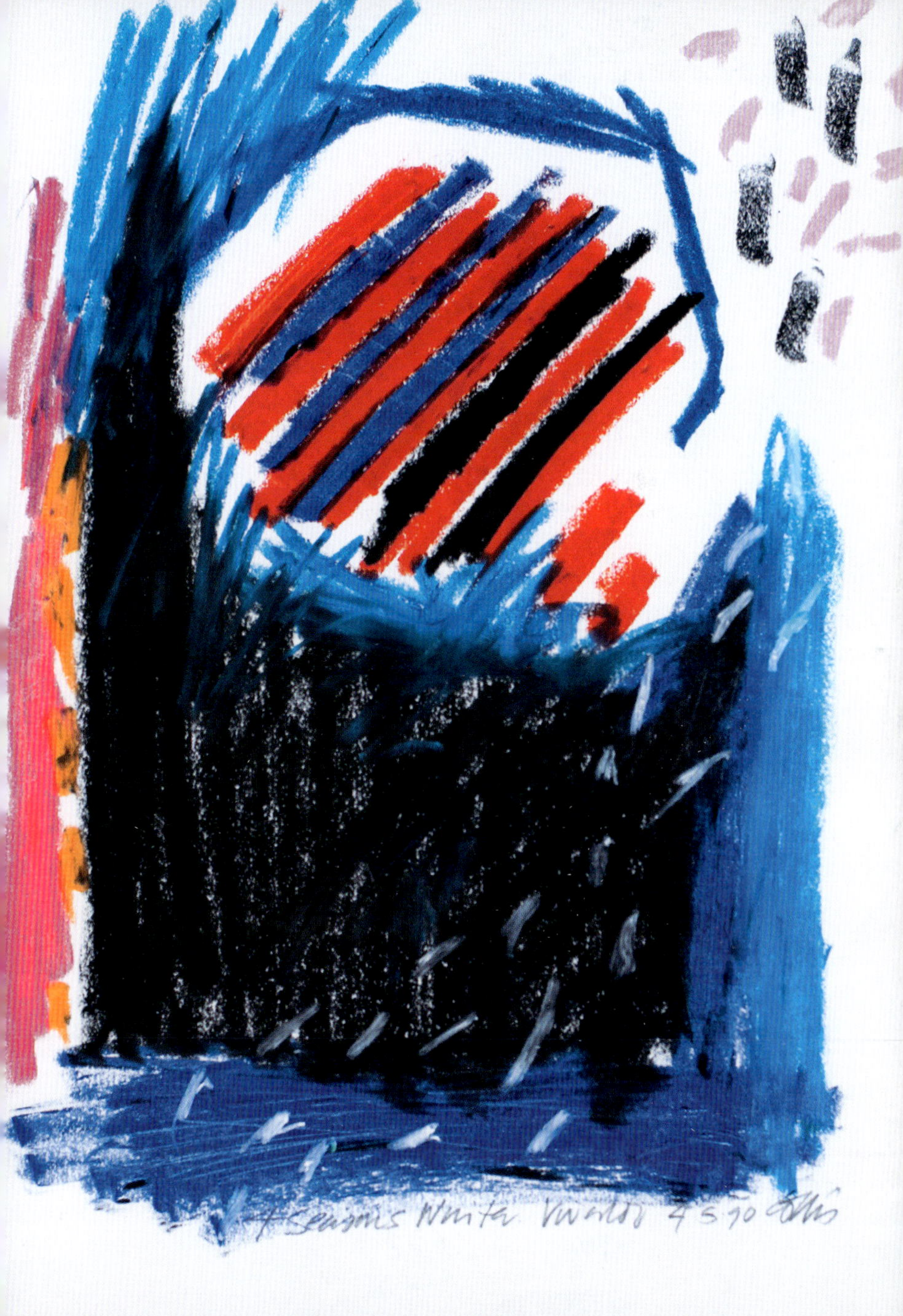
4 Seasons Winter Vivaldi 4.5.90

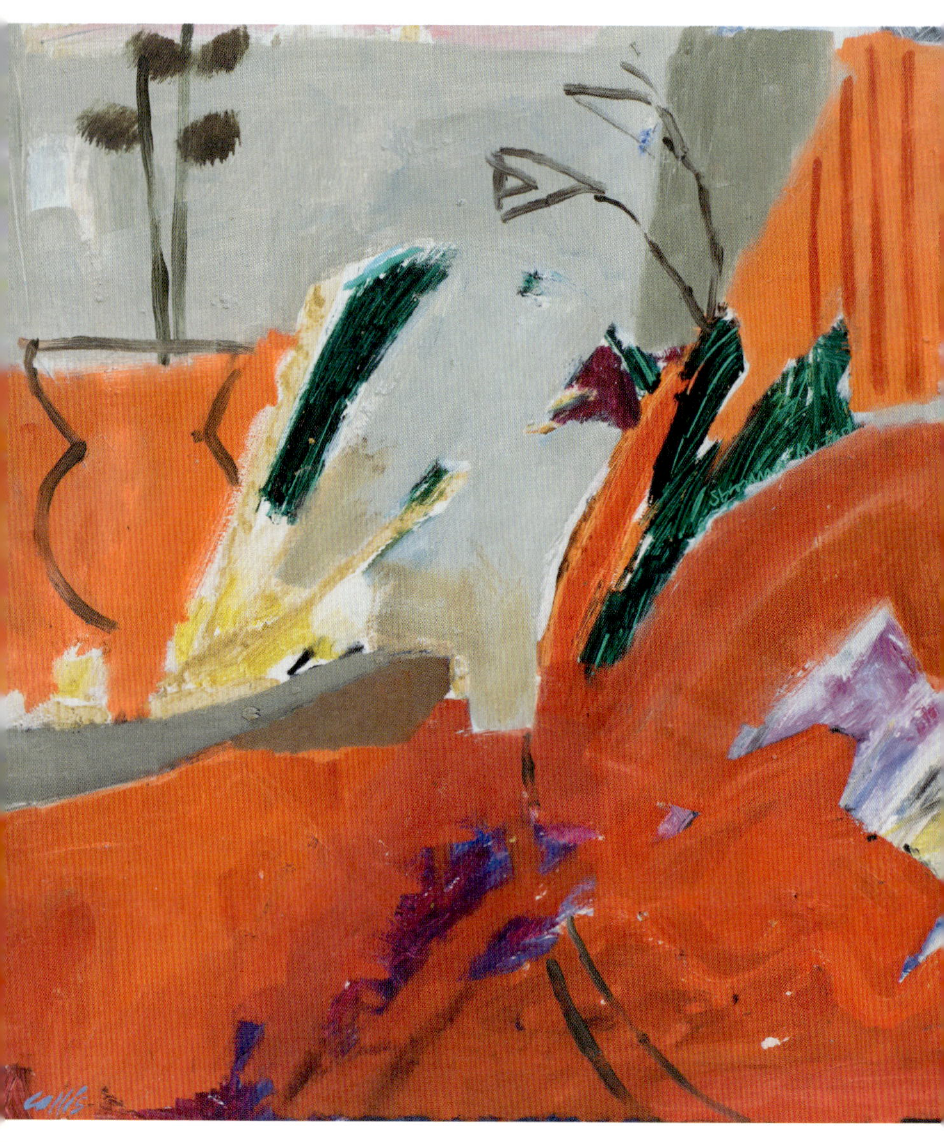

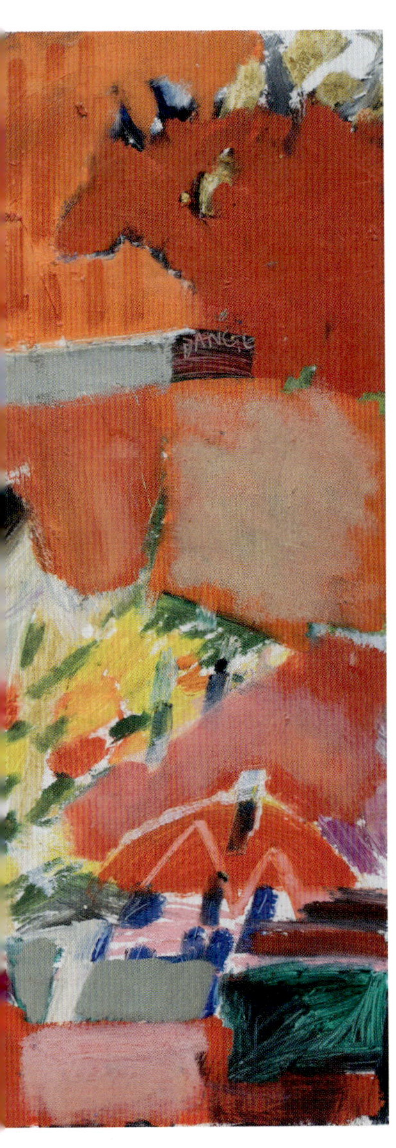

Day 198
Untitled, oil on cardboard

A large piece currently in storage,
where a lot of my work languishes.
I had nowhere to put it after we
moved house.
I like the composition of this effort,
the balance and the colour.
I am looking for the right studio,
as I am presently still working in a
small hut in a friend's garden.

Day 199
Perspex

Acrylic on Perspex, which is why it is
so bright. The plastic refracts the light,
and the work is lit from inside. The idea
was (but it did not happen) to cook the
Perspex over the gas flame, which would
bend the plastic into wonderful shapes.
(One has to wear a mask, so as not to
inhale the fumes.) I liked this so much
I never cooked it! The heating of
the plastic was an idea I pinched
from my most and very creative friend,
Stups Gollmer, whom I regard as
the best and most creative artist
that I know personally.

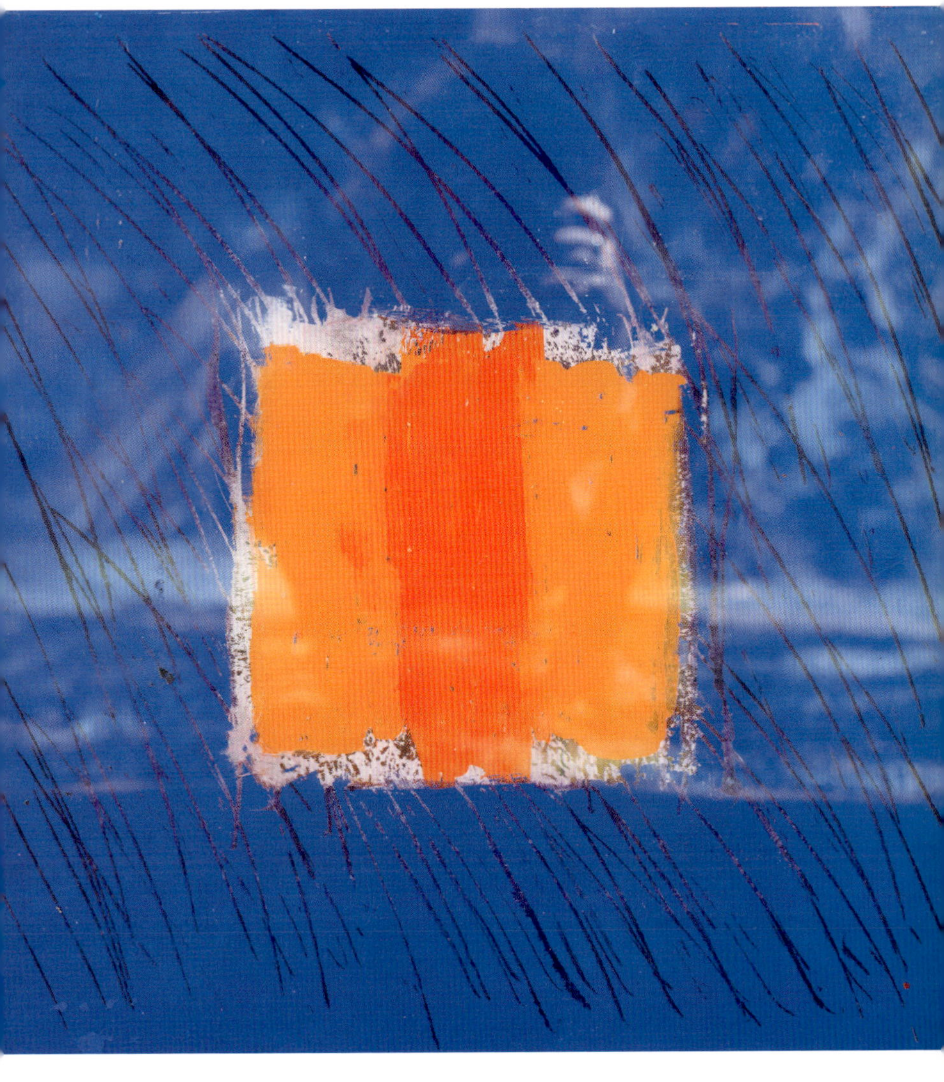

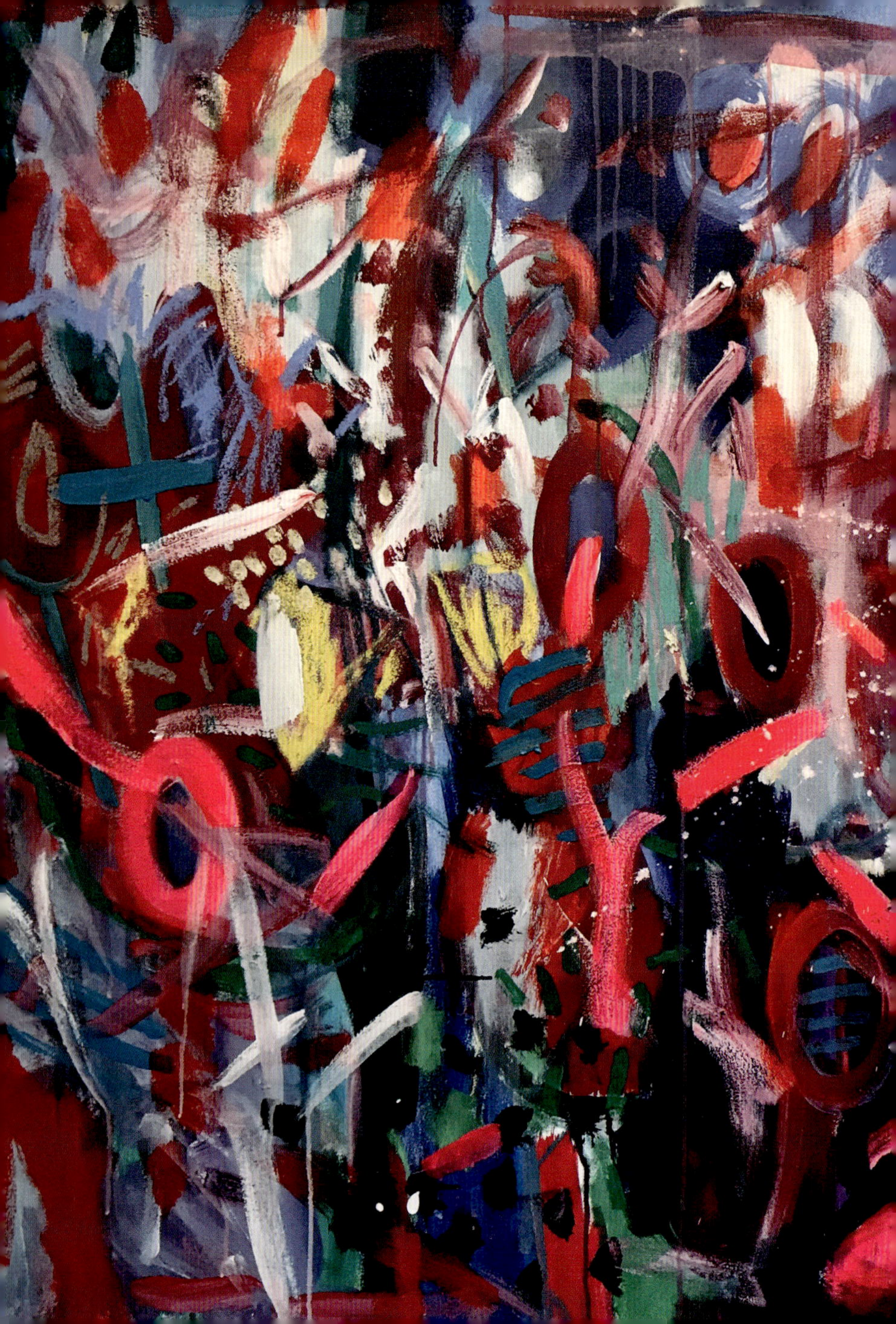

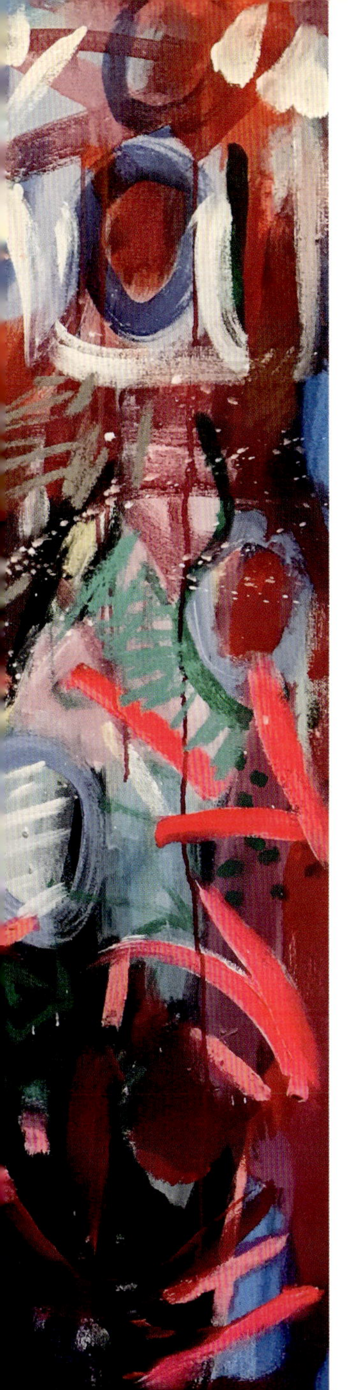

Frustration at the continued lockdown and restriction of movement. What has happened to normal people? I am worrying about common sense and what is becoming of us all. For the first time in the history of mankind, healthy people are quarantined for a 'virus' that is highly survivable. Painted for an exhibition called 'Artists Against Hunger'.

The following six works belong together as The Clusterfuck Series. In the Lockdown Diary they appeared as they were completed during the year. For this book, I have put this latest series together as if they were being exhibited in a gallery. Action painting is an emotional way to paint, where one paints a feeling on to the canvas and waits for the 'feeling' to speak back. The theory is that the painting paints itself.

Day 201
The World Looks Better ...
(Through Rose Colour Grasses)

The first of the 'Clusterfuck' paintings,
completed after weeks and weeks,
off and on, working on it. Acrylic and oil on
heavy canvas. I found some acrylic pens in
the Japanese shop in Nairobi, which added
to the mark-making and helped pull
the whole thing together.
I asked my friends on Facebook to name
this painting (title inspired by Jolene Wood).

128 x 128 cm
The Clusterfuck Series

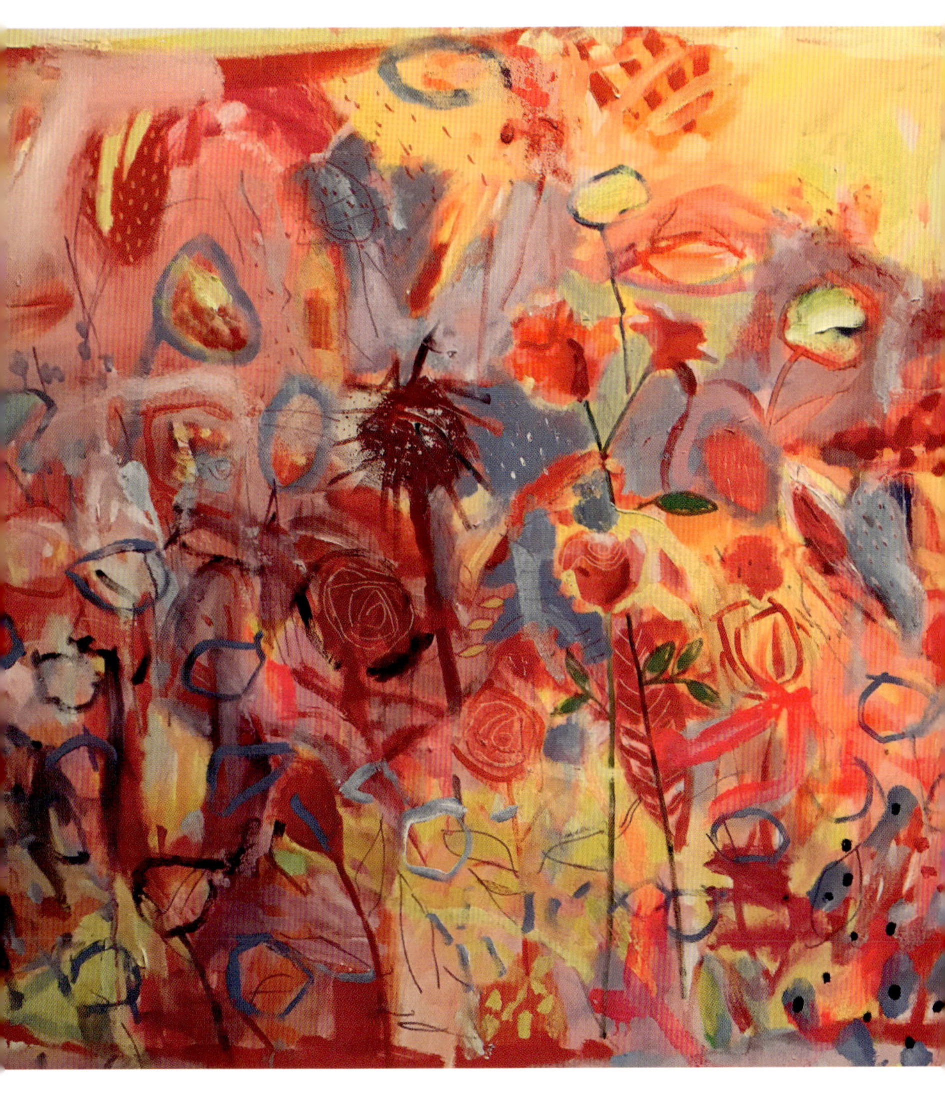

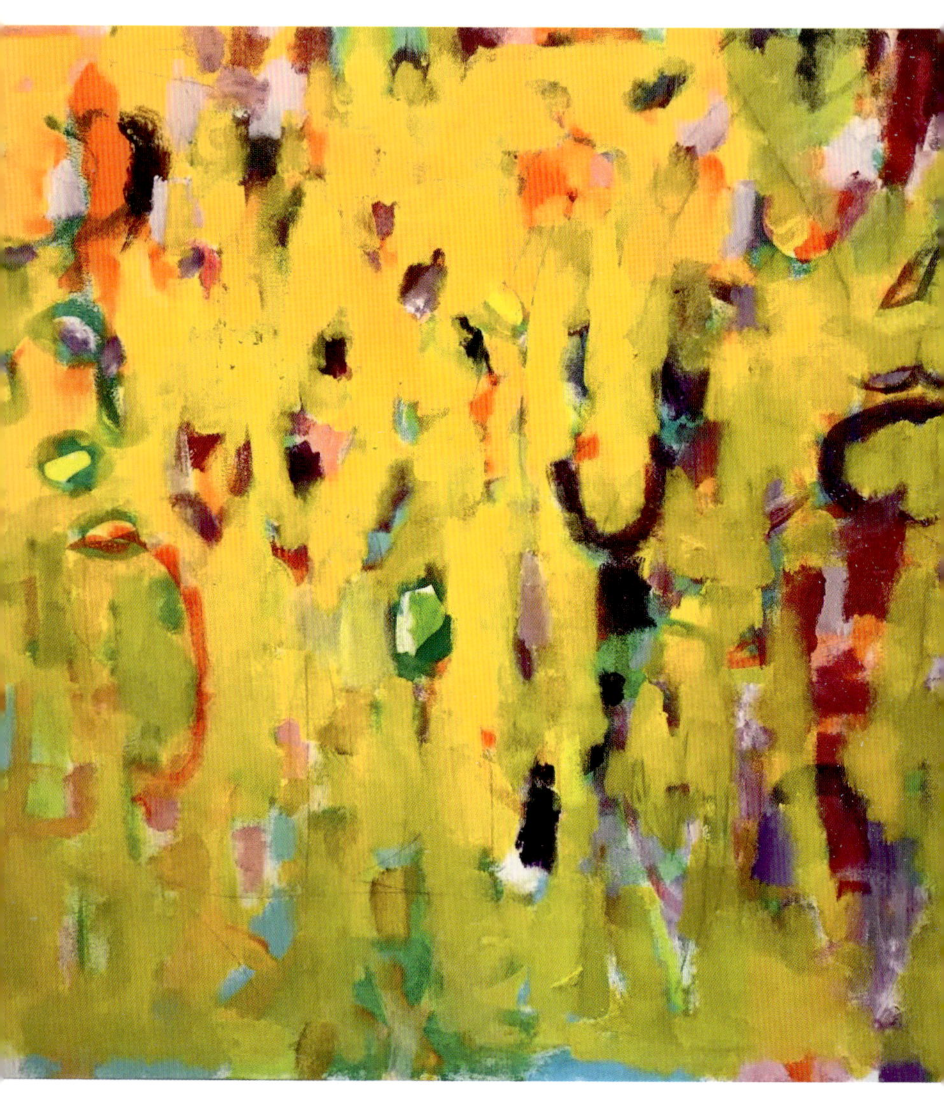

WAITIKO

I have been painting up a storm in my
studio; this is the eighth composition of the
'Clusterfuck' series that I have been working on
since all our lives were altered in a most weird
and uncommon way, over a virus that has a
death rate of 0.04% (at the time of writing).
I like to think that these particular yellows are
slightly sickly and uncomfortable to look at.
'WAITIKO' is a word the First Nations people
used to explain a brain blindness, sometimes
achieved by a hallucinogenic drug.

The Clusterfuck Series

Day 203
Clusterfuck

I heard this excellent expression
recently and thought it was perfect
to title this latest work of mine.
It describes a world which is wearing
a bit thin on me at this moment
in time: 24 July 2020. I understand
why some people feel deceived and
misinformed by the mainstream
media and governments, the
suspicion that this is actually about
a technocratic coup d'état, with the
'virus' as a manipulation tool and
not the main issue. This painting
is huge, like the mess.

The Clusterfuck Series

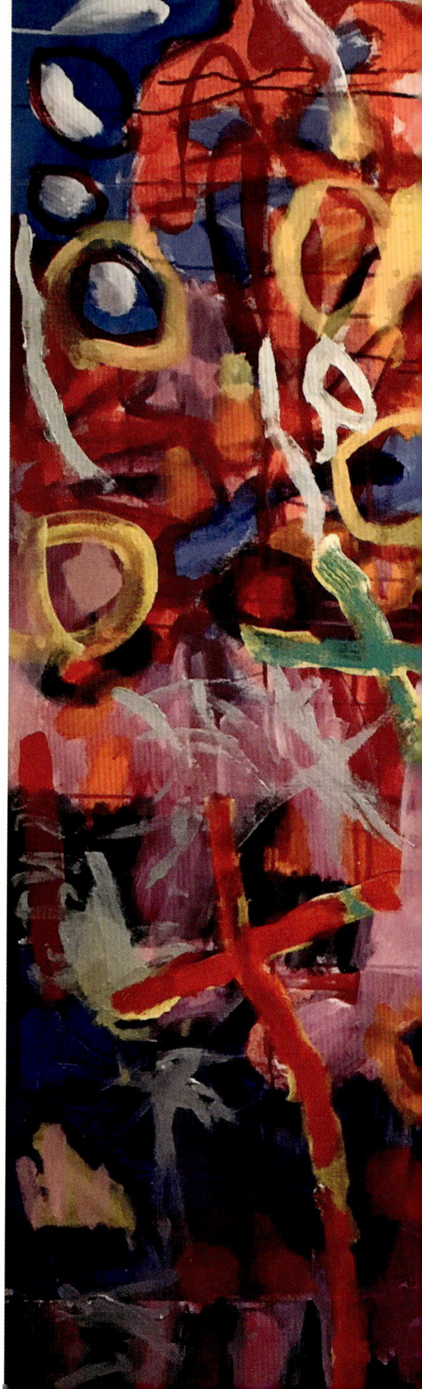

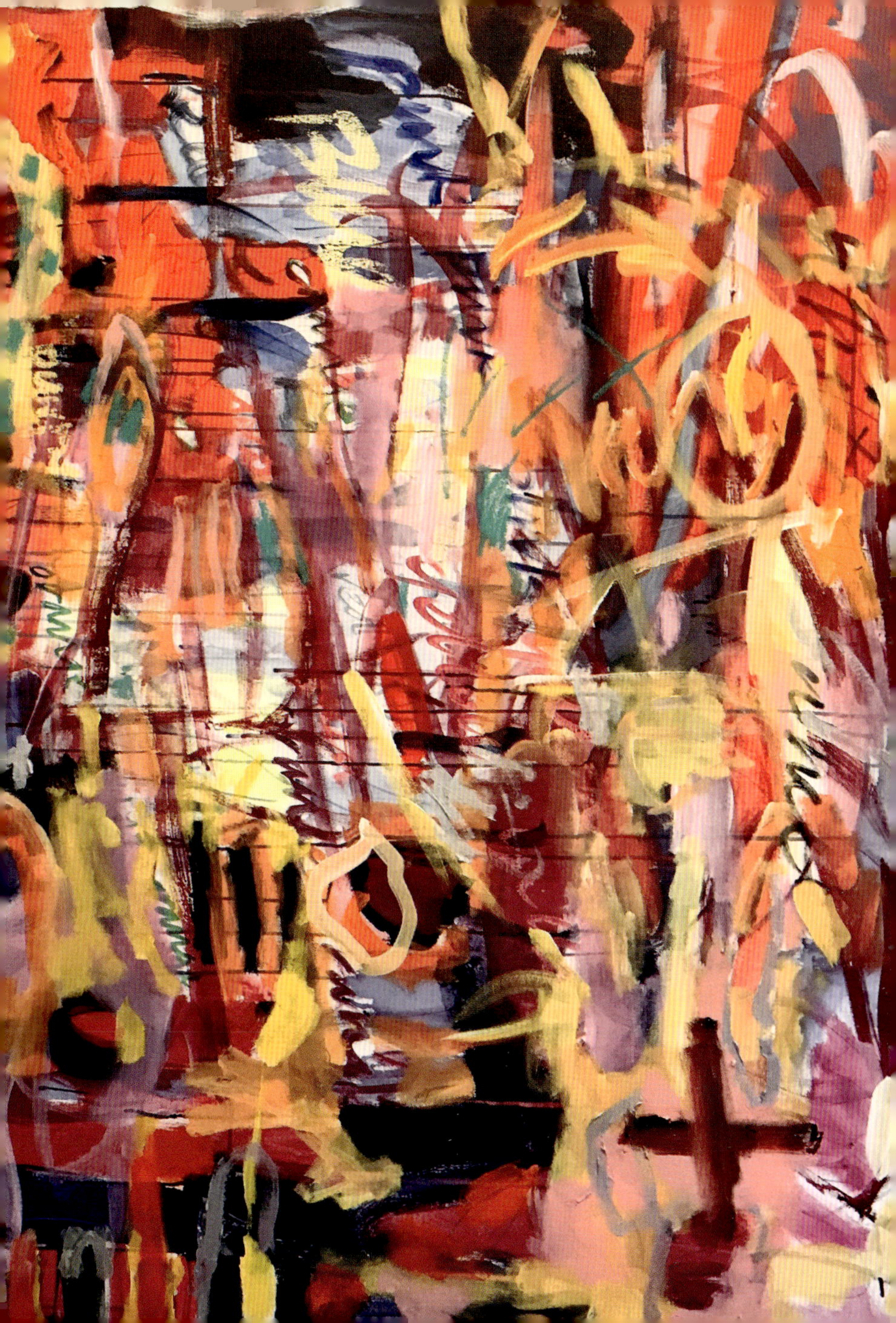

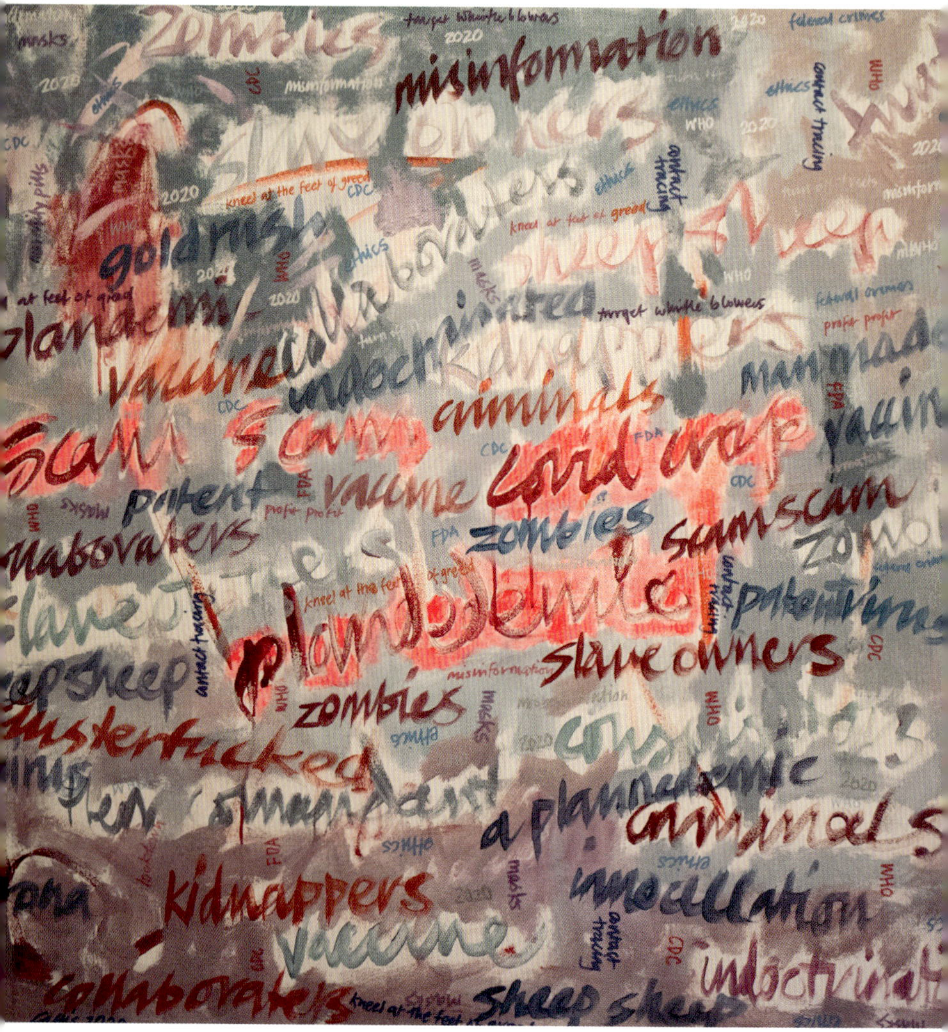

zombies 2020
masks
2020
ethics
CDC
misinformation
target whistle blowers
2020
misinformation
2020
federal crimes
ethics
WHO
ethics
2020
contact tracing
WHO
2020
misinform
slave owners
monthly pills
WHO
contact tracing
ethics
CDC
kneel at the feet of greed
kneel at feet of greed
sheep sheep sheep
misinfo
goldrush
at feet of greed
2020
WHO
ethics
2020
masks
target whistle blowers
federal crimes
profit profit
plandemi-
vaccine
indoctrinated
man made
FDA
CDC
scam scam criminals
CDC
FDA
covid crop
vacin
patent
FDA
profit profit
vacine
FDA
zombies
scam scam
ZOMBI
labovaters
WHO
masks
FDA
kneel at the feet of greed
patent virus
CDC
slave
plandemic
WHO
misinformation
slave owners
sheep
contact tracing
zombies
masks
ethics
misinformation
2020
clusterfucked
mandate
cows
a plandemic
criminals
FDA
ethics
masks
2020
contact tracing
ethics
inoculation
WHO
kidnappers
2020
ANA
CDC
vaccine
contact tracing
CDC
indoctrin
collaborators
kneel at the feet of greed
masks
ethics
sheep sheep
scam
ethics 2020

WHO?

This is an unpleasant work, horrid colours about a despicable subject. I risk losing a few supporters. What happened, that we cannot all get along in-spite of our opinions? Divide and rule. There are many people keeping their staff inside their compounds, for months, at the time of writing. I would understand it better if they themselves were self-incarcerated. Generally they move about whilst their staff remain trapped. I have to ask, what has happened to normal people?

The Clusterfuck Series

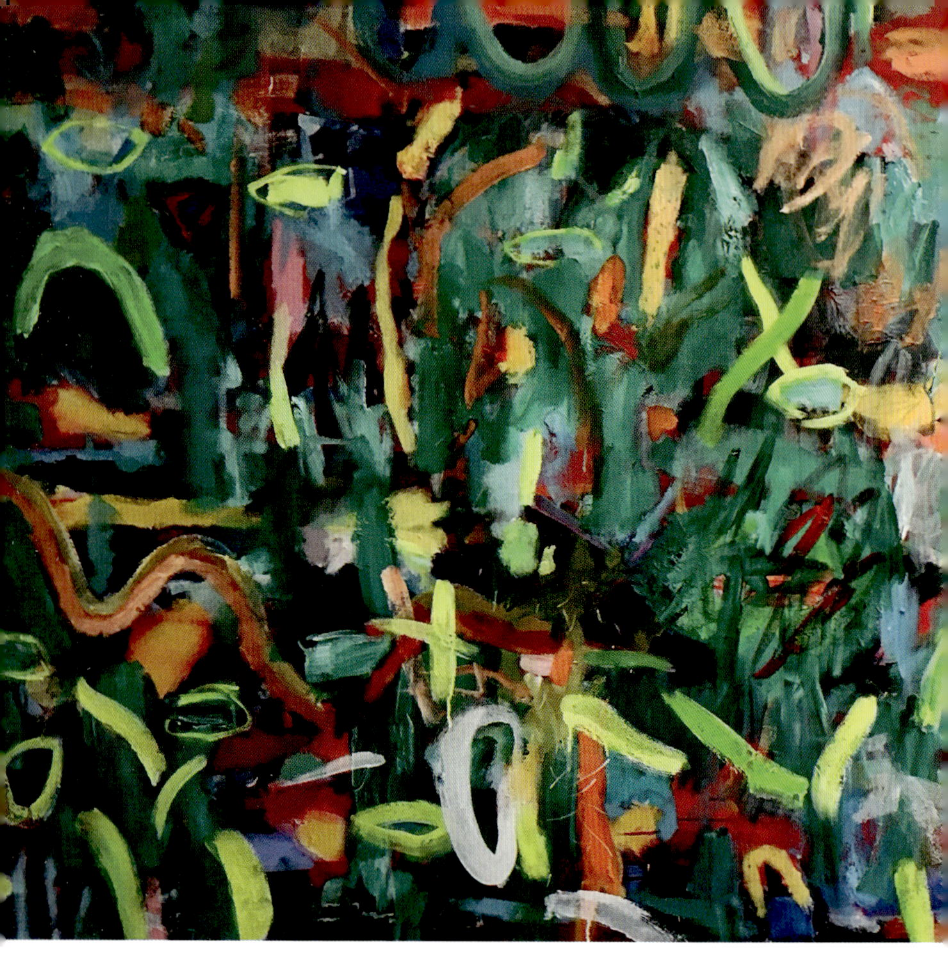

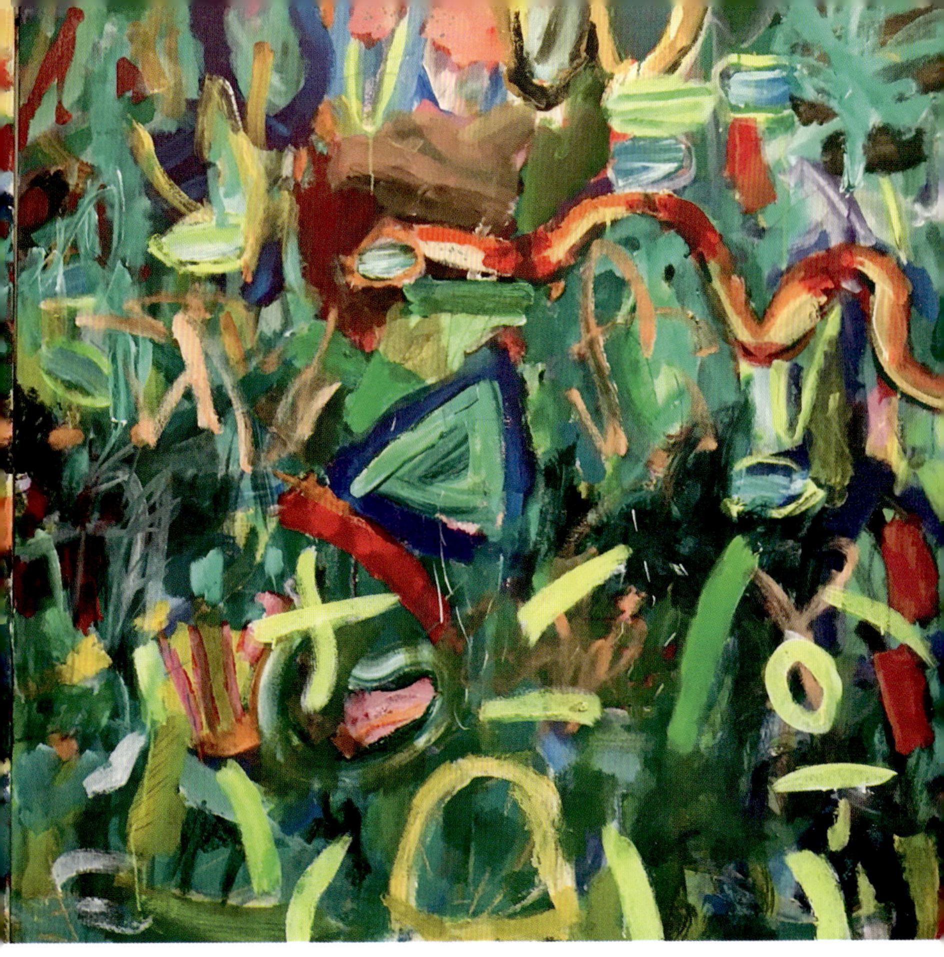

Day 205
AGENDA

For anyone who would like to know what this painting is all about, please check out the UN non-binding charter, 'Agenda 21'. All 400+ pages of it. The Wikipedia version is shortened and very 'sweetened'.

7ft-wide acrylic diptych
The Clusterfuck Series

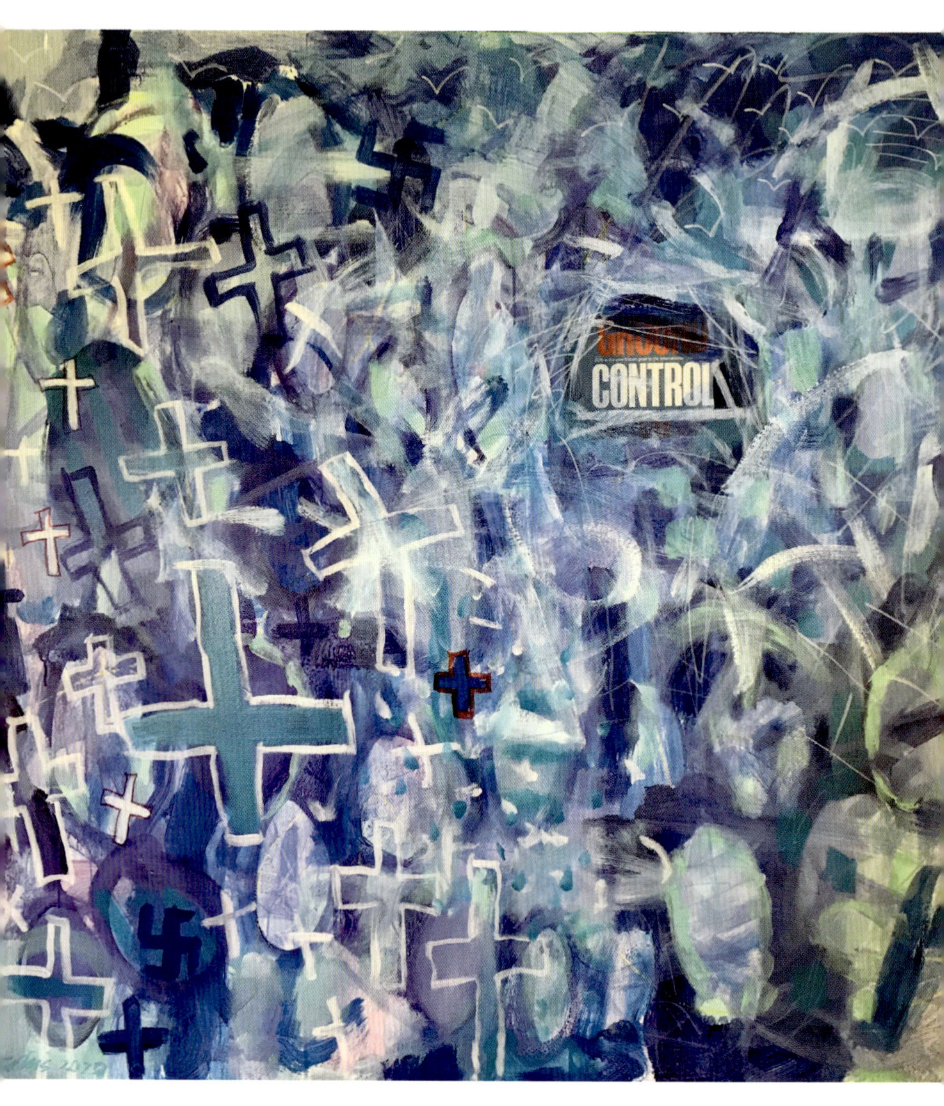
CONTROL

Tyranny

It seems to me that many in the world have
unwittingly sold their soul to the Globalists.
Are governments propagandising against their
people? Many believe they are fighting a virus
when the real virus feels like tyranny.
Anti-social distancing, muzzles, lockdowns,
no church, no schools, big Pharma and
vaccines. Crimes against humanity.
The longer people continue to cooperate with
their own enslavement, the longer the tyranny
will prevail. UK, Canada, Europe, Australia,
Israel, South Africa and now America are all
being subjugated, at the time of writing.
The world has never known the like before.

The Clusterfuck Series

DAY 207
THE ROAD HOME

Our road in Kibagare Valley,
a constant source of inspiration,
especially in October, when the
whole valley is in blossom.
I painted it every year for forty years.
This was a very early one and it was
shown in London at a one-woman
show at the Mall Galleries, courtesy
of the McEwan Gallery, and the
greeting card company of that time,
Medici, made it into my first card.

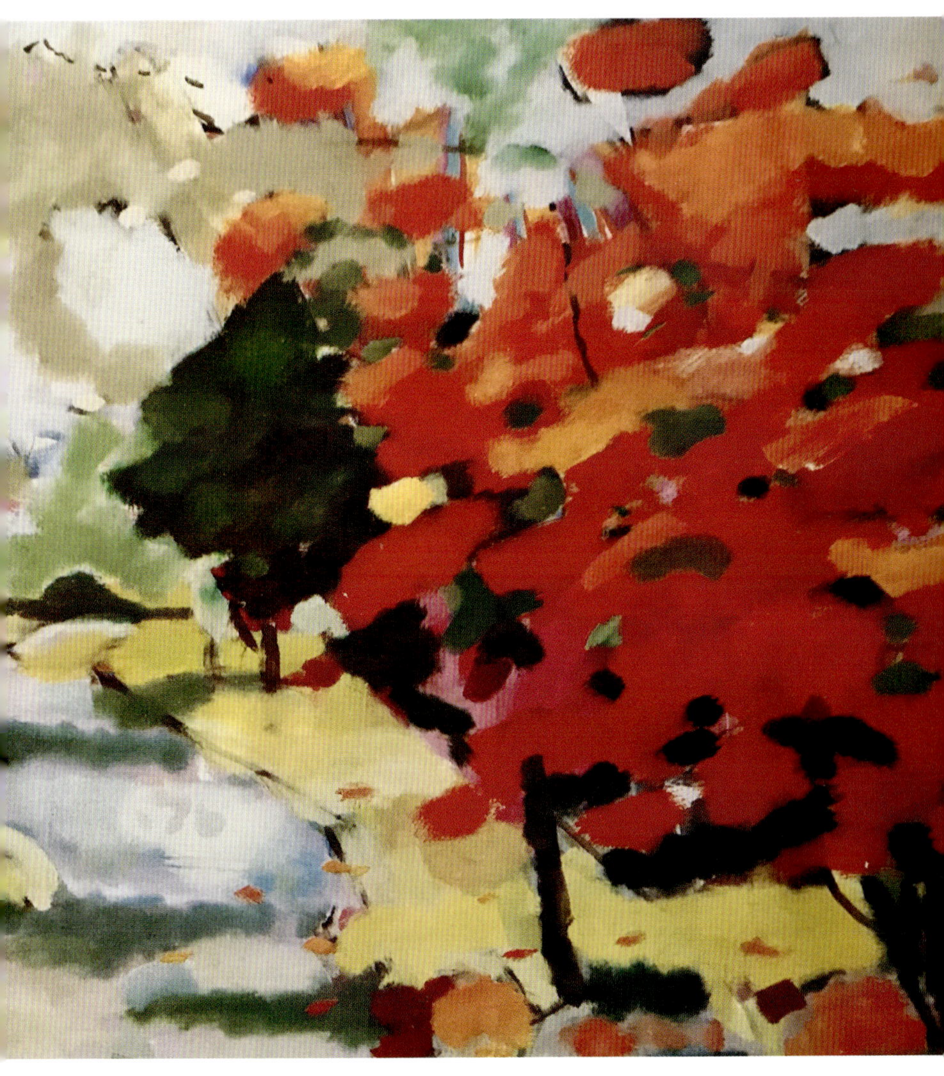

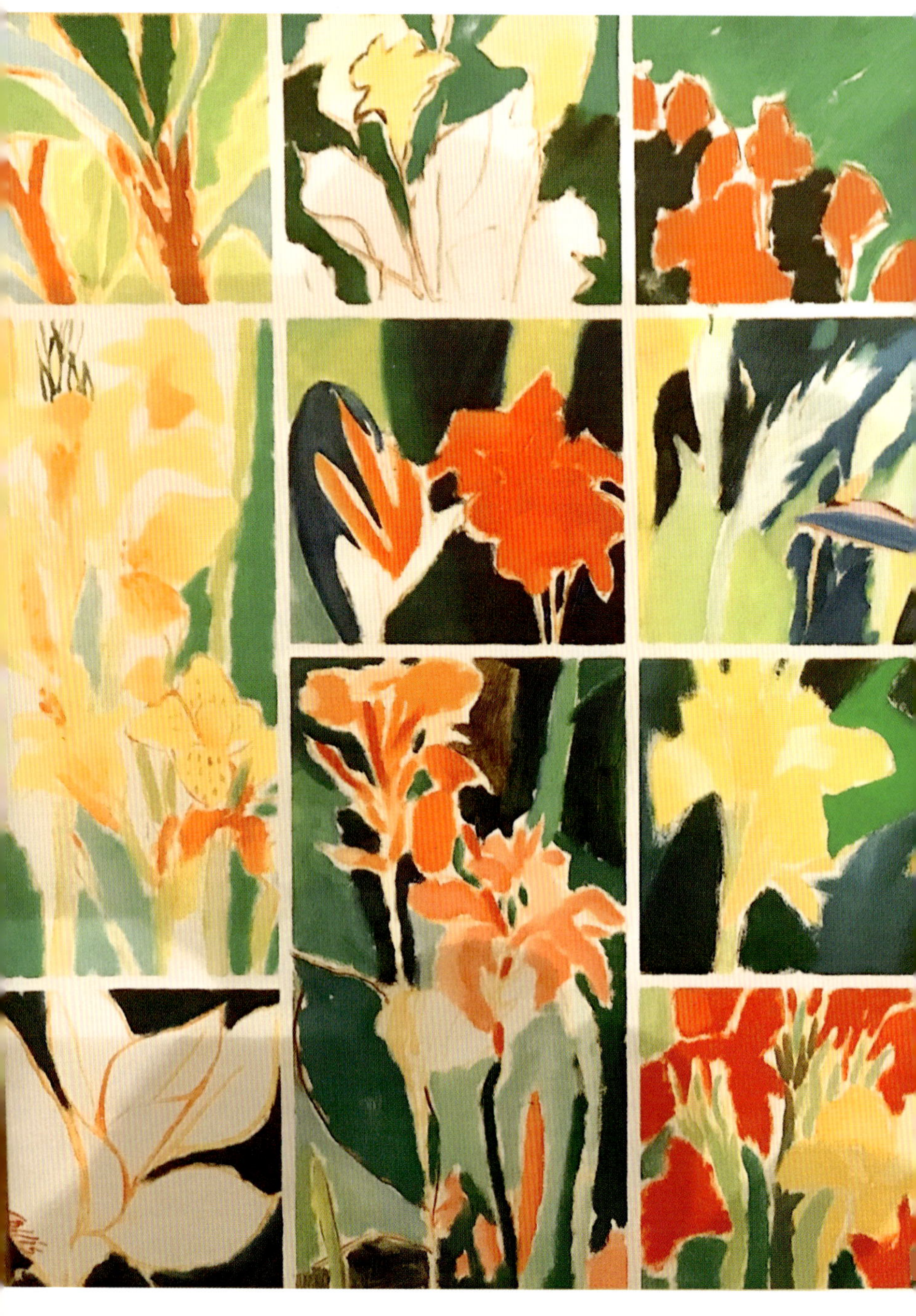

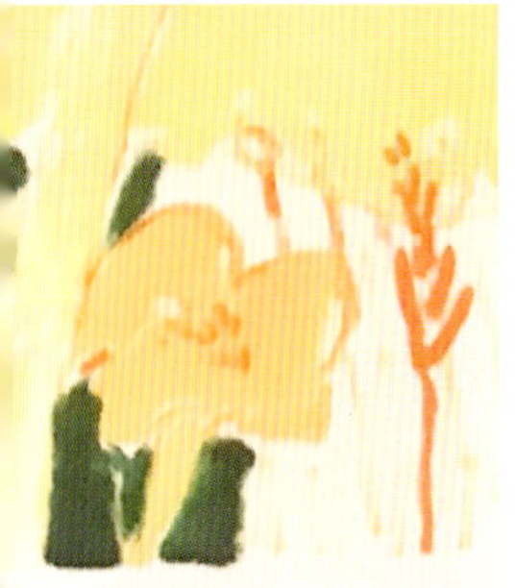
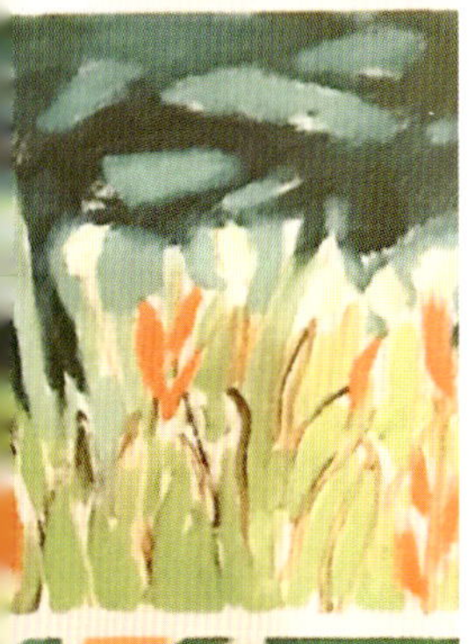
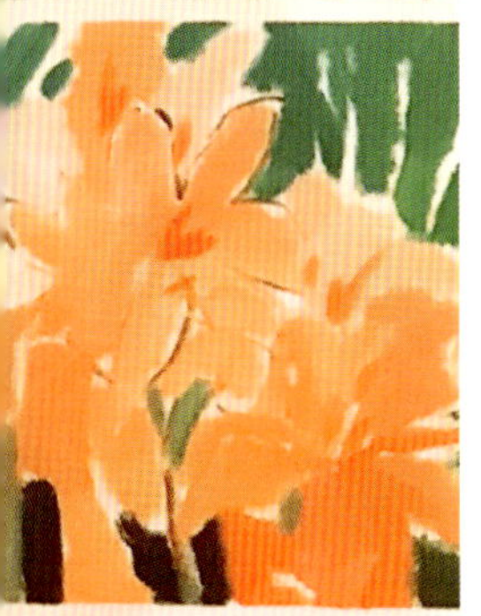
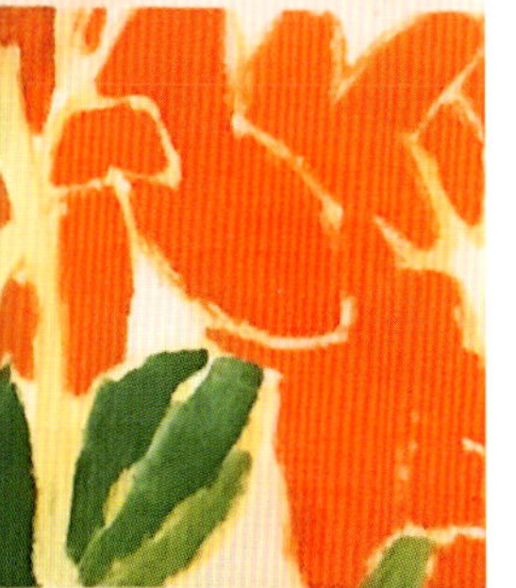

DAY 208
CANNAS

The 'Canna' series was my first sequence.
I painted them for two years. There comes
a time where a particular flower blooms in
spectacular fashion and the cannas were
immense those two years in East Africa.
I made them into cards, gift tags and prints,
and other people 'borrowed' them and made
them into trays and tablemats, and did not ask
my permission ... never mind. This grid
is an oil on canvas, separated by masking tape
to make a straight edge in between.
I noticed a most interesting occurrence.
The green leaf of an orange canna did
not 'suit' another spotty orange canna.
It occurred to me that each flower was in a
perfect marriage with its leaf, and one could
not mix them up, the greens being so subtle.
Jules and Jenny Larby bought this painting.

DAY 209
CANNA

Drawn with coloured pencils.
I worked in situ this entire series
whilst standing in front of the
flowers. The range of oranges/pinks
kept me spellbound. So many warm
and cold shades in an overall look of
orange. I have found that a little bit of
untouched paper (in this case white
paper) around the flower gives the
object space to breathe. A little trick.

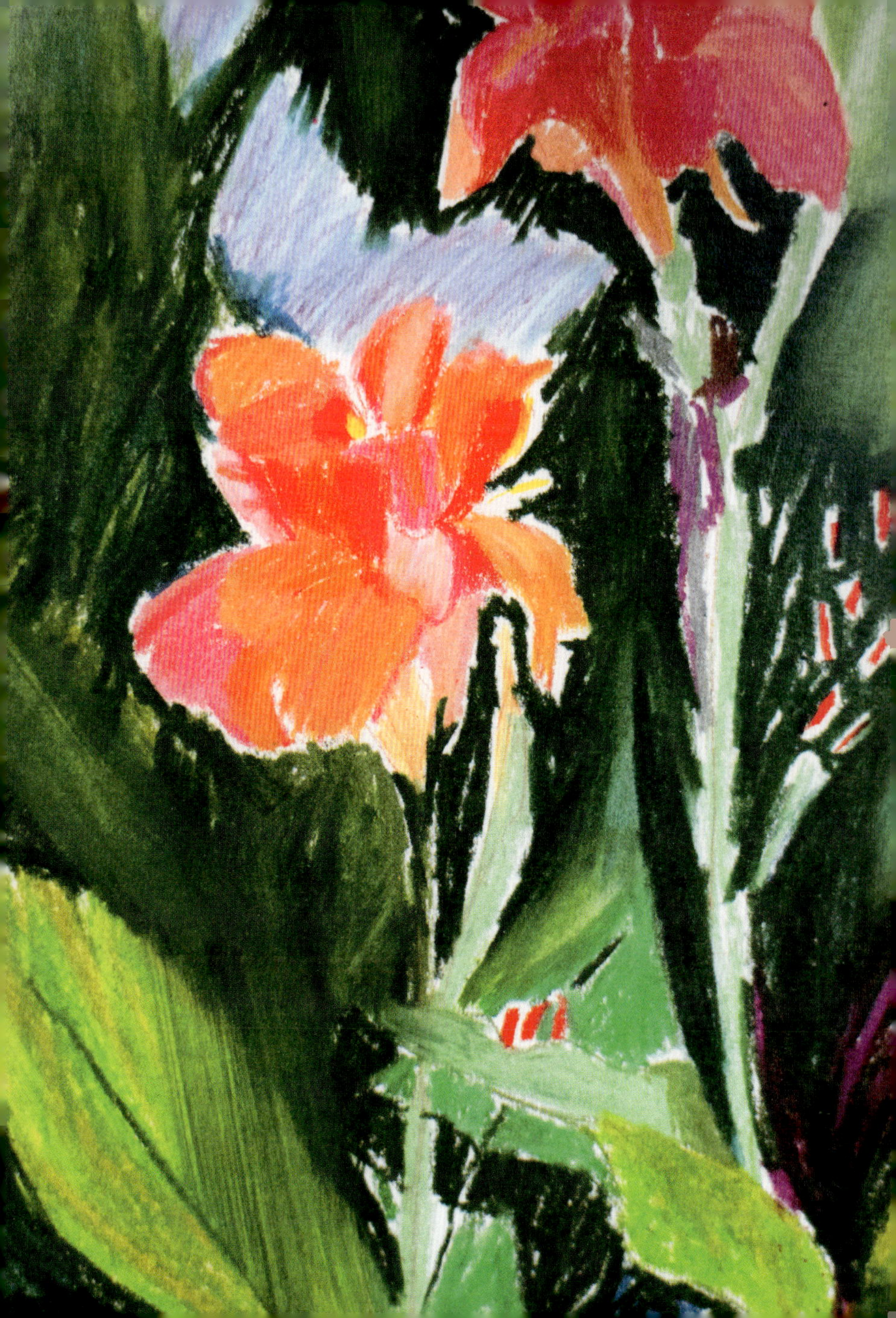

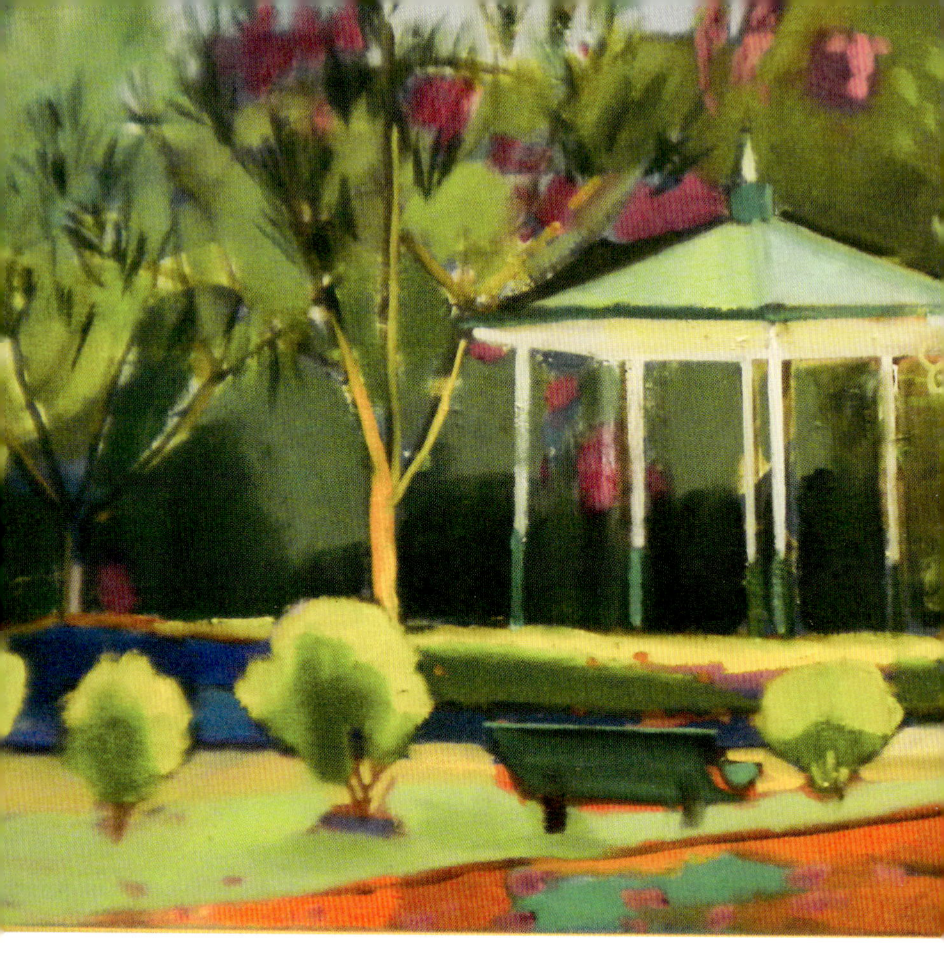

DAY 210

I was asked by the committee of the Friends of City Park to paint this commission to bring attention to the park's vulnerability and its restoration. I was astonished to find the old bandstand that had been there when I was a child. Our family would go there on Sunday afternoons and listen to the police band. Although it looked a bit sad

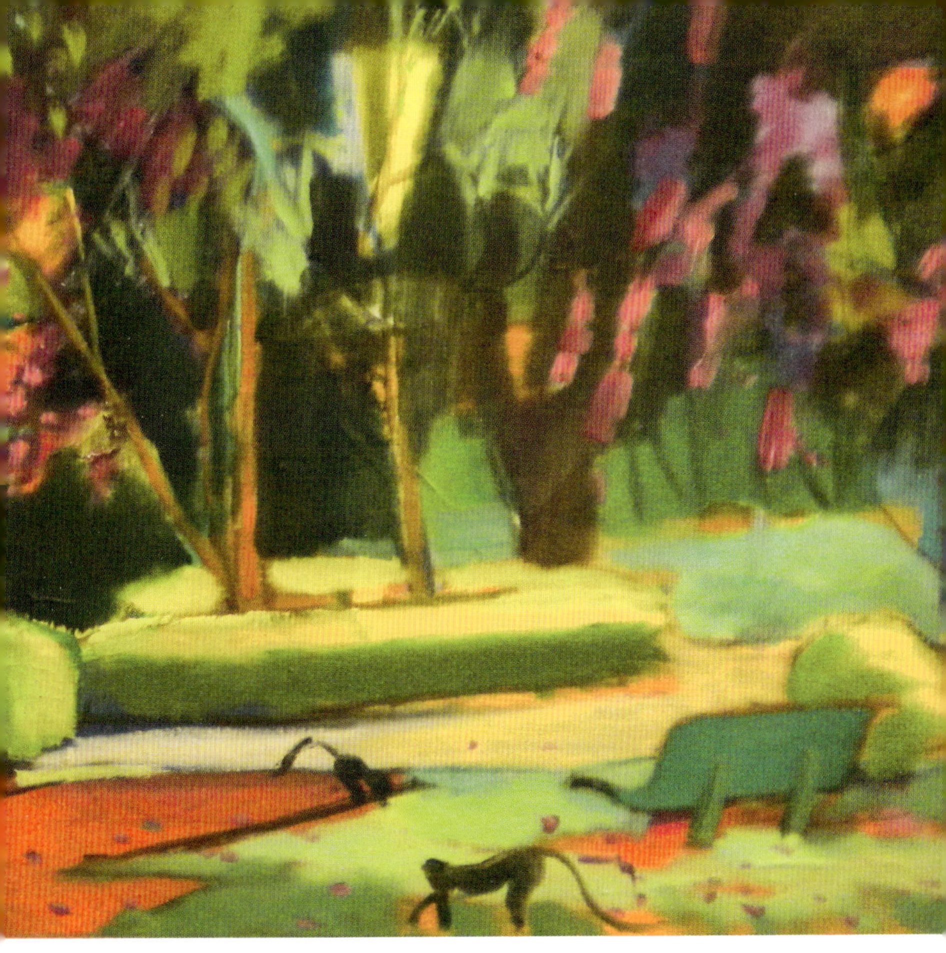

and dilapidated, there were quite a few people enjoying the quiet away from the adjacent Limuru Road, and many Sykes' monkeys were hoping for scraps from workers' lunches. The painting was auctioned and a card was made to raise money. City Park forgot to credit me on the card. This is a second painting of the park in the late afternoon.

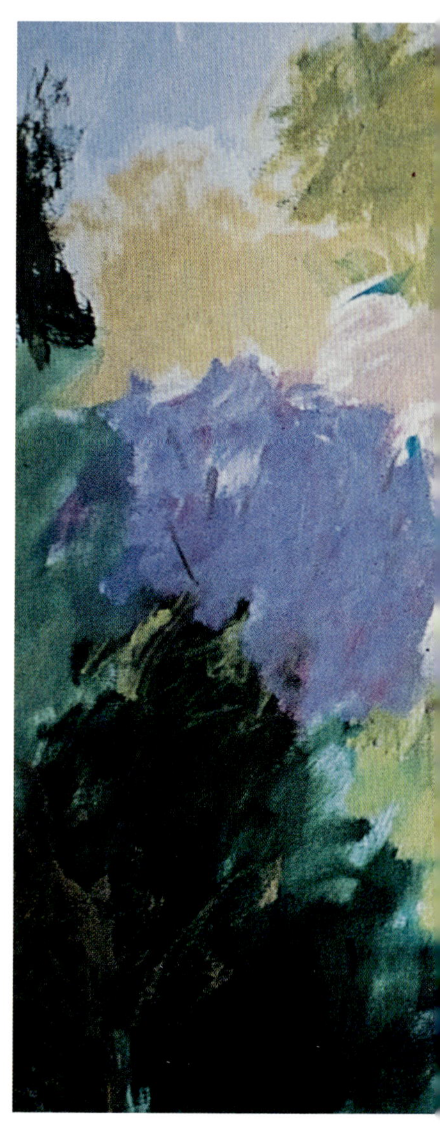

Day 211
My Valley

I am posting another painting of the trees in my valley in Kibagare. The reason for this is that today I have been to see Camille Wekesa's stunning paintings of trees at the Red Hill Art Gallery on the Limuru Road. If you have not seen this show, those living in Kenya should go, it is outstanding. There is a masterpiece in the show, which belongs in a museum. Helmuth Rossler (owner of the gallery) bought it, of course. A good buy.

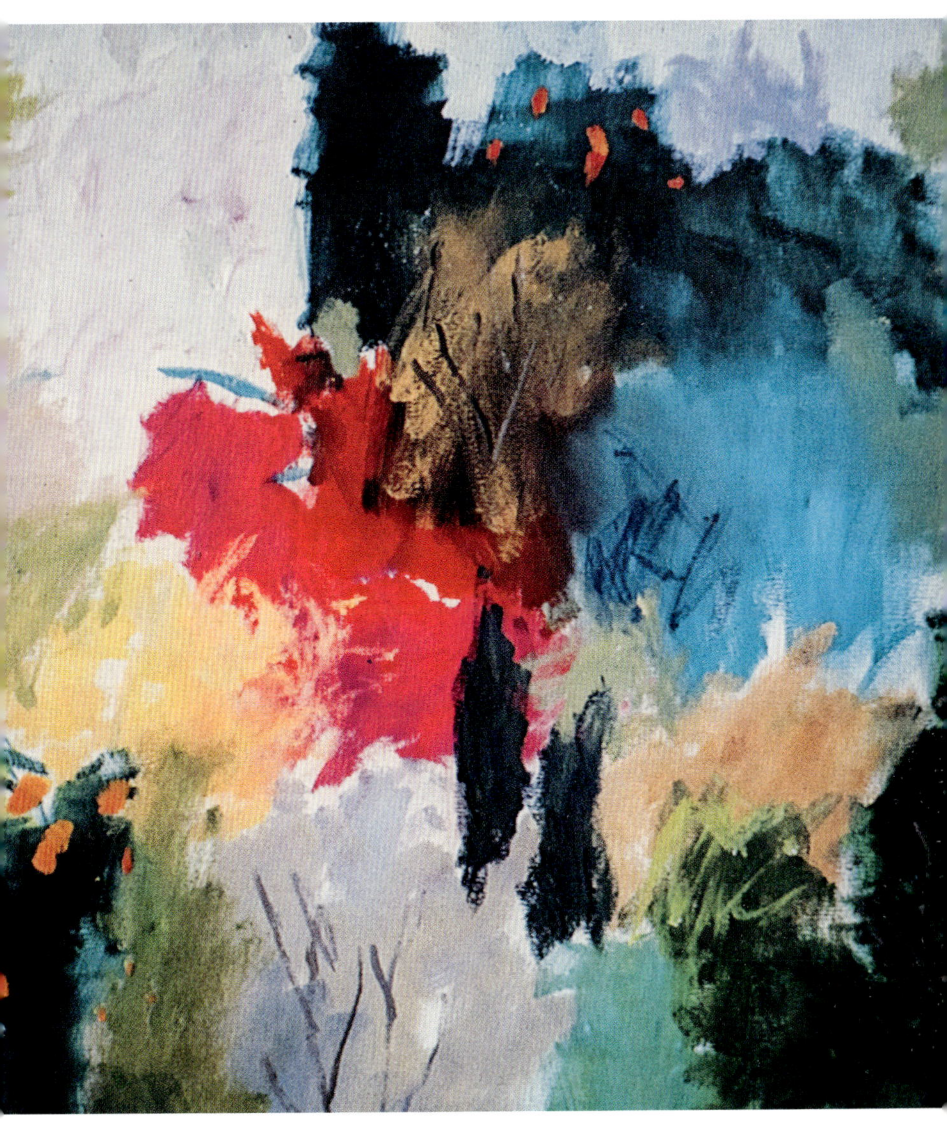

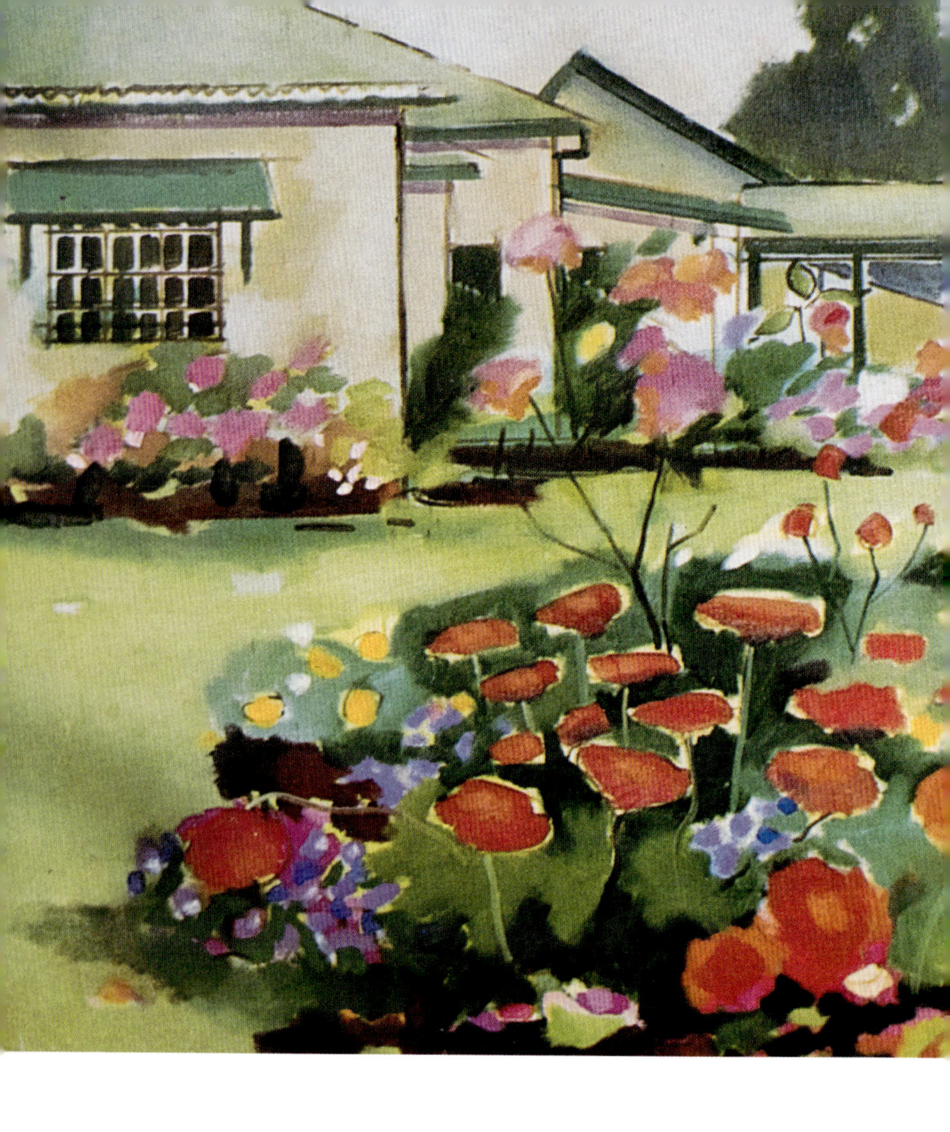

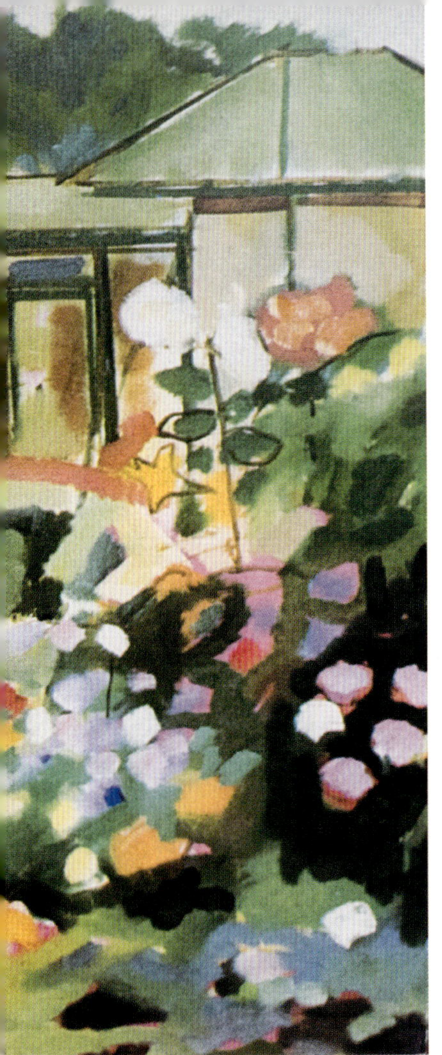

Day 212
Makuyu

When our son and daughter were very young, we would often spend a weekend with friends up the Thika Road. Kay was a gardener, which was a delight for me, though I painted this because of that typically extended Kenyan farmhouse … with the covered corridor leading to the outside kitchen. The whole building was under the painted tin roof, matching the greens of the flowerbed in the foreground.

Day 213
Crescent Island

Lake Naivasha in the Rift Valley, Kenya. We had a boat in those days and most weekends we would go fishing on the lake. This painting of a day out in the very hot sun with my two small children has remained in the family. It belongs to my sister, Sally Kampf. My children are standing on the causeway that once connected the island to the shore. There is an animal sanctuary on Crescent Island, which is smaller now than it used to be. At present, the water in the lake is the highest it has ever been, swallowing many trees along the shore and changing the shape of the lake.

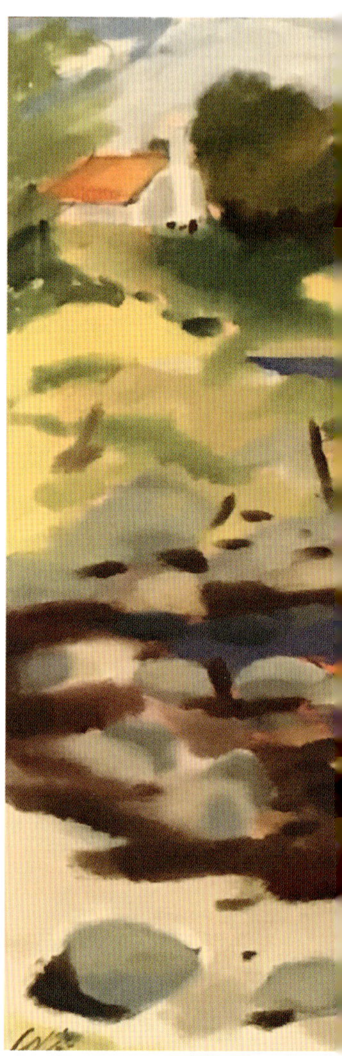

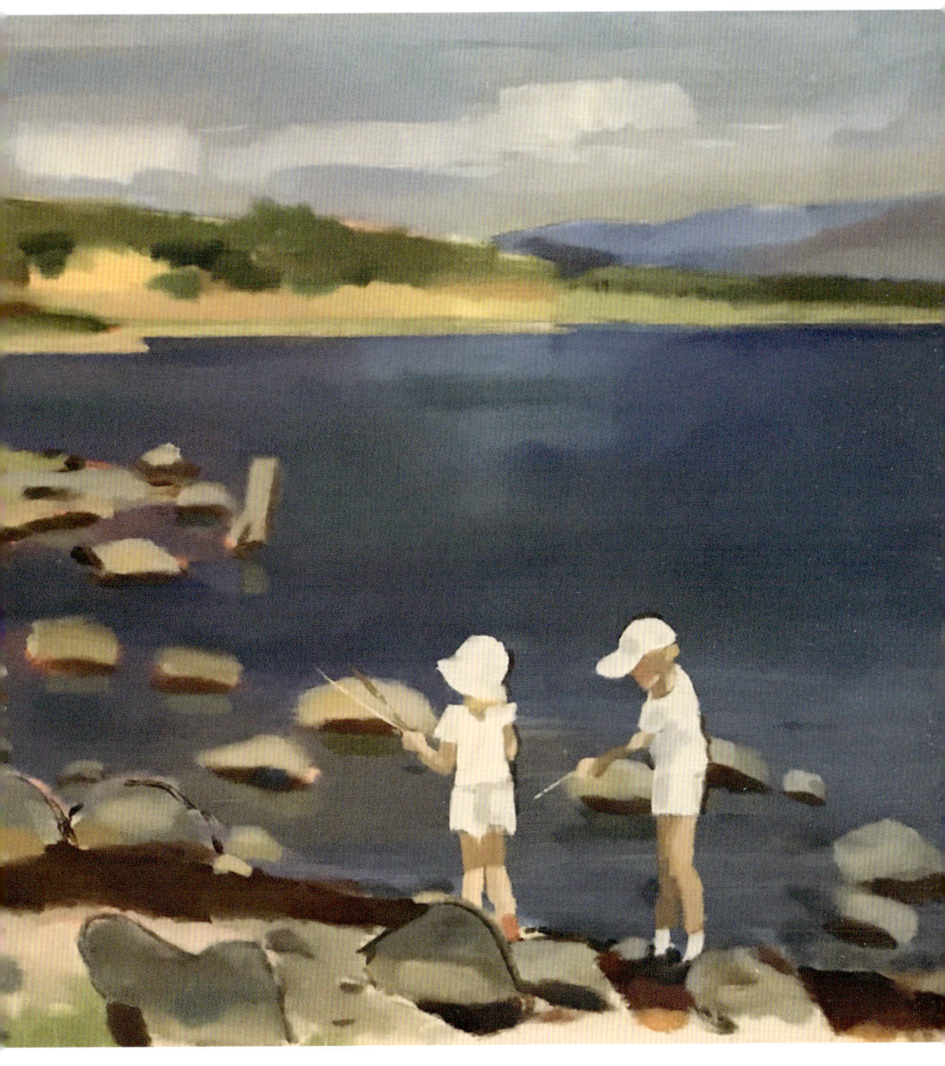

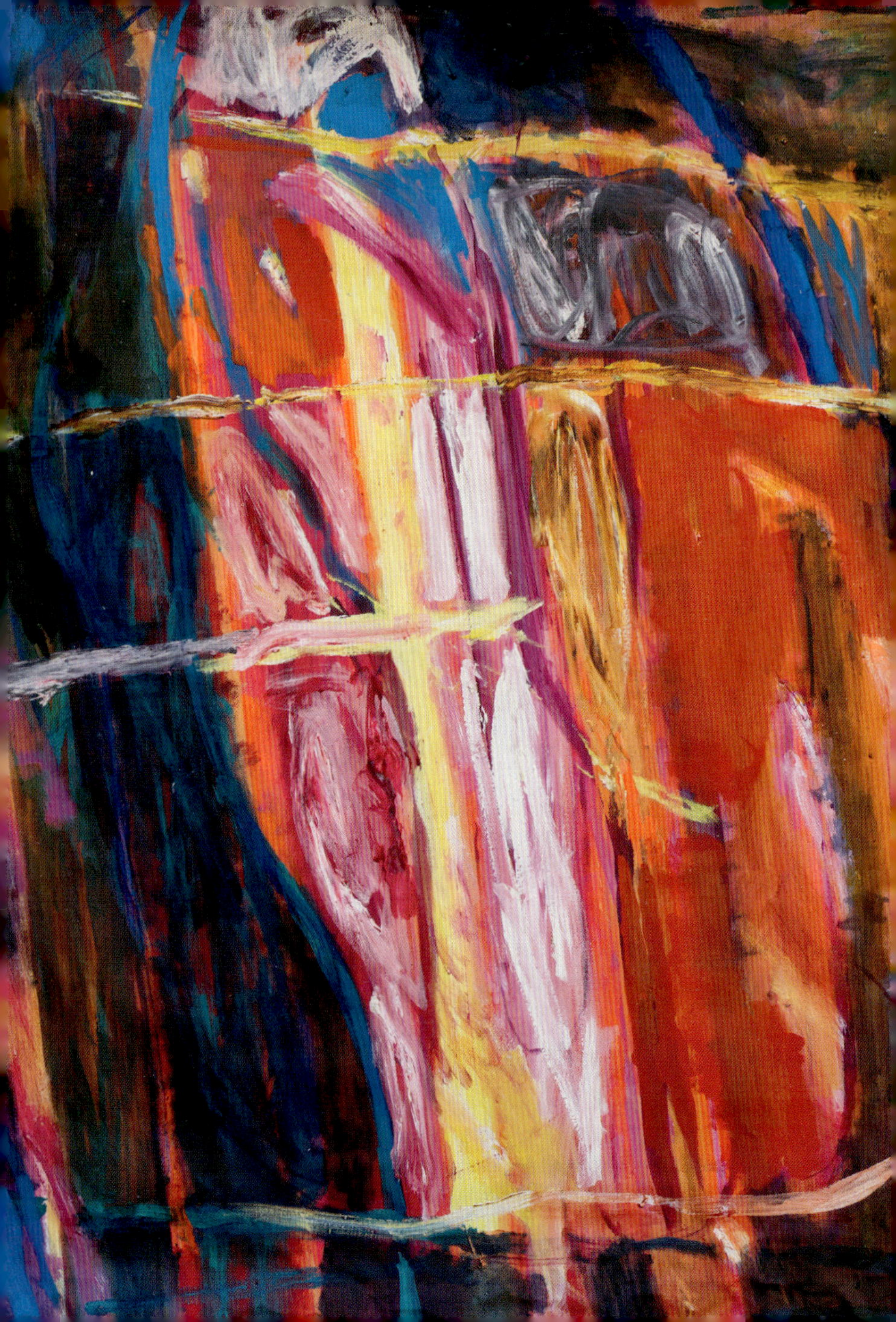

Day 214
Freedom Corner

Today, 20 October 2020, is Mashujaa Day.
It means Hero's Day. It used to be Kenyatta Day,
for the father of independent Kenya. This was
painted when Robert Maxwell (the press baron)
was wanting to build a sixty-four-storey skyscraper
on the corner of Uhuru Highway, taking up a
huge chunk of Uhuru Park in downtown Nairobi.
Our hero, and indeed she was, Wangari Maathai,
organised a sit-in in the cathedral just down the
road. Many women joined her, taking over the
crypt and the nave for a few weeks. They won.
The Maxwells and the Moi government retreated,
and the corner has ever since been known as
Freedom Corner. Professor Maathai was a true
hero for all of us in Kenya. She endured prison
so all the residents of Nairobi could enjoy the
Karura Forest. Deep thanks to her. In 2004
she won the Nobel Peace Prize.
Collection of Radha Upadhyaya

Day 215

The title of this eludes me. It's painted
over another work and allows the colours
below to come through. It reminds me
slightly of the sculptor Tony Cragg, who
will lay out on the floor or wall plastic
found objects, with equal spacing in
between. A Turner Prize winner, his work
is about examining relationships between
the material world and people. There is
a huge variety in his work, and it is often
marked by a singular colour, excepting
the plastic pieces which might follow a
rainbow of colours, with a lot more order
than here. A bit of 'social distancing'.

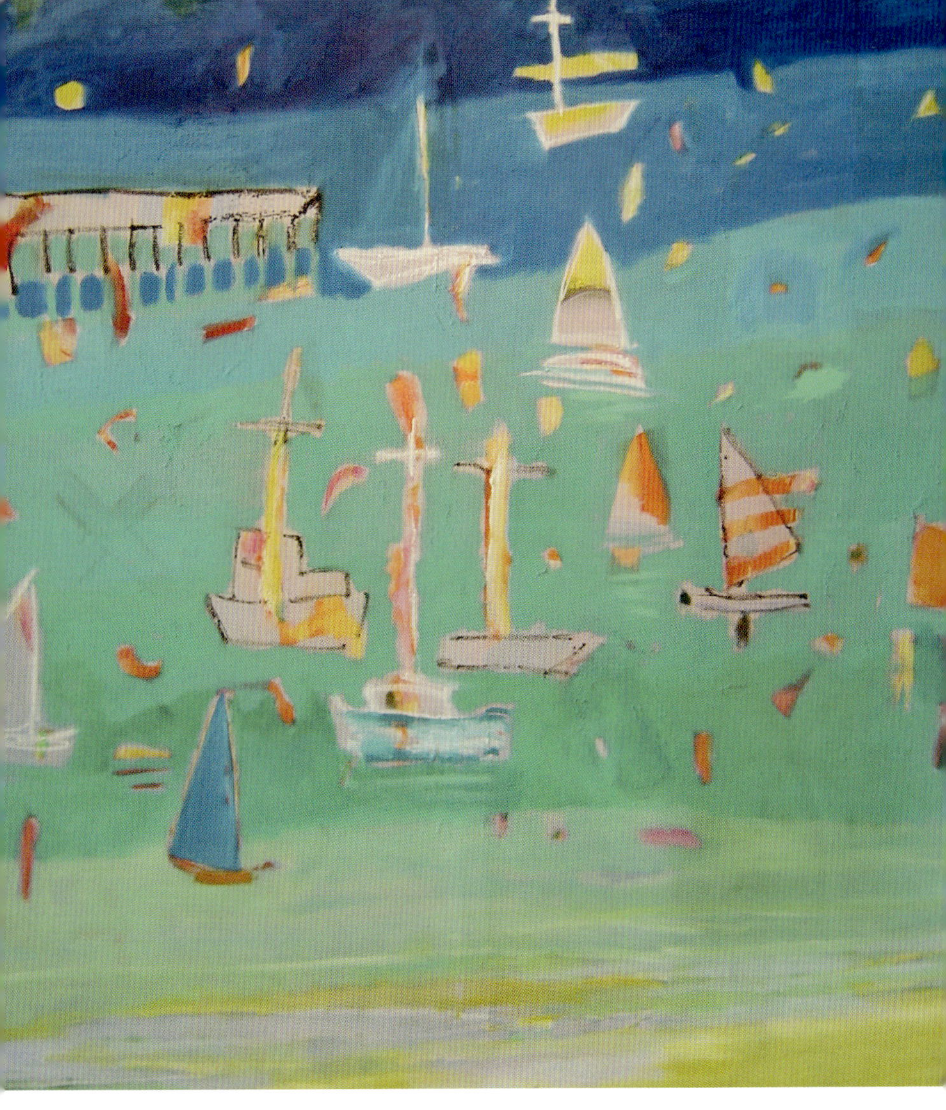

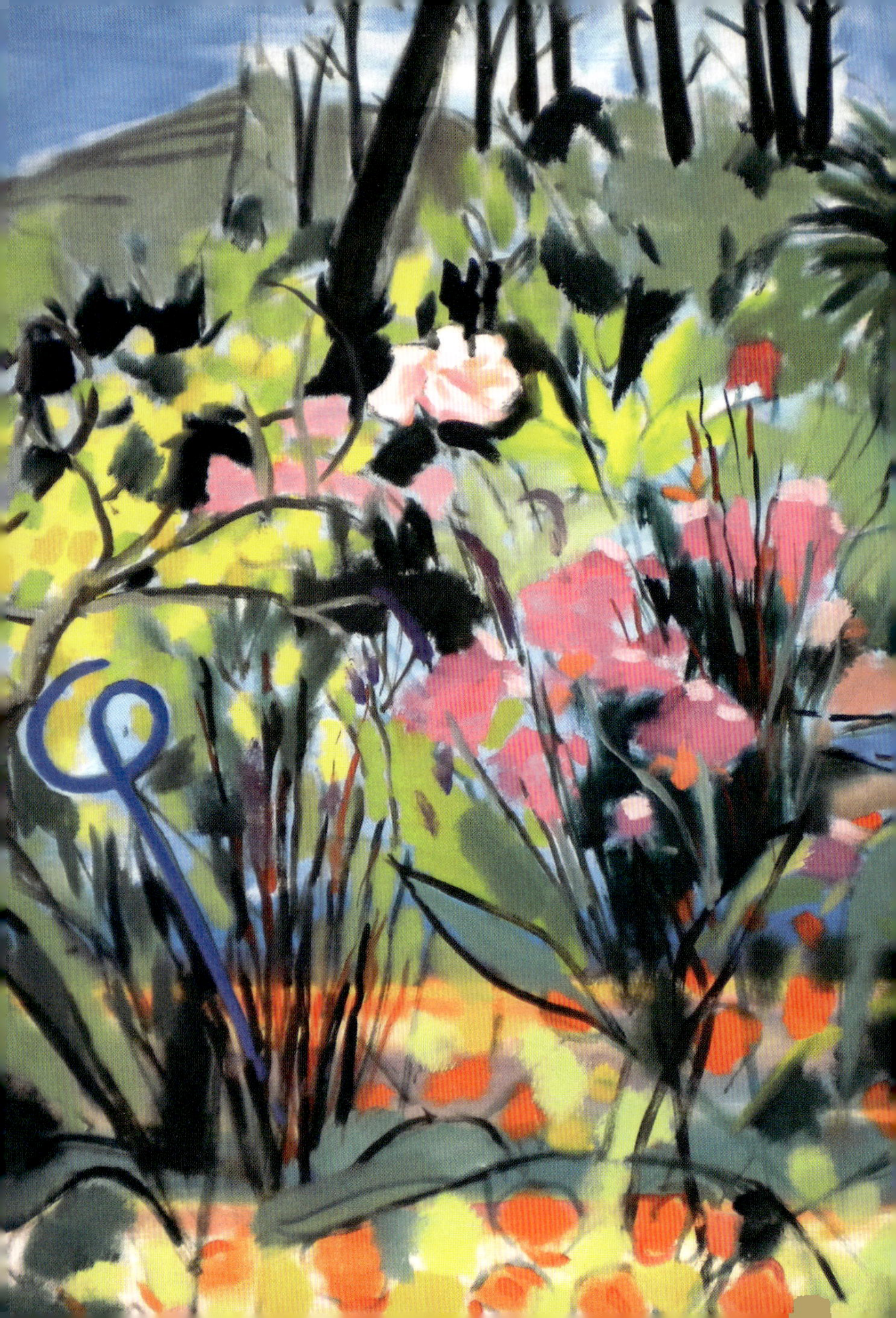

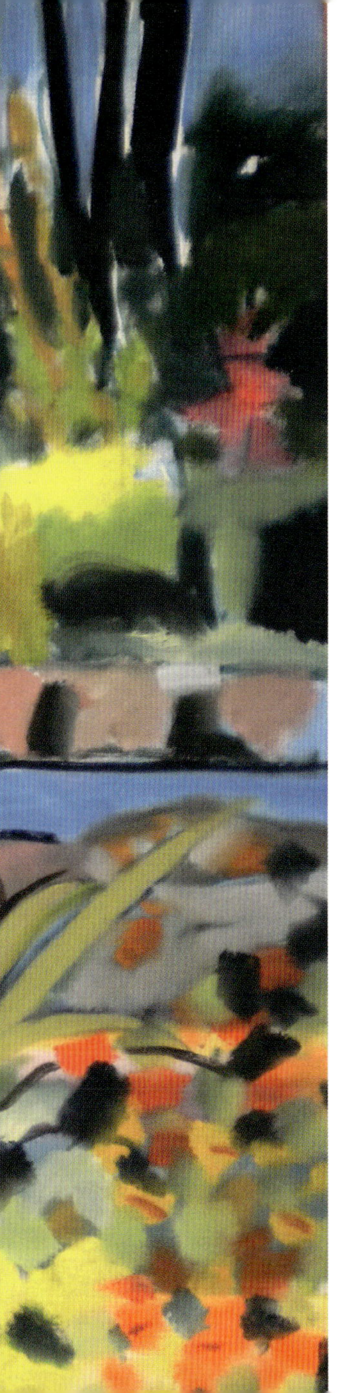

Day 216
Judy's Shamba

I have an artist friend in
the Cape whose garden is
her canvas and it is forever
changing. I walk around and
enjoy her creativity for longer
each time I go there.
Judy Conway bought some
stony ground behind the
mountain and turned it
into Eden. She adds the
quirky, in that it is endowed
with coloured balls and
Perspex fences in mauve
and magenta, marbles,
much sculpture and two
mannequins lying in a baby
pool, to name a few. Judy has
filled an empty space and
furnished it with a presence.

Day 217
A page from my sketchbook

This is derived from the Japanese Sumi_e brushstroke, only I have used colour and black ink. The art of ink painting (Sumi_e brushstroke) is about the quality of line and the ink. The Japanese have the most beautiful brushes. One cannot buy a cheap quality brush, as one would become quickly disillusioned. I have several of these wonderful brushes and occasionally will have another try at the perfect line. The breathing is essential to this art and meditation, and with that, the energy comes through the arm to the hand to the brush. To be absolutely authentic, one should have the Japanese paper, which I don't. The work is then displayed as a hanging scroll.

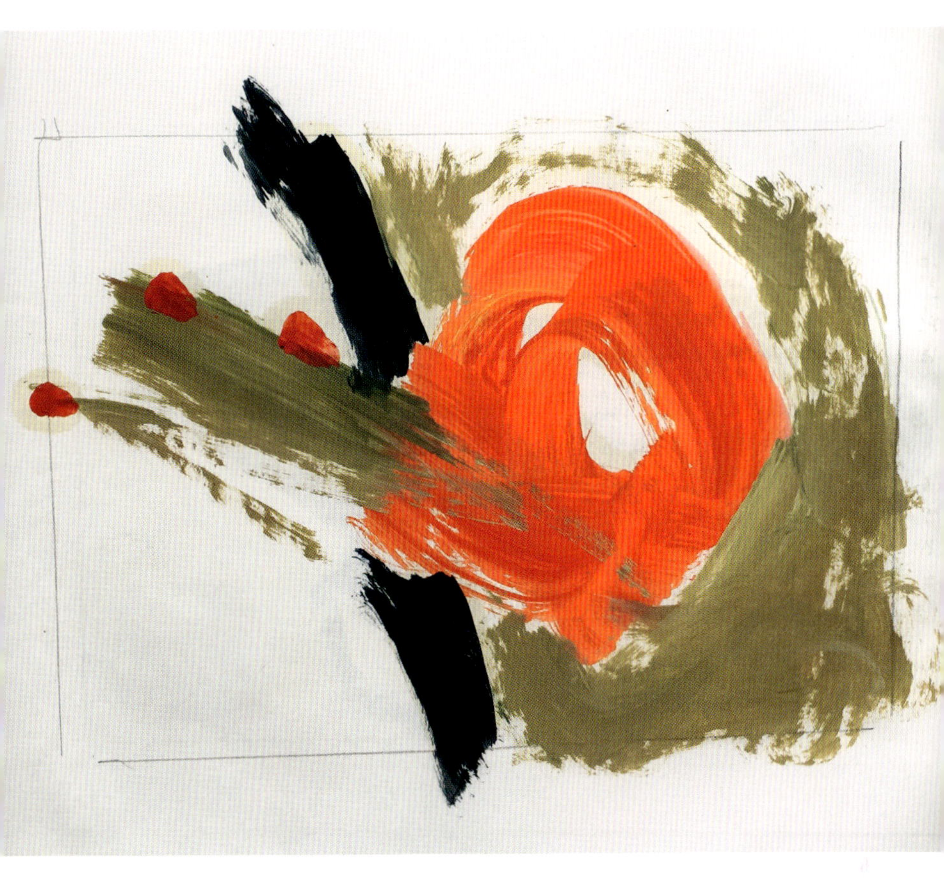

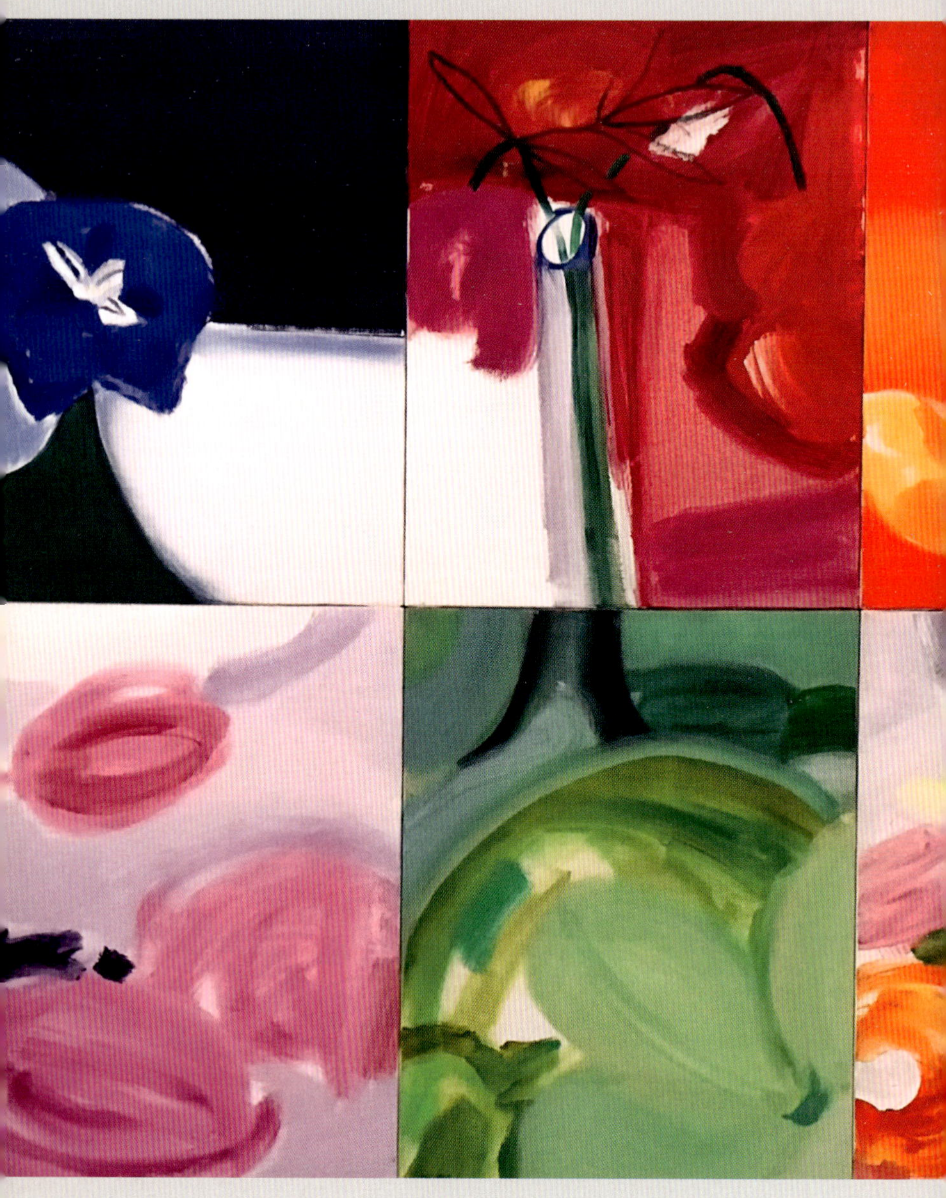

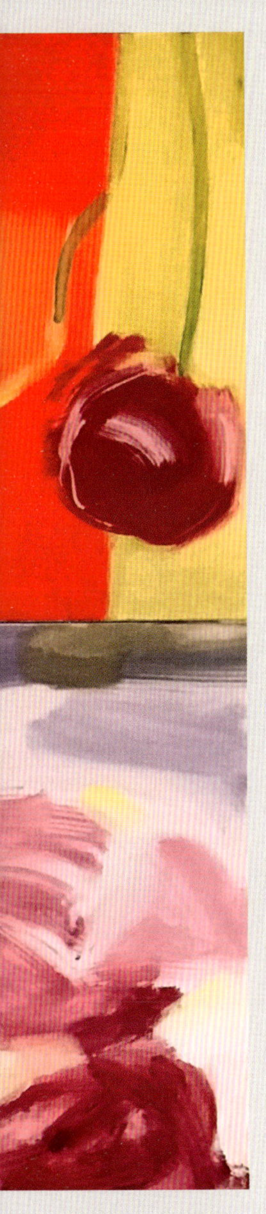

Day 218
All is One

The Seven Spiritual Truths series

There are seven truths, the last one being 'All is One'. The work encompasses all six panels: Truth, Generosity, Love, Honour One Another, Forgiveness, Intention. I borrowed these colours from the interior designer, Tricia Guild, and the splendid way she puts them together. Her range is different from mine. Each panel represents a truth through the colours, helped by the images. There are many interpretations of the Seven Truths by different philosophers, as I suspect there are many interpretations of colours and their meanings.
Collection of Jeremy and Alexandra Pike, UK

Day 219

Another from The Seven Spiritual Truths series

Multi-media, collage, gold leaf, acrylic and oil on top.
There are seven of these paintings in this series, unfortunately
split up and spread all over the world. The Spiritual Truths
are a subject that I return to again and again.
This one belongs to the collector, Anis Pringle, in Nairobi

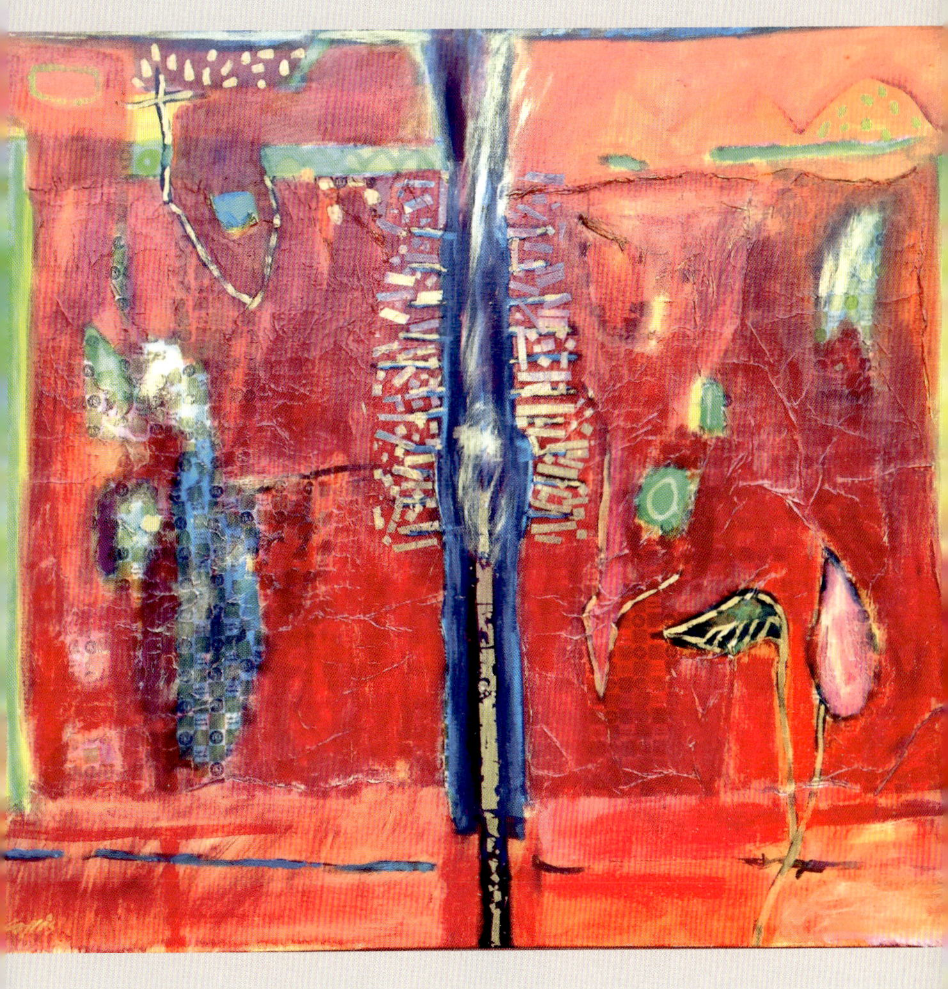

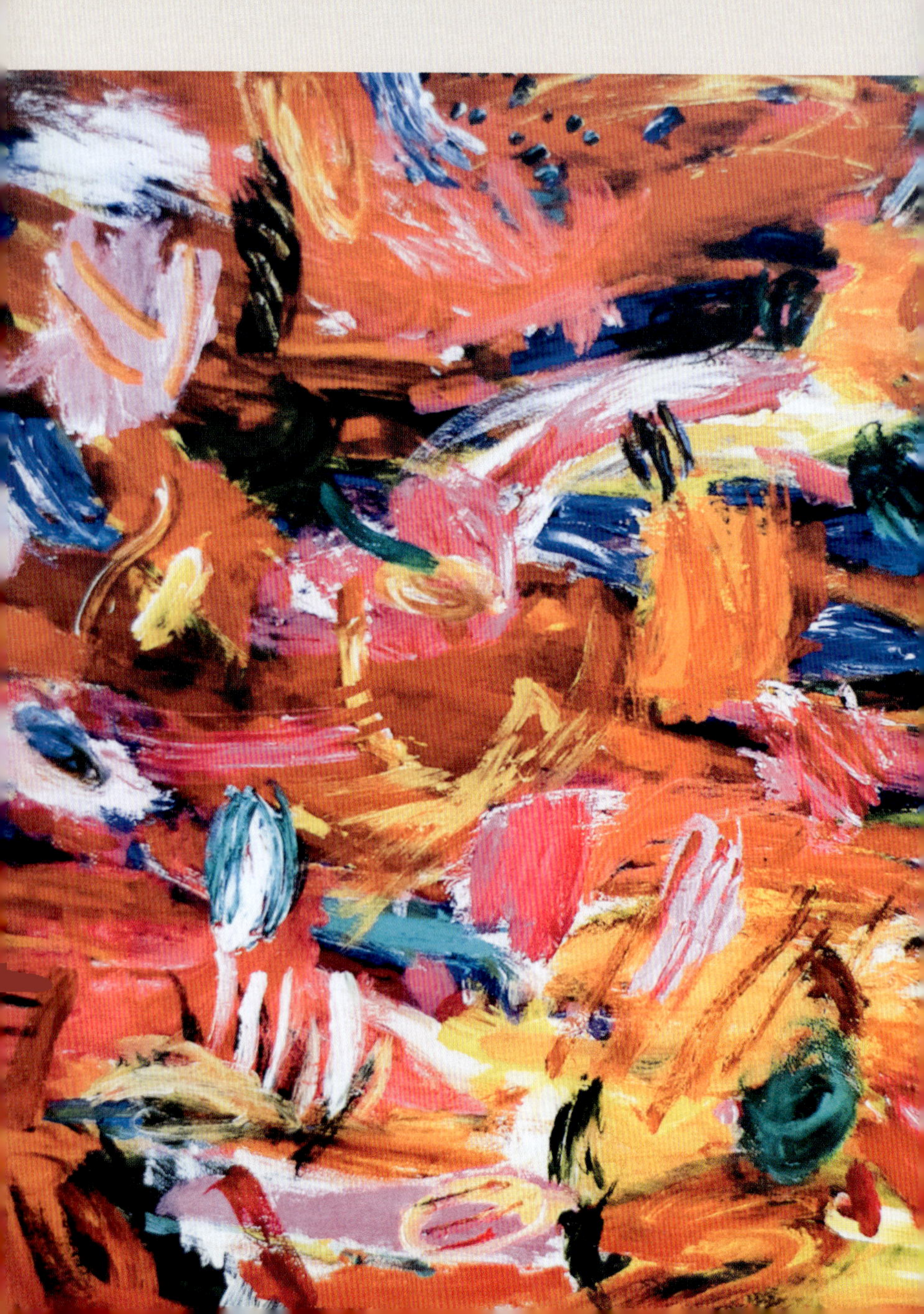

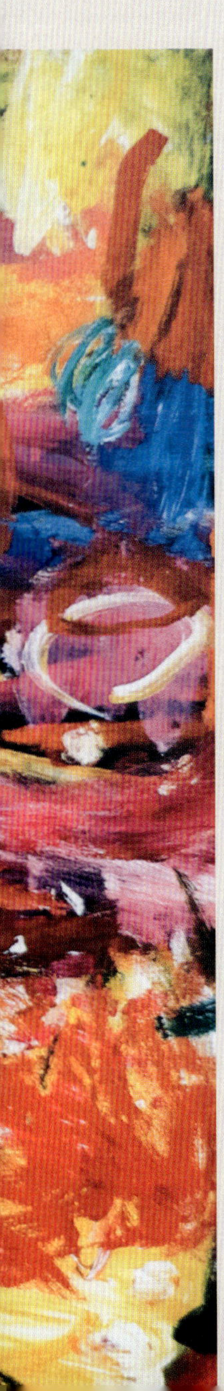

Day 220
Riotous Assembly

One of my personal favourites, it was
printed on a blank card to raise money for
Thomas Barnardo Homes, but reproduced
on its side. I have corrected that error here,
although it is quite alright, as a really good
abstract ought to work any way up.
Perhaps because it has no immediate focal
point, the viewer's eye is forced round.
I like to think one sees the depths first,
there are a few brushstrokes that definitely
come forward. It has a lot of energy and
there is a circular movement. There is no
picture here. This is about brushstroke,
movement, action and process, and that is
quite enough to understand.

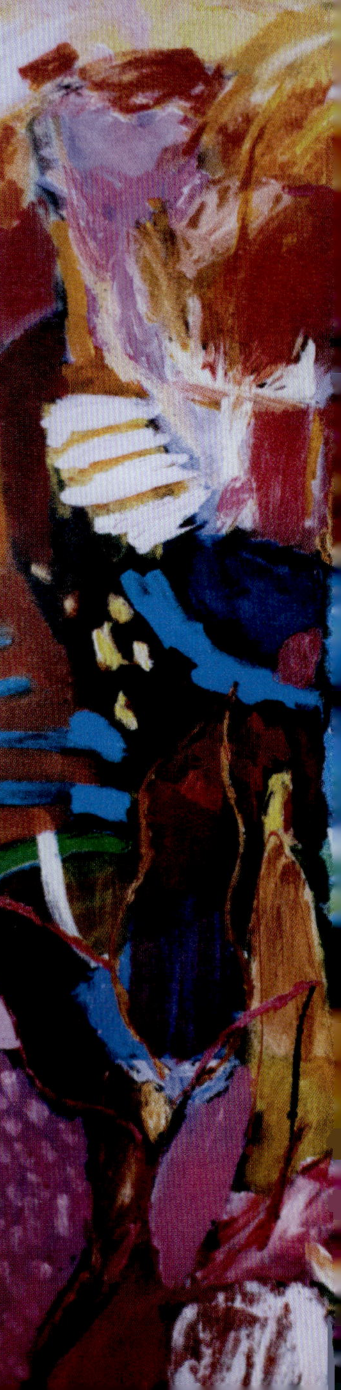

Day 221
Spirited Dance

6 ft screen hinged, three panels,
mixed media – mostly acrylic.

This painting took me a long time.
I kept losing it, as it has so many
elements. Along the bottom are two
horizontal lines where I changed the
colour ever so slightly to give it a
stability. Look carefully and you might
find other horizontals that help too.
In those days, my medium was almost
always oil paint and it had all got a
bit 'slick' for my liking. With acrylics,
having to work much faster, I found
a gauche mark, which I like, and it set
me off on another trajectory.
Private Collection

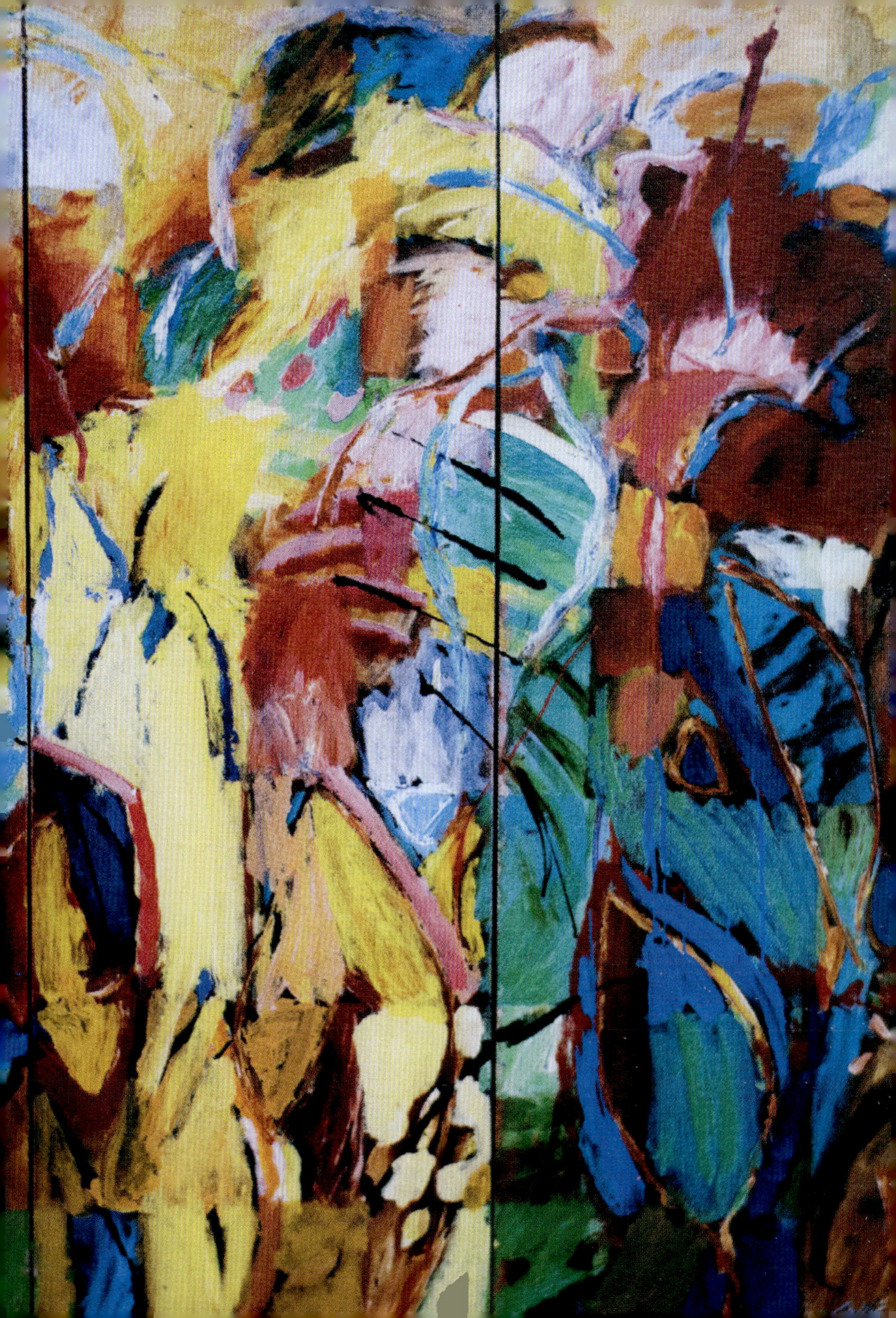

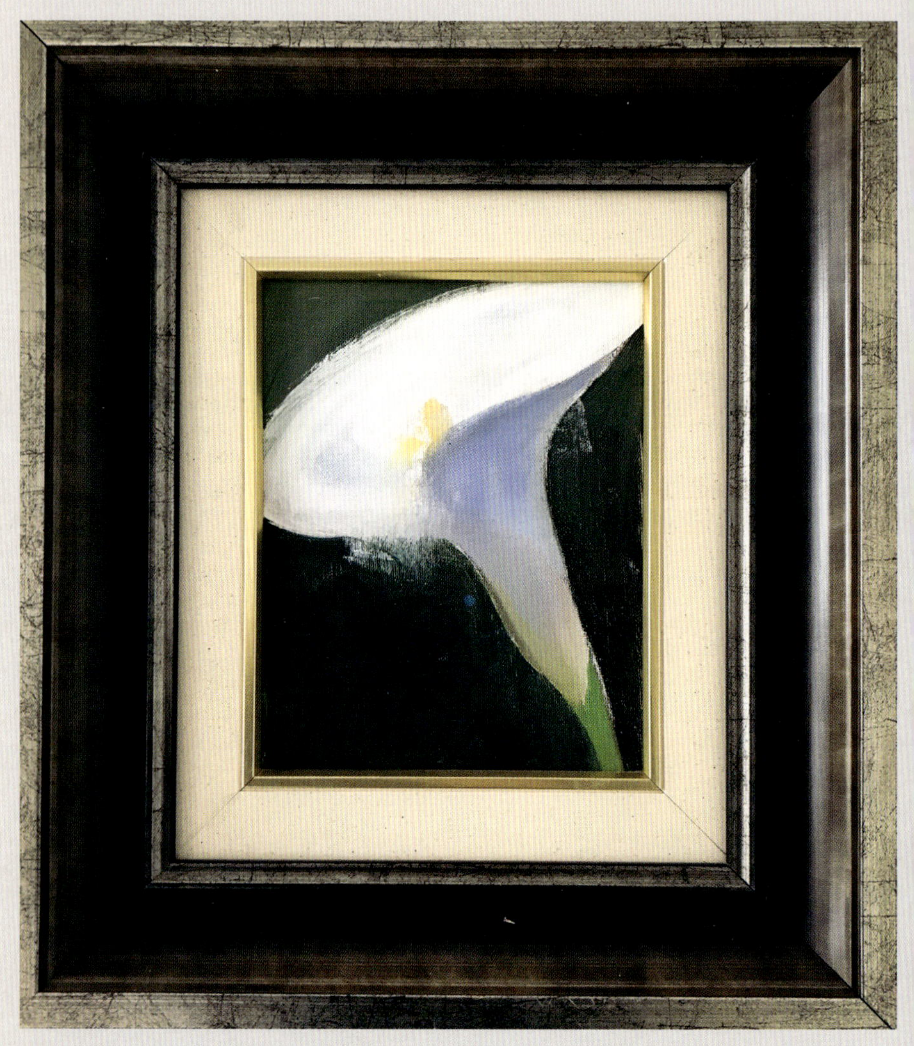

Day 222
Renaissance Lily

The 'Lily' series was painted after my father died in
August 1993 and was made in his memory. There were
drawings, monoprints, oils, acrylics, stone sculpture,
a tall metal lily that Kioko made for me, glass bowls
and two of these Renaissance lilies. The lovely frames
form part of the whole. Kioko is a well-known Kenyan
metal artist, his public sculptures are all over Nairobi.
Sometime during the making of this prodigious series,
I surprised myself when I realised that the works had
covered just about the whole history of art, from
the Renaissance to Minimalism of the day. It was a
discovery and, as sometimes happens when one is
working well, a bonus.

Day 223
Framed Flowers

These roses are in our bedroom, although they belong to a friend who lives in New Zealand. She left them with me for safekeeping. One never knows when inspiration strikes. I have been talking about frames ... and this one is a painting of roses that were in front of the window in front of a small, framed painting on an easel. The curtain is top right. I loved the greys and the soft yellow and peach. It is a large oil on canvas of 50 x 44 in.

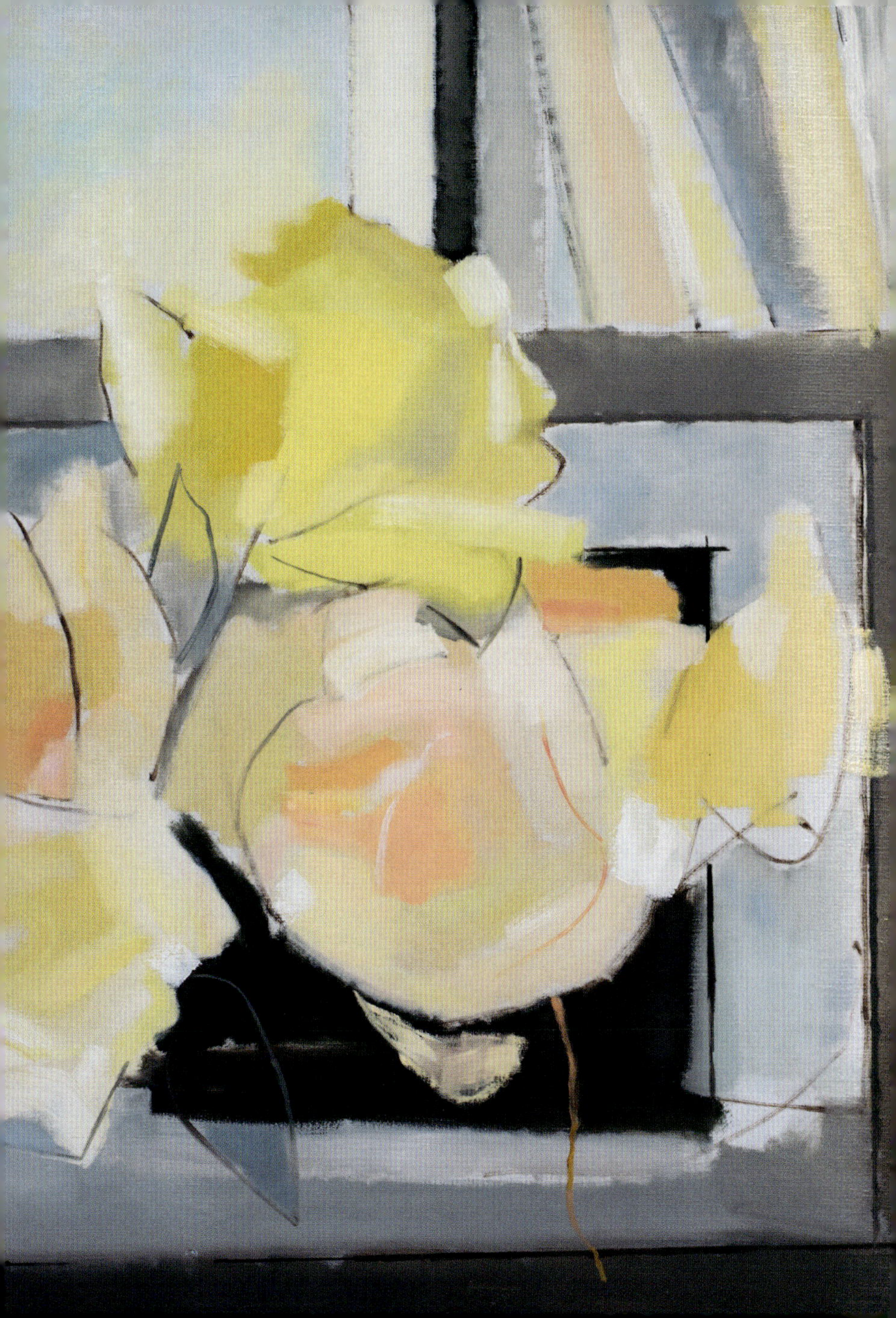

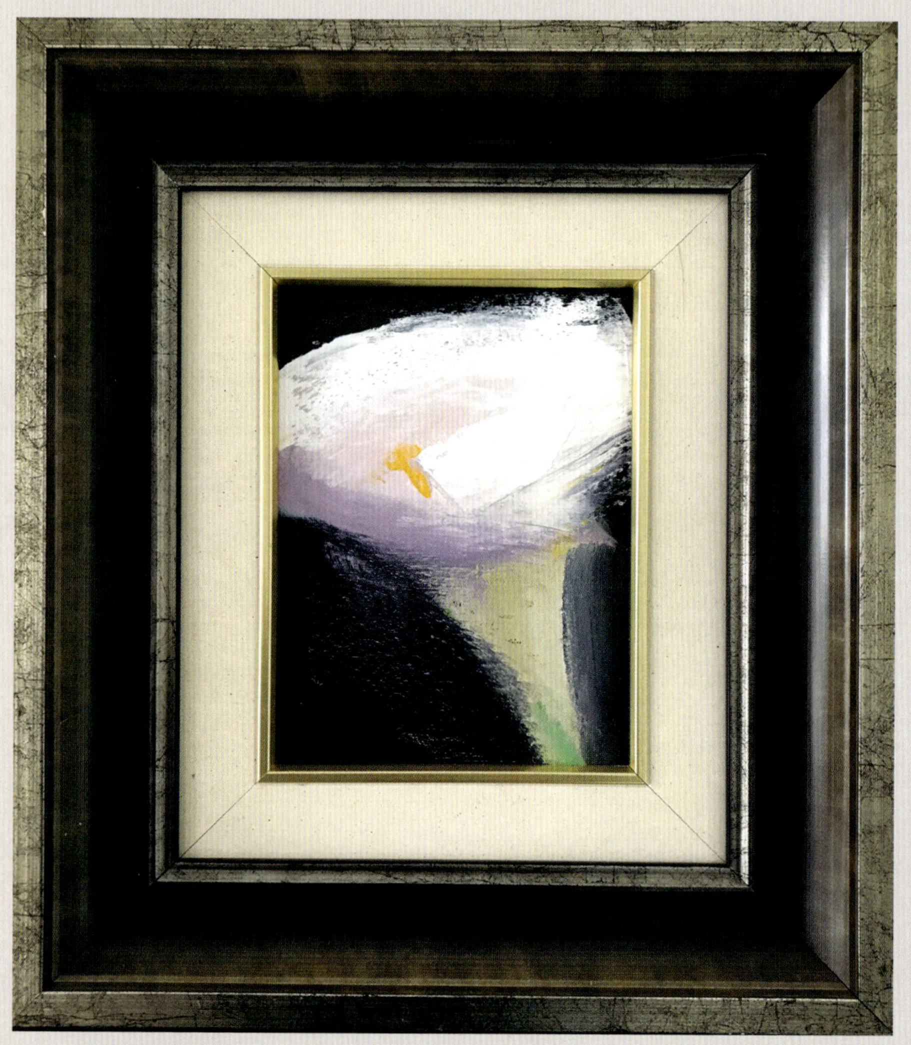

Day 224
Renaissance Lily II

A painterly lily in this wonderful frame. The 'Lily' series was
shown in two countries. First, in Kenya at the One Off Gallery
which was then on Waiyaki Way. The guest of honour was
the Netherlands ambassador, HE Robert Fruin.
Many years later, the series was shown in Holland for a month
in a most beautiful gallery in a park, and where the Kenyan
ambassador to the Netherlands was the guest of honour.
The coincidence just occurred to me whilst writing this
paragraph. I would have liked the series to stay together but,
inevitably, it was separated. My youngest sister, Gillian Meijer,
who at that time lived in Holland, bought several of the works,
which she kindly left to family when she died, and so once
again I own these two Lilies.

*Consider the lilies, how they grow. They toil not, neither
do they spin; yet I say unto you, even Solomon in all
his glory was not arrayed like one of these.*
Luke 12.27

Day 225

A Long View to Lake Naivasha

This was painted from the
Green Park Golf Course on
a dull day, with the orange
murram road holding the eye,
and searching for the bunker
in the foreground which is in
a similar hue. I have a rule that
in every landscape there must
be a marriage somewhere
of colour or shape.
The painter, Dale Webster,
owns this work.

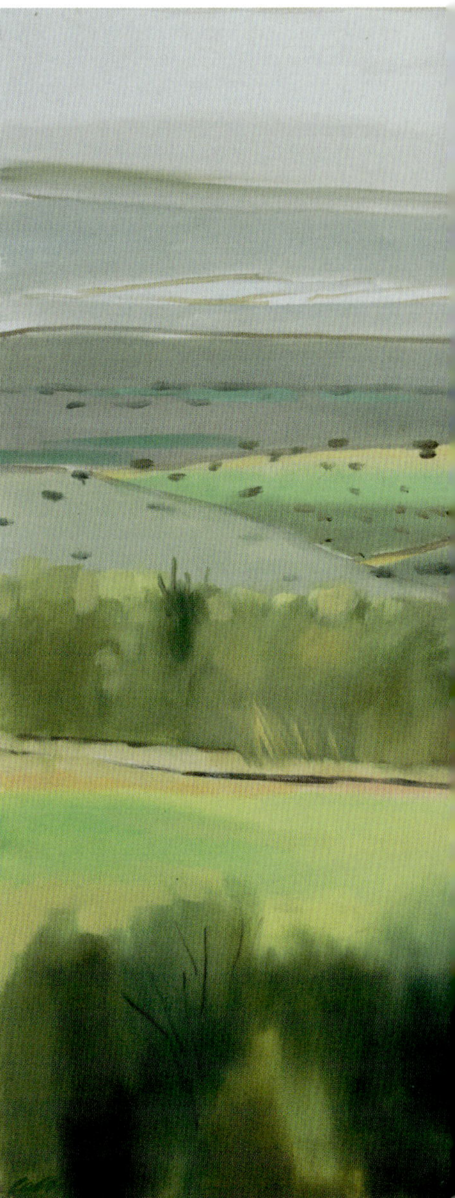

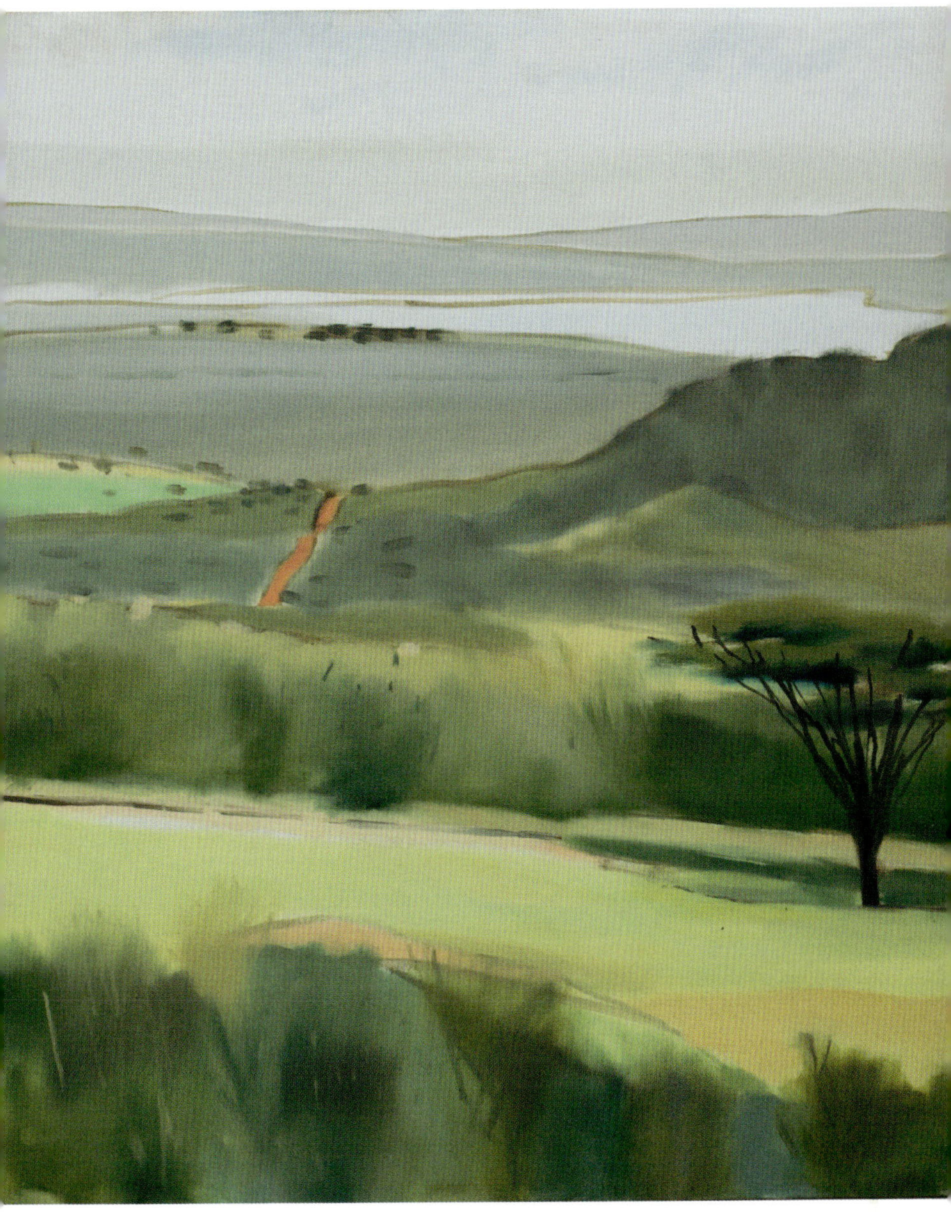

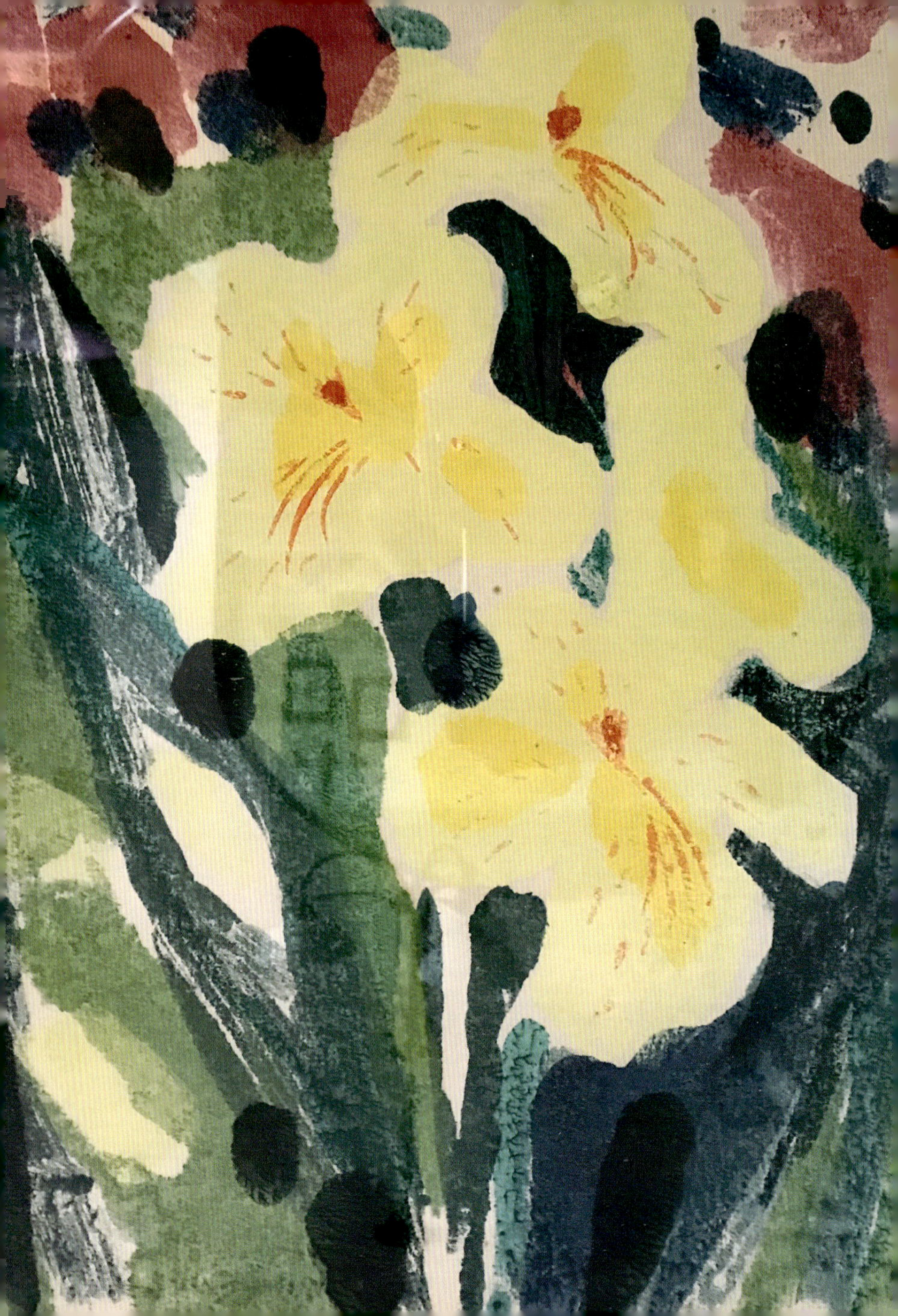

Canna

This week I am showing sketches,
watercolours and monoprints.
Smaller work is essential to the daily effort,
though most of it lives in drawers and
I rarely show them to anyone. Great friends
have a few, and I am always surprised to
see them framed and cherished.
This monoprint of pale yellow canna lilies
belongs to George and Carol Zibarras.

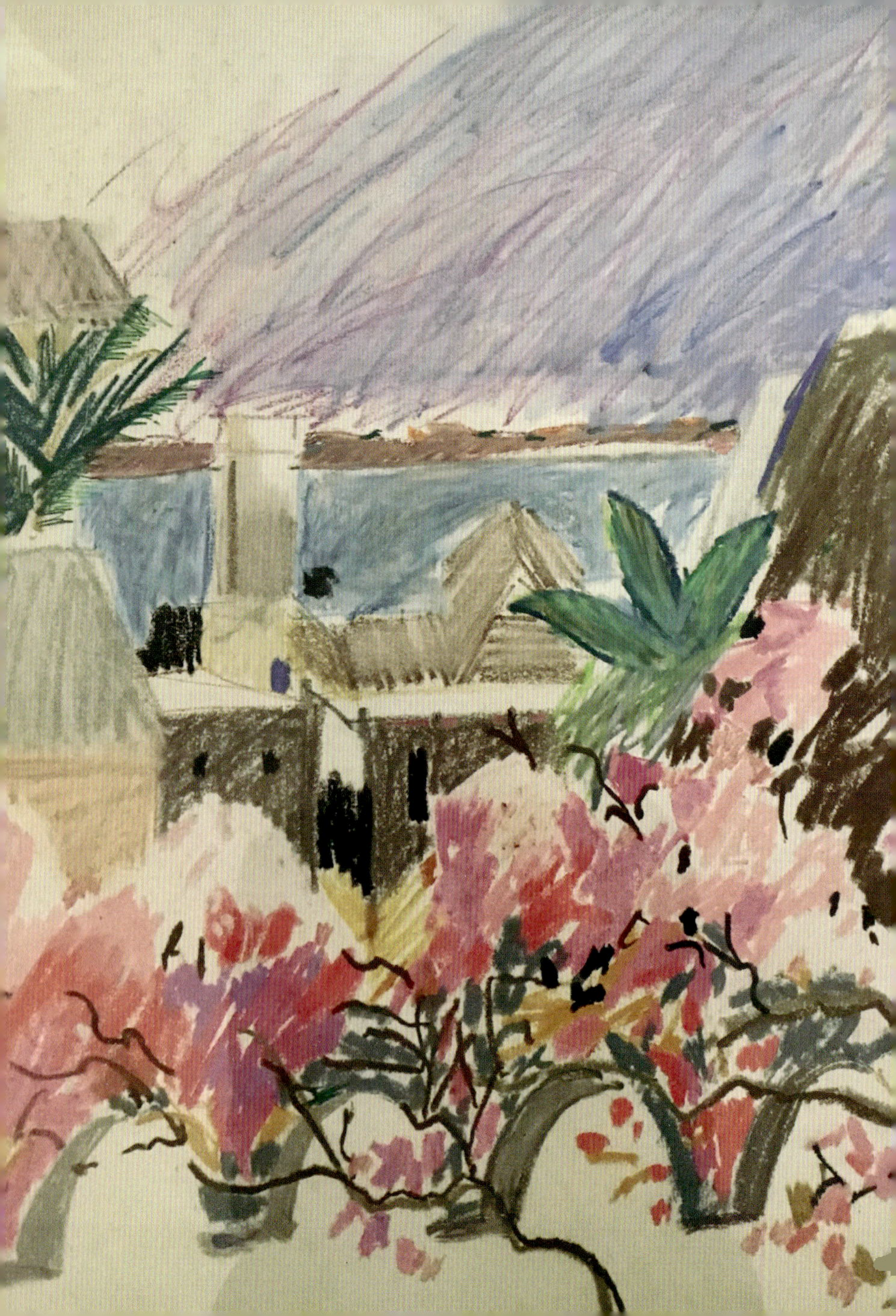

A drawing with coloured pencils
from a rooftop of the Arab town
of Lamu, north Kenya coast.
The extravaganza of bougainvillea
in the foreground contrasts the
straight lines of the horizon
and the buildings.

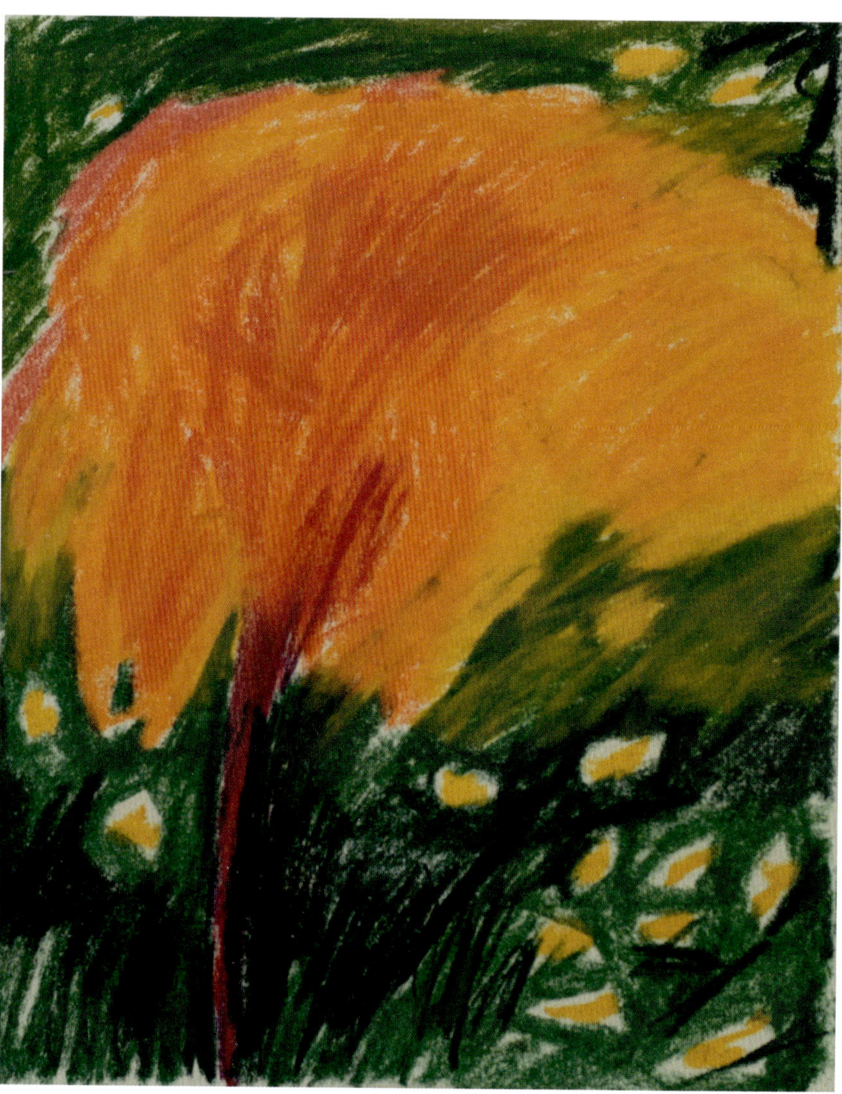

Canna Lily

This small work is in oil pastels
on handmade paper, which
absorbs the paint so beautifully.

A drawing from Erica's Garden

I recognise the little island in the middle of that magical flowerbed. Oil sticks on paper with a bit of smudging with turpentine. Sally Kampf, my sister, owns this coloured drawing. It was drawn in 1992 and is fading a bit.

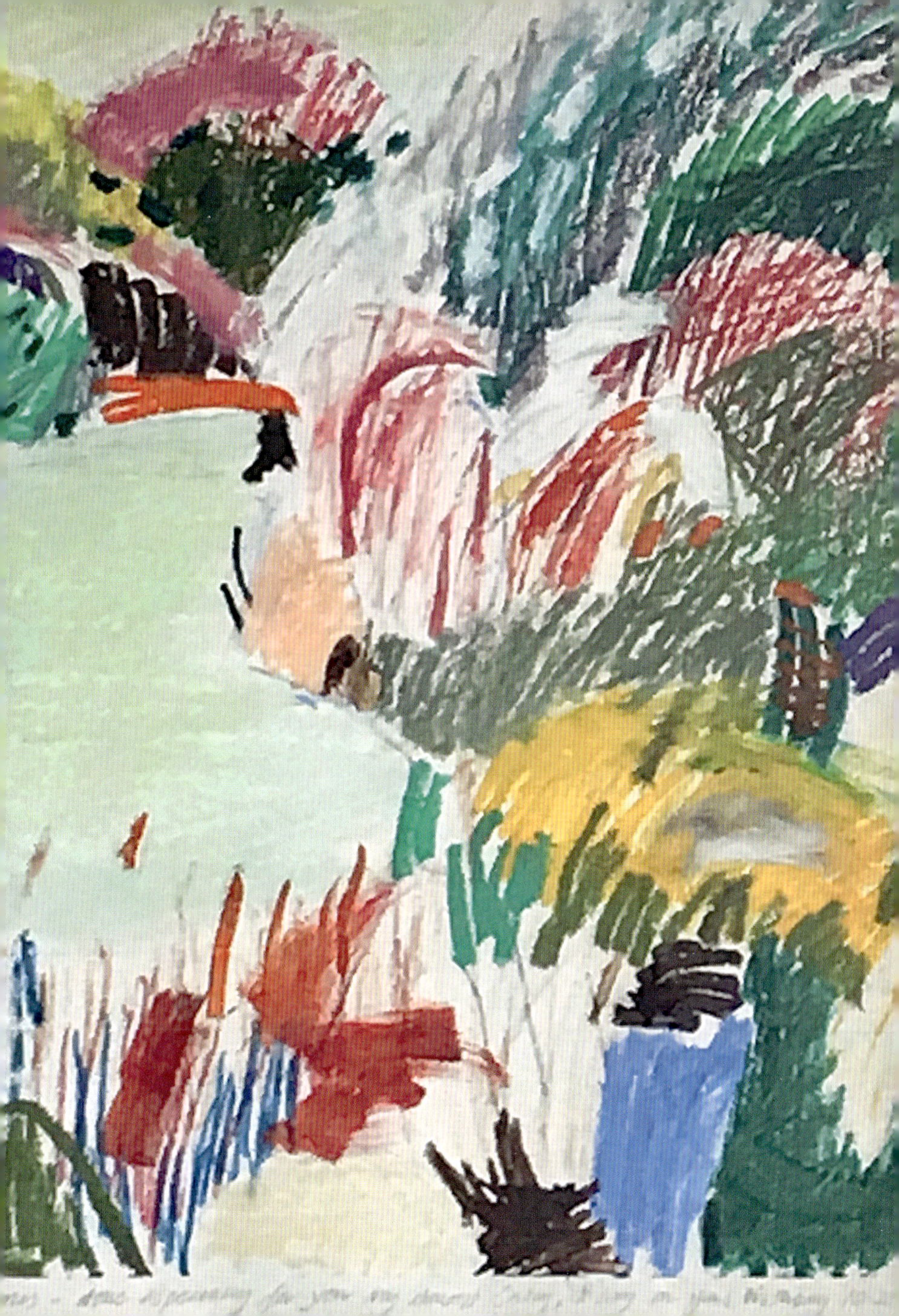

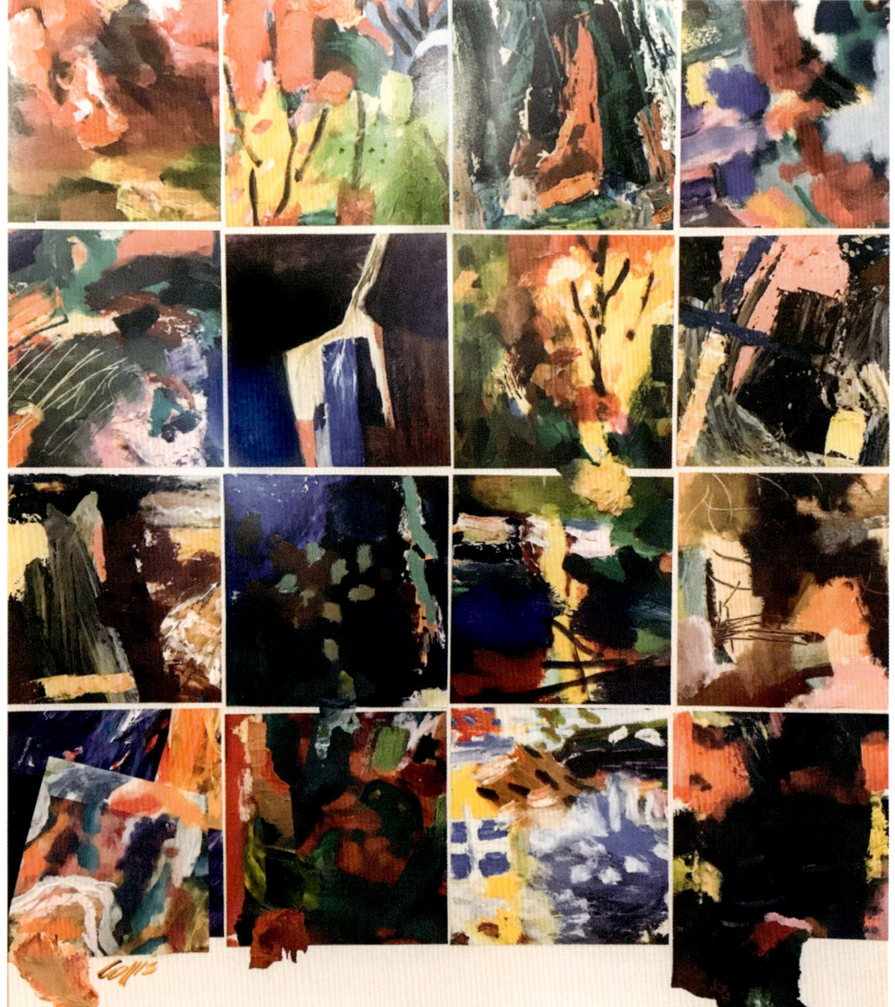

Secrets

A grid format which works on paper.
Occasionally I will go through my drawers
where all the drawings or thoughts on
paper are stored. I cut them up into smallish
squares, and re-arrange them, as here,
glued on to card and framed under glass.
There is power in a repeat shape and a
stability with un-attachment to the end
result. The painting leads me. It is the
master and I am 'doing what I am told',
which is a lovely way of functioning.
Collection of Jan and Azmina Janmohamed

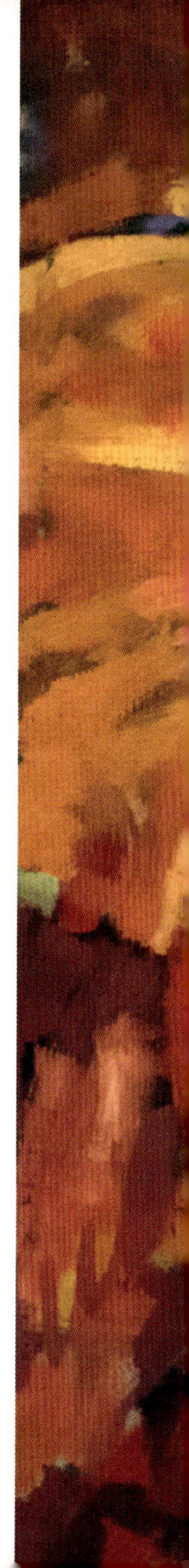

Day 231

Canna Fairy

A very early work, one of the first of
the series of the canna lilies. I gave
this to my friend Vicky Chignall.
There is a little fairy in this painting.
I hope you can spot her?

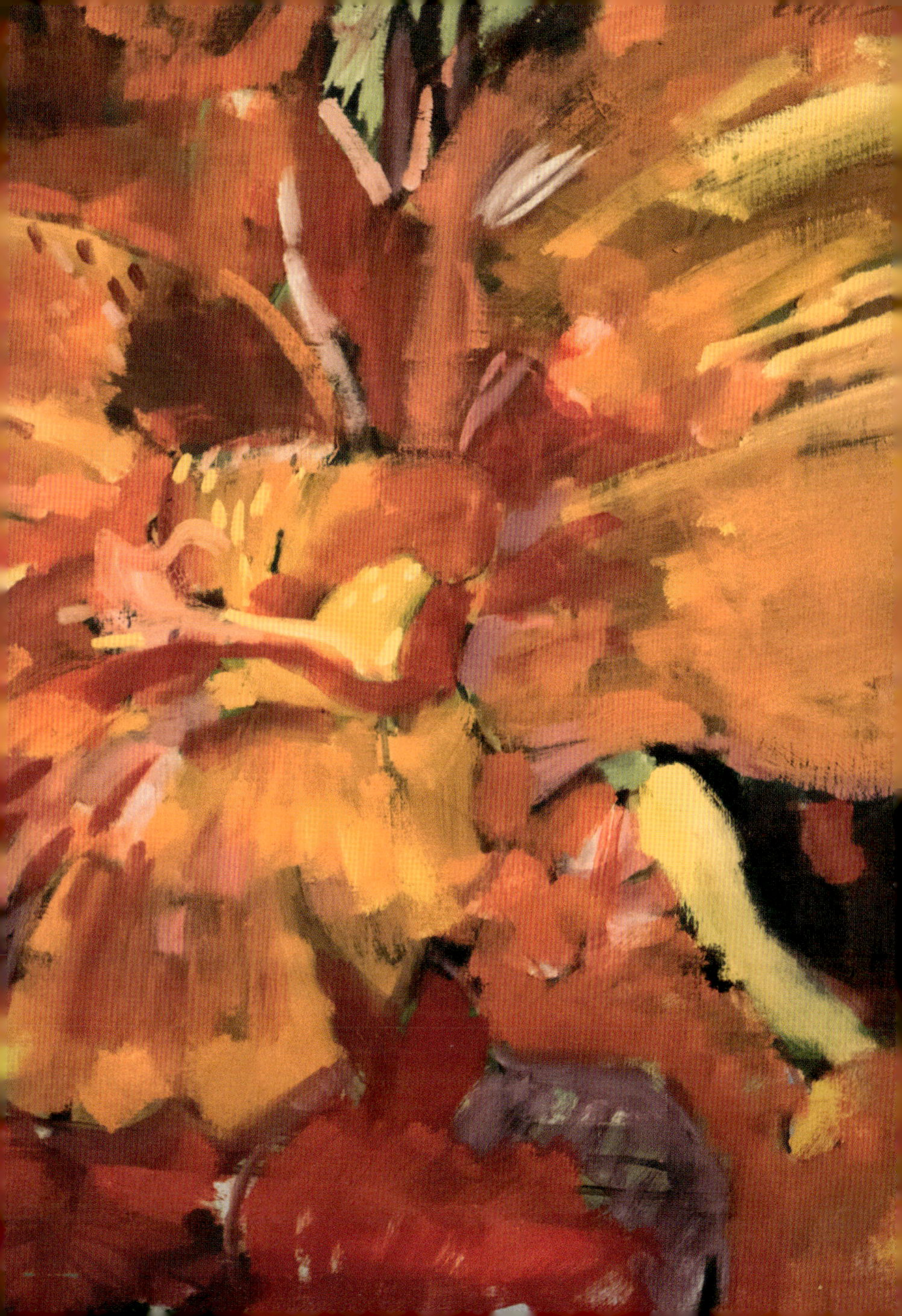

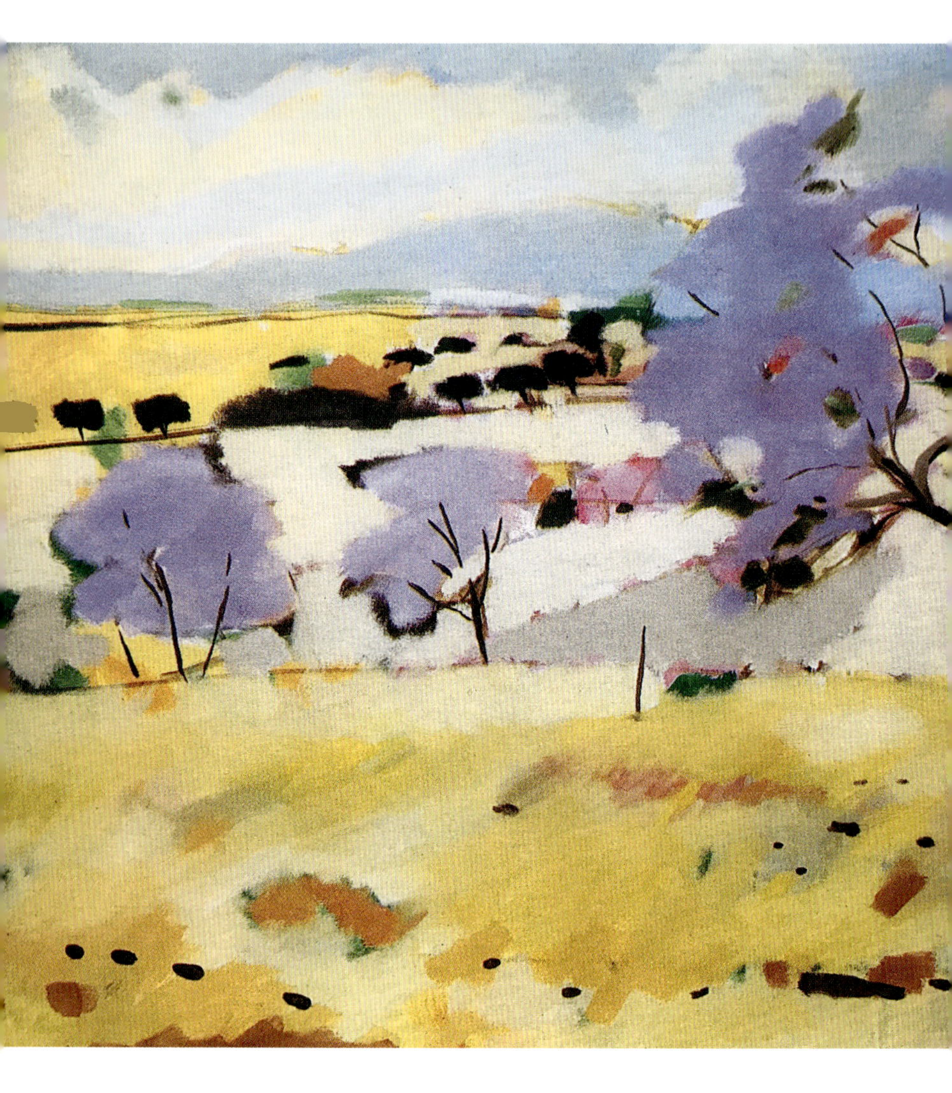

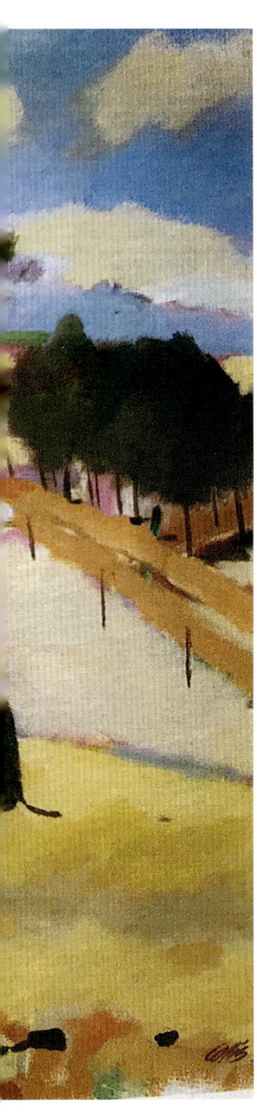

Farm at Makuyu

This canvas of a jacaranda tree, bent by the
wind, was sold in a one-woman show in London,
organised by the McEwan Gallery from Ballater,
situated in the heart of Royal Deeside.
The exhibition was at the Mall Galleries, London.
In 1991 the Medici Society bought the rights to
reproduce this picture in an address book.
Private Collection of Sir John Madejski OBE

Canna

A quick colour rendering
on absorbent paper. I like the
composition of this one, as it
reminds me of my favourite
artist, Mark Rothko.

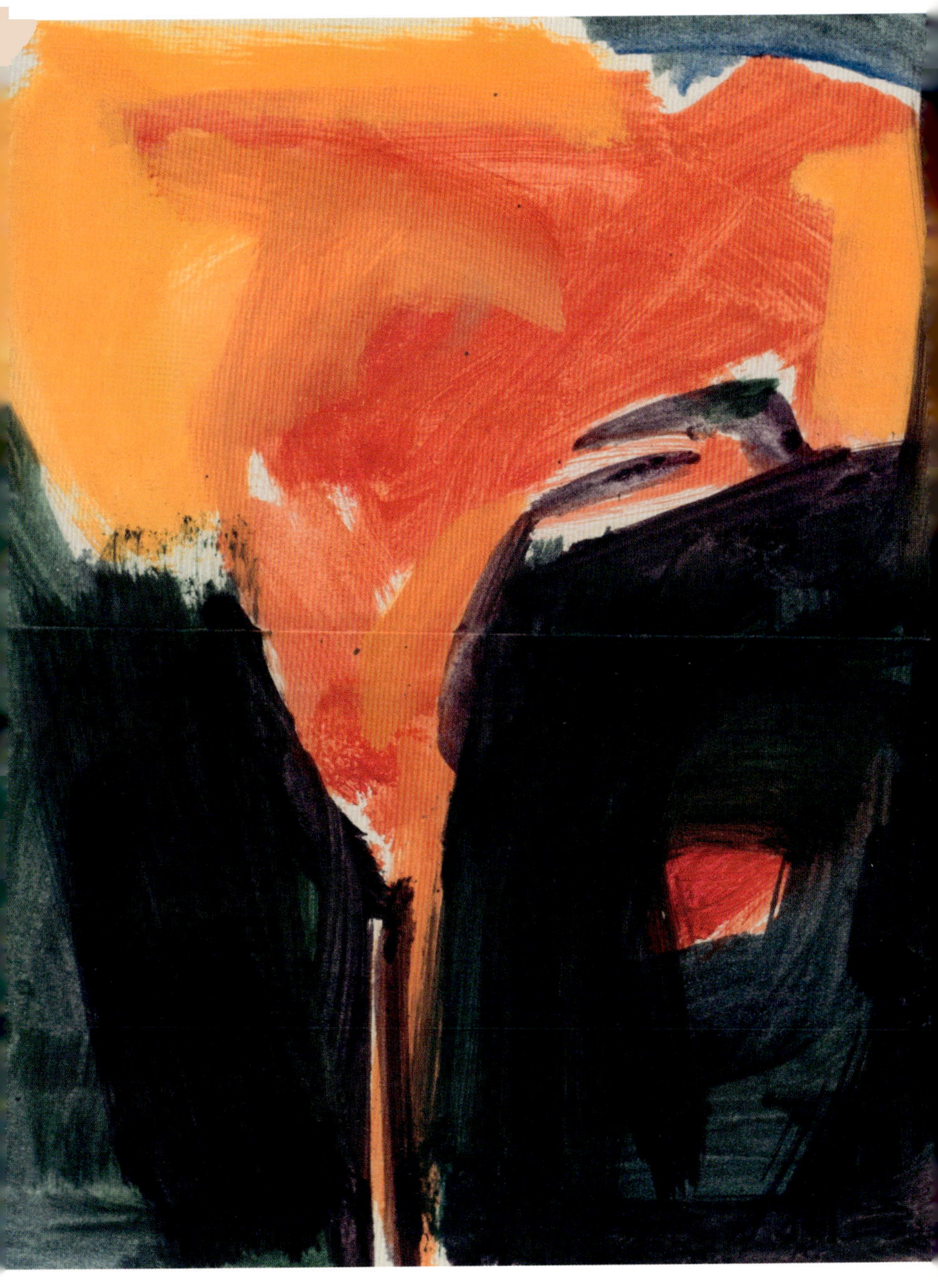

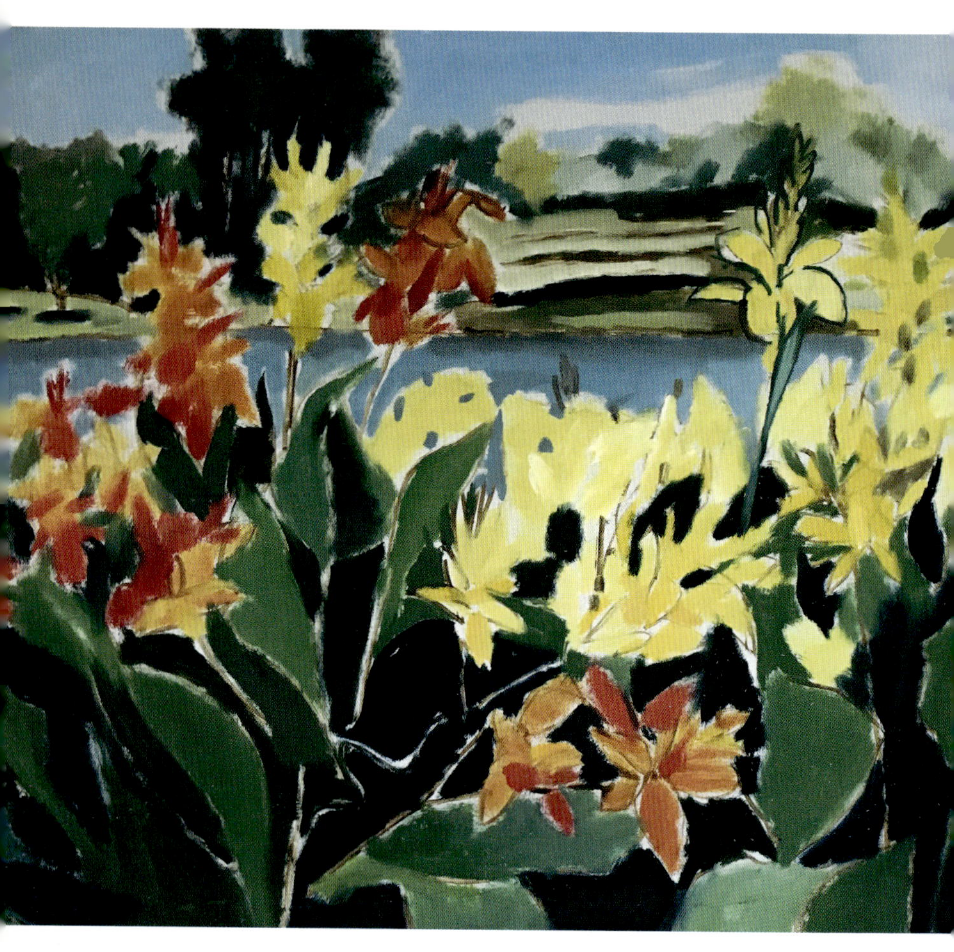

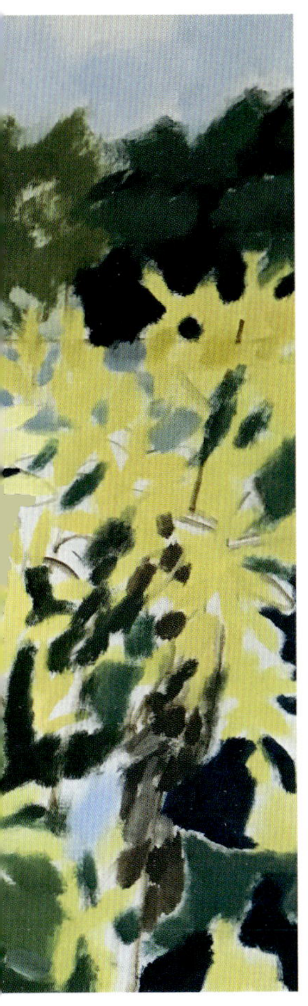

Canna Lilies

Set against the little lake at the bottom of
the golf course in Limuru. It was a dull day
and these pale cream-yellow cannas are very
unusual. Native to Central America, Mexico,
the Caribbean and tropical South America,
cannas were introduced and naturalised in
East Africa and are sometimes considered an
invasive species. I think they are beautiful,
I love the different colour lilies and I love
the leaves that are many different shades of
verdigris; some are striped and some are copper.
Collection of Mike and Sheila Barker, London

Waters Edge,
Simon's Town

A secret beach where the locals go to swim
in a natural pool, I painted this in a gale,
40 mph winds whistling, a disturbing sound
and which somehow misses this water's edge,
as you can see by the calm waters. However,
there was a sudden gust and the canvas flew
off my easel into the sea, and I was resigned
to wave it goodbye. A man from Zimbabwe
was sitting on a bench nearby.
He jumped into the water and rescued the
painting. I could not believe how kind and
selfless some people are. Oil does not mix with
water, so the paint was wet but undamaged.
The poor man was soaked. I had had enough
by that time, packed up and went home.
The work is unfinished.

... my soul is full of longing
For the secret of the sea,
And the heart of the great ocean
Sends a thrilling pulse through me.
Henry Wadsworth Longfellow

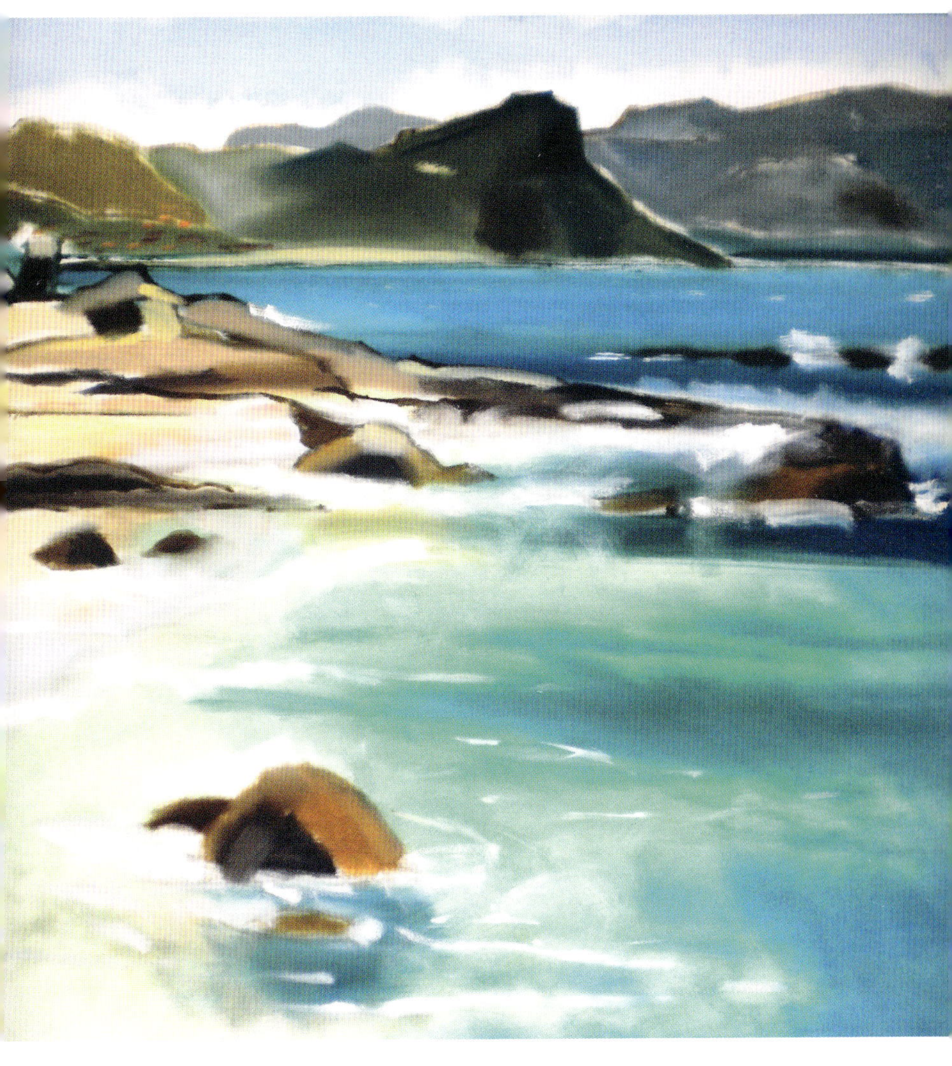

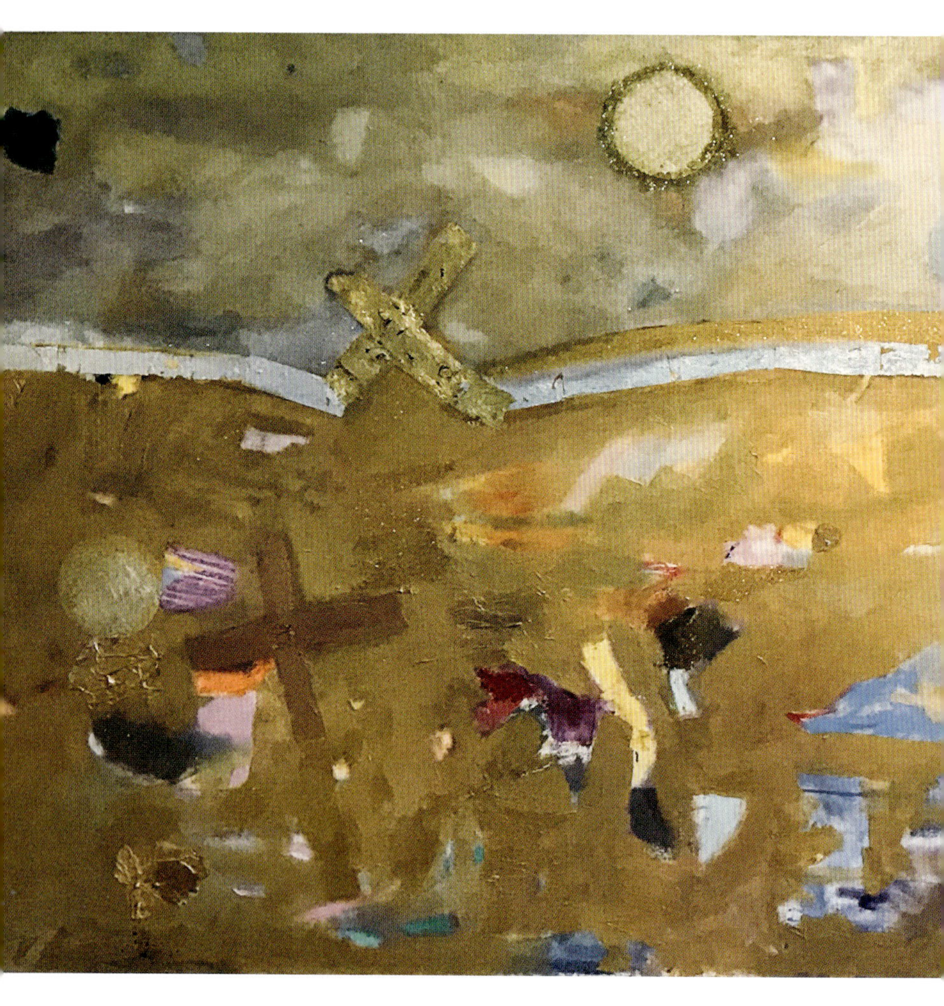

Golden Means

Mixed media on canvas: acrylic, gold and silver
foil, gold glitter, collage and oil on top.
A new, large gold painting has moved on today.
Silence is golden beneath a starry sky.
I am happy.

Golden Shamba

This painting is in a tube and on its way to Colorado. There are some people in this world who are special to me, and Marcia and Bill Levy can lift the day from afar. Xx

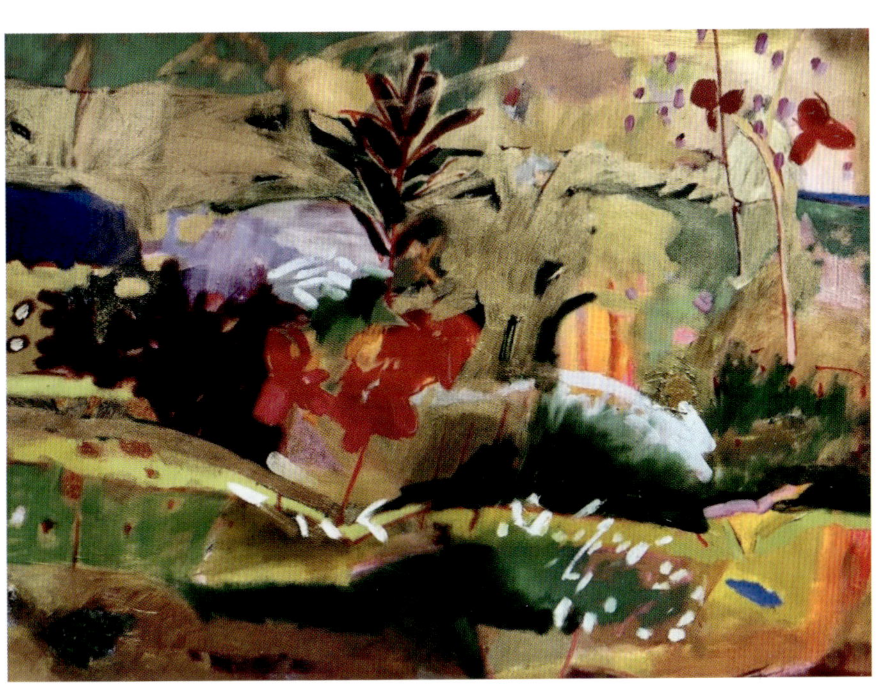

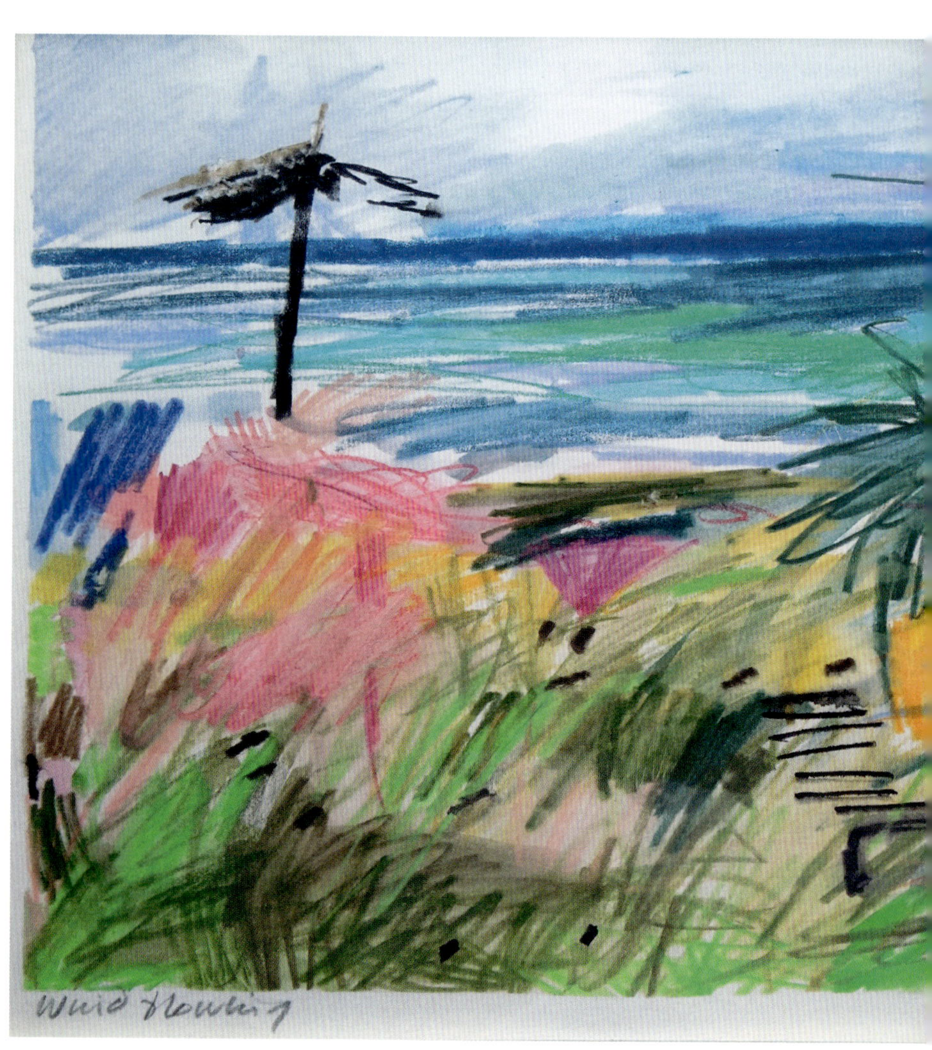
Wind blowing

Wind Blowing, Watamu

One of the really lovely things about this long
daily Covid exhibition on Facebook is that
I have made friends with people I did not know
before. Naveed Awan sent me this little sketch
which he purchased at RaMoMA (Rahimtulla
Museum of Modern Art).
The wind is really blowing! Every line in this
rough drawing is a testament to that wind.
It has real movement, as you will see from
the edges, the paper which was firmly stuck
to the board to stop it blowing away.

Pages from a notebook

Here are little vignettes of a holiday at
Watamu on the north Kenyan coast.
The yellow umbrellas of Hemingway's Hotel
feature, although we were staying in a
spectacular villa very close by. These are quite
small, coloured drawings done on the spot as
I saw them. The square on the golden section
is a wind sock that looks like a fish.

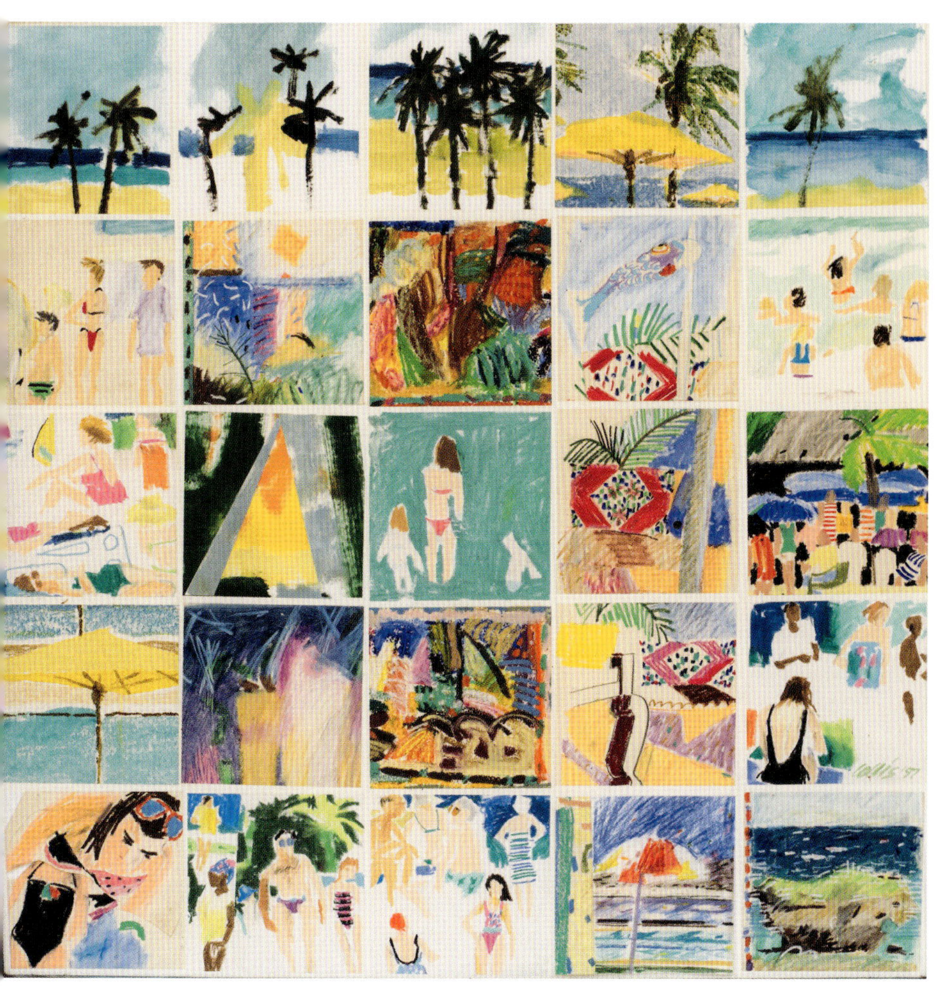

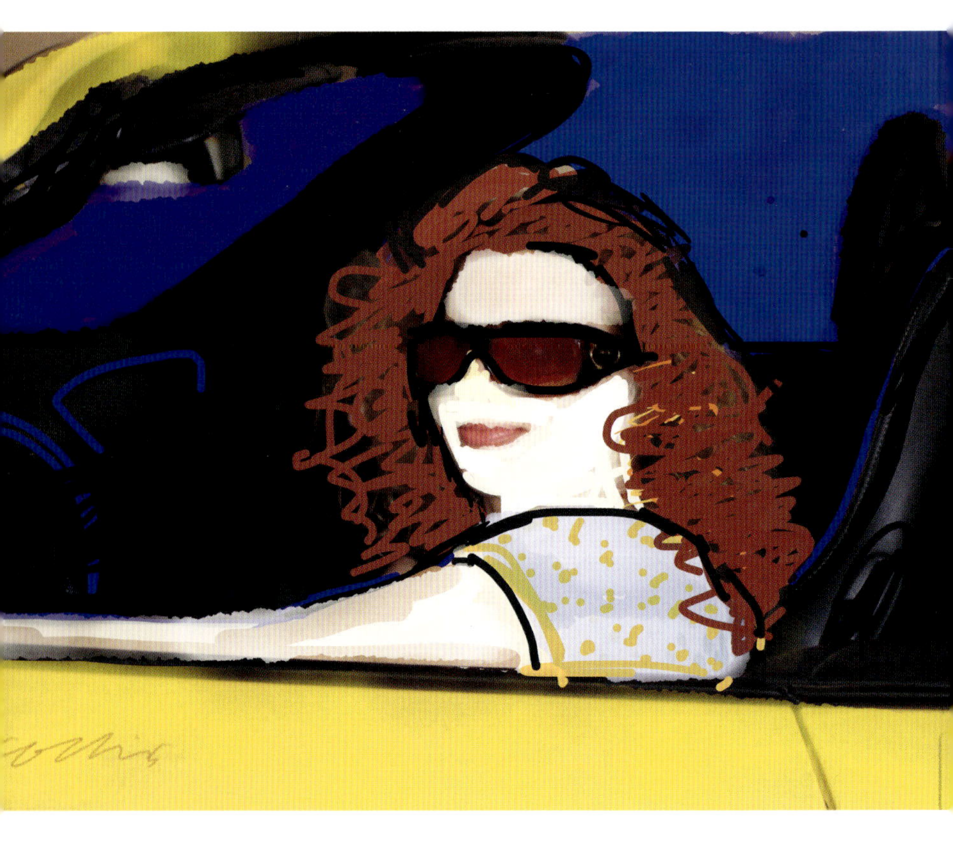

Day 240
Gillian

My youngest sister who sadly died
three years ago, aged fifty-nine.
She had an incredible life of wealth
and success. A real character who lifted
everyone she spoke to. There are four
girls in our family: Sally, Elizabeth,
Gillian and me, the eldest. This is a
drawing done over a photograph on the
computer and it has caught her essence.
I miss her.

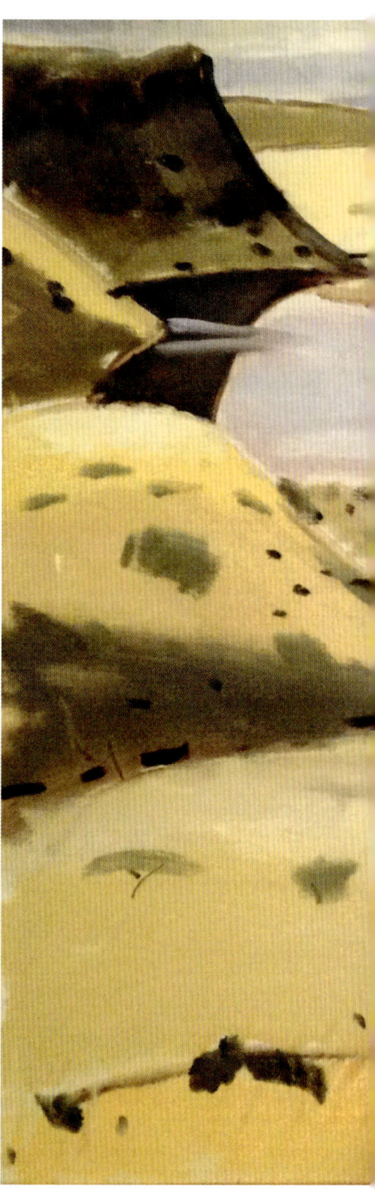

Day 241
Lake Magadi

A salt lake in the Great Rift Valley.
Scott and Isla Lindsay are friends who
lived on Lake Magadi and we would
often stay with them at weekends.
Scott was the best bagpiper I have ever
heard. On this particular evening, he
played the pipes as the sun went down
and I finished this desolate painting of
almost no vegetation, it was so dry,
on the pink lake. A very wistful and
haunting memory. We all cried.

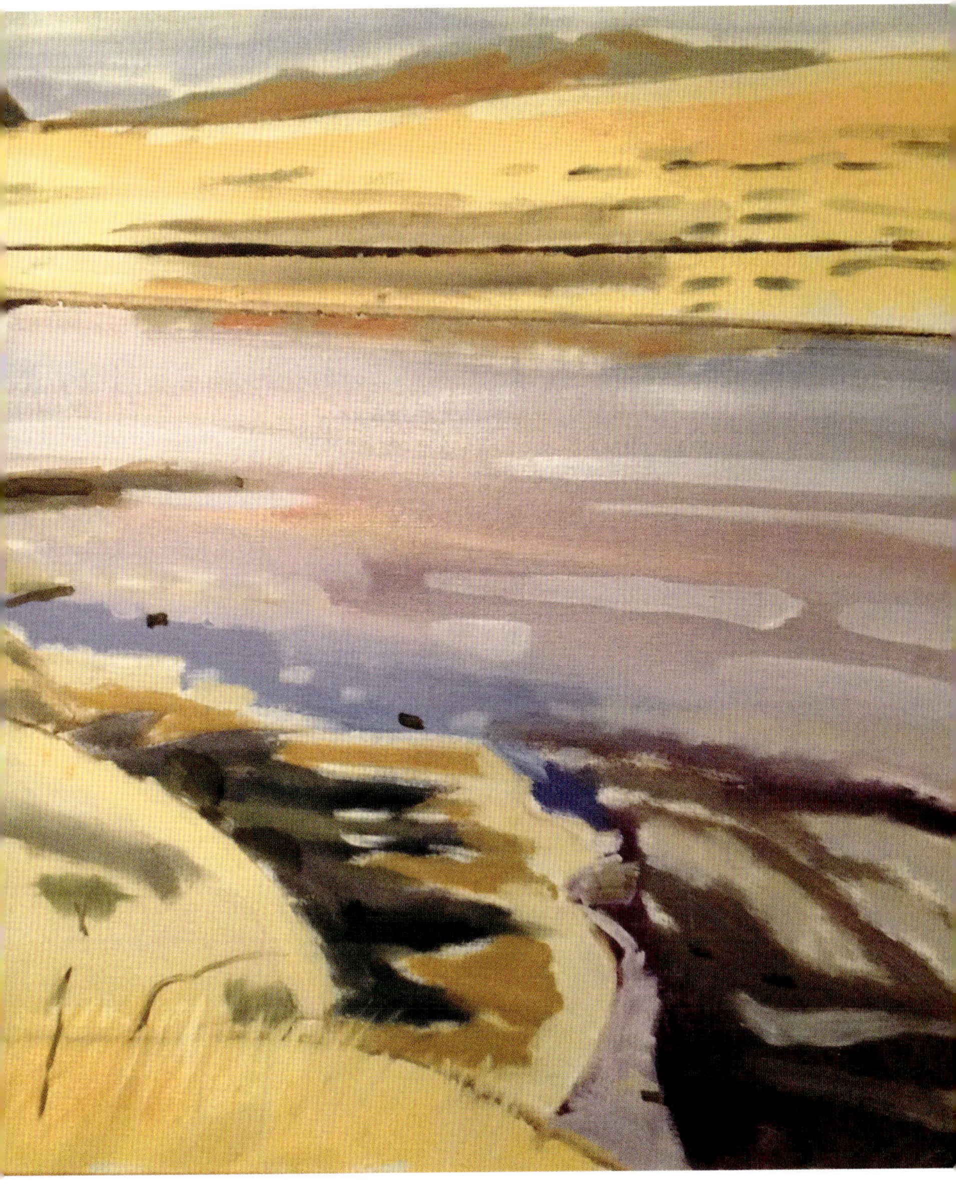

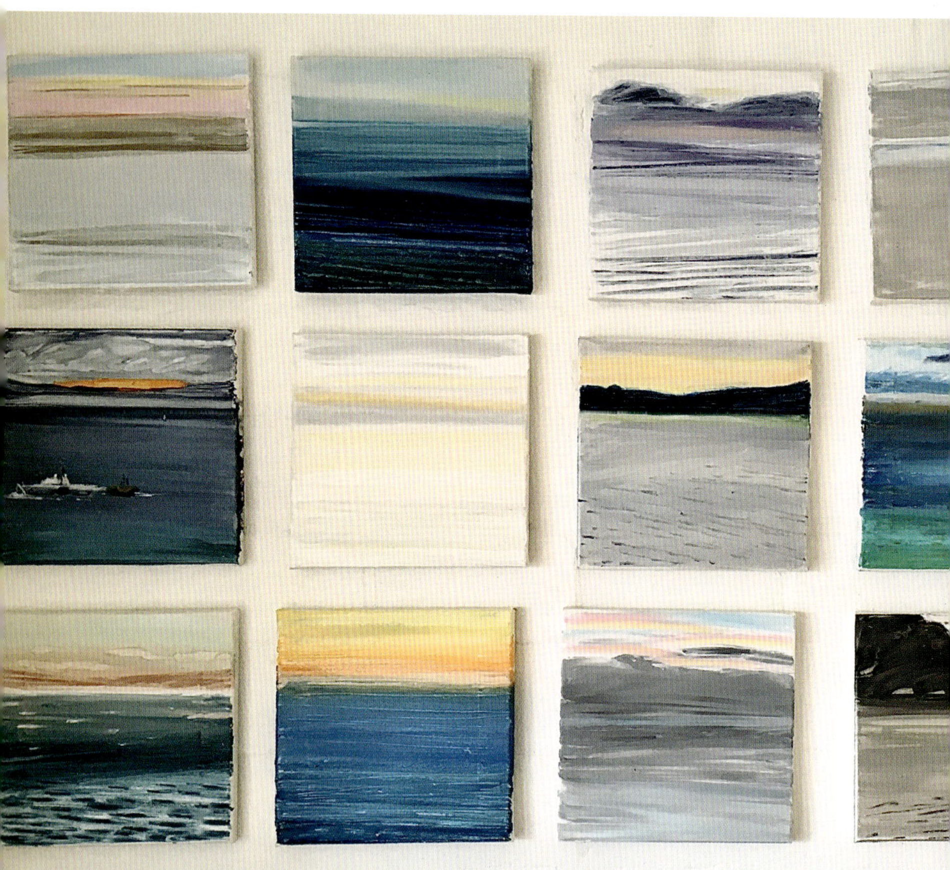

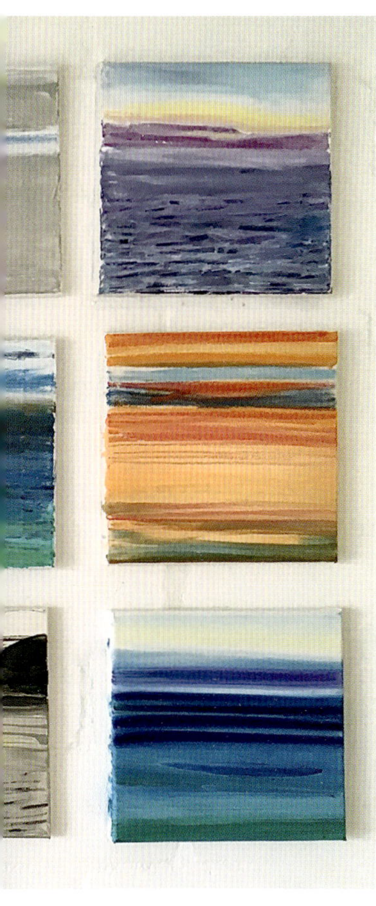

Day 242

This is a snap shot of a wall in the lounge.
Our apartment in Simon's Town is small.
This is where the paintings dry, on the wall
just after I do them. The sequence changes
daily. The dry ones go into a cupboard
where they form pillars of paintings
taller than me.
Next week we are flying off to the
Glorious Cape for the first time in a year.
This Facebook exhibition is coming to an
end in two more days. I want to thank you
all for supporting me. What started out as
only a desire to 'lift the day' for us all has
made me realise the variety of painting
I have done in my life. I had no idea. It has
put me in touch with friends and collectors
from all over the world. Forgotten works
have come to light. Memories from each
work that I had no idea were there.
Friendships with people I did not know
before. And a book deal, a publisher of
art books, in London.
Such kindness, I want to thank you all
for solace and moral support during this
insane year, 2020.

Day 243
Erica's Garden
'Erica's Garden' series

Steps ascending to Erica's outside dining room.
This painting is in Hermanus on the south west
coast of South Africa, and Lindsay Hooper has
just sent it to me. I always enjoy seeing work
from that wonderful garden. There are so many
paintings from this series. The colours in this
work are not exaggerated, though I did allow
that blob of yellow from a failed painting below
to shine through. It holds the painting together.

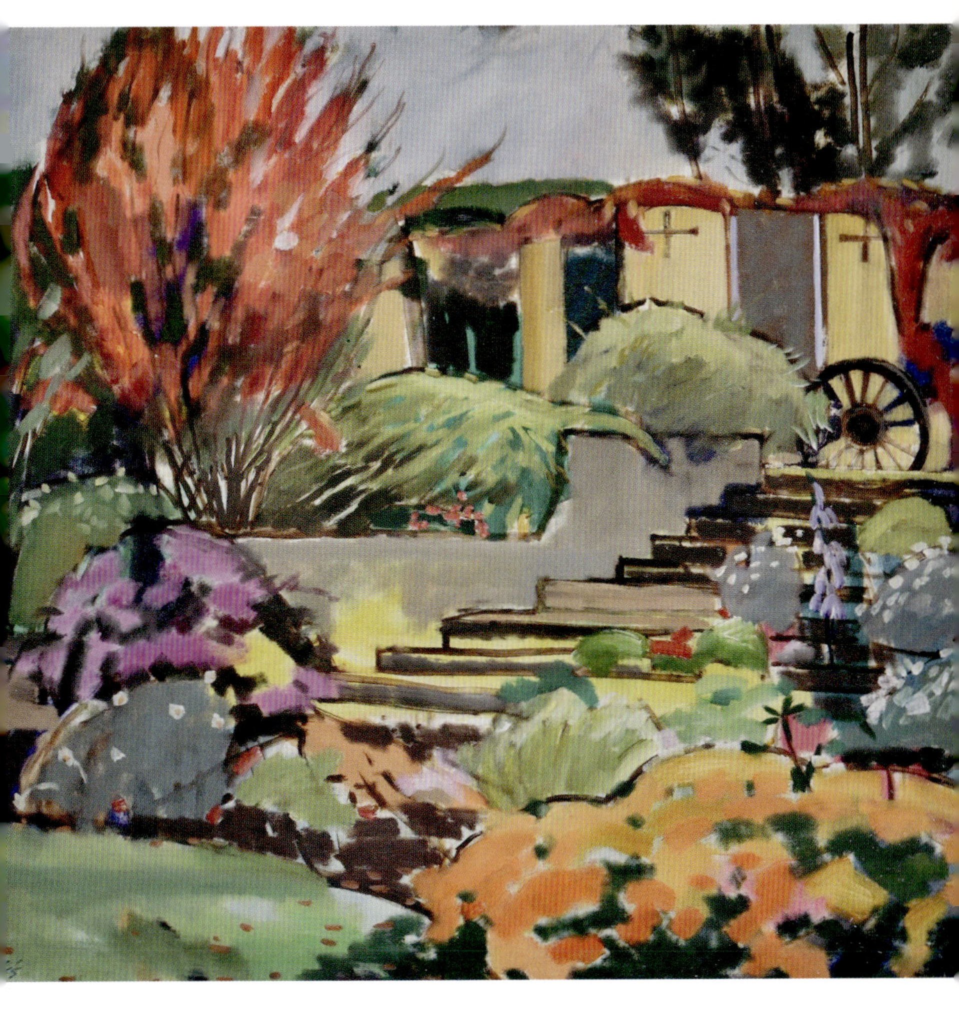

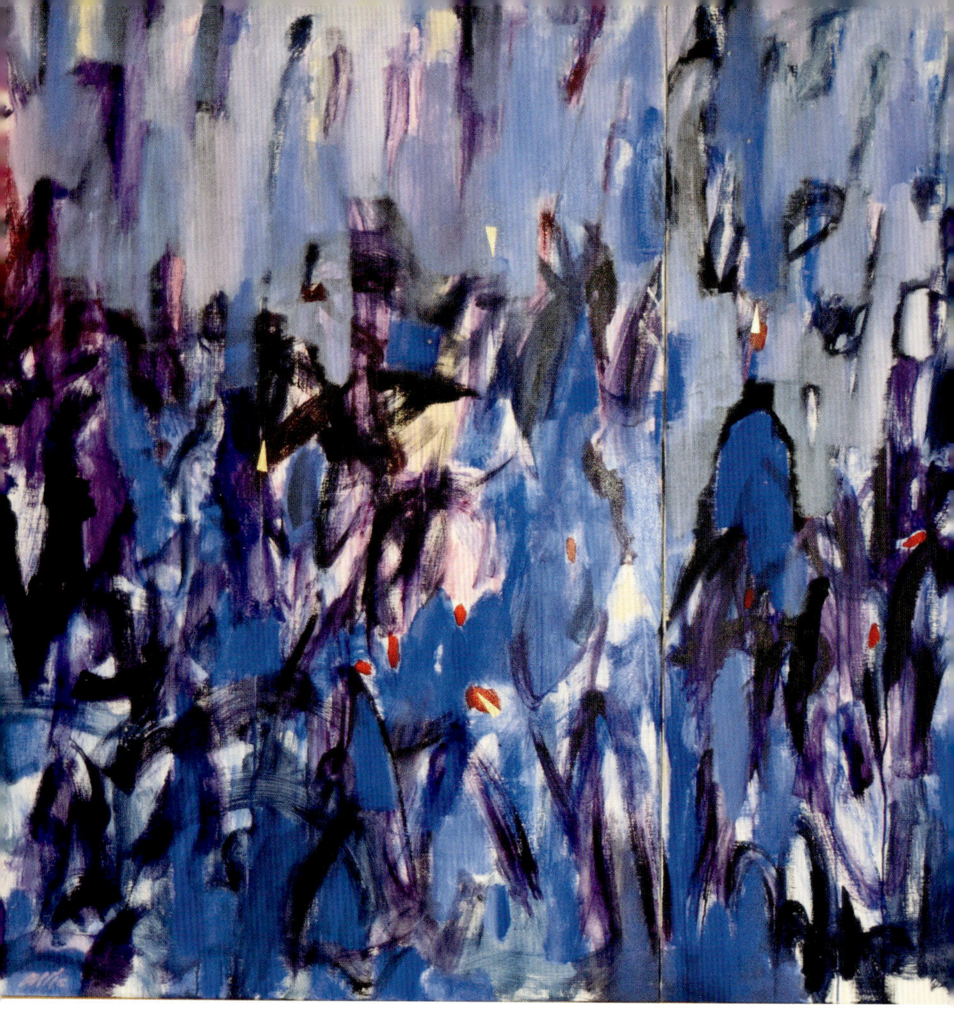

Day 244

How Long Will I See Girlhood in My Daughter?

Inspired by the beautiful poem *The Blossom* by the Irish poet
Eavan Boland. I was feeling very blue, realizing Mia, no longer a
girl, was leaving home again so soon, after living a year in Nepal.
The Abstract Expressionist Joan Mitchell works from poems
and inspired this 7ft diptych.

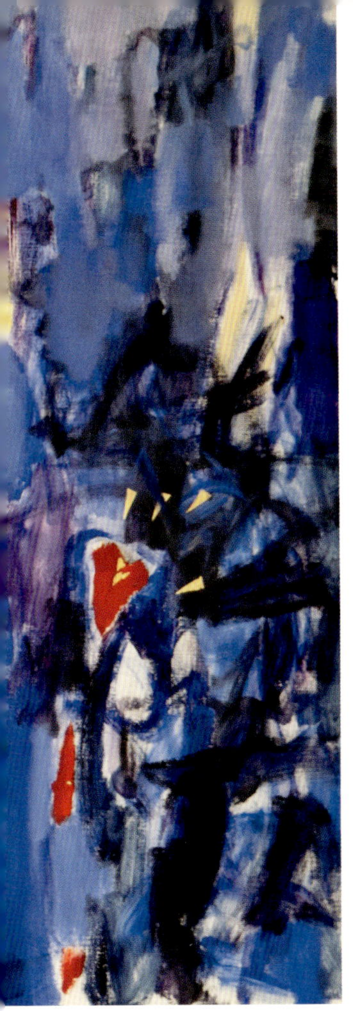

The Blossom

A May morning. Light starting in the sky.
I have come here
after a long night.

The blossom on the apple tree is still in shadow,
its petals half white and filled with water at the core,
in which the secrecy and freshness of dawn are stored
even in the dark.

How much longer will I see girlhood in my daughter?

In other seasons,
I knew every leaf on this tree.
Now I stand here almost without seeing them

and so lost in grief
I hardly notice what is happening
as the light increases
and the blossom speaks

and turns to me with blond hair
and my eyebrows and says –

Imagine if I stayed here
even for the sake of your love.
What would happen to the summer? To the fruit?

Then holds out a dawn-soaked hand to me
whose fingers I counted at birth
years ago

and touches mine for the last time

and falls to earth.

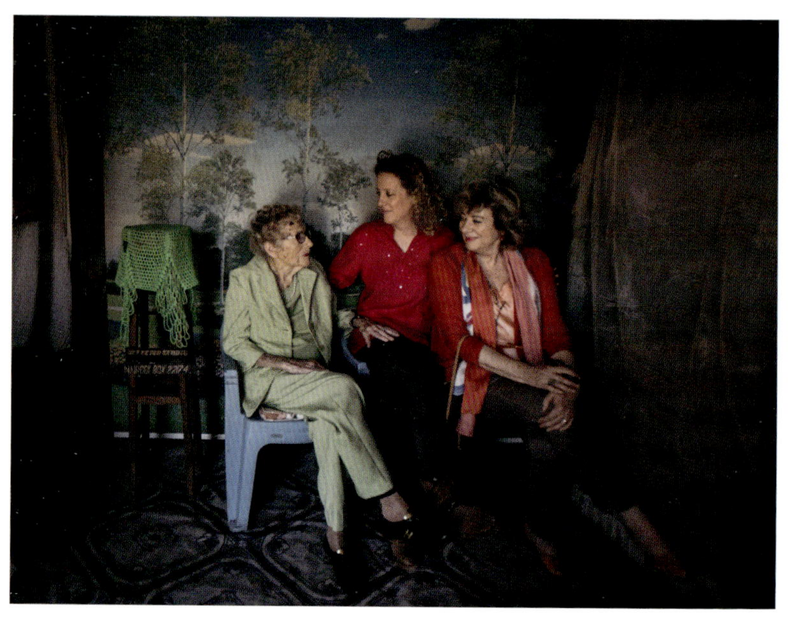

Three generations.
My Mother, my daughter Mia and me
in the Weekend Studio in Kibera.

I would like to dedicate this book to my mother, Brenda Kampf,
who died on 29 November 2020. She was ninety-eight.

Nothing can stop what is coming.
I choose to believe it will all work out.
Good always trumps evil.
Thank you all for your comments and
support, and for following me on this path.
Your encouragement has sustained me
and lifted my day.

This is the End.

Praise for the Facebook Lockdown Exibition

Sandeep Desai, Nairobi
Stunning. A potent expression. Beautiful.
Have truly enjoyed viewing such a remarkable body of work.

Pauline Proudfoot, Cape Town
Thank you for a unique masterclass experience.
I shall treasure what I've seen and learnt.

Celia Howe, Guernsey
Thank you for all your time and hard work putting your wonderful
works all together and sharing. It has been inspirational.

Don Young, Indonesia
Thank you for your dedication both to your journey
as an artist and in gathering together this quite incredible
body of work to share with your devoted friends and fans.

Liz Pannet, New Forest, UK
Thank you for uplifting the day every day. I love both your
paintings and your illuminating comments on your working
thoughts and inspiration.

Maureen Albrecht, Kenya
Such a wonderful story of paintings.
Bringing colour and light during some dark and difficult times.

Elizabeth Hilken Wackman, Washington, USA
Every day I've looked forward to seeing your wonderful work.
Day by day – a moment to stop and enjoy another beautiful
painting. It was a real gift to us this year.